D1598454

The Cults
of the
Roman Empire

The Ancient World

General editor: **T. J. Cornell**

Professor of Ancient History, University of Manchester

The Ancient World series exists to publish works combining scholarship with accessibility on central aspects of the political, cultural and social history of Europe, the countries of the Mediterranean, and the Near and Middle East from the origins of human society to the period of Late Antiquity. The books are designed to appeal both to students and to the wide range of readers with a serious interest in the field.

Titles in print

* Published in the USA by Harvard University Press

The Cults
of the
Roman Empire

Robert Turcan

Translated by Antonia Nevill

BLACKWELL
Oxford UK & Cambridge USA

Copyright © Société d'édition, Les Belles Lettres 1992
English translation ©Antonia Nevill 1996
First published as *Les Cultes Orientaux dans le monde Romain* in 1989
by Société d'édition Les Belles Lettres. Second edition published 1992.

First published in English 1996
2 4 6 8 10 9 7 5 3 1

Blackwell Publishers Ltd
108 Cowley Road
Oxford OX4 1JF
UK

Blackwell Publishers Inc.
238 Main Street
Cambridge, Massachusetts 02142
USA

British Library Cataloging in Publication Data

A CIP catalogue record for this book is available from the British Library.

Library of Congress Cataloging-in-Publication Data
Turcan, Robert.
    [Cultes orientaux dans le monde romain. English]
    The cults of the Roman Empire/Robert Turcan; translated by Antonia Nevill.
      p. cm. – (The ancient world)
    Includes bibliographical references and indexes.
    ISBN 0-631-20046-0 (alk. paper). – ISBN 0-631-20047-9 (pbk.:
alk. paper)
1. Cults-Rome. 2. Rome-Religion. I. Title. II. Series:
Ancient world (Oxford, England)
BL805. T8713 1996
292.9-dc20   96–7500
                                                        CIP

Typeset in 10/12 Palatino by Photoprint, Torquay, Devon
Printed in Great Britain by T.J. Press Limited, Padstow, Cornwall

Contents

Plates

Figures

Abbreviations

AA	*Archäologischer Anzeiger*
AE	*Année Épigraphique*
AJA	*American Journal of Archaeology*
ANRW	*Aufsteig und, Niedergang der römischen Welt* (= Festschrift J. Vogt, ed. H.Temporini and W.Haase)
BCH	*Bulletin de Correspondance Hellénique*
BEFAR	*Bibliothèque des Écoles Françaises d'Athènes et de Rome*
CCCA	M.J. Vermaseren, *Corpus cultus Cybelae Attidisque* (EPRO, 50), Leiden, 1979ff
CCID	M. Hörig und E. Schwertheim, *Corpus cultus Iovis Dolicheni* (EPRO, 106), Leiden, 1987
CCET	Z. Goĉeva *et alii*, *Corpus cultus equitis Thracii* (EPRO, 74), Leiden, 1979ff
CIL	Corpus inscriptionum Latinarum
CIMRM	M.J. Vermaseren, *Corpus inscriptionum et monumentorum religionis Mithriacae*, I–II, The Hague, 1956–60
CIS	Corpus inscriptionum Semiticarum
CRAI	Comptes rendus de l'Académie des Inscriptions et Belles-Lettres, Institut de France
EPRO	Études préliminaires aux religions orientales dans l'Empire romain (dir. M.J. Vermaseren)
Ggr	M.P. Nilsson, *Geschichte der griechischen Religion*, I–II2, Munich, 19 55–61 (re-edited)
IBIS	J. Leclant, *Inventaire bibliographique des Isiaca. Répertoire analytique des travaux relatifs à la diffusion des cultes isiaques*, 1940–69 (EPRO, 18), Leiden, 1972ff
IG	*Inscriptiones Graecae*
IGVR	*Inscriptiones Graecae Vrbis Romae*
JMS	*Journal of Mithraic Studies*
JRS	*Journal of Roman Studies*

LIMC	*Lexicon iconographicum mythologiae classicae*, Zurich–Munich,1981ff
LSAM	F. Sokolowski, *Lois sacrées de l'Asie Mineure*, Paris, 1955
MEFR(A)	*Mélanges de l'École Française de Rome (Antiquité)*
OrRR	M.J. Vermaseren, ed., *Die orientalischen Religionen im römischen Reich (EPRO, 93)*, Leiden, 1981
PGM	*Papyri Graecae magicae*
RA	*Revue Archéologique*
RAC	*Reallexikon für Antike und Christentum*
RAE	*Revue Archéologique de l'Est et du Centre-Est*
REA	*Revue des Études Anciennes*
REG	*Revue des Études Grecques*
REL	*Revue des Études Latines*
RGVV	*Religionsgeschichtliche Versuche und Vorarbeiten*
RHR	*Revue de l'Histoire des Religions*
RM	*Mitteilungen des deutschen archäologischen Instituts, Römische Abteilung*
RO⁴	F. Cumont, *Les religions orientales dans le paganisme romain*, 4th edition, Paris 1929 (re-edited)
SEG	*Supplementum epigraphicum Graecum*
SIG	W. Dittenberger, *Sylloge inscriptionum Graecarum*, 3rd edition

xii

NORTH SEA

Hadrian's Wall
Cataractonium (Catterick)
Eburacum (York)

BRITANNIA
Londinium

Colonia Agrippina (Cologne)   GERMANIA

GERMANIA
INFERIOR   Augusta Treverorum (Trier)
Nemetacum (Arras)   Moguntiacum (Mainz)
BELGICA   GERMANIA
SUPERIOR

ATLANTIC OCEAN

Lutetia (Paris)   Argentoratum
LUGDUNENSIS   Lauriacum   Carnuntum

Augusta Vindelicorum   Aquincum
(Augsburg) NORICUM   Savaria (Budapest
Alesia   RAETIA   Virunum
Augustodunum (Autun)   Geneva   PANNONIA
AQUITANIA   Lugdunum (Lyon)   Emona
Burdigala (Bordeaux)   Vienna (Vienne)   Mediolanum (Milan)   Tergeste Siscia   Dr
Vesunna   Verona Aquileia   Sirmium
(Périgueux)   Alba Arausio   Cremona   Senia   Vimin
NARBONENSIS   (Orange)   Ravenna   DALMATIA
Asturica   Tolosa (Toulouse)   Rhône   Bononia (Bologna)   Iader   Salonae (Split)
Augusta   Legio   Narbo (Narbonne)   Massilia   ITALIA
Bracara Augusta   Clunia   (Marseille)   Pyrgi   MACEDO
Aquae Flaviae   Emporion (Ampurias)   Arelate (Arles)   (Santa Severa)   Teate   ADRIATIC SEA
TARRACONENSIS   Nemausus (Nîmes)   Roma   Corfinium
Olisipo   LUSITANIA   Ostia   Puteoli (Pozzuoli)
(Lisbon)   Norba   Tarraco (Tarragona)   Neapolis (Naples)   Beneventum   Brundisiu
Augusta Emerita   Metellinum   Saguntum   Pompeii & Herculaneum   Tarentum   (Brindi
(Merida)   (Medellin)   Valentia   SARDINIA   Corcyra
Pax Iulia (Beja)   BAETICA   TYRRHENIAN SEA
Corduba
Hispalis (Seville)   Panormus (Palermo)   Rhegium
Gades (Cadiz)   Carthago Nova (Cartagena)   Segesta   Tauromenium (Taorm
Utica   Henna   Catana
Iol Caesarea   Cirta   Bulla   Carthago   Acrae   Syracusae
Volubilis   Sitifis   Zama   Leptis   SICILIA
Augusta Emerita   Lambaesis   Theveste
TINGITANA   MAURETANIA   (Tébessa)   NUMIDIA   MEDITERRANEA
CAESARIENSIS

Leptis Magna
Sabrata
TRIPOLITANA
AFRICA

Note: Great Greece (Magna Graecia) is a term applied to the Greek cities of southern Italy.

xiii

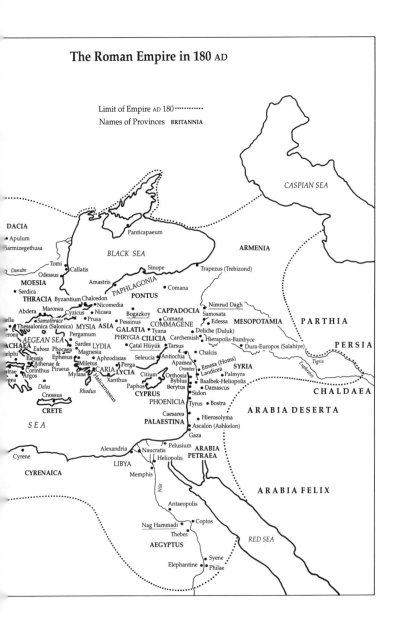

The Roman Empire in 180 AD

Limit of Empire AD 180 ·············
Names of Provinces BRITANNIA

CASPIAN SEA

DACIA
• Apulum
Sarmizegethusa
⌇ Danube   • Tomi
            Odessus• Callatis
MOESIA
• Serdica
THRACIA Byzantium Chalcedon
Abdera Maronea   • Nicomedia
ella • Samothrace   • Prusa
   Thessalonica (Salonica) MYSIA ASIA
eroea   Pergamum
ACHAEA Euboea Phocaea Sardes LYDIA
elphi Eleusis Ephesus   Magnesia
    Athenae &   • Aphrodisias
trae Corinthus Piraeus Miletus Perga
gea • Argos Mylasa CARIA LYCIA
        Delos   Xanthus
        Cnossus   Rhodus
CRETE

SEA

Cyrene

CYRENAICA

Panticapaeum
BLACK SEA

Amastris
Cyzicus • Nicaea   Bogazkoy
PAPHLAGONIA
PONTUS   • Comana
        Sinope
Trapezus (Trebizond)

ARMENIA

CAPPADOCIA Samosata
Pessinus Comana • Nimrud Dagh
GALATIA • Tyana • Edessa MESOPOTAMIA
PHRYGIA CILICIA Carchemish • Hierapolis-Bambyce
• Çatal Hüyük • Tarsus • Doliche (Duluk)
Seleucia • Antiochia   • Dura-Europos (Salahiye)
        Apamea   Chalcis
        Orontes Emesa (Homs) SYRIA
Citium Orthosia Laodicea • Palmyra
       Paphos • Baalbek-Heliopolis
       Byblus • Damascus
CYPRUS Berytus• Sidon
PHOENICIA Tyrus • Bostra
       Caesarea
PALAESTINA • Hierosolyma
       • Ascalon (Ashkelon)
       Gaza

Alexandria • Naucratis • Pelusium ARABIA
           Heliopolis   PETRAEA
LIBYA
    Memphis

Nile

Antaeopolis

Nag Hammadi • Coptos
    Thebes
AEGYPTUS

Elephantine • Philae
       • Syene

PARTHIA

PERSIA

Tigris

CHALDAEA

ARABIA DESERTA

ARABIA FELIX

RED SEA

Introduction

W
HEN, at the corner of a busy shopping street in the heart of
Paris, one comes across several shaven-headed men, shaking their belled tambourines, their filmy pinkish robes
contrasting with the commonplace of urban life as if they were
apparitions from another planet, one experiences something of the
impact that must have been made on diehard Romans by the worshippers of the Egyptian Isis, parading to the sounds of sistra, heads
bare to the sun, in the immaculate whiteness of their linen garments,
or the eunuchs of Cybele, dancing to the harsh and doleful noise of
the Phrygian *aulos*. When the building of a mosque arouses the
reactions of a district or township, it brings to mind the destruction of
the first Isiac chapels which had been established near the Capitol at
the instigation of slaves or freedmen of Alexandrian origin, even
though the historical and social traditions are completely different.
Nowadays, the proliferation of sects which are often foreign, mystical
and (or) fanatical, the ill-defined success of occultism and fringe
attachments and the noisy and provocative fervour of followers of
Krishna, irresistibly recall the multicoloured spectacle presented by
the cosmopolitanism and religious diversity of the Rome of the Severi,
in the third century AD. The situation alternately hidden from and
revealed to us by the great cities of western Europe is not fundamentally foreign to the subject of this book.

Whether speaking of antiquity or modern, contemporary times, one
must describe and analyse civilizations or traditions not (or not only)
by themselves, in isolation from one another, but in their historical
relationships of conflict, osmosis or symbiosis.

The Mediterranean basin has always been, and still remains, a
favoured point of contact between the civilizations of three continents,
but also (and correspondingly) of clashes between heterogeneous
traditions. Great civilizations often result from the meeting of several

traditions which have fused to emerge as richer syntheses in which the originality of the component elements is not immediately or necessarily obliterated. Assimilation does not take place in one direction only, despite the external appearance of language, law or culture. When the term 'Romanization' is used about Gaul or Africa, the word is misleading and in fact concerns only a linguistic, administrative and political facade. Anyone who journeys through the sites of the ancient 'Roman' world gets the feeling of a civilization that is uniform in the architecture, amenities and structure of its towns, (with their baths, temples, theatres and amphitheatres, the arrangement and settings of daily life, the imagery of the gods and classical mythology), and which is omnipresent and almost trivialized by a repetitive art. But a closer look at the layout of sanctuaries, their cultic furnishings, the introduction and local adaptation of civic or religious monuments, often reveals the vitality of the indigenous heritage. This is even more true in the provinces of the East, where the Greek language and Hellenistic architecture convey a range of varying beliefs. The centuries-old dialogue of 'cultures' which meet, or even confront one another, as individuals and societies, gives rise to fusions in which the dominant characteristic is merely a manner of speaking. Greek civilization was a daughter of the East, as Roman civilization was the product of Greek education:

> Graecia capta ferum victorem cepit et artes intulit agresti Latio
> (Horace, Epistles, II, 1, 156–7)

'Defeated Greece conquered her fierce victor and brought the arts to rustic Latium.' Later, when conquering the rest of the East, Rome was to fall under its spell.

But that same Greece which had polished the rough edges of the Latin peasant would nevertheless bear the mark of the victor, as Greek architecture and sculpture of the imperial period bear witness, to say nothing of the literature, notably of Plutarch, who adopted almost the soul and style of a Roman by dint of keeping company with the sons of the She-wolf ... By serving to express Roman ideas and values, Greek art became partly Romanized – or rather, that is how a true Roman art was created and given its form. Here as elsewhere there was interaction and reciprocity. In Gaul itself, to take an example which is closely connected with French national roots, the representation of deities and of Celtic or pre-Celtic myths benefited from Graeco-Roman art. But this expression in the plastic arts could not be achieved without repercussions on the authenticity of the indigenous world of the imaginary, which nevertheless remained present, lively and vigorous in content as well as in form.

The eastern religions which spread through the ancient Mediterranean world pose similar problems and call for the same type of examination.

Terminology

Since the work of Franz Cumont,[1] the term 'Oriental religions' has been understood to mean the Egyptian, Syrian and Anatolian cults whose spread in Rome and the Roman West is borne out by archaeology, epigraphy and literary tradition. Besides Isis and Serapis, Cybele and Attis, Adonis and Atargatis, the Baals of Heliopolis, Damascus and Doliche, Cumont also took account of a Greek god (in an appendix on the mysteries of Bacchus), but one whose Thracio-Phrygian ancestry linked him to the East and whose initiatory ritual was structured later in Asia Minor or Ptolemaic Egypt in a period when Levantine cults were beginning to seduce the Hellenic world. Christianity and Judaism were naturally omitted, as only *Oriental Religions in Roman Paganism* were being surveyed. On the other hand, certain aspects of magic and astrology, whose Egyptian or Babylonian ancestry we know, were the subject of a substantial and significant chapter in this justly celebrated book.

The expression 'Oriental religions' passed into the language, and M.J. Vermaseren definitively established it in the title of a collection founded to promote research in this field.[2] Apart from implying a limitation in being applied only to pagan cults, it contains at least two ambiguities.

It supposes, in fact, or leads one to suppose that these religions were imported just as they were and that they remained purely eastern in a western milieu. Moreover, this all-embracing terminology tends to place these cults in a fairly homogeneous category of mystery liturgies inspired by the same ultimate goal, as 'salvation religions' which would thus have responded in the consciousness and sensibilities of the Graeco-Roman world to the same appeals, the same deep needs, as Christianity or its heterodox variants.

The eastern gods did not all arrive together at the same time, carried by a great wave that is easily datable and historically determinable. The times, conditions and means of their migrations largely elude us. But we know that some of them had reached the ports of Africa Minor (or the 'Maghreb'), Sicily, Spain and southern Gaul before the Roman conquest. Others did not become implanted in the West until the second and third centuries AD. Some made their way slowly, others came on the scene officially and triumphantly, helped by a crisis or thanks to an emperor. Some, like Melqart of Tyre, had gained a foothold in Gades (Cadiz) several centuries before Christ, and perhaps even in Rome, under the name of Hercules, in the Forum Boarium. Phoenician and Carthaginian traders prepared the way for later expansion, as did the Greek sailors and colonists who came from Asia Minor. When they founded Massalia, the Phocaeans installed near the Rhône delta an Artemis related to the Anatolian Mothers, and Strabo (*Geography*, IV, 1, 5p, 190C) informs us that the idol of Diana on the Aventine in Rome resembled that of the Massaliots. This hill dominating the Forum Boarium doubtless witnessed the arrival at the Tiber port of goddesses of love from afar. That is no reason for supposing that Cybele landed 'with the first Etruscan vessel' . . . some six centuries before her official reception in the temple of Victory on the Palatine . . . '³ Astarte had worshippers at very early times in Punic Africa and Sicily, notably where she would assume the name of Venus on Mount Eryx. The inscribed gold tablets of Pyrgi have revealed that around 500 BC the Etruscan king of Caere identified in Astarte the deity *Uni*-Juno.[4] Where the Greeks supplanted the Phoenicians and Carthaginians, their Herakles, a civilizing and colonizing god, quite naturally replaced Melqart, but this nominal Hellenization did not totally annihilate the personality of the Semitic god. A whole process of settlement and interpenetration, of which we know little, was the prelude to the great religious invasions of the Roman era. These early contaminations obviously altered the character of the immigrant deities.

To start with, purely geographical reasons explain a preliminary Hellenization of several eastern cults. Greece's natural and necessary relations with Asia Minor allowed Cybele a very early introduction into the Peloponnese, where effigies of the Mother with the lion cub testify to her presence even in the sixth century BC. The Syrian Adonis inspired Sappho of Lesbos to moving ritual lamentations (if the verses are really hers), and Astarte's lover even gave his name to a catalectic dactylic dimeter, henceforward known as *versus Adonicus*. The Egyptian gods were familiar to Greek travellers and philosophers well before they were known to the Romans. In the classical period, the Thracio-Phrygian Sabazius had his frenzied worshippers and nocturnal mysteries in Athens.

Later, the conquest of the East by Alexander, then of the Mediterranean world by Rome, brought about other contacts, other exchanges, other inflows and outflows producing crises that encouraged the renewal of national religions, in differing forms, in both East and West. Seeking first to dominate part of the seas, in the Aegean or Magna Graecia, the Ptolemies of Egypt contributed to the peregrina-tions of Nilotic deities, but ones which were vastly different from those which had travelled several centuries earlier with the cargoes of Phoenician or Greek navigators. The mobile and very disparate populations of the Hellenistic world – mercenaries, adventurers, traders, wandering philosophers and orators, businessmen and exiles – would carry with them their hopes, hallowed by a variety of gods, in all directions. The masses of slaves originally from Egypt, Syria and Asia Minor, who were sold at Delos and taken to Italy, would in their turn import something of their beliefs to the West, as would the Cilician pirates captured by Pompey in 67 BC.

Later still, in the imperial era, not only Alexandrians, Anatolians and Levantines of all classes came seeking to make their fortune in Rome and the ports, but Roman officials and legionaries, won over to the cults of regions where they had served, or to the gods venerated by their companions in arms, strengthened the movement. The 'Pax Romana' which the Fathers of the Church were to hail in retrospect as providential for the expansion of Christianity, was favourable to the dialogue and mutual intercourse of polytheisms. The intermingling of men and attitudes, representations and ideas, produced – with differing degrees of intensity depending on circumstances – an extraordinary ferment throughout two or three centuries.

This brew and ferment could not fail (any more than earlier sedimentary deposits) to have a resulting impact on the nature of the imported gods. When Cybele reached the banks of the Tiber at the end of the second Punic War, and Isis landed less than a century later at Pozzuoli, their forms of worship did not arrive in the pure and raw state of their country of origin. They had to a greater or lesser extent undergone the effects of Hellenic filtration, both in their imagery and the form of their liturgy, even in the very structure of their initiatory ceremonies (if, that is, Isiacism had already taken the form of a mystery cult).

The mysteries of Eleusis, which alone held firm in the civic and religious revolution of minds in the time of the Diadochi,[5] exerted the influence of their universal prestige on the founders of initiatory sects, whether Dionysiac, Isiac or Mother-worshipping. A priest of Eleusis, the Eumolpid Timotheus, was consulted as an expert by Ptolemy I, when this king of Egypt instituted the worship of Serapis in his country. The same Timotheus wrote a work on the myth and religion of Cybele, who was readily identified with Demeter, the patron goddess of the Eleusinian initiations.

In Asia Minor, Greek-speaking rulers such as Mithridates VI Eupator, who was inspired by the Greek hero Perseus, and 'Hellenized' magi, believers of ancient Iranian origin who were faithful to certain ancestral representations but congenitally in contact with Greek civilization, pioneered the *interpretatio Graeca* of the 'Persian' Mithras. Antiochus I of Commagene, who claimed a double ancestry, Iranian and Macedonian, identified Mithras with Helios, Hermes and Apollo. Some generations later, Philo of Byblos, claiming to translate a book of Sanchuniathon, explained the theogony of the Phoenicians by giving their gods Greek equivalents. That is broadly what had been done about 500 years earlier by the great Herodotus, father of history and comparative religion.

Far from jealously guarding the secrets of their local traditions, indigenous priesthoods were eager to emphasize in Greek the prestige of their antiquity by a sort of literary advertising. Were the books attributed to the Babylonian Berosus, priest of Belus, and to the Egyptian Manetho of Heliopolis, forgeries? At all events, they were the work of Hellenized Orientals. Other apocryphal writings gave a flavour of sanctity to Greek astrology and the mysterious *aura* of Egyptian exoticism, such as the work of the alleged pharaoh Nechepso with whom the (no less allegedly) famous Petosiris[6] is said to have collaborated. As we know, the Hellenes had readily and for a long time laid claim to the knowledge and wisdom of the 'barbarians'. Around 300 BC, Hecataeus of Abdera ascribed to Orpheus the importation into Greece of Egyptian beliefs concerning the Underworld.

In the Roman era the priests of Syrian sanctuaries who informed and guided visitors gave the backing of their priestly authority to this *interpretatio Graeca*. In return, the Greeks gave astrological legitimacy to the myth of Derketo-Atargatis by placing the zodiacal fish (*Pisces*) among the stars. In the story of the gods assuming the appearance of animals to escape Typhon, they also justified the theriomorphism of the Egyptian pantheon which alternately aroused the indignation or mirth of the philosophers. All this labour of adaptation and contamination had extensions elsewhere. It was accompanied by an acclimatization to western surroundings every time that Easterners who settled in Piraeus, Delos, Sicily and Campania founded a line and grafted their devotions on to a Hellenic main stem or in a Hellenic environment.

The consequences and tangible evidence of this Hellenization are revealed in the language and images relating to the representations of the divinities themselves; that is, at a deeper level than that of occasional translations or transcriptions. The hymns to Cybele were chanted in Greek, as were those to Isis, all of whose cult names remained Greek. The festivals in the Isiac liturgical year had Greek names. Similarly, the terminology of the initiatory hierarchy in the mysteries of Mithras was Greek. Certainly, at that time Greek played the role – now filled by English – of an international language: so it was also the liturgical language of the first Christians. Thus the common ground of all cults was the Greek language. Similarly, the iconography of the eastern religions was Greek. In paintings and sculptures Isis bears the stamp of Greek art, like the images of the Phrygian Great Mother and her consort Attis. Serapis was the creation of the Greek sculptor Bryaxis. The bull-slaying Mithras was represented by adapting the Greek model of the sacrificing Victory which decorated the balustrade of Athena Nike on the Acropolis.

To be more precise, rather than 'Oriental religions' one should speak of religions of eastern *origin*, or of *Graeco-Oriental* religions, which had been coated, or even penetrated, by a Hellenic veneer, sometimes for two or three centuries before their arrival in the Latin West. In the case of the Egyptian gods, several waves of migration had successively and variously covered the first layers of religious transplantation. Other gods, like Elagabal or Jupiter *Dolichenus*, who were later comers, did not take lasting root but reinforced what appears to us as a tidal wave in the period of the Severi. This very relative orientalization of the Roman Empire around the 200s was merely a confluence of the currents which crossed the Mediterranean world, and had done so for a long time, as the result of a series of accumulations and syncretisms which transformed the 'Oriental' religions by detaching them from their roots, as people change when they leave their own country.

Typology

The overall designation 'Oriental religions' for a phenomenon that is complex and diversified (in space as well as time) always carries the risk of implicitly simplifying their nature and range, reducing the aspects of the various cults to an abstract typology, or even one that is unhistorical. In fact, from the time of Cumont (and in this regard as in so many others this book pays tribute to the master) there has been a tendency to take 'Oriental religions' *en bloc* and to consider them as species of the same genus: that of religions with 'mysteries' which, proceeding from nature- or animal-worshipping cults that were originally fairly rudimentary, evolved towards a spirituality that was variously shaded according to ambiance or individuals, but which generally exhibit an underlying doctrine of the soul freed after death from bodily ties and promoted henceforth to a happy celestial eternity.[7]

The ever-intriguing mirage of pharaonic Egypt and the East, and of Asiatic literature and wisdom, may have contributed in modern times to the idealization so brilliantly formulated by Cumont. The ambivalences of 'mystical' Frenchmen have also, to a certain extent, sometimes distorted the picture one has of the initiations. In the imagination of cultured Europeans, such as Nerval, and Villiers de l'Isle-Adam or Merejowsky, the *Golden Ass* and the *Magic Flute* continue to colour their vision of the ancient mysteries. A certain confusion tends to haunt Romantic imaginations, even those fed on classical studies. Thus in the brilliant reconstruction of his *Memoirs*, the emperor Hadrian recalls the bloody baptism of the Mother-cult taurobolium in the belief that he is recounting the memory (in any case concocted) of an initiation into the mysteries of Mithras.[8]

It has to be said that Graeco-Roman literary tradition – the Neoplatonist philosophers and the Fathers of the Church bear a large share of responsibility on this point – inclined historians to apply in retrospect a uniformity to the rituals and theologies. The solar theosynscrasy of Macrobius in his *Saturnalia* gives the impression that all pagan cults, whether properly Roman or Syrian, Phrygian or Egyptian, have the same significance and the same finality. But he was writing in the early fifth century AD!

However, the idea of forming a distinct category of cults of eastern origin separately in order to attack them jointly goes back to Firmicus Maternus, a fourth-century Christian polemicist, freshly converted after having been a Neoplatonist and astrologer. In his *Error of Profane Religions*, he accuses the Egyptians of worshipping water, the Phrygians earth, the Syrio-Phoenicians air, and the Persians fire: in other words, Isis and Osiris, Cybele, Tanit-Astarte and Mithras. This geotheology of the four elements which already systematizes a sort of typology of the eastern cults visibly impressed Cumont. It is revealing that he should write on this subject: 'In the common danger threatening them, formerly rival cults . . . looked on one another as divisions of the same church, whose clergies formed, if I dare say so, the congregations'.[9] There is nothing to justify speaking of 'the same church' or even 'churches' (whether or not they are similar to one another). But all in all, Firmicus Maternus appears to have inspired a topic for research and publication that has prospered for the past century.

I fear, however, that this way of combining the cults of the Levant for the purposes of argument (as does the author of the *Error of Profane Religions*) has left its mark on modern historians and has sometimes led them to neglect the respective particularities. Isis had her mysteries; but Isiac initiation seemingly had nothing to do with Mithraic initiation, whose planetary hierarchy and ideology had no equivalent in any other 'eastern' religion. The Eleusinian ritual must have served as a model for the Isiac as well as for the Mother-cult mysteries; yet the two liturgies were not alike, as far as we know. The concept of salvation extolled in the caverns of Mithras was as different from the posthumous bliss promised to the worshippers of Isis and Osiris as it was from the 'rebirth' guaranteed by Cybele's bull sacrifice or the eschatology taught by the priests of the Syrian Baals. It is true that in the later period there would be syncretisms and contaminations which the last pagans echoed in literature, but which must not give rise to illusions. The fact that Firmicus Maternus denounces the justification of these cults by a *ratio physica* which relates them all to contemporary solar theology betrays a belated and artificially unifying reconstruction, perhaps elaborated by the school of the Neoplatonist Porphyry. The ceremonial itself of these *profanae religiones* (as Firmicus calls them), which were not all initiatory, differentiated them from one another materially and noticeably enough to make categorical generalizations unacceptable.

Of course Isis and Serapis are seen associated with Juno and Jupiter Dolichenus on this or that figured monument,[10] as if the two couples coincided in the minds of their followers. But in no way can it be inferred that the two cults were interchangeable. When Apuleius recognized in the mythical bride of Osiris, 'queen of the sky', the same fundamental mother-goddess as Artemis of Ephesus, Cybele or the Eleusinian Demeter (*Metamorphoses*, XI, 2 and 5), he was well aware of what positively characterized each one; otherwise he would not have sought all the sacred rites which in another work he boasts of having received (*Apologia*, 55, 8: *Sacrorum pleraque initia in Graecia participavi*). The relationships of these cults with one another – proximity, rivalry, even cohabitation – do not allow us to assimilate one with the other in the same 'vulgate'. There are plenty of epigraphic and literary testimonies to prove that the same men and women participated in several forms of devotion at the same time; but it is also proof that each of these devotions had its specific interest or value, and that a follower of Isis might wish to find other emotions, other revelations, in Mithraic crypts, the pit of the taurobolium or the banquets of Sabazius.

We must compare in order to make distinctions, and distinguish in order to understand. That does not prevent us from perceiving that eastern religions imposed themselves on the West in a whole range of historical, sociological and psychological contexts which all either simultaneously or successively favoured their success. Indeed, these religions satisfied – each in its own way and for a variety of reasons – the more or less conscious aspirations and fairly refined sensibilities of that fluid and very mixed world of the Roman Empire.

Externa superstitio

The Romans talked of religions that were not exactly 'eastern' but 'foreign'. They did not distinguish the East from the West: apparently at least, for in fact the Levantine cults were the only ones involved, because they alone threatened the religious integrity of the *Urbs*. Every ancient city defended its national identity by imposing its gods. In the Hellenistic world, the decline of the city-state upset that fundamental tradition, and Rome in its turn was to feel the effects over several centuries, when it became an empire and its *civitas* reached the dimensions of the universe. But for men like Varro or Cicero, it was sensible to hold fast to the religion of one's country, the official forms of worship. 'Let no one have separate gods, either new or foreign, unless they are officially allowed', wrote Cicero in the *Laws* (II, 19). Varro[11] was indignant that the gods of Alexandria should be revered in Rome: it was a nonsense! Two centuries later, Juvenal had the same xenophobic reaction, nor was he alone in showing this aversion.

But it should not be imputed only to the Romans of Rome, as if they were narrow-minded nationalists. Paradoxically, a Hellenized Syrian such as Lucian of Samosata enjoyed mocking the debasement of Olympus, invaded by immigrant gods: 'This Attis, this Corybas, this Sabazius, where do they all come from? Who is this Mede Mithras, with his *kandys* (Persian garment) and his tiara? He doesn't know a word of Greek . . . And you, dog-faced Egyptian: how can you pretend to divinity? What does this spotted bull from Memphis want with us? . . . ' (*Assembly of the Gods*, 9–10). Elsewhere, Lucian gives us the arrival of an astronaut in the realm of Zeus, in a banqueting hall where Hermes seats him alongside Corybas, Attis and Sabazius, 'resident aliens in heaven and dubious gods' (*Icaromenippus*, 27).

In Rome, *religio* (national and authentic) was readily contrasted with *superstitio* (exotic and suspect). Anything that deviated from the ritual taught by the ancestors and legitimized by tradition smacked of *superstitio*, chiefly the fringe practices of prophecy and occultism, the techniques of mental exaltation, of direct contact with the supernatural and the sacred, where people ventured in times of moral crisis or epidemics, without the mediation of pontiffs, flamines and augurs. Today, as then, one finds in the Roman church the same kind of mistrust towards anything that evades the necessary mediation of the institutional Church. Christianity was a 'depraved superstition' in the view of Pliny the Younger (*Letters*, X, 96, 8), 'disastrous' in the eyes of his historian friend Tacitus (*Annals*, XV, 44, 5). The Christians would not hesitate to turn the same defamatory word against the pagans! By definition, every 'superstition' is irrational in proportion to its dissidence.

The automatic hostility to the *externa superstitio* particularly affected the eastern cults, firstly because their irresistible expansion, like an overflowing wave, created a feeling of dizziness and panic among Romans anxious about their national identity. These devotions were alien, especially to the Roman mentality and temperament. They helped to alter, to adulterate, the attachment to the 'custom of the ancestors' or *mos maiorum*, to perturb spirits and change the nature of sensibilities by making the city of Romulus cosmopolitan. 'Since we have taken into our hearth and home peoples with their disparate rites, their exotic cults or no cult at all [an obvious allusion to the first Christians], this murky horde can be kept in check by fear alone', Tacitus makes an anxious senator say (*Annals*, XIV, 44, 5). When denigrating the Christians, whom he combines with fanatics of other eastern forms of worship, this same Tacitus denounces Rome as the meeting point of every sort of horror, 'where every kind of infamy converges' (*Annals*, XV, 44, 5). This image of a foreign flow or confluence also obsessed Seneca (*Consolation to Helvia*, 6, 2) and Juvenal (*Satires*, III, 62).

The exotic cults deplored by the above-mentioned senator for their penetration into the hearts of the great houses were imported by slaves who had remained faithful to their ancestral religions just as the old Romans claimed to be towards their own gods. But the traditionalists were more seriously worried by the sympathy, the attraction, even the fascination which these cults inspired in the true Romans of Rome. 'Who would dare to drive from his doorstep one whose hand shakes the sonorous sistrum of Pharos? When, before the Mother of the gods, the flute-player sounds his curving horn, who would refuse him alms of a copper coin?' (Ovid, *Letters from the Black Sea*, I, 1, 37ff). Such charity towards the alms-collectors would not have mattered if their liturgies had not impressed the Roman citizens, and chiefly their mothers, wives and daughters. One gets the feeling that, in his famous evocation of the festivals celebrated in honour of Cybele, the Epicurean Lucretius (*On the Nature of Things*, II, 601–32) cannot help a contagious emotion, any more than Tibullus (I, 7) in his Osirian aretalogy. Seneca was distressed to see Isiac prophets, Cybele's eunuchs or the fanatics of Bellona arouse the enthusiasm of curious onlookers (*The Happy Life*, 26, 8).[12] Juvenal had nothing but sarcasm for feminine credulity, victim of a priest who 'wearing the mask of Anubis, secretly derides the lamentations of the populace' (*Satires*, VI, 534).

How, then, are we to explain why, despite a fundamental allergy to the *externa superstitio* and the irrationality of the 'cults that disturb the souls of men', as the Latin jurists[13] maintained, eastern religions won the contest so successfully that in the fourth century AD the last pagans of Rome had integrated them into the national heritage?

The Romanization of Foreign Gods

In the first place it must be remembered that the fierce and haughty nationalism of the Romans did not prevent them from integrating men and gods from outside into the *Urbs*, the first by the freeing of slaves or or the granting of citizenship, the second by consultation of the Sibylline Books or the ritual of the *evocatio*. A college of specialists, whose duty was to preserve the Sibyl's famous oracles which had formerly been purchased by Tarquin the Proud from the prophetess of Apollo, interpreted them (with the agreement of the Senate) to give oracular backing to the adoption of new cults. Fifteen in number from the time of Sulla (whence their title *quindecimviri sacris faciundis*), they had 'naturalized' notably the Greek Asclepius, the Semitic Aphrodite of Mount Eryx and the Phrygian Great Mother. The town that Romulus was said to have populated by way of a handful of stateless people (according to the famous legend of the Capitoline *asylum*) still had the vocation to assimilate heterogeneous elements. That was true both politically and legally. Rooted in a visceral patriotism, the *civitas Romana* would one day be enlarged to world dimensions: '*Urbem fecisti quod prius orbis erat*' – 'You have made a city of what was formerly the universe,' the Gaul Rutilius Namatianus was to proclaim after the sack of Rome by Alaric's Goths (*On his Return*, I, 66).

It was also true from the religious aspect. By giving Latin names to the foreign gods, the *interpretatio Romana* implicitly recognized them and thus contributed to suppressing religious xenophobia while preparing for the future. But the procedure of the *evocatio* went as far as annexing the enemy's gods into the national pantheon. It consisted of gaining their benevolence, charming them in order to entice them and enthrone them in Rome, by means of an almost magic formulary. This happened with the Etruscan *Uni*-Juno from Veii and Tanit-*Caelestis* from Carthage.[14] Even in the *mos maiorum* itself there were thus regulatory and traditional ways of circumventing it. Not all the eastern gods felt the benefit. Most remained on the fringes of divine high society. But in the end they would all enter *Romanitas*.

For the crises spawned by the very expansion of Roman power, and ultimately by the imperial regime which it had made necessary, opened the roads to Romanization for these gods, as for their human compatriots.

Before the end of the second Punic War, which had so gravely tested the morale and nerves of the Roman people, the Senate had to cut its losses. It came to an agreement with the king of Pergamum to send from Pessinus the black stone of Cybele, whose worship was made official in 204 BC. Less than twenty years later the affair of the Bacchanalia erupted, introduced to Rome by a mysterious Greek who had come from Etruria, and then developed thanks to the support and complicity of uprooted Campanians.[15] With the prelude to the political and social disturbances following the third Punic War and the conquest of Greece and Asia, there was a proliferation of sects and trends that were alien to the official doctrine. In 139 BC, the Chaldaeans and other charlatans of eastern astrology had to be expelled from the *Urbs*, then the worshippers of Sabazius, whom the authorities likened to, or who were confused with, the Jews.[16] Four years afterwards, exasperated by the inhumane treatment they received, the masses of Syrian slaves deported to Sicily rose up behind a certain Eunous who invoked the goddess Atargatis.

The civil wars troubled not only the state, but also people's consciences. The rugged Marius, who affected the air of an old peasant-soldier faithful to the values of the rural people, believed in the predictions of a Syrian woman named Martha, who accompanied him everywhere, wearing priestly adornments, and whose slightest instructions he scrupulously observed! His adversary, Sulla, was not to be left out. He called on Mâ-Bellona, a Cappadocian Mother, whom he saw in a dream handing him a thunderbolt to strike his enemies. The 'pastophori' of Isis ascribed the organization of their first Roman fraternity to Sulla. A little later, the rebel Spartacus had his prophetess, whom the Thracian Dionysus put into a trance, as Eunus of Apamea had fired his fellow-slaves in Sicily, and the Cilician pirates called for the aid of Mithras the Invincible in their struggle against Roman imperialism.[17] It is not hard to imagine the fierce energy that religious feeling can breathe into a leader and his followers.

In Rome itself, freedmen of eastern origin played a growing part in the urban plebs who, in 'clubs' or *collegia*, guaranteed political agitators an ideal body of supporters to exploit. They were not content merely to make speeches and applaud; they disrupted elections and assemblies of the people. Armed gangs, really 'tough' professional commandos, controlled and terrorized the streets, freed Catiline's accomplices, restored the Isiac altars banned by the Senate, and blocked the execution of legal orders. Clodius and his *populares* exploited the religious militancy of the Alexandrian slaves. Religion

and politics were mutually involved in the last confused shudders of
the Roman Republic, even though A. Alföldi seems to have over-
interpreted the Egyptian-style symbols of contemporary coinage as
signs of revolutionary propaganda.[18] At all events, the leaders of the
political class made no mistake. They knew how to 'seize the moment'
in order to win over the masses by significant deeds. If we are to
believe Servius, Caesar reintroduced the Bacchic mysteries to the *Urbs*.
After his death, the Triumvirs (who had Cicero murdered) decided in
43 BC officially to erect a temple to Isis and Serapis. But twelve years
later, passing himself off as the restorer of national values, the same
Octavian who had taken part in the triumviral decision would be
fighting Cleopatra with her Nilotic gods and the 'barking Anubis',
latrator Anubis (Virgil, *Aeneid*, VIII, 698)!

Nevertheless, under the Empire eastern cults continued to benefit
from both the Romanization of the Mediterranean world and the
political crises inherent in the personal power of the *imperatores*.
Augustus and Tiberius repressed the religious expansion that was
taking place at the expense of the ancestral cults. But Antony's great-
grandson, Caligula, had an affection for Egyptian gods. Claudius,
however, favoured Phrygianism. Nero, on the other hand, was interested in the Syrian Goddess and the doctrines of the magi. Otho took
part in Isiac processions, and in the crisis of 69 the Levantine cults
revealed themselves strongly in various ways. Proclaimed in Alexandria, Vespasian received his divine consecration from Serapis. Domitian escaped the massacre on the Capitol in Isiac disguise. Charged
with carrying a message of loyalty to the emperor Galba in Rome,
Titus did not fail to make a pilgrimage to the temple of Venus-Astarte
at Paphus in Cyprus. In October 69, at the Battle of Cremona, the
Syrian soldiers of the IIIrd 'Gallica' legion hailed the rising sun
according to eastern custom.[19] And before the celebration of their
triumph over Judaea, Vespasian and Titus spent the night in the
sanctuary of Isis on the Campus Martius. The Flavians would not
forget how much they owed to the gods of the Nile.

A hundred years later, the assaults of the plague, the Quadi and the
Marcomanni inflicted the first cracks in the Roman Empire, heralding
what E. Renan called the 'end of the ancient world' (the subtitle of his
Marcus Aurelius). The philosopher-emperor resorted to the services of
the Egyptian theurgist Arnouphis and had two lions drowned in the
waters of the Danube, complying with the instructions of a Paph-
lagonian charlatan, Alexander of Abonuteichos, high priest of the
serpent Glycon. With the end of the Antonine dynasty and the
military anarchy that followed, and with the African and Syrian
emperors of the Severan dynasty (193–235), the gods of the armies

recruited in the East were still further entrenched in Rome and on the frontiers, in the social and urban fabric of the *Orbis Romanus*. Sometimes they were even officially imposed owing to the initiative of a legionary legate or an employee in the imperial customs service. In its competition for sovereign power, the army carried a weight that had religious repercussions in all regions where the Empire had a military and administrative presence. It is true that the barbarian incursions, harassing the Rhine and Danube fronts, also sometimes ruined places of worship (the *Mithraea* in Germania for instance) or challenged the faith of the vanquished gods in the person of their worshippers. But the anguish, the general insecurity and feeling of precariousness which silently undermined the Roman world supplied further ammunition to the mystery religions which, while tightening the solidarity of the sect's members, guaranteed them the firm hope of divine protection in this world and the next.

Society and States of Mind

In between the great crises which put the populations of Rome and the Empire to the test in various ways, the facilities and even the joys of the *Pax Romana* were favourable to the slower, more diffuse, but often deeper and more motivated, penetration of the eastern cults. The movement of soldiers and civil servants, their acclimatization to the provinces of the East or West, the mobility of men on official assignments or in search of hefty profits, orators, mendicant preachers and sophists, the dynamism and commercial aggressiveness of Levantine businessmen, were a wonderful stimulus to foreign religions. As a result they very quickly gained a hold on people, to the great despair of men like Seneca or Tacitus, and soon Juvenal. Easterners embedded themselves in the ports, the houses of the wealthy, the antechambers, kitchens and offices of the imperial palace. Everywhere they turned their *savoir-faire* to good account. They went up the valleys to set up stalls and shops near army camps. They opened kinds of dubious 'bars', which were nevertheless frequented by the decadent aristocracy, in the suburbs of Rome.[20] They undertook the type of work that was repugnant to Roman citizens. Moreover, they provoked indignation that they should have acquired wealth and astonishment that their gods were in dangerous rivalry with those of the Capitol . . . Not everything can be explained by the economy. But the activity of men demands, and often advises, the presence of the gods.

Government took a hand in it. The whims of men like Commodus and Caracalla or the loud missionary militancy of Heliogabalus had no truly lasting results, except ultimate rejection. However, other Caesars (for instance, Caligula, Domitian and – despite what the *Augustan History* says[21] – Hadrian) gave a more effective welcome to the Alexandrian deities, whose festivals would eventually be inscribed in the official calendar of the liturgical year. But the anonymous mass of individuals receptive to the attractions of these exotic forms of worship is of more importance to us, even though the secrets of their souls remain forever inaccessible. What reasons did they have for rallying to religions so deeply alien to their national and family traditions?

Over three centuries, in differing historical circumstances but with the same moral consequences, Roman society experienced the same effects, and the same intellectual revolution, as Greek society did when the conquests of Alexander and the great monarchies that came after him set the seal on the decline of the city-state. As we know, the Greek city clamped the individual in an iron girdle that dominated his existence and beliefs. The gods of the defeated and annexed towns did not defend them. In the immense and shifting realms of the Diadochi, the individual was thus set free, but abandoned to his own devices and therefore bewildered. Within this troubled and drifting world, people travelled about, emigrated, became expatriates. The horizon opened up and widened further to exotic civilizations, those eastern cults which, not being bound up with defunct or decadent regimes, lost nothing of their vitality even when their allegiance was pledged to temple-states like Hierapolis-Bambyce, Comana or Pessinus. Henceforward people felt all the less attached to their local gods because philosophical criticism – Epicureanism, Euhemerism, the probabilism of the Neo-academicians, scepticism and Pyrrhonism – relativized traditional piety. Only the mysteries of Eleusis preserved their prestige intact, because they already enjoyed a supranational sphere of influence and opened a perspective on the beyond. But they were limited in both time and space, immovable and strictly periodic. When the condition of a citizen in this or that city lost, or almost lost, a large part of its importance, the individual sought another status, by way of his integration in another more durable city, in a society hallowed by the gods and initiation. It is a well-known phenomenon, recognized by sociologists: when a community becomes debased and disappears, the members of the 'diaspora' create new bonds for themselves in another place or another way.

The multiplication of communities with secret doctrines, chiefly Dionysian to begin with, satisfied the concern of migrants who wanted to rediscover a family, an identity, on the fringes of a disintegrating society. Sailors, mercenaries, roving intellectuals, stateless philosophers who wished to be so (the wise man is a 'stranger' everywhere, according to Aristippus of Cyrene[22]) needed universal gods who would be omnipresent and, if they were pious, cults that they could practise in the ports where they landed and when they stayed there, at any time of the year. Eastern religions had their sacred sites and their specific local forms of worship, but the Greeks and Hellenized Easterners knew how to transport and adapt them, and make their diffusion and celebration more flexible in order to meet the aspirations of all these uprooted people.

The same phenomenon was repeated and amplified in the imperial Roman era. The vast majority of Roman citizens did not live in Rome, were not ethnically or physically linked with Rome, took no part in the affairs of the city, above all from the time when *civitas* was conferred on all the Italians, then on the inhabitants of Cisalpine Gaul, followed by numerous Transalpine Gauls, Greeks and Africans. The *Urbs* became the *Orbis*.[23] Rome was the great political and legal fatherland, cosmopolitan and generous, but it was no longer a 'city' properly speaking: it was an idea. The imperial regime released the ordinary citizens from their political obligations. They decided nothing, no longer voted (since Tiberius) for the election of magistrates, no longer deliberated on the affairs of the *Urbs*. This void was favourable to the formation of marginal groups. Where the individual no longer plays an active, direct and personal part in the running of the city, he inevitably loses interest and seeks responsibilities elsewhere, in other solidarities, other 'fraternities'. Religious micro-societies and 'mystery' sects assure him of a kind of reintegration and existence, when traditional frameworks and institutional authorities are in decline or failing in their mission.

Even those with official, administrative responsibility, in the emperor's service (civil servants, officers, soldiers transferred to distant postings, the borders of the Sahara, Scotland or the banks of the Rhine), needed transportable gods, mobile or mobilizable, cosmic and omnipotent, who could journey beyond the indigenous and localized horizon of the classical religions. They needed cults in which they knew one another and met together to share the same ideal, the same sense of the world and life, the same bread. There is no strong grouping without the solidarity of the sacred and secret[24] which preserves the singularity of the brotherhood, its moral cohesion and its loyalty.

The urbanization of the Roman world helped to cut the individual off from his roots and to demoralize him. Relatively speaking, the tragedy of housing schemes is not peculiar to the twentieth century. Bread and circuses did not guarantee personal happiness or security.

In Rome, as in Ostia, residential property reached four or five storeys.[25] Juvenal's *Satires* convey a feeling of dread and oppression. Tertullian compares the 'skyscraper' of Felicula to the interlocking spheres of the world imagined by the Valentinian Gnostics.[26] In terms of cosmological phantasmagoria, this vision of a dizzying pile transposes something of the anguish that urban concentration aroused in those theosophers. In the Rome that Athenaeus of Naucratis believed he was extolling when he called it *Uranopolis* (universe-town),[27] many people suffered from loneliness and anonymity. In the shadows of the Mithraic crypts or Egyptian sanctuaries they found the comfort of the shared meal and the supernatural. The success of Gnostic sects in Rome, Lyon, Carthage and Alexandria may be partly explained by the same reasons. The theme of the 'Stranger' is typical and significant in the Gnosis, whether it be of the soul or god.[28] For the Gnostic, existence is conceived as an exile. That was the reality experienced by many in the Roman Empire.

Attraction and Efficacy of the Liturgies

In a blasé and weary world, eastern religions also offered the attraction of strong feelings and emotions. Their liturgies excited and aroused the senses of those who were henceforth left cold by the strictly formalist worship of the Roman gods. In sound alone, the wild and frenzied rhythms of the Egyptian dances (plate 1), the harsh and strident noise of the Isiac sistra, the hoarse cries of the priests of Atargatis or Bellona, the timbrels of the galli and the insistent tones of their oboes left no one indifferent. In contrast, this sonorous exoticism was not a characteristic of Mithraic ceremonies; but beneath the vault of the Persian caverns, the hymns sung in chorus, like those of which a few lines may be deciphered under the church of Santa Prisca on the Aventine, must have resounded with a moving beauty.

There were also more colour and visual contrasts in the public or secret celebrations of these foreign religions than in Roman ceremonial. The dazzling whiteness of the linen tunics or the black robes of the priests in the Isiac processions, the saffron-yellow or purple-striped robes worn by the itinerant clergy of the Syrian Goddess, the sumptuous and symbolic garments of the Mithraic hierarchy left an undying memory on spectators and participants.

In the crypts of the 'invincible' god, the play of colours (chiefly purples and gold) was emphasized by the effects of light and shade. Nocturnal liturgies, mystical evenings and initiations into the mysteries of the next world led to quite hallucinatory performances that

Plate 1 Relief from Aricia (Rome, Museo delle Terme; photo. Inst. All. de Roma)

left an indelible mark on people's souls. After hours of prostration and lamentation in the dark, the lighting of lamps or torches gave the believers the impression of being born into a new life.

These cults also had a sense of festival. The Isiac opening of the sailing season in March gave rise to a sort of carnival. A colourfully dressed masquerade marked the 'Hilaria' (or 'joys') of 25 March in honour of Attis. The masks intrigued the eyes of curious spectators by their unusual theriomorphy, like that of the jackal-headed Anubis in Egyptian ritual. In the Mithraic feasts, the 'Ravens' and the 'Lions' sometimes wore heads appropriate to their degree. Such disguises altered the way in which the faithful viewed their humanity. Other details underlined and displayed adherence to an order, the concern to differentiate oneself from the secular world. If the Isiac pastophori had shaven heads, in contrast the galli of Cybele and fanatics of Bellona let their hair grow like women (as did the priests of Atargatis). Others were branded or tattooed.

The painted or sculpted decor of the sanctuaries, the sacred menagerie of the Egyptian temples, their statues of monkeys, crocodiles of marble and sphinxes of dark granite, the star-spangled firmament in the Mithraic caverns, their unusual idols, notably the lion-headed god spitting fire (sometimes in reality) held a fascination for the neophytes. On this theme St Jerome speaks of 'monstrous statues', *portentuosa simulacra* (*Letters*, 107, 2). Entering a Greek or Roman temple of the classical tradition did not produce the same religious frisson. The realm of imagination of the eastern cults took one into another world, and that special emotion was experienced within the sacred building, rather than in public before the temple, as was the case in the official Roman rite. In this respect, O. Spengler was not wrong to comment (in *The Decline of the West*) on 'the sensation of the crypt'.

But outside the sanctuaries, the display of gestural rites and the noisy processions went beyond the level of the senses or of mere spectacle. In the public rituals of Isiacism and Phrygianism, the pathos had a direct, if not lasting and profound, impact on the crowd, and not only on the initiates. The evocation of the death of Attis or Osiris (in March and November), the funeral lamentations followed by an explosion of joy celebrating the rediscovery, awakening or resurrection of the suffering gods struck the attendant crowds with collective contagion. The very violence of Cybele's galli, the priests of Bellona or the Syrian Goddess slashing their arms after a stunning sabre dance, the spurting of hot blood, the castration of candidates for consecration to the Mother-worshipping cult may certainly have caused some revulsion among the uninitiated. But that violence itself also gave rise to irresistible vocations.

In some initiations, the testing of candidates for initiation (mystae) by fear, the knife, fire and bloodshed actually strengthened their resolve – far from putting them off or discouraging them. Sacrificing oneself (and not animal victims), feeling a wrong that needed personal expiation, even a sort of confession of sins, graven in stone in some Lydian inscriptions, were deeply alien to the inventions of Roman ritualism, which was henceforth unsuited to the way in which attitudes of mind were evolving. Many Romans did not understand why the followers of Osiris bruised their chests with increasingly violent blows from pine cones, or why those of the Anatolian Mothers slashed their flesh. But when Ovid (*Letters from the Black Sea*, I, 1, 51ff) witnessed a man prostrating himself at the foot of Isiac altars, confessing aloud that he had offended the goddess, or a blind man shouting in the streets that he had thoroughly deserved to lose his sight because of his impiety, the poet was visibly impressed. Juvenal mocks a female devotee who, naked and shuddering, trailed on her bleeding knees on the Campus Martius (round the temple of Isis) after plunging into the icy waters of the Tiber (*Satires*, VI, 522ff). But the cult of the gods to whom he was so attached aroused no such physical heroism. Four centuries earlier, the Athenian comedy writer Menander seemed not insensitive to the self-inflicted penances of a Syrian who had partaken of fish: exhibiting the swellings on his body, chastized by Atargatis, he publicly implored the goddess's pardon (Porphyry, *Abstinence*, IV, 15).

Besides the rhythms (which have been likened to the success of 'negro' music after the Great War), the sounds, colours and sufferings, nearly all the oriental liturgies, although in different forms, possessed the effectiveness that was bound up with the daily, weekly or seasonal regularity of their offices. This was particularly true of the Isiac cult, which was ruled by a precise timetable personified and controlled by the *horologos*. The morning opening of the temple, followed by worship, hymns, sacrifices, and the kind of 'vespers' sung before closing, held the believer spellbound, just as among the Mithraists, Sabaziasts and devotees of Jupiter Dolichenus communal repasts strengthened mutual bonds and adherence to the service of the god. In the Egyptian, Phrygian and Syrian sanctuaries, the steadiness of a full-time clergy guaranteed the constancy of the *ordo*. In the caverns of the Persian cult, priestly functions were carried out by laymen who at the same time had various occupations in the 'profane' world; but the time and trouble they devoted to the cult of Mithras were not occasional like the priesthoods of official Roman religion. All these religions had their 'permanent' staff.

Without assuming the responsibilities of a cleric properly speaking, practising followers were closely associated with the priestly ministry. In the Egyptian cult, kinds of hostelries or monastic annexes allowed the faithful to take retreats and increase their attendance at services. The pastophori and anubophori formed a sort of 'third order', bound by strict obligations and a specific way of life. The rigours of abstinence and continence, rules regarding clothing, the precision and assiduousness demanded by eastern religions thus kept their adepts in a state of psychological tension favourable to proselytism and conversions. These cults met a need for the absolute.

The devout follower was joined intimately and intensely with the deity through the mortification of the flesh and the sorrows endured by the believers, the kind of perpetual adorations of the Isiac neophyte, as mentioned by Apuleius,[29] the emotional participation in the 'passions' of Attis or Osiris, or the militant ardour maintained by the example of the bull-slaying god which was present everywhere in Mithraic crypts. An uncrossable frontier had formerly separated the immortal and happy Olympian gods from humankind, which was obviously mortal and unhappy. But Dionysus, Attis and Osiris themselves had undergone mutilation, suffering and death; and they had triumphed over it. For mortals that was a reason to hope, all the more so because the gods and goddesses of the East let men share in their deeds by receiving them into their holy 'militia' (Apuleius, *Metamorphoses*, XI, 15, 5), personally adopting them as individuals. They often had the epithet *epekooi*, meaning that they listened attentively and answered prayers. Their solicitude matched their demands. They were close to their devotees. They broke down the barriers of a very ancient segregation between heaven and earth.

Theo-cosmologies

A religion is successful only if it can monopolize the individual totally: body and soul, mind and senses. If the impoverishment, indigence or inanity of the liturgy engender indifference, divorce between knowledge and religion undermines or relativizes belief. In order to be stimulating and full of dynamism, a faith must provide an all-embracing explanation of man, the world and life.

The Roman gods had strictly defined attributes, and people called upon them according to their respective abilities.[30] This splitting-up of the divine powers legitimized a precise, specific and finicky ritualism which avoided a frenzy for the supernatural but also correspondingly excluded any cosmic view, any response to intellectual queries, especially from the time when in the second century BC Greek philosophy arrived to shake up the calmly legal attitude of the Roman pontiffs. So in the mind of Cicero (and probably many others), a fundamental agnosticism dwelt side by side with a practical pietism, respectful of civic tradition. The juxtaposition of the *numina* did not constitute a rational and coherent theology. Even at the beginning it involved no kind of hierarchy. It made nothing clear about the finality of the universe or the fate of the soul after death. The same applied, in any case, to the other cults of the Roman West.

We thus find that the Iberian, Celtic, Germanic, African and Latin gods had scarcely any influence in the Mediterranean world. Only Janus played a role in Roman colonies, as mythical king of ancient Italy and thanks to the Calends of January, which remained a popular festival in both the East and the West.[31] Certainly, Epona, the Gallic goddess of horses, was known and honoured in Cisalpine Gaul, Transylvania and Rome itself, but only among the horsemen or circus charioteers, because of either her worshippers' ethnic origins or their professional activities: there is no sign that this divine patroness of stables, any more than the mother-goddesses of German or Danubian horsemen, reached all strata of urban and Romanized society, as did Isis and Mithras. Nor is there any evidence that specifically Roman gods imposed themselves as such in the East. The opposite happened. Apart from the official or festive demonstrations under the patronage of provincial assemblies and governors, the cult of the goddess Roma made no deep impact. That of the emperors succeeded for a while only because it had Graeco-Oriental roots. It emerged, moreover, from initiatives that had come from Asia Minor. In the colonies Jupiter Best and Greatest was identified, as at Baalbek-Heliopolis, with the indigenous god of cosmic sovereignty.[32] The Zeus of Doliche, too, was decked out with the superlatives of Jupiter Capitolinus. But in both iconography and forms of worship the Syrian Baals eclipsed the Latin god.

The superiority of the East and Graeco-oriental religions was connected first of all with their rich and powerful clergy, who had thousands of years of theological tradition behind them, a theology intimately bound up with a cosmology which Greek philosophy and astrology often helped to legitimize, even to rationalize. Different schools of intellectual Hellenism (notably Stoicism and Neoplatonism) thus gave a kind of backing to the cults of Levantine origin, even though the Greeks inevitably had a tendency to distort the significance of the religions in which they took an interest. In Syrian and

Egyptian temples, fairly complex theogonies and cosmogonies were taught, which were used to explain the peculiarities of divine imagery or indigenous ritual. The Hellenic philosophers at the time marvelled at these symbolic doctrines and the myths that were so intriguing to decode: for instance, Plutarch (in his treatise on *Isis and Osiris*) or Porphyry (in his book on *Statues*). The traditionalism of the eastern cults mingled with a remarkable faculty for adaptation to the great ideological currents and to the science of their time. Now, the last word in science in the imperial Roman era was astrology, that total and totalitarian explanation of the fate of beings in a world dominated by the movement of the planets, and notably the sun, in the zodiac. Solar theology was linked to astrology to give cults as diverse as that of Jupiter Heliopolitanus, Isiacism, Phrygianism and Mithraism a semblance of cosmic coherence which gave the individual an account of his place in the world and the functioning of the universe.

Thus linked with the phases of the sun's annual revolution, the myths of emasculated Attis, dismembered Osiris, Mithras slaying the bull, Adonis dead and lamented by Astarte, assumed the guise of eternal truths. The seasonal liturgies illustrated and ritually confirmed this correspondence. We know the importance of the equinoxes and solstices to the Mithraic cult. We also know the cosmic dimension conferred on the sacrifice of the bull by the planets or signs of the zodiac represented in the arc of a circle above or around the Bull-slayer.[33] Each placed under the tutelage of a star, worshippers of the 'invincible' god knew that the Mithraic story of salvation coincided with celestial order. The initiates of Isis, too, knew that the goddess commanded the course of the planets and that her power would prevail if necessary over that of the constellations. Jupiter Heliopolitanus wore stars on his girdled breast. Sabazius amassed symbols and attributes attesting to this sovereign power.

Everywhere these gods were the absolute masters of the animal, vegetable and sidereal world. Their supremacy supernaturally transposed the imperial monarchy reigning here in the inhabited world, the Oikoumenè, just as their supranationality matched the heterogeneous universality of the *Orbis Romanus*. Their worship accorded not only with a theocosmology appropriate to the spirit of the time, but also with the state of the world and society.

Soteriology

A religion that helps man to understand the world, and himself in the world, would not be enough for his uneasy conscience unless it guaranteed him divine protection in return for unswerving obedience to the celestial will. Prayers were said to gods to obtain their power and favour, or at least so as not to suffer the effects of their anger. That is what the Greeks and Romans did.

But the powers of the Greek, and above all Roman, gods were often limited both in scope and in function. In rural settings, in the case of a nature-worshipping cult, a sanctuary connected with a spring or a hilltop, a tree or a rock, as in artisanal circles, in the case of gods who were patrons of the work of carpenters or blacksmiths for example, such specialization presented no challenge to religious feeling. But for a mixed and roaming population of slaves or imperial freedmen, civil servants, legionaries, auxiliary cavalrymen frequently being transferred, even technicians (architects, surveyors, army doctors) required here and there, or even *negotiatores*, travelling philosophers and lecturers, cults and gods were needed whose power extended beyond such a narrow setting. Certainly, from preference traders honoured Hermes or Mercury, doctors Asclepius, and soldiers Mars. But one realizes that these gods were at that time becoming cosmopolitan and acquiring a dimension that largely exceeded their original field of power.

Assuredly, too, it is found that when soldiers and officers were sent to Germany or Britain they sought to win over the favours of local gods,[34] sometimes associating them with the gods to whom they remained attached, which was the prelude to some very strange religious grafts.

But many others preferred anyway to call on the omnipotence of Isis, Mithras or Jupiter Dolichenus. The risks and dangers of military campaigns or commerce, the precariousness of situations which seemed secure but were always liable to change because of the very uncertainties of the imperial regime, periodically exposed to wars of rivalry, inspired a need for an absolute divine safeguard, and not only for occasional or limited favours. Already in the Hellenistic period, the Dioscuri Castor and Pollux, the Cabiri or gods of Samothrace, and above all Isis, were held to protect sailors. Asclepius-Aesculapius (frequently assimilated to Serapis) saved people from illness. But the idea of 'salvation' was very early enriched by the concern to be preserved even after death from the punishments of hell or punitive and distressing reincarnations (in Orphism and Pythagoreanism). In truth, the preoccupations of present life were often linked to those of the life hereafter.[35]

In a world where human beings seemed at the mercy of astral powers or the caprices of *Tyche*, the goddess of 'Good Luck' who tended to supplant the traditional gods in the time of the Diadochi,

and whom traders would soon couple with Mercury under the name
Fortuna, it was important to resort to providential divinities who
merged with a benevolent Fortune or even prevailed over the fatalism
of the stars, like Isis. In the face of the upheavals which the gods of the
city had not spared their fellow-citizens, and above all in the face of
the hazards confronting migrants far from their local religions, 'saviour' gods were necessary to take the individual into their care, and
for all eternity.

Eastern religions offered their followers various forms and concepts
of 'salvation'. But their liturgies and especially their initiations were
deemed to ensure protection in this world and the next, without
breach of continuity. Isis, Mithras, Cybele and the Syrian Baals each
enjoyed a supremacy which transcended the Roman perspective of a
propitiation that was well-defined but had no future. These divinities
guaranteed total security of the soul both inside and outside the body.
The recomposition and revitalization of Osiris, the awakening or
revival of Attis, the survival of Adonis, thanks to the love of goddesses
who were wives or mothers (or wives *and* mothers), were the pledges
of a victory over misfortunes and death. Their myths, reenacted by a
deeply moving ritual, each year renewed the 'good hope' of future
felicity. 'Here you are in the haven of Rest', says the high priest to
Lucius, on the day when his remetamorphosis from donkey into man
prefigures his initiatory rebirth and his entry into the harbour of
Salvation.[36]

In space as well as time, the cosmic and sovereign gods of the
Hellenized East in some way gave their worshippers an unrestricted
prospect, while remaining close to their all-too-human preoccupations. These gods were simultaneously personal, personally attentive
to the fears or aspirations of individuals, and universal, responsible
for the immense terrestrial and supraterrestrial world, which inexpressibly surpassed them. More intimately and constantly present
than the gods of the classical pantheon in the heart of their worshippers, but endowed at the same time with a boundless power that
was without either geographical or potential frontiers, each was all
things to all men in the great Everything over which they had
sovereign domination.

But if they were able to seduce some sectors of the Roman West,
which had become heterogeneous, it was also because they were
different. Their invasion was a chance of escape. Their exoticism
brought the Romans or Romanized circles a new tremor of the divine
and sacred because they were something 'completely different'.

However, this 'otherness' also took on a share of Roman-ness.
Several eastern gods were partly 'Caesarized', though they remained

foreign, such as Apis, and the Baals of Doliche or Heliopolis. They donned the imperial breastplate, but the first kept his bull's head, the second his calathus and starry girdle, and the third his two-bladed axe and his *pileus*. Their often-hybrid iconography reflected a multicultural world and mixed societies where they recruited their worshippers.

Chapter 1

The Great Mother
and her Eunuchs

T HE Tyrian Melqart, who became the Hercules of the Cattle
Market in the river port of Rome, perhaps made his first entry
into the *Urbs* in the company of Phoenician traders.[1] But the
first deity from the East to be officially consecrated by the Romans
within their walls was Cybele of Pessinus.

Origins

She arrived from Asia Minor where, for centuries if not millennia,
matronal and nurturing goddesses, often accompanied by wild animals, had been revered and regarded as protectresses of the dead
whom the earth reabsorbed into its bosom. They lived in rocks,
mountains and woods, had command over the animal and plant
world, and were the secret and inexhaustible sources of fecundity.
They were sometimes worshipped in the form of sacred stones,
baetyls that in some instances were refined into busts which were
clothed and laden with finery, as coins from the Roman era bear
witness. Some of these Mothers, such as the Artemis of Ephesus and
many others, were many-breasted; they were shown standing, stiff,
hieratic and flanked by animals of the deer family, at least in Graeco-
Roman times when their iconography spread.[2] Elsewhere, they were
enthroned, powerful and round-faced, between two lions.[3] Monuments in rock, which have been interpreted as tombs, were dedicated
to them.

The eastern Mediterranean world had long known images of goddesses mastering wild animals. Cretan and Mycenaean gems already
presented curious examples. But the oldest representation (around
6000 BC) is a terracotta found at Cátal Hüyük, near Konia in Phrygia
(now in the to Anatolian Museum in Ankara).[4] It features a Mother

with enormous breasts and thighs, seated with dignity between two great cats. We do not know the name she bore at that time. *Kubab* (*Kubebe*) or *Cybele* did not appear until much later, in the classical era. Its precise meaning remains unclear to us. The Byzantine Johannes Lydus likened it to the word 'cube' because of the black stone which represented her at Pessinus.[5] Hesychius – another Byzantine – speculated on the etymology *kubba/kumbe*, 'cymbal'.[6] R. Eisler went so far as to compare the 'ka'aba' of Mecca, which is also a black stone – and quadrangular (a cube!).[7] The repetition of the syllable *ba/be* is, in any case, characteristic of children's terms of endearment, like 'papa' and 'mama'. The name Kubaba can be read on Hittite inscriptions.

This Kubaba may be seen in profile on a relief from Carchemish at the beginning of the first millennium BC, wearing the tall *polos* or cylindrical headgear and holding a pomegranate.[8] We find her again in statue form in the seventh century BC at Büyük Kale (Bogaz Köy, in Turkey),[9] standing between a flute-player and a lyre-player, which suggests that there was already a liturgy with music.

It seems that in very early times the Mother of Pessinus had no companion god. A large number of images showing her on her own, and even fairly late Hellenic versions, which ignore or play down the cult of Attis, justifiably suggest a sort of initial Mother-worship monotheism. The figure and legend of Attis, and the orgiastic dances and rites associated with him, may have been imported into Phrygia, with the cult of Sabazius, by tribes of Thracian origin before 600 BC, as has been conjectured. But where does the eunuch priesthood of the galli of Pessinus come from? Was it of Semitic tradition? Had it been borrowed from the cult of the Syrian Goddess as practised at Hierapolis-Bambyce, as H. Hepding would have it?[10] The argument continues. At all events, Herodotus does not mention galli when writing (IV, 76) of the sacred evenings and festivals celebrated at Cyzicus in honour of Cybele.

The Great Mother and the Greeks

The goddess with the lions reached Greece, and even Magna Graecia, in the sixth century BC. She appeared in a chariot drawn by a pair of wild animals in the Gigantomachia of the Treasure of Siphnos at Delphi (around 525 BC). A series of Cypriot terracottas datable to the same century shows her seated with a child in her arms who is wearing the cap of Attis. She was found at Marseille tucked into a small cell in the form of a chapel (*naiskos*), sitting with a lion cub on her lap. This image spread through the Hellenic world from Ionia, where it is attested at Phocaea, the mother-city of Massalia.[11]

In Athens, the construction of a temple in homage to the Mother (*Metrôon*) was said to have been in expiation for throwing one of her roaming priests or 'metragyrtes' into the barathrum (a ravine into which criminals were hurled), which had provoked the anger of the goddess and brought the plague.[12] Some years later, in 415 BC, a man leaped on to the altar of the twelve gods and castrated himself with a stone, as the galli of the Roman period would do. Such violence against nature was repugnant to the Greeks, and this incident was taken to be an evil omen before Alcibiades' expedition to Sicily.[13]

We know nothing of the cult practised at that time in Phrygia, or of the recruitment of their priests, who were probably eunuchs, like the Megabyzes of the Ephesian Artemis. But at Athens, service to the Mother was purely Greek. The goddess was traditionally identified with Rhea or Demeter.

When Attis set foot in the islands (notably Thasos) and mainland Greece, his cult remained confined to the ports, among immigrants. But already in the fourth century nocturnal ceremonies were being celebrated, to cries of 'Hyès Attès, Attès', with Sabazian rites that curiously prefigured the Bacchic mysteries.[14] We have seen that Attis had arrived in Phrygia with Sabazius, who would later (like Attis) be taken to be the child of Cybele (Strabo, *Geography*, X, 3, 15). The Greeks were struck by everything that related Mother-cult dances to Dionysiac orgies. In Euripides, when the god who is the hero of the *Bacchae*, having come from Asia, appears with his boisterous rabble of worshippers, we hear him proclaim:

> Raise your native Phrygian timbrels
> invented by Rhea, the Great Mother, and me . . .
> *(lines 58–9)*

Even today, watching the peasants of Hierapolis (Pamukkale) whirl wildly to the rhythm and accents of native percussion instruments, we can feel something of the effect on the nerves that 'corybantism' must have had. The name Corybants was given to the armed acolytes of Rhea-Cybele, who danced to the sound of timbrels and cymbals, clashing their swords against their shields. Corybantism was said to have the same effects as Maenadism. A goddess of the mountains (*Oreia*) and nocturnal frenzies, Cybele like Dionysus, inspired *mania* or madness of divine possession (Euripides, *Hippolytus*, 141–4). 'To rave with the followers of Bacchus' (συμβαχχεύειν) was synonymous with 'to be carried away with the Corybants' (συγκορυβαντιαν). In a celebrated page from Plato (*Euthydemus*, 277 d–e), Socrates compares the specious argumentation of the sophists to the dizzying dances performed by the Corybants around the neophyte seated on a 'throne' (*thronismus*), before his consecration.

We are talking, however, of literary images and evocations. In Greece, Corybantism, even more than Dionysism, was on the fringes of public cults and would remain so, even when in the Roman era Cybele came into official favour.

Cybele and Agdistis in the Hellenistic World

To the problem of the origins of Mother-cult eunuchism can be added the myth of a divinity who is sometimes associated, sometimes confused, with Cybele: Agdistis.

In an inscription from Sardis, brilliantly discussed by L. Robert,[15] a copy of a ruling by the Persian governor has been recognized, dating back to the fourth century BC and relating to the 'mysteries' of Agdistis in which the priests of Zeus did not have the right to take part. A relief from Piraeus dated to *c.* 300 BC shows us Attis seated facing an 'Angdistis' with the profile of Cybele.[16] Another stele (provenance unknown, but Greek) bears a dedication to Agdistis, with the portrayal of a goddess with a *tympanum*, standing between two lions, who has all the appearance of the Phrygian Great Mother.[17] Consecrations to Agdistis increase in the third century BC. But a priest of Eleusis and a poet of love gave this local deity her Greek credentials.

The first was the Eumolpid Timotheus, the man who conducted enquiries in Pontus (and therefore Asia Minor as well) on behalf of the king of Egypt, Ptolemy Soter, in order to prepare the new cult of Serapis. This renowned theologian (the Christian apologist Arnobius tells us *c.* AD 300) had devoted to Cybele and the origins of her cult a learned work based on the study of ancient books that were inaccessible to the layman (*ex reconditis antiquitatum libris*), and of the 'profound mysteries' of priestly knowledge of which the galli of Pessinus were the guardians. At least that is what he claimed or implied (*quemadodum ipse scribit insinuatque*).[18] For he had not been able to resist Hellenizing the indigenous tradition rather tendentiously, which was a preparation for the future. In any case if, in order to denounce contemporary Phrygianium, Arnobius invoked the authority of a text almost six-centuries old, it was probably because the clergy of Cybele were still harking back to it in the Roman West, even though by way of Latin exegetes.

Here, according to Arnobius (*Against the Nations*, V, 5–7) is the Pessinuntian foundation myth as set out by Timotheus as follows.

In Phrygia there was a rocky eminence called Agdos, from which Pyrrha and Deucalion were said to have taken the stones which they threw behind them to reconstitute the human race after the deluge. From this living stone was formed the Mother whom Jupiter vainly tried to seduce.

Faute de mieux, he was said to have impregnated the rock which gave birth to a bisexual child, Acdestis (Agdistis). This hermaphrodite, who had the violence of both masculine and feminine instincts, erupted without regard for either gods or men. Worried by and weary of his excesses, Olympus resolved to limit the effects of this savagery by removing at least one of the two sexes. After rendering him drowsy with wine, Dionysus bound his testicles and attached the cord to his feet. When he arose, on waking, Acdestis automatically emasculated himself, and from the blood reddening the ground was born a pomegranate tree laden with fruit.

Nana, the daughter of King Sangarios (the name of the river that flowed at the foot of Mount Dindymus, equally celebrated for its cult of Cybele), enchanted by the sight of a pomegranate, picked one and put it on her bosom, which made her pregnant and aroused her father's anger. Sangarios then locked Nana away, depriving her of food. But the Mother of the gods was watching over her and fed her by mysterious means. Nana bore a child which the king had exposed in the wilds. Fed like a kid among the ibexes (which the Phrygians called *attagis*), he was given the name Attis.

Cybele adored the boy; but she also loved Acdestis – and passionately – although he was a eunuch, or because he was a eunuch (?). One day, too much wine caused Attis to confess the affection Acdestis had for him. Midas, king of Pessimus, tried to dissuade Attis from such a shameful liaison by promising him his daughter's hand in marriage. To avoid any kind of disturbance that would upset the joys of the wedding, Midas had the town walled and locked. But the Mother of the gods, 'knowing the destiny of the youth and that he would never be safe among men unless he could escape the bonds of marriage', broke through the ramparts with her head 'which from then on and for this reason was crowned with towers'. Acdestis, enraged, suddenly burst into the midst of the festivities and imparted a collective madness to the assembled guests. The bride cut her breasts, her father castrated himself. As for Attis, beside himself and in a state of almost Dionysiac trance (*perbacchatus*), he fled out into the wilds and fell at the foot of a pine tree after cutting off his genitals, crying: 'Here, Acdestis; take those parts because of which you have caused such great tragedies through madness!'

He died, and from his blood sprang the violets used to adorn the sacred pines of Attis. The Great Mother gathered up, washed and gave precious burial to the *virilia* of the dead youth. His fiancée mingled her tears with those of Acdestis and killed herself on the corpse which was piously wrapped in woollen cloth. The colour of her blood passed into the brilliance of the purple violets. From her body, buried by Cybele, grew the almond tree, bitter symbol of mourning. Vainly implored by Acdestis to revive Attis, Jupiter agreed only to what destiny allowed: his body would escape putrefaction, his hair would continue to grow and his little finger to move. In his honour Acdestis instituted an annual cult and a body of priests.

Shortly before 300 BC (approximately the same period as Timotheus, to within 10 or 20 years), the poet Hermesianax recorded a 'Lydian' version of the myth which said nothing of the castration of Attis, but made him impotent.[19] Having become a missionary of the Mother-worshipping cult, the young man attracted the jealousy of Zeus: a maddened boar killed him, together with several Lydians. This version obviously recalls the story of Atys, son of Croesus, as narrated by Herodotus (I, 34–45). The 'Father of History' does not speak of the Mother of the gods. But Pausanias (VII, 17, 10) tacks on to the Lydian version an account which he ascribes to the local tradition of Pessinus and which corresponds in broad outline to that of Arnobius. The difference lies in a few details (Zeus impregnates the earth while he sleeps, an almond tree and not a pomegranate emerges from the blood of the emasculated Agdistis, Attis does not die of his mutilation) and chiefly, in Pausanias, the absence of the Great Mother.

In fact it is all as if Timotheus had separated the Phrygian goddess into two, Acdestis in his account assuming the negative and violent aspects of the Mother who is in love with Attis. In Arnobius, Cybele plays a normalizing role. Acdestis at first embodies the disorder resulting from the irrepressible concupiscence of Jupiter, who sires a destructive monster.[20] This split may be indigenous and very old, for certain dedications from Asia Minor distinguish Agdistis from the 'Mother'.[21] But Agdistis – who is to be found sometimes as a god, sometimes as a goddess – doubtless also preserves the memory of a primordial androgynous deity, probably marginalized in favour of Cybele-Kubaba from Carchemish, recalled perhaps by the image of an androgynous and many-breasted Zeus (like the Artemis of Ephesus) who is well-attested in Caria.[22] The cult of Agdistis is sometimes associated, sometimes contrasted, with that of the sovereign god. In Philadelphia in Lydia, Agdistis in the first century BC had nothing of the savagery attributed to him by Timotheus' version. This deity demanded a strict morality from his followers; he condemned adultery, as well as murder and abortion.[23]

The castration of Acdestis legitimized eunuchism. But the Great Mother also opened up the town to Acdestis so that the dementia let loose by his initially androgynous double should put an end to the dramas of love by the emasculation of Attis. Clearly, Timotheus had to explain the mutilation of the galli by their wish to avoid subjection to sexual instincts. Unlike the eunuch-priests, Attis died of it. But this death is necessary to the dramaturgical scenario of a mystery religion.

The presentation of the myth given by Timotheus must have been peppered with aetiological considerations: the turreted head of Cybele, the flute of Attis, the violet that sprang from the blood of Ia, Midas's daughter (since *ias* in Greek is the word for this flower), even the ritual of the pine, unless the explanation of the ritual in Arnobius comes from a Roman commentator on Timotheus.[24] In fact, the Christian apologist incidentally quotes a 'Valerius *pontifex*' regarding the name Ia. This Valerius is unknown to us, but a Valerius Messala *augur* (whom Arnobius may have confused with a pontiff) had been interested – as we know from Macrobius (*Saturnalia*, I, 9, 14) – in the etymology of Janus. We also know from Johannes Lydus that this same Valerius Messala had annotated the Pythagorean monad, underlining the *ia-mia* equivalence.[25] Much later, it is true, but not without having scoured much gibberish from the Pythagorean tradition, the emperor Julian would justify the emasculation of Attis as putting an end to the indeterminate plurality of generation and a return to oneness. Julian recalls the example of the hierophant of Eleusis who denies herself any offspring.[26] Perhaps the Eumolpid Timotheus had already made the same comparison.

Similarly, the story of the pomegranate must have reminded him of the one which Aidoneus offered to Persephone (the Kubaba of Carchemish held a pomegranate; did the legend inspire the iconography, or vice versa?). The relationship of Attis to corn was also ready made to suggest certain analogies with 'the ear of corn harvested in silence' (Hippolytus, *Philosophoumena*, V, 8). Were not the Phrygians said to call Attis 'the ear of corn harvested green'? It is not only the request of Agdistis to Jupiter for the survival of Attis that brings to mind Demeter's plea for her daughter, carried off by the god of the dead. The mention of King Midas[27] opposing Cybele's plans is all the more curious because Plutarch (*Life of Caesar*, 9, 4) makes him the actual son of the Great Mother. Lastly, the 'invincible strength' (*robur invictum*)[28] of the monster born of the rock recalls Mithras, the god who was petrogeneous and *invictus*.[29] An enormous amount of comparative study and reflection, if not syncretism, is involved in this text by Arnobius, not to mention the Hellenizing of the names in the myth by those of Jupiter, Liber-Dionysus, Pyrrha, Deucalion and Themis.

Cybele and the Republic

Attis is present in Hellenistic art (notably on the noble and moving relief of Venice,[30] dated at the latest to the second century BC), but far less often than the Great Mother, who has a prominent place on a lion's back on the great altar of Pergamum.[31] Even Greek literary tradition clearly found it repugnant to acknowledge and include the castration of Attis. At the end of the third century BC, the poet Dioscorides (*Palatine Anthology*, VI, 220) sings of the 'chaste Atys', prey to madness but without the slightest exhibition of gore, who promises Cybele a place of worship (*thalamè*) on the banks of the Sangarios because she had made a lion flee by striking her timbrel. Even in the 'orgeones' or religious associations of the Piraeus,[32] the Mother had priestesses and not galli. In the euhemeristic version transcribed by Diodorus Siculus (III, 58–9) in the first century BC, Cybele is a 'Mother of the Mountain', the protectress of livestock and the newborn, resembling Demeter. Her father has Attis killed because she has been enjoying a clandestine affair with him. But Agdistis, sexual violence and emasculation do not come into it. The Pessinuntian myth is expurgated. Paradoxically, it was Rome that would bring it to the fore, although with variations, and in Rome that the violence of the galli, after being strictly regulated, would end in public display in the March festivals.

In 205 BC the war with Carthage was still dragging on. Hannibal was no longer at Rome's gates, but persisted in being a source of anxiety in the south of Italy. Prodigies and notably showers of stones terrified the populace, who were in danger of sinking once more into *externa superstitio*. As always in similar circumstances, the Sibylline Oracles were consulted. They predicted that the enemy would be driven from the peninsula on condition that 'the Idaean Mother of Pessinus' was brought to Rome. There were two Mount Idas, one in Crete, the other dominating Troy. From the forests of the Trojan Ida, Aeneas and his companions had taken the wood for the vessels that had brought them to Italy. The Idaean Mother had therefore already watched over the distant ancestors of Romulus, and was identified with the Cretan Mother, as Apollo of Delos reminds Aeneas in Virgil (*Aeneid*, III, 94–8). Until that time a stranger to the official religion, the goddess was not so to the mythical tradition of the *Urbs*.

Pessinus came under the authority of the king of Pergamum, Attalus (who bore in his name that of Attes-Attis). It was a theocratic principality that had been formerly independent like many temple-states of the Near East, but which had become a vassal of the Attalids, as it was later to be a vassal of the Roman Republic, then of the emperor until 25 BC. At the head of the priests or galli of Cybele were an 'Attis' and a 'Battakès'. The Attis presided as high priest, and the Battakès played the role of vice-president of the priestly community.[33] The pre-eminence of the Attis – apart from the name itself which made him the incarnation of the companion god – is confirmed for us by the correspondence of the kings of Pergamum carved on three marble tables discovered in the Armenian cemetery of Sivri Hissar.[34] The Attalids apparently treated this priest-king on equal terms; but in fact Pessinus was under their protectorate.

Because of the war waged together with Attalus against Philip V of Macedon, common interests united Rome with the king of Pergamum, who for obvious geo-political reasons was unable at the time to refuse anything to his powerful allies. One may rightly be surprised that Pessinus should have allowed itself to be dispossessed of the precious fetish, a black stone, an aerolith, the mysterious dwelling-place of the Mother, and that Attalus himself yielded to the Roman demand. To tell the truth, a version echoed by the poet Ovid mentioned the king's initial resistance. But an earth tremor is supposed to have indicated the irritation of Cybele, whose voice prophesied: 'Rome is worthy to become the meeting-place of all the gods.' To which King Attalus is said to have replied: 'Go, then! You will remain ours. For Rome boasts of Phrygian ancestors' (*Fasti*, IV, 265–72). According to Livy (*History of Rome*, XXIX, 11, 7), Attalus himself accompanied the Roman ambassadors to Pessinus to have the sacred stone handed over to them. It has been conjectured that in fact the king might already have transferred it to Pergamum. However that may be, in this affair (as in so many others) religion and politics were wonderfully in accord: external politics, needless to say, but also internal, since resorting to the Great Mother permitted the soothing of minds distracted by the supernatural, while at the same time making careful use of the prestige of the national religious heritage.[35]

To be on the safe side, the Senate's delegates had in passing questioned the Delphic oracle. Apollo had reassured them; but they had to ensure that the goddess was welcomed by the best man in Rome, *vir optimus*. Publius Scipio Nasica – nephew of Africanus, soon to be Hannibal's conqueror – was deemed worthy of this honour: here again, politics undeniably played a part. On 4 April 204 BC, he went to Ostia with all the matrons of the senatorial 'gentry'. He took the stone from the boat to give it to the women to carry. Later, it would be said that the vessel had at first run aground in the mud of the port which was beginning to silt up. Then a young matron, whose reputation had been tarnished by her elaborate hairstyles, elegance, and a tongue that was a little too ready at the expense of the austere old men, removed her girdle and tied it to the boat, freeing it easily. Her name was Claudia Quinta and she was descended from the illustrious *Atta Clausus*, whose name was linked with that of Attis. This test of chastity would render her famous in literature and art.[36] She would be made a Vestal!

With the matrons passing the stone from hand to hand, the goddess made her entry into the *Urbs* amid joyous invocations and clouds of incense rising from the perfume-burners that the citizens had set up in front of their doors. Cybele was provisionally installed on the Palatine, in the temple of Victory (which she guaranteed to the Romans), while awaiting the building of her very own sanctuary. Henceforth, each year from 4 to 10 April festivals and spectacles or 'Megalesian games' commemorated the arrival of the Great (*Megale*) Mother on this sacred hill of Romulus. The results of the transfer were not long in coming. Singularly abundant harvests that year and, above all, Scipio's triumph at Zama were a dazzling revelation of the divine favour.

On 10 April 191 BC, the temple especially pledged to Cybele was 'dedicated' (today we would say 'inaugurated', but the Latin *inaugurare* means the preliminary consecration of the site, according to the auspices or signs given by the gods in the sky). The victim of fire, it was rebuilt in 111 BC, then AD 3. The edifice, of which the podium and a few architectural remains can be seen on the Palatine, dates from the Augustan era. But thanks to excavations, the first phase of building and use is known to us from the vestiges of foundations and, chiefly, the terracotta votive deposits which tell us much of popular devotions.[37] The dark aerolith from Pessinus was adapted as the head of the cult statue.[38] Like Artemis of Ephesus, Cybele was a black 'virgin'.

She had not come alone. Her eunuchs had accompanied her. But the Senate confined them to the enclosure of the sanctuary. A priest and priestess from Phrygia took charge of the clergy, who would continue to be recruited outside Rome, in the East. No citizen had the right to castrate himself like the galli, or even to enter the annexes occupied by these eunuchs and take part in the frenzied 'orgies'. Once a year, during the April festivals, the galli were permitted to dance through the streets of Rome to the sounds of *auloi* and tambourines, in their exotic 'get-up', with their feminine garments, long hair and amulets.

At that time they were allowed to make door-to-door collections, for the upkeep of the temple and its emasculated staff. Afterwards, they were not seen again until the next year. Passers-by skirting the enclosure of the Mother-cult monastery would notice the sounds of barbarian voices, the clash of cymbals, delirious singing.[39] In honour of the goddess, aristocratic associations or 'sodalities' organized banquets. But citizens were rigorously prohibited from donning the colourful garb of the eunuchs or taking part in their ritual practices. The Chief Pontiff, responsible for Roman religion, kept firm control over all cults of foreign origin, liaising with the decemvirs *sacris faciundis*, the custodians and interpreters of the Sibylline Books. When the cult of Cybele was made official, its priests were effectively marginalized.[40] But in spite, or because, of these restrictions the Mother-cult temple excited curiosity.

The *Megalesia* or *Megalensia* aroused popular enthusiasm. The sanctuary was open to the public on 4 and 10 April. People brought dishes of *moretum*, a mixture of cheese and pounded herbs, to the Mother. Curule aediles offered the Romans not only theatrical shows in front of the Palatine temple (several of Terence's comedies were presented on this occasion), but also chariot races in the Circus Maximus where the statue of Cybele was taken in procession in the company of the gods.

At the end of March, a procession had triumphantly carried the goddess to the banks of the Almo (a tributary of the Tiber) where the high priest, with his white locks, clad in a purple robe, solemnly bathed the idol and sacred objects (*Lavatio*). Lucretius – the sworn enemy of the devotions that torment humankind – vibrantly evokes the spectacle of these liturgical jubilations:

The taut timbrels thunder as palms beat them, the concave cymbals clash around the statue, the trumpets blare their threatening harsh noise and the Phrygian rhythm of the flute fills hearts with madness ... As soon as the silent image of the goddess, carried through the big towns, favours mortals with her mute protection, bronze and silver are strewn over the whole road along which she passes, the generous offerings of her worshippers. It snows roses, which shadow the Mother and the company escorting her ... (*De Rerum Natura*, II, 618–28).

For the celebration of the Megalesian Games, the idol was borne 'on the necks of the galli' (Ovid, *Fasti*, IV, 185), by means of a kind of stretcher, as so many statues of saints are still carried on their feast day in Italy, Sardinia and Sicily. During the *Lavatio* procession, the goddess was enthroned in a chariot pulled by heifers, under a rain of spring flowers (ibid., 345–6).

Certainly, her cult and priests were not safe from hostile reactions. During the war of the Cimbri and Teutones, the Battakès of Pessinus came one day to announce to the Romans that from the depth of her sanctuary the Great Mother had predicted their victory; but she demanded public expiations, for her Palatine temple had been sullied! Apparelled in his prestigious priestly garments, wearing his massive golden crown and leaf-patterned robe covered with gold embroideries, which gave him the appearance of a king, the Battakès intended to harangue the people in the Forum. But the tribune Aulus Pompeius drove him from the rostra, calling him a charlatan, and the crowd, as unfavourably impressed by the priest's threatening tone as by his crown, heaped insults upon him. Then, the tribune was seized by a burning fever and lost his voice, dying three days later . . . The Battakès therefore reappeared in the Forum, his head held higher than ever, and the repentant populace honoured him with magnificent gifts.[41]

It was in this period that the turreted effigy of Cybele made its appearance on official coinage. It would often be re-issued on the Roman *denarii* of the last century of the Republic, especially on those which the aediles ordered to be struck to commemorate the organization of the *Megalensia* for which they had responsibility. The goddess figured in 78 BC in a chariot drawn by two lions, on coins bearing on the obverse the image of one of those Corybants[42] whose armed dance around the Lady with the wild animals is celebrated by Lucretius.[43]

With his violent gangs, Publius Clodius (Cicero's enemy), who had violated the mysteries of the Good Goddess, caused disturbances and profaned the *ludi scaenici* of 56 BC. The Great Mother showed her anger by rumblings in the ground in the Roman countryside, where people believed they heard her galloping in her lion-drawn chariot, with her noisy retinue. Two years earlier, this fanatical demagogue had scandalized the Romans by auctioning the native priest of Pessinus: a priest had been snatched from his altars and the sacred furnishings ransacked, 'all those objects which Antiquity, the Persians, the Syrians, and all the kings who have ruled Europe and Asia have constantly honoured with the greatest respect!' (Cicero, *The Replies of the Haruspices*, 28).

In his *Menippeae* (*Eumenides*, XVI–XXVII),[44] Varro makes fun of the Phrygian horn with its lugubrious strains, the feminine apparel and raving chants of the galli, the high-priest's dawn-coloured alb and crown resplendent with gems. But, like Lucretius, Varro is careful to account allegorically for the eunuchism and corybantism as well as the religious imagery. The tambourine symbolizes the earthly disc; the towers crowning the goddess refer us to the inhabited towns which she sustains and protects; people move around her as around the earth which remains immobile and to imply to the peasants that they should never rest ... She has eunuchs in her service, for those with no seed must cling to the earth which contains all seeds. The clash of the cymbals brings to mind the noise of agricultural implements. The tamed lion to be seen at her side suggests that there is no soil so hard or barren that it cannot be mastered and cultivated ... etc. This *ratio physica* was appropriate to the Roman peasant (Augustine, *City of God*, VII, 24). Lucretius (*De Rerum Natura*, II, 60ff) develops a less simplistic, but moralizing, explanation, inspired by Stoic ideas.[45] For the poet, the galli embody 'those who have outraged the divinity of the Mother' and who, ungrateful towards their parents, must be deemed 'unworthy to bring to the light of day living descendants'. The concern felt at that time in Rome to explain the turbulent and shocking aspects of Phrygianism tended to sanction its literary and intellectual integration, something that is scarcely to be found in Greece itself.

Catullus did not hesitate to put into verse the story of a beautiful ephebe drawn by Mother-worship dementia to commit the irreparable act, a repentant Attis: 'Henceforth I am but a ruin of myself, a eunuch!' (*Poems*, 63, 69). This mixture of sentimental refinement and pathetic horror reveals a strange attraction matched by revulsion for sexual ambiguity. Unlike Diodorus, too, Ovid (*Fasti*, IV, 223–44) is careful not to omit the tragedy of the emasculation of an Attis who, because he has deceived the Mother with the little nymph of the Sagaris (the daughter of Sangarios in Timotheus' version), goes mad and cuts himself with a stone, crying, 'With my blood I pay the punishment I have deserved. Ah! Let those parts perish which have caused my downfall.' Here we recognize the theme of the unmanning which puts an end to the distractions of love, but with no mention at all of the disturbing figure of Agdistis.

Attis did not as yet come into public ceremonies, but among the innumerable ex-votos discovered in the excavations of the Mother-worship temple on the Palatine,[46] a whole range of figurines representing Cybele's young companion have been identified, and many were discovered at the earliest level. So, contrary to the hypotheses that would delay the introduction of Attis into Roman Phrygianism until the imperial era, we find that the god already had his place in popular piety in the second century BC. The Palatine statuettes are a foretaste of the brilliant future cult of the Great Mother's mythical castrated lover. Slaves and freedmen of eastern origin must have numbered among the dedicants of moulded terracottas mass-produced in a very cheap material. But it is not inconceivable that Attis may already have recruited worshippers among the urban plebs, even outside the compatriots of the Anatolian goddess.

The cults of close or kindred goddesses were linked with that of Cybele. In fact, the wars waged in Asia Minor against Mithridates had put legionaries in contact with other Mothers, and among the captives brought back to Italy many remained loyal to their local divinities. The two temple-states of Comana (one in Pontus, the other in Cappadocia)[47] revered a goddess Mâ, whom the Romans identified with Bellona. Her priests (plate 2), who were known as *fanatici*, indulged in armed dances whose bloody frenzies recalled those of the galli. Clad in black, like the priests of Cybele they wore gem-studded crowns and long strips of woollen cloth. Their hair flying, they pirouetted brandishing their two-edged axes. At the height of the dizziness excited by the beating of timbrels and the sinister wailing of the trumpets, they hacked their arms to sprinkle the idol with red splashes, before predicting the future to the dumbfounded spectators. The future dictator Sulla's propaganda had profited in this way from the promises of victory given by a Cappadocian slave in the grip of prophetic delirium.[48] Tibullus had evidently witnessed a scene of this nature when he wrote (*Elegies*, I, 6, 45–50):

> Once set in motion by the action of Bellona, neither the bite of fire nor blows from a whip frighten this distracted woman. With her own hands she wounds her arms with an axe, and her flowing blood sprinkles the goddess, yet she feels no pain. Standing, her side pierced by a spear, standing, her bosom torn, she chants the future as told to her by the powerful goddess.

The Christians would claim that initiates of Bellona were made to drink human blood, as was said of Catiline's accomplices (Tertullian, *Apologetica*, IX, 10).

Whatever the truth of the matter, the Anatolian Bellona remained linked with Cybele, whose *pedisequa* or 'follower' she was said to be (*CIL*, VI, 30851), in worship as in the imagination of poets and novelists. Juvenal (*Satires*, VI, 511ff) unites the two Mothers in the same obscene and noisy brotherhood. In Apuleius (*Metamorphoses*, VIII, 25, 3) the galli of the Syrian Goddess, when making a curse, associate Bellona with the 'Idaean Mother with her Attis'. The 'Berecyntian' of Beneventum (*CIL*, X, 1596) is a Cybele who bears the name *Minerva*, thus a warrior Mother related to Bellona. Under the Empire, 24 March – 'the day of blood' – would be a date as dear to the fanatics of Bellona as to the followers of Attis.[49]

Plate 2 Cistophorus of Bellona (Rome, Museo Capitolino)

Decidedly, this Rome which was so austere, so imbued with moralizing seriousness and authority, appeared to be more receptive than Greece to violent and disturbing liturgies. It is true that the *Urbs*, capital of a cosmopolitan empire, was becoming the meeting-place of the human race.

Imperial Phrygianism

With the accession to sovereign power of a member of the *gens Iulia* which was descended from Aeneas, the Great Mother of Ida acquired a revived legitimacy. So she appears on several occasions in the *Aeneid*. On the prow of the vessel carrying the founding hero in company with Pallas, the son of Evander, who would give his name to the Palatine, a pair of Phrygian lions symbolizes the Mother's divine protection (*Aeneid*, X, 157). It is she whom Aeneas invokes for victory, as the Romans would do to drive Hannibal from the Peninsula. It is she who, on the Vienna *Gemma Augustea*, crowns with laurels the emperor, in the guise of hero, accompanied by the goddess Roma.[50] Another cameo from Vienna shows us Livia as Cybele, with her crown of towers, leaning on the timbrel beaten by the dishevelled galli, and adorned with the effigy of a lion.[51] The Great Mother also figures prominently on the base of Sorrento, a monument erected under Augustus' reign in honour of the imperial family: she is to be seen enthroned beside a Corybant who dances, brandishing his shield.[52] In AD 3 August had the *Metrôon* on the Palatine rebuilt, as we are shown on a relief from the Villa Medici; on the tympanum of the temple a throne occupied by the turreted crown may be recognized, placed between two galli and two lions, while Corybants twirl at the base of the two oblique sides.[53] On the pediment of a sanctuary close to the imperial residence, this iconographic homage to Cybele's mutilated servants implied that their devotion mattered to the state. But the historian Dionysius of Halicarnassus (*Roman Antiquities*, II, 19), writing under Augustus, notes that Phrygian orgiastic practices are not publicly on display in Rome, as they are in the East. At the same time, it has been found that priests of the Mother-cult were recruited from among the household staff of the Palatine. Two freedmen of Augustus and Livia are known to have become respectively priest and priestess of the Great Mother (*CIL*, VI, 496). However, although on the above-mentioned relief Attis's cap symbolically crowns the summit of the temple, the castrated god is not seen to have enjoyed a cult before the reign of the emperor Claudius.

This grandson of Livia belonged to a family whose clan name Appius/Attius went back to the famous Sabine Atta Clausus and recalled the very name of Attis ('Papa'). Claudius took great interest in the mysteries of Eleusis, which he tried in vain to bring across to the *Urbs*,[54] and his erudition – encouraged by the historian Livy – had perhaps led him to read the work of Timotheus on the religion of Pessinus. Among the freedmen of Graeco-oriental origin whose influence and activities were growing stronger at that time in the imperial court,[55] many came from Phrygia where the assets of the imperial treasury were considerable. Apart from the palace and civil service, Anatolians must have been numerous at Ostia, where the cult of Cybele would experience increasing success during the following century.

At all events, it was apparently Claudius who instituted and had inscribed in the Roman calendar a ceremony which, after a fashion, opened the 'holy week' of the god Attis: the Entry of the Tree (*arbor intrat*). Henceforth, on 22 March, the brotherhood of woodcutters or 'dendrophori' (which traced its foundation to a 1st of August, Claudius' birthday!) carried in procession to the Palatine temple a pine tree felled in memory of the tree at whose foot Attis had destroyed his virility. This festival implies at least part of the cycle of celebrations which, in later calendars, mark the second fortnight in March. For, like the procession of the Tree, they liturgically re-enacted the phases that were indissociable from the foundation myth.

On 15 March, the brotherhood of Cannophori went in procession through the streets, carrying reeds cut from the banks of the Almo, and leading a six-year-old bull which the high priest sacrificed for the fertility of the mountain fields. It is not certain whether the reeds were meant to recall the infancy of Attis, exposed on the banks of the Sangarios (his grandfather) or the Gallos, or his infidelity to Cybele with the nymph. In the first instance, the festival would underline the solicitude of the Mother for the child she had saved from the water. But the dalliance of the Phrygian shepherd with the daughter of the river, unleashing the wrath of Cybele, demanded all the resources of dramatic art ...

That was the beginning of nine days of penitence, a sort of 'Lent'. People abstained from bread, pomegranates, quinces, pork, fish and probably wine as well. Only milk was drunk. Perhaps it was also a time of obligatory sexual continence.

On 22 March, a pine had to be cut before the end of the night, and a ram sacrificed, its blood bathing the roots of the tree. The felling (*ektomè* in Greek) took place in a wood sacred to Cybele. The procession (*pompè*) went through Rome, like a funeral cortege, to the sound of canticles intoned by the dendrophori and probably taken up by the mass of worshippers thronging the streets. In concert with the galli, the weeping devotees beat their breasts. Once the sanctuary was reached, the pine was exposed to the adoration of the crowds (*prothesis*). An image of Attis had been attached to it, decorated with the violets that his blood had caused to grow, according to the legend. On that day (*dies violae*), people went to lay flowers on the tombs.

The whole of the next day was given over to mourning lamentations. On 23 March, the Salii, priest dancers of the god Mars, went in procession sounding their sacred trumpets, which received their annual blessing (*tubilustrium*) on this day. Like Corybants, they leaped about, striking their shields.

But 24 March – the day of blood (*Sanguis*) – marked the peak of the mournful cycle. Then the high priest with his galli gave the signal for a wild dance around the sacred pine. He flagellated himself and them with a whip hung with knucklebones, to the sound of curving clarinets and cymbals. The timbrels were beaten furiously, but people also beat their naked breasts with pine cones; they cut their shoulders and arms with knives; they made their blood spurt over the tree and the altars, emitting screams and yells that were echoed in the crowd. For a feverish trembling seized those among the spectators who were suffering from the effects of the ritual fasting and devotional stress. They entered the dance and, beside themselves, in paroxysms of frenzy slashed their testicles with a piece of broken glass or a flint. In their turn they became Attides. After the emasculation, the lower bellies of the galli were tattooed,[57] which confirmed their adherence to the goddess, henceforward imprinted in their flesh (like the mark of the sacred slaves in certain temples of the East). Sometimes, it seems, gold leaf was applied to the healed wound of the mutilation.[58]

After cutting the Tree, 'on the third day, the holy and ineffable harvest of Gallus was cut', as the emperor Julian would write (*Discourse on the Mother of the Gods*, 9, 168 d). The pine, festooned with strips of cloth and flowers, was then buried, as Cybele had done with the corpse of Attis. On that day, the high priest had prayers said for the protection of the emperor and the Empire. Tertullian (*Apologeticus*, XXV, 5) may jeer at 'this very respectable archigallus' who, eight days after the death of Marcus Aurelius, 'made libations of impure blood by ripping open his arms' and ordering public invocations for an already-dead sovereign, or wax ironical about Cybele and the oracles she inspired in her excited priests; in this regard, Montanism had the same genuinely Phrygian roots.[59] In fact, it is known that the disciples of Montanus claimed to prophesy in the name of the Paraclete, but their fasts and hallucinatory ecstasies were somewhat akin to Mother-cult practices. It was not by chance that this heresy was playing havoc in the Church (and as far as Lyon) at the very time when, in paganism, the cult of Attis was enjoying its greatest success.

The funeral ceremonies of the pine-Attis were probably followed by a kind of vigil, which was distinct from the 'midnight' (*Mesonyctium*) celebrated on 9 December 160 in Lyon for the consecration of the archigallus.[60] We do not know what this liturgy consisted of. A famous page from Firmicus Maternus (*The Error of Profane Religions*, XXII, 1) has been connected with the Mother-worship cult:[61] the Christian pamphleteer recalls a night of prayers and lamentations chanted rhythmically in the shadows until the moment when a light shines; the priest then anoints the bosom of the worshippers attending, murmuring slowly:

> Have faith, O believers: god is saved!
> And for us salvation will emerge from his suffering.

But what follows and the context plainly show that the ceremony must rather be connected with Osiris.[62]

On the following day, 25 March, the resurrection of Attis was proclaimed, at least as the fourth-century texts tell us; but a bas-relief of the Antonine era, found at Ostia,[63] shows us, beside the dead Attis at the foot of the pine, a little Attis standing and in some sense 'reborn'. This was the day of the 'Hilaria' or popular 'rejoicings', 'the first day when the day is longer than the night' (Macrobius, *Saturnalia*, I, 21, 10), a festival of spring and life rediscovered. In the time of Commodus, it would take on the air of an exuberant carnival. Behind a triumphal procession where, in front of the idol of Cybele and the emperor, were carried the most prestigious works of art lent by the sovereign and the Roman aristocracy (gold and silver wine bowls, costly candelabras and statues), knights and senators, freedmen and dignitaries could be seen in procession, made up, masked and clad in the most unexpected disguises. Flute-players, trumpeters, drummers and chanters of the Mother-cult brotherhood, with others, helped to add sound to the masquerade which was followed by lavish feasting. On that day, even the sober and frugal Severus Alexander (222–35) ate pheasant! It was under cover of this festival that the terrorist Maternus, dressed as a soldier of the guard, thought he could assassinate Commodus in 187. But his evil designs were thwarted, and he was immediately beheaded. With even more jubilation than before people celebrated the goddess who had saved the emperor's life.[64]

After nine such days of testing the endurance of bodies and nerves, there was a real need for the *Requietio* (or 'Rest day') of 26 March. On the next day, 27, the procession of the 'Bath' (*Lavatio*) assumed even more solemnity than in the Republican period. The priests whose duty was to guard and consult the Sibylline Books took part officially in the ceremony. The silver idol with the black stone for its head left the Palatine in a chariot harnessed to heifers to go to the Porta Capena and the Appian Way. 'Important personages in togas walked barefoot before the *carpentum* of the Idaean Mother' (Prudentius, *Hymns*, X 154–5). When they arrived at the banks of the Almo (now the Acquataccio), the high priest, draped in his purple robe, plunged the goddess into this tributary of the Tiber and rubbed her with ashes. The chariot and all the religious furnishings, sacrificial knives and vessels, were also washed. The Mother was asked if she agreed to return to Rome. We do not know how she replied, but the procession then performed a U-turn to music, under a shower of blossoms, amid dances and pantomimes. Goddess of the earth and harvests, Cybele gave the countryside her blessing for abundant crops.

Eight days later, on 4 April, the Megalensia began, as in the Republican period, celebrating the arrival of the black stone by a sort of new term for the theatres after over four months without any *ludi scaenici* (the last in the civil year were given on the occasion of the *Ludi Plebei*, on 17 November). But under the Empire, hardly any classical comedies in the style of Terence's works were presented. The crowds were kept amused by mythological pantomimes or lyric dramas, among which the loves of Cybele and the 'passion' and death of Attis prominently featured.[65] We are not sure whether it was during the April spectacles, but Nero put himself on stage to warble a lament for Attis which he had put into verse, and which was mocked by Persius (*Satires*, I, 93ff). The taste for blood, violence and horror which invaded Roman theatre at that time extended the effects of the *dies sanguinis*. Tertullian said that he had been present at the castration of an Attis, and also at the death of a Hercules who was burnt alive (*Apologeticus*, XV, 5).

Everything came to an end on 10 April, the anniversary of the temple. The people were entitled to chariot races in the Circus Maximus, where a statue of Cybele riding on a lion's back stood in the middle of the track beside the central obelisk. Before the competitions started, in the *Pompa Circensis*, she went in procession in a lion-drawn chariot carried on a litter, in company with other great gods.[66] This 'solemn procession of the Circus', led by the magistrate who presided over the games wearing a toga embroidered with palm leaves, had the appearance and brilliance of a triumphal procession.

Phrygianism was thus well and truly officialized. It became popular and imperial. Claudius and his freedmen played a decisive role in this respect, even though the Romanization of the March cycle was confirmed only in the following century by the solemnity of the Hilaria. In 69, many were offended because the emperor Otho hastened his departure without regard for religious prohibitions, writes Suetonius (*Otho*, 8, 5), 'on the very day when worshippers of the Mother of the gods were beginning their groans and lamentations' (that is, on 24 March, the 'Day of Blood').

In Hadrian's time, the prolific writer Arrian of Nicomedia – where he was a priest of Demeter – recalled that in Rome Attis was mourned according to the funeral rites of the Phrygians (*Tactics*, 33, 4). That was precisely the period when Cybele reappeared on Roman coins or, more exactly, on the medallions[67] with the form of the large sesterces which the emperor perhaps had distributed, in this case, on the occasion of the Mother-cult festivals (plate 3). The goddess would be found again during the second century AD on coins honouring the empresses Sabina, Faustina the Elder and Faustina the Younger, and Lucilla (the wife of Lucius Verus). The imperial medallions show Cybele, sometimes alone on a lion, sometimes seated in company with Attis. She is also featured arriving by boat at the mouth of the Tiber or in the procession of the 'Bath'.[68] On the sesterces commemorating the apotheosis of Faustina the Elder (d. 141), the goddess is given the title *Salutaris*; this is in some sort 'Our-Lady-of-Salvation'.[69] But on common coinage, the eunuch shepherd does not figure at her side. Under

a   *b*

Plate 3 (a) Medallion of Sabina; (b) Medallion of Lucilla (cast, Paris, Bibliothèque Nationale, Cabinet des Médailles)

Commodus, the image of the Mother sidesaddle on her wild beast reflects in the coinage the emperor's gratitude to her for having preserved him from Maternus' crime. As for the coinage of Julia Domna (wife of Septimius Severus) and Julia Soaemias (mother of Heliogabalus), it honours in the Mother of the gods the model of the empresses who gave birth to princes destined for deification. Nevertheless, Cybele again suffered an eclipse after the Severan dynasty, to re-emerge in the fourth century AD only on contorniate medallions.[70]

Claudius did not stop at incorporating the deeds of Attis into the calendar. He may also have reformed the official priesthood by instituting the office of archigallus, if one agrees with the reasoning of J. Carcopino[71] (still valid in my opinion). There is no reliable mention to be found of an archigallus before the Antonine era, at least in epigraphy (but the alleged 'archigallus' of Parrhasios in Pliny the Elder, *Natural History*, XXXV, 70, is more than suspect). As high priest (*summus sacerdos*) of the Mother-worship cult, the archigallus was a Roman citizen. He thus had an official duty that was incompatible with castration, which Roman law forbade its nationals. The galli consecrated themselves to Cybele by sacrificing their manhood to her. How, therefore, could an archigallus be 'ordained' without breaking the law? Here we meet and have an explanation for the taurobolium which, in ancient documentation, is often the accompaniment of the archigallic title.

The first epigraphic attestation of a Mother-cult taurobolium is dated to AD 160.[72] But we are told of the forms of the ceremony only by fourth-century Christian authors, Firmicus Maternus and, chiefly, Prudentius (*Hymns*, X, 1006–50), writing around 400. A man descends into a pit or trench, wearing a toga of which one fold covers his ribbon-adorned head. The pit is covered with an openwork platform or flooring with many holes in it. A bull is then brought and its chest hacked with blows from a spear.

> The huge wound spouts a flood of hot blood . . . which seethes in all directions . . . Through the countless channels provided by the perforations a stinking torrent falls. The priest enclosed in the pit gets the full force of it, exposing his befouled head to every drop; his robe and his whole body reek. Worse is to come! He tilts his head backwards, exposing his cheeks, his ears, his lips and nostrils, even his eyes. Without sparing his palate, he soaks his tongue in it, until his whole body is impregnated with this horrible, dark blood. (Prudentius, *Hymns*, X, 1028–40)

The victim is removed, the cover taken off, and then 'the pontiff, dreadful to see' is extracted from the pit. He is hailed 'with the idea that vile blood ... has purified him while he was hidden in these shameful depths' (see fig 1).

The etymology of the word *taurobolium* (Latin transcription of a Greek word) has aroused hypotheses about kinds of 'corrida' which may in the early days have been the prelude to the slaughter. Prudentius speaks of a throwing weapon, *venabulum* or hunting-spear. Yet monuments show us a long, hooked knife (*harpè*).[73] In fact, it was a matter of striking the bull and then enlarging the wound with the hook in order to obtain a plentiful flow of blood. Cumont emphasized the invocation to Artemis 'Tauropolis',[74] whose savage rites were said to have been imported by Orestes from Tauris to Comana in Cappadocia (Strabo, *Geography*, XII, 2, 3). But the origins of the taurobolium, of which Cybele did not have a monopoly, elude us.

At any rate, in the Roman era the process consisted of being immersed in the spilt blood in order to identify oneself ritualistically, though imaginarily, with the victim. It was a substitution sacrifice.

Figure 1 Taurobolium (from M.J. Vermaseren, *Cybele and Attis*, p. 106).

Inscriptions inform us that the slaughtered bull's testicles were cut off and buried beneath an altar, just as the *vires* of the castrated galli were ritually interred. Prudentius quite rightly makes the martyr denouncing the repugnant performance say: 'It is my blood that you see, not that of an ox' (*Hymns*, X, 1007). Now the subject of the taurobolium of which he speaks is the *summus sacerdos consecrandus* (ibid., 1011–12): the one who is to be consecrated as high priest, or in other words, the archigallus. So he was hailed and worshipped, and ended with the conviction that he was 'purified'. The Great Mother was given satisfaction by the castration of the sacrificed bull. Henceforth, the archigallus wore the crown and the *occabus* or heavy gold bracelet.[75] Invested by the quindecimvirs *sacris faciundis*, he belonged to the official hierarchy of the Roman priesthood.

At first carried out in the port of Ostia, from the time of Antoninus Pius the taurobolium was celebrated in a new Phrygian sanctuary built in the Vatican, and is possibly shown to us in a contorniate medallion (plate 4) struck in homage to the memory of Faustina the Elder.[76] Archigalli were 'ordained' there, sacrificing a bull for the safekeeping of the emperor and the imperial family. Apart from future archigalli, others could go through the same ceremony, standing in the pit to receive the bloody benediction, 'for the preservation' (*pro salute*) of the emperor. The fact that on Faustina's coins the Great Mother

Plate 4 Contorniate medallion (*Phrygianum* according to T.D. Donaldson, *Architectura Numismatica*, No. 21)

bears the epithet 'salutaris' is probably connected with the imperial officialization of the ritual and the site. Furthermore, the placing of a *Phrygianum* in the Vatican may be explained by the 'vaticinations' of the archigallus, who recommended the execution of taurobolia in the name of the goddess. Not just anybody – not even the emperor – could take the initiative. A taurobolium was carried out on the command (*ex imperio, ex iussu*) of Cybele, who most frequently expressed herself by means of the voice of her high priest, sometimes also (though rarely) as the fulfilment of a vow. However that may be, from the middle of the second century AD, the Vatican sanctuary was the Mecca of Mother-cult consecration. It lay in front of the present-day St Peter's Basilica, where in the early seventeenth century a remarkable series of taurobolic altars was discovered.[77]

The taurobolium was nearly always accompanied by a 'criobolium', the sacrifice of a ram, whose testicles were also removed. It was thought that the taurobolium honored Cybele and the criobolium was specifically for Attis.[78] That is not obvious. Before quoting the formula of Mother-cult initiations, the Christian apologist Clement of Alexandria (*Protreptikos*, II, 15, 2) recalls a myth of Zeus snatching the two testicles of a ram and 'throwing them right into Ge's lap, thus deceptively paying the penalty for his shameless violence, as if he had mutilated himself'. This is the very definition of a substitution sacrifice. Moreover, Zeus' violence to Ge, or the Earth Mother, reminds us of the impregnation of the rock Agdos. Lastly, the very name of Ge implies a connection with the Eleusinian mysteries and thus brings us back to Timotheus. In these conditions, the criobolium legitimized in this way by a 'Phrygio-Eleusinian' myth may well be far older than is generally believed.

The participant in the taurobolium is 'reborn', like Attis, born to a new life (hence the word *natalicium* found inscribed on some taurobolic altars). In 376, a follower declared himself 'reborn for eternity'[79] and two inscriptions from Turin are consecrated *viribus aeterni*, that is to say to the 'forces' (vital, sexual) of the 'eternal', in commemoration of a taurobolium.[80] In fact, we know that this bloody 'baptism' was held to regenerate for twenty years the man or woman who descended into the pit. The Latin *aeternus* indeed implies durability rather than transcendental eternity in the Christian sense.[81] It seems that only one emperor had himself 'taurobolized' (if we are to believe the *Augustan History*):[82] Heliogabalus (218–22); but in order to gain possession of the black stone, something which is historically unconfirmed.

Against the date 28 March in a fourth-century calendar is the note *Initium Caiani*, which tends to be translated as 'initiation [of the circus] of Gaius', or 'Caligula's circus'. It was a ceremony celebrated in the Vatican *Phrygianum*, but not necessarily to be confused with the taurobolium. When they attack the mysteries of Cybele, the Fathers of the Church teach us about initiation. Clement of Alexandria and Firmicus Maternus even give us the text of the 'symbol' that the neophyte had to utter for his consecration. This symbol was clearly influenced by that of the Eleusinian mysteries, and here again perhaps we find traces of a syncretic action attributable to the Eumolpid Timotheus. But Clement and Firmicus do not keep strictly to the same formula. According to Clement (*Protreptikos*, II, 15, 3), the initiate had to say: 'I have eaten from the drum, I have drunk from the cymbal, I have carried the sacred vessels, I have plunged beneath the curtain'. In Firmicus (*The Error of Profane Religions*, XVIII, 1), one reads: 'I have eaten from the drum, drunk from the cymbal, and learnt in depth the secrets of religion'; but in Greek: 'I have eaten from the drum, drunk from the cymbal, I have become a priest of Attis'. Apparently, therefore, according to Firmicus, one becomes a priest of Attis by receiving the complete revelation (*perdidici*) of the mythico-religious arcana (*religionis secreta*).

This revelation could be matched by the priest's final declaration according to Clement, if 'plunging beneath the curtain' had a metaphorical sense, of an unveiling or explanation of the holy images, for instance. But *pastos* ('curtain') may be applied to the marriage bed, the chamber of the goddess, and thus be concerned with a sacred marriage identifying the initiate with Attis, Cybele's mythical lover.[83] Where Firmicus speaks of an instruction (*perdidici*) Clement would appear to mention a rite of mystical union with the Great Mother, in a sort of 'holy of holies' or *adyton* (which is also alluded to in *The Error of Pagan Religions* after the quotation of the symbol).

But in Clement of Alexandria the neophyte also declares: 'I have carried the sacred vessels'. This describes the *kernos* which is a tray bearing kinds of jars, and which seems to have played a part in the Eleusinian mysteries. In the period when Timotheus lived, the poet Alexander of Aetolia alluded to this Mother-cult rite (*Palatine Anthology*, VII, 709, 2). It also arises in taurobolic epigraphy. Perhaps the blood of victims was poured into them?[84] But as Firmicus Maternus does not breathe a word about them, nor of a priestly marriage with Cybele, it may be supposed that his formula concerns first-degree initiates or priests of Attis, whereas Clement refers to the symbol of higher-degree initiates – such as the epopts of Eleusis – or priests of Cybele. The liturgy of the mysteries may also have included local variants, notably at Alexandria.

However that may be, what was the meaning of 'eating from the drum' and 'drinking from the cymbal'? Were they real or symbolic food and drink? The first hypothesis has been disputed on the grounds of the abstinence imposed on the faithful before the Hilaria. P. Boyancé[85] emphasized two passages from the Jewish philosopher Philo of Alexandria on corybantic enthusiasm and the mystical perception of celestial harmony, which fed the soul through the ears, and musical intoxication, as provided by the drums and cymbals. But we know that in Antiquity there was no mystery cult without food and a holy feast. Symbols of the type quoted by Clement and Firmicus may be connected with the foundation myth, but are never properly speaking metaphorical. We therefore have to admit that candidates for Mother-cult initiation did not absorb imaginary nourishment through their ears by way of a rite of musical purification. We do not know what was presented to them on the drum or in the cymbal. People drank milk before the Hilaria, but the mysteries of Attis are not to be confused with the 'holy week' of the god who dies and is resurrected.

In parallel with the public or initiatory cult, more or less marginal groups called on the Cappadocian Mother at the same time as Cybele. Juvenal (*Satires*, VI, 511–21) leads one to believe that, with their charlatanesque arguments, certain eunuch priests competed with the archigallus:

> Here comes the raving brotherhood of Bellona and the Mother of the gods, with a gigantic eunuch, presenting a venerable face to his obscene underlings. It is a long while since he cut his flabby testicles with a piece of broken glass. He takes precedence over this hoarse cohort and the drummers. His Phrygian tiara is tied under his plebeian chin. He makes a great to-do and decides there is cause to fear the approach of September and the Auster [south wind], unless by way of purification he is presented with one hundred eggs, with old robes in a dead-leaf shade. The threat of this fearful and sudden peril will disappear in their folds, and at a single stroke the entire year will be exonerated from sin![86]

It may be imagined that in this cosmopolitan Rome of the Antonine period, a number of mendicant galli scratched a living in the shadow of the sanctuary. We know, moreover, that the Great Mother of the gods often extended hospitality to the wandering sect members of Bellona and the Syrian Goddess.

Outside, but in the environs of Rome, there are quite a few monuments that bear witness to the sphere of influence and importance of Phrygianism. Near Albano, at *Bovillae*, a college of dendrophori gave itself the title *salutare* (like the Great Mother on the coins of Faustina who had died six years earlier).[87] That epithet was all the more apt as the brotherhood had been allocated land for a plantation of pines, the trees which the dendrophori carried to the Palatine on every 22 March. In 1736, between *Lanuvium* and Genzano, the marble bas-relief of the Capitoline Museum was discovered,[88] preserving for us the fascinating portrait of a Mother-cult priest, his head laden with sacred medallions and adorned with long strings of pearls, beside the whip of little bones with which he scourged himself on 24 March.

But above all at Ostia Cybele and Attis had a renowned religious centre,[89] well worthy of the historic tradition which celebrated the arrival of the goddess at the mouth of the Tiber in 204 BC. There the temple of the Mother rose on a high podium with lateral vaults, at the end of an immense triangular campus which was cut off from the profane world by an enclosing wall and covered an area of 4500 sq m. At the eastern point of the triangle (connected with the temple by a long portico), a partly vaulted excavation that has been wrongly identified as a taurobolic pit (*fossa sanguinis*) was close to a temple to Bellona and a little sanctuary of Attis. In this *Attideum*, two Pans guarded the entrance to a chapel with an apse. The temple of Bellona (incorporated with the *area* of the campus but separated from the buildings of the Phrygian cult) gave on to a closed courtyard where the *fanatici* of the Cappadocian Mother could indulge in their bloody gambols; it communicated with a room where the 'lance-bearers' (*hastiferi*) gathered. From the *Metrôon* at Ostia come several notable sculptures like the reclining statue of Attis (today in the Vatican Museum), where the god combines with the attributes of the Sun and the Moon those of harvests and fruitfulness.[90]

As a Roman colony, in March of every year Ostia celebrated the same cycle of festivals as Rome. One has to imagine the display of moving and colourful processions, the pulsating and resonant dances, the cries and the flagellations of the *dies sanguinis* on the triangular ground that opened out, as it were, facing the temple and perhaps had a symbolic value. In the port itself Cybele had many worshippers, either settled or passing through. In the Isola Sacra (the port's cemetery) a sarcophagus lid was found which shows the recumbent figure of a priest whose bracelet bears the picture of Cybele.[91] The same person appears, carrying out his sacrificial functions (plate 5) on two reliefs with the same archaeological origin. In the port's taverns,

Plate 5 Priest of Attis (Museo di Ostia)

aristocrats who liked to mingle with the riff-raff would spend the night 'higgledy-piggledy with sailors, thieves, fugitive slaves, amid executioners, pall-bearers and the silent drums of a gallus flat on his back' (Juvenal, *Satires*, VIII, 172–6).

The Expansion of Mother-worship

Cybele and Attis are present all over Italy, although in a fairly sporadic manner.[92] Our information, too, is largely due to chance. The Mother and her companion were honoured in the ports, especially at Brindisi (where their priest was also in the service of Isis and the

Syrian Goddess), at Pozzuoli (where Cybele had her *religiosi*, dendrophori and kernophori), at Aquileia (where Danubian and Levantine influences met). But Phrygianism prospered equally in the hinterland, on the great estates where slaves of eastern origin toiled; in the *municipia* where it was official; in the mountainous or forested areas where the goddess of Ida felt at home; where the woodsellers – along the high Apennine valleys or in the foothills of the Alps – cultivated the material for rendering homage to the god of the tree; near lakes and springs, and in thermal spas where, as in Asia Minor, she remained the goddess of the waters. Evidence of devotion ranges from the marble statue to the modest popular ex-voto in terracotta. The goddess was as important to peasants anxious for good harvests as she was to the businessmen in the ports or to the woodcutters in the mountain forests. She also watched over the dead who became reincorporated with the Earth Mother.

Everywhere her idol was sumptuously displayed to the adoration of her faithful. At Corfinium, (Pentima), where as often happened elsewhere she was associated with Bellona, she had a gilded statue which gleamed in the shadows of the temple, in the company of a golden-haired Attis who, as Mên Tyrannus, wore a big silver moon behind him.[93] At Formiae, her marble idol (now kept in the Ny Carlsberg Glyptothek in Copenhagen) wore a blue-painted robe, an expensive necklace, bracelets, rings and, in her pierced ears, dazzling gold pendants or pearls.[94]

Monuments of the Mother-worship cult are particularly dense in Campania, at Baiae, Cumae, around and south of Vesuvius, Pompeii, Herculaneum, Stabiae. At Capua, Diana Tifatina, like Cybele the mistress of wild animals and mountains, seems to have reconciled her native tradition with that of the Mother from Pessinus. From a deposit of ex-votos (*favissa*) connected with her temple, several figurines of Attis were recovered.[95] People have wondered whether the religion of Demeter and Dionysus (with its orgiastic rites) may have paved the way for Phrygianism in southern Italy. The fact remains that the chronology of the finds gives no grounds for supposing that the cult of Cybele could have taken root in Campania before the arrival of the black stone in Rome. The earliest taurobolium known through epigraphy is dated to AD 134 by a dedication at Pozzuoli (*CIL*, X, 1596), but there it was a matter of a sacrifice offered to Venus Caelestis, the Syrio-Phoenician Astarte: was she at that time implicitly identified with the Great Mother, following a syncretism that is attested elsewhere?

In Magna Graecia, Hera and Demeter seem to have defended their local origins. Mother-cult discoveries there are somewhat scattered. Nevertheless, in Sicily, west of Syracuse, *Acrae* had a vast rocky sanctuary, whose figures sculpted directly into the rock have kept the name *Santoni*, 'the Saints'. On the hill close to a sacred spring can be seen a dozen or so niches two to three metres high, housing the richly adorned image of Cybele. She appears in company with Attis and Hermes (like the Hermes *Propolos* of Greek iconography) or enthroned between Hermes and Hecate. This open-air holy place, highly suitable for reminding people of the power of a deity of stone and water, must have been carved in the third century BC.[96] But it was frequented until the end of Antiquity and even later. Formerly in Calabria on Holy Thursday groups of young people held the 'Saint Jerome' race (*di San Girolami*), cutting their flesh with broken glass and lancets, like the galli and their emulators on the Day of Blood.

Roman Africa gladly incorporated the Great Mother into its public and private pantheon.[97] In Tripolitania, she is hardly to be found except at Leptis Magna (homeland of the emperor Septimius Severus), where the proconsul inaugurated her temple in AD 72 on the old Forum, with the financial aid of a native notable. But Phrygianism extended its influence chiefly from Proconsularis to Mauretania Caesariensis: all along the coastline, in the ports; in colonies of Roman citizens, where it was a part of civic loyalism and the imperial cult; in the hinterland, along the great communication routes that penetrated active and Romanized centres. The criobolium and taurobolium for the safekeeping of the emperor or private individuals were practised in Carthage, Utica, Makthar, Zana, Announa and Tipasa. Utica had its 'initiates' (*sacrati*), Setif and Cherchel their 'devotees' (*religiosi*). A magnificent statue from Cherchel (plate 6) represents a Mother-cult priest garbed in the fashion of the third century AD who may be identified with the archigallus of this town, whose status as a Roman colony dated back to the emperor Claudius. Like Utica, Philippopolis and, of course, Carthage, Makthar had its college of dendrophori. At the other (western) extremity of Africa, Banasa, as a colony, had to have a temple to Cybele.

In Carthage itself, the Great Mother on a lion's back recalled the cult image of the *Dea Caelestis*, the Latin name for Tanit, popularized in the coinage of Septimius Severus.[98] In the Sousse Museum there are two statues of seated deities which probably come from Carthage, one showing us Saturn and the other Astarte enthroned, like Cybele, between two lions. Even in the fourth century, St Augustine (*City of God*, VII, 26) acknowledges the success of the Mother and her eunuchs:

They were seen yesterday, their hair moist with perfume, their faces covered in make-up, their limbs flaccid, their walk effemi-

Plate 6 Archigallus of Cherchel (photo. kindly provided by P.-A. Fevrier)

nate, wandering through the squares and streets of Carthage, demanding from the public the means to subsidize their shameful life

(in other words, collecting on the occasion of the Megalensia). The bishop of Hippo admits:

We enjoyed the infamous games offered to the gods and goddesses, to the Celestial 'Virgin' [Tanit] and the Berecyntian, mother of the gods.

Obscene ham actors mimed disgusting acts in front of her litter 'in the presence of an immense throng of spectators and listeners of both sexes'. At the end of the century, paganism survived semi-clandestinely in the chapels to household gods in private homes. A mosaic of this period presents two women and a little girl bringing offerings to an Attis ensconced in his shrine.[99]

The Iberian peninsula does not appear to have been so receptive to the cult of Cybele.[100] Contrary to all expectations, Mother-cult epigraphy is concentrated in the western half, in Baetica and, above all, Lusitania, where there were large numbers of slaves of eastern origin. The army did not play any outstanding role here. In contrast, the indigenous religion of the goddess *Ataecina* may have been the prelude to the adoption of the Great Mother. The trade that Lisbon and Merida maintained with the central and eastern Mediterranean similarly encouraged it. The relative popularity of Attis appears more clearly in the south and east of the peninsula. But Phrygianism does not seem to have put down any deep roots. It was the affair of colonists and freedmen.

In colonies like Cordoba, Merida, Beja (*Pax Iulia*) and Medellin (*Metellinum*), it is not surprising to find mention of taurobolia and criobolia. In AD 234 at Cordoba, a private citizen of Graeco-Oriental origin had the sacrifice carried out for the 'preservation' of the emperor Septimius Severus, and a woman gathered up the ram's testicles. Four years later, the taurobolium and criobolium were repeated on a 24 March 'Day of Blood'. This time again a woman received the consecration of the criobolium. But in Merida, Valeria Avita took the benedictions of this bloody 'baptism' for herself alone, for her birthday, with the ministrations of an archigallus bearing the name Mysticus. Besides the March festivals celebrated normally, as in Rome, in towns with the status of colony Attis played a chiefly funereal role, as protector of the dead and the divine embodiment of their posthumous hopes. The tomb known as that of 'the Scipios', near Tarragona, provides a fine example.[101]

Phrygianism came into its own in the Gauls.[102] No other region in the Empire has yielded so many taurobolic altars (over sixty). It is true that as early as the sixth century BC a Mother from Asia Minor had landed at Marseille with the Phocaeans, as some fifty votive monuments datable to that period bear witness. C. Picard even believed he could recognize Attis on one of these reliefs. The worship of the mother-goddesses and the Earth Mother, notably in the southern half of Gaul, could also have encouraged the naturalization of Cybele, to say nothing of the distant ethnic links of this western Gaul with the Galatians of Asia Minor, who had taken a very close interest in the priesthood of Pessinus; or of the Gallus or galli whose name and graphic symbol of the cock coincided with those of the Gaulish people. However, even though for nearly a thousand years indigenous traditions may have provided the link between the pre-Celtic Mothers, the Phocaean Mother and the Great Mother of the gods, the first testimonies to Phrygianism properly speaking are hardly earlier than the time of the Antonines. But they reveal an extraordinary infatuation, perceptible for over a century, its prolongation still to be discerned in rural paganism at the end of Antiquity.

In the township of Lectoure (*Lactora*) alone, near Condom in the Gers, there were no fewer than twenty-one taurobolia, four of which were celebrated on 18 October 176 and nine on 8 December 241, some for the safekeeping of the emperor and some privately. Women were not behindhand in their passion for the bloody benediction – they were even in the majority! The *dies sanguinis* was celebrated in Lectoure with as much fervour and frenzy as in Rome. On 24 March 239, a wealthy Gallo-Roman lady carefully gathered up the testicles of Eutyches who, on that day, had castrated himself; she consecrated them in the temple and paid for the building of an altar to commemorate the event. In Narbonne, the capital of a province where Attis often watched over the deceased, taurobolia increased at the end of the Antonine period and during the time of the Severi. They were celebrated officially in colonies with Roman or Latin all along the Rhône valley, but also in the region of Die where Cybele met the local goddess Andarta, the mistress of bears and victory.[103] At Dea Augusta, as elsewhere, the Mother of the gods strengthened the religion of the Augusti. On 30 September 245, the permanent pontiff in charge of the imperial cult took part, with two women (mother and daughter), in the bloodbath achieved by the sacrifice of three bulls, for the preservation of the emperor Philip the Arab, his son and the empress. Fellow-celebrants in this memorable ceremony were the priests of Orange, Alba and the City of the Vocontii, as well as a priest of Liber Pater.

A special feature of the Die altars is that, alongside the heads of the bull and ram, the sickle and musical instruments, they show us the caduceus of Mercury. Apparently, the intention was to give prominence to this attribute of the conductor of souls into the afterlife or their regeneration by means of the taurobolium.[104]

Near St-Rémy-de-Provence, Glanum had its dendrophori, and a simply carved relief shows the death of Attis (plate 7) which the March festivals must have re-created in this town with Latin rights. There Cybele was associated with the Good Goddess whose ears (sculpted on an altar) were not addressed in vain, or so it was believed. Dendrophori served the Mother-worship cult in Vienne, where the Great Mother seems to have given refuge to the Syrian

Goddess,[105] in a town where Easterners must have been as numerous as in Lyon. But the archaeological site of the Old Hospital has nothing to do with a 'theatre of mysteries', a type of building of which no positive example is known, either in Gaul or the rest of the Roman Empire.

The great centre of the taurobolic cult was the capital of the Gauls, Lyon, Colonis Copia Claudia, from the name of the emperor Claudius who was born there on the very day of the inauguration of the altar to Rome and Augustus. Phrygianism which worked liturgically for the 'safeguarding' of the Caesars was hand in glove with the religion of the sovereign. So the *seviri Augustales* in charge of it frequently took a hand in the organization of taurobolia. Through Arles and the Rhône Valley, Lyon had steady relations with Ostia. The college of dendrophori celebrated the anniversary of its foundation there on 1 August, the day when the Gaulish peoples gathered at the federal sanctuary of the Croix-Rousse and also the *dies natalis* of Claudius, an ardent supporter of Cybele and Attis.

The earliest known dated taurobolic altar belongs to Lyon (*CIL*, XIII, 1751). But it commemorates a taurobolium carried out in 160 in the Vatican *Phrygianum*, most probably to consecrate the first archigallus of Lyon, ritually invested in Rome by the quindecimvirs *sacris faciundis*. The ceremony was followed by a 'midnight' (*Mesonyctium*) on 9 December of the same year, a vigil perhaps marked by an initiatory liturgy. The enthronement of the Lyonnais archigallus must have coincided with the inauguration of Cybele's sanctuary, which has not yet been identified with certainty behind the great theatre of Fourvière. Though Lyon's Mother-worship fervour went hand in hand with imperial loyalism, there is no evidence that the martyrs of the 'pogrom' of 177 (whose most notable victims were Pothinus and Blandina) were suffering the results of Phrygian fanaticism. Neither the *Letter* of the Christians in Lyon and Vienne 'to the Churches of Asia and Phrygia' (Eusebius, *Ecclesiastical History*, V, 1, 4–63), nor contemporary patristic texts denounce the cult of Attis as especially persecutory. Nor is there cause to extrapolate on the hypothetical coincidence in that year of the Christian Holy Week with the March Mother-cult cycle.[106]

Farther east, Phrygianism reached the region of Belley (Ain), perhaps grafting itself on to an indigenous worship of health-giving waters. But very often Cybele coexisted and cohabited with the local

---

Plate 7 Attis (Glanum, St-Rémy-de-Provence; photo. kindly provided by M. Euzennat)

Mothers or the springheads associated with them, without being confused with them.

In the south-west and the centre of Gaul, taurobolia are attested either epigraphically or iconographically (by the victims' heads) at Bordeaux, Périgueux and Texon (Haute-Vienne). The Périgueux altar (plate 8) shows us the bust of Attis on a block draped with a fringed tapestry, beside a bull, and from the god's head a tree appears to rise – is it the pine of 22 March? – on which are hung the whips used to scourge the galli. The richly embroidered headgear of the archigallus is featured above a set of pan-pipes. This iconography is strong confirmation of the symbolic and fundamental relationship of the mythical sacrifice of Attis with the taurobolic consecration of the high priest. The dedicant was the son of a priest of Rome and Augustus at the federal sanctuary of the Three Gauls. He must have imported the Phrygian ritual from Lyon to the Petrocorii. Like the designation of the flute-player in the Lyonnais dedications, the featuring of the timbrel, cymbals and straight and curved flute on several altars demonstrates the importance of musical stimulation and sound accompaniment in the ceremonial.

Cybele and Attis are present elsewhere through images or dedications in public or private chapels, on tableware (as decorative medallions), on and in tombs. But their cult appears to have scarcely touched the north-west. In the north and north-east, as well as isolated taurobolic monuments (at Metz and Vesoul), a few representations of the Mother and her castrated lover were found, notably at Bavay. Near the *Castrum* of Arras, in a house that was rearranged around the late third century for religious gatherings, two figures of Attis (one an idol in porphyry) were recently discovered, not far from trenches over-hastily interpreted as signs of taurobolic celebrations.[107] In the Rhine sector, funerary Attises chiefly indicate the spread of Romanized beliefs from Asia Minor. Pine cones and terracotta figurines of Cybele found at Trier and Cologne accompanied the dead in their last resting place. The Great Mother is linked with other deities, either local or of eastern origin, like Mithras or Bellona. At Kastell, (opposite Mainz) the 'lance-bearers' consecrated an altar to the imperial cult in 224, the actual day 'of Blood', 24 March. Twelve years later, they restored for Bellona a tumulus where they 'vaticinated' like the archigallus of Cybele, and which, for that reason, bears the name 'Vatican'.

The Mother-worship religion was rooted so strongly in the 'heartland' of Gaul that even in the fourth century, in Autun, on the day of the *Lavatio*, the statue of the 'Berecyntian' goddess was paraded on an ox-drawn chariot, to bless the vineyards and fields, with an escort of

Corybants and cymbalists who were as frenzied as the galli in Rome. Cybele had blended in so well with the local Mothers that at Fontaine-la-Mère (near Autun) an ex-voto homage of cymbals was given to the goddess of the place. People have tried to decipher allusions to her worship in the *Life of St Martin* (a great attacker of dendrolatry).[108]

The Phrygian couple crossed the Channel, with traders and soldiers, but without introducing the taurobolium.

Similarly, there is no evidence that the ritual bloodbath was practised along the Rhine or Danube,[109] in the provinces where Mithras and Jupiter Dolichenus dominated the religious field in garrison towns. The alleged *fossa sanguinis* of Neuss (*Novaesium*)[110] arises from a hypothesis which no epigraphic indication has yet confirmed, even though the cult of Cybele (plate 9) may have taken over from that of the matronal goddesses. Raetia and Noricum (present-day Switzerland and Austria) were not seduced by the Great Mother. Farther east, in the two Pannonias (Hungary and the north of ex-Yugoslavia), Cybele was honoured by local worthies in the large centres lying along military routes, in more or less close correlation with the civic religion of the sovereign. Official Phrygianism continued to go hand in hand with Romanization, but that did not rule out a certain popularity, chiefly in urban milieux. In Dacia, Roman colonists or soldiers helped to implant it. At Romula and Drobeta, Cybele was worshipped as protectress of the Aeneadae, in memory of the Trojan legend of the origins. But on the shores of the Black Sea, in Lower Moesia and Thrace, she had been settled for a long time with the Greek colonists, and people remained faithful to her in the Roman era.

Dalmatia has yielded a great deal of evidence relating to her cult. It was even thought possible to identify a taurobolic pit at Zecovi, near Prijedor (in Bosnia).[111] Foreigners populated the ports of the Adriatic coast, notably Salonae, *Iader* (Zara Zader), *Senia* (Senj) and the island of Arba. Salonae had its archigallus. At Senj the cathedral dedicated to the Virgin approximately occupies a site formerly consecrated to the Great Mother.[112] Freedmen of eastern, and more precisely Anatolian, origin served the Mother-cult at the same time as that of the emperors, which very often occurred elsewhere. In the early 1970s, in the countryside around Medvida, a life-sized head of Attis was found, provided with holes in which gilded bronze rods could be fixed, thus likening the image of the dead and revived god to the Sun.[113] This region was the meeting-place for influences that arrived by sea, but also by the roads and valleys connecting it with the Danubian provinces.

Plate 9 Cybele (from Neuss? photo. Mannheim Museum)

Syncretisms and Theosophical Allegories

A remarkable phenomenon was the growing importance of Attis, whose cult at first had vegetated somewhat clandestinely in the shadow of the Great Mother in the Palatine sanctuary. This increase in the popularity of the suffering companion god went hand in hand with a whole series of identifications that allowed him to absorb the powers and fields of influence of other divine personalities, and not only the minor ones.

In Anatolia, the Moon-god Mên bore the Lydian title of 'Sovereign' (*Tyrannos*). He exercised his sovereignty over the celestial, terrestrial and subterranean universe. He was lord of the animal and plant kingdoms, generation and fructification, the living and the dead. Like Attis, he wore a Phrygian cap, but also, behind him, a crescent which showed him to be the lord of nighttime, a major symbol in a period and among people where the day began at sunset, at an hour when

---

Plate 8 Taurobolic altar of Périgueux

one started to come alive again after a long ordeal of overwhelming heat ... An inscription from Lydia proclaims with an almost monotheistic conviction, 'There is only one god in the heavens, the great celestial Mên'.[114] This god had won worshippers in Greece and Italy. By annexing the attribute of the crescent moon, Attis incorporated with the prerogatives of the god Mên those that were recognized as belonging to the night star in the matter of growth and germination. The fourth-century-BC dedications addressed him as *Menotyrannus*. But in the second century BC at Ostia, his cap was crowned with the crescent moon under a star or two corn-ears, as a sign of celestial omnipotence over harvests.[115] In other words, he tended to take over the responsibilities first held by Cybele.

Although wrongly, the epithet *Menotyrannus* was probably related to his reign over the months. Indeed, a god could hardly die and be reborn annually, at the spring equinox, without having some connection with the cycle of solar revolutions. So the head of Attis was endowed with rays which he wore at the same time as the crescent of Mên. Such is the case of the statue found at Ostia in the *Attideion*. The recumbent god holds a bunch of corn-ears, pomegranates and pine cones; he wears a crown of fruits under a cap decked with rays and a moon. He therefore already appeared (in the second century AD) as a universal deity, responsible for heaven and earth.[116] The archigallus's tiara, which likened him to an Attis, was studded with sparkling stones, some of which in the shape of stars or moon refer us to a cosmic omnipotence.[117] It was already the starry cap, 'the star-spangled tiara' with which Cybele crowns her beloved in the prose hymn that the emperor Julian devoted to her (*Discourse on the Mother of the Gods*, 165 b, 171 a).

This syncretic fermentation went beyond the circle of official Phrygianism. In Gnostic circles, where various theosophies inherited from pagan tradition were wildly embroidered onto Christian Scriptures, the Naassenes who, without practising eunuchism, eschewed all sexual relations, sang hymns to Attis 'for he is Pan (= the great 'All'), he is Bacchus, he is the pastor of the twinkling stars'. These Gnostics significantly harked back to Eleusianism as well as to the Phrygianism of which Timotheus had been the exegete. In the time of the emperor Severus Alexander, around 230, the Christian Hippolytus, denouncing the sect, quotes an example of the kind of canticle intoned in the theatre to a harp accompaniment (*Philosophoumena*, V, 1):

Hail to thee, Attis, unhappy victim of Rhea's mutilation! In Assyria thou art called Adonis; in Egypt, Osiris; in Greece, the

Celestial Crescent of the Moon [allusion to the god Mên] ...
and in Phrygia, sometimes Papas, sometimes ... the cropped
green ear of corn or the flute-player.

On the myth of Attis the Naassenes advanced a theory which oddly
enough prefigured the one to be developed by the emperor Julian. The
Mother of the gods castrated the Phrygian shepherd 'although she
had him for her lover; it was because, on high, the blessed Nature of
beings who are above the world and eternal wants to make the
masculine virtue of the soul rise towards her'. Attis cut off his testicles
in order to break with the baser and material world and gain access to
immortal life, where there is no longer either male or female (*Philosophoumena*, V, 7).

Curiously, Roman sarcophagi of the third century AD which represent the Genii of the Four Seasons, personifications of the cycles of
eternally fecund and regenerative nature, sometimes show us Winter
looking like Attis.[118] One would rather expect him to embody Spring.
Perhaps this representation arises from a confusion in the model
books, but a confusion that reveals the extent to which this god filled
the imagination, or even the religious thinking, of contemporaries.
'The Phrygians', wrote Plutarch, 'in the belief that their god sleeps
through the winter and awakes in the summer, celebrate with Bacchanalia his winter drowsiness and his reawakening in summer' (*Isis and
Osiris*, 69). But Plutarch does not tell us the name of the god connected
with the annual alternations.

However, the myth of Cybele and Attis also intrigued the philosophers who tended to see in it the confirmation of their doctrines.
Plotinus (*Enneads*, III, 6, 19) interprets the Great Mother as the image
of Matter who receives the forms of the intelligible world, but who is
sterile, like the eunuchs who serve her. In his treatise on *Statues*, which
allegorically gives an account of an entire polytheistic iconography,
Porphyry makes Attis the symbol of flowers which appear in the
spring but wither and fall before bearing fruit: 'hence the emasculation attributed to him, when the fruits have not matured' (Eusebius,
Praeparatio Evangelica, III, 11, 12). Other exegetes deciphered in the
Phrygian legend the story of corn cut and stored for the winter or
buried, sown, in the autumn to germinate into rebirth in the spring.
But this *ratio physica* of Stoic inspiration (denounced and denigrated
by Firmicus Maternus, a former Porphyrian converted to Christianity)
could bring no satisfaction either to minds animated by a cosmic
mysticism or souls tormented by the problem of their incarnation and
vocation in this world here below!

From the end of the third century, and chiefly during the second half of the fourth, taurobolic monuments reveal the passionate adherence of pagan aristocracy to Mother-worship, at the same time as Isiacism and Mithraism. The construction of St Peter's Basilica, then the antipagan laws of Constantine and his sons upset the religious service of the Vatican *Phrygianum*.[119] But after a long 'night' lasting twenty-eight years, as we are reminded by the dedication of a priest who made 'the offering of his actions, his intelligence and his life' to the Great Mother, it was once again possible (thanks to the usurper Magnentius) to lead the bull and the ram to sacrifice, 'the sign of felicity'.[120] And when the Arian Constantius II once more became master of the West, he had to turn a blind eye to the liturgies of Roman polytheism so as not to alienate a party that remained powerful in the Senate of the *Urbs*. The last dated taurobolia belong to 390. A poem against Nicomachus Flavianus – 'the last of the Romans' (E. Stein) – deplores the fact that members of the nobility escort the silver chariot of Cybele, take part in carrying the pine tree, and that senators are proud to keep their stained togas, sullied by the blood of the taurobolium.[121]

In 295 the augur and 'clarissimus' Scipio Orfitus consecrated the memory of a taurobolium by an altar on which we see Cybele triumphant in her lion-drawn chariot, opposite Attis standing against a pine. Probably twenty years later he repeated the beneficial act of the bloody sacrament, and commemorated the event on another altar, where Attis' Phrygian cap is crowned with an eagle's head, the Jovian bird symbolizing celestial sovereignty.[122] In fact, fourth-century dedications qualify the young god with 'Very High' (*hypsistos*) or 'Invincible' (*invictus*), like Mithras and other divinities of eastern origin. Attis is 'holy' (*sanctus*). With Cybele, he is 'all-powerful' (*omnipotens*). In 370, after receiving the 'baptism' of blood, the clarissimus Petronius Apollodorus, who was a pontiff, quindecimvir *sacris faciundis* and 'Father' in the Mithraic cult, celebrated Attis in Greek verse as 'he who unites and maintains the universe', an expression applied elsewhere to the Sun as lord of the heavens.[123]

The Christian apologists Arnobius and Firmicus Maternus were most indignant that anyone should dare to identify with the radiant star an emasculated shepherd over whom there was much noisy lamentation in the theatre and the streets every year in March. How could anyone '*Attin castratum subito praedicere Solem*', 'suddenly proclaim the castrated Attis "Sun"', to take a line from the pamphlet published against Nicomachus Flavianus.[124] That however was the identification illustrated one or two centuries earlier on monuments of popular piety, and coupled in dedications with the lunar qualification

Menotyrannos. Far from constituting a decisive objection, the mourning of 22–24 March before the Hilaria served as an argument for exegetes of Phrygianism. It was claimed that the confirmation of this cosmic syncretism could be discerned in the slightest details of the cult. The varying notes of the flute played by Attis were interpreted as the winds themselves 'that take their very substance from the Sun' (Macrobius, *Saturnalia*, I, 21, 9). The Phrygian shepherd's crook symbolized the omnipotence of the celestial *khoregos* (we may recall that the Naassenian Gnostics called him 'pastor of the twinkling stars'). For Macrobius, the proof that the March ceremonies were related to the sun was that, according to Mother-cult ritual, at the end of the revolution in the southern hemisphere or 'katabasia' of the day star

> when the simulation of mourning was over, the rebirth of joy was celebrated on the eighth day before the kalends of April. This day is called 'Hilaria', the first when the hours of sunshine are longer than those of night. (Macrobius, *Saturnalia*, I, 21, 9)

Thus in their liturgical year, as well as in the myth and holy iconography of Attis, the followers of the Great Mother were able to recognize a sort of coherence granted to their vision of the universe.

But from their questioning of the mythology and religious traditions some intellectuals of mystical and theosophical paganism drew something other than an explanation of the material world. Such was the case of the emperor Julian and his friend Sallustius, the prefect of the East. Contrary to Plotinus, the man known as 'the Apostate' regarded Cybele not as passive and negative matter, but as Providence, Mother of the 'intellectual' gods who were directly issued from the intelligible world. 'Mistress of all life and cause of all generation', she possessed the causes of the forms imprinted in matter. In Attis she animated 'the demiurgic and generative cause' of living beings. She therefore invited him to give birth 'in intelligible order, turning towards her . . . to avoid advancing towards matter'. Attis blossoms 'like a flower' on the banks of the Gallus which Julian identifies with the Milky Way where souls founder in the corporeal world. Cybele then places on his head the spangled cap that makes him sovereign of the skies. But Attis goes down into the shadowy cave and falls in love with the Nymph, the embodiment of the humid principle of matter. Now, the Lion, which represents the igneous principle – in other words, the part of Attis concerned with the celestial fire – warns the Great Mother, and her young lover mutilates himself in order not to multiply corporeal forms indefinitely.

Attis' adventure with the Nymph thus corresponds to the movement of divine generosity that illuminates the dark matter of the lower

world, like the sun's rays, but without ever falling into total compromise with it. Castration is the mastery of the demiurge who keeps
his distance from the object he determines while at the same time
giving it form. The divine rushes passionately towards its becoming,
but breaks its inclination to infinity in consideration of the defined
forms of the intelligible world. Attis is identified with this demiurge
who contains all the principles of sublunar creatures and who 'engen-
ders everything to the last degree' without ceasing to contemplate the
divine matrices of the Great Mother and without dissipating himself
in the multiplicity of evolution (*Discourse on the Mother of the Gods*, 166
a–169 d). This is a far cry from Porphyry's botanical and restricted
interpretation.

Sallustius takes up the same doctrine in the sort of pagan catechism
he compiled at the request of the emperor under the title *The Gods and
the Universe* (IV, 7–9). Attis is the demiurge of developing beings, who
are born and destroy themselves. By loving the Nymph of Gallos, he
becomes enamoured of the very world that he animates and creates,
rather as God falls in love with his own image in the *Poimandres*
(*Hermes Trismegistus*, I, 12) or as primordial Man falls in love with
Nature over which he has full power (ibid., 14). But generation has to
be stopped, and by mutilating himself Attis 'casts off the generative
powers of becoming to return to a communion with the gods'.

It is not merely a matter of elucidating creation which, unlike
several variants of the Gnosis, is not a disastrous fall but the expression of overflowing fruitfulness. The exegesis of the myth is applied to
the incarnate soul, 'for we too have fallen from the heavens and live
with the Nymph' (Sallustius, *The Gods and the Universe*, IV, 10), and
'these events took place at no precise moment', as Julian's friend
reminds us: 'they still exist' (ibid., 9). So the phases of the March ritual
are all related to our salvation. The felling of the Tree (the pine of 22
March) and the subsequent fast 'represent our removal from the
ulterior progress of generation; after that, drinking milk shows our
rebirth; lastly come the joys of the Hilaria . . . like reascending to the
gods' (ibid., 10).

This 'ascent' (or *epanodos*) of souls that turn and go back to the skies,
is embodied by Attis, not only for Julian and Sallustius but also on
contemporary monuments. Many of the contorniate medallions that
Rome's polytheistic aristocracy had cast and distributed in the second
half of the fourth century, to mark pagan festivals, show us the Mother
and her beloved in their lion-drawn chariot. Attis is the 'driver of her
chariot', Julian tells us (*Discourse on the Mother of the Gods*, 171 d). A
precious and significant item is the silver dish of Parabiago,[125] preserved in Milan in the Pinacoteca di Brera (plate 10). This splendid

piece, with a diameter of nearly 40 cm, represents the triumph of Cybele and Attis in a quadriga drawn by lions, accompanied by Corybants, flying above land and water deities, opposite the Genius of Eternity in his zodiacal circle, beneath the chariots of the Sun and the Moon. *Putti* personifying the four seasons dance below the big cats, above Ocean and a Nereid. This *lanx* from Parabiago, which has sometimes been dated (without good reason) to the Antonine period, is a demonstration of the enthusiastic devotion to the Phrygian gods' cosmic omnipotence.

Their triumph is that of souls over death, at least in the view taken by Sallustius, but also implied by Julian, for there is no other life than a return to the divine. A century later, the Neoplatonist philosopher Isidore of Alexandria, dreaming at Hierapolis in Phrygia that he was Attis and was celebrating the Hilaria, gathered from this dream the conviction that he had been 'saved from Hades', in other words,

Plate 10 Parabiago Dish (Milan, Pinacoteca di Brera)

promised to a happy eternity (Photius, *Bibliotheca*, 242, 131). The god of ephemeral blossoming, or rather, tragic deflowering, has become the guarantee of immortality, of which the funerary Attises of the preceding centuries had already given a foretaste.

In the name of the sacrifice of their virility, which had made them become Attides, the galli especially aspired to this felicity in the afterworld. Hence the indignant reaction of St Augustine (*City of God*, VII, 26):

> In order to have a happy life after death, must one consecrate oneself to these gods when by doing so one cannot live decently before death, subject as one is to such repugnant superstitions and linked with such obscene demons?

The dendrophori were not officially suppressed until 415. The victory of Theodosius over the pagan rhetorician and usurper Eugenius in 394 had put paid to the public practice of the Mother-worship cult. Serena, Theodosius' niece, having made her way into the temple on the Palatine, seized Cybele's necklace to put it round her own neck; so the Great Mother's faithful were not much surprised to learn one day that the princess had died of strangulation ...

Phrygianism would still hold its ground for a while in some localities and in theosophical cenacles. In the East, Neoplatonists like Damascius continued in the sixth century to incorporate Attis in their theology as generator of the sublunar world.[126] Proclus devoted a 'Mother-cult' book to Cybele in which, like Julian, he justifies the myth of Attis by way of lofty speculations on the soul and the cosmos.[127] He takes pains not to forget him in his *Hymn to Helios*,[128] any more than the esoteric encyclopedist Martianus Capella in the invocation to the Sun that he ascribes to Philologius (II, 192). The biographer of Proclus, Marinus of Neapolis, informs us that every month his master underwent the purifications of the Phrygian ritual.[129]

Absolutely remarkable is the development of the Neoplatonist exegesis applied to Cybele, and chiefly to her 'divine offspring' as he is called in the previously mentioned inscription of Petronius Apollodorus. This mythical model of the scorned galli – neither men nor women – benefited from an advancement that was all the more paradoxical because the eunuch god had taken on the aspect of a demiurge! But it was Cybele who survived in the *Theotokos*. It is known that the Nestorians rejected the epithet which permitted a parallel between the Mother of God and the Mother of the gods. In the early fifth century, Isidore of Pelusium took the trouble to examine this comparison. Did not Julian himself give the goddess the title of 'Virgin' (*Discourse on the Mother of the Gods*, 166 b)?

Chapter 2

Isis of the Many Names, or Our Lady of the Waves

E GYPT always exerted a sort of fascination over the Greeks. They were the first to recognize not only analogies between Egyptian religion and their own, but the former's influence on their own beliefs and some of the liturgies they held most dear. At a very early period the 'holy' accounts (*hieroi logoi*) of the Heraion of Argos identified Io with Isis, and Epaphos with the bull, Apis. Aeschylus took his inspiration from it in his tragedy, *The Suppliants*. In the middle of the fifth-century BC, Herodotus stressed the agreement of Egyptian 'taboos' with Orphic and Bacchic rules (*History*, II, 81), which actually came directly from Egypt (II, 49). Comparing the Isiac festivals with the Thesmophoria in honour of Demeter, he had no hesitation in writing: 'It was the daughters of Danaos who brought these rites from Egypt and taught them to the women of the Pelasgi' (II, 171). The *Helen* of Euripides again leads us back to the Delta. In the *Phaedrus* (274 c–275 b), Plato places his myth of the invention of writings under the patronage of the god Thoth. If we are to believe certain traditions which were developed chiefly during the Hellenistic period, Orpheus imported from Egypt the ritual of the mysteries and the representations relating to the tortures of hell.[1]

Curiously, this theory re-emerged not so long ago with the hypothesis upheld by P. Foucart on the Egyptian origin of Demeter, the mysteries of Eleusis and Bacchus.[2] No one believes this any longer. But the fact remains that the Greek world had very early, and precociously 'cultural', relations with the Delta. The Greeks of Naucratis, and probably the Phoenician sailors before them, had traded scarabs, amulets, ushabtis (small funerary figures intended for work in the afterlife), moulded vessels and other cheap goods, of course, but stuff that spread the imagery of the Nilotic gods through Sicily, Sardinia and as far as Spain.[3]

Thus exchanged for cash along the shores of the western Mediterranean, then illustrated by geographers, historians, philosophers and poets, the mirage of Egypt could not fail to have religious extensions after the conquest of Alexander. 'There is no other country in the world that the Greeks would rather hear about', declares a priest from Memphis in the *Aethiopica* (II, 27, 3) by Heliodorus, the novel about 'Theagenus and Chariclo' which captivated the imagination of the young Racine.

For their part, the Egyptians who traded with Greece installed Isis in Piraeus, with the consent of the local authorities, as early as 333 BC.[4] The theophoric name *Isigenes* ('born of Isis') had already been given to an Athenian who must have been born around 400 BC. Travel, trade and war gave rise to the somewhat uneven relations between these two worlds that were so drawn to each other. The Athenian mercenaries who fought for Nectanebo I, then those of Agesilaus sent to help Takhos, must have been impressed by the land of pharaohs and pyramids. But historically, the occurrences of religious interaction did not take shape until after the enthronement of the Macedonian dynasty of the Ptolemies.

Zeus-Serapis and Hellenized Egypt

One of Alexander's generals, Ptolemy (who would bear the divine name of *Soter*, 'saviour'), took possession of Egypt and made Alexandria its capital. As successor to the pharaohs, he was king by divine right and legitimized by the word of Isis, as Roman emperors would be later. Soter and his descendants adopted the indigenous religion on their own account and to their own advantage, not without attempting to restrain the endemic power of the Egyptian priesthood, while at the same time generously endowing their temples. But the priestly class held firm and ultimately took advantage of the gradual weakening of political power.[5] The heartland of Egypt would not give up a single one of its rites. Eventually it was to impose itself morally and psychologically on the dynasty as on Greek colonists. Ptolemy Philadelphus married his own sister, as former pharaohs had often done, and this custom was observed by his successors, on the model of Isis and Osiris, the divine archetypes of sovereignty. Royal spouses were constantly identified with these two deities, and consequently a king's son with Horus.

What did the Greeks think? It seems that the Ptolemies strove to reconcile the Nilotic tradition with Hellenic piety by instituting the cult of Serapis.[6] Etymologically, *Sarapis* transcribes the Egyptian *Osor-*

Hapi or 'Osiris-Apis', in other words, the dead Apis become Osiris, god of the afterlife. That is why the Greeks thought they could discern the name 'coffin' (*soros*) of Apis.[7] Iconographically, Serapis has the majestic and fearsome aspect of a Pluto, king of Hell and the underworld. He is shown seated, accompanied by Cerberus, his head crowned with a receptacle overflowing with fruit (*modius* or *calathus*), which symbolizes his chthonian omnipotence. There is apparently nothing of an Osiris about him, but he possesses all the latter's powers, whether in matters of fruitfulness, agricultural fertility or protection of the dead. In statue form he is purely Greek. It was attributed to Bryaxis, although this sculptor's activity predated the creation of the model by at least a half if not a whole century.[8] But a statue by Bryaxis may have inspired the iconography of the Ptolemaic god, unless we are speaking of a sculptor with the same name.

The institution of the Serapian cult, which would appear to date back to Ptolemy I Soter or Ptolemy II Philadelphus, is submerged in a swirl of confused and contradictory legends. According to Plutarch (*Isis and Osiris*, 28), the first-named saw in a dream a statue of Pluto; but according to Tacitus (*Histories*, IV, 83, 1), it was a 'young man'. The god ordered him to come and seek for him at Sinope, in Pontus. Why Sinope? In Egyptian, *Sen-Hapi* means 'the dwelling-place of Apis', which would send us back to the cult of the dead Apis in his tomb. Stephanus of Byzantium also quoted the name *Sinopion* given to a hill in Memphis[9] where the cult of Apis and Osor-Hapi had developed before the arrival of the Macedonians. The priests of Memphis may therefore have been able to suggest their explanation. But as was customary with the Greeks, they would have embroidered on to the Egyptian place-name a story justifying the iconography of this Pluto, perhaps influenced by an idol originating from Asia Minor. In the Roman era, a god appeared whose attributes allow us to identify him with Dionysus-Sabazius, crowned with the vessel, like Serapis, and it is known that Sabazius had been worshipped in Anatolia for a long time.[10] But it is probably pointless to try at all costs to take account of piously fabulous traditions, of which Clement of Alexandria (*Protreptikos*, IV, 48) provides us with variants. Later, Christians would even explain the name *Sarapis* as that of Joseph, 'son of Sarah' (*Sarras pais*, in Greek).[11]

Erected under the aegis of Ptolemy III in honour of Serapis and Isis, the Serapeum of Alexandria was among the most prestigious sanctuaries in the ancient world.[12] The temple gave onto a courtyard, in the centre of a complex of buildings and annexes housing the clergy and all the serving priests of the cult, even including 'recluses' making their retreat. Incubation (sleeping in a holy place to obtain dreams

78   Isis of the Many Names, or Our Lady of the Waves

from the gods) was practised there so that a medical prescription could be received in a dream, since Serapis had the same authority over the health of the living as over the fate of the dead. Sacred banquets were also held there. But there is no evidence that they proceeded to initiations before the imperial Roman era.

The idol of the seated god seemed all the larger because it touched the walls of the *naos* with both hands. It was made of wood, metal and added stones whose colours contrasted with one another as with the interior tonality of the temple. From the overall dark blue the white of the eyes stood out, the ears of corn in the *calathus*, the gold of the sceptre, the silver of the draperies and sandals.[13] Clement of Alexandria (*Protreptikos*, IV, 48, 5–6) claims that for the execution of his work Bryaxis mixed filings of gold, silver, copper, iron, lead and tin, as well as many fragments of sapphire, haematite, emerald and topaz. 'He ground them all, mixed them and tinged them with blue ... then after thinning the whole mixture with drugs left over from the embalming of Osiris and Apis, he shaped his Serapis ... '

It is noteworthy that – according to Plutarch and Tacitus – for the institution of the cult of Serapis, Ptolemy consulted the very same Eumolpid Timotheus who had taken an interest in the myth of Cybele and Attis. At the same time he is said to have enlisted the able advice of Manetho, an Egyptian priest from Sebennytos, where Isis was revered. It would seem that the goddess was no stranger to Timotheus, whom the king 'had brought from Eleusis in his position as priest of the mysteries' (Tacitus, *Histories*, IV, 83, 3). A district of Alexandria had the name Eleusis, and it has been conjectured that the Ptolemies had envisaged setting up a 'branch' of the celebrated sanctuary there.[14] At the time, Callimachus wrote a *Hymn to Demeter* for a procession of the *calathus*, which Alexandrian coinage still attested in the Roman era. In Egypt, the goddess of the earth and corn was Isis, whom Herodotus had already assimilated to Demeter. Timotheus therefore collaborated with Manetho to help one of the Ptolemies (either Soter or Philadelphus) found a syncretic Graeco-Egyptian cult, in which a Serapis-Pluto who was similar to Dionysus-Sabazius but nominally assumed the Underworld functions of Osiris, was associated with an Isis who was identified sometimes with Demeter, and sometimes even with her daughter Kore, who became Proserpine in the realm of the dead.

The myth and the powers of the Egyptian Isis allowed both interpretations. The name of the goddess could mean 'seat' or 'throne', a metaphor especially appropriate to a mother deity, so often represented with the infant Horus sitting at her breast. This maternal function was popularized in Graeco-Roman art and would remain fundamental in the devotion of her faithful followers.[15] Like Demeter, she was first and foremost a mother. Also like Demeter, she suffered, but through losing a husband, not a daughter carried off by the king of the Underworld. Curiously, Isis would be confused with Demeter in the role of a goddess seeking traces of a loved one, but with Kore-Proserpine in the role of wife of the king of the dead, and the 'passion' of Osiris would be likened to that of the infant Dionysus mutilated by the Titans.[16]

We know the story of the 'good god', victim of his unworthy brother, Seth or Typhon, who embodies evil.[17] Osiris, shut up in a casket, is carried by the waves of the Nile, then tossed about on the sea, to come ashore at Byblos at the foot of a tree that enfolds him in the wood of its enormous trunk. The king of the country has the tree cut down to be used as a pillar in his palace. But the mourning Isis is divinely guided to Byblos, where she becomes the nurse of the little prince. During the night she burns the mortal part of his body, as Demeter in the palace of Keleos deified the infant Demophon by fire. The mother is panic-stricken, and Isis, then revealing her power, demands the opening of the trunk that has become a pillar in order to recover the casket containing Osiris. But Seth recaptures it and cuts the corpse into fourteen pieces (twenty-six in the version reported by Diodorus Siculus, I, 21), scattering them hither and thither. So Isis once again sets out on a quest for her husband, who is now dismembered. She accords funeral honours to each portion of the corpse as if it were the whole man, hence the number of 'tombs of Osiris'. But the goddess was also said to have reconstituted her husband and magically restored him to life. Thanks to his hunting instincts, Anubis, the jackal-headed god, had guided her in her search. Horus and Thoth had also taken part in finding Osiris.

This was the myth that provided the staging of the *heuresis* or 'discovery' of Osiris in the Roman era. The watery wanderings of the future patroness of sailors reminded the Greeks of Demeter's search through the world for Kore, while the dismemberment of Osiris recalled Zagreus torn to pieces by the Titans. As in the Mother-worship cult, it was the goddess who revived a dead god. Timotheus and the Alexandrian clergy must have played a preponderant role in the Hellenic reinterpretation of the Egyptian myth. This reinterpretation (contaminated by a budding syncretic Dionysism) and the Ptolemaic expansion in the eastern Mediterranean as in Sicily and Cyrenaica contributed to the spread of the new Nilotic cults beyond the Delta.

As Goddess of the Lighthouse of Alexandria, it was Isis *Pharia* who protected and guided those convoys of sailors who, with the thalassocracy of the Ptolemies, transported the lively and spirited image of *Pelagia*, mistress of the seas holding in both hands a sail swollen by the wind.[18] After the quest for Osiris, she went off to conquer men and souls. It is true that, by resuscitating her husband, she offered her worshippers, who were uneasy about their fate in this world and the next, the pledge of a victorious omnipotence over evil and death. So to begin with, her cult asserted itself in Egypt as possessing more impact – and in all circles – than that of Serapis. It must be said that the vigour of local traditions there favoured the many incarnations of the goddess, whether as a lioness (*Sekhmet*), a cow (*Hathor*), a cat (*Bastet*) or a snake (*Thermoutis*).[19] Numerous minor and major gods who were cherished in popular piety gravitated around her, such as Horus, Anubis, Bes, Ptah and the crocodile Sobek. By his name alone Hermanubis illustrates the occasional fusion of the Greek Hermes with the jackal-faced god. Countless terracottas bear witness to these devotions.[20]

Similarly, the plurality of Isiac powers facilitated the different aspects of Graeco-Egyptian syncretism, as both in her cult and in the plastic arts she adapted equally well to the Hellenic type of Demeter (chiefly the Eleusinian Demeter who was often accompanied by a snake) and those of Fortune (*Tyche*) or Aphrodite. Statues and statuettes in marble, bronze or clay spread an imagery which was no longer purely indigenous or wholly Greek. Frequently the goddess, draped in Hellenic fashion, wears between her breasts the distinctive folds of the Isiac knot which reproduces the hieroglyphic sign for life (*ankh*), and on her head, with or without the horns of Hathor, between the two ears of corn that liken her to Demeter, the *basileion*, royal emblem of a disc together with plumes, an uraeus or a lotus-flower. Elsewhere she is seen naked like Aphrodite or immodestly lifting her garment, wearing on her head an immense *calathus* stamped with the basileion. In the Roman period, she is also to be found wearing a little cloak over her tunic, or nobly draped in the folds of a large embroidered scarf, like the priestesses of her cult. But in parallel with this burgeoning popularization of a polymorphous Isis, a faithfully Egyptianizing and hieratic iconography persisted, which made a much greater impression on travellers and would always be exported with success.

In very ancient times, Isis tended to assume a universal sovereignty, or at least to encroach on the prerogatives of Osiris. The god was identified with the water of the Nile which made the land of Egypt fertile.[21] But at an early stage Isis was assimilated with the idol Sothis, that is, Sirius, whose heliacal rising coincided with the day when the river flooded. Isis-Sothis (who would be represented astride the astral Dog) 'made the Nile flow in its time'. She was therefore 'mistress of the stars' and the heavens at the same time as of the earth and the waters. At the end of Ptolemaic times, the hymns of Isidore carved at the entrance to the Isiac temple of Medinet Maadi express (two centuries before Apuleius) the polyvalency and omnipotence of the 'queen of the gods': for the Greeks, she was Demeter, Aphrodite, Rhea, Hestia; for the Thracians, Cybele; for the Lycians, Leto; for the Syrians, Artemis or Astarte. She was already the Unique and the Many-named, *numen unicum multiformi specie*, who would be exalted by her worshippers in the Antonine period.[22]

From the Nile to the Mouth of the Tiber

The myth of an Osiris travelling through the world with a triumphant army to teach man viticulture dates back to the Ptolemaic era.[23] This euhemerist and pseudo-rationalist or utilitarian reinterpretation turned the gods into the benefactors of the human race as educators or inventors of the amenities of life. These were the deeds of a missionary Dionysus, tamer and civilizer of the East, the divine archetype of Alexander, but also of Ptolemaic expansion in Syria, Asia Minor and, more generally speaking, in the eastern Mediterranean.[24]

In the third-century BC, the Ptolemies controlled part of the Greek islands and towns of the Greek mainland, towns in Asia Minor, even Cyrenaica for a time. One would think that the Graeco-Egyptian cults might have benefited from this to some extent, complementing the military, political or economic presence of the Ptolemies, since these cults went hand in hand with the dynastic religion. Actually, what we know of the circumstances of their implantation does not in every case justify explaining the success of Isis and Serapis by that reason alone.

In Athens and Piraeus, it owed nothing to Ptolemaic imperialism.[25] Thanks to Lycurgus, nicknamed the 'Ibis', whom Aristophanes mocks in the *Birds* (1.1296), in Piraeus Isis was receiving the homage of Egyptian merchants in the fifth-century BC, long before the decree allowing the building of a temple there. Three centuries later, the goddess had her sanctuary on the slope of the Acropolis, and her prestige eclipsed that of Serapis. But the associations of followers of Serapis in Athens itself also showed their vitality. Priesthoods there were annual in conformity with Greek rules, whereas in the port – peopled by foreigners – there was loyalty to Egyptian traditions. Unlike the situation in other social contexts, the Nilotic cults in Attica reached the well-to-do. On coins of the second-century BC, representation of the Isiac *basileion* and the goddess herself holding a corn-ear or lotus set the seal on the officialization of her cult in the city of Athena.

During the third and second centuries BC, we find that the gods of the Delta spread in various sectors of the Hellenic world, mainly in the islands and ports, but also in the interior.[26] They were to be found around Delphi, in Corinth, Argos, Sicyonia, Methana and Mantinea. But in all they had little impact in the Peloponnese. At Eretria in Euboea, Isis had a temple and large number of priests.[27] As at Delos, she preceded the arrival of Serapis. Sailing festivals there perhaps foreshadowed the *Navigium Isidis* of the imperial epoch.

Farther north, in Macedonia, Thessalonica was an active centre of Nilotic religion after the founding of the port under the aegis of Cassander (in homage to his wife *Thessalonike*). There an Osiris *Mystes* was worshipped, an epithet borne also by the infant Dionysus, as a model for all initiates. At Maronea in Thrace, an aretalogy celebrated the 'virtues' of Isis.[28] With Serapis, the goddess reached the shores of the Black Sea. They were honoured on Thasos which had long-standing relations with the Delta, on Lesbos, Cos, Rhodes (where the Isiac *basileion* on coinage was henceforth associated with the rose), at Smyrna, Ephesus (where the establishment of a temple was contemporary with Egyptian domination under Ptolemy Philadelphus), at Halicarnassus (where coins bore the effigy of Serapis), Priene (also occupied for a time by the Egyptians, and where the city maintained a kind of cloistered religious group, known as the 'possessed', who devoted themselves to the adoration of the gods),[29] on Crete and Cyprus, the base of the Alexandrian fleet.

The case of Delos is singularly revealing.[30] There Serapis had three sanctuaries, but Isis, who had preceded him, enjoyed absolute pre-eminence and influence. She was identified with Victory, Justice, Fortune (*Tyche*), Nemesis, Aphrodite, even with the Great Mother of the gods. The inventories of offerings and, notably, adornments or robes intended for the divine idols are impressive. The cult there was served by a large and specialized priestly personnel, and by groups of the faithful organized to assist the clergy, men and women who formed a kind of 'third order' which was subject to rules regarding lifestyle and vestments. So we find on Delos as on Cos 'melanophori', wearers of the black robe of Isis which later would distinguish monks in the East.

But on this island Serapis experienced some difficulties at the start, recounted in a chronicle carved under the direction of his priest on a pillar of the first temple.[31] There we learn that Serapis had to be content for a long time with a private chapel, before acquiring a modest temple (thanks to the subscriptions of his faithful) at the site of a dumping-ground which was a source of dispute between the Delians and this metic god. His trouble was that he gave his divine support to Ptolemaic imperialism. But Serapis won the case by miraculously shutting the mouths of his accusers. The god may have been a victim of his own success at Delos, for conflicts seem to have brought the sanctuaries of rival cults into opposition.

However, the island's geographical position and the current political situation, in the second-century BC, facilitated its contacts with Rome and conferred on it a role that was not exclusive but certainly decisive in spreading Nilotic religions as far as Italy. Its Apollonian sanctuary earned it a privileged position on the international map. The status of free port that Delos owed to the Romans made it the centre of a slave trade, fed by wars and piracy. Italian speculators, brokers, bankers, tax-gatherers dominated the commercial traffic. In this cosmopolitan milieu, western *negotiatores* were not insensitive to the attractions of the Egyptian gods, to judge by the inscriptions involving the various Romans and Italians installed on Delos.[32] Many of them subscribed towards the construction of a *Serapeum*. Others made offerings to Isis and Anubis. It was more especially the goddess who captured their attention and devotion. Some dedications bear witness to relationships between Italians and Egyptians. Lastly, slaves purchased on the island for or by Romans were able to import their beliefs and gods into Italy. Delian epigraphy gives us precise information about those Isiac worshippers of slave status who belonged to Romans.

Several devotees of Nilotic cults on Delos had connections with Magna Graecia. Sicily maintained commercial and political, if not cultural, relations with Egypt and Rhodes.[33] The Syracusan Theocritus sings the praises equally of Hieron II, 'tyrant' of his native town, and Ptolemy Philadelphus; but he breathes not a word of Isis and Serapis. The purely religious consequences of Agathocles' marriage to the daughter of Ptolemy Soter in 306, and the good diplomatic and economic relations between Hieron II and Philadelphus have been overvalued. There is no testimony to confirm that the Nilotic deities reached Sicily by that route and in that period. But at the end of the third-century BC, after the capture of Syracuse by Marcellus and his Romans, the bronze coins of the great Sicilian port show us the effigy of Serapis on the face and Isis with her sistra on the reverse, or the profile of the goddess on the face and her *basileion* on the reverse.[34]

Tauromenium (Taormina) at that time had a temple to Serapis, endowed with an altar offered to Hestia by a 'neocor' from Cyrenaica.[35] Sicily, like Delos, was then actively trading with Pozzuoli and Campania where Alexandrian cults had made a solid impact at a very early date. Naturally, Rome too had direct, but mainly official, contacts with the Ptolemaic Delta, even though Roman traders were dealing with Alexandria as early as the second-century BC. Slaves of Egyptian stock soon made their way into the families of the *Urbs*, notably in the time of Cicero and Caesar.

As in Sicily and Sardinia (Tharros for instance), scarabs and amulets brought to the coasts and offshore islands of Campania[36] something of Egyptian magical beliefs, as they are to be found in seventh-/sixth-century BC graves on Ischia and at Cumae. The Alexandrian gods were enthroned in the port of Pozzuoli before 105 BC in a sanctuary facing the sea and richly endowed by sailors.[37] The sacking of Delos in 88 BC during the war with Mithridates and the ravages suffered by the holy island twenty years later at the hands of Cilician pirates eventually stripped the the great place of its international role to the benefit of Pozzuoli, whither sailors and businessmen flocked in droves. The building of the first great Pompeian *Iseum* probably dates to the end of the second century BC.[38] Naples, which traded with Delos, perhaps had its *Serapeum* similarly at that time. Natives of Capua are attested on Apollo's isle. But apart from Pozzuoli, all these budding exotic forms of worship would flourish and expand only in the imperial period.

The moment Delos, afflicted by wars (and their consequences on the market), lost its interest, the Italians deserted it, to the advantage of the Campanian ports, where they transferred a religious imprint which would strongly stamp the region and which explains the favour, even the fervour, of municipal notables towards the Alexandrian gods. It is also found that henceforth Egyptian sailors and merchants went straight to Pozzuoli. Papyri even mention Egyptians from the interior doing business in the Peninsula. This movement would become more definite and stronger under the Early Empire. But very soon Ostia took over from Pozzuoli, and Nilotic cults experienced a great success.[39] However, in the time of Seneca, *Puteoli* still played a major role in Italy's relations with the Delta.[40]

Roman expansion in the East favoured Isiac expansion in the West. The gods of the Delta took advantage of the economic situation and commercial currents, because Isis also guided the boats laden with slaves and corn, in the persona of 'Our-Lady-of-the-Sea' (*Pelagia*). As for Serapis, this calathophoric god, lord of earthly prosperity at the same time as guarantor of the wellbeing of his faithful and their posthumous destiny, saviour of the living and the dead, the *negotiatores* honoured in him the majesty of a Jupiter, simultaneously fearsome and benevolent, with the biocosmic powers of a Dionysus. He made the crops grow and protected those who transported them. The divine couple had worshippers among both the profiteers and the victims of the slave trade.

Paradoxically, the deities who benefited from the boom in the slave market would recruit a large part of their 'militants' in Rome among the slave classes or those of slave origin.

Religion and Politics: from the Streets to the Palatine

In 88 BC Delos was captured by Archelaus, an admiral of Mithridates. The Italians and Romanized Greeks who escaped from the island before the massacre of some 20,000 inhabitants rendered thanks to Sulla who 'liberated' it. The future dictator had his Venusian cult of Fortune and liked to be known as the 'beloved of Aphrodite' (*Epaphroditos*). It has been conjectured that Sulla's Venus *Felix* could have been no stranger to Isis *Fortuna* or *Tyche*, so dear to the sea traders.[41] The *Fortuna Primigenia* of Praeneste was, as we know, richly endowed by the dictator after the reconstruction of the town, which became a colony for his veterans. Now, on Delos Isis bore the names *Tyche Protogeneia*, which put into Greek the titles of the Praenestine goddess, and in Praeneste itself a hall with an apse, paved with a remarkable mosaic of Nilotic themes, bordered upon the sacred area (people have tried to see it as an Iseum).[42]

At Pompeii, which also became a Roman colony under the name *Veneria Cornelia*, Venus had the attributes of *Felicitas*. In any case, if there is no explicit testimony to the slightest devotion to Isis on Sulla's part, we at least know through Apuleius that the college of 'Pastophori') claimed that its founding dated back to Sulla's time.[43] Delos had a *Pastophorion*, that is, probably a kind of religious hostel suitable for the 'retreats' of already initiated followers who lived their life following a rule.[44] The conqueror of Mithridates and Marius had returned from the East with slaves and freedmen of Graeco-oriental stock who had perhaps been won over to the Isiac faith.

During the first two or three decades of the first-century BC, the Egyptian gods made a more or less underground progress in Rome in lower-class milieux. They would become involved in the troubles of the Republic's death-throes. It is surprising to see, on the official denarii of an auxiliary mint around 90 BC, the appearance of Egyptianizing emblems like the *basileio* and lotus-flower, then around 79 BC, the sistra of Isis.[45] These were marks distinguishing the dies used to strike a set number of copies each. These official differences in coinage, which did not necessarily have a religious significance, were paralleled elsewhere by completely secular symbols (tools or objects of domestic life). The same marks are to be seen on Ptolemaic money, and it may be that slaves of Alexandrian origin worked among the employees of the Mint. However, the mint on the Capitol (beside the temple of *Iuno Moneta*)[46] has been wrongly emphasized, with much said about Isis *Capitolina*, attested by an inscription, and the precarious existence of an *Iseum* which the authorities had to have destroyed. (Recently, the disturbances about this Capitoline Isis have been related to the activities of slave traders, who had formed an association with headquarters in this sector, *Collegium Capitolinorum*.)[47] A. Alföldi tended to overemphasize the importance of the Egyptian symbols, seeing them as the expression of an indirect monetary propaganda orchestrated by immigrants who had infiltrated revolutionary clubs.[48] But the fact that the Romans in charge of the *Moneta* could have allowed designs linked with an alien cult to pass into the national coinage intrigues historians, the more so because this marginal imagery showed itself in a period when the Egyptian gods were alternately arousing and being subjected to violence.

Their cult was not permitted within the sacred confines of the *Pomoerium*. So it is doubtful whether Isis and Serapis figure in a temple with 'lotiform' capitals on a denarius of C. Egnatius Maxsumus struck in 75 or 73 BC, as P.F. Tschudin and J.G. Griffiths have suggested.[49] But before 58 BC statues and altars had been erected clandestinely on the Capitol. The Senate had them demolished. On 1 January in the same year, a band of Isiac militants had disturbed the performance of a solemn sacrifice, while the consul Gabinius was ritually proceeding with an examination of the victims: the magistrate was blamed for having done nothing on behalf of Isis and Serapis! Immediately after the demolition, the devotees of the Alexandrian gods replaced the altars.[50] There is something surprising about the audacity and pressure exerted by these Isiac 'commandos'. But they must have had the benefit of a certain amount of backing from within the Senate, and have taken advantage of the conflicts splitting the political class at that time. This was the period when Clodius and his clubs (*collegia*), real gangs of fanatics, ruled the streets and the Forum. These bands were recruited from the same mixed populace of slaves and freedmen as those accomplices whom, five years earlier, Catiline had led in rebellion. 'All wars are about religion' (Alain). In effect, the Isiac agitators of the *populares* seemed to want to thwart the party of the Great Mother of the gods embodied by the Senate in its traditionalist majority. We have seen how Clodius profaned Cybele's Games.

As they lacked official authorization, followers of the Egyptian gods erected private chapels. The Senate had these destroyed in 53 BC. At that time Rome was still the stage for the disturbances organized by

Clodius, who served Caesar so well but was wiped out by Milo and his supporters on 1 January 52. Nevertheless, the relentless pressure and obstinacy of the Isiasts gave the guardians of the *mos maiorum* no respite. They restored their places of worship, and in 50 BC the Senate once more had to decree their demolition. Here there is a revealing anecdote: none of the workmen required to tear down the holy walls of Isis and Serapis dared to lift a hand to them. Then the consul in person, P. Aemilius Paulus, had to lay aside his embroidered toga, seize an axe and set about the doors of the forbidden temple (Valerius Maximus, I, 3, 4). Two years later it was necessary yet again to destroy the walls of sanctuaries that had been set up on the Capitol itself in homage to the gods of the Delta.[51] Like the Christian faith later, Isiac perseverance was forged and strengthened in persecutions. Indisputably, it seems to have enjoyed wide popular support.

Anxious to gain this support for themselves, the triumvirs Mark Antony, Lepidus and Octavian (the future Augustus) decided in October 43 BC to have a temple built in honour of Isis and Serapis. To escape their proscriptions, the aedile M. Volusius donned the jackal-headed mask of Anubis and the linen garment of Isiac devotees: 'Can there be anything more deplorable', wrote Valerius Maximus (*Memorabilia*, VII, 3, 8), 'than a Roman magistrate having to disguise himself in the trappings of a foreign religion?'. It was a sign of the times, and in any case the proof that the celebration of Egyptian festivals was then nothing out of the ordinary in the streets of the *Urbs*. In the next century, the future emperor Domitian would also owe his physical safety to an Isiac disguise.[52]

The Egyptian sanctuary promised by the triumvirs did not materialize on Roman soil, at least not immediately. The last of the Ptolemies and her gods were apparently defeated at Actium in 31 BC. Antony, who had presented himself as a reincarnation of Osiris or Dionysus,[53] and Cleopatra who had taken the title 'New Isis', both committed suicide; and though Octavian on his return to Alexandria paid homage to Serapis, he refused to go to see the Apis of Memphis. In 28 BC Egyptian cults were prohibited in the *Urbs*, but it would appear that a blind eye was turned to private chapels. This probably explains a subterranean recrudescence of Isiacism within families, and chiefly among women. Propertius and Tibullus grudgingly put up with the periods of continence observed by their mistresses in the name of the goddess. But although Propertius had nothing but sarcasm for Isis and the 'swarthy sons' of Egypt, Tibullus (*Corpus tibullianum*, I, 3, 23ff) invoked her for his own health and composed in Latin verse a vibrant outpouring to Osiris (I, 7, 23–54). M. Valerius Messala, his powerful protector, perhaps brought back from the Delta in 29 or 28 BC the cult

of an Osirian idol which he kept in his household shrine, together
with his *Penates*. Ovid must have been converted by his beloved
Corinna, for whose recovery he begs with the fervour of an ardent
neophyte (*Amores*, II, 13). 'Who can tell what influence maidservants
from Antioch or Alexandria acquired over the mind of their mistress?'
wrote Cumont:[54] who can say what influence the 'mistresses' of the
demi-monde exerted on their lovers?[55]

   In 21 BC troubles assailed Rome while Augustus was in Sicily.
Agrippa, his son-in-law, restored order and drove from the *pomoerium*
the Egyptian cults 'which were again invading the City' (Cassius Dio,
Roman History, 54, 6, 6). At that time they were even banned from the
suburbs within a radius of seven and a half *stadia* (1.330 km) of the
Urbs. But in the Trastevere Agrippa himself shared with Julia the
amenities of a villa, discovered in 1879 under the present-day Villa
Farnese, where painted or stuccoed Egyptianizing motifs recalled the
characters and landscapes of a Hellenized Nilotic mythology.[56] Augustus' daughter must have enjoyed encouraging an imagery which
contrasted so strongly with the official religion and, in her eyes,
offered a sort of aesthetic escape.

   But on the Palatine itself, the *Aula Isiaca* distinguished by a similar
decor of Alexandrian inspiration is dated to the 20s BC (the period of
prohibition outside the suburbs). Yet it was part of the emperor's
dwelling![57] In the paintings in Livia's House, where curious 'baetyls'
rendered the ambience sacred, people have thought it possible to
discern the signs of an Egyptianizing solar theology.[58] Terracotta
plaques (called 'Campana') showing Isis between two sphinxes were
discovered in the temple of the Palatine Apollo, which adjoined the
residence of Augustus.[59] We must assuredly give consideration to a
certain Egyptomania.[60] But just as much as the domestic staff of the
imperial household whose Isiac 'graffiti' can be deciphered on the
palace walls,[61] ornamental iconography introduced into the lives of
the Caesars an ambience and world of imagination that were propitious to the Egyptian gods. Nor must we forget that when Mark
Antony married Octavian's sister he had two daughters by her,
Antonia Major, great-grandmother to Nero, and Antonia Minor, who
would be mother and grandmother to two emperors: Claudius and
Caligula. With them, a little of Alexandrian devotions could not fail to
enter the imperial family.

   But the stern Tiberius, haughty guardian of public order, again
banned the Egyptian rites from Rome, forcing the adepts of these
'superstitions' (says Suetonius)[62] to burn their holy vestments and all
their religious trappings. The Jews were embraced in the same repression which resulted in the deportation to Sardinia of 4,000 freedmen

'infected by these superstitions'. It was then that Seneca's father alerted his son who, faithful to Pythagorean-style vegetarianism, subjected himself to abstinences which might be suspected of compromise with the foreign devotions.[63]

In actual fact, a resounding scandal hit the already fairly tarnished reputation of the Egyptian cults. Like Flora, Isis was the patroness of courtesans, but that meant calling the virtue of matrons into question! A knight, Decius Mundus, was smitten with a woman of the aristocracy, Paulina. She proudly rejected his advances, and even the offer of 200,000 drachmae for a single night. In despair, the unhappy Decius went on hunger strike, when one of his father's freedwomen offered to gain the lady's favours for a sum four times less, but by means of a subterfuge. We learn, in fact, that Paulina frequented the sanctuary of Isis. Then a priest came to see her on behalf of the god Anubis who, 'conquered by love, invited her to visit him' (Flavius Josephus, *Jewish Antiquities*, XVIII, 72). Delighted and flattered, she told her husband, who saw nothing untoward, knowing that his wife's virtue was above suspicion. The lady therefore went to the temple at nightfall. Once the doors were closed and the lamps extinguished, the knight had no difficulty in taking the place of the jackal-headed god. When she returned home, Paulina recounted the marvellous adventure and boasted of it to her friends. But Decius Mundus was incautious and vain enough to confess his crime to the over-beautiful devotee who, disillusioned and desperate, denounced herself to her husband, who in turn denounced Mundus to Tiberius. The emperor then had the go-between freedwoman crucified, the temple of Isis razed and her idol thrown into the Tiber. The knight was merely sentenced to exile . . . This story, probably exaggerated by the authorities, none the less demonstrates the credulity of the faithful and the lucrative complicity of the clergy.

But ridicule does not kill, any more than scandal, and the Nilotic cults had a no less resounding revenge in the reign of Caligula. Antony's great-grandson had the *Iseum* that had been demolished on Tiberius' orders rebuilt on the Campus Martius. His chamberlain, the Egyptian Helicon, exerted a constant influence on the emperor.[64] We know that Caligula 'busied himself with initiations and celebrated the rites of foreign mysteries' (Suidas).[65] On the day of his death, preparations were being made for a spectacle that evening at which Ethiopians and Egyptians would enact scenes relating to the Underworld.[66] Other indications lead one to think that he celebrated the Isiac ceremonies that were officially attested later and inscribed in the Roman calendar from 28 October to 3 November. Henceforth the Alexandrian gods would not have to suffer the slightest snub from the authorities. The famous Isis of the Capitol probably dates back to this period,[67] her hair styled in the fashion of Agrippina the Younger, the last (and murderous) wife of the emperor Claudius.

Nero's tutor was the Stoic Chaeremon, a great connoisseur of hieroglyphs and Osirian theology.[68] His expert astrologer, Balbillus, took an active interest in the Nilotic cults. Poppaea was the cousin of a Poppaeus Habitus, known at Pompeii for his Isiac household shrine where the goddess featured in company with Osiris, Harpocrates and Anubis.[69] In his *De clementia*, Seneca celebrates Nero as a sun in his east and in terms that have been likened to pharaonic hymns.[70] Otho, the intimate friend of the emperor and Poppaea's first husband, wearing linen robes, took part in the offices of the Isiac cult.

The Egyptian adherence was so strong that in 69 – the year of such a grave crisis for the Empire and the regime – Vespasian, proclaimed emperor by the army of the East, received from Serapis a kind of consecration and supernatural recognition. The Nile flooded on the day he entered Alexandria. In the name of the calathophoric god, he restored a blind man's sight and healed a cripple. In the Serapeum where the priests left him alone with the god, Vespasian enjoyed an oracle and a miracle. He was acknowledged by Serapis before the Senate did so.[71] In AD 70, returning to Rome with his son Titus, he spent the night in the temple of Isis on the Campus Martius, before celebrating next day his triumph over Judaea. The façade of this *Iseum Campense* occupies the reverse of the large sesterces struck the following year in the name of the Senate (plate 11).[72]

Nor did Domitian forget that the Isiac costume in which he had fled the burning Capitol, on 19 December AD 69, had shielded him from the attack of Vitellius' partisans.[73] He had the *Iseum Campense*, which was burnt in 80, rebuilt and embellished. To commemorate this rebuilding, an obelisk, specially cut and engraved on the orders of the emperor, was erected in the sanctuary. On it Domitian is shown, crowned by Isis, and the accompanying hieroglyphs glorify the accession of the *autokrator* 'beloved of Isis and Ptah: may he live like Ra!' This is the obelisk of the Piazza Navona.[74]

The fragments of statues and reliefs found on the Palatine in the *Domus Flavia*[75] allow us to suppose that a chapel of Egyptian cults there housed the imperial devotions which seem to arouse the indignation of Pliny the Younger (*Panegyric of Trajan*, 49, 8). Officially, Domitian chiefly honoured Minerva. But the Isis-Neith of Sais was an armed goddess likened to Pallas. Near the *Iseum Campense* there was in fact a temple to *Minerva Chalcidica*, whom Domitian celebrated on his coins, and the goddess appears below the opening of the *Arcus ad*

Plate 11 Coin of Vespasian showing façade of the *Iseum Campense*

Isis, the monumental entrance to the Egyptian sanctuary, on the famous funeral monument of the *Haterii*.[76]

Egypt and its gods fascinated the emperor Hadrian, who had constructed in his Tibur (Tivoli) villa a model Canopus leading to a 'Serapeum', a sort of cavern where fountains cooled the atmosphere for sacred banquets, modelled on those celebrated in Alexandria.[77] The Villa Adriana has yielded a whole series of Egyptian or Egyptianate statues[78] representing Isis, Osiris, Harpocrates, Apis, naophoric priests and Antinous as an Egyptian god (plate 12). Coins struck in Rome towards the end of the reign show us Isis on the dog Sothis, as on the pediment of the *Iseum Campense*. Other coins show the emperor and empress being welcomed to Alexandria by Isis and Serapis.[79]

Less than forty years later, Hermes-Thoth features in his temple with a half-moon tympanum on sesterces glorifying the *religio* of Marcus Aurelius and referring us by allusion to the 'miracle of the rain', which the Aurelian column also celebrates.[80] The Egyptian magus Arnouphis, who was supposed to have encouraged the god's intervention to save the legions on the Danubian front, belonged to the imperial entourage.[81] But the philosopher-emperor did not go so far as to take part in Isiac processions, as his unworthy son would do. Commodus had himself shaven like the pastophori. He joined the *pausarii* who carried the idol from one resting-place to the next,

Plate 12 Antinous-Harpocrates (Vatican Museums)

through the streets of Rome. He dressed up in the canine mask of
Anubis and amused himself by hitting the heads of his team mates
with it. A statue shows him between a bull and a cow, i.e., probably as
Horus, between Osiris-Apis and Isis-Hathor.[82] Such exhibitionism did
not give rise to vocations, only emulation among his courtiers. Thus
the legate of Syria, Pescennius Niger, displayed himself carrying the
sacred objects of the Isiac cult on the mosaic adorning a portico in the
imperial gardens.[83] A short time before the death of Commodus,
people believed they saw the idol of Anubis move, as if the Egyptian
gods were condemned and compromised by their scandalous de-
fender.

But the Severi confirmed imperial favour towards them. On the
denarii of Julia Domna, Isis suckling Horus, with the legend SAECVLI
FELICITAS ('Felicity of the Age') made allusion to the prosperous and
beneficial maternity of the empress.[84] Though it is doubtful whether
the curly hair and beard of Septimius Severus intentionally likened
him to Serapis,[85] the emperor was fascinated by Egypt which he
assiduously visited, together with his family. His son Caracalla
pledged a special cult to Serapis as god of health,[86] who figured each
year on the reverse of his coins, beginning in 212. He made a retreat in
the Serapeum at Alexandria, and was officially given the title of
Philosarapis, the 'beloved of Serapis'. On the Quirinal in Rome itself
Caracalla dedicated a gigantic temple to his god, traces of which may
still be seen in the Villa Colonna. Enormous fragments of stonework
give some idea of the size of this colossal sanctuary, to which access
was gained from the Campus Martius by two monumental stairways.
On this site (henceforth within the *pomoerium*), at this altitude and
with these proportions, the temple of Serapis almost dominated that
of Jupiter Capitolinus.[87] Later, the *Augustan History* and Aurelius
Victor would state that Caracalla introduced Egyptian cults to Rome,
for in fact he was the first to consecrate them on this side of the
augural wall. This was the period when, in the Baths of Caracalla, an
inscription proclaimed: 'One and only [is] Zeus Sarapis Helios, invincible master of the world'.[88] But after 217 the name of Sarapis was
hammered out to be replaced by that of Mithras. However, the
Alexandrian god willingly cohabited with Mithras in several crypts of
the ancient Persian cult, like that of Santa Prisca.[89] Moreover, it was in
the *Mithraeum* of Caracalla's Baths that the above-quoted inscription
was found, its rear face preserving a dedication to Serapis the 'saviour' identified with Mithras. But after his death Caracalla's 'philoser-
apism' may have unleashed some ill-humoured reactions.

At all events, his young cousin Severus Alexander enhanced the
Iseum Campense, like the Serapeum, with bronze statues from Delos

and hieroglyphic monuments. The Egyptian gods remained present in the official coinage of Gordian III and Gallienus. Plotinus, the philosopher friend of Gallienus and the empress Salonina, is said to have been present at the summoning of his own daemon in the *Iseum Campense*, for – declared the Egyptian priest presiding over the operation – 'no other place that was pure could be found in Rome' (Porphyry, *Life of Plotinus*, 10).

In parallel with the evidence of imperial favour, epigraphic testimony reveals the progress and the strength of Isiac devotions within the emperor's entourage, on the Palatine. Slaves and freedmen of Egyptian origin were relatively numerous in the imperial household, where they often exercised a hefty influence.[90] Inscriptions preserve for us the memory of their homage to the Nilotic gods. A servant of Titus married a priestess of Bubastis (the cat-headed goddess). One of Galba's freedmen was a sacristan of Isis *Pelagia*. The Cretan Mesomedes, known as the author of a hymn to Isis, became chapel-master of the emperor Hadrian. Many of the domestic staff on the Palatine bore theophoric names which placed them under the patronage of Horus, Harpocrates, Serapis, Apis (*Epaphus*), Thermoustis (Isis with a snake's body) or Ammon. Outside the palace and secondary residences of the emperor, Isiacism reached different milieux in Roman society, from the humblest strata of immigrants to the highest officials. Already around AD 70, Pliny the Elder (*Natural History*, XXXIII, 41) noted that 'even men are taking to wear on their finger the effigy of Harpocrates and images of Egyptian gods'.

A typical example is one of a community of faithful who met together in premises on the Aventine set up in the time of Marcus Aurelius or Commodus, to the north-west of a complex of buildings where the church of Santa Sabina would be erected three centuries later.[91] This long vaulted corridor belonged to a house occupied by one of the emperor's accountants. Decorated with paintings relating to the Osirian myth, this meeting-place still bears some primitive or coarse graffiti scratched on its walls by the 'mystae', with their names, the direct and spontaneous expression of their customary talk: a trivial and rudimentary Isiacism, in sharp contrast to the mysticism which mistakenly captivates the embellishing imagination of the Moderns. But this vulgarity in no way detracts from the sincerity of the feelings and denotes a remarkable adaptation of Egyptian-style piety to all levels of intellect and sensibility. Whether enthroned on the Palatine or in the prestigious temples of the Campus Martius and the Quirinal, the religion of the Delta retained its hold on the masses and the minds of the people.

The Conquest of the West

Apart from the two great sanctuaries just mentioned, other temples housed Isiac worship,[92] notably near the church of SS. Pietro and Marcellino, perhaps on the Capitol but in any case on the Caelian where the little stone vessel of Santa Maria 'in Navicella', not far from a barracks (*Castra Peregrina*), reminds us of those ex-votos offered by soldiers to Isis-of-the-Sea (*Pelagia*) when they had safely arrived in port. But a number of statues were also set up in kinds of public or private chapels in every quarter of the *Urbs*.

Italy was unevenly affected by the Isiac trend. Generally speaking, this entrenched itself in ports, especially Ostia,[93] where the bustling population was as cosmopolitan as that of Rome, and in Campania,[94] in Naples and Pozzuoli where trade with the Delta remained active despite the swiftly triumphant competition of the *Portus Augusti* on the mouth of the Tiber. In the north-east of the peninsula Aquileia,[95] which had direct and sustained contact with Egypt, was a flourishing centre in the imperial period from which Isiacism spread its influence along the military routes to Pannonia on the one hand and, via Verona, to Milan and the Alpine passes on the other. On the archaeological map of finds, the two coasts of the Adriatic are studded with *Aegyptiaca*,[96] from Brindisi to the Veneto and from Trieste to Salonae, where several statuettes of Osiris and numerous ushabtis ('stand-ins' for the dead which were supposed to work in their place in the afterlife) demonstrate the vitality of genuinely Nilotic beliefs. Certain Egyptian or Egytianizing communities had their cemeteries, as is evidenced, for example, by the discovery of a Canopic vase near Pozzuoli, on the Capua road.

From the coastal towns of Dalmatia, and chiefly from Salonae, roads provided soldiers, officials, Italian and Graeco-oriental traders with the means of conveying the Alexandrian gods to Siscia (Sisak) and Sirmium (Srijemska Mitrovica).[97] From Aquileia one could go directly to Emona (present-day Ljubljana), where on the occasion of the autumn festivals cake moulds in the shapes of Isis and Serapis turned out goodies for popular delectation.[98] One could also reach Poetevio (Ptuj), where the customs post recruited Mithraists at the same time as worshippers of the Egyptian gods. By the same route Savaria (in Hungary) could be visited, where Isis had a flourishing sanctuary, or Aquincum, on the banks of the Danube (near Budapest), where the discovery of mummies bears witness to the immigrants' loyalty to their funeral traditions.[99] In the Danubian provinces Isiacism prospered remarkably, and the relative frequency with which statuettes of Osiris have been recovered confirms the strongly Egyptianizing nature of the cult.[100] From the Adriatic to the Black Sea, at Salonae as at Tomi, Alexandrian shipowners contributed to the diffusion or strengthening of Serapian worship. But outside urban and administrative centres, the Nilotic religion scarcely appears to have taken root except along the major trunk roads and great trading routes. It never really 'got its teeth' into the hinterland that was little or poorly Romanized.

Even in Italy, apart from Latium, Campania and the North-east (Venetia, Aemilia), Isiacism penetrated only to a limited extent. The south of the peninsula (Lucania, Bruttium, Calabria) and even Picenum were scarcely affected. Around Rome and the large ports the cult expanded partly into the rural areas. In the early fifth century people would still joyfully celebrate the rediscovery of Osiris, honoured as god of vegetation.[101] But Isis had hardly any followers in rural circles.

Nevertheless, in and around towns one finds a remarkable attachment to the exoticism of the ceremonial and representations. This leaning went as far as making pseudo-Egyptian monuments, like the famous Isiac Table of Turin (probably originating from Rome)[102] or the base from Herculaneum whose hieroglyphs are a product of the wildest flight of fancy.[103] This Egyptomania influenced pictorial fashion, notably in the Third Pompeian style. More than the Greeks, the Romans had a penchant for the Egyptianate type of Isis, which in any case enjoyed an absolutely clear pre-eminence in the Peninsula. Despite his temple on the Quirinal, in Italy Serapis had far fewer worshippers than the goddess of Fortune, whose power prevailed over destiny and who was easily identifiable with so many sovereign, maternal or helpful goddesses. Isis, in fact, was the embodiment of various aspects of divine femininity that were familiar to the Romans in the imagery of their family household shrines (*lararia*), at the same time as the 'mystery' and 'complete otherness' in hieratic idols of Memphitic tradition.

The Roman West by no means frowned upon her.

Cyrenaica which, in the 200s BC, sent a worshipper of Serapis to Taormina,[104] had for a long time maintained an Egyptian style of worship that did not fail in the imperial period. Cyrene had an *Iseum* that was richly endowed with statues.[105] A polychrome statue was found there which perhaps represents a female initiate enveloped in strips of cloth like a mummy and wearing on her head the solar disc with the snake (uraeus), which likens her to Isis. Among the sculptures, one in particular is noteworthy: a priestess carrying a heavy garland of fruits slung across her shoulder, as Apuleius attributes to the goddess when she appears to Lucius (*Metamorphoses*, XI, 4, 1). In the (unfortunately fragmentary) iambic aretalogy of Cyrene, Isis is revealed as 'the greatest among the goddesses in the heavens'. In Tripolitania, at Sabratha, the Serapeum dominated the Forum, but Isis had her temple outside the walls.

In the west, in Africa Proconsularis as in Numidia and the two Mauretanias, evidence is spaced out unevenly along the coast, from Carthage to Volubilis by way of Cherchel.[106] Egyptian art had already influenced the iconography of the Punic gods. Carthage maintained its trading relations with Alexandria, and Serapis was especially honoured there. At Cherchel (where the temple of Isis housed a crocodile), the Egyptian gods must have benefited from the marriage of Juba II, king of Mauretania, to Cleopatra *Selene* or 'Moon', the daughter of the great Cleopatra and Mark Antony. Garrison towns like Tebessa, Lambaesis and Auzia did not escape the Isiac trend. In AD 158 the legate of the IIIrd Augusta legion himself publicly made an act of piety at Lambaesis, by having the temple of Isis and Serapis enlarged and embellished. The sanctuary yielded a number of curious objects, notably an altar decoration with Horus-Harpocrates between two anguipede deities, and sacred animals (Apis, uraeus, cat- and dog-headed).

Outside the ports and military camps, the Egyptian gods variously penetrated the hinterland by the most frequented routes in Proconsularis: in towns like Cirta (which had its temple and priestess of Isis), El Djem, Dougga, Makthar and Bulla Regia; in more modest localities like Membressa (Medjez el Bab), Vallis or Choud and Battel. J. Toutain, who (like too many historians) attached importance only to epigraphy, underestimated the success of the Nilotic cults in Roman Africa.[107] It appears that Serapis was particularly venerated in Proconsularis (roughly present-day Tunisia). There he was assimilated to Baal-Hammon and Saturn and (as in a dedication from Aquincum) Neptune as god of aquatic fruitfulness, which presumes identification with Osiris, the fertilizing water of the Nile. On a bas-relief from Makthar the god wears the solar rays of *Heliosarapis*. In the Louvre a fragment of a large sculpted panel may be seen, on which Isis is featured in company with Serapis and Bacchus, behind Horus-Harpocrates: this monument came from Henchir el Attermine (Tunisia). Dionysus perhaps corresponds to Osiris. We find Anubis associated with the goddess on the two faces of a large base discovered at Dougga. Finally, we must not forget that an African from Madaurus, Apuleius, ended his novel *Metamorphoses* or *The Golden Ass* with an emotive profession of Isiac faith.[108]

In the Iberian peninsula,[109] the Mediterranean ports and huge valleys assisted the immigration of men and their gods. At Emporiae

(Ampurias), which was in communication with Marseille and Alexandria, a republican period temple was discovered, whose *adyton* flanked by lateral stairways, in a closed courtyard bordered by a portico, recalls the layout of the Pompeian *Iseum*. On the road going along the coast from the Pyrenees to Gades (Cadiz), Tarragona, Saguntum and Valentia preserve evidence of Isiac devotion. At Saguntum, a faithful believer fulfilled his vow to the Mistress of the Sea (*Pelagia*). At Valentia, a company of slaves honoured the goddess. Between Ampurias and Tarragona, the spa *Aquae Calidae* (Caldas de Monbuy) attracted pilgrims seeking divine and curative favours. Farther south, in Baetica, along or near the valleys of the Guadalquivir and Guadiana, there was a proliferation of *Aegyptiaca*, chiefly at Seville, *Italica* and Cordoba, on the one hand; Beja, Badajoz, Merida and Santa Amalia, on the other.

One of the earliest dated sites is the camp of Metellus, near Caceres (*Norba Caesarina*), where the piety of merchants who were perhaps of Alexandrian origin is displayed (to judge by the style of the terracotta pillar erected in their sanctuary around 79 BC).[110] The density of finds in Baetica is explained by the activity of Iberian ports which did business with both the eastern Mediterranean and Italy. Along the valley of the Ebro and the road which, via *Legio* (Leon) and *Asturica Augusta* reached the Atlantic at *Bracara Augusta* (Braga), the Egyptian gods widely penetrated the north-west of Tarraconensis. *Clunia*, Valladolid, *Aquae Flaviae* (Chaves, still a cosmopolitan spa) preserve traces of homage to Isis, who was prayed to and represented in statuary more than Serapis. In a minor town in Tarraconensis, *Acci* (Guadiz, near Granada, at the foot of the Sierra Nevada), the goddess wore on her legs, arms, neck, little finger, ring finger, diadem and sandals, dozen upon dozen of precious stones: emeralds, diamonds, to say nothing of a hyacinth, a carbuncle and two 'lightning stones' (*cerauniae*).[111] All in all, Isis was better adorned than a Spanish Virgin! The Guadiz inscription, incidentally, gives her the title *puellaris*. In the fourteenth-century BC, a text from Abydos had her say, 'I am the great Virgin'.

The instance of the Iberian peninsula, like that of Africa, challenges the over-general conclusions of J. Toutain. The spread of Isiacism, in fact, went beyond port and Romanized zones to reach the indigenous population in several sectors. Even if Graeco-Egyptian elements contributed to the introduction of the Alexandrian cults, Isis and Serapis were eventually incorporated into the local pantheon.

They enjoyed enormous success in Gaul, initially around the Golfe du Lion mainly, in the delta and along the Rhône basin, but also on the Atlantic and Channel coasts. Their cult flourished as it followed the major river and road traffic routes. In this respect the Rhône–Rhine axis (via the Saône and the Langres–Trier route) played a decisive role.[112] But this penetration branched out in inner Gaul, above all in the sanctuaries at springs where the saving and healing gods of the Nile Delta united with and strengthened indigenous worship. The Alpine routes, road junctions, relay posts, trading towns, even some large isolated villas in the south-west like those of Montmaurin and Chiragan did not escape the current of Isiacism. As in Spain, we find that after a preliminary wave dominated by Graeco-oriental immigrants, but also by Italian *negotiatores* and colonists originating from regions that were already impregnated with Alexandrian devotions (Campania), the Egyptian gods seem to have conquered certain rather superficially Romanized regions of Gaul.

At a very early stage the Phoenicians and the Greeks from Naucratis imported *Aegyptiaca* from Gaul to the Mediterranean coast. In this respect the Ptah Sokar of Villemagne (north of Béziers) is more significant than the scarabs and other tawdry Nilotic specimens. The concentration of finds in the Narbonensis sector, around Narbonne and Toulouse, demonstrates the importance of the Garonne basin and the 'Gaulish isthmus', as it is called. But the Egyptian or Egyptianate objects found on the Gironde side[113] lead one to think that sailors arriving from the Atlantic must also have played a part, although more limited. Rebuilt in the fourth-century AD, the famous villa of Montmaurin (Haute-Garonne) yielded a gilded bronze head of Serapis-Helios, perhaps identified with Jupiter and honoured in a polygonal chapel of indigenous tradition that was found at the entrance, in the main courtyard: a notable instance of integration with domestic worship?[114]

We know that, in the Rhône delta, the ports of Marseille and Arles had a cosmopolitan population, which explains the proliferation of evidence in that region of Gaul. The ushabtis and funerary bronze Osirises are especially plentiful all along the Rhône valley, from Arles to Lyon, and in the hinterland that was opened up to traffic by Roman roads. Nîmes, a colony founded for veterans from Egypt, as was recalled by its coinage stamped with representations of the crocodile and palm tree (still present on the town's coat of arms), had its temple to Isis, and the lighthouse of Alexandria perhaps inspired the architecture of the Tour Magne.[115] There was a flourishing papyrus trade. Among the significant discoveries was the tomb of a priest, containing his sacerdotal attributes. Like Ostia, Nîmes had its pastophori and *pausarii*, who were responsible for processions and altars of repose.

An 'anubophoros' is known in Vienne, and appliqué terracotta medallions from the Rhône valley, which in relief adorned semiluxury tableware, confirm by their imagery that Isiac festivals were popular in those parts. In fact, they represent not only Isis and Serapis face to face or the goddess endowed with pantheistic attributes, but processions of the faithful wearing liturgical masks. The medallions of Moulins, Vichy and Clermont-Ferrand eloquently illustrate the spread of this cult iconography in central Gaul.[116] In Marseille, Arles and the large river ports (perhaps including Lyon itself) people must have celebrated the opening of the sailing season in March (*Navigium Isidis*). But the lamps, like the one from Marseille (plate 13), which show us Anubis beside Isis must have been sold and lit on the occasion of the great autumn festival: the *Discovery of Osiris*.

The Egyptian funerary tradition of the 'answerers' (ushabtis) seems to have been imported with such success that imitations had to be

Plate 13 Lamp from Marseille (photo. kindly provided by M. Euzennat)

manufactured, whose misrepresented hieroglyphs are void of mean-
ing, as in several examples from Avignon, Orange and Caderousse.[117]
In contrast, the ushabti found near Annecy at *Boutae* (in a first-century
AD context) is authentically Egyptian and bears the name of General
Potasimto, who died in 530 BC. Another was exhumed *c*.1950 near
Aime, on the road linking Italy with Geneva.[118] The burial areas of
Lyon and the bed of the Saône have yielded several ushabtis and
statuettes of Osiris. Effigies of Isis-Ceres and Serapis-Helios ornament
the belly of jugs that were probably offered on the occasion of vows
pronounced in March for the festival of the Rhône and Saône boat-
men. *Lugdunum* possessed if not a sanctuary, at least a chapel consecrated to the goddess in the upper town, not far from Fourvière. Lead
seals and little tablets found in 1858 in the bed of the Saône near the
river port (St Paul quarter) confirm the relations of the Gaulish
metropolis with Alexandria.[119]

From Lyon the Egyptian cults expanded westward, towards the lands
of the Arverni, the Loire and the Allier (where the spas of Vichy and
Néris welcomed the exotic deities with open arms), then by the
Aquitaine route to Limousin. In the north, the valley of the Saône is
studded with indications extending into Morvan (at Autun) and Côte-
d'Or (at Dijon and Vertault). East of Lyon, in the Ain region, Sermoyer,
Pont-d'Ain, Bourg-en-Bresse and Bugey have revealed Osirises in bronze
appropriate to the protection of the dead. In the south-east, in Alpine
Gaul, there is no lack of evidence, although it occurs in more sporadic
fashion (at Entrepierres, La-Bâtie-Montsaléon, Die and Grenoble).

In the north-east, Isis declares her presence at Besançon, Trier and
Metz. Various parts or detachments of the VIIIth Augusta legion,
which came from Moesia (in eastern Europe), doubtless contributed to
this propagation. But in this instance, their occasional piety did not
carry any decisive weight. On the banks of the Rhine, Strasbourg, the
headquarters of this Eighth legion, and its cosmopolitan suburb of
Königshofen, were exposed to the infiltration of foreign religions. The
soil of *Argentoratum* effectively surrendered a whole range of Egyptian
or Egyptianate objects.[120]

In the two Germanies and the valley of the upper Danube, the
number of indications, together with the quality or particularity of
certain remains, are a good illustration of the flexibility with which the
Alexandrian cults settled in and adapted.[121] Writing of the Suebi,
Tacitus says that some of them sacrificed to Isis:

What is the explanation, the origin, of this foreign cult? I have
not been able to discover, unless the emblem itself, shown in the

likeness of a Liburnian boat, denotes an imported religion.
(*Germania*, 9, 2)

In truth, the motif of the vessel, or what would have been taken for
a vessel, proves nothing, even if it suggests a connection with Isis
Pelagia. But the goddess had numerous followers west of the territory
occupied by the *Suebi*. In the land of the Batavi, the Roman military
presence that inevitably gave rise to the surrounding and profitable
activity of non-native traders explains the importation of Isis, Serapis
and Harpocrates via the Rhine and, starting from Cologne, along the
road leading to Leiden, passing through Nijmegen. Isiac statuettes
have been found even in Friesland and Groningen (still farther north,
and even in Scandinavia). In Cologne, the density of finds allows us to
postulate the existence of a sanctuary. Other pieces of evidence denote
a strong presence there of Graeco-Oriental elements. The temple of
Serapis (if there was one, as may be presumed) must have comprised
annexes where ritual banquets were held, as at Alexandria and several
other towns in the Greek Orient.[122] In fact, a dedication instances a
table-bed (*clinè*) consecrated to the god. There Serapis is likened to the
Sun, as is often the case in Gaul. The same type of cultic feasts must
have been practised at Augsburg in Raetia, where a terracotta cover
represents the god on his symposial couch. But it was an exception in
the West. At Cologne two epitaphs for Alexandrians are known, one a
sailor named Horus.

Mainz, Karlsruhe, Baden-Baden and Augst (apart from Strasbourg,
mentioned earlier) stand out on the map of *Isiaca*. Several sites where
Mithraism prospered have similarly revealed traces of Nilotic worship: Dieburg, Stockstadt, Heddernheim. But Mithras, despite his
relative elitism, seems to have gathered more worshippers than the
Egyptian gods. Isis and Serapis did not manage to recruit quite so
many faithful among the soldiers of the Raetian-Rhine *limes*. It is true
that the Egyptian gods had no kind of civic solidarity with the
imperial cult.

North Italy had economic relations with the two Germanies (by way
of Aosta and Geneva) and the Danubian provinces, and similarly with
Narbonensian Gaul. In the Isiac expansion along the Raetian-Rhine
limes, the routes linking towns like Turin, Milan, Verona, and thus the
Veneto with the Alpine valleys and passes played a role that must not
be underestimated.

But maritime traffic also transported these influences by way of the
Ocean, as testified by the *Aegyptiaca* recognized along the Atlantic
coastline, even if the discoveries were somewhat sporadic. In the west
and north-west of Gaul, the Breton coasts,[123] the Seine valley and even

Paris,[124] Nord/Pas-de-Calais, Anvers and Tournai have provided indications: figurines of Osiris, Isis, Serapis, Anubis, Harpocrates, the god Bes, the bull Apis, ushabtis, to say nothing of all the 'junk goods' of Nilotic inspiration whose religious scope obviously remains open to question. Unfortunately, the contexts are insufficiently well known to us to allow inferences to be drawn. Many of these objects were conveyed or lost for reasons that elude us. Others may have been used as amulets. The Osirises and 'answerers' exhumed from burial sites denote the hope of a posthumous security, but we know nothing of the origin or condition of the deceased. The pseudo-hieroglyphs, the confusions committed by the moulders or casters of statuettes and ushabtis, who frequently mixed up the respective types of Osiris and the 'answerer', giving the first the attributes of the second, and vice versa, prove that these were often regional products which had nothing to do with Egypt; but these objects are thus all the more significant of the spread outside Alexandrian circles. They are sometimes to be found mingled with attestations of the Mother-worship cult, for example the ithyphallic baboon discovered at Arras with a porphyry Attis and other problematic monuments.[125]

Unlike Phrygianism, Isiacism does not appear to have benefited directly from official backing or, generally speaking, to have enjoyed solidarity with the imperial cult, although from time to time a sevir augustalis made an act of homage to the goddess of the Delta. Mass production of objects and especially the finding of moulds used to make large numbers of lamps, figurines and appliqué medallions demonstrate that Gallo-Roman craftsmen must have met the demand of customers who by far exceeded the clientele of restricted, notable or marginal circles. As in Spain, Isis was invoked and represented more often than Serapis. But in Gaul, Osiris occupied a relatively important place as protector of the dead.[126]

Southern England was quite rich in testimony,[127] mainly in London (which had an Isiac chapel as early as the first-century AD and the mouth of the Thames, the south-west of the island and York, where a temple was consecrated to Serapis, probably in the time of the Severi. Farther north, in the Roman fort of *Bravionacum* (Kirkby Thore), the Alexandrian god was honoured with an altar. But no trace of the Nilotic cults has been found along Hadrian's Wall, where Mithras and the Syrian gods gained a foothold. Traders proved to be the principal carriers of Isiacism in Roman Britain, but it does not appear to have penetrated as widely or deeply as in Gaul.

Generally, Italy served as a staging-post between the Greek Orient and the western provinces. Many religious representations and formulations underwent the effects of a Roman mediation rendered commonplace by syncretism. Isis-*Fortuna* was the patroness of traders and sailors as well as of officials and soldiers on postings. Serapis watched over their health as well as their crops and the dead. For others, Dionysus-Harpocrates embodied the joys of wine and life. This relative Romanization must not efface the particular instances of transplantation of rites peculiar to Alexandrian Serapism, the sacred banquets for instance. But the historically significant phenomenon is that this religion of immigrants, whether we are speaking of Graeco-Egyptian followers or of colonists from Campania, conquered other milieux, even outside the heavily urbanized zones, without challenging indigenous attachment to local deities.

Scenes, Acts and Actors of Isiacism

The originality of Isiac piety is made plain first in the architecture of the sanctuaries, which immediately conditioned the sensibility of the worshippers and functionally corresponded to the particular features of the liturgy.

Around AD 200, in a famous page that Hippolyte Taine would apply in a pungent fashion to the false prestige of the revolutionary government of Year II,[128] the Christian Clement of Alexandria denounced the settings (and psychological staging) of the Egyptian cult:

> The people of this country have given a great deal of care to propylaea and forecourts, woods and sacred enclosures. The courtyards are encircled by innumerable columns. The walls are resplendent with stones imported from abroad ... Gold, silver, vermilion give lustre to the temples which sparkle in the shimmer of precious gems from India and Ethiopia. Thanks to gold-embroidered curtains, the sanctuary remains in shadow ...

But all this pomp is merely to hide a foul beast: a crocodile wallowing in the purple! (*Paidagogos*, III, 4).

The first fundamental distinction contrasting with Graeco-Roman sanctuaries is the fact that, instead of opening directly onto the street, forum or any other public place, the Egyptian temple was generally isolated, separated from the profane world by an enclosing wall. Thus the *Iseum* at Pompeii (figure 2) rose in the centre of a courtyard closed by a perimeter wall. It was matched on the interior by a covered portico, which had no communication with the street running along the wall except by a single rather narrow gateway, which was situated not in the middle of the blind facade, but at the north corner.[129]

One did not enter the domain of the Egyptian gods 'like going into a mill'. Independently of conditions for initiations, the cult's daily service was terminated early in the afternoon by the closing of the gates. In Rome, the *Iseum Campense* with the *Serapeum* formed an ensemble that was materially and architecturally autonomous,[130] to which access was by two gates that were certainly monumental, one on the east (the *Arcus ad Isis* represented on the tomb of the *Haterii*) and the other on the west, and straightaway gave the visitor the sensation of penetrating a separate world (see figure 3). Moreover, these two gates opened only onto the interior courtyard separating the *Iseum* and *Serapeum*, and access to either could be gained only by a

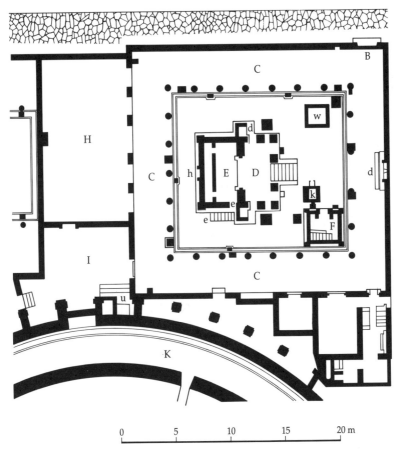

Figure 2 Temple of Isis, Pompeii (from E. La Rocca, M. and A. de Vos, *Guida archeologica di Pompei*, p. 160).

relatively narrow entrance. The sanctuary was not accessible to hoi polloi. There was a sort of 'enclosure', as in real monasteries.

In fact, Egyptian temples in the Roman world did not only harbour divine idols; they included annexes for the accommodation of clergy, 'recluses' (*katochoi*), devotees or pilgrims making their retreat, and also for the accomplishment of initiatory rituals, far from the gaze of the impious or, at least, strangers to the Isiac faith.[131] At Pompeii, behind the *Iseum* a large hall called the *ekklesiasterion* opened out onto the courtyard and was used either for the presentation of new priests on

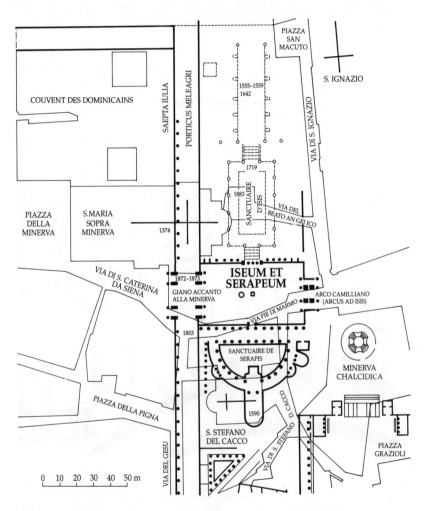

Figure 3 The *Iseum Campense*, Rome (from M. Malaise, *Inventaire prélimi-naire*, Plan 3).

a dais (according to the liturgy of which Apuleius tells us), or (or perhaps at the same time) for the feasts consecrating the incorporation of the initiates. To the south-west, another adjoining room, but with far more restricted access (the *sacrarium*), may have served as sacristy or premises for the celebration of the sacred mysteries. Other buildings to the south and south-east (one of which is a tiered room) probably formed the *pastophorion*, where the priests lived and guests making retreat could stay. At the south-east corner of the portico surrounding the *area*, a small edifice covered a stairway descending to a subterranean chamber that has been related to rites of incubation or preliminary purification, but was more likely to be used for storing the holy water presented to the worship of the faithful before the morning lustrations: indeed, on the pediment of the pavilion one can make out a vessel between two kneeling persons.[133]

The furnishings of the cult, too, were more complex than that of Roman temples. As well as the main altar erected east of the stairway rising to the *pronaos*, two others were raised on the podium facing niches housing the idols of Harpocrates and (probably) Anubis, and six others may be seen unevenly spaced between the columns of the portico surrounding the *area*. Ordinarily, facing Roman temples, a single altar was used for sacrifices performed specifically for the named deity. But the daily *ordo* of Isiac services required completely different liturgical equipment.

In short, the morning ritual called for a very special temple architecture. At the rear of the Pompeian *Iseum*, a little staircase allowed the clergy to enter the *cella* discreetly in order to open the leaves of the gate from the inside. This *cella* was not deep; strictly, it served only to house the two idols of Isis and Serapis set up on two pedestals above a podium, high enough to be seen by the crowd of faithful assembled facing the temple stairway. The Pompeian *Iseum* was not a house that one visited like the Graeco-Roman temples to see, for example, as well as the official statue of the cult, all kinds of sculptures, paintings, offerings and various works of art. The Isiac *naos* was a sort of tabernacle or great monstrance where the divine image could be adored until two o'clock in the afternoon.

While working its way into the urban fabric, and in a lay context, the *Iseum* of Pompei thus constituted a kind of foreign entity in the town, like the one on the Campus Martius in Rome; not a resistant enclave, but singular and concerned about, if not jealous of, its singularity. The Serapeum in Alexandria on its enormous platform, with its body of lodgings occupied by the pastophori, 'the priests who had taken a vow of chastity' (Rufinus, *Ecclesiastical History*, II, 23, 294) and the sacristans, around an inner courtyard where the temple properly speaking rose, must have resembled a fortified monastery around its abbey church. Though not as prestigious as the one at Alexandria, the Quirinal Serapeum – which included quite a considerable area of buildings – could in this regard make just as much impression on those men and women who were tempted to try another religion.

The decorative context disorientated people's senses (plate 1). The exotic imagery of sacred animals and zoomorphic gods must have made just as striking an impression on Roman or, more generally, western candidates for Isiac initiation. On entering the *Iseum* at Pompeii, on the inner walls of the perimeter, painted in the the taste of the Fourth style, one at first identified the figures of the different priests astrologer, scribe, lychnophoros, spondophoros, anubophoros – as they were seen filing past in the annual processions.[134] Admitted into the *sacrarium*, the mysta deciphered on the walls, or had explained to him, the images of Bes, the ibis, Apis, Isis in a boat pulling by a rope the vessel 'Sokaris', with its casket containing the corpse of Osiris. The frescoes of the *ekklesiasterion* would show him the adoration of the mummy of Osiris in its human-shaped sarcophagus surmounted by a phoenix, beside a sycamore, amid the little buildings of a sacred island. He would also see there the myth of Io welcomed by Isis wearing the uraeus encircling her arm and standing with both feet on a crocodile.[135] Sphinxes, gryphons, dolphins and sea monsters would certainly remind him of the motifs of the mythical repertoire into which the painters and stuccoists of wealthy Roman houses were wont to delve. But such marginal decor counted for little at the sight of this other Nilotic world to which his astonished imagination escaped. Everywhere in the Isiac sanctuaries and their annexes, idols, paintings, reliefs, offerings peculiar to Egyptian worship intrigued his curiosity, and one may easily imagine that the sacristans would have no hesitation in arousing it so that they could reap the benefit of satisfying it.

Anyone venturing into the *Iseum* on the Campus Martius in Rome (figure 3) through the *Arcus ad Isis* would first find himself in a vast courtyard centred on Domitian's obelisk, mentioned above. The giant statues personifying the Tiber (in the Louvre today), the Nile (in the Vatican) and the Ocean evoked the universal power of the gods over sea and river waters. On the left, in the middle of a blind wall, a small door opened onto the *area* of the Serapeum. This must have had the aspect of a huge oracular grotto like the Serapeum of the Villa Adriana, with its internal semi-circular gallery broken at the summit of the curve by a large, deep apse housing the gigantic idol of the god.[136] Other deities belonging to the Serapian family were in niches in three subsidiary apses. This architecture was conceived with the aim of giving visitors a sensation of the sacred.

To the north, the three-columned entrance to the *Iseum* properly speaking faced a stairway probably reserved, as at Pompeii, for the appointed clergy of the temple. To attend the services one had to go round the edifice, passing through the long forecourt opposite the temple. The *Iseum* had marble columns with campaniform capitals carved to simulate enormous bunches of papyrus. Some had their shaft enveloped in stylized leaves, others a base of pink granite with bas-relief representations of the priests and servers of the cult (plate 14) each standing on a stool and holding a censer, palm leaf or other sacred emblem, papyrus flowers, canopic vases with the head of Isis, Osiris or Anubis.[137] On the line of the temple, two obelisks marked the entrance to a prestigious *dromos*, where one moved forward between two rows of statues: Horus in black granite, Apis in marble, lions and sphinxes in dark basalt and dog-headed figures in grey granite.[138] Even the strange figures carved on the paving-stones reverently trodden by visitors and worshippers would, in the middle of the town, transport them to the land of the pharaohs.

Opposite the temple, they could contemplate the carving in the half-moon tympanum (another feature of Isiac sanctuaries) of Isis riding sidesaddle on the dog Sirius amid the stars of the sky, under the curve of a pediment bristling with falcons crowned with a pshent. The roof was edged with antefixes showing the Isiac headdress between two snakes. A winged solar disc dominated the lintel of the door which opened above a stairway flanked by two hieratic statues accompanied by sphinxes (plate 11). As at Pompeii, the *naos* itself covered a limited area and served only to house the idol, well situated to be revealed to the veneration of those attending, who were grouped in orderly fashion on the forecourt of the *dromos*. Only the priests could get in through the rear to open its gates from the inside.

As well as the sacred animals and zoomorphic iconography, certain motifs such as ears (symbols of the attentive hearing given by Isis to the prayers of her believers) or the votive feet commemorating the intervention of Serapis – and sometimes honoured, it would seem, like St Peter's foot in the Vatican[139] – contrasted sharply with what Romans had been accustomed to see in temples conforming to the *mos maiorum*.

The daily services that continually animated the life of the sanctuary and ordered its structure strengthened the fervour of the neophytes. Isis had her dressers (stolists or hierostoles), chambermaids (*ornatrices*) who every morning robed and adorned the idol and arranged its coiffure before presenting it to the faithful. The costume

and adornments of the goddess doubtless varied, at least on the occasion of festivals. The inventory of the temple of Nemi (*CIL*, XIV, 2215) and the previously mentioned inscription of Guadiz (to say nothing of other epigraphic testimony like that of Delos and Pergamum) refer to the existence of wardrobes that were as rich as those of the imperial palace. A whole symbolism must have determined the costume and choice of jewellery. 'The garments of Isis', wrote Plutarch (*Isis and Osiris*, 77) 'are dyed in rainbow colours, because her power extends over multiform matter that is subjected to all kinds of vicissitudes'. The doctrines concerning the gods are ambiguous, partly clear and brilliant, partly obscure. The Hierostoles 'dress the idols in sacred garments which reveal these different aspects' (ibid., 3). Plutarch dedicates these considerations to a female initiate of the Osirian mysteries. The Naassenian Gnostics similarly explained the seven black robes of Isis corresponding to the seven ethereal spheres with which 'nature is clad' (Hippolytus, *Philosophoumena*, V, 7).

On the bosom of the goddess her male and female dressers had the art of making the famous Isiac knot that also distinguished her priestesses. Apuleius describes the 'cloak of intense black resplendent with a sombre brilliance', its hem falling in layered folds beneath a knot comparable to the *umbo* of a toga (*umbonis vicem*): this garment undulated like the waves of the sea beneath a scattering of stars . . . (*Metamorphoses*, XI, 3, 5).

Once the idol was ready, the priests pushed open the leaves of the door.

Anxiously [Lucius confides], I watched the morning opening of the temple. When the white curtains were pulled back on either side, we worshipped the venerable image of the goddess. Meanwhile, the priest going round the altars set here and there [as in the *Iseum* of Pompeii] performed the divine service with acts of thanksgiving and poured a libation of water taken from the depths of the sanctuary, (Apuleius, *Metamorphoses*, XI, 20, 3–4)

This water was piously kept in store, 'holy' water said to have come from the Nile. Private individuals who celebrated the Egyptian cult at home in their own chapel kept amphorae full of it, like those discovered at Pompeii in the house of D. Octavius Quarto (the house known as 'of M. Loreius Tiburtinus').[140] Some of these receptacles

Plate 14 Relief of columns from the *Iseum Campense* (Rome, Museo Capitolino)

unearthed in various sectors of the town bear the indication 'gifts of Serapis'. The water of the god-river was thus presented for veneration by devotees, while the altars were lit and purificatory scents were burnt on them (plate 15).

Then, to the sound of flutes and sistra (those kinds of wire rattles still in use in Coptic churches), the hymnodist standing on the threshold of the temple awoke the goddess in the Egyptian tongue. The liturgy of water and fire was therefore considered to bring the idol back to life by means of ritual invocations. There then rang out 'announcing the first hour of the day, the voice of the faithful [*religiosi* who greeted the return of light' (Apuleius, *Metamorphoses*, XI, 20, 5). This office of the reborn day, which coincided with the resurgence of the god (Serapis-Helios), continued well into the heart of the Roman era the joy of primitive man distressed by the uncertainty of whether or not the sun would triumph over the dark of night.

After singing and chanting their homage and gratitude to the divinity, the worshippers adored and prayed at length to its idol. It is notably Isiacism that seems to have introduced this form of piety to the West. Lucius again informs us:

Plate 15 Painting from Herculaneum (Naples, Museo Nazionale)

I fully enjoyed the ineffable pleasure of seeing the divine image.
(*Apuleius, Metamorphoses*, XI, 24, 5)

Chaeremon, Nero's Stoic tutor, had stressed that in Egypt priests
'devoted their entire life to the contemplation of the gods' (Porphyry,
Abstinence, IV, 6). But they were the only ones who could actually do
so face to face. When it spread, Isiac piety became more flexible,
adapting itself to the pressing demand of many converted Greeks and
Romans. Henceforward, the faithful had the right to worship the idol
directly, by means of a kind of pre-initiatory arrangement. But in any
case adoration remained limited in time as in place. At the eighth hour
(around two in the afternoon), after a kind of 'vespers' intoned by the
officiants and taken up in chorus by those in attendance (Martial,
Epigrams, X, 48, 1), the curtains were drawn, the doors closed, and the
statue remained out of sight until the next morning.

The timetable that strictly governed daily worship explains and
justifies the office of *horologos* mentioned by Chaeremon (Porphyry,
Abstinence, IV, 8): it was his duty to determine the exact moment of
opening and closing the sanctuary, as well as the different times of the
great annual ceremonies. Water-clocks or fragments of them (including three from the *Iseum Campense*) found on the consecrated sites, and
sundials dedicated to the goddess met this need. That is also why the
Delian inventory of Metrophanes mentions a clock offered to Isis.[141] A
similar discipline in devotions, which prefigured that of cloistered
monks, radically transformed the customs of pagan worship. It was
no longer a matter of sacrificing once a month or once a year to this or
that god.

With sustained application, gentle calm and exemplary silence,
day after day I attended the celebration of the sacred service
[declares Lucius]. (Apuleius, *Metamorphoses*, XI, 22, 1)

It appears that Egypt taught the West a certain spirituality in observance and meditation.

A sense of asceticism and rule went hand in hand with the
discipline of the timetable. The continence to which even women of
easy virtue submitted themselves caused some irritation to their
lovers. Of course, there were arrangements that could be made for the
wife at fault:

The silver snake has moved its head: it was seen! But thanks to
his tears and knowing paternosters, the priest manages to per-
suade Osiris not to withhold his pardon. A plump goose, a

dainty cake . . . and the god lets himself be corrupted! (Juvenal, *Satires*, VI, 538–40)

But consciousness of failing towards the goddess called forth public confessions (Ovid, *Letters from the Black Sea*, I, 51) and displays of penitence. Seneca bears witness to the impression that could be made on a well-brought-up Roman by the sight of a woman devotee shrieking as she dragged her knees over the paving stones in the streets (*Happy Life*, 25, 8).[142] Juvenal (*Satires*, VI, 522ff) was appalled to see a woman duck her head three times under the ice of the Tiber and tear her knees around the *Iseum Campense*:

'If the white Io [= Isis] orders it, she will go to the depths of Egypt and bring back water drawn from near torrid Meroe to sprinkle the temple of Isis . . . She is convinced that the goddess in person has intimated this command to her. See with what kinds of souls and imaginations the gods would converse during the night!

Indeed, together with the divine service, dreams occupied a large part of the lives of Isiac believers.

In order to conform to the conditions of such a strict form of piety and persevere in them, worshippers who could do so moved into an annexe of the sanctuary. It was 'the better to enjoy the sweet presence of the goddess' that Lucius booked 'lodgings within the temple enclosure itself' and temporarily established his dwelling there, 'taking part, though still as a private citizen, in the service of the goddess, closely associated with the life of the priests and perpetual worshipper of the august divinity' (Apuleius, *Metamorphoses*, XI, 19, 1).

Public Solemnities and Mystery Rites

Two great festivals, one in spring, the second in autumn, gave a rhythm to the liturgical year: the *Navigium Isidis* and the *Inventio Osiridis*.

The first, the 'Vessel of Isis', on every 5 March, marked the opening of the sailing season, in which the protectress of sailors, more than any other deity, had a direct interest.[143] It recalled how Isis had once set off over the waves in search of her murdered husband. The 'navarchs' and 'hieronauts' of whom there is epigraphic evidence at Eretria, Tomi, Byzantium, Tenos, Nicomedia and Seleucia of Pieria took part in this festival of sailing in those capacities. Apuleius gives us a vivid and colourful description (*Metamorphoses*, XI, 8, 17).

The day began with an exuberant procession of costumed groups, a kind of carnival featuring men in women's clothing, some dressed up as soldiers or gladiators, some as hunters or magistrates, fishermen or philosophers. A bear attired as a matron carried in her litter; a monkey was rigged out as Ganymede; a donkey was fitted with false wings; a mock Pegasus was accompanied by an aged Bellerophon: the people making fun of both human and divine society . . .

Behind this pantomime, clad all in white and crowned with flowers, walked the women, some strewing the ground with petals, others miming with their ivory combs the art of dressing the goddess's hair, sprinkling the streets with unguents and perfumes. They were followed by the faithful, armed with lamps, torches, candles 'to propitiate the origin of the celestial stars'; then, to the sound of pan-pipes and flutes, came a choir of young singers followed by the musicians of Serapis who, 'on their oblique instrument extended towards their right ear, played a tune familiar to the god in his temple'. Next arrived 'groups of initiates to the divine mysteries, men and women of every age and rank, in all the immaculate splendour of their linen robes', the women veiled, the men shaven-headed, 'terrestrial stars of the august religion'. They shook their sistra of bronze, silver or gold. This concert of metallic stridency announced the ministers of the cult, tightly clad in white linen, like the priests who, on a famous fresco from Herculaneum, preside over the ceremonies preceding a procession of the holy water (plate 15).

All carried symbolic attributes. The one who led the procession (the lychnophoros) held a lamp carved in the shape of a small boat, its flame signifying the light of Serapis-Helios, its shape the power of Isis over the sea waves. The second held with both hands a small altar called 'succour' to remind people of the providence of the helpful goddess. The third carried a gold palm-leaf and a caduceus which characterized him as 'astrologer'. The fourth showed a hand of justice and a small golden vessel, rounded in the shape of a breast, which was used to pour out libations of milk: this was the stolist (in the Pompeian *Iseum* a large open-palmed hand was found which was used precisely in the solemn procession).[144] The fifth had a winnowing basket laden with gold branches (one tradition held that Isis laid the mutilated limbs of Osiris in just such a basket). Lastly, a sixth dignitary presented the amphora which probably corresponded to the hydria of the 'prophet' in the list detailed by Clement of Alexandria (*Stromateis*, VI, 4, 37, 1).

Following the priests came the gods, 'deigning to walk on human feet': an anubophoros holding the idol or the mask of the cynocephalus god, with a black face and a gilded face (in his role of mediator, like Hermes-Mercury, between the two worlds, infernal and celestial): the sacred litter-bearers of the cow Hathor; a cistophorus whose basket 'hides within it the mysteries of the sublime religion'. Lastly, 'the venerable image of the sovereign divinity' appeared in the guise of a gold vessel whose handle bore 'an asp with twisting coils', the uraeus of Isis (Apuleius, *Metamorphoses*, XI, 11, 4). According to inverted hierarchic order, still observed in the Catholic ritual, the high priest brought up the rear.

The procession reached the port where a brand-new boat waited, decorated with Egyptian-style paintings. The high priest then uttered a solemn prayer, purifying the boat's hull with a torch, an egg and some sulphur. On the white sail phrases of good omen were embroidered in gold lettering. The vessel was laden with spices, libations of milk broth and all sorts of offerings, before the mooring-ropes were cut: and off drifted the boat! Everyone then returned to the temple where the high priest, his servers and the initiates replaced the idols after the procession. Standing in front of the door, from the height of the podium the scribe, or 'hierogrammatos', crowned with two plumes, summoned the pastophori (that is, the category of priests who formed a kind of 'third order' or auxiliary liturgical team). Following a sacred book, he pronounced the annual and traditional vows for the emperor, the Senate, the equestrian order and the Roman people, but also for sailors and ships subject to the laws of the Empire. In Greek he announced the opening of the sailing season (*Ploiaphesia*) to the acclamations of the crowd, who climbed the steps of the sanctuary to adorn the silver idol of the goddess with flowers and green branches, kissing her feet. The *Navigium Isidis* must have varied from one port to another. But everywhere this spectacular festival of springtime renewal mobilized the municipal authorities and popular enthusiasm.

Unlike the *Navigium*, the autumnal Isiac solemnities occupied several days. Like the festivals of March commemorating the death and resurrection of Attis, the *Discovery of Osiris* in effect formed a cycle of alternating grief and joy from 28 October to 3 November.

The correspondence of these dates with the movable Egyptian calendar and the Alexandrian calendar, as with the data of literary tradition, raises thorny argument.[145] But we know that, in the Delta, the festivals began on the 17th of the month called *Hathyr* and that in AD 40–3 this day coincided in the West with 28 October, a date which remained constant in the Roman holiday year until the fifth-century. This occasion was thus very probably officially written into the calendar at the time when Caligula recognized Isis and had her temple rebuilt on the Campus Martius. In Egypt it was the moment in the year when, Plutarch tells us (*Isis and Osiris*, 39), 'the Nile disappears into the earth and leaves the ground bare. The nights become longer, darkness increases, the power of light is dulled and seems to be vanquished'.

The river's fertilizing water and the sun which makes the seed germinate were together deified in the figure of Osiris, who was then held to have died as victim of Seth. In the West as in the Delta, the faithful shared in the mourning of Isis, whose priestess perhaps played the role by donning her attributes. Black was worn (hence the name 'melanophori' borne by members of the brotherhoods vowed to this funereal commemoration) and statues of the goddess were veiled

Plate 16 Priestess of Isis (from Rome; Karlsruhe Museum)

in black. Priests, priestesses (plate 16) and initiates of both sexes and all ages (even children, singled out by a tress of long hair behind the right ear and thus likened to Horus) ritually participated in the 'passion' of Osiris and the anguish of Isis, chanting laments, but also uttering piercing cries of grief, beating their breasts with pine cones until blood ran from the bruised skin. A statuette preserved in the Museum of Turin shows us a dishevelled Isis whose arms and body express pain, as some members of the priesthood and liturgical teams must have done.

The search for the god was mimed in the sanctuary enclosure, following a route probably laid down in advance. According to a passage from Firmicus Maternus (*The Error of Profane Religions*, XXII, 3), it would seem that a physically dismembered idol of Osiris was used, its various parts being scattered like those of the body torn apart by Seth. They were reassembled before it was proclaimed that he had been found (hence the name of the festival: *Inventio* – or rediscovery – of Osiris). A priest or mysta would don the mask of Anubis to mime the god who, thanks to his sense of smell, had helped the goddess, like a good hunting-dog, to detect the remains of the divine corpse.

On 3 November everyone emerged from the sanctuary, and a joyous procession went through the streets of the town to celebrate the 'Hilaria', matching those which on 25 March fêted the revival of Attis. People shouted 'We have found: we rejoice' (or 'let us rejoice'), frenetically shaking their sistra. People in the countryside also sang and danced, for the rediscovered Osiris gave life to the seeds of future harvests. They made images of the god, fashioned out of a block of damp earth that was decorated with seeds and placed in a hollowed-out pine trunk. These figurines have been found in tombs, pledges of survival under the sign and protection of the'good god'. This rite of the 'vegetating' Osiris, originating directly from Egypt, enjoyed a success in the West that exasperated Christians.[146] The god was identified with wheat, and his rebirth guaranteed good harvests: 'It is on this day that Osiris, at last restored to life, raises the fertile seeds of new crops' (Rutilius Namatianus, *On His Return*, I, 375f). Matrons took a lively and noisy part in the moving scenes of the autumn *Isia*.

Some, like Seneca and the Fathers of the Church, deplored the hypocritical passion of the actors and 'bit-players'. But the decoration on lamps and vases that were moulded and surmoulded to be offered on the occasion of these festive displays illustrates their success, which apparently went beyond the circle or cenacle of the mystae.

As well as these two high points in the Isiac year, the *Pelusia* of 24 March celebrated the infant Harpocrates emerging from the alluvial soil on a lotus, his finger on his lips.[147] People coated their faces with a mush that was then applied to passers-by as a remedy for their pains. A month later, the *Serapia* of 25 April were consecrated to the great Alexandrian god and perhaps in Rome commemorated the dedication of one of his temples.[148] On 12 August a nocturnal festival known as 'the lighting of the lamps' (*Lychnapsia*) was probably incorporated into the official Roman calendar around AD 38–9, in the reign and at the instigation of Caligula, for at that time this day corresponded with the anniversary of Isis which was solemnized throughout Egypt.

In parallel with public liturgies, private citizens celebrated Egyptian liturgies in their own homes. For example, in Pompeii a property-owner had constructed a 'Euripus' (or artificial canal) in his garden, bordered with statuettes, which was filled by means of a waterfall and fountains to represent the annual inundation of the Nile.[149]

Those men and women whom this festive Isiacism attracted but without satisfying them or assuaging their need for revelation, the absolute, and intimacy with the divine, aspired to initiation. After serving in a college of worshippers (*cultores*) of Isis and Serapis, *Anubiaci* or *Isiaci*, by dint of observance and perseverance one could be 'called' by the goddess. For initiation did not depend on the follower's own wish, or even that of the high priest. The goddess herself gave them a sign when she judged the time was right.[150] It even happened that at certain festivals Isis would not admit anyone at all. At Tithorea in Phocis, only the men and women she accepted by appearing to them in a dream were allowed to take part in the ceremonies. It was said that an intruder to whom the goddess had not given an invitation had died, the victim of his casual curiosity and sacrilege. 'I heard about the same thing from a Phoenician', wrote Pausanias (*Description of Greece*, X, 32, 18) concerning the Isiac sanctuary of Coptos. The divine *dignatio* has something of providential grace, and one must know how to wait for it. It was a foremost and fundamental test of the mysteries. In a dream Isis jointly informed the candidate and the priest charged with his or her initiation, who confirmed the good news:

> O fortunate Lucius, what happiness is thine, thou whom the august divinity deems worthy of her favour! (Apuleius, *Metamorphoses*, XI, 22, 5)

The postulant acknowledged by the goddess immediately received preliminary instructions drawn from a book of hieroglyphic writings (*ibid.*, 8), the expression of a wisdom from time immemorial which conferred a supernatural legitimacy on these regulation arrangements.

Accompanied by the 'pious cohort' of mystae, he was led by the priest to some baths near the temple where, once bathed, following the Egyptian ritual, he was sprinkled with purifying water said to have come from the Nile. After this preliminary purification, the priest advised the candidate to have ten days of abstinence (wine and meat), but probably also of sexual continence.

When evening came, the one to be initiated was offered presents. The profane were kept out of the way. The initiate was dressed in a linen robe never previously worn; then the priest took him by the hand to lead him to 'the remotest part of the sanctuary' or *penetralia*, the Latin equivalent of the 'Holy of Holies'. What took place next? Apuleius (*Metamorphoses*, XI, 23, 5–7) speaks of it only in veiled terms and, curiously, the Christians who gladly denounced or derided Mother-cult or Eleusinian rites say barely a word about the Isiac mysteries. It seems that after taking an oath, the mysta carried out an imaginary astral and infernal journey that was supposed to reveal to him the power and the aspect of the gods:

> I approached the frontiers of death and, having walked on the threshold of Proserpine [i.e., of the Moon, the abode of the dead], I returned thence carried through all the elements ... I approached the gods of below and the gods of on high. I saw them face to face and adored them close to.

The neophyte was probably shown statues that were concealed from the gaze of ordinary followers.

Other testimony confirms the importance of the representations relating to the Underworld, over which Osiris reigned, but where Isis exercised the same total sovereignty as in the heavens. In this regard, the words she addressed to Lucius before the miracle that restored his human body to him prefigured the meaning of the initiation:

> Thou shalt find me shining amid the gloom of the Acheron, and thyself living in the Elysian Fields will assiduously render homage to my benevolent divinity. (Apuleius *Metamorphoses*, XI, 6, 6)

To enjoy this foretaste of the next world, the mysta obviously had to 'die' to his former life.

The following morning, after a night during which hallucinations perhaps aided by lack of food played a part (however they were brought about), Lucius donned twelve consecration robes which apparently symbolized the zodiacal constellations ruled by Isis, like

all the stars in the heavens, unless they were intended as the twelve
zones of the night traversed by the Sun in the lower world (or austral
hemisphere), as they had been by the candidate in the realm of the
dead.[151] In the middle of the sanctuary, a platform was set up which
the new initiate mounted, this time clad in an embroidered linen robe
decorated with Indian dragons and hyperborean gryphons, creatures
of the Other World. When the curtains were drawn, he was revealed
'like a statue', crowned with palm-leaves and armed with a flaming
torch, for the admiration of the faithful, who filed slowly past his feet.
Henceforth, he was a new man, the initiation representing a 'volun-
tary' death (*ad instar voluntariae mortis*), as the high priest had informed him (Apuleius, *Metamorphoses*, XI, 21, 7). He was honoured
almost like a new Osiris, saved and regenerated as the god had been
through the ineffable powers of Isis. The palms radiating from his
head were the sign of the Sun triumphing over death.

A communal banquet then consecrated the incorporation of the
mysta and his birth into the religious life, *natalem sacrorum*. Two days
later, a sacramental meal concluded this first ceremony. Two other
initiations, to Rome itself and to the mysteries of Osiris 'the Invincible,
Supreme Father of the Gods', completed the consecration of Lucius.
These initiations were still prepared and ordered by divine appearances in dreams. Lucius had his head shaven and entered the college
of the Pastophori. From then on he knew true happiness. He had the
assurance of 'salvation' in this world and the next. Pledged by oath
into the 'holy militia' of Isis and Osiris, he lived under the gaze of
their tutelary omnipotence.

It was even more true of those men and women who consecrated
themselves to the priesthood (sometimes in their childhood or adolescence) in the cult of the 'Many-named'. An epitaph from Megalopolis
in Arcadia celebrates a woman who at the age of fifteen answered the
call of the goddess, and served her for nearly half a century until she
died, when she was coiffed, dressed and buried in the likeness of the
goddess.[152] The dignity and calm of Isiac faith had something to
impress anxious or fickle pagans who were beguiled by the murky
occultism of the sects or the pandemonism of the magicians.

The Twilight of the Gods

The *Asclepius*, a Latin translation of a Greek original of about AD 300,
makes Hermes Trismegistus say, 'Egypt is the image of heaven',

But there will come a time when it will seem as if the Egyptians
have vainly honoured the divinity with a pious heart and

constant worship . . . The gods, leaving the earth, will regain the heavens; they will abandon Egypt . . . Then this very holy country, the homeland of sanctuaries and temples, will be completely covered with sepulchres and the dead. O, Egypt, Egypt! Nothing but fables will remain of thy cults, and later thy children will not believe in them. All that will survive will be words carved on stones, recounting thy pious deeds. (*Asclepius*, 24)[153]

Even making allowances for the prophetic genre and, incidentally, Egyptian or Iranian doctrines about the end of the world and its cyclic renewal, this 'apocalypse' coincided remarkably with the religious situation of the Nilotic country in the fourth-century AD, and Christians did not fail to cite it, just as they made use of the Sibylline pseudo-oracles or Virgil's IVth Eclogue.

Outside Egypt, however, Isis and Serapis retained many worshippers in the period of the Tetrarchs. Their images had been made official on coinage of the second and third centuries, but no public monument showed them alongside the emperor. In vain have people claimed to see a likeness to Serapis in Septimius Severus on the Arch of the Moneychangers in Rome or on the Arch of Leptis in Tripolitania.[154] In contrast, on the Arch of Galerius erected at Salonica in 303 after the victories of the Eastern Caesar over the Sassanid Persians, Isis and Serapis are recognizable among the gods surrounding the Tetrarchs, and were henceforth incorporated into the public pantheon.[155] Their presence was all the more opportune because the *Vicennalia* were being celebrated at that time, twenty years of Diocletian's reign, and on this occasion vows were made for the supreme happiness of the Empire (we have seen how these vows were solemnized in March for the opening of the sailing season). A whole series of coins commemorating the *Vota Publica* was struck then and would continue to be so in Rome, even under the Christian emperors.

The same Diocletian, who was so attached to traditional religious values, had a new sanctuary of Isis and Serapis built in Rome, but its exact location remains uncertain. In his palace at Spalato (Salonae), fragments of eight sphinxes and various Egyptian or Egyptianate monuments have been found.[156]

In the *Urbs*, the aristocracy displayed a devotion that contrasted considerably with the scorn evinced less than two centuries earlier by senators and writers. The 'clarissimus' Scipio Orfitus reconsecrated to Jupiter Capitolinus, identified in this instance with 'Sarapis-Sun', an altar on which one of his ancestors (?) had had himself represented astride the bull Apis for his last journey to the bosom of Mother

Earth.[157] In 299, on ground offered by a former consul, four Egyptians erected in honour of Serapis a glistening marble, chapel to house the image of the god 'dazzling with rays of gold' (*IG*, XIV, 1026). Serapis also took part in the war of the gods that brought Maximinus Daia, the Caesar of Galerius who became Augustus in 308, into conflict with Constantine and Licinius. Between 310 and 313 his coinage broadcast the image of Helios holding the head of the calathophoric god with the legend: 'to the Invincible Sun'.[158]

The antipagan laws of Constantine and his sons without doubt hampered the practice of the Isiac cult to some extent. But after 357 a kind of 'gentleman's agreement' between Rome's polytheistic aristocracy and Constantius II led the Christian emperor to turn a blind eye to manifestations of idolatry. Julian 'the Apostate', however, unequivocally showed his favour to Serapis-Helios, 'the great and very holy god', who especially contributed to entrusting him with 'the right to rule the world' (*Letter to the Alexandrians* = *Ep.*, 60). Julian did not have money struck in Alexandria in the likeness of his wife Helena represented as Isis, as was formerly supposed.[159] But a whole range of bronze coins issued between 362 and 363 bear the image of the bull Apis on the reverse.[160] In a letter to the prefect of Egypt against the antipagan militancy of the bishop. Athanasius, the emperor swears 'by the great Serapis' (*Ep.*, 6).

Around the same period or, at any event, in the second half of the fourth-century, contorniate medallions distributed on the occasion of great festivals represent the bust of Serapis on the obverse, and on the reverse Isis *Pelagia*, standing on a vessel and holding the sail which is bellied out by the sea wind.[161] In 376 the three Christian emperors, Valens, Gratian and Valentinian II, gave their patronage to the restoration of a temple of Isis and its portico in the port of Ostia. It was perhaps one of those buildings with a half-moon pediment that are to be seen on the reverse of the sesterces featuring the *Portus Traiani*.[162] Several eminent members of the Senate and their wives displayed their adherence to the Isiac faith, notably Vettius Agorius Praetextatus and Ceionius Rufius Volusianus, former prefect of Rome, later the praetorian prefect Nicomachus Flavianus, on whom an anonymous rhyming pamphlet (the *Carmen contra paganos*) heaps sarcasm because, shaven-headed, he makes supplications to the 'goddess of the Lighthouse':

> ... *calvus ad aras*
> *sistriferam Phariam supplex cum forte rogares.* (v. 98f)

Another anonymous poem appended in the manuscripts to the works of Cyprian,[163] but composed by a Christian polemicist also in the late fourth century, denounces a senator who, having fallen back into the path of idolatry, had his head shaven and, shod with papyrus, took part in processions with the canine mask of Anubis. Until 394, each year on the occasion of the public vows, the polytheistic aristocrats of the *Urbs* had bronze coins struck showing Isis *Pharia*, Serapis crowned with rays, Harpocrates and the jackal-headed Anubis, the barking god reviled by Virgil, Lucan and Juvenal before being so by the Fathers of the Church. Before 379, those who sponsored these propagandist money issues pushed provocation to the point of having the effigy of Christian emperors reproduced on the obverse. From that date, the busts of Isis and Serapis occupied the face.[164]

A priori, it is difficult to explain how an enlightened and cultivated class, passionately interested in a literature which defended the *mos maiorum* at the expense of Nilotic superstitions, could have become so besotted with bird-, jackal- or dog-headed gods. Until the second-century AD Egyptian zoolatry remained an inexhaustible topic of mockery or indignation among Rome's pagans. With even greater reason there was astonishment at the cult of plants! 'Egypt invokes garlic and onions among the gods in its oaths', lamented Pliny the Elder (*Natural History*, II, 101). 'It is sacrilege to insult the leek and the onion by sinking your teeth into them. What devout populations, whose deities grow in vegetable gardens!' continued Juvenal (*Satires*, XV, 9–10).

But in the fourth-century, people also read Apuleius, who figures on the face of several contorniate medallions; and above all, the work of the Neoplatonist Porphyry, *On Statues*, gave an account philosophically, and sometimes astronomically, of the minutest peculiarities of Nilotic idolatry.

> In the town of Elephantine, reverence is paid to a statue ... seated, dark blue in colour, with a ram's head and a diadem with goat's horns surmounted by a discoid circle ... By its ram's face and goat's horns it signifies the meeting of the sun and moon in the sign of the Ram; the dark blue colour, that by this meeting the moon brings rain ...

Elsewhere, we see a white statue with a falcon's face which, with its spear, overcomes a Typhon in the form of a hippopotamus:

> The whiteness symbolizes the light of the moon; the falcon's face signifies that it receives light and breath from the sun ... As for the hippopotamus, this means the pole of the setting sun, because it swallows up passers-by. (Eusebius, *Praeparatio Evangelica*, III, 12, 12)

The Egyptians

> consecrated to the moon the bull they call Apis, he too blacker
> than the rest, with the signs of the sun and moon ... The sign
> of the sun is the blackness of the body and the knot under the
> tongue; the symbol of the moon is the division (of the spine) into
> two equal parts and its double gibbosity. (Ibid., 13, 2)

Naturally, the Egyptians were not so stupid as to look upon animals
as gods. They simply took them to be 'the images and symbols of the
gods' (ibid., 12, 6). Plutarch had already explained the zoolatry for
which they were unduly blamed.[165] But Porphyry made himself the
careful and zealous popularizer of an allegorization directly inherited
from the Stoics. In this view, Isis, Osiris and Serapis were *a fortiori*
justified in their iconography as in their myths and liturgies. The
crimson tunic of Serapis

> symbolizes the light that has come down to earth; his broken
> sceptre, his subterranean strength; the shape of his hand, his
> passage to the invisible. (Ibid., 11, 28)It is Isis who nourishes and
> makes the shoots rise from the ground; the Osiris of the Egyp-
> tians represents the force of fruitfulness which they propitiate by
> lamentations when it disappears into the soil at seedtime and
> when we eat it to feed ourselves. (Ibid., 50)

Osiris represents the Nile that fertilizes and

> is believed to descend from heaven: mourning is performed for
> him too, in order to propitiate the force which declines and is
> consumed. (Ibid., 51)

In fact, the fall in the Nile occurred at the time when shortening days
gave the impression that the sun was becoming correspondingly
weaker.

Firmicus Maternus bears witness to the success obtained among
pagan circles by both the *ratio physica*, likening Osiris to the buried
seed, and the solar syncretism which the cult of Attis similarly
enjoyed. In the early fifth century, Macrobius was probably still
inspired by Porphyry's treatise *On the Sun*, when he referred to the
symbolism of the hieroglyphs (already used by Chaeremon) in support of heliac theosyncrasy. With the same attitude, Macrobius gives
an explanation of the idols of Horus, whom the Egyptians represented
with his head shaven except on the right side:

The hair that is retained [the lock of Horus] shows that the sun never conceals itself from the eyes of nature; the hair that is cut off, yet with the roots persisting, signifies that, even during the period when we do not see it, like the hair this heavenly body preserves the property of reappearing. (*Saturnalia*, I, 21, 14)

As for the bull Apis:

it is asserted that he changes colour every hour and that the hair lies in the opposite direction to that of all other animals. So he is deemed to be an image of the sun, which travels in the opposite direction to the stars. (Ibid., 21)

In the basket of the calathophoric god Macrobius discerns the proof that Serapis is identified with Helios: it

symbolizes the height of the star and the power of its capabilities, so that all terrestrial bodies drawn by the heat it gives out return to its bosom. (Ibid., 20, 15)

Despite all these fine speculations, which are often naive and artificially acrobatic, or perhaps actually because of the sophisms that exasperated the Christians, Egyptian cults were condemned in Egypt itself, where passions were more violently exacerbated than elsewhere. The Serapeum in Alexandria remained a fortress of paganism for a long time, but finally had to yield before the end of the fourth century.

One day when the bishop Theophilus had had the effrontery to close down a former *Mithraeum* for the benefit of his flock, the Christians taking possession of the premises had profaned it and ridiculed the remains of the religious furnishings. It would appear that skulls were exhumed in order to denounce the human sacrifices said to sully the nocturnal liturgies! Beside themselves, the pagans counterattacked. They hurled themselves on the profaners: there were blows and wounds, bloody confrontations. The affair took a nasty turn, the polytheists withdrew to the Serapeum, from where they made sorties to seize hostages whom they forced to sacrifice to the idols. Their position was too well fortified for them to be easily dislodged, even using troops. The philosopher Olympius, who was besieged with them, galvanized their energies.

Powerless or hampered, the prefect of Alexandria and the military governor of Egypt referred the matter to the emperor Theodosius, who pardoned the pagan resistants, but advised the extirpation of the evil in other words, the destruction of idolatry. Confronted with the pagans who were downcast by this reply, the Christians exulted. Immediately roused to fanaticism by the bishop, they mounted an attack on the Serapeum, breaking, pillaging and sacking everything that fell into their hands. The doors were forced and broken down. There remained the gigantic idol whose two arms were said to touch the temple walls. If anyone dared to attack Serapis, it was believed that the earth would open and the sky fall. But Theophilus ordered that an axe should be taken to it. Even the wildest of the mob hesitated, when a soldier delivered the first blows to the jaw of the god, smashing the statue, which was made of fitted sections. At once thousands of rats fled from the worm-eaten statue, to the vengeful cries of the populace (Théodoret, *Ecclesiastical History*, V, 22, 5). The dismembered idol was then set on fire. And it was not the end of the world: quite the reverse, that year's harvest was said to be better than harvests in preceding years!

As a result, a crowd of pagans appears to have been converted, perhaps terrorized by the strong-arm monks and shock-troop Christians. Rufinus (*Ecclesiastical History*, II, 29) tells us that the priests of Serapis themselves humbly made a pretence of recognizing in the looped cross or *ankh* (hieroglyphic sign for life), a prefiguration of the Christian emblem of salvation. In polytheistic circles the event had painful repercussions. It inspired Eunapius to write these bitterly ironic lines:

Men who had never heard of war boldly attacked stones and walls. They demolished the Serapeum! Victors without a battle and without enemies, they made war on offerings. Courageously, they gave battle to the statues until they had vanquished and robbed them. Their military tactics consisted of stealing without being seen. As they could not carry away the pavement because of the weight of the stones that could hardly be moved, when they had tumultuously overturned everything in sight, these great and valiant warriors, whose hands, though rapacious, were not stained with blood, declared that they had triumphed over the gods. They gloried in their sacrilege and impiety. In these sacred places 'monks' were installed, those creatures who resemble men but live like pigs . . . In that period anyone who wore a black robe had despotic power! In the abode and in place of the gods, henceforward worship was rendered to the skeletons of a few wretched ex-convicts, slaves who deserved the whip: the 'martyrs' . . . (Eunapius, *Lives of the Sophists*, revised text of 1878, ed. J.F. Boissonade, p. 472).

All the busts of Serapis which adorned and were formerly supposed to protect the walls, doors and windows were systematically broken and hammered. They were replaced by crosses. Egypt rejected its god, as Hermes Trismegistus had 'prophesied'.

However, in Rome and its environs, Isiacism held firm. On 3 November 417 the Gaulish writer Rutilius Namatianus could still witness at Falerii 'crowds of peasants rejoicing' (hilares), celebrating the Hilaria of Osiris at the crossroads of this rural township.[166] In Egypt itself, Isis still had worshippers in university circles at the end of the fifth century, as is borne out by Zachary the Scholastic. At Menuthis, near Canopus, the pagans had hidden idols brought from Memphis in a house with a double wall, into which the priest could get by a narrow window-shaped opening to sacrifice secretly to the goddess. The patriarch of Alexandria had statues of all kinds discovered there (cats, monkeys, snakes and crocodiles). It was then learned that the polytheists were paying the Christian clergy of the village not to take any notice. Everything was confiscated and destroyed (Zachary the Scholastic, Life of Severus, in Patrologia Orientalis, II, Paris, 1907, p. 27ff).

Damascius confirms the relative vitality of the Graeco-Egyptian traditions in Neoplatonist circles. He tells us of a Heraiscus who emerged from his mother's womb with a finger glued to his lips, like Horus-Harpocrates. When he was to be mummified according to the Osirian rite, the hieroglyphs written on the strips of cloth were illuminated, surrounded by 'divine apparitions' (Life of Isidore, 107, in Photius, Bibliotheca, 242, 343 a).

In his Life of Proclus (19) Marinus of Neapolis informs us that at that time (in 486) Isis was still honoured in her sanctuary at Philae. Her cult was not definitively abolished and banned until 535. Narses, who was then in command of Justinian's troops in Egypt, put the priests of Isis in prison and had the idols sent to Constantinople. The carved walls were plastered over and the pronaos became a church.

Small pagan splinter groups persevered clandestinely until the end of the sixth-century.[167] Individually, idolatry kept its obstinate adherents. Around 570 a notable of Antaiopolis in Thebaid (where Isis and Horus were supposed to have overcome Seth) dedicated chapels to the gods and sacrificed to them. Even under Arab domination, in the eighth century, a magician of the Faiyum continued to invoke 'Isis and her son Horus', or 'Isis and Nephthys, the two sad and afflicted sisters'. Isis of the Many Names, 'the initial progeny of worlds' (Apuleius, Metamorphoses, XI, 5, 1) was a long time a-dying.

She survived in those of her idols that were used as madonnas. All in all, the refrigerium animae Christianized the invocation to her husband, which was carved on tombstones: 'May Osiris give thee cool water!' And when, for the feast of the Epiphany,[168] after a solemn blessing of the water at midnight, the Christians in Egypt went with their pitchers to the banks of the Nile to draw from the beneficial flow, they were simply repeating in their own fashion a very ancient action of their pagan ancestors.

Chapter 3

The Orontes Pouring into the Tiber

'THE Syrian Orontes has been disgorging into the Tiber for a good while now,' proclaims Juvenal (*Satires*, III, 62), with the same alarmed indignation that makes elderly Parisians quiver when they see this or that part of the capital occupied by Asians or North Africans.

> It has conveyed to us the language and customs [of Syria], girl flute-players, slanting harps, exotic timbrels and maidens whose instructions are to loiter near the Circus. Go to them, then, you who love these barbarian she-wolves with their gaudy head-dress! (Ibid., 63–6)

Vice was being let loose on Rome with these Orientals who were to be found in places of ill repute, at the doors of shady taverns, as skimpily clad as might be expected and proffering their bottle to the passer-by . . . (Juvenal, *Satires*, VIII, 162).

The poet was writing in the reign of Hadrian, who was derisively nicknamed the 'little Greek' (*Graeculus*). This is the very word that describes Juvenal's *bête noire*, *Graeculus esuriens*, the 'half-starved Greek', or in other words, the Greek-speaking Levantine, who could turn his hand to anything and was therefore capable of anything, who adapted to any surroundings and jobs, notably those that the Romans did not want to perform: repairing public buildings, keeping rivers clean, clearing out sewers, funeral services, 'farming' mines or customs, trade of all kinds and at all levels. These people were equally successful as roving orators, litter-bearers and accountants! The Roman citizen who no longer wanted to work and aspired to live as a landowner, or a client of the wealthy, was soon outstripped. In the houses of the great, the Orientals competed with and supplanted him, by virtue of their flexibility, resourcefulness and spirit of initiative.

In commerce they were unbeatable and ubiquitous: in the Aegean and in the North Sea, in the valleys of the Rhône, Danube and Rhine. These worthy descendants of the Phoenician sailors had a flair and a passion for profit which made them travel the world, braving every kind of danger (St Jerome, *Commentary on Ezekiel*, 27, 16), but which also earned them an odious reputation (St Ambrose, *Duties*, 11, 14, 67). Even in the fifth century, the Christian Salvian of Marseille was denouncing 'these hordes of traders, all Syrian, who have taken over the greater part of all the cities': their life is nothing but deceit and they 'look on any betrayal as a singular source of gain' (*The Government of God*, IV, 69). In Merovingian Gaul, they retained enough financial clout to be able to obtain episcopal thrones. In 591 Eusebius, a merchant of Syrian race, got himself elected bishop of Paris by means of handing out many gifts; upon which 'he sacked all his predecessor's staff and employed Syrians of his own race to serve in the ecclesiastical palace' (Gregory of Tours, *History of the Franks*, X, 26): a prime example of 'spoils-system'! Syrian could be heard spoken in Arles or Orléans, where King Gontran had himself acclaimed 'here in the Syrian language, there in the Latin tongue, and elsewhere also in the language of the Jews ... ' (Ibid., VIII, 1).

These intrepid Levantines also served in the army, mainly as archers, footsoldiers and cavalry, in Africa as well as on the banks of the Rhine and Danube. Commagenians, Emesians, Ituraeans and Palmyrenians formed an elite body. Some of their compatriots followed the cohorts and set up shop near the camps where the Baals of Doliche, Emesa and Baalbek-Heliopolis were worshipped. Their indefatigable ubiquity, their active and multiform proliferation gave the Quirites, imbued with ancestral prerogatives, some cause to lose their sangfroid. Livy (*History of Rome*, XXXIX, 6) had already denounced an initial wave of lubricity and harmful luxuriousness that had arrived from Asia in 187 BC, with the consul Manlius Vulso whose triumph imported female players of the harp and sambuca into the *Urbs*. At the time when Nero enjoyed mixing with the riffraff of courtesans and flute-players of the Circus Maximus, Lucan (*Pharsalia*, VII, 405) was bemoaning the fact that Rome was becoming depopulated of its own citizens but filled with 'the dregs of the universe'. Less than a century later, there were numerous Orientals in the Senate.[1] They were also in the Palatine, in the corridors of power and the imperial domestic scene (if not in close intimacy).[2]

'The Orontes overflowing into the Tiber' suggests a cataclysm. This imagery of rivers abandoning their natural course to flood other valleys obviously brought to mind certain apocalyptic visions of the end of the world, as found in the Sibylline Oracles, or even in Seneca, in the character of Cremutius Cordus (*Consolation to Marcia*, 26, 6: *flumina avertet*). It was again the metaphor of the overflowing wave that came to Seneca's mind concerning the immigrants who had come from all over the world to crowd into Rome (*Consolation to Helvia*, 6, 2: *confluxerunt*), and in Tacitus (*Annals*, XV, 44, 5) regarding this town 'where all the vices flow together'. But above all, the Orontes had symbolic value where Syrian cults were concerned. It had its source in the Bekaa, to the north of and not far from Baalbek-Heliopolis, whose breastplated god would soon reach Italy, Africa and the Danubian provinces. It passed close to Emesa (which would send empresses and a high priest of Elagabal to Rome), then Apamea, the birthplace of a prophet who stirred up Sicily in the name of the Syrian Goddess. The Orontes watered Antioch, whose port, Seleucis of Pieria, was not far from Mount Casius, consecrated to a famous Baal who was celebrated in both Spain and Germany.

Not all Syrians imported their country's gods or, at least, they did not always make a display of their beliefs. The subject of a bilingual epitaph found at Genay, near Trévoux, was a Syrian who kept a shop in Lyon for articles from Aquitaine (*CIL*, XIII, 2448). His name was Thaïm, which means 'servant', but of which god? The inscription says nothing about it and speaks only of his economic activities.[3] These immigrants often sought to integrate themselves and knew how to conciliate the local gods at the same time as indigenous opinion. For example, there is the Syrian lady living in Besançon (*CIL*, XIII, 5373), who paid for the restoration of the ruined temple of a Gaulish Mercury, *Cissonius*, the god of travellers and therefore of trade. It is also to be seen that soldiers and officials endeavoured to win the favours of the deities connected with the places to which they were posted, notably in the sanctuaries of springs. But one gets the impression that sailors and, above all, soldiers showed a more faithful devotion to the pantheon of their native East. Exposed to the perils of the sea or war, they needed mighty and vigilant protectors, saviour gods who were often armed, like themselves, in Roman style, but also like them originating from Lebanon, Palmyra or Commagene.

Alongside these cultic pockets, gods like Adonis, who had long since been incorporated into Graeco-Roman mythology, or Marnas at Ostia, merited festivals which mobilized some participation on the part of the populace as well as their Levantine compatriots, such as the *Navigium Isidis* or the March Mother-cult ceremonies. However, generally speaking, the Syrian or Syro-Phoenician religions were far from having the same impact on public life as the Egyptian gods or the Great Mother. Although the Syrians were to some extent omnipresent in the Roman world, in the fields of pottery, painting and sculpture their gods were not in the same league as Cybele, Attis, Isis and Serapis. Apart from the Baal of Emesa, who was pushed to the forefront of the imperial scene by his high priest Heliogabalus (but only during a reign that was as fleeting as it was scandalous), they did not have their place in the sun of official cults, even if Nero 'flirted' temporarily with the Syrian Goddess or, on the occasion of a journey to the Orient, Hadrian sacrificed to the baetylic Zeus of Mount Casius. For the most part, the Syrian gods remained on the fringe and were the object of strictly local homage in sanctuaries frequented by migrants or resident foreigners.

Syrian cults were further singled out from other Graeco-oriental religions by their relative plurality and disparity. The various Baals and Baalats who were patrons of the towns in the Semitic Orient preserved the local particularities of their attributes, their costume, their animal environment or, sometimes, their 'aniconic' cult. The Levantine *diaspora* was coupled with a diversity of idols and deities who could be distinguished by their ethnic forms of invocation.

From this patchwork a goddess first emerged in the history of Rome, two centuries before the Baals of Heliopolis and Doliche, whom their worshippers would assimilate to Jupiter Capitolinus.

Dea Syria

It was Atargatis of Hierapolis-Bambyce who was commonly known by this generic title. She had a prestigious sanctuary which was the subject of a small work composed in the second century AD, a kind of publicity notice which slipped into the works of Lucian and testifies to a perhaps feigned (?) credulity, but one which is strangely foreign to the style and caustic wit of the pamphleteer from Samosata.[4]

The 'Sacred Town' (*Hierapolis*) was indeed consecrated to a sovereign goddess whom the Greeks identified with Hera, wife of Zeus, master of the heavens, as was Hadad, Atargatis' companion, who was known as *Derketo* at Ascalon. The founding of the temple was said to date back to Deucalion, like Noah a survivor of the Flood, for the goddess of Hierapolis-Bambyce had power over water and fertility. According to Plutarch (*Life of Crassus*, 17, 10), she was seen as 'the cause or the nature which has drawn from moisture the principles and seeds of all beings, she who has made man know the source of all that is good'. Twice a year, water taken from the sea was brought to the temple, and not far from the sanctuary sacred fish were kept in a pool. The story went that Atargatis fell in the pool and was saved by the fish: hence the rule forbidding their consumption. Derketo of Ascalon

was a fish-woman who, according to local legend, was the mother of
Semiramis.[5] To justify the confusion that mixed Astarte, goddess of
love, with the cult of Atargatis, one myth held that an egg laid by the
fish on the banks of the Euphrates and hatched by doves gave birth to
the Syrian Goddess. Astrology was to hallow this story, together with
the respect due to fish, by the zodiacal constellation of Pisces. The
Christian Arnobius jeered at the 'Syrian gods hatched from their eggs'
(*Against the Nations*, I, 36). With the simplism of a Voltairean ahead of
time, Cicero mocked these 'ignorant' (*imperiti*) people who 'venerate a
fish!' (*The Nature of the Gods*, III, 39). But for them the dove had equal
right to divine honours for having fed the child of a fish-woman
(Diodorus Siculus, *Bibliotheca Historica*, II, 4).

Apart from the prestige of a fabulous antiquity, the temple of
Hierapolis-Bambyce had wealth and a large priesthood: over 300
clergy who, robed in white, officiated under the guidance of a high
priest clad in purple and with a gold tiara on his head, amid a throng
of various musicians, galli and 'distraught women, with deranged
minds' (Lucian, *The Syrian Goddess*, 43). As in Egyptian sanctuaries, a
daily service assembled all the personnel of the temple. There were
sacrifices twice daily: in silence for Hadad, the companion of the
goddess; to the sound of flutes and castanets for Atargatis. As in
Cybele's cult, galli ritually consecrated their manhood to the goddess
and offered her their blood with sweeping swordstrokes, slashing
their arms to the rhythmic beat of the native drum. She also received
the sacrifice of children, who were enclosed in sacks before being
hurled down from the propylaea. Lastly, because Atargatis, like many
of the oriental Mothers, was mistress of wild animals, great oxen,
eagles, bears and lions (tamed however) were to be seen in the
sanctuary courtyard. Festivals and pilgrimages attracted many people
and offerings: from Arabia, Phoenicia, Babylonia, Cappadocia and
Cilicia. The temple's treasures made visitors marvel.

If not missionaries properly speaking, the goddess at least had
followers who told the Greeks about her demanding cult and impressive liturgies. In the late fourth century BC, the comic poet
Menander evoked the strange appearance of those Syrians who,
suffering from swollen feet and belly, wallowed in dung because they
had broken the taboo of the sacred fish (Porphyry, *Abstinence*, IV, 15 =
Menander, *Fragments*, 754, 73). Hellenization started at Delos where
Hieropolitans landed and set up a sanctuary to serve their national
gods. A hundred or so texts inscribed on stone there relate to Syrian
gods whose cult was flourishing in the second century BC. The Delian
sanctuary of the Syrian Goddess neighboured on that of the Serapians
(*Sarapieion C*) who came to an agreement with the Hieropolitans for

the enlargement of their temple.[6] It comprised a gallery in the form of a theatre from which, so it seems, the faithful could watch the processions of divine images which took place on a broad terrace. It also contained banqueting rooms suitable for the kind of ritual gatherings that were held in Syria. The first people in charge of the sanctuary came from Hierapolis. But from the end of the second century BC, the priests were Athenians who honoured the goddess under the name of *Hagnè Aphroditè*, the 'chaste', the 'holy' Aphrodite.[7]

Around 118–17 BC, a statue of this 'holy Aphrodite' was consecrated for the wellbeing of the Athenian and the Roman people. At that time Roman citizens themselves formed an important group in the Syrian sanctuary of Delos, in fact a majority, at least if we are to judge from epigraphic data. They were Romans by enfranchisement, or Italians trading with the Orient.[8] For their part, the Syrians of Delos did business with Campania, and among the worshippers of Atargatis we find, for example, a banker from Ascalon who ended by becoming a citizen of Naples.[9] Among the numbers of the faithful there were also many slaves, the victims of the wars that set Rome against the rulers of Hellenistic Asia. Nearly all those who, on the great estates of Sicily, would swell the troops roused to fanaticism by Eunus, must have passed through the island that was a centre for the slave trade.

Certainly, the cult of Atargatis did not enjoy the same range of influence as that of Isis. But as early as 333 BC, an Attic decree authorized the foundation of a sanctuary of Aphrodite *Urania* (the 'Celestial'), imported by sailors from Citium in Cyprus (*SIG*, 280). She was to be found revered in the third century as much at Beroea in Macedonia or Phystion in Aetolia as in a Greek colony in Faiyum where her devotees associated her with Aphrodite 'Berenice' (the wife of the king Ptolemy Euergetes).[10] She is attested at various points of the Aegean (at Cos, Thera, Scyros, Astypalaea, Nisyros, Syme) and in western Asia Minor, notably Smyrna, where a sacred law protected her fish and threatened any contraveners with being devoured by them![11] In the second century BC, the Syrian Aphrodite – the 'Celestial' – cohabited in the Piraeus with the Mother of the gods in a sanctuary which her orgeones built for her in the port.[12] In the imperial era, she had a priestess for herself alone. Pausanias mentions temples at Thurii in Messenia and, on the Achaian coast, at Aegira where access to the *naos* was forbidden to the public (*Description of Greece*, VII, 26, 7).

In Sicily, there was an association at Syracuse (but in the Roman era) which rendered homage to the Syrian Goddess.[13] The Phoenician Astarte had long occupied part of the religious terrain in the west of the island. A carved dedication at Segesta for 'Celestial' Aphrodite must refer to the Punic goddess rather than Atargatis properly speaking. The Venus of Mount Eryx – whom the Romans would be able to append to their legend of the Aeneadae and their Trojan origins – concealed the same devotion to the oriental Astarte. The consuls and generals passing through Eryx did not fail to render homage to this Punic Aphrodite:

> Stripping off the insignia of their authority, they joyfully took part in the games and gatherings of the women, convinced that it was the only way to make themselves agreeable to the goddess ... (Diodorus Siculus, VI, 83)

In other words, Roman government quite officially showed indulgence towards the sacred prostitution of Semitic tradition, in the very name of national tradition ... In 215 BC, Venus Erycina had her temple on the Capitol.

But unlike Isis or Cybele, the Syrian goddess did not often benefit from a settled cult, above all in the West. After the defeats of Antiochus III, king of Syria, at Thermopylae (191 BC) and Mount Sipylus near Magnesia (189 BC), when the first waves of captives reduced to slavery reached Italy and Sicily, these uprooted masses retained no links with their ancestral religion except through the occasional passage of mendicant priests, like those referred to by Lukios of Patras in the *Ass* of the Pseudo-Lucian and Apuleius in the *Metamorphoses*. They went from town to town, prophesying in the name of the goddess, rather like those Chaldaean fortune-tellers, also from Syria or Babylonia, who made their appearance in Italy in the second century BC. Cato the Elder (*Agriculture*, V, 4) puts the Romans on their guard against these charlatans who were always likely to put ideas in the heads of rural workers, whose hard life understandably needed to be relieved by dreams now and then.

Events proved him right.

On the great Sicilian estates, barely fed and clothed, worked herds of slaves of oriental stock to whom the Syrian Goddess gave a hope of life as well as the energy to rebel. Round about Henna, where the rising started (in 135 BC), Eunus, a slave from Apamaea, 'was regarded as a magician and miracle worker. He pretended to receive divine commands in his dreams, and to predict the future' (Diodorus Siculus, XXXIV, 2). He delivered oracles, spitting out fire. To achieve this, Eunus filled with sulphur a nutshell with a hole at each end, which he hid in his mouth: all he needed to do then was to blow gently in order to emit showers of sparks when he spoke, thus imparting a supernatural prestige to his utterances. He prophesied, calling on Atargatis, his hair as wild as that of a Sibyl in a trance. The goddess announced to him that he would be king, and in a sense the prediction was fulfilled. For, exasperated by the cruelty of a pitiless couple, Damophilos and Megallis, their slaves received divine backing from Eunus. Immediately, 400 slaves assembled, hastily armed themselves and fell upon Henna, led by Eunus emitting flames from his glowing mouth. Damophilos was beheaded with an axe, Megallis hurled from the top of a tower and the master of Eunus executed. The Syrian slave then donned the diadem, had himself proclaimed king under the name Antiochus and his companion in slavery proclaimed queen. In three days he recruited over 6,000 men, armed with scythes, billhooks, slings, roasting-spits and sticks hardened in fire. Elsewhere a Cilician raised 5,000 slaves. Other rebels joined them, and soon there were 20,000, then 200,000, desperadoes. Rumour of their success had contagious effects as far as Attica and Delos, where the compatriots of Atargatis were sold. Even in Rome a slave conspiracy broke out.[14]

The blaze in Sicily was quickly extinguished, like a straw fire, and Eunus perished, gnawed by vermin. But this affair showed the revolutionary strength of the eastern religious ferment. Thirty years later, the flute-player Tryphon and the astrologer Athenion would once more galvanize slaves on the island by their prophecies of liberation.[15]

Meanwhile, oriental prophetism also made its way into the confidence of the Roman government, at that time embodied by Marius.

> There was, in fact, a Syrian woman named Martha who, it seems, pronounced oracles and whom Marius took with him everywhere, having her borne in pomp in a litter, and he offered sacrifices only upon her instructions. Previously she had been driven from the Senate when she aspired to speak to the senators about these events [the invasion of the Cimbri who were threatening Italy] and predict the outcome of the war. But she had gained access to the ladies of Rome and had provided them with proof of her talents.

When Martha left her litter to be present at the sacrifices, fastening her purple double cloak about her, she carried a lance regarded as sacred because of the garlands and strips of cloth tied to its shaft (Plutarch, *Life of Marius*, 17, 2–5). Which deity was she invoking? Marius affected a singular devotion for Cybele:[16] bearing in mind the cultic connections of Hierapolis with the Mother-worship religion, it is not unbelievable that Martha might have hived off some of the consul's piety (or credulity) to the advantage of Atargatis.

All the same, the goddess of Hierapolis remained on the fringes for a long time before attaining a certain prosperity in Rome. She did so only belatedly and in a restricted fashion, with a temple attested by the writer known as 'the Chronicler of 354', but its exact location remains unknown.[17] In the meantime, Atargatis journeyed with her itinerant and ill-famed galli. Apuleius draws us an edifying portrait of

> those creatures from the dregs who go through the streets, from village to village, carrying the Syrian Goddess and forcing her to hold out her hand for alms.

Having reached a village,

> they wear garments of many colours, painting their faces with a hideous clay make-up, outlining their eyes with greasepaint. They wear little turbans, robes of saffron yellow, fine linen or silk. Some wear red-striped white tunics that undulate in all directions and are belted tightly at the waist. On their feet they wear yellow boots. (*Metamorphoses*, VIII, 24 and 27)

The hero of this adventure, who has been changed into a donkey, thus transports 'the goddess dressed in a silk robe'. Then begins the bloody performance of prophesying by which she and her holy eunuchs make their living:

> They hoist their sleeves up to their shoulders, brandishing enormous two-edged swords and axes, leap about shouting to the notes of the flute which excite them to dance like men possessed. After going from door to door in a few dilapidated dwellings, they reach the villa of a rich landowner. At the entrance they make a fearful row with their cacophonous yells, hurling themselves about like madmen. They bend their heads and lewdly twist their necks so that their long hair flies out in circles. Now and then they bite their own flesh before finally cutting their arms with a double-edged blade. But one of them surrenders to an even more frenetic delirium and repeatedly heaves profound sighs from the depths of his being: as if filled with the numinous breath of the divinity, he simulates a dementia that exhausts him, as if in truth the presence of the gods did not improve the condition of men, instead of making them weak or sickly!

Apparently the African orator had no greater appreciation of this exhibitionism by the mentally deranged than did the Spanish Seneca.[18] Like Juvenal, they similarly failed to comprehend what one might be tempted to call a penitential masochism:

And see what fine recompense he receives by the providence of heaven! Noisily prophesying, he forges a great lie. He rails against and accuses himself as if he has committed some sacrilege against his holy religion. He goes to the extent of inflicting his just punishment on himself with his own hands. Finally, seizing the attribute that suits these emasculated creatures, a whip whose long-fringed thongs of woven wool are strung with many sheep's knucklebones, he scourges himself with these many knots, amazingly armoured against the pain of his wounds by his proud endurance. You could see the soil soaking up the foul blood of these effeminates, under the slashes of the swords and the blows of the whips ... When at last, at the end of their strength and in any case surfeited with sufferings, this butchery came to an end, the people vied with one another to offer bronze, even silver, coins which they gathered in the ample folds of their robes, to say nothing of a pitcher of wine, milk, cheeses, and a certain amount of flour and wheat. Some even gave barley to the ass carrying the goddess ... They greedily raked everything in, thrusting it into sacks brought for the purpose which they then loaded on my back [It is still the ass speaking]: I thus became both temple and itinerant larder. (ibid., 28)

This final picture is typical of the nomadic cult and its wandering clergy, who lived on alms collected from day to day. Apuleius, or rather Lukios of Patras,[19] was inventing nothing. An inscription from Kefr-Hauar in Syria introduces us to a slave of Atargatis who declared himself proud to have brought back seventy sacks from each of his missionary tours (*BCH*, 21, 1897, p. 60). Apuleius shows us these galli, who identified their goddess just as much with Cybele and Bellona as with Venus-Astarte in order to win over various clienteles of devotees, gladly risking journeys into the mountains to woo credulous peasants. In this manner, by means of a favourable prediction, they demanded 'a good fat ram whose sacrifice will appease the Syrian Goddess' (*Metamorphoses*, VIII, 29, 12). On occasion, she found shelter in a temple of Cybele. But her starveling priests took advantage of it to help themselves to some precious object from the religious furnishings, for instance a gold cantharus 'purloined from the very cushions of the Mother of the gods', which the galli subsequently claimed was offered by Cybele to 'her sister the Syrian Goddess as a gift of hospitality' (ibid, IX, 10).

The Mother-worship cult, officially recognized, enjoyed the benefit of an established sanctuary and financial support for the celebration of the annual festivals, from which the religion of the sovereign derived some reward. This explains why, even in towns where the Orientals were relatively numerous, the Syrian Goddess lived in the shadow of her great Anatolian sister. We have seen that in the second century BC the Great Mother had made room in her temple in Piraeus for the oriental Aphrodite. It is also understandable that the two Mothers, of Syria and Phrygia, were sometimes the object of the same homage. The same priest could minister in different cults. An epitaph is known at Brindisi, of a *sacerdos Matris Magnae et Suriae Deae et sacrorum Isidis* (*CIL*, IX, 6099), which implies a fairly remarkable 'ecumenism'. In the Rhône valley, the immigrant population of Vienne contained many Levantines. Not long ago I interpreted the bas-relief figure of a woman with a mirror as an indication of the association of the Syrian Goddess with the Mother-worship cult.[20] Cybele's temple in Vienne may have housed the idol of an Atargatis-Astarte. To tell the truth, there was little to choose between her galli and those of the Great Mother, and the 'Day of Blood' was no more repulsive than their sabre dance.

This syncretism may have acted in favour of Astarte-Atargatis, despite all the disgust that her pilfering and begging eunuchs inspired in the Greeks. In a metrical inscription found in England at Carvoran (*Magnis*), on Hadrian's Wall, a tribune who had been promoted to prefect by imperial favour honoured a goddess whom he identified with Ceres, the Mother of the gods, Peace, *Virtus* and the Syrian Goddess, who is described with the attributes of Justice, but whose zodiacal constellation – Virgo – calls to mind the apotheosis of Julia Domna (*CIL*, VII, 759).[21] It was fairly uncommon for an officer in the Roman army to express himself in verse with such fervent enthusiasm as Lucius glorifying the Many-named Isis in Apuleius' *Metamorphoses*. Doubtless of oriental origin, and in any case very attached to the family of the Severi, this tribune whose rank of prefect was owed to the favour of the emperor (perhaps Heliogabalus?) acknowledged *Dea Syria*'s total sovereignty over both the earth and the skies. Still at Carvoran,[22] a prefect of a cohort in command of Syrians known as the *Hamii* (i.e., from Hamah-*Epiphania* on the Orontes) made a dedication to the Syrian Goddess, whom another inscription celebrates as *Dea Hammia* (or *Hammiorum*).[23] It was again a soldier who offered an altar to the Syrian Goddess in the north of Yorkshire, at *Cataractonium* (Catterick).[24]

At the other northern extremity of the Roman world, at Romula in Dacia,[25] the plinth of a clay figure was found which bears, in Syrian, the remembrance of an offering to Atargatis for the health of an immigrant: Ragysbl. The goddess had followers elsewhere in Dacia (at *Micia*), in Macedonia (at Philippopolis), in Pannonia (at *Aquincum*, near Budapest), on the shores of the Adriatic (at Salonae) and naturally at Pozzuoli, where so many other oriental divinities disembarked.[26] She even had some in central Italy, at San Vittorino (*Amiternum*), near L'Aquila in the Abruzzi.[27] We have seen that she was not unknown in Gaul, even if her presence there remained very modest and marginal. As in Britain, it was a soldier, the former prefect of a cohort stationed in Syria, who rendered homage to *Leucothea*, whose priest he was, and who, as 'white goddess', was identified with Astarte:[28] her dazzling beauty matched that of the star to which the prefect of Carvoran alludes.

At Pozzuoli the cult of the goddess had certain strikingly singular features. A waterpipe with a lion's face (appropriate for a Lady flanked by wild beasts) was dedicated to her, and this was to be used as a fountain:[29] an offering which was well suited to the aquatic functions of Atargatis at Hierapolis-Bambyce. Similarly at Pozzuoli, *Venus Caelestis* had a temple, and taurobolia were carried out in her honour. The one held on 5 October 134 (*CIL*, X. 1596) is the oldest known in the Roman world, but in homage to a deity who was not usually the recipient of this sacrifice, which was peculiar to the Mother-cult. A dedication recounts the gifts consecrated to the goddess: a gemstone mounted in a gold setting, moons adorned with stones, a sun and palm in gold, a gold figure of Venus, sceptres and cloak of silver, silver dishes and lion heads ... [30]

In Rome itself, the worshippers of the Syrian Goddess must have gathered in the Trastevere district where many Levantines lived, more precisely near the Porta Portese in an area also frequented by Palmyrenians. Two statues, one dedicated to the goddess, the other to Jupiter Heliopolitanus, for the safeguarding of an emperor who may have been Nero, come from this quarter (the former Mattei Gardens).[31] It is known that Nero, who 'despised all forms of religion, for a while had eyes only for *Dea Syria*, but afterwards showed her such disdain that he soiled her with his urine' (Suetonius, *Nero*, 56), when he became caught up in another cultic fad. From the same Mattei Gardens comes a votive altar, bearing the sculpted image of the goddess seated between two lions (plate 17): wearing a tall conical headdress topped with the crescent moon, from which hangs a long veil, in one hand she holds the mirror of Venus-Astarte, and in the other a distaff.[32]

She also features, perhaps, as Tyche-Fortuna, with the horn of plenty and the tiller, between two lions, on a pillar consecrated to Jupiter Heliopolitanus.[33] In the triad of Baalbek on the Palatine, we find a veiled Venus whom people tended to confuse, in fact, with the

Plate 17 *Dea Syria* (Rome, Museo Capitolino)

Syrian Goddess, as is borne out by the mirror on the Mattei altar, now kept in the Museo Capitolino. As for the lions, they would suggest a comparison with Cybele. Macrobius, writing in the early fifth century AD (but drawing on Porphyry, who lived in the second half of the third century and went through a vast quantity of literature), interprets the two rayed statues of Hadad and Atargatis by attributing to them respectively responsibility for heaven and earth, as is shown by the wild beasts accompanying the goddess 'by the same reasoning that led the Phrygians to represent the Mother of the gods – in other words, the earth – carried along by lions' (*Saturnalia*, I, 23, 20).

In the *Urbs* Atargatis had a temple attested by the *Chronicler of 354*, but which does not necessarily match the famous 'Syrian sanctuary of the Janiculum', which we shall deal with later. This section of the Trastevere was in any case rich in springs and for that reason under the patronage of the Nymphs known as *Furrinae*, who had a sacred wood there.[34] As the goddess of Hierapolis was a divinity of fruitful and fructifying waters, one can understand why the Syrians were able to honour her more specially in a district well watered by fountains. A dedication (*CIL*, VI, 422) precisely associates with the *Genius Forinarum* (for *Furrinarum*) Jupiter Heliopolitanus, whose companion goddess was related to the Syrian Goddess.

Ovid, narrating the myth of Dione in the *Fasti* (II, 461–73), shows her to us fleeing in company with Eros on the banks of the Euphrates and invoking the Nymphs before plunging into the river. Two fish, who would become the famous constellation Pisces, took her on their backs: 'So the superstitious Syrians hold it a sacrilege to serve it at table and refuse to soil their mouth by eating fish'. We may recall that this was the story of Atargatis. Philo of Byblos (Eusebius, *Praeparatio Evangelica*, I, 10, 35) identified Dione with Baltis, the 'Lady' of Byblos. This Baltis (Baalat, the female equivalent of Baal) was to be found invoked in Pannonia and associated with the Syrian Goddess or assimilated to the Carthaginian *Caelestis*.[35] She corresponded to Astarte.

It was this Syrian Venus who was said to have wept over the death of Adonis.

Adonis and Salambô

Everyone knows the story of the handsome adolescent born of the union of a father with his daughter, Myrrha, who was changed into the tree of the same name whence the child emerged miraculously. Mortally wounded by a boar provoked (so it was said) by the jealousy

of Ares, Adonis survived by virtue of the all-powerful love of Aphrodite (Salambô, in the Orient). But he passed only six months of the
year in her arms, the queen of the Underworld keeping him for the
remainder. He was formerly the Dumuzi of the Sumerians, the
Tammuz of Ezekiel (VIII, 14), the lover of Ishtar who wept for him
annually according to the *Epic of Gilgamesh*. Passing by way of Cyprus,
where the legend of Myrrha, daughter of Cinyras, is placed, he would
reach the Hellenic world under the name *Adoni*, 'my lord'.

He made an early appearance in art and literature, as in the
religious and festive life of the ancient Greeks.[36]

He is dying, O Cytherean, the tender Adonis! What shall we do?
Beat your breasts, young maidens, and tear your tunics!

This threnodic fragment (Fr. 152) is attributed to Sappho, who is said
to have invented 'Adonic' verse, a dactylic dimeter consonant with the
ritual cries of the women when they sang in chorus the mourning of
Aphrodite. The poetess is supposed to have hurled herself from the
height of the Leucadian rock for love of Phaon, like Aphrodite for the
love of Adonis.

In the classical era, Athenian women fêted the young god on the
rooftops. In 415 BC, in his *Lysistrata* (392f), Aristophanes evokes the
figure of a popular orator's wife, intoxicated and dancing, to the cry
'Aiai Adonis', on the roof of her house. Plato's *Phaedrus* (276 b) refers
us to the success of the fleeting 'gardens of Adonis' which bloomed
suddenly in July to wither almost as quickly. The *Adonia* were
sufficiently popular to have impressed the contemporaries of Alcibiades as a bad omen when they were making ready for the expedition to Sicily, at the very moment 'when women displayed the earthen
images of the dead they carried ... beating their breasts and singing
funeral hymns' (Plutarch, *Life of Alcibiades*, 18, 5; cf. *Life of Nicias*, 13,
11).

Paintings show the chipped vases containing these rapidly germi-
nating plants (fennel, barley, corn, lettuce).[37] But for the *Adonia* of
Alexandria described by Theocritus in the *Syracusan Women*, the
queen Arsinoe used silver baskets placed, with other offerings (jars of
perfumes, bowls of fruit and various cakes), at the foot of a silver bed,
before a tapestry picturing the dead god in all his dazzling beauty. A
renowned woman singer performed a ritual lamentation. The ceremony ended with a celebration of Aphrodite, to whom 'the dainty-
footed Hours bring back Adonis, with the twelfth month, from the
everlasting Acheron' (Theocritus, *Idylls*, XV, 103). After these funeral
ceremonies – comparable but not identical to those of Attis or Osiris –

there was the prospect of the cyclic return of this huntsman god, killed by a boar's tusk. Throwing the figurines of Adonis into the sea, the women of Alexandria besought his benevolence for the coming year. 'And when thou returnest,' they said, 'we will greet thee as a friend' (ibid., 144).

These obsequies were not followed, like those of Attis or Osiris, by explosions of joyfulness hallowing his resurrection, but had the aim of propitiating the god for the prosperity of later harvests:

Thou who hast succumbed to the love of Persephone . . . come, blessed one, come and bring thy mystae the fruits of the earth! (*Orphic Hymns*, 56, 9–12)

In fact, and contrary to what the rite of the gardens may make us think, Adonis symbolizes 'The gathering of fruits which have reached maturity' (Porphyry, *The Statues*, 7).[38] It is true that his death coincided with the period in which the ripe corn was cut. But for Origen (*Selecta in Ezech.*, VIII, 12), Adonis represents 'the fruits of the earth for which we weep when they are planted, but which rise and by their growth bring joy to the farmers'. Cyrillus of Alexandria (*Commentary on Isaiah*, 18, 1–2) writes that Aphrodite was represented re-ascending from Hell with Adonis, and that a choir rejoiced with her, dancing: 'This scene was played in the temple of Alexandria up to our own day'. However, literary tradition generally mentions only the lamentations and mourning. So, when the emperor Julian made his entry into Antioch in July 362, to the funereal sounds of the *Adonia*, he took it as an ill omen for his campaign against the Persians (Ammianus Marcellinus, XXII, 9, 15).

The myth of Adonis filled the imagination of Etruscan artists as early as the second half of the fourth century BC, to judge by the mirrors of that period and later. A terracotta sarcophagus from Tuscania represents the dead god, wounded in the left thigh and watched over by his dog.[39] Plautus (*Menaechmi*, 143–5) bears witness to the frequency in Rome itself of murals showing Adonis being carried away by Venus. In the imperial period the death of the young god was commemorated there as in other towns in the West. *Adonia* were held on the Palatine,[40] near the spot where the sanctuary of Elagabal would be erected, that Baal from Emesa whose high priest-become-emperor mimed (so it seems) the desolation of Salambô 'with all the lamentations and gesticulations of the Syrian cult' (*Augustan History, Life of Heliogabalus*, 7, 3). According to the lexicographer Hesychius, Salambô was a Babylonian name also to be found in the form Salambas, 'a female demon who is in a state of perpetual agitation, when she wanders

around weeping for Adonis' (which corresponds to the ritual gesticulations of Heliogabalus). Her name may have meant 'image of
Baal'.

We know about the ceremonial of the *Adonia* celebrated at Seville *c*.
287 thanks to the account of two martyrs preserved in a breviary from
Evora (published at Lisbon in 1548),[41] namely Saints Justus and Rufina
who were persecuted and tortured under Diocletian. The festival
began with women parading an idol of Salambô through the streets of
Seville and making a collection. They stopped at certain places and
danced around the goddess before asking for alms, like the galli of
Cybele and Atargatis. They begged from the residents an offering of
pots for the famous 'gardens'. The faithful then took part in a great
barefoot procession through the countryside, after which dolls of the
dead Adonis were thrown into a sacred well. For having refused the
gift of a vase for the god and broken his idol, the two Christian
women were arrested and forced to walk with the devotees before
being imprisoned and condemned. The Roman governor had the
body of Justus thrown in a well. In the monastery of the Holy Trinity
near Seville, a cave and hole where the saint is said to have perished
are on view. The festival of the two martyrs falls on either 17 or 19
July; that is, the precise period when the *Adonia* were celebrated.

The theosophical sects of the gnosis, which incorporated some of
the Graeco-oriental paganism by reinterpreting its tragic myths of
loving and suffering divinities, were as interested in Adonis as in Attis
or Endymion. For the Naassenians, 'when one speaks of Adonis, it is
really the soul for which, under this name, Aphrodite burns with
love'. Adonis with Persephone is 'the soul exposed to death, because
it is parted from Aphrodite, in other words deprived of generation'
(Hippolytus, *Philosophoumena*, V, 7). Thus in the Severan period when
this priest of Rome was writing, one could attend the *Adonia* while
thinking of the drama of beings 'yearning for a soul'.

The story of Adonis also inspired the marble-carvers who worked
for the dead. A series of sarcophagi which extend chronologically
from the first half of the second century to the beginning of the fourth
reveal the love and death of Adonis, the grief of Venus who clasps the
wounded youth in her arms, and whose love which is stronger than
death, gives hope for a happy afterlife.[42] This funereal imagery
certainly conveys something of the performances given in the theatre
on this theme, with all the success achieved there, as we know, by
pantomimes on erotic and moving subjects (blood, voluptuousness,
death . . .).[43] The myth applied to young people whose life was cut off
in its flower, and we know the importance of the iconographic
heroization accorded to the *ahoroi* or prematurely dead. At all events,

where the gods were portrayed in the likeness of the deceased it was the expression of an analogy or, at least, of an idea commonly illustrated in Antiquity (and not only proverbially stated by the poet): *omnia vincit amor.*

Heliacal syncretism did not spare Adonis. Macrobius, who seems to have made use once again of a treatise on the sun by Porphyry, gives an explanation in his *Saturnalia* (I, 21, 1–6). It must be said that the version according to which Adonis spent half the year with Venus and the other with Proserpine was adapted to the daystar's revolutions passing alternately from one hemisphere to the other:

Therefore among the Assyrians or Phoenicians, the goddess [Venus] is represented in mourning when, in its annual course following the twelve signs of the zodiac, the Sun enters the lower hemisphere . . . The days shorten and Venus is believed to be in mourning, as if the Sun were lost, carried off by a temporary death and held by Proserpine, goddess of the lower hemisphere and the antipodes.

Conversely, Adonis is restored to Venus when, at the spring equinox, the sun returns to the northern hemisphere, and the days lengthen. The death of Adonis is blamed on a boar because this animal, which likes damp, cold places, is the symbol of winter. Macrobius describes an idol of Venus on Mount Lebanon, 'veiled, with a sad look, resting her shrouded face on her left hand, and appearing to shed tears'. She was supposed to represent 'the earth during winter when, veiled with clouds and widowed by the Sun, it is in a state of torpor'. Then the springs flow abundantly (like Venus' tears). But when the sun emerges once more and crosses the limits of the vernal equinox, the goddess is beautiful and happy, the fields are covered with crops, the meadows with grass and the trees with leaves:

'That is why our ancestors consecrated the month of April to Venus!' Macrobius here rejoins the properly Roman tradition. But his argument does not tally very well with the calendar of the *Adonia.*

Was Adonis the subject of an initiatory cult? That has been conjectured in connection with the villa of P. Fannius Sinistor at Boscoreale, where the 'room of Aphrodite' with its painting of the divine couple may have been used as *telesterion;* the mystae would have attended the representation of the myth.[44] According to P. Lehmann, the lighting of the frescoes would suggest a source of light corresponding to the star that in the Orient signalled the celebration of the *Adonia.* We know, in fact, that at Aphaca (on the road from Byblos to Heliopolis) it was recounted that on a certain day, after an invocation, there leaped like a star from Lebanon's summit a flame that descended to plunge into the river 'Adonis'; this shooting star was given the name Aphrodite Urania (Sozomenus, *Ecclesiastical History*, II, 5). But no text, either explicitly or implicitly, indicates the existence of a true mystery ritual. Firmicus Maternus (*The Error of Profane Religions*, XXII, 1), recalling the funeral of an idol that could be taken to pieces and reassembled, was speaking of Osiris,[45] not Adonis. As for the bronze statuette taken from a triangular coffer in the 'Syrian sanctuary' of the Janiculum, far from illustrating Firmicus' theme and being identified with Adonis, it shows us a sheathed deity of Egyptian appearance, entwined in the coils of a snake, which has nothing at all to do with the suffering lover of Venus-Salambô.[46]

Constantine had the temple at Aphaca, said to be the haunt of prostitutes, closed down. In the late fourth century St Jerome (*Letters*, 58, 3) was able to write:

> Bethlehem which is now ours, the most august place in the universe ... was shaded by the sacred wood of Tammuz, that is, Adonis. And in the grotto where the newborn Christ once cried, there were tears for the lover of Venus.

However, until the Middle Ages Harrân in July would resound to lamentations over the death of Tammuz.[47]

Jupiter Heliopolitanus and the triad of Baalbek

We rediscover Atargatis-Astarte in a triad, as wife of a god whose origins are obscure and whose composite iconography already intrigued the Ancients: the Baal of Baalbek, identified with Jupiter, and even Jupiter Capitolinus 'Best and Greatest' (Optimus Maximus).[48] He was said to originate from the land of the pharaohs because of his hieratic type and the vessel he wore on his head, like Serapis.

> The Phoenicians have yet another cult which is not Assyrian but Egyptian. He was imported from Heliopolis [in Egypt] to Phoenicia. (Lucian, *The Syrian Goddess*, 5)

For his part, Macrobius (*Saturnalia*, I, 23, 10) imputes the same Nilotic heredity to the cult statue:

> The Assyrians [frequent term for the Syrians] in the city named Heliopolis sumptuously honour the Sun, under the name Jupiter,

whom they call 'Heliopolitan Zeus'. His idol was taken from a town in Egypt also called Heliopolis, in the reign of Senemura who is perhaps identified with Senepos.

The last name is significant, for it recalls the story of a Serapis who supposedly came from Sinope, because of the expression *Sen-Api* ('abode of Apis') applied to a god who, just like the Baal of Heliopolis, was a calathophor, at least in the imperial Roman period.

For though the author of *The Syrian Goddess* regards her cult as prestigious and 'ancient', in reality it emerged only belatedly, just conceivably in the era of the Seleucid kings, in any case round about the first century AD. In fact, it was the establishment firstly of a Macedonian colony and secondly (and crucially) of a colony of Roman citizens founded by Augustus for the veterans of the Vth Macedonian and VIIIth Augustan legions which seems to have brought about the success of this god and his triad. All in all, it was as paradoxical a phenomenon as the Mithraism spread by Roman soldiers.

Initially, it appears that Baal Hadad and his wife Atargatis were honoured, as at Damascus.[49] But once it had become the *Colonia Iulia Augusta Felix Heliopolis*, the town of Baalbek, like every colony, felt it should have a Capitol on the Roman model. By adding to Jupiter, and the kind of Juno-Venus whom Atargatis-Astarte represented for the Syrians, a local deity likened to Mercury, a group was obtained that took the place of the Capitoline triad. It was the partial Romanization of this cult that promoted it and explains its relative expansion, together with the favour bestowed on it by the imperial government.

Despite the strictly geographical epithet 'Heliopolitan' which gave this god a connection with a certain place, like the Latin Jupiter he had a sort of supranational sovereignty, on a par with the Roman Empire. The cosmic attributes written into the symbols with which his idol was laden corresponded with the astrological or astrolatrous pre-occupations of contemporaries as opportunely as with the universalism of the *Orbis Romanus* and the mobility of its armies.

Several types of this god are known which assimilate him directly to Zeus carrying a sceptre, or make him a kind of anthropomorphized baetyl. He is sometimes featured also by a symbol, notably the hand holding a thunderbolt, or by a foot. But the type that reached the Roman West is a more complex idol.

Jupiter Heliopolitanus is almost always represented standing, full face, on a plinth which sometimes has the appearance of a temple, between two bulls which seem to be walking alongside the motionless god. Most often, too, he is crowned with a vessel or basket which opens out fairly widely at the top and is decorated with corn-ears, foliage, pearls or an eagle. But occasionally his wavy hair is crowned by a small Egyptian-style pshent. Clad in an ankle-length tunic whose pleats may be seen above his feet, which are together, the god's body is tightly encased in a compartmentalized robe which, on the upper part of the torso, has the appearance of a cuirass with shoulder armour and epaulettes, like those of Roman officers. Generally, with his raised right hand he brandishes a whip; in his lowered left hand he holds ears of corn. He often wears a neckband with, in exceptional cases (such as the Marseille stele: plate 18), its curve formed by two dolphins holding a disc flanked by two Egyptian snakes (*uraei*).

The fixed full frontal aspect of this type, which summons up a rough and fascinating manifestation of the god, and the base itself of the Jovian image give good authority for seeing it as the fairly faithful reproduction of a cultic idol. The walking bulls flanking it may lead to the assumption that it originates from a representation of the god in a chariot, cracking his whip, like some near-eastern storm deities. Similarly, a likeness seems apparent to those goddesses surrounded by animals, including the Artemis of Ephesus, whose swathed rigidity is strangely akin to that of Jupiter Heliopolitanus. A revealing piece of evidence like the bronze Sursok (in the Louvre Museum), by virtue of the perforations in the base, proves that the idol was carried on a litter,[50] following a fairly common practice in the Orient, attested by figured monuments and confirmed by Macrobius in the precise instance of the Heliopolitan Baal (*Saturnalia*, I, 23, 13).

In this iconography various influences can be detected which combine differently depending on the variants. The Hadad of Damascus already appears as a swathed god on the coins of the Syrian king Antiochus XII, around 87–86 BC. But this portrayal most likely originated in Asia Minor. Onto this basic Anatolian type – analogous with those of the goddesses worshipped at Ephesus and Aprhrodisias or of Zeus Labraundos[51] – were grafted Syrian and Hellenistic-Roman motifs which render the idol a fine illustration of the cultural confluences and coalitions that were advantaged by historical circumstances.

The first testimonies barely allow us to go back beyond the first century AD; that is, to a period and in a context which rule out the existence of a strictly local prototype. The vessel worn on the head and adorned with ears of corn has a dual ancestry, of the Assyrian tiara and the Alexandrian calathus. But these emblems of fertility refer us less to earth than to the skies, as is shown by the eagle – Jupiter's bird – with which the calathus is sometimes decorated. He is the god of storms and rain who makes the crops grow. His whip symbolizes

Plate 18 Jupiter Heliopolitanus (Avignon, Musée Calvet; photo. kindly provided by the Curator)

lightning, and on occasion he carries a thunderbolt. The whip could also bring to mind the instrument of a charioteer. Now, some gems show us Heliopolitanus with rays,[52] and the Greek name of the town proves that this solar explanation does not date from Macrobius. The author of the *Saturnalia* (I, 23, 12) precisely describes the god as a charioteer, his left hand holding the thunderbolt and ears of corn 'all attributes which show the associated power of Jupiter and the Sun'.

But the original feature that singles out the god of Baalbek is that his idol combines the cuirass with a celestial garment. The compartments of his garment are occupied by busts or symbols of the planetary gods, sometimes beneath a winged globe or, as on the Marseille stele (plate 18), under the disc flanked by Nilotic *uraei*. The arrangement of the sidereal figures varies from one instance to another, but normally the Sun and the Moon open the series from the top. In the astral pattern, a lion mask may represent Saturn or, at any rate, the celestial fire. In the longitudinal line of the garment, a pillar *en hermes* of Mercury may indicate the importance of the son-god in the Heliopolitan triad. Zodiacal divinities can also be discerned on a statuette from Venice.[53] On the other hand, the five divine busts (Poseidon, Demeter, Athena, Artemis and Herakles) who occupy the reverse of the bronze of Tartous,[54] together with the seven planetary busts on the obverse, form a group of twelve which does not match that of the official Graeco-Roman pantheon.

This star-studded idol brings to mind a vision of Plotinus:

One perceives the sky as a great and beautiful statue animated or produced by the art of Hephaestus, with stars twinkling on its face, others on its breasts and placed wherever appropriate. (*Enneads*, III, 2, 14).

The founder of Neoplatonism is apparently remembering something seen somewhere in a temple in the Orient or Rome. I believe he is speaking of an idol of Zeus Heliopolitanus.[55] Porphyry had doubtless spoken of it with the Master before writing his treatise on *The Statues*, in which he strove to render an account of the more disconcerting oddities of pagan iconography. In this instance, the astral mantle clearly signified the cosmic omnipotence of this Hellenized and Romanized Baal. The two luminaries almost always figured at the top of the starry breastplate, not only because they opened the planetary week, but because they symbolized eternity: now, eternity (*Aiôn*) was for certain theosophers identified with the star-spangled sky or the soul of the sky.[56]

Jupiter Heliopolitanus probably proceeded in part from a Syrian
god of vegetation or from the fertilization of the earth by the sky. But
astral mysticism and Graeco-oriental speculation caused him to assume all the prerogatives of absolute sovereignty. So he was clad in
the imperial cuirass, which had the further advantage of recalling the
military origin of the colony whose divine patron he became. In the
second and third centuries AD, armed gods enjoyed a success which
may be explained by way of certain indigenous heritages but also
because of the 'clientele' of officers and soldiers who sought their
protection. Nor was the imperial cult, or at least the idea that the god
reigned as universal *imperator*, foreign to this representation. Such a
relationship was materialized in a statue of Severus Alexander
(222–35) found at *Carnuntum*, near Vienna, where Jupiter Heliopolitanus had a temple: the god of Baalbek is shown in relief on the
imperial cuirass, between his two bulls, above a couple of Victories
wearing crowns.[57]

Officially endowed with the same epithets ('Best and Greatest') as
Jupiter Capitolinus, like him the Baal of Heliopolis was at the centre of
a triad formed with Venus and Mercury.
    Venus Heliopolitana is seated and flanked by sphinxes, like the
Aphrodite of Aphrodisias or the Artemis of Perge.[58] On her head she
bears a calathus, but a veil envelops her whole body down to her feet,
sometimes forming a sort of mandorla around the goddess and even
her acolytes: we see her thus on the octagonal altar of Fikè or the
Palatine relief.[59] Often, with her right hand open and facing the
viewer, she seems to be making a gesture of greeting and solicitude
towards her faithful (we know the importance of the hand in the
Orient, and can understand why it surmounted some legionary
standards). But this right hand may also hold a whip. Like Jupiter's,
her left hand holds ears of corn.
    Like Jupiter, the Heliopolitan Mercury has his body enclosed in a
generally compartmentalized girdle, but has the appearance of an
armless bust in continuity with its pedestal (term).[60] Sidereal motifs
(discs, rosaces, stars) occupy the compartments of the squared pattern.
But on the above-mentioned Palatine relief one can make out beneath
his collar the chariot of Helios pulled by a gryphon. Gryphons also
decorate the lower registers of his Hermaic statue on a monument
from Antioch, now kept in the Louvre. This fabulous beast confers
solar power on the Heliopolitan Mercury. The god is also to be found
erected on a plinth flanked by rams, which make him akin to the
Palmyrenian Malakbêl, a god linked with the Sun. Bearing on his head
a calathus which may appear quite clearly as a basket of fruit, he

embodies the spirit of vegetation. So he was likened to Bacchus, if not
Adonis. Lastly, this son-god was worshipped as a protector of children. This is an example of the complexity of the interwoven syncretisms. His powers over fruitfulness, and thus prosperity, in Roman
eyes confirmed his Mercurial responsibility and solidarity with the
'Fortune' or *Tyche* of Heliopolis.

The Caesars were unstinting in their generosity towards the sanctuary
of Baalbek, which was one of the most noteworthy in the Roman
world.[61] A Sibylline oracle attributed its construction to Tiberius and
Caligula. In its initial state it was not completed until the end of the
first century AD. The Byzantine chronicler John Malalas ascribes its
glory to Antoninus Pius (138–61), because this emperor endowed the
temple with a vast porticoed courtyard and a monumental altar.
Probably from the time of Marcus Aurelius (161–80), a projecting
hexagonal courtyard and propylaea gave this sacred complex its
definitive appearance. Other edifices – a temple to Mercury–Bacchus,
another to the Heliopolitan *Tyche* – contributed to the religious prestige of this district. After the Antonines, the Severans continued to
favour Heliopolis which had connections with Emesa, the cradle of
the Syrian dynasty.

The sanctuary of Zeus, which occupied an enormous area (270 m
long by 120 m wide) comprised four large main buildings oriented
towards the east. Three flights of stairs, each of seven steps, led to the
Propylaea: a broad façade and arcatured gateway between two high
towers, as at the entrance to other famous sanctuaries in the Hellenized Orient, made known to us through coins. From a first courtyard,
hexagonal and surrounded with porticoes, one entered a second,
rectangular and much more vast. This contained two pools and two
altars (including the one that Antoninus had built between two
columns). Next, by a triple flight of stairs, one gained access to the
temple proper. It rose to about seven metres above the level of the
propylaea, which already stood at that height in relation to the level of
the forecourt. The paving of the temple thus dominated the surrounding terrain from a height of some fourteen metres. As he walked
towards the idol the faithful follower went upwards: the line of the
sanctuary corresponded to an ascent.

The two columns framing the colossal altar represented the gate of
heaven. This altar was used for sacrifices of the 'holocaust' type which
were characterized – apart from the total incineration of the victims –
by a concern to celebrate the offering on high, nearer to the firmament.
These tower-altars, reached by stairways, were to be found elsewhere
in the Orient. It is known that the kings of Judah erected altars on the

terrace of the temple in Jerusalem 'to the whole army of heaven'. As for the small altar, it must have been used for common sacrifices or communion (with partial consumption of the victims' flesh).

The successive and closed courtyards preceding the temple itself follow a lay-out from the Semitic world. Comparison has been made with the aforementioned temple of Solomon.

According to Macrobius (*Saturnalia*, I, 23, 12), the idol of the god of Baalbek was of gold, which does not mean to say that it was solid gold. As often occurred in the Greek Orient, it must have been a wooden statue covered with gold, an appropriate colour for the solar aspects of Jupiter Heliopolitanus. Macrobius again (ibid., 13) tells us that the idol was paraded on a litter, the bearers were among the province's notables, their heads were shaven, and that a long period of continence had purified them and rendered them worthy of this office:

Guided by divine inspiration, they bore the statue not where they willed but where the god directed them.

Before making war on the Parthians, Trajan was pressed by friends 'of very firm piety' to consult the Baal on the outcome of the campaign. Probably sceptical, the emperor sent the god a communication to test the oracle. Zeus commanded a sheet to be sealed without anything being written on it: that was in reply to the tablets that Trajan had left blank. Convinced, the emperor asked if he would return to Rome. The god had a centurion's baton, chopped in pieces and wrapped in a shroud, sent to Trajan. Less than four years later, the remains of the *Optimus Princeps* were brought back to Rome.

The base of a statuette kept in the Louvre, Paris (Sursok bronze) contains a circular orifice. If this bronze reproduces the cultic model of Baalbek, one can imagine that the faithful slipped written questions to the god into this hole. It has even been suggested that a priest was concealed under the idol and answered on its behalf.[63]

The cult of Zeus Heliopolitanus spread its influence especially in Syria itself, but with uneven effect depending on the area. Naturally it had a strong presence around Baalbek, in the Bekaa. It was also found particularly in Beirut, an Augustan colony founded at the same time as Heliopolis and sharing religious solidarity with it. The Beirutans in Pozzuoli contributed to the expansion of the cult in Italy. Beirutans similarly consecrated votive monuments to this god at Syene (in Egypt), Nîmes (in Narbonensian Gaul), Stockstadt (in Germania).[64]

Nearly all Beirutan manifestations of Heliopolitan devotion emanated from Roman citizens, whether or not they were descendants of the founding colonists. Very often they were soldiers.

Other ports on the Phoenician coast were affected by this sphere of influence, not Tyre or Sidon, but Byblos which perhaps in its turn exerted an influence on Heliopolitan religion (with sacred prostitution and the tendency to recognize Adonis in the Mercury of the triad). In the south, the coinage of Ptolemais bears witness to the official success of the Heliopolitan god, starting with the Severi, and the Baal of Mount Carmel (which was subject to Ptolemais) was even identified with that of Baalbek on a votive foot offered by a colonist of Caesarea. In the north, intaglios and tesserae indicate his worshippers at Emesa, which also had its heliacal Baal. They were to be found at Apamea, Antioch and, much farther east, at Palmyra, in the Roman camp of Sohne and at Dura Europos, a garrison town and great caravan city.[65]

In Cilicia, Jupiter Heliopolitanus reached the port of *Aigeai* and probably had a temple at Kadirli, where the god was given the title *hypatos* or 'supreme commander'. But apart from this very limited sector, which was close to Syria, Asia Minor was no more concerned with the cults of Baalbek than was Greece, except in Athens where a Heliopolitan speculator, known through a Latin dedication of Heliopolis for the 'safeguarding' of Antoninus Pius, occasionally showed his devotion. As we have seen, after the economic decline of Delos, the axis of major trade had shifted westwards, to Pozzuoli and the large ports of the Italian peninsula.

Despite the unbeatable competition of Ostia, Pozzuoli continued to play an active role in trade between Egypt and the Mediterranean Orient in the first two centuries AD. In 116, worshippers of Jupiter Heliopolitanus originating from Beirut and resident in Pozzuoli honoured the emperor (*CIL*, X, 1634). They had their warehouses, hostelries, places of worship and cemetery there.[66] They had a temple which was allocated to the worship of their god, and restored in the second century thanks to a private citizen who called himself 'sacristan', and priests who sometimes conferred on their Baal the title 'Lord'. People known as 'lucophori' took part in the services. The name gives rise to difficulties: it has been interpreted as meaning either 'bearers of wolves' (because the wolf appears connected with the solar god Apollo), or bearers of torches, *lycophoroi* then being a hybrid Graeco-Latin word for *Luciferi*.[67] The second hypothesis is the more likely, and implies the celebration of nocturnal processions with flaming torches.

Connected with the cult of Jupiter Heliopolitanus, a dedication from Pozzuoli (*CIL*, X, 1578) mentions a chapel of the *Geremellenses*, a Latin adaptation of an expression which, according to E. Renan, meant 'worshippers of the god'.[68]

At Ostia, around the end of the reign of Marcus Aurelius – 177/80 – the god of Baalbek bore the title *angelus*, explained by virtue of his oracular power: the dedication (*CIL*, XIV, 24) was the deed of a M. Antonius Gaionas, who is to be found in Rome in 176, where he offered a paving-stone (*mensa*?) to Jupiter Heliopolitanus and Venus *Caelestis*, and in 186 associated the emperor Commodus with the homage of a little column used for the idol's base. This Gaionas arranged sacred banquets in the Trastevere district, where Jupiter Heliopolitanus had a temple, perhaps connected with the indigenous cult of the *Furrinae* Nymphs.[69] This is not the only example of the grafting of a Syrian devotion onto a spring sanctuary.

The god of Bekaa was not completely alien to the *Urbs*. In solidarity with Jupiter Capitolinus, he was equally so with imperial loyalism. Gaionas was an 'augustal' priest, and there is nothing surprising in a centurion originating from Heliopolis (*CIL*, VI, 423) offering a pillar crowned by the goddess with the lions in homage to a god who watched over the wellbeing of the Empire (*conservatori imperii*) 'of our Lord Gordian', i.e., Gordian III, who reigned from 238 to 244.

The two Baals of Heliopolis and Doliche were together venerated in the port of Aquileia, where oriental religions prospered. The Jupiter of Baalbek does not appear to have penetrated into the heart of Italy, but Italians serving in the army had contacts with his followers who converted them to the cult: for instance, the prefect from *Teate* (Chieti) who encountered the Heliopolitan god at Lambaesis in Numidia (*CIL*, VIII, 2628). The IIIrd Augusta Legion which happened to be camped there included Syrians, and Jupiter *Dolichenus* also had his worshippers.[70]

The two divinities were associated in Pannonia:[71] at *Aquincum* (near Budapest), *Carnuntum* (near Vienna), *Neviodunum* (Dernovo) and Trebnje in former Yugoslavia. At *Carnuntum*, two freedmen honoured the 'Genius' of Jupiter Heliopolitanus 'on the god's order' and for the safeguarding of the emperor Commodus (180–92). On the breastplated statue of Severus Alexander (222–35), probably erected in the praetorium of the camp, the image of Baal was deemed to protect the emperor.[72] Evidence of devoutness almost always concerns soldiers, but there were some civilians too. Among the latter may be discovered Orientals and traders who, in the vicinity of the camps, persuaded legionaries and auxiliaries to spend their pay.

Soldiers seem to have imported the god into Dacia.[73] At Sarmizegetusa, a dedication reveals the faithfulness of one of these Heliopolitans who believed they lived under the protective surveillance of their breastplated Jupiter. At Nîmes, in Narbonensis, it was a primipilus centurion, native of Beirut, who made an offering of a cippus to the god of Baalbek, joining him with *Nemausus*, the name of the beneficial spring (*CIL*, XII, 3072). Another man from Beirut, a prefect of the Ist cohort of the Aquitani, paid homage to the Heliopolitan triad in an inscription dated AD 249 and discovered in the foundations of the church of Zellhausen. At Nasselfiels, an ordinary soldier left us the epigraphic evidence of his piety. In Britain,[74] on Hadrian's Wall, the Syrian gods were invoked by their compatriots serving in the army, notably as archers. Jupiter Heliopolitanus had his worshippers at *Magnis* (Carvoran) and Corbridge on Tyne.

In the Iberian peninsula, where the Levantine gods received a pretty warm welcome, the god of Baalbek is missing. Among the western Mediterranean ports, Marseille alone yielded a Heliopolitan monument: the stele preserved in the Musée Calvet in Avignon (plate 18). Unfortunately, we know too little of the context of its discovery to be able to deduce any convincing evidence.[75]

Other Syrian triads were akin to that of Baalbek. At Niha, Jupiter Hadaranes was coupled with a *Dea Suria*, and he had a minor companion similar to the Heliopolitan Mercury, to judge by a votive hand that may be seen in the Louvre in Paris: in the hollow of the palm, which must represent the omnipotence of the father-god, sits the *herma* of a swathed and cuirassed Mercury, flanked by two rams.[76] Here the son-god truly appears as messenger or 'angel' of Jupiter, the expression of his paternal omnipotence.

The Antiquarium of the Palatine houses a small fragmentary relief bearing the images of the Heliopolitan triad: the god of Baalbek between Simios-Mercury and Astarte. This very modestly-sized monument (27.5 cm wide) may have been used in the devotions of a domestic servant in the imperial palace or a group of Syrian faithful. In a period when Christians were beginning to occupy the civilian household of the Caesars, Jupiter Heliopolitanus made a somewhat more discreet appearance.[77]

Immigrant Italian colonists adopted and partly Romanized the god of Baalbek who, in his turn, migrated with their descendants to the Roman West. But he put down no lasting roots there. By contrast, in Heliopolis itself his cult long outlived the official triumph of Christianity. In 579 it took no less than a military operation ordered by the emperor Tiberius II to gain the upper hand over the tenacious local aristocracy who still supported idolatry.[78]

Jupiter Dolichenus

He, like Jupiter Heliopolitanus, was a breastplated god whose ethnic epithet vied with his celestial sovereignty, but who did not benefit from the same imperial favours although he also bore the two superlative titles (*Optimus Maximus*) of Jupiter Capitolinus.[79]

He owed his name to Doliche (today Duluk in Turkey), a small town in Commagene situated at the crossing of several roads leading from Asia Minor to the great towns of northern Syria. Traders who had business at Samosata or Edessa, and soldiers on their way to the frontier of the Euphrates to defend it against the Parthians, or later the Persians, inevitably passed through the town. Yet literary tradition makes no mention of the name Doliche, which one reads for the first time in the second century AD in the *Geography* of Claudius Ptolemaeus. Strabo breathes not a word of it.

A temple has been recognized there, and the Greek dedication of an imperial legate for the 'safety' of the emperor and his family. An altar erected in the reign of Nero has also been discovered. Earthen seals found *in situ* and datable to Augustus or Tiberius show us the image of a local Zeus, wearing a Phrygian cap, clasping the hand (*dexiosis*) of an *imperator*! following the same schema as on the monuments of Nimrud Dagh, which I shall discuss again in the chapter on Mithras. Another seal imprint represents the Dolichean god standing on his bull, facing a classical Zeus armed with a sceptre. But this was probably a more recent seal.[80]

The canonical type of Jupiter *Dolichenus* did not make its appearance before the imperial Roman period; that is to say, before the emergence of his cult outside Asia Minor. But the stele of Zeytintepe perhaps dates from the first century AD: it represents the god with a Roman-style cuirass and wearing a horned tiara, brandishing the double-bladed axe with one hand and the thunderbolt with the other; each foot rests on a bull.[81] In the same indigenous style, two reliefs from Kurcuoglu (in the Antioch Museum) show us Jupiter and his consort *Juno Dolichena* standing, one on the right on a bull, and the other on the left on a deer, as they would be found in the West in the second century AD.[82] This iconography comes from the type of Teshub, a Hurrian storm god adopted by the Hittites.

The double-headed axe (*bipennis*) had a long Anatolian ancestry. It has been recognized in the hands of the Zeus *Stratios* of Mylasa, the Amazons and the Heracles Sandan of Tarsus (also perched on a bull). In the east this motif reached the Mesopotamian world, and in the east the Creto-Aegean world (the two-bladed axes of Knossos were famous as symbols of a divine power as yet foreign to the human form). It was found on cylinders (seals) of northern Syria, in the hand of a storm god not holding the thunderbolt. One therefore gets the impression that the bipennis and the thunderbolt were two ways of representing the same fulminatory function, the same striking power of a celestial god. As for the bull, this embodied the fieriness and fury of wind squalls, the bellowing of tempests and thunder.

The double cutting blade brandished by Jupiter Dolichenus seems also to have something in common with a phrase that defines the god as coming from the place 'where iron is born' (*ubi ferrum nascitur* or *exoritur*).[83] There were indeed ferruginous deposits near Marash (*Germanicia*) in Commagene, north-west of Doliche. The metal from which weapons were forged (the working tool, so to speak, of legionaries who followed the cult of *Dolichenus*) was believed to be formed in the bowels of the mountain, itself connected so closely and naturally to the religious conception of storms: who knows whether they established some sort of relation between the 'birth' of the mineral ore and the flashes of celestial fire, which seemed to penetrate the earth through the peaks? At all events, a god of iron could not fail to attract the attention and devotion of military circles.

So he donned the cuirass and lambrequins of Roman officers, like Jupiter Heliopolitanus. And although Doliche by no means had the status of colony, its divine patron was given the title *Optimus Maximus* like Jupiter Capitolinus. Like him, indeed, he protected the army and granted victory. It is not surprising, therefore, to see him accompanied by an eagle, even though for Syrians the bird evoked mastery of the firmament and cosmic omnipotence more than the eagle of the Latin god. Nor is it surprising to find that, alongside the properly Dolichean figures, this Jupiter also appears in the traditional aspect of the Roman god, full face and standing, with a bare torso, leaning on a sceptre and holding a thunderbolt.

His companion, the Dolichenian Juno, is descended from a similar Hittite or Syrio-Hittite line.[84] The Hurrians, who left such a strong mark on the Hittite pantheon, had already honoured a goddess Hebat or Hepet, associated with Teshub, and whose iconographic variants reveal contacts with different deities – Mothers and mistresses of wild beasts – worshipped in early Asia. The Juno of Doliche is generally shown standing, like Jupiter, but turned to the left and on the back of a hind, a goat, a deer or sometimes an ox, or in exceptional cases a lioness. Most often veiled, she sometimes wears a calathus (like other oriental goddesses) or a diadem, like the Graeco-Roman Juno. Besides the sceptre, as a characteristic attribute she sometimes holds a mirror, which some sculptors interpreted as a patera for libations (a motif dear to the Roman Juno), but which in the eyes of her oriental worshippers made her akin to the Syrian Goddess. She may also (though rarely) hold a sistrum in place of a mirror: for example, on a bronze triangle from Heddernheim[85] (which identifies her with Isis). But on two stelae from Rome,[86] the Dolichenian couple frame Isis and Serapis (plate 19), which does not give grounds for ascribing certain apparently nonsensical variations to the whims of the craftsman. In the same way as Jupiter, his consort occasionally figures with the features of the classic Juno, accompanied by her peacock, and the confusion of the mirror with a patera was all the more avoidable because *Iuno Regina* holds the latter (not raised but extended towards the altar). Queen Juno had the same prerogatives of sovereignty as the Juno of Doliche. She dominated the earth, as Jupiter dominated the heavens.

On cultic reliefs, the Dolichenian gods are coupled with the Sun and the Moon, sometimes Isis and Serapis and often the Dioscuri, Castor and Pollux. The two symbols of light do not evoke only the alternation of day and night, but also symbolize eternity, as the Roman coins of Vespasian, Trajan and Hadrian bear witness.[87] Inscriptions qualify Jupiter Dolichenus with *Aeternus*, an epithet applied to other Syrian gods of sidereal sovereignty. The Baal of Doliche was, in fact, the master of Time, whose cyclic phases were marked by the stars. In other words, *Sol* and *Luna* were the Graeco-Roman expression of a belief which originated in the Orient.

The busts of Isis and Serapis feature on a relief from the Aventine, above an eagle with spread wings which holds the Jovian thunderbolt in its talons (plate 19). This representation implies the similarity of Serapis and Jupiter. As for the flames of the altar carved below the thunderbolt, they refer us to the celestial fire possessed by *Dolichenus*, but which is not unconnected with Isis-Sothis or Isis-Selene, 'queen of heaven', as Lucius calls her (Apuleius, *Metamorphoses*, XI, 2, 1), who 'fixes the course of the stars'. The aretalogy of Maroneus (lines 18–19) says of her and Serapis:

The world blazed under your countenances, placed in the gaze of Helios and Selene.[88]

It must also be pointed out that, on the Aventine, the sanctuary of the Dolichenian gods adjoined the sector of the vaulted passage where the Isiacs, as we have seen, gave vent to their fervour which was inevitably mingled with profane joys and supernatural hopes.

The two hemispheres of the world were commonly recognized in the Dioscuri, materially represented by the ovoid caps of Castor and Pollux (allusion to the cosmic egg whose two halves corresponded to

162

Plate 19 Juno Dolichena (relief discovered in the Aventine sanctuary; Rome,
Museo Capitolino)

the sky and the earth). But the myth that the twins came to life on
alternate days had grafted onto the symbol one of a perpetual cyclic
alternating recommencement. That is why in the third century and
even the beginning of the next, on both money and sarcophagi, Castor
and Pollux personified eternity, not absolute and transcendental like
Christian eternity, but the everlastingness of the *renovatio temporum*, of
astral revolutions and the apocatastasis.[89] But here again, this Graeco-
Roman iconography transcribed a motif of indigenous oriental origin.
Although, for example, in Rome the Dioscuri appeared in Dolichenian
art as they are found elsewhere, two horsemen holding their mount by
the bridle, on triangular plaques from Budapest and Heddernheim we
see two torsos of breastplated gods emerging from the ground or on a
pile of stones. They then appear as companion deities arising from the
rock (in the manner of the petrogenous Mithras) or as the hypostases
of a mountain-god. On the silver tetradrachmas of Antiochus VIII
Grypus, king of Syria between 125 and 96 BC, two sorts of baetyls can
be made out, on either side of a god brandishing the bipennis and
standing on his bull, like *Dolichenus*. In this case, it was Heracles
Sandan of Tarsus. But the pair of rugged blocks bears witness to the
antiquity of motifs which were reinterpreted as the caps of the
Dioscuri, and thus as the two halves of the universe.

With Jupiter Dolichenus in his capacity of military god and protector of combatants, Mars and Minerva were sometimes associated,

together with Hercules, the valorous hero honoured at Tarsus in the aspect of a *Dolichenus*. The *Nikè* wearing a crown also quite naturally accompanied the god who granted victory. For the same reason, a crown of laurel occupied the central part of a triangular plaque, between Jupiter and Juno.

These bronze triangles, together with votive hands and little plaques in beaten silver, formed a noteworthy speciality of Dolichenian cultic artefacts.[91] It was formerly supposed that the triangular plaques were grouped in threes to form pyramids, images of the mountain filled with the divine force of the Dolichenian Baal. Here again, one obviously thinks of the baetyls flanking the god of Tarsus on the above-mentioned coinage of Antiochus VIII. In the view of A.H. Kan, the pyramid evokes the rite of the *chammanim*, those stones placed as boundary markers on the altars of the Baals or beside Syrian idols.[92] But these plaques were not found in threes, and some – with two faces – for this reason rule out such a hypothesis. But it by no means rules out the symbolism of the mountain. The faithful would also have seen in them, and perhaps more so, the point of a lightning flash, the fire of heaven, at the same time as the spear, the weapon of the fighting god and protector of fighting soldiers.

Like many small-sized Mithraic reliefs, the Dolichenian plaques bear an iconography which gathers together and syncretizes in a minimum of space a maximum of significant motifs and attributes. The one from Jasen (Bulgaria) shows us a sacrificer (apparently a soldier) clad in a hitched-up tunic, putting incense on a lit altar between two military ensigns.[93] These plaques therefore had a cultic function. They must have been carried on poles in order to present the gods to the adoration of the faithful during ceremonies. A relief preserved in the Pecs Museum (Hungary) represents the personification of *Terra Mater* holding a sacred triangular ensign, like those used in the Dolichean ritual.[94]

The purpose of the silver plates was quite different.[95] Some bore the stamp of Jupiter, with the aspect of either the great Capitoline god, or of the Dolichenian Baal. But the majority have only a plant ornamentation. They are cut in a flower shape, like an open lily at the tip of a sort of palm. These were offerings, votive plaques consecrated by soldiers by way of prior homage or evidence of gratitude. Their shape and decoration made them appropriate emblems for the god of victory.

The Dolichean bronze hands usually had an open palm, the fingers extended and the thumb separate (unlike Sabazian hands which have two fingers curled inwards).[96] The ones from Myszkow (Ukraine) and Catunele de Sus (Romania) hold a globe between the thumb and forefinger; this globe must have been surmounted by a Victory. The Dolichenian hand of Bizone-Varna (Bulgaria) effectively allows such a replacement. Other hands bear the image of the god or the bull in the hollow of the palm. All are hollowed out and pierced in the wrist section so that, like the triangular plaques, they could be fixed onto a pole. An open raised hand is an oriental symbol of justice, protection and omnipotence (as we have seen in the instance of Jupiter Heliopolitanus). It was a gestural motif that characterized the Sun, notably, and the emperor in the late period. This sign of salutation was a prerogative of anyone who had the power to ensure safety. The acrolith of the Dolichenian sanctuary on the Aventine[97] was a colossal full hand which had a different use from the bronze hands, but the same meaning.

Plaques and hands presuppose a ritual involving processions.[98] Sanctuaries must have had their bearers of sacred insignia, comparable to the *hastiferi* of Mâ-Bellona at Mainz and possibly Vienne (Isère). The plaques had the advantage of forming cultic images that were easier to handle and transport than idols properly speaking or stelae. They could be lifted and displayed to the assembled worshippers without difficulty, as the phrases of the liturgical *ordo* were uttered. Similarly, when they were posted to different places or subject to various other changes, soldiers of Dolichenian communities could transfer their cult objects as expeditiously as possible.

In a large fixed temple like the one on the Aventine, the idol was solemnly paraded. Hence the title *Lecticari dei*,[99] carriers of the god in his litter. This ritual was connected with an oriental tradition, as was found concerning Jupiter Heliopolitanus and as we shall see in the instance of Elagabal. But the Dolichenian cult does not appear to have paraded through public thoroughfares – at least in the towns – like the Isiac and Mother-cults. These processions must hardly ever have passed beyond the confines of the sanctuary.

The worshippers (*cultores*) of Jupiter *Dolichenus* gathered in religious communities where they addressed one another as 'brother'. Alongside a fabric committee responsible for the material existence of the sanctuary, *candidati* or 'aspirants' to the priesthood had to play the role of deacons in the charge of a 'father' (*pater candidatorum*).[100] Among them were the two *lecticari* of the Dolichenian temple.

Banquets were the high point of the celebrations. At these the faithful probably ate the meat of the sacrificial victims. On a relief from the Aventine (plate 20), we see a priest leading a bull and holding the patera used for the preliminary libations, as in an ordinary Roman ceremony. But this server in the Dolichenian cult wears an oriental tiara and a long, sleeved garment which distinguishes him from official Roman celebrants. The flesh was carved up on a stone table like that of Zugmantel (Germany), which still bears traces of the knives.[101]

It has been conjectured that by consuming part of the bull that had been ritually slaughtered to a god of whom it was the animal attribute, his devotees were absorbing 'a little of the divine essence' (P. Merlat).[102] At all events, the horns and skulls of bulls discovered in the Dolichenian temple of Stockstadt confirm that there was a liking for this kind of victim. Following a practice attested in both the traditional Roman and Mother-worship cults, the defleshed heads or 'bucrania' of the sacrificed bulls were displayed on the altars or walls of the temple. Communal meals explain the epigraphic references to *cenatoria* and *triclinia*. In the main room of the Aventine *Dolocenum*, two parallel stone benches have been recognized, comparable to those found in Mithraic crypts. As in certain *Mithraea*, too, one reached one of these table-beds by two steps. To the east, a room strictly isolated from this dining-room held a sort of swimming-pool appropriate for preliminary purifications.[103]

Plate 20 Jupiter Dolichenus (relief discovered in the Aventine sanctuary; Rome, Museo Capitolino)

However that may be, the particular features of the cult justify the fairly complex lay-out of the sanctuaries, which is not confined to a simple *cella* – with or without *pronaos* – as in the classical temples. A temple of Jupiter *Dolichenus* was not merely the god's dwelling, but also housed the devotions of a group of duly qualified 'mystae' around the permanent priest or priests.

The Dolichenian priesthood seems to have been solidly organized in liaison with laymen who looked after the functioning and financing of the sanctuaries. Every consecration was performed on the command and in the name of the god; that is to say, through the mediation of the clergy. The priests were normally of oriental lineage and ensured respect for tradition.[104] We know of one named *Barlaha* ('Child of God'), *Baradados* or *Barhadadus*[105] ('Child of Hadad'); others who, with the name *Basus* or *Bassus*, bear an oriental title of priesthood to be found in the first *cognomen* of the emperor Heliogabalus (*Bassianus*), also borne by Caracalla: both were descendants of high priests of Emesa.

We see the officiating priests in the Dolichenian cult join together to build a temple. Military recruitment of the followers led them to devote themselves at the same time to the imperial cult. In exceptional circumstances, in the period of the Tetrarchs (?), Dolichenian priests of Pannonia held a kind of council for 'the entire province', perhaps to confront Christianity, at a time when pagans were mobilizing against the new religion. But it was supposed that this 'council' rather had as its object a communal prayer of thanksgiving for the emperor Septimius Severus, who in 202 had presided over the reconstruction of a Dolichenian temple.[106] Whatever the truth of the matter, this initiative postulates the existence of an active and soundly structured clergy.

Sociologically speaking, Jupiter *Dolichenus* had followers mainly in the army. Among them some traders may be picked out, one of whom, at Beroea (in Thrace), became a priest; but they do not seem to have played a decisive role in the spread of the cult. Essentially, soldiers from the Orient made the major contribution to it, in Italy, Africa, on the Danube and the Rhine. The names of oriental or Graeco-Oriental origin and the recruitment itself of legions in which this religion prospered are eloquent testimony.

In certain cases, it rapidly reached the highest echelons of the hierarchy.[107] In the reign of Hadrian (around 131–3), the legate of the IIIrd Augusta legion stationed at Lambaesis presided over the building of the Dolichenian sanctuary. Under Caracalla, it was the legate of Lower Germania who had Cologne's sanctuary restored. In Britain, it was again an imperial legate who rendered homage to the god. Many were the officers and NCOs of all ranks (prefects of legions or cohorts, tribunes, centurions) who manifested their piety. But it must be admitted that three-quarters of the inscriptions emanating from the army were due to subalterns. People often contributed to collections for expensive consecrations performed on behalf of a body of troops (legion, cohort, detachment) or a group of veterans. We also find slaves and freedmen, a military doctor, municipal magistrates, priests of the imperial cult, knights, a procurator and even two personages of consular rank (senators). At Lambaesis, the families of legionaries in the garrison took part in the Dolichenian cult. In comparison with the Mithraic cult, the importance of women is worthy of note, as inscriptions show them named on an equal footing beside their father or husband; but they could not enter the priesthood.

The annexation of Commagene in 71, and doubtless also the posting to the West of legions who had fought in the Orient against the Jews or Parthians, should have been a determining factor in exporting Jupiter *Dolichenus* at the end of the first century AD. In fact, he did not appear in either Africa or Pannonia (at *Carnuntum*, near Vienna) before the time of Hadrian. It was rather the participation of certain legions in Trajan's campaigns against the Parthians which seems to have brought about the spread of the cult, then conversions among soldiers of Italic, or at least western, origin. The success of the Dolichenian Baal took shape more clearly in the time of Marcus Aurelius, to reach a sort of climax under the Severi, in the first few decades of the third century. In Rome, it affirmed itself in the middle of the second century with the establishment of the Aventine sanctuary, which was modified in the Severan era and under Gallienus (253–68). Another sanctuary was in use on the Esquiline at the end of Commodus' reign (*c.* 191–2).[108] We know of freedmen of Trajan and Antoninus Pius who honoured *Dolichenus* with a dedication.[109]

Outside Rome, his followers hardly emerged in Italy except in the ports (Naples, Pozzuoli and Misenum, a naval base), during less than half a century, from Commodus to Severus Alexander.[110] This cult did not penetrate or expand as much as that of Mithras, and its *floruit* was far more ephemeral. We find it entrenched in the frontiers of the Euphrates (under the Severi), Africa (in the second and third centuries at Lambaesis and *Castellum Dimmidi*, Ain Wif), Britain (Hadrian's Wall, from Antoninus to the Severi), the Rhine (also from Antoninus to the Severi) and above all in the Danubian provinces: Pannonia, Moesia and Dacia. Sporadic attestations indicate it at *Leptis Magna* and, in the Iberian peninsula, at Villadecanos and Saldanha (where its followers were still army men). In the lower valley of the Rhône, the rare monuments connected with it do not mean that the god enjoyed an established cult there: the statue found in the port of Marseille may have been destined for another region of the Empire.

Apart from the *Urbs*, therefore, it did not reach the large cosmopolitan centres or, *a fortiori*, the hinterlands of western provinces. Both ethnically and sociologically, its impact was limited. But the religious vitality of those groups who did worship *Dolichenus* sustained the morale of military circles. Former soldiers entered the Dolichenian clergy. In Dacia, in the third century, a priest and an adherent who bore the names of the Dioscuri (*Castor Polydeuces*) saw an eagle swoop down on three snakes: but a viper coiled itself round the eagle, which the two worshippers rescued from danger, with thoughts of Jupiter's bird (*CIL*, III, 7756). Did they feel they were participating in the victorious power of the Dolichenian god? It should be noted that several of his priests had the Latin name for eagle (*Aquila*).[111]

This Jupiter intervened in the lives of men by various signs, in dreams or apparitions. Many inscriptions mention divine order (*ex iussu*). The god also gave oracles. Some plaques bearing the Greek or Latin alphabet must have been used for composing prophecies by stringing together letters pointed out in succession by a priest with closed or blindfolded eyes.[112]

Was there a myth connected with the Dolichenian Baal? Nothing in the reliefs of this cult resembles the painted or sculpted narrative sequences of the *Mithraea*. Yet the two cults were often neighbours: for example at Stockstadt in Upper Germania, *Brigetio* (Oszoni) and *Carnuntum* in Upper Pannonia. At Dura Europos on the Euphrates, one and the same sanctuary housed Mithras and *Dolichenus* (as well as the 'Lady', an anonymous goddess). They had the same military clientele, but neither seems to have rubbed off on the other. Perhaps the Dolichenian iconography of the god with the bull and the goddess with the deer, together with their attributes and divine environment, was explained to the followers as a story, a theo-cosmogony (?). Literary tradition is absolutely silent on this point, as it is on the very name of this oriental Jupiter.

Nor is there evidence that his cult was conspicuous for an eschatology or soteriology properly speaking. The consecrations 'for the safeguarding' of this or that person (*pro salute*) are in no way concerned with 'salvation' in the next world. Like the Baal of Heliopolis this god, whose inscriptions sometimes evoke his Commagenian origin, assumed the cosmic dimension of absolute master of the heavens, above and beyond History, and who as such could do without any mythology. These local gods from the Semitic Orient possessed a sort of transcendence that was alien to the anecdotes and vicissitudes on which the Greeks were so keen.

Other City or Local Gods

Different Baals and other Syrian gods emigrated to various points in the Roman West, despite their original and fundamental attachment to one city or one place. Perhaps it was even because of this local patronage that they were able to achieve transplantation without difficulty. In fact, their followers felt a religious patriotism which, despite the surrounding syncretism, remained strongly rooted, and they were more willing to accept the confusion of their local Baal with a Greek or Roman god than with the Baal of another Syrian town.

The *Melqart* (or 'king of the town') of Tyre had long before conquered the shores of the western Mediterranean. Under the name Hercules, the god of Tyre formerly imported to Gades (Cadiz) by the Phoenicians was popular in the Iberian peninsula. Trajan and Hadrian, who had family connections in Spain, did him the honour of putting him on their coinage. The Punic Melqart had landed at the mouth of the Tiber perhaps seven or eight centuries earlier, or even disembarked near the future Forum Boarium. The numerous ports with the name of Heraclea had often inherited it from the holy patron of Tyre, conveyed thither by his sailors. Cavalaire may have preserved in its early name (*Heraclea Caccabaria*) the memory of a consecration to the Phoenician god. In the imperial era, he was worshipped at Pozzuoli, and as far from Rome as the north of England.[113]

As for the Gades sanctuary,[114] at the time it kept the particular features of the Punic ritual. It was an aniconic cult (despite the coins of Trajan and Hadrian which show the god in the likeness of the classic Hercules). His priests were obliged to observe strict continence. They remained faithful to the Phoenician costume, with a purple-bordered linen tunic. Their feet were bare, their heads shaven and encircled with a ribbon. A flame burned permanently on the altars. Entry to the temple was forbidden to pigs and women (Silius Italicus, *Punica*, III, 21ff)

The sanctuary lay not in Cadiz itself, but 18 km to the south-east, beside the sea, on the island of St Peter, which at that time was connected to the town by a roadway. In front of the entrance stood two columns, said by Posidonius to be bronze, and by Philostratus (*Life of Apollonius*, V, 5) to be an alloy of gold and silver, but whose brilliance must in any case have been used a landmark by sailors. Originally there were probably two baetyls comparable to those of the

Tyrian sanctuary and like those to be seen elsewhere in Syria (even in Cilicia, on either side of Heracles Sandan). The Gaditan sanctuary was also made special by some prestigious relics: the girdle of Teucer, the baldric of Ajax, the golden olive tree of Pygmalion, the famous sculptor who fell in love with his ivory Aphrodite ... Another famous feature of this Hercules-Melqart was his oracular ability. His temple drew pilgrims: people came to dream there in order to know the future. Caesar had a dream at Gades (the rape of his mother) which for him was a presage of ruling the world.

The Baal of Tyre had followers in certain ports who adhered to the national religion. In AD 174, the Tyrians of Pozzuoli, no doubt hit like other shipowners by the economic crisis which the Roman world suffered under Marcus Aurelius, asked their mother-city for an annual subsidy of 100,000 denarii for the maintenance of their local sanctuary and the financing of the ancestral cult.[115] The senate of Tyre replied favourably: tradition had to be preserved 'in the interest of the homeland'. The inscription tells us that the Tyrians in Rome pre-viously supplied the same amount to their compatriots in Pozzuoli. Apart from the material links maintained by the migrants with their native city, this gives us outstanding proof of the sizable expenditure on sacrifices and cultic amenities supported by the piety of expatriate Tyrians.

The Hercules-Melqart of Tyre had worshippers at Corbridge (*Corstopitum*) on Hadrian's Wall, where his altar would later be used as a font in the Christian church.[116] There women were not excluded from the cult, since the monument was consecrated by an archpriestess of the god.

Some idols were taken directly from their place of origin. It was thus on 29 May 79 (under Vespasian) that 'the holy god of Sarepta' arrived at Pozzuoli by boat from Tyre (brought by a member of the *Elim* at the god's command'.[117] It may have been a solar god whose priestly dignitary accompanied the statue to Campania's great port to ensure that immigrants could practise their national religion.

Again at Pozzuoli (*CIL*, X, 1576), the Baal of Damascus, under the name *Iupiter Optimus Maximus Damascenus*, had a temple served by several priests, including a decurion, aedile and Roman knight, who was promoted to equestrian rank by the emperor Antoninus (138–61). His brother held the same priesthood, which seems to have been a family affair, in a circle of oriental freedmen who were well integrated with the municipal notables. It may be recalled that this Hadad of Damascus, who also had followers in Rome, was featured on the tetradrachms of Antiochus XII of Syria, in 87/6 BC. There the god had the hieratic type of Jupiter Heliopolitanus: standing between two bulls, holding an enormous ear of corn. Coins struck some years earlier in the name of Demetrius III *Eukairos* (96–55 BC) represented his companion Atargatis, flanked by two tall corn ears.[118] The mosque of the Omayyads at Damascus today occupies the remains of his temple: in the courtyard, pigeons appear to enjoy the same respect as the doves of Aphrodite once did.

The god of Berytus (Beirut), Balmarcodes or 'Lord of the dances' had hardly any followers in the West.[119] But in May, for the god of Gaza, Marnas, in the port of Ostia and in Rome itself, people celebrated the Maiumas, a popular festival which consisted of plunging into the water and competing to splash one another, rather as the Neapolitans celebrate Santa Lucia by merry frolicking in the sea opposite Castel dell'Ovo. If we are to believe the *Augustan History*, the Syrian emperor Severus Alexander would sometimes give vent to exclamations calling on the name of Marnas.[121]

The holy patron of Apamea, Belos, was renowned afar for his oracle, which was consulted by several emperors, Septimius Severus and Macrinus, perhaps Hadrian. An altar from Vaison-la-Romaine bears two inscriptions, one in Greek (*IG*, XIV, 2482), the other in Latin (*CIL*, XII, 1277), which consecrate the remembrance of the offering dedicated by one Sextus to Belos, 'ruler of Fortune' (*Fortunae rector*). Formerly, L. Renier thought he could detect in the dedicant's forename that of Varius Marcellus of Apamea, the husband of Julia Soaemias (mother of the future emperor Heliogabalus). Whatever the precise identity of this person, the bilingual dedication clearly indicates the conception preserved by a Syrian in Gaul of his Apamean Zeus – absolute master of destiny, i.e., the sky and the stars that fix its course.[122]

Among the gods of the highlands, the Baal of Mount Casius had a prestige that spread its influence in the Greek world at Delos, Athens, Epidaurus and Corcyra (where a merchant offered him a stone vessel).[123] Nero began his singing tour amid the Greeks before the altar of Zeus Casius at Cas(s)iope, whose name had doubtless facilitated the Syrian god's acclimatization to Corcyra. He had a temple in Egypt near Pelusium,[124] where his idol had the aspect of young man holding a mysterious pomegranate (Achilles Tatius, *Leucippus and Cleitophon*, III, 6), an attribute borne on the reverse of coinage of the Pelusian nome. Hadrian made the ascent of Mount Casius to contemplate the rising sun and perform a sacrifice there. Early in this century, an American missionary saw the Ansariya (Nusayris), a

Shi'ite Syrian people, worship the daystar there and perform certain special rites. This god-mountain was honoured in the form of an aerolith, as shown to us on the coins of Seleucia, near Antioch. Like the baetyl of Emesa, that of Mount Casius must have benefited from a solar cult.

In the West, besides Nero, Trajan and Hadrian, he had his devotees at Heddernheim on the Rhine frontier, *Carnuntum* on the banks of the Danube and Cartagena in Spain where, in 1905, about thirty lead anchors were retrieved from the sea: some bore the engraved names of Roman shipowners, but two others had the names of Zeus Casius and Aphrodite.[125] The god and goddess are termed 'saviours'. Like Isis and Serapis, Zeus Casius, although linked to a place, but also by reason of his cosmic and sidereal powers had in this instance become the protector of sailors. At *Carnuntum* it would seem that the miracales of lightning and rain were ascribed to him (as the Egyptians attributed them to Thoth and the Christians to their God).[126] At all events, Zeus Casius was identified with Horus-Harpocrates in his capacity as solar god, and like so many other oriental Baals, he possessed the fulminatory power of the great celestial gods.

Another god of the heights had followers at Trier, in Dacia, at Rome: Turmasgad, whose name means 'mount of adoration'.[127] Like other Syrian Baals he was assimilated to Jupiter: hence the eagle embodying his divine force on the altar that an imperial freedman offered to him in the *Urbs*. Soldiers recruited in Commagene seem to have imported his cult to the territory of present-day Romania. He is to be found associated with Mithras in a chapel of the *Dolichenum* at Dura Europos.

In lower Galilee, the god of Mount Carmel, dear to the Philistines, received a visit from Vespasian in 69 when he was in command in Judaea. 'This god', wrote Tacitus (*Histories*, II, 78, 6), 'has neither statue nor temple, only an altar and worshippers'. Through the voice of his priest Basilides, he promised the first of the Flavians – who was sacrificing to him – the imperial future that Serapis would soon consecrate in Egypt. Lastly, over Lebanon reigned a Hadad *Libaneotes*, also termed *Acroreites* (god 'of the mountain peaks'), who was not to be confused with Jupiter Heliopolitanus, but was found in Rome honoured in the same cultic sector of the Janiculum.[128]

At Beirut and Rome there was evidence of a Baal called the August Jupiter *Maleciabrudes*, 'sovereign (malec-) of Iabruda' (a place situated east of Heliopolis-Baalbek).[129] The same epithet (*Optimus Maximus*) was applied to him as to Jupiter Capitolinus.

Palmyrenian Gods

A caravan city enriched by the trade between Central Asia and the Roman world, Palmyra (Tador) possessed some prestigious sanctuaries.[130] Although incorporated in the Empire, the palm grove benefited from a relative autonomy:

The oasis is hemmed in on all sides by the sands and nature has cut it off from the rest of the world. It enjoys a privileged state, between two great empires, Roman and Parthian: both sides appeal to it as soon as their conflict is renewed. (Pliny the Elder, *Natural History*, V, 88).

Phoenician, Arab, Babylonian and also Graeco-Roman religious influences met there, were grafted on to one another and combined. By providing Rome with excellent archers, Palmyra made its gods known along the borders of the African desert and in the mountainous regions of northern Pannonia, where they rubbed shoulders with other oriental gods.

Love and motherhood hardly count at all in this masculine and warlike pantheon. Gods of water and vegetation, strength and the heavens, we find them often grouped in triads from the first century AD.[131] The first triad is attested in AD 32 by an inscription commemorating the inauguration of the temple which was consecrated to it at that time. To the god Bêl it joined two companions named Iarhibôl and Aglibôl. The name of the god Bêl is of Akkadian origin (Bel-Marduk). Originally he must have been called Bôl. Like the Belos of Apamea, he was the absolute master of the cosmos and time, represented by the two luminaries flanking him.

Iarhibôl, 'good god', was initially the 'baetyl of the spring', as he is designated in a dedication by Palmyrenian archers. This Efka spring was vital to the city. But Iarhibôl means 'master of the months', and his radiate head makes him equivalent to the Sun, which the Greek version of his name confirms. Aglibôl or 'calf of Bôl', for his part, was a lunar god wearing the crescent behind his head (frequently likened to bull's horns). Selenic humidity gave him power over plant growth and fecundity.

A second triad was dominated by Baalshamin, Syrian god of the skies and storms, thus the rain so precious to farmers. Unlike Bêl, who was clean-shaven, he had a beard and sometimes held a thunderbolt. He was accompanied by Aglibôl and Malakbêl, 'angel of Bêl', who had rays like Iarhibôl. But in this other triad the Moon-god had precedence, since he was shown on the right of the sovereign god, in keeping with an ancient tradition which acknowledged that the nocturnal star had a determining power over living beings.

The two triads present a frontal view of the gods, who are armed and breastplated in Roman fashion. The acolytes of Bêl and Baal-shamin are haloed, and both Aglibôl and Iarhibôl or Malakbêl have rays coming from their head. In the Roman era, the two sources of light symbolized (as around Jupiter Dolichenus) celestial eternity at the same time as the benefits of warmth combined with humidity. The formation of the triads apparently had nothing to do with a Semitic heritage, but was the result of a Hellenistic 'updating' linked to astral mysticism.

The military equipment of the Palmyrenian gods can be explained, not by virtue of a theology of celestial armies, but in relation to the religion of the sovereign and imperial power as the incarnation of a universal royalty. Such iconography was just as appropriate to the gods venerated outside Tadmor by Palmyrenian soldiers. However, Malakbêl does not wear a cuirass unless he is the counterpart of Aglibôl, on the left side of Baalshamîn. On his own, or facing Aglibôl, he wears Persian trousers and a sort of kaftan. Following a process which is by no means exceptional in the history of religions, Malakbêl in his role of 'messenger' of the supreme god, and thus mediator, eventually took on a dominant role in the devotion of the Palmyr-enians. He was even found confused with Bêl in an inscription from Rome,[132] and he was the one most gladly invoked by his compatriots when they were exiled by military service, together with Iarhibôl, another name for the Sun. The visible image of the great invisible god, the angel of Bêl tended to supplant him. Conversely, at Ostia Jupiter Heliopolitanus was invoked as *angelus*.

Aglibôl and Malakbêl were worshipped as the 'two holy brothers'. At Palmyra itself – where the emperor Hadrian personally paid them homage by conferring on the town the status of free city – they were fêted by singing, dancing and other popular rejoicings that lasted twelve days. We find Iarhibôl and Malakbêl chiefly honoured wher-ever Palmyrenian archers were stationed: Coptos in Upper Egypt, Africa and Dacia. At Lambaesis, the cult of Iarhibôl was secured in the camp of the IIIrd Augusta legion by an annual priesthood. Malakbêl had his place there in the temple of Aesculapius, and he was wor-shipped under the name of Mercury by the Palmyrenians of Biskra and El Kantara.[133] His cult is well attested to the north-east of Lagouat, at *Castellum Dimmidi* (north of the Sahara), where the cavalrymen had set up their Palmyrenian chapel in a room in the barracks.[134] We find Malakbêl associated with Iarhibôl under the title 'Mercury, Genius of the army'. He had his followers at Sarmizegetusa in Dacia, where his temple was equipped with a kitchen (*culina*) for the sacred banquets.[135] With Bêl Hammon, Benefal and Manawât, he benefited from homage to 'the national gods'. Manawât is a plural perhaps designating certain goddesses of destiny dear to the Arabs of the south. Benefal is unknown elsewhere, unless he is confused with Beellefar who had his followers in Rome among the horsemen of the imperial guard (*equites singulares*).[136]

This attachment to the *dii patrii*, similarly found in Rome, was peculiar to Syrians in general and to Palmyrenians in particular. At *Apulum* (Alba Iulla) in Transylania, Iarhibêl was the object of a dedication. On the Euphrates frontier, at Dura Europos, Bêl had a temple for soldiers of the Palmyrenian detachment and the traders of the agents' office that had been established there. The soldiers had their chapel, with their accredited *hiereus*, who figures on a work noticeboard as priest *ad signa* (assigned 'to the ensigns'). One thinks of that priest of Jupiter Dolichnus whom an inscription makes known to us as *ad legionem*.[137] Apparently the Palmyrenian archers had their 'chaplains'. The one at Dura had the same name, Themes, as the Palmyrenian priest of Sarmizegetusa (*CIL*, III, 7954). It was also the name of a trader installed in Lyon, Thaïm, who did business with Aquitaine.[138] It means 'servant', 'server' or 'servitor'. In this instance, it had all its functional value in the case of the supreme service formed by the priesthood. A magnificent fresco in the temple of the Palmyrenian gods at Dura shows us priests making a sacrifice, clad in long pure white albs and wearing tall conical mitres, which are similarly white.[139]

In Rome, the Palmyrenians honoured their gods in Trastevere, at the foot or on the slopes of the Janiculum.[140] The exact site of their sanctuary is unknown, perhaps on the side of the Porta Portese, where a fragmentary relief with a biligual dedication carved in honour of Bêl and Iarhibôl was found. From the same district come an inscription dedicated to the Palmyrenian Mars (the Arab god Arsu), for the safekeeping – *pro salute* – of the emperor Hadrian, and the regulations of a chapel consecrated to *Beheleparus*. Another relief found in this sector shows Malakbêl and Aglibôl shaking hands in front of a cypress. The bilingual dedication (in Greek and Palmyrenian) dates the monument to 235; the dedicant, T. Aurelius *Heliodorus* bears the name of the Sun itself in his Greek surname.[141]

Even richer in significance is the altar consecrated to the 'very holy Sun' by a family of imperial freedmen connected with the activities of the river port and, more precisely, the *horrea Galbiana* facing the Porta Portese, on the other bank of the Tiber.[142] Judging by their names, they must have been former slaves freed by Nero, which would date the monument to the Flavian period (end of the first century AD). On the facade, above the Latin dedication, the bust of the Sun with rays, (seven, an allusion to the planetary week) and a halo, is shown carried on an eagle, the image of celestial power. On the short sides, to the left, above the Palmyrenian inscriptions, is Helios crowned by Victory in a quadriga drawn by gryphons, those Apollonian quadrupeds of the fabulous Orient; on the right, the veiled head of Saturn, god of Time, but also the Sun of the night for Chaldaean astrologers. On the back of the altar a beribboned cypress is carved from which a child emerges carrying a kid on his shoulders. This is one of those rare illustrations of Palmyrenian mythology, which seems to make Malakbêl a herdsman god or 'good shepherd', born of a tree (like Adonis) and protector of flocks (like the Heliopolitan Mercury).

It may be recalled that the young god of the Heliopolitan triad had on his breast the image of the heliac chariot drawn by a gryphon (Palatine relief). Now, Mercury-Simius, like Malakbêl, was a messenger or mediator god. As much for his middle position in the chorus of the planets as for his function of giving life and revealing the supreme god, the Sun 'shepherd of the dazzling stars', as the Gnostic Naassenes invoked him (Hippolytus, *Philosophoumena*, V, 9) under the name Attis, had the same vocation as Malakbêl in Graeco-Roman imagination.

We know that after his triumph over Zenobia in 272, the emperor Aurelian consecrated the statues of Bêl and Helios, which were part of the booty brought back from Palmyra,[143] in his gigantic temple of the Sun in Rome (near the present-day Piazza San Silvestro). The gods of Tadmor were thus officially enthroned in the very heart of government, under cover of a cult which would initially have the favour of the first Christian emperor, Constantine, then of the last pagan emperor, Julian the Apostate. But another oriental Sun, who was deemed to have given Aurelian victory over the queen of Palmyra, had for a time scandalized and revolutionized Rome: the *Sol Invictus* of Emesa.

Elagabal

On the road from Palmyra to the sea, at the crossroads with the one leading from Heliopolis to Apamaea, then to Antioch on the Orontes, from an unknown time a cult had been established at Emesa (Homs), worshipping a black aerolith called *Elagabal* or 'god of the mountain'. This sugar-loaf-shaped baetyl was taken to be a sacred image of the

'Invincible Sun' (*Sol Invictus*). Several coins show him in his temple behind an eagle which, as in the case of other Syrian gods, symbolically embodies celestial sovereignty. On other coins, the eagle is seen perched on the aerolith, which was dressed (so it seems) on the occasion of certain ceremonies in a cloak circled with garlands and gleaming with gemstones. A monumental altar bearing the figures of many gods subordinate to this god – who was identified with both Zeus and Helios – stood in the sanctuary courtyard. His high priest danced there in a gold-embroidered purple tunic, his head crowned with jewels of myriad colours. The baetyl was fêted to the sound of flutes and trumpets.[144]

Since the end of the Seleucids' reign (64 BC) an Arab dynasty of priest-kings had ruled in Emesa, and in the first century AD had acquired Roman citizenship by virtue of their loyalty towards the ruling power and services rendered (notably in Corbulo's war against the Parthians, then Vespasian's and Titus' war against the Jews). This kind of priestly principality had kept a semblance of autonomy, by dint of providing Rome with horsemen and archers (like Palmyra), until the reign of Antoninus Pius. The temple and its clergy were rich. Elagabal attracted a good many pilgrims and visitors, motivated by devoutness or curiosity:

The god is not worshipped by the natives alone. All the barbarian kings and satraps in the neighbourhood annually send him as many magnificent offerings as he could desire. (Herodian, *Roman History*, V, 3, 5)

However, the prestige of the black stone of Emesa did not go beyond the Ports of the Levant until the day when the high priest of Elagabal married one of his daughters to the Roman governor of Lugdunensis, the future emperor Septimius Severus. He had stayed in Syria when in command of a legion there. Like others, he had made the pilgrimage to Emesa, probably as a tourist; but this African from Leptis – who was also fascinated by Egyptian gods – was not immune from all religious disquiet. His accession as *imperator* in 193 made an empress of Julia Domna, who with her sister Julia Maesa was heiress to the priestly dynasty.

It is then that one sees the epigraphic evidence of the Emesian migrants' fidelity to their ancestral god. Their cohorts of mounted archers stationed in Pannonia (chiefly at *Intercisa* on the banks of the Danube) or in Africa (at El Kantara, on the edges of the desert) paid him emphatic homage, the expression of a religious patriotism strengthened by the enthronement of an Emesian woman in the palace of the Caesars.[145] In Rome itself, late second-century inscriptions[146] bear witness to the presence of a college of priests and an organized cult outside the pomoerium, probably in the Trastevere district where – like several other Levantine gods – *Sol Invictus Alagabalus* (sic) had a chapel. In AD 201 a priest, T. Julius Balbillus, consecrated the image of an eagle to the god. Nevertheless, Julia Domna was not seen to encourage, still less promote, the religion of her forefathers in the *Urbs*. This cultured great lady, who presided in the Palatine over a court of Greek and Latin writers and intellectuals, seems to have shown no kind of attachment, either personal or family, to the worship of the baetyl. She doubtless preferred to be compared by the poet Oppian to the 'Uranian' Aphrodite or Venus-Astarte.[147]

But Julia Domna had a sister, Julia Maesa, whose two daughters would each have a son. When Caracalla got himself assassinated in 217 at the instigation of his praetorian prefect, Julia Domna, his mother, died of starvation or a cancer brought on by despair. Julia Maesa and her daughters remained alone in the running to confront the usurper Macrinus who had financed Caracalla's murder. They alone personified a kind of dynastic legitimacy, simultaneously imperial and priestly.

Julia Maesa's two grandsons, Bassianus (the son of Julia Soaemias) and Alexianus (the son of Julia Mammaea) thus inherited the priesthood of the temple of Emesa. In the full bloom of his adolescence, the elder (Bassianus) attracted the notice of the soldiers who had come to make their devotions to the black stone. They found him as handsome as Bacchus when they saw him dancing around the altar in his Phoenician robe of purple and gold, his arms and head studded with jewels. We know the rest of the story . . . His grandmother, who loathed her exile to her native country, far from Rome and the court, took advantage of the enthusiastic piety of the legionaries to bribe them and rouse them against Macrinus, spreading the rumour that Bassianus was Caracalla's adulterine son. The youth was then proclaimed emperor under the names of his alleged father: Marcus Aurelius Antoninus. Macrinus was defeated and killed.

But the boy wanted to remain a priest, and as he could not stay in Emesa itself, since an emperor could truly be so only in Rome (to which his grandmother was eager to return), the new ruler would go only if accompanied by the baetyl, which was carried in a processional chariot drawn by four horses, like the quadriga of the Sun. This lengthy journey, which took a year, was interrupted only by stops in various towns where the Pseudo-Antoninus tirelessly attended to the service of his god. Coins and inscriptions commemorate the passage of the black stone through Asia Minor, celebrated by the gesticulations and sacred orgies of its high priest to the exciting rhythm of the timbrels.[148]

His grandmother obviously feared that this strolling entertainer of an emperor, attired in eastern fashion, ran the risk of making a disastrous impression on the aristocracy, and even the populace, of Rome. So, in order to prepare them for the priestly entry he would make into the city, he sent the Senate a portrait of himself in the costume of a sacrificer. The picture was placed in the meeting chamber, above the statue of Victory, at the foot of which each member of the Curia burned incense and poured wine on the altar: from then on it was impossible to accomplish this preliminary rite without paying homage to the crowned high priest. The god of Emesa was henceforward invoked before all the others: such was the command of the emperor who was nicknamed 'Heliogabalus' to mock his exclusive and exclusivist devotion, not without a play on words which turned this Graeco-Latin hybrid into the equivalent of an insult like 'scoundrel of the Sun'.

Immediately upon his arrival in Rome, Heliogabalus had a sanctuary (Elagabalium) set up for his baetyl, almost next door to the imperial palace, where the church of San Sebastiano now stands.[149] Every morning he came out to slaughter bulls and a vast quantity of sheep. On the altars the blood of the victims mingled with exotic aromas and intoxicating wines. The emperor went about among hecatombs and libations, with the women of his country playing their cymbals and timbrels. Knights and senators, clad in trailing tunics with long wide sleeves, purple girdles and flaxen footwear 'like the soothsayers of Phoenicia' (Herodian), were not behindhand in participating in the liturgical frolics. On their heads they carried golden vessels containing the entrails of the sacrificed animals and they conformed strictly to the Syrian ritual. The emperor's mother and grandmother danced and sang with him in the language of the Bedouins who had previously installed their cult of the Sun at Emesa. What a spectacle for the old Romans, or at least those who claimed to be!

That is to say nothing of the behaviour and sexual or culinary extravagances of the crowned anarchist (as A. Artaud called him): there were worse things than these barbaric exhibitions, so unworthy of an *imperator* – in the view of a senator who was from the Greek Orient himself, the historian Cassius Dio. Heliogabalus aspired to make his god pre-eminent, at the expense of Jupiter Capitolinus, the guarantee of Roman sovereignty and victory. By doing so he subverted the very foundations of imperial government. The *Augustan History* accuses him of having wanted to centralize the most sacred

pledges of its universal domination and durability that the gods had
given Rome: the flame of Vesta, the Palladium (a crude idol of Pallas-
Athena brought back from Troy by Aeneas, the ancestor of the twins
suckled by the She-wolf), the shields of Mars, the black stone of
Pessinus enclosed in the head of Cybele ... Heliogabalus was said to
have burst in on the Vestals, guardians of the 'perpetual fire' that he
wished to extinguish, and because he could not lay hands on the
genuine receptacle of the *sacra* he broke the imitation one offered to
him by the Great Vestal as a sop to his rage. He was also said to have
submitted to the taurobolium and tied his testicles in order to pass
himself off as a Gallus of Cybele and penetrate her temple to steal the
goddess. This fanatic's intentions (it appears) would not have stopped
short of transferring to Rome the idol of the Tauric Artemis (previously carried off by Orestes at the same time as Iphigenia)![150]

Elagabal's high priest thus seems to have possessed a single and
totalitarian priesthood, incorporating all cults into one alone, including those of the Jews, Samaritans and Christians (claims the *Vita
Heliogabali*, which is obviously suspect). He was even accused of
planning to authorize only the worship of the sole and unique god of
Emesa: a *Sol Invictus* like the Sun of Constantine before his official
conversion to Christianity. Apparently the pagan biographer (who
wrote around the end of the fourth century AD at the earliest) charged
Heliogabalus with all the sins of Constantine,[151] who was guilty of
having almost imposed his monotheism on the Roman world.

In fact, the contemporary historians of the 'mad Caesar', Herodian
and Cassius Dio, do not refer to the assembling of the Roman religion's
venerable relics in the *Elagabalium*. Heliogabalus was said only to have
transported the statue of Pallas to the Palatine in order to wed her to
his god: a crime which, by itself, was sufficiently grave, as no one had
the right to move her, except in case of fire (and even then ... the Great
Pontiff Caecilius Metellus had been struck blind – hence the name *Caecus*
– for saving her from the flames in 241 BC!). Then, on the pretext that
a warlike and ever-armed goddess was displeasing to her husband,
Heliogabalus is supposed to have brought another spouse from Carthage:
Juno *Caelestis*, the Punic Tanit. Indeed, the union of the Sun and the Moon
was absolutely 'comme il faut' (Herodian).

In reality, Pallas and Juno with Elagabal must have formed a triad of
the kind worshipped in Syria. The iconographic proof is provided for
us by a capital found in the Forum but probably torn from the
Elagabalium on the Palatine. It shows the baetyl with an eagle, between
an armed goddess and a divinity identifiable with Juno (plate 21).[152]

Coins and medallions also inform us of the general appearance of
the sanctuary (plate 23):[153] a monumental temple in the centre of a vast

courtyard isolated by an enclosing wall from the profane world and even from the imperial palace, although directly neighbouring on the *Domus Augustana*. On the reverse of certain coins Heliogabalus is shown sacrificing to his god, dressed up in his rich priestly garb (baggy Persian trousers, loosely belted tunic under a little cloak). The emperor holds a kind of thick, knotty stick, perhaps a piece of cypress wood, a tree consecrated to the Sun.

The daily liturgy on the Palatine was interrupted each year at the climax of the Dogstar (in July) by a grandiose procession to a secondary sanctuary, built in the summer residence that the Severi had begun to arrange for themselves in a suburb to the south-east of

Plate 21 Capital from the *Elagabalium* (Rome, Antiquarium Forense)

Plate 22 Medallion of Heliogabalus (eagle and baetyl in a chariot)

Rome (between San Giovanni Laterano and the Porta Maggiore): the Sessorian palace.[154] In the Orient, carrying the idol or baetyl on a litter on men's shoulders or in a sacred chariot was a part of the periodic and festive rituals. In the case of Elagabal, this solemn moving of the solar aerolith significantly coincided with the moment in the year when the star exerted its power with maximum intensity (plate 22).

It was therefore a Sun festival, marked also by various spectacles, chariot races (in the purpose-built *Circus Varianus*), gladiatorial games in the *Amphitheatrum Castrense* (still visible near the church of Santa Croce in Gerusalemme), dances and banquets offered to the populace. The procession itself, from the Palatine to the *Sessorianum*, in some respects illustrated the theology of the priest-Caesar. The baetyl, placed on a chariot sparkling with gold and gems, was deemed to steer the team, guiding the emperor who walked backwards holding the reins, his eyes fixed on his god, along a path scattered with gilded grain. The crowd ran along on both sides of the chariot waving torches and throwing flowers. The Invincible Sun was preceded in the procession by statues of the gods, the insignia of imperial power, and soldiers and horsemen of the praetorian guard. The other gods thus processed in homage to the one honoured by Heliogabalus as a supreme god, the manifestation of a henotheism quite different from the intransigent monotheism imputed to him by the last pagans, who caricatured him as a precursor of Constantine. The *Augustan History* is nearer the religious truth when it attributes to him the statement that all the gods were in the service of his own (*Life of Heliogabalus*, 7, 4).

After the sacrifices, the emperor ascended the towers (probably comparable to those flanking the propylaea of several Syrian sanctuaries) from the top of which, to placate the delirious crowds below, he threw jars of gold or silver, expensive materials, and live animals which people tore from one another, getting themselves crushed or impaled on the praetorians' spears in the process: this caused a number of deaths, which added to the ritual victims . . .

The imperial promotion of Elagabal among the sons of the She-wolf naturally encouraged roving Emesians, above all those serving in the army, to redouble their devotion to their national god. A legate from Raetia, apparently connected with the family of the high priest, C. Julius Avitus Alexianus, was at that time (around 219–20) anxious to show his piety by a dedication to the *deus patrius* that was found at Augsburg (*AE*, 1962, 229). A Greek inscription from Cordoba,[155] unfortunately mutilated, celebrates the Great Sun Elagabal, Cypris and Athena Allath as benevolent to their worshippers and attentive to their prayers; this is a triad similar to the one represented on the capital of the *Elagabalium* mentioned above, except that the Syrian *Caelestis* (Cypris or Venus) is substituted here for the Punic *Caelestis*. But we know that they tended to be identified with each other.

Heliogabalus' excessive zeal did not gain many followers for his god, apart from his faithful courtiers. The populace of the *Urbs* appreciated only the wild extravagances and annual revels of the Emesian cult. The emperor eventually wearied even those close to him, and worried his grandmother Maesa who, in order to maintain power, showed no hesitation in having one grandson assassinated so that the other, Alexianus, could be proclaimed ruler. He would reign under the name Severus Alexander, and his most urgent task was to send the baetyl back to Emesa and reconsecrate the temple on the Palatine to Jupiter the Avenger (plate 23).[156]

But the god bore no grudge against Rome for having repatriated him, at least if we are to believe the *Augustan History*. In fact in 272, in the thick of the battle that set him against Zenobia's Palmyrenians, Aurelian, in difficulties, received the favour of a divine apparition which urged him on to victory and, when he entered the temple at Emesa, the emperor acknowledged Elagabal (*Life of Aurelian*, 25, 5): a strange anticipation of the famous vision that Constantine would have forty years later before the battle of the Milvian Bridge. However that may be, Aurelian made official the cult of a *Sol Invictus* which had nothing to do with that of the Syrian aerolith.

Other Arab Divinities

We have seen that a Palmyrenian Mars, the Arab god Arsu, gained a foothold in the Trastevere. Allat the warrior goddess, who with

Plate 23 Medallion of Severus Alexander (*Elagabalium* consecrated to Jupiter 'the Avenger')

Caelestis served as companion to Elagabal and whom the Palmyrenians had also incorporated in their pantheon, had the same lineage. Inscriptions carved on rocks in the desert remind us of the cameldrivers' invocations: 'O Allat, safety and booty!' or 'O Allat, vengeance!'[157] Aziz was associated with Arsu. Aziz was a god of Edessa (?) and certainly of Emesa. Princes of the Emesian priestly family bore his name. With Monimos, he accompanied Helios, according to the emperor Julian who in this instance draws on the Neoplatonist Iamblichus in recognizing Hermes (Monimos) and Ares (Azizos: literally, the 'Strong' god) as the companion gods of the Syrian Sun.

A solar and armed god, Aziz was honoured by soldiers in the Danubian provinces.[158] He was the *Bonus Puer Conservator* assimilated to *Phosphorus*, the Morning Star whose counterpart was the Evening Star (*Hesperus*). He was invoked at *Intercisa* (Dunapentele in Hungary) for the safekeeping of the emperor Severus Alexander and his mother; at Potaissa (in Dalmatia) for that of Valerian and his son Gallienus. At *Intercisa* the cult of Aziz – the work of a Syrian – seemed at one with the Emesian religion: there the god was given the title *Invictus*, like Elagabal. Other dedications to the *Bonus Puer* or *Puer Phosphorus* concern the same oriental 'Lucifer'. We even find him identified with Apollo in Dacia (*CIL*, III, 1133; 1138). But he was also given the name Mars, as Monimos was called Mercury, to judge by epigraphic consecrations of a Syrian which were found at Potaissa: the proof that the fairly learned explanations of someone like Iamblichus tallied well with popular syncretism, most likely inspired by the clergy.

But in literary tradition, it was Dusares who appeared as the great god of the Arabs.[159] Tertullian, claiming on behalf of the Christians the right to have their God (*Apologetica*, XXIV, 8), enumerates those which the Romans acknowledged for different peoples:

Syria has its Atargatis, Arabia its Dusares ...

Like Elagabal or the Baal of Mount Carmel, Dusares – whose name designated him a 'lord of the mountain' – was a baetyl, 'A cube-shaped black stone resting on a ground covered with gold sheets ... ' (Suda, *s.v. Theusares*). Porphyry (*Abstinence*, II, 56) also tells us that the Arabs of Dumatha annually sacrificed a child at the foot of an 'altar which they used as an idol', which again suggests a quadrangular form. Indeed, it is thought today that among the Nabataeans the baetyl was erected on a cubic block serving as an altar, the *môtab* (or 'throne') in Aramaic.

Coins from Adraa and Bostra show, in the first instance, a rounded block and, in the second, three baetyls similar in outline to that of Elagabal, but surmounted by discs: one on each lateral baetyl and seven on the central one (formerly interpreted wrongly as a 'press', because of the common assimilation of Dusares with the god of wine, or even as 'shewbreads' piled on top of one another).[160] It would seem that several baetyls were the object of a cult in Arabia. Hence the reputation for litholatry which characterized it in Graeco-Latin imagination. The Arabs 'worshipped a shapeless stone' wrote Arnobius (*Against the Nations*, VI, 11), echoing Clement of Alexandria (*Protreptikos*, IV, 46, 1): 'The Arabs prostrated themselves before a stone'.

For Stephanus of Byzantium (*Ethnica, s.v.*), 'Dousares' is the name of a rock, 'the highest peak in Arabia'. This appears to have been a mountain in the Hedjaz, covered with vines and sugar canes, In fact, the *interpretatio Graeca* made Dusares the equivalent of a Dionysus. Already for Herodotus (III, 8) the Arabs invoked only two divinities: Dionysus (Orotalt) and *Urania*, goddess of the sky whom the Father of History calls Alilat (otherwise known as Allat). But he does not speak of Dusares. In Strabo (*Geography*, XVI, 1, 11) as in Arrian (*Anabasis*, VII, 20), the same divine duo are found, but with a masculine sky corresponding to Zeus. In contrast, Origen (*Against Celsus*, V, 37) draws on the same tradition as Herodotus: the Arabs worship 'Urania as the female and Dionysius as the male'. In the Roman world, the cult of an indigenous Dionysius was chiefly accepted.

The Nabataean Arabs took advantage of the trade in spices, incense, gemstones and silk with the Middle and Far East to gain certain profitable markets in the West or with the West. In their company, Dusares made himself known as an object of worship in Miletum, Cos and Delos, where a bilingual dedication to 'Zeus Dusares' was carved in 9/8 BC in a sanctuary which, despite the island's economic decline, was still operating at the end of the first century AD. This consecration to 'Zeus Dusares' would lead to the supposition that the above-mentioned Greek authors (Strabo and Arrian) made a distinction between two deities (Zeus and Dionysus) who perhaps constituted only one for the Nabataeans.

Dusares is to be found at Pozzuoli, where the god had had a temple since 54 BC (thus shortly after the ruin of Delos).[161] This sanctuary, which also appears to have functioned as a meeting-place, was restored in the reign of Augustus (AD 5), as a Nabataean inscription testifies. Another, similarly Nabataean, inscription informs us that Zaïdu and Abdelge, sons of Thaïm (a significant name which we have already met) made an offering of two camels to Dusares in AD 11. Were these camels alive or votive (i.e., carved or statues)? Some people believed it possible to state that on the occasion of the 'festivities of AD 11', the two Arabs paraded the two camels 'before the astonished gaze of the people of Pozzuoli'.[162] Apparently they were the processions celebrating Cybele ... This hypothesis cannot stand up to scrutiny. Even admitting that the camels were offered alive, they could have been consecrated to the god merely to browse in the sacred enclosure in Pozzuoli, as around certain temples in Arabia. But the epigraphy is more likely to refer, like that of a Sabaean monument (CIS, II, 184), to two statues or statuettes of camels. For its consecrators, the offering had a double symbolic value. The camel evoked their home country and, above all, the animal that the Arabs called 'ship of the desert' was the tool of their profitable trade with Central Asia; it carried the precious goods which the sea vessels transported to Campanian shores to satisfy the luxurious tastes of decadent Romans.

At Pozzuoli, too, an altar and three bases dedicated to Dusares were found.[163] The bases present some unexplained singular features. One, which has the oblong shape of a large altar table, has on the front of its upper surface seven notches into which kinds of stelae were inserted (four are preserved). Each of the other two bases has three notches. As for the stelae, they have the contour of baetyls. One may imagine that the large base with seven notches was flanked by the other two to form an ensemble comparable with the baetylic triad figured on the reverse of the coins of Bostra. V. Tran Tam Tinh has suggested a parallel with the ritual observed by Arab parties to a contract, according to Herodotus (III, 8): seven stones placed between the two men were anointed with their blood, while Dionysus and *Urania* were invoked.[164] The monument may therefore have been used for deals engaged in by Nabataean traders in their Pozzuoli sanctuary. More recently, a parallel with the 'parapegmes' has been advanced; that is, the kinds of perpetual calendars provided with holes in which the symbols of the days, and thus the gods of the week, were placed. Dusares, the master of the seasons and vegetation, would have been held to rule the planets. This argument of P.G.P. Meyboom[165] does not take account of the bases with three notches, but would sit well with Dusares's acknowledged solar function at that time. It is not out of the question that a stele matching the god of the day should have been set up each day; the large base would then have served as a liturgical calendar.

At all events, it appears that Dusares was contaminated by solar syncretism. Cumont insisted on this in reference to a Mithraic relief found at Si (Djebel Druze), not far from Kenawât (*Canatha*) in the Hauran, in front of the temple of Dusares itself.[166] According to Ephiphanius (*Panarion*, 51, 22), on 25 December the Arabs of Petra celebrated the birth of Dusares, as the *Natalis Solis Invicti* had been fêted, since Aurelian's time, on this date in Rome, and already the birth of Christ also shared this day. The bishop of Cyprus even wrote that Dusares was hymned by the Arabs as the son of a virgin named Khaamu or Khabu (?), which obviously brings to mind the Ka'aba, or black stone of Mecca.

This testimony is suspect. But we know that the Arabs dedicated a cult to the Sun which would explain both the actual data and the Christian interpretations. The actual data are of the literary and numismatic kind, and are concerned with litholatry. A stone baked during the day by the sun's burning rays preserves a little of its heat after nightfall, as if the Sun remained present in it. It was thought that, like the black stone of Emesa, that of Dusares was worshipped as a heliac idol. Vines love the sun, and thus the stones which heat the earth. Like the Graeco-Roman Dionysus, Dusares who caused the grapes to ripen had powers matching those of the Daystar, and in the fourth century, in a period when the Christians were emphasizing the Word as the Light of the World and the Sun of Justice, it is understandable that Epiphanius should have commented tendentiously on the god of the Nabataeans, just as after the destruction of the Alexandrian Serapeum, the cross was deciphered in the Isiac hieroglyph for 'Life'.[167] Apologists at the time liked to demonstrate that certain pagan cults represented a distortion of the Revelation or a foreknowledge of the new religion.

The Syrian 'Sanctuary' of the Janiculum

It has been noted that in Rome, in the Trastevere districts (where Christians also gathered), the Syrian and Palmyrenian cults left traces on the slopes or at the foot of the Janiculum, mainly around the sacred wood of the *Furrina* or *Furrinae*, deities of the waters that welled up on the eastern flank of the hill. Jupiter Heliopolitanus was combined with the 'Genius of the *Forinae*', as a statue plinth found near the church of San Crisogno (*CIL*, VI, 422) bears witness.

In 1720, a tunnel excavation in Cardinal Ottoboni's gardens (which would become those of the Villa Sciarra) unearthed a statue of Hercules with the hydra of Lerna, together with bronze figurines of frogs and snakes, votive objects connected with the water cult.[168] C. Fea's research in 1803 resulted in the discovery of a triangular base (today in the Louvre, Paris), which apparently related to Mithraic worship, and a pillar dedicated to Jupiter Heliopolitanus and surmounted by the image of a turreted Fortune between two lions (Atargatis?). A century later, the American diplomat G.W. Wurts, who had become the owner of the Villa Sciarra, had a caretaker's house built in the sector of the *Lucus Furrinae*. The foundation works brought about the discovery of a number of significant 'finds': an altar consecrated to Zeus *Keraunios* ('of the thunderbolt') and the 'Phorrines' Nymphs; another bearing three dedications to Hadad; a third a dedication to Jupiter *Maleciabrudes*, already mentioned.

In 1908–9, almost immediately north of the caretaker's house, P. Gauckler, aided by G. Nicole and G. Darier, discovered what is customarily called, following their lead, the 'Syrian sanctuary of the Janiculum'.[169] What exactly was it?

The excavators recognized three stages of construction:

- an east–west wall and rows of amphorae which may have corresponded with an initial temple of the age of Nero;
- with the same orientation, structures comprising rooms paved with mosaics which appear to date to the second half of the second century;
- with a noticeably different orientation (SE–NW), a very long edifice stretching slightly less than 45 m, with a lay-out dating back to the fourth century, perhaps to the period of Julian the Apostate (361–3).

This last complex architectural construction was composed of three parts (figure 4). One entered it by a closed central courtyard from which, through a vestibule flanked by two 'chapels' one passed into a sort of temple with a triple *cella*: the central nave had a semicircular apse at the back of which, enthroned in its niche, was the marble idol of a seated god, of Jovian or Serapean type (the condition of the statue, which was decapitated, does not permit its identity to be ascertained); the two small lateral naves, accessible through the central *cella*, each had a rectangular niche. In the centre of the main nave, a triangular base scooped out in a half-moon shape, facing east, was perhaps used to support a lamp rather than a triple statue. Under the niche in the apse where the supreme god was enthroned, a rectangular cavity held a human half-skull. This top of the skull must have been sliced off and ritually placed under the idol to render the latter sacred.[170]

East of the interior courtyard was an equally tripartite building complex, but here two pentagonal chapels flanked a *cella* which broadened out strangely in the form of an octagonal room. This *cella* had an apse in which there was a niche probably housing the basalt pharaonic statue discovered nearby. In line with the apse, in the centre

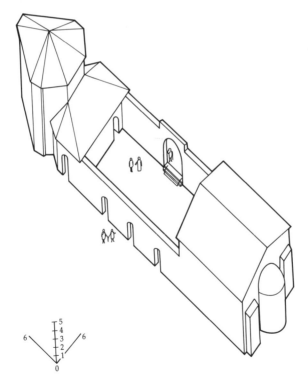

Figure 4 The 'Syrian sanctuary of the Janiculum' (reconstruction drawn by R. Meneghini: *L'area del 'santuario siriaco del Gianicolo'* p. 56; see note 33).

of the octagon, a kind of triangular masonry vat contained a recumbent bronze statue, with the feet to the west. It is of a man, his feet
together and his arms against his body, wrapped in a sort of shroud.[171]
A snake entwines him in seven coils and rears its jagged crest above
the idol's hooded head. Seven hen's eggs were placed between the
reptile's coils. A dried root made a necklace for this enigmatic deity,
and seeds were recognized on his chest. In one of the two pentagonal
chapels a mutilated group of three female persons on a triangular base
was found (the three Hours?) and, buried in the ground, a marble
statue of Dionysus.

Indisputably destined for cultic use, this building presents several
singular features which do not permit it to be placed in a known
category. Certainly, the central courtyard enters a sort of temple (to the
west) and a polygonal structure at first sight makes one think of the
Baalbek sanctuary mentioned earlier. But at Baalbek, the hexagonal
building was an initial porticoed courtyard used as a vestibule to the
large inner courtyard where the altars stood. There is no interruption
from the propylaea to the temple properly speaking, and the line of
the heliopolitan sanctuary makes it differ radically from the one
excavated by Gauckler. One cannot fail to be struck by the triplicity of
the buildings, both east and west, and by the triangularity of the cultic
furnishings facing both the western apse and the apse of the eastern
cella. These special features suggest the cult of a triad, but was it
actually the Heliopolitan triad?

The seated god, with a nude torso like Jupiter or Serapis, cannot be
identified positively with the Zeus of Baalbek, and the other items of
sculpture and statuary do not match any of the divine figures in the
Heliopolitan triad.

True, the two inscriptions found in this area are the work of a
certain Gaionas, known for his devotion to the Syrian gods.[172] One is
carved on a plaque that is perforated to serve as a fountain mouth:
Gaionas describes himself as an organizer of (sacred) meals, which is
confirmed by his epitaph. It is an amenity allowing the celebration of
offerings to the gods thanks to the water of the Lucus Furrinae. Which
gods? In 176 another stone slab used as a mensa was dedicated by the
same Gaionas to Jupiter Heliopolitanus and Venus Caelestis. But this
slab was re-used as a threshold, in the entry to the vestibule that was
crossed in order to reach the central nave of the building in which the
Jovian idol was enthroned.

According to Gauckler, this dedication belonged to the 'temple' of
the second phase. But the structures corresponding to this phase have
nothing to justify their being regarded as a temple, and the re-use as

a threshold of an epigraph expressly consecrated to the divine couple of Heliopolis would ill accord with a reconsecration to the same gods. As for the fountain mouth, it was discovered outside the fourth-century sanctuary, on the occasion of work carried out in the Villa Wurts. Neither the Egyptian pharaoh, nor the seated god, nor the statue of the three Hours (?) has a place in a Heliopolitan temple.[173]

There remains the bronze idol in which (in regard to the Baalbek triad) some people have believed it possible to discern a Mercury-Simius who could be assimilated to Adonis.[174] The death, burial and resurrection of the young god would have been celebrated before his reburial in the triangular casket. But the statuette has none of the features which characterize either of them. The type of Heliopolitan Mercury is sufficiently well known[175] for him not to be recognized in this statue. As for the image of Adonis, whatever the variants may be he is never represented as a swathed mummy. The snake reminds one of the Mithraic god of Time and the spirals of the solar revolution in the ecliptic (it has indeed been compared with the reptile's sinuous movement). But the idol has nothing of the Mithraic lion-headed god. Nowhere in the caverns of the Persian cult has any figure of this type been found. Might it then be the *Aiôn* of Alexandria? The Graeco-Egyptian god is seated and nude. Equally foreign to the Janiculum statuette are the monstrous representations of the Orphic Chronos, as described by Damascius.[176]

The only really enlightening and pertinent parallel to have been put forward is that of certain Graeco-Egyptian 'magic' intaglios which show a mummy entwined in the coils of a snake. On two of the known examples, the reptile's head overhangs the mummy's, as in the case of our idol.[177] The stones in another series bear the image of a mummy lying in the curve of a snake, and the shape of this image corresponds to the hieroglyph meaning 'eternity' (*ḏt*).[178] The figure wrapped in its shroud and encircled by the serpent with a radiate head was apparently identified with Osiris, who conquered death thanks to the rites of mummification instituted by Isis. He was assimilated to the Sun, whose serpent, as we have seen, symbolized the annual circumvolutions of the diurnal star. The seven coils obviously refer to the planetary hebdomad of which Osiris-Helios was the celestial *choregus*.

Bearing in mind the placing of the idol in its triangular receptacle, it is possible that the death and resurrection of Osiris were celebrated in the sanctuary on the Janiculum, as was done at Cyrene, Pompeii, and Eretria where graves of similar dimensions – though not triangular in shape – have been recognized.[179] In the Isiac *telesterion* in Cyrene, the *bothros* contained eggs, an offering which evokes both the origin and rebirth of the world. The seeds scattered on the bronze statue also bring to mind the ritual of 'vegetative' Osiris (p. 118).

But the religious site on the Janiculum does not come into the category of Isiac sanctuaries properly speaking. The religion observed there must have incorporated certain Egyptian rites into the framework of a syncretic cult practised clandestinely by the last pagans, away from the city centre where temples remained closed and sacrifices were prohibited. The cultic furnishings (statues of pharaoh and Bacchus in particular) make one think of salvaged idols, such as those found in a Dionysian building of *Cosa*.[180] Being unable to honour the idols that had been consecrated for centuries in official temples which were henceforward inaccessible – and the idols themselves having often been destroyed or mutilated by the Christians – hardened polytheists re-used statues or statuettes which had once served to adorn private houses.

These circumstances would explain the disparate nature of the sculptures discovered on the Janiculum. In the late fourth century, the eminent members of the senatorial aristocracy who had stayed loyal to the *mos maiorum* willingly displayed their adherence to the different priesthoods of Dionysus, Hecate, the Sun, Mithras, Isis and Cybele. The triangular base dedicated by a Mithraic 'Father', discovered by C. Fea in 1803, may well come from the site.[181] The sanctuary may thus have gathered together the followers of those cults brought into solidarity by the nostalgic pietism of the idolatrous *clarissimi* and the intolerance of the Christian emperors. In the octagonal temple they adored Osiris at the same time as Dionysus, another dead and revived god who, like the husband of Isis, embodied the annual cycle of plant regrowth. The western building (with three naves) must have been consecrated to the cult of Jupiter-Serapis enthroned between two companion divinities (Isis and Harpocrates?). The triplicity of the chapels, the 'Hours' or Hecates (?), the triangularity of the bases (examples of which are found in Mithraic crypts) and notably of the casket containing the bronze idol justify making a connection with the doctrine that Servius (*Ecl.*, V, 66) ascribes to Porphyry: the same god is Sun in the heavens, Liber Pater (or Dionysus) on earth, Apollo in the Underworld.

This is the same kind of belief that the devotees on the Janiculum might have celebrated. This Porphyry on whom the last pagans of the Roman 'gentry' so eagerly drew, took pleasure in commenting on the trimorphism of Hecate as well as the attributes of the 'Hours' or the identity of Dionysus with Horus-Harpocrates as well as with the Sun, the master of the seasons or *Horai*.[182] What is known about the sanctuary gives the feeling that it was suited to a theosophical circle of

Neoplatonist inspiration. The sacralization of the Jovian idol by a human half-skull refers us to the mysterious rites of the initiatory cults in which polytheists with Neoplatonist leanings took such an interest.

So the last ones to cling to traditional religion seem to have retreated to the hill which had previously offered asylum to the cults of the Levantine *Diaspora*.

What an astonishing destiny for the Syrians, who were as passionately religious in spirit as they were actively realistic when it came to occupying terrain, whatever it might be! It was all very well for Plutarch (*Superstition*, 10) to mock these people who were convinced that the Syrian Goddess 'eroded the legs, burned the body with ulcers and destroyed the liver' of anyone who dared to eat pickerel or loach. Atargatis enjoyed success among her worshippers.

To tell the truth, and contrary to what Cumont states, the gods of the Semitic Orient did not 'impose themselves on the West'. But they travelled about with their fellow-nationals. They were expatriated, often with their clergy, without ever losing anything of their fundamental originality of form or ritual. The extraordinary mobility of the Syrian gods went hand in hand with an indestructible religious patriotism, as frequently evidenced by the expression *di(i) patrii* and the ethno-geographic determinants: *Dea Syria, Di Syri, Di Samariae, Dea Hammiorum, Iuppiter Heliopolitanus, Dolichenus* or *Damascenus*. Even the local Baals of Carmel, Casius or Lebanon were able to move from their native land without ever losing their prerogatives.

This attachment to their own small homeland, to an iconography and a cult that escaped being made commonplace by the 'cosmopolitics' of the Roman Empire, did not prevent these gods from being 'at home' everywhere they went, in their role of masters of the heavens, and being in harmony with the spirit of the times by incorporating astrolatry, and doubtless also astrology, in the devotions of their followers.

The primitivism of the oriental litholatries was not incompatible with homage to a universal and absolute sovereign who was often not too far removed from the Biblical God. It is understandable that Syrian Baals should have been called 'eternal'. Some dedications to the *deus aeternus* keep the secret of his identity.[183] Starting from the second century AD, there is a noticeable tendency to honour a supreme god who is superior to any name. Apuleius (*The World*, 27; cf. *Plato and his Doctrine*, 12) calls him *exsuperantissimus*, a superlative that, on the coins of Commodus, is found applied to the Roman Jupiter, but is also borne by the Jupiter of Doliche at about the same period (*CIL*, IX, 948).

In the Orient, the *Theos Hypsistos* was a Zeus who was identified with the Palmyrenian Baalshamîn. But the Jews also gave this superlative epithet to Jehovah who, in an inscription from *Intercisa* (*CIL*, III, 10321), may be concealed behind the name *deus aeternus*. At all events, despite appearances and the diversity of Syrian cults, these gods who reigned over space and time were preparing the way for Christian monotheism.

Although in Heliopolis, Emesa and Gaza, local paganism had a hard time in the fourth and fifth centuries, the Syrians who travelled and traded around the Mediterranean were effortlessly converted. In Ravenna as in Arles, they henceforth piously chanted in the churches. But they continued to be successful in their business ventures (for instance in the wine trade), and if need be they knew how to make their way in the ecclesiastical hierarchy! In the Orient, the aerial asceticism of the 'Stylite' monks, as illustrated by Simeon, in fact Christianized a practice that was already famous at Hierapolis-Bambyce. The Syrian Goddess had devout followers there who stayed for eight days at a stretch perched on giant phalluses, some 55 m high. People were convinced that 'from this elevated spot, man converses with the gods' (Lucian, *The Syrian Goddess*, 28).

Chapter 4

Beneath the Rocks of
the Persian Cavern

T HE story of Mithras is remarkable and paradoxical. It is
remarkable, because this god, who was alien to the pantheon of
the Greeks and Romans, had not been so to their distant Indo-
European ancestors. When they welcomed a god of foreign appearance, with Persian trousers and a Phrygian cap, the sons of the
She-wolf were in fact linking up again, at least partly, with a very
ancient religious genetic inheritance; but the cult of Mithras, as it was
received by the Latin West, had also incorporated a share of Greek
culture. Although the god kept his Asiatic costume, his myth and
surroundings of symbolic images, he had taken his place in the
syncretic pantheon of the Hellenized Near East.

At the same time, the paradox lay in the destiny of this god who,
honoured in the first instance by Rome's enemies, became (with
others) an idol of the Roman legionaries. After inspiring and embodying resistance to the ruling power in Asia Minor, Mithraism two
centuries later was to sustain and legitimize certain values of 'Roman-
ness'.

But vast shadowy areas surround this story and fragment the vision
we have of it today, after over a century of remarkable research and
discoveries. In particular, the passage of the Iranian god into the
Greek world and the many mutations he must have undergone, both
in rituals and in the conception of his worshippers, before becoming
the mainspring of a mystery cult, for the present almost entirely elude
us. A hiatus of some two thousand years separates the Vedic Mithras
from the first known representations of Mithras the bull-slayer. Making due allowances, Cumont could say that our knowledge of Mithraism is as problematical and full of lacunae as our knowledge of
Christiantiy would be if we had at our disposal nothing but the Old
Testament and the carved iconography of the cathedrals. The illustrated data that the sanctuaries have yielded are for us like a book of

Beneath the Rocks of the Persian Cavern

pictures with the text missing. The theology and soteriology which these pictures illustrated for the faithful are accessible to us only through inference and conjecture.

Lastly – again a paradox – the most ancient religious representations of Mithras, those of the Vedic tradition, are on the whole far clearer and better known to us than those of the Hellenistic god, in the very period when he was to become a saviour god in the limited framework of initiatory cenacles. Despite all we know, or think we know, of the mysteries of Mithras, the circumstances and reasons of the mystery ritualization of the cult continue to puzzle us.

Indo-European Heredity and Iranian Protohistory

The name Mithras comes from a root *mei- (which implies the idea of exchange), accompanied by an instrumental suffix. It was therefore a means of exchange, the 'contract' which rules human relations and is the basis of social life. In Sanskrit, mitra means 'friend' or 'friendship', like mihr in Persian. In Zend, mithra means precisely the 'contract', which eventually became deified following the same procedure as Venus, the 'charm' for the Romans.[1] We find him invoked with Varuna in an agreement concluded c. 1380 BC between the king of the Hittites, Subbiluliuma, and the king of Mitanni, Mativaza. The text of this treaty was discovered in 1907 at Boghazkeuï, in the royal archives of the ancient Hittite capital, some 150 km from Ankara. It is the earliest evidence of Mithras in Asia Minor.[2]

The sacralization of the engagement committing two parties was fundamental for every community. In Vedic literature,[3] Mithras is the one 'who brings people together'. Correspondingly, he watches over respect for the rules of good conduct. 'He takes care of his peoples' and plays his role in the cosmic order, since he 'sustains heaven and earth' (a curious prefiguration of the Atlas Mithras to be found twenty centuries later on reliefs and paintings of the Roman era). He sees everything, like the sun which is his great eye. He is a benevolent god, close to men, a luminous and just god who gives abundant vegetation, harmony and health. In the minds of his Graeco-Roman initiates he would continue to be the guarantor of a pledge, as well as the protector and promoter of animal and plant life.

In Vedic theology Varuna and Mithras correspond to two aspects of the Indo-European function of sovereignty which G. Dumezil wanted to recognize in the first two kings of Rome, Romulus and Numa.[4] The first embodied terrible and magical strength; the second, justice and priestly law. But as there is no justice without the strength demanded by the application of and respect for the law, the Indo-Iranian Mithras tended to assume certain prerogatives of Indra, the Vedic god of the second function – war.

In Avestan literature,[5] the Xth *Yasht* or 'hymn', which is dedicated to Mithras, invokes him as 'a god of fighters . . . the terror of those who bear false witness . . . armed with the thunderbolt feared by Angramainyu' (Ahriman, the spirit of evil). He was then a 'warrior with white horses and swift arrows . . . whose long arms everywhere reach those who violate a contract'. We shall later recognize this sagittarian god in the cultic paintings and reliefs of the Roman era. He already appears also in this Xth *Yasht* as a solar god, 'of the dawn that rises over Mount Hara and embraces in his gaze the whole country of the Aryans'. This vision of light emerging from behind a stony summit prefigures the image of the petrogeneous Mithras, arisen from the rock with his sword and torch. The same hymn shows him to us passing before Verethragna, the *yazata* or 'genius' of victory, who has the shape of a boar: yet another view of the huntsman god who reappears in the *Mithraeum* of Dura-Europos, for instance. This concept has been regarded as typical of the 'Männerbund', that is, companies of men united by the exercise of strength and communal feasting around the slaughtered game, as later we shall see Mithras and the Sun at table behind the carcase of the bull. If one adds that Mithras was celebrated as master of the fertilizing rain and prosperity, 'watchful over live-stock and fruitfulness', this *Yasht* (of which the version known today dates back to the reign of Cyrus the Elder, or the sixth century BC) gives us the impression that a fair proportion of the components of the future god of the mysteries was already firmly in place in the believers' imagination.

The rosace carved on the pediment of Cyrus's tomb at Pasargadae has been interpreted as a solar symbol of Mithras.[6] It is certain that in old Persian *Missa* would fit the *Mithra* of the Avesta. Mithra is a form preserved in the language of the Medes. Cyrus would thus appear to have remained loyal to the cult of a Medic god. The name Cautes, the dadophor of the rising sun in Mithraic iconography, seems equally to have Medic ancestry. In fact, it is in the north Iranian sector and on the borders of Armenia that Mithras appears to have enjoyed a lively and tenacious tradition. People have also compared the myth of Diorphos (a son of Mithras, who like him issued from rock), that the Pseudo-Plutarch (*The Rivers*, 23, 4) places on the banks of the Araks, with the Ossetian legend of Sozryko, the substitute for an ancient solar god. At the end of the seventeenth century, the traveller Jean Chardin saw in a monastery in Mingrelia (western Georgia) a ceremony which strangely recalled the myth of Mithras the bull-slayer.[7] There it was announced that Saint George had stolen a bull (this was the 'cattle stealer' god or *bouklopos* of the mysteries). 'At once a young man . . . dragged the bull out of the church, killed it and cut it into pieces'. According to a popular Armenian legend, on the shores of Lake Van there is an opening in the rock. In the cavern, Meher (Mithras) on horseback and his black raven stay enclosed until Ascension night when manna falls from heaven. Then Meher emerges to gather the manna and live on it for the rest of the year in the cave, which closes behind him. Two candles burn beside him (like the two torch-holders which flank him on the cultic panels in Roman *Mithraea*). When the wheel of the universe, which turns day and night before his eyes in the cave, stops, Meher will emerge and his reign will come in time to coincide with the end of the world.[8] It brings to mind the Mithraic ladder whose seventh door is of gold and corresponds to the era of the Sun (Origen, *Against Celsus*, VI, 22).

However, the Medic god suffered a sort of eclipse with what might be called the 'white revolution' of Darius, whose father Vistaspa had the same name as the protector of Zoroaster. Henceforth, the great god was to be Ahuramazda.[9] The Zoroastrianism of the early Achaemenids marginalized popular polytheism. But Mithras retained a solid impact in traditional piety. In the Xth *Yasht*, the expression Mithra-Ahura, parallel with the Vedic Mitra-Varuna, still reveals his pre-eminence. This same *Yasht* glorified him as 'the sovereign who imparts the well-being of law and Sovereignty'. In fact, Plutarch tells us that, even in the Achaemenid era, the kings believed themselves invested by a *Mesoromasdes*, in which S. Wikander has rightly deciphered the names Mithras (*Mes-*Missa*) and Ahuramazda,[10] who were precisely the gods of sovereignty. The *Tale of Alexander* describes Darius as 'sharing the throne of Mithras'. This special relationship of Mithras with royal office is confirmed by the festival of the *Mithrakâna* (*Mihragân* in the Parsee year), the only day on which the *Basileus* had the right to get drunk; elsewhere wine was known as the royal drink *par excellence*. In the famous trilingual inscription from Xanthos, the Aramaic version gives for the name of Apollo the designation *Hshatrapati* or 'lord of power' and the solar god might correspond to Mithras (?).[11]

In any case, the god reappears in the official epigraphy of the Persian kings dating from Artaxerxes II Mnemon (405–359 BC). Mithras and his companion Anahita were then invoked in addition to Ahuramazda as protectors of the ruler against evil. Under his successor Artaxerxes III, Mithras alone is associated with the supreme god, which reminds us of the duo implicit in *Mesoromasdes*.

Anahita was probably already identified with the Moon, and Mithras with the Sun. It was because of this divine couple that Herodotus (I, 131) mistakenly gave the name Mitra to the Persian Aphrodite. She also assumed the warrior aspects of an Athena, and it was in her temple at Pasargadae that Artaxerxes II had himself consecrated king. In Asia Minor, she would easily be assimilated to an Artemis.[12] As for Mithras himself, his light was invoked in oath-taking, which allows us to see him as the vigilant day-star (Plutarch, *Life of Alexander*, 30). In Quintus Curtius (*History of Alexander*, IV, 13, 12), we see Darius III Codoman pray to 'the Sun, Mithras and the eternal fire' before the decisive battle, so that they might inspire in the Persian soldiers a courage worthy of their forefathers against the Macedonian aggressor. Mithras (at least in the historiographic tradition on which the Latin writer relied) remained well and truly a god of armies and also of divine justice called as witness, as in the time of Cyrus the Elder. He would remain so in the camps and along the frontiers of the Roman Empire.

Hellenistic Mithras

The epigraphy of Persepolis and biographical material on the royal family or dignitaries attached to the Achaemenid court show us that Mithras had numerous and fervent followers there. Theophoric names prove that people eagerly sought his divine patronage.[13] This religious tradition parallel with the official cult survived the collapse of the Persian Empire as it did the upheavals following Alexander's conquest. The Iranian colonies and aristocracies of Asia Minor in particular preserved their identity. Many local dynasties would claim the prestige of an Achaemenid line of descent. Mithras figures notably in the pantheon of the kings of Armenia, Cappadocia, Pontus and Commagene. The Parthian dynasty of the Arsacids, who came from the north-east of Iran, sometimes included him in the names of their kings, beginning with Mithridates I the Great, to whose reign some people would like to date the writing of the above-mentioned Xth *Yasht*. Kings of Pontus, Bosphorus and Commagene bore this sacred anthroponym, which means 'given by Mithras', as formerly in France the name 'Dieudonné' or 'Déodat' was bestowed on ardently wanted children.

According to Cumont, in Babylonia the Magi were under the influence of Chaldaean astrology.[14] More recently the most suspect arguments in compared iconography have been highlighted: petrogeneous Mithras is said to proceed from the Akkadian imagery of Shamash emerging from the mountain: the lion-headed Time, from the Mesopotamian Nergal; the identification of Mithras and Hermes in Commagene is explained by the connections of Nabu with the planet Mercury, and the *Mithrakâna* tie in with the Babylonian calendar . . . [15]

Actually, up to now nothing proves that the Mithraic cult took over astrology on contact with the Mesopotamian clergy. The ladder Celsus speaks of which was shown to initiates had the planetary week as its foundation, which is not of Chaldaean origin.[16] The Stoics too attached great importance to astrology, and one can just as easily point to traces of their doctrine concealed in Mithraism. The Iranian god had worshippers at Tarsus where the teachings of the Stoic 'Painted Porch' prospered.[17] It is in Asia Minor that we have to seek the crucible in which, under the dual influence of north Iranian traditions and Greek culture, the Mithras of the mysteries was formed.

Unfortunately, and despite a few rare and unequally enlightening indications, we have to rely on conjecture.

Cumont earlier insisted on the influence of the 'Magusaeans' or Magi who had emigrated to Anatolia.[18] In Cappadocia, Strabo (*Geography*, XV, 3, 15, 733) witnessed these worshippers of a fire that was tended as scrupulously and ritually as Vesta's. Coins from Hierocaesarea and Hypaipa in Lydia show us the fiery altars that were honoured according to the Persian cult. In the early second century AD, the orator Dio Chrysostom (*Discourse*, 36, 39–60) comments on a hymn 'sung by Zoroaster and the children of the Magi' when they celebrated certain 'ineffable mysteries', in which Cumont tried to discern an allusion to the initiatory religion of the Bull-slayer.[19] But the latter is not named by Dio, or by Strabo in connection with the Magusaeans. This hymn of the Magi, evoking the quadriga of the four elements and the final blaze of the world, has only a distant link with the known representations of Mithraism, despite the attempted comparison with a bifaced relief from Dieburg where the myth of Phaethon is depicted.[20] The Mithraists doubtless harked back occasionally to the Magi and Zoroaster, to whom Eubulus quoted by Porphyry (*Cave of the Nymphs*, 6) ascribes the consecration of the first 'mystery' cavern. An inscription names the Magi in the *Mithraeum* of Dura-Europos, where Zoroaster and Ostanes perhaps figure in Persian costume on the frescoes painted on either side of the chancel.[21] A graffito in the cavern built into the Circus Maximus in Rome mentions 'magic' activities.[22] But the title 'magus' is not found in the priestly hierarchy. The only unchallengeable (though isolated and inexplicit) testimony is that of one Sagarios in a rock inscription of Rhodandos (Farasha) in Cappadocia: it reminds us that he has celebrated a 'magic' ceremony (ἐμάγευσε) in honour of Mithras.[23] The datings of this text waver between the third century BC and the first century AD. It is not known if this Sagarios, who was a 'strategus' and apparently of Iranian ancestry, had the services of a Magus or if the verb *mageuein* means simply 'to sacrifice'. We shall see the Magi again with Tiridates, who is said to have initiated Nero to their sacred banquets.

In Commagene,[24] King Antiochus I (69–34 BC), the son of a Mithridates made illustrious by a dual heredity, Persian and Macedonian, had himself portrayed on the Nimrud Dagh shaking hands with Mithras. The god has the radiate head of the day-star and the Phrygian cap with flaps, as he would two centuries later on Roman reliefs. This clasping of hands (*dexiôsis*), or oath of alliance, here characterizes the union of Mithras and the Sun. But in the sanctuary of Arsameia on the Nymphaeum, a rocky corridor has unduly aroused comparisons with future Mithraic caverns. The inscriptions of the Nimrud Dagh add to Mithras' name those of Helios, Hermes and Apollo as so many equivalents. They would be found again in the Roman West of the second and third centuries AD. But neither at the Nimrud Dagh nor on the sites of Samosata, Selik or Arsameia can one decipher the slightest reference to the bull sacrifice that would be at the centre of Mithraic mysteries and crypts.

The king of Pontus, Mithridates VI Eupator (despite his name) did not take his inspiration from the Iranian god, but from Dionysus in his role of liberator god of the Greeks in the face of the Roman dominators.[25] On his coins, as on those of the towns of Pontus and Paphlagonia struck during his reign, Pegasus and Perseus have the starring roles. For the Greek hero was taken to have founded the Persian nation and even instituted fire worship. The coins of Mithridates and Panticapaeum (where the king died in 63 BC), like those of Amastris in Paphlagonia, bear on the obverse an effigy wearing the Phrygian cap, which has been identified as Mithras, while Dionysus is shown on the reverse. Others represent the head of Bacchus or Apollo. It was at Panticapaeum also that terracotta statuettes were discovered, datable to the first century BC, showing a child wearing the *pileus* like Mithras:[26] now, like Mithras, he is overcoming a bull, a knife in his hand . . . But, curiously, this bull-slayer has the costume and look of an Attis! These figurines (one example of which was found in the tomb of a woman) do not demonstrate that Mithraism penetrated the Bosphorus from Trapezus (Trebizond) in the reign of Mithridates Eupator.

On the other hand, we know that Mithridates' officers were in command of the Cilician pirates who, according to Plutarch (*Life of Pompey*, 24, 7), were the first to celebrate the mysteries of Mithras. They attacked sailors, ravaged the islands of the Aegean and even the coasts of Italy, pushing their audacity as far as to carry off Roman magistrates or their children. It is conceivable that groups of 'irregulars', organized clandestinely to resist Roman imperialism, should have felt the need to galvanize the combatants' energies in a cult sacralizing their adherence by an initiatory vow and a communal banquet. If Plutarch is well informed, Mithraism would appear to have germinated and grown in the framework of military terrorism and masculine groups armed against the occupying power.

It was at Tarsus, in Cilicia (from where the first initiates to the mysteries came), that coins were struck bearing the effigy of the emperor Gordian III (238–44), with the bull-slaying Mithras on the reverse. A Heracles Sandan, the sacrificer of bulls, was worshipped at Tarsus, at the same time as Perseus glorified (as we have seen) on the money of Mithridates, who upheld the pirates' action. Pegasus, the winged horse of Perseus and Bellerophon, figures only in exceptional cases in the imagery of the caverns – on a stele in the Museo Torlonia[28] – despite the connection of his name with the 'spring' (*pege* in Greek), which plays an important role in both the myth and the liturgy of Mithras. However, Perseus also wears an Asian cap and, on the map of the skies, brandishes his sword above the Bull. An astronomical explanation has therefore been proposed for the incorporation of Perseus into Mithraism.[29] The precession of the equinoxes had caused the spring equinox to fall back from the sign of the Bull into that of the Ram. The Stoics of Tarsus would seem to have allegorized the representation of Perseus, assimilated in this instance to Mithras, so as to read into it the ousting of the zodiacal Bull. The frequent image in the Orient, and later in the West, of the lion bringing down a bull would correspond to that of the lion-headed Time in the *Mithraea*. It is not the only sidereal explanation applied to the Bull-slayer, nor is it the most convincing. But in the development of Mithraic theocosmology, astrology and Stoicism seem to have had their share, together with Mithridates and the Cilician pirates.

In the psychological war orchestrated by the king of Pontus, Dionysian propaganda may have been coupled with prophecies like the famous oracles of Hystaspes, which inspired hopes of the coming of a saviour, 'great king', sent by Zeus as 'leader of the holy militia'. His reign would coincide with that of the Sun at the end of a cycle matching that of the Mithraic ladder with seven doors, i.e., a sidereal week.[30] The Mithras of the mysteries, 'Invincible Sun', would also appear as the protagonist of a *sancta militia*. Had Nigidius Figulus, who borrowed from the Magi the prediction of a reign of Apollo or the celestial fire setting the universe ablaze (like the ekpurosis of the Stoics), and the Virgil of the IVth Eclogue (*tuus iam regnat Apollo*), perceived echoes of that apocalypse in which the name of the Sibyl was involved?

We know that, after crushing the pirates, Pompey installed a few of them as peasants in Apulia, and the old man of Tarentum celebrated by Virgil (*Georgics*, IV, 125ff) is none other than one of those Corycians recycled into beekeeping (later Porphyry would comment on bees in connection with Mithraic mysteries). Why should not these first worshippers of the Bull-slayer have planted the earliest seeds of beliefs which – it is true – would not come to full fruition until fifteen decades later? When the Roman Republic was in its death throes, a whole spate of oracular literature flourished confusedly in a mingling of heterogeneous trends which are very difficult to detect today among the scraps of later scholiasts or in the allusions of poets. We have to believe that Mithraic tradition was not extinguished with the repression of the Cilician terrorists. It survived on the fringes of cultic expression, whether public or private, in the Roman world, in conditions that are impossible to grasp. Really, though it was *ab origine* a 'mystery' religion, one realizes that it was able to make its way and take shape obscurely, like other secret societies.

However that may be, neither in Rome nor in Italy can any concrete evidence of it be found before the end of the first century AD.

Mithras in Italy

Painting with broad brushstrokes a picture of Roman religion in Caesar's time, J. Carcopino stated: 'Mithras . . . then recruited his first followers'.[31] For his part, Cumont, comparing the Iranian *diaspora* to that of the Jews, imagined the Mithraists being implanted somewhere in the Trastevere district, while admitting that they had no more hold at that time than similar small groups of Buddhists had in pre-1914 western Europe.

In reality, we have to wait until the time of Nero to pinpoint certain signs which have been avidly exploited by historians. After eight years of war between Rome and the Parthians, the latter acknowledged the emperor's sovereignty over Armenia, whose king, Tiridates, agreed to come to the *Urbs* to be crowned by Nero in 66. According to Pliny the Elder (*Natural History*, XXX, 17), the king, who was of Arsacid lineage, had himself accompanied by Magi and 'initiated' the emperor to their 'banquets' (*magicis etiam cenis eum initiaverat*). When Tiridates came to prostrate himself at the emperor's feet, he saluted him as his 'god', giving him the name Mithras (Cassius Dio, *Roman History*, 63, 5, 2).

We know of the heliac and Apollonian pretensions of Nero, whom a colossal statue some 35 m high represented as the Sun in the vestibule of his Golden House (the colour of a *solar* palace). Is that enough to permit the supposition that Mithraism had then penetrated Rome and the imperial court? If the 'magic' banquets Pliny mentions already matched those of the Mithraic caverns, it would be necessary to believe that the ritual of the mysteries had taken shape among the Parthians, since Tiridates was the brother of their king, Vologeses I . . . something that seems suspect. In fact, these meals must have had a connection with the coronation of Persian kings in which, according to Plutarch (*Life of Artaxerxes*, 3, 1–2), the Magi participated. The sovereign had to taste a fig cake, chew terebinth and drink a goblet of whey. As for hailing Nero as 'Mithras', that can be explained by the very fact that the emperor conferred on Tiridates the consecration of royal power of which Mithras was still the divine guarantor.

Furthermore, Corbulo's campaigns, which had resulted in this homage from an Arsacid to the sovereign Caesar, may well have contributed to Mithras' infiltration into the Roman army. The batches of recruits raised in Galatia and Cappadocia, and the legionaries' prolonged contacts with Armenia and troops stationed in Commagene – where the god had his hereditary devotees – must certainly have had some connection with the effective emergence of Mithraism in the West. In 71 or 72, the transfer of the XVth *Apollinaris* (significant name) legion to Carnuntum had restricted, but religiously very precise, effects along the banks of the Danube. A centurion of foreign origin named 'Barbarus' would soon consecrate an altar to Mithras there. Certain bricks used in building the *Mithraeum* of Deutsch-Altenburg bear the mark of this same legion which, in 114, returned to the Orient – there to revitalize the Persian cult perhaps on the banks of the Euphrates, owing to a war against the Parthians. Vespasian ordered the return to Moesia (Dobroudja) of the IVth *Macedonica* legion, which had also fought the Parthians, then the Jews, and whose officers later showed their piety towards the 'Invincible Sun'. Lastly, the IInd *Adiutrix* legion, raised in 69–70 and recruited partly from freedmen of Asiatic origin, served in Britain before being posted, under Trajan, to Aquincum on the Danube where Mithras had many followers. During the first century AD, the annexation of vassal kingdoms such as Cappadocia, western Pontus, Commagene and Armenia Minor favoured these presumed currents of influence (there is no way of verifying them).

Here again, as in the case of the Egyptian and Syrian cults, slaves who had come from the Orient following the campaigns of Corbulo and Titus must have had some part in the Romanization of the Iranian

god who had been Hellenized in Anatolia. One of the earliest epigraphic attestations is the bilingual dedication (in Latin and Greek) of
an imperial freedman, a former slave who had entered the service of
Titus, then probably of Domitian.[33] Around the same period, or a little
later, an agricultural slave of Tiberius Claudius Livianus (who became
praetorian Prefect in 101) dedicated 'to the Sun Mithras' a sculpted
group which is housed today in the British Museum (plate 24). It is the
oldest known and dated example of the Bull-slayer.[34] Two other slaves
belonging to the same Claudius Livianus are celebrated by the poet
Martial (*Epigrams*, IX, 103) when he compares them to Castor and
Pollux. Apparently there were some pretty influential persons in the
imperial entourage.

Another court poet of the same generation, Statius, inaugurated
reference to the Bull-slayer in literary tradition. Statius was the author
of a *Thebaïd*, published in 92 at the latest, after twelve years' work. The
first of the epic's twelve cantos, composed and even read in public
before 83 (Juvenal, *Satires*, VII, 82ff) ends with an invocation by
Adrastus, king of Argos, to Apollo:

Whether thou wouldst rather bear the bright red name of Titan
In the tradition of the Achaemenid people,
Or of fruitful Osiris, or of him who beneath the rocks of the
Persian Cavern twists the horns of the stubborn bull: Mithras!

This is the last name in the first canto of the *Thebaïd*, as the first
canto of the *Iliad* ends on the name of Hera, and the first canto of the
Odyssey on that of Athena ... [35] Adrastus is descended from Perseus,
and the adjective *Persei* applied to the Mithriac cavern refers us as
much to the Greek hero as to Persia (we have seen that Perseus
perhaps had a hand in the shaping of Mithraism in Asia Minor). The
lines of Statius, in any case, bear witness that Mithras with Osiris is
henceforth incorporated into solar syncretism. In this regard, the
prayer of the Perseid remarkably actualizes the terms of the Theban
epic: it is a real 'aggiornamento' of the classical pantheon. The stories
of Osiris and the heliac prerogatives of the Alexandrian Serapis were
not unknown to the readers of Statius, above all in a period when the
Egyptian gods were enjoying imperial favour.

The poet explains himself at greater length and in particular about
Mithras, whose final naming arises like an epiphany, a revelation, or
the solution of a puzzle. This god is a newcomer, but Statius' description suggests the view of a painting, a relief or a sculpted group in the
niche of a sanctuary vaulted to look like a grotto (*sub rupibus antri*). We
are speaking of a picture that was apparently familiar to his public,
which was by no means a coterie of initiates, for the *recitationes* of

Statius attracted large numbers of people, if we are to believe Juvenal (*Satires*, VII, 82–6).

This evocation synchronizes two moments in the mythical sequence: when Mithras grasps the bull's horns and then when, overcoming the animal, twisting (*torquentem*) and mastering it like a toreador, he drags it into the cave to sacrifice it. The poet fixes one's attention on the instant prior to the act of salvation. But his synthesizing description implies all the earlier deeds, the valour and the *ponos* of the invincible god. This 'pseudo-Virgilian' religiously actualizes the genre of mythological epic, soon to be mocked and decried, according to beliefs which intrigued his contemporaries. We must not forget that Statius was Neapolitan, from a region where the oriental gods were, so to speak, well established.

Rome was to become a dynamic centre of Mithraic art. Although craftsmanship developed in the provinces (to serve local communities), in the production of stelae and styles peculiar to the Rhine and Danube territories, the greatest inspiration frequently came from the *Urbs*.

Places of worship multiplied then in Italy, first of all in the south. The painted crypt of Capua may have been created in its original state before 140 or 150.[36] Mithras gained a foothold in the ports of Sicily (Syracuse, Catana, Palermo) and Campania (Naples, Pozzuoli), in the islands of Ponza, Ischia and Capri, at Antium and Ostia on the Tyrrhenian Sea, and Aquileia on the Adriatic where the Alexandrian gods were already anchored. Even in the interior of the peninsula, around Rome, in Latium, southern Etruria, but also in Umbria, in Cisalpine Gaul along the major traffic routes and sometimes even on the fringes of townships in some secondary localities, evidence mounts up from the Antonine era to the dawn of the fourth century.[37]

The *Urbs* may have contained a hundred or so *Mithraea*.[38] Around twenty have been identified on the site that is currently known and cleared at Ostia, where the earliest are datable to the reign of Antoninus Pius (around AD 150–60).[39]

The Mithraic Diaspora in the West

With a much lower density, Mithraic communities became located in the Roman Maghreb, in the ports as in Italy but also in the hinterland

---

Plate 24 Mithras the Bull-slayer (from Rome; London, British Museum)

by reason of the road network, urbanization and the military presence. At the end of the second century, Tertullian, the son of a centurion of the urban cohort who had perhaps been initiated into the mysteries, bears witness to the impact of Mithraism in Carthage and the esteem it aroused even among Christians. In the legionary camp of Lambaesis in Numidia, Mithras was side by side with Jupiter Dolichenus and the Syrian gods. Around 190, he had followers as far as Volubilis, in Tingitana (Morocco). But as a whole, apart from Carthage and Lambaesis, the *Mithraea* were somewhat scattered in this sector of the western Mediterranean.[40]

Also sporadic were the finds relating to this cult on the coasts of the Iberian peninsula,[41] but they were often original and significant. Thus at Troia (Setubal) south of Lisbon, a relief was discovered which belonged to a sort of triptych reredos representing the banquet of the Sun at table with Mithras. Apart from occasional consecrations, the god penetrated the interior of the country chiefly by way of the Guadalquivir valley in the colony of *Emerita Augusta* (Merida). In 155 a quartermaster-sergeant of the VIIth *Gemina* legion offered him an altar surmounted by Mithras emerging from the rock. The same year, the 'Father' or priestly superior of the community dedicated to him a statue of Mercury, which seems to represent Mithras as the supreme mediator, beside a lyre symbolizing celestial harmony. In the Merida *Mithraeum* two statues of a god could be seen, each enlaced in the coils of a snake: one with a lion's head, the other with the face of a young man (but with a leonine mask on his chest). This brotherhood seems to have been rich and active in the Antonine era.

Perhaps Mithras reached Bordeaux via the Atlantic coast, even though the Garonne valley and the 'Gaulish isthmus' played a notable role in Narbonne's commercial relations with Aquitaine. Under the Carmelite convent at Bordeaux a *Mithraeum* was recently discovered whose dimensions justify its being regarded as the most important of this type of sanctuary in Roman Gaul.[42] A niched stele there housed an idol of the lion-headed god holding a key. At Eauze (Gers), a clothes-seller from the north-east, from Trier where the Persian god had a strong following, seems to have introduced his cult. The Rhône valley and the Alpine routes contributed to its expansion in the eastern half of Gaul. The links of the Rhenish *limes* with Lyon by way of the Moselle, Langres and the Saône also played their part.

Near to its circus Arles had a *Mithraeum* that was richly provided with marble statues, like the one of Time entwined by a coiling snake between the signs of the zodiac. Nearly two centuries ago a remarkable statuary group of Mithras slaying the bull was unearthed at La Bâtie-Montsaléon (Hautes-Alpes), a much-frequented staging-post between the Alpine passes and the Rhône basin. A rock sanctuary can still be seen at Bourg-Saint-Andéol, where the Bull-slayer carved in the rock dominates the running stream of the Tourne. Orange perhaps, certainly Vienne and Lyon had their crypts. In the capital of the Gauls, it lay not far from the barracks housing the garrison, and again a quartermaster-sergeant showed his piety by his offerings.[43]

Ascending the Rhône, one would meet Mithras along the edges of the valley, in the town of Vieu (*Venetonimagus*), where a doctor of Graeco-oriental origin probably incorporated him into the operation of his baths complex, associating him with Apollo, the Gallo-Roman god of healing waters. On the banks of Lac Léman, he was to be found at Nyon and Geneva, perhaps in connection with the main road linking the Helvetian town to the Rhinelands by way of Mandeure, where his cult is attested (*CIL*, XIII, 11556).

In the Rhône's extension northwards, the Invincible God can be found in isolated spots such as Dyo (Saône-et-Loire) but also in the crossroads-towns such as Entrains, where indigenous cults coexisted with religions of foreign origin.[44] In the resort of Les Bolards (near Nuits-Saint-Georges), whose ancient name is still unknown, a *Mithraeum* was the almost immediate neighbour of a temple consecrated to a Gaulish deity. Mithras was also present in the chief town of the Mandubians, Alésia, where he may have blended in with local devotion to the healing god, Apollo Moritasgus. The Gaulish pottery of Lezoux incorporated him into their decorative repertoire.[45]

The west and north-west of Gaul appear to have been hardly touched, but the unearthing of a *Mithraeum* at Septeuil (Yvelines) recently proved that archaeology can lead us to review inferences drawn from present documentation – which remains provisional. At all events, the cippus of Lillebonne showing a bust of the Sun does not come from a Mithraic crypt, and the two Dioscuri of Boulogne have nothing at all to do with the dadophori of the Bull-slayer.[47]

In contrast, Britain (in the Roman sense of the word, i.e., England) had several fairly richly endowed sanctuaries, notably in the south-east and along Hadrian's Wall.[48] A veteran of the IInd *Augusta* legion who had been freed at Orange consecrated in the London *Mithraeum*, in the time of Marcus Aurelius (?), a relief showing the Bull-slayer circled in the orb of the zodiac, with the Ram in the East. Dionysus figured in the sanctuary with the inscription *hominibus bagis bitam*, or in other words: '[gives] life to roving men', a probable allusion to those migrants among whom Mithras recruited a goodly number of his followers.

It is on the Germanic frontier[49] and in the Danubian provinces,[50] in central and eastern Europe, that the density of discoveries is greatest.

Mithras is found in Rhineland-Pfalz and Baden-Württemberg chiefly, between Cologne and Strasbourg, but in fact as far as Augst, in the valleys of the Main and Neckar, two notable areas of concentration – close to the *limes* – where the god appears in bas-relief on monumental stelae which number among the finest in the Roman world: especially at Heddernheim (Nida), Rückingen, Gross-Krotzenburg, Neuenheim, and Osterburken. The great cultic reliefs of Sarrebourg (*Pons Saravi*), Mackwiller and Königshofen (Strasbourg), which belong to the same typology, bear witness to the influence of this Mithraic art (plate 25). Teams from Italy clearly contributed to this sculptural flowering.

Plate 25 Cautopates from Königshofen (Strasbourg, Musée Archéologique)

In the Moselle valley, Trier seems to have been an active centre for the Persian trend.[51] This town probably had several *Mithraea*, including one which was constructed around the late third century in a house built on a theatre destroyed by the first invasions, in a period when Trier attained the rank of administrative capital of the Gauls, not far from the Roman defence line on the Rhine. In Germania, not all manifestations of Mithraic worship stemmed from the army, but the establishment of *Mithraea* there often remained connected with military camps. Their size and capacity were generally in keeping with the large stelae mentioned above. Apparently, they housed the devotions of communities that were more numerous than those of Rhodanian Gaul, for example. As in Gaul (Vieu, Septeuil, Alésia), the Bull-slayer there was sometimes associated with worship of springs.

Farther east and south, in Raetia, *Mithraica* are more random, but at Mauls we find a cultic relief with many scenes of the Rhenish type (plate 26).[52] The concentration is much more striking in Noricum, on the Danube, at Linz and Lauriacum, and above all in Carinthia in the region of Klagenfurt, notably at Virunum where imperial administration gives us several indications of its backing in favour of the Persian cult. The road connections of this sector with north Italy, and of Milan (where there is no lack of signs of Mithraic piety) with the port of Aquileia, must have played as decisive a role as the military routes along the Raetio-Danubian *limes*.

The Mithraic Diaspora in Eastern Europe

The establishment of Mithras is even more distinct and tightly packed in the two Pannonias, whose territory occupied part of present-day former Yugoslavia, Austria and Hungary.[53] Two zones of special density are situated, one at Ptuj-Pettau (Poetevio) on the Drava and south of Ljubljana (Emona) and Sisak (Siscia) in particular; the other in the Danube valley between Vienna and Paks, notably at Carnuntum and Aquincum (near Budapest).

Poetevio lay at the crossing of roads that were much frequented by traders and officials or troops moving from one posting to another. A road passed through there linking Aquileia, and thus the Adriatic, to Carnuntum. It is punctuated with explicit testimonies. At Sisak as at Ptuj, the names of the Mithraists often betray their eastern origins. A camp was called *Commagena* (or *Comagenae*?) to the north-east of Noricum: there Mithras was the recipient of a dedication 'for the safeguarding of the Commagenians'. We have seen that the XVth *Apollinaris* legion came from Commagene. On the other hand, a 'wing'

212   Beneath the Rocks of the Persian Cavern

of Commagenian cavalry took up its position on the Danube in
Trajan's time, in 106.

But at Virunum and Poetevio above all, Mithras recruited his
followers among the slaves and freedmen of the financial administration service. If his cult was imported there, conversely a native of Putj,
the legate Marcus Valerius Maximianus (who may have been touched
by the grace of the Invincible only in Dacia) subsequently exported it
to the Lambaesis camp in Africa.[54]

In Dacia and two provinces of Moesia (present-day Romania and
Bulgaria),[55] both north and south of the Danube and on its lower

Plate 26 Stele from Mauls (Sterzing-Vipiteno)

reaches as far as the Black Sea, *Mithaica* proliferated: they account for some 400 numbers in the corpus of M.J. Vermaseren, without counting the discoveries that have been made over the last twenty or thirty years, and which continue to be made. Evidence of devotion is especially plentiful at Apulum (Alba Julia) and Romula. Sarmizegetusa, the old capital of the Dacian kings, had one of the most spacious crypts in the Roman world. Syrians seem to have played a role in this promotion of Mithraism in Roman Dacia, if not actually in its Danubian acclimatization, for we know of a corps of Commagenian cavalry (the Ist *Flavia Commagenorum* cohort) that was part of the army installed in the province which had been newly annexed and organized under Trajan. Soldiers, civil servants, tax collectors and administrators of the saltworks, municipal elites which had been created from Trajan's veterans, all declared their devotion to the Bull-slayer. In Lower Moesia, discoveries abounded as far as the mouth of the Danube and, here again, it has been verified that the Persian cult was imported relatively early, at least judging by a relief representing Cautes and Cautopates, dedicated by Melichrisus, the slave of one Publius Caragonius Philopaestus, customs farmer in Illyria around AD 100.[56] In the port of Histria, the foundation of a Mithraic crypt dated to the very year when the imperial legate was the eponymous priest of Apollo *Hietros* (or 'Doctor'), demonstrates the zeal of local notabilities who had the support of the provincial authorities.[57]

The originality of Danubian Mithraism lies in its cultic reliefs.[58] Unlike the great stelae of the Rhine *limes* which show the Bull-slayer between two pilasters with historiated compartments beneath a sort of lintel occupied (like the lateral registers) by episodes from the divine *gesta* and the assembly of the Olympians, the small Danubian panels, which are often arched and sometimes carved in the shape of medallions, give a somewhat confused impression. They are characterized by two registers that unfold above and below the salvific sacrifice, but it sometimes happens that the images overflow to right and left below the upper register and overlap one another. These stelae present analogies with those showing a goddess between two horsemen (equally typical of Danubian countries), or even with certain Sabazian reliefs like that of Plovdiv (Philippopolis). At all events, it is a matter of local adaptation of canonic iconography, with the bull figuring in a kind of crescent moon-shaped boat (*scapha lunata*), which symbolically underlines the relationship of the victim's blood with Selenic humidity. This model was also found in Thrace, at Philippopolis and Serdica (Sofia), where a *Mithraeum* was brought to light.

To the west, coastal and interior Dalmatia – where the other cults of eastern origin met with a mixed reception – did not escape Mithraic infiltration, notably in Salonae where a very curious marble medallion encircles the Bull-slayer, between a snail, a lobster, a crocodile and a dolphin: symbols of the humid element released by Mithras' sacrifice. From the *Mithraeum* of Konjic [c] in Herzegovina, comes a bifaced relief whose reverse side recalls the archetypal repast served by initiates wearing Lion and Raven masks.[59]

To the east, Macedonia was only sporadically involved. Greece itself was even less so, and seems to have remained resistant. The alleged *Mithraeum* of Eleusis is still very open to question, even though the historian Eunapius stresses the personal connections of an Eleusinian hierophant with the Persian initiation in the fourth century AD.[60] Actually, the only unchallengeable monuments – of Patras and Andros – bear Latin dedications by Roman soldiers! When Plutarch, in the age of Trajan speaks of Mithraic 'consecrations' whose tradition had been preserved until his time (*Life of Pompey*, 24, 7), he is not dealing with ceremonies of which he would have had direct knowledge in Boeotia, but rather – so it would seem – of observations made in Rome, where he went in 92, at the very time when Statius published his *Thebaïd* and introduced the name Mithras into Latin poetry.

The Crimea's military relations with Moesia may suffice to explain why traces of the Iranian god are found there. Detachments of the Ist *Italica* legion and the IXth *Claudia* were, indeed, stationed there for a period. It is doubtful whether they found the source of a Mithraism which then spread its influence through the Danubian provinces, as has been conjectured.[61] The Crimea certainly had links with Trebizond, where imperial coins show us Mithras on horseback between the dadophori. But in Asia Minor, overall, the harvest of *Mithraica* is likely to disappoint historians, even though the earliest known dedication to Helios-Mithras (which is datable to AD 77/8) comes from Savçilar (on the borders of Lydia, Mysia and Phrygia). It was believed that a *Mithraeum* had been identified at Pergamum, and a sanctuary of Cybele and Mithras at Kapikaya.[62] But there is neither epigraphic nor even iconographic evidence to confirm such hypotheses. Generally speaking, the western, heavily Hellenized, coast did not adopt the Bull-slayer any more than did Greece itself. On the other hand, Cilicia has not yet yielded all its secrets. If the official coinage of Tarsus under Gordian III made a place for Helios-Mithras, together with the Moon – at the very moment when the emperor was leaving to fight the Persians – we have to believe that his cult preserved a traditional prestige there.

At all events, it took hold in the Syrian Orient, on the Euphrates (at Dura-Europos) and on the coast (at Caesarea in Palestine, Tyre, Sidon, and Laodicea). When he recalled the XVth *Apollinaris* legion to Syria to fight the Parthians, Trajan may have contributed to sowing the seeds of Mithraism in those parts. In Egypt, the impact was fairly weak, outside the Delta (the alleged 'Liturgy of Mithras' of the famous papyrus commented upon by A. Dieterich, when all is said and done, has nothing whatsoever to do with the god of the mysteries).[63] But a representation such as that of the lion-headed Time bears the mark of an Alexandrian heritage.[64] Lastly, up to the present Libya and Tripolitania have revealed only rather tenuous and problematical indications.

One therefore gets the feeling that Mithraism, as an initiatory religion, was developed and shaped away from its original setting, owing to this migration itself. For by expatriating itself with its followers, it had all the greater need for a 'mystery' structure. A rank like that of 'Persian' made sense only outside Persia or the Iranianized Orient (unless the name refers to Perseus? . . .).

In his astrological chronography, Ptolemy (*Tetrabiblos*, II, 3) attributes central and southern Asia, from India to Assyria, to the power of Aphrodite-Isis and Kronos-Mithras, while the Phoenicians and Chaldaeans were concerned with the Lion and the Sun. In fact, we find Mithras under the name Miro (or Mirro) as far as on Kushan coins.[65] As regards his cult, the god had followers almost everywhere, from the Indus to Scotland, from Germania to the edges of the Sahara, but they were more numerous in Rome and Ostia, on the one hand, and in the lands of the Rhine and Danube, on the other: at the centre of government and in the camps or garrison towns which watched over the safety of the Empire.

A Religion of the Crypt

People have often quite justifiably emphasized or suggested the fundamental relationship of a religion and the representation of the world it implies with cultic architecture. O. Spengler insisted on it in the terms of a daring comparativism:

All these religions, Christian, Judaic, Persian, Manichean, syncretist . . . , whatever their doctrinal particularities . . . , are imbued with an equal religiousness that is expressed in an equal experience of depth, generating a suitable spatial symbolism. Christian basilicas, cults of Baal, of Hellenistic Jews, of Mithras, the fire of Mazdan temples, mosques, all express an equal mental attitude: the feeling of the crypt.[66]

There is truth in this *a priori* alarming list, and more precisely in the case of the *Mithraea*.

Unlike the other religions of oriental origin, Mithraism included no public ceremonies. People could take part in the festivals of Attis or Isis without being initiated or incorporated in the priestly body. So Cybele's sanctuaries and those of the Egyptian gods had their place in the town among the other sacred buildings, even if they were in theory isolated from the profane world by an enclosing wall. Certain rites were secretly celebrated there by the priests, for their consecration or the initiation of mystae. But a large part of the worship was periodically open to the popular masses, often with the backing and co-operation of the official authorities and the great state bodies, on whom the solemn vows and divine benedictions reflected.

Mithraists, too, prayed for the safety of the emperor and the Empire. But their worship was hidden. It was carried out on the fringes of the temples and places frequented in broad daylight by ordinary pagans. Mithras was honoured only among initiates, and initiation immediately attached them to a priestly hierarchy. They were engaged *ipso facto* in a 'militia' in the service of the god and the community. This deliberate marginalization rendered them even more suspect than the other polytheists in the eyes of Christians, who accused them of having an affection for shadowy caverns.[67] Did not some followers of the Mithraic crypt bear the name *cryphii*, the 'hidden ones'?

Indeed, the *Mithraea* were not open to all and sundry. Admission was reserved for previously consecrated devotees, and the premises were of a singular kind, not like temples, and sometimes situated outside towns, in the open countryside, but also frequently in the centre of town, in a private house or even in the shadow of a public building. Like the Mithraists themselves, several of their caverns were physically incorporated into, but religiously foreign to, the urban environment.

In parallel with the earliest Christian places of worship, they often benefited from the generosity of a private individual (who offered his land and even financed the building work and decoration of the *Mithraeum*) or from his kindness in allowing his co-religionists to use his own dwelling. Several crypts are known in Rome that were organized in premises belonging to this or that rich *domus*; for example, under the church of Santa Balbina, in the home of Lucius Fabius Cilo, prefect of the *Urbs* in 203, or in a complex of buildings which seems to have belonged to Trajan's private residence under the church of Santa Prisca. The *Mithraeum* of the Palazzo Barberini, celebrated for its painted panel, occupied a rearranged room in the house erected on that spot in the first century AD. At Ostia, the Mithraists of the 'Casa di Diana' met in a room that was set back in the rear of the house. The *Mithraeum* of Vulci stood against the House of the Cryptoportico, in a sector corresponding to the domestic outbuildings.[68] The two sanctuaries in Aquincum were absorbed into the urban fabric, linked with local dwellings. At the foot of Mount Cefalo, between Itri and Gaeta, the cryptoportico of a Roman villa was reused as a *Mithraeum* and, in this instance as elsewhere, advantage was taken of the water inflow system for the needs of the cult.[69] At Marino, not far from the Alban lake, it was again in a Roman villa that the Bull-slayer found shelter, this one magnificently decorated with frescoes.[70]

He was also to be found receiving worship in commercial premises in the river port area of Rome; or in the stables of the 'Greens' faction at San Lorenzo in Damaso; or in the Circus Maximus, in the head-quarters of a company connected with chariot races. One recalls that the *Mithraeum* at Arles was housed in an annexe of the circus. Others in Rome were in the outbuildings of the Baths of Titus, Caracalla and Constantine, at Ostia in the Baths known as those 'of Mithras'. The complexes of certain administrative buildings offered equal possibil-ities which the Mithraists did not hesitate to make use of when the occasion arose – above all when they were in the employ of the state – with the benevolent tolerance of the imperial authority: for instance, under the basilica of San Clemente or the Hospital of San Giovanni (near the Lateran) where the water supply of a former cistern was carefully collected for liturgical uses.[71] Lastly, several barracks were commonly the setting for their chaste banquets, starting with the barracks of the Praetorians, then those of the horsemen or *equites singulares* of the imperial guard, of the Vigiles and the *Castra Peregrina* (under the church of Santo Stefano Rotondo).[72]

On the Danube or the Rhine, or along Hadrian's Wall in Scotland, the *Mithraea* were close to the camps and fortified posts of the Roman legions. It also happened that they were installed at the gates of the town, in an area frequented by travellers and where the soldiers got their supplies, as at Königshofen near *Argentoratum* (Strasbourg). But it seems that people also liked to honour the god amid natural surroundings, against the wall of a cliff cut for this purpose and sculpted to show the Bull-slayer in relief, as at Bourg-Saint-Andéol (Ardèche) or Schwarzerden (Germany), but preferably bordering a watercourse or near a springhead. At Zlodjev Grabeen or 'Devil's Rock', in Slovenia, the *Mithraeum* occupied a real grotto. A sanctuary confined on three sides by natural rock, in the middle of the forest, has been recognized at Rožanec. At Modrič (west of Ptuj), men working in the mines and quarries of Pohorje clubbed together to set up their place of worship in a grove, above a fast-running stream.[73] On the western flank of the Halberg, near Sarrbrücken, a small *Mithraeum* dominating the Sarre, not far from the Roman fortress, must have welcomed officers and men from the garrison in the evenings.

Other rock sanctuaries have been recognized at Tirgusor (Romania), Cavtat (Croatia) and Nefertara (Bosnia). They answered a certain mythical tradition legitimized by Zoroaster. According to one Eubulus, the author of an 'Inquiry into Mithras' quoted by the Neoplatonist Porphyry (*The Cave of the Nymphs*, 6), the famous Iranian prophet was said to have consecrated the first Mithraic cavern in the heart of the mountains, amid springs and flowers.

In principle, the *Mithraeum* thus had the appearance of a grotto (*spelaeum*) or a crypt. Hence the recovery of cryptoporticoes or half-buried buildings, service passages, cisterns (under the San Giovanni Hospital, for example), outbuildings of boiler-rooms (in the Ostian Baths 'of Mithras') and other well-sheltered premises. When this possibility was unavailable, or there was not even the opportunity to rearrange a rocky surface outside a town, Mithraists simply dug into the ground to create the imitation of a crypt and the illusion of descending beneath the level of the ordinary world. In such a case, the *Mithraeum* would have the appearance of a house covered with a double-pitched roof, or even the aspect of a Christian basilica, like the London sanctuary of Walbrook.

But inside, in every case, the ceiling was constructed in the form of a vault thanks to a system of beams and fliers, carefully plastered to give the sanctuary the look of a grotto. If necessary, bursts of pumice stones or gravel cemented here and there above the cultic image, in the sanctuary chancel, helped to evoke the memory of the Zoroastrian cavern.

Above all, the intention of the *spelaeum* was to remind the faithful of the grotto into which Mithras dragged the bull, before sacrificing it and eating the flesh of the victim off its carcase in the company of the Sun. Mithraists gathered to re-enact this archetypal meal. Their sanctuaries therefore had the functional structure of an ancient-style dining-hall; that is to say, equipped with benches on which the guests reclined. But unlike the Roman *triclinia* or semi-circular dining rooms (*sigma*), the *Mithraea* contained two parallel stone beds on either side of a central aisle, which was often paved with mosaics, where the cult's priests could move around. Slightly tilted towards the walls, these *podia* generally had a rim that was wide enough to accommodate the receptacles of food and drink. The Mithraists would half recline on these benches, slantwise, their faces turned towards the rear of the crypt where gleamed the painted or sculpted image of Mithras slaying the bull – they did not kneel, as Cumont wrote. The chancel was sometimes built like a niche above a sort of platform (or *bema*), which was mounted by a few steps. In front of and below the cultic idol, tables or kinds of counter could be set up for the consecration of the food which was subsequently distributed to the members of the community. Flames lighting the god and his worshippers burned on braziers or altars. Sometimes a simple hanging, a painted canvas, represented Mithras and various episodes of the myth, the light shining through from behind. But when those in charge of the crypt acquired the wherewithal, they replaced the painted cloth with a marble relief (*CIL*, XIV, 4314). Other sculptures featured Mithras emerging from the rock, or a lion-headed god (plate 27); or the Bull-slayer's two acolytes (Cautes and Cautopates) surrounded the cultic image. But often, too, Cautes and Cautopates flanked the entrance to the nave.

The crypt was not always entered directly; it was generally preceded by a *pronaos*, a forepart of the building, or even a simple fairly spacious room where costumes were donned appropriate to the various grades of initiation. Bathing pools and various devices about which we know few details (because of the destruction they suffered, notably in the fourth century, at the hands of the Christians) were used for preliminary purification, and also for the trials to which candidates had to submit themselves. When there was no running water in the vicinity, they had to be content with a basin, or even a large jar that was often fed by water channelled from a cistern or diverted from an aqueduct. As Mithraists always needed a store of water, it is easy to understand why on occasion they gladly set up their crypt close to bathing establishments.

Sizes of *Mithraea* varied considerably. Although, including the *pronaos* and annexes, some sanctuaries attained a length of 40 m or more, the crypt itself rarely exceeded 20 m in length. Most of the *Mithraea* were much shorter and often narrow. That of the 'Casa di Diana' at Ostia, mentioned above, is only 6 m wide by 4 long. It could barely contain ten or a dozen guests. The one unearthed around 1979 near Biesheim in Alsace (Colmar arrondissement) could hardly have housed a larger number.[74] Generally speaking, to judge by the capacity of known caverns, the 'clubs' of Mithraists never assembled more than around forty, or exceptionally fifty, people. The average must have fluctuated around twenty.

We are therefore speaking of a religion of small groups, where people knew one another personally and where links were very close and strengthened by the perhaps daily practice of the communal meal.

Plate 27 Lion-headed Idol (Rome, Villa Albani; photo. Alinari)

Hence the proliferation of *Mithraea*. Those who wanted to belong to the 'club' of a sanctuary whose capacity had reached saturation point had to take steps to occupy and equip a new crypt. This multiplication of caverns was a phenomenon which, in ancient paganism, had its equivalent only with Dionysian societies whose places of worship, like the *Mithraea*, often flourished in private homes. We know that the same thing would happen with the first Christian churches.

In Rome, only some twenty crypts have actually been recognized. But a number of other finds, isolated or not, connected with cultic goods, allow us to place about fifty *Mithraea* on the map of the *Urbs*, and bearing in mind sectors that have as yet been inadequately examined, M.J. Vermaseren was able to estimate their number at around one hundred. However, other estimates multiply that by seven,[75] and the mass of Roman Mithraists properly speaking may thus have reached some ten or twenty thousand followers in the third century AD. This figure is obviously exaggerated (like those advanced for the total population of the *Urbs*). I do not think that Mithraism ever mobilized more than one or two per cent of the population. At Ostia, fewer than twenty crypts have been brought to light. What has been excavated of the town perhaps permits the figure to be put at around forty. Some 300 or 400 people may have worshipped the Bull-slayer there in the Severan era, out of a population of 20,000 or 30,000 inhabitants; that is to say, a noticeably similar proportion. The abundance of *Mithraea* on the map of discoveries relating to oriental cults in the Roman Empire may create an illusion. But although the sanctuaries proliferated for a while, the sacremental banquets for the most part gathered together only very small groups.

Myth and Mythography

The ritual celebrated in the caverns was founded on the deeds of Mithras which were its model and legitimized their re-enactment. These deeds were written into a history of the world and creation illustrated by reliefs and painted panels, on which sequences of pictures comparable to our strip cartoons surrounded the Bull-slayer. Unfortunately, these pictures have no captions and do not follow any constant order. But this is the narrative cycle which it is thought possible to reconstruct approximately, chiefly following the great stele of Osterburken.[76]

Originally, there emerged from chaos a god who was identifiable with the old Saturn, then the Earth and the Sky supported by Atlas. The three Parcae, goddesses of destiny, already dominated the world.

But then Saturn's reign was succeeded by that of Jupiter, who received from his father's hands the ultimate weapon: the thunderbolt. It was immediately used to lay low the snake-footed giants who, in the name of a maleficent power (the possible equivalent of the Iranian Ahriman), sought to take possession of the world. The Mazdean Scriptures told how the demons of the shadows had tried to mount an attack on the light. From then on Saturn rested.

But another god would take charge of Creation, which the evil spirit was perhaps trying to force into a decline through drought and thirst. This saviour god was Mithras, who miraculously rose out of a rock. Henceforth he was responsible for the Cosmos, as is signified to us by the images of Mithras holding the orb of the zodiac, on a stele from Trier,[77] or Mithras as Atlas on the Neuenheim relief (plate 28) and on the fresco in the Palazzo Barberini.[78] With his bow, at the shot of an arrow, he makes the spring leap forth at which the parched shepherds greedily slake their thirst. The trees produce fruits which the god gathers, and the fields corn which he harvests (Dieburg relief).

But the world remains under threat, it seems, for want of the moisture that passes from the Moon into a bull. The animal which possesses this vital substance (and which we see lying in a lunar boat, *scapha lunata*, on Danubian stelae) at first escapes Mithras. The god must set fire to the house where the bull has taken refuge and hidden itself, so that he can force it to come out and be able to capture it. Mithras gets a grip on the animal, overcomes it, sometimes getting astride it like a tamed horse, and hauls it on his back by its hind legs, its head hanging down. Mithras taurophorus (*qui portavit humeris iuvencum*, says a metrical inscription of Santa Prisca) thus fulfils the rite of 'passage', *transitus dei*, like all the other Mithraists, soldiers, officials, slaves or itinerant traders, who carry their burden.

The victorious god then goes into a grotto to put the bull to death, following the command of the gods that is transmitted perhaps by a raven, the messenger of the Sun. Immobilizing the beast by holding its muzzle with one hand and pressing his right foot down on its pastern, he plunges his knife into the hollow beneath its shoulder. No sooner has the blood spurted from the wound when a snake and a dog hasten to lick it up, while a scorpion and sometimes a crab attack the victim's genitals. Frequently a lion approaches the bowl into which the blood has flowed. Trees seem to grow and branch out around the bull. The entire animal and plant creation thus appears to profit from the sacrifice.

Plate 28 Stele from Neuenheim (photo. Karlsruhe Museum)

On several painted or carved panels, we see a ray leave the Sun (shown as a bust above the grotto) to strike the Bull-slayer, whose gaze is directed towards the day-star. Apparently the Sun is co-operating in the action of the saviour god, who is inspired by the Olympians, to be seen on several stelae presiding over the sacrifice. But one gets the impression also that a sort of rivalry at first sets him against Mithras, who is trying to mount his chariot: to supplant him? From the fact that Mithras bears the name 'Invincible Sun' (*Sol Invictus*) on the dedications, it is justifiable to suppose that by his deeds he acquires the Sun's prerogatives: so on some monuments he is depicted with rays from his head. At all events, the Sun must make an act of allegiance, whereupon Mithras confers a kind of accolade on him. Holding his head with one hand, with the other he brandishes an often indistinct object which has been variously identified as a Phrygian cap, a rhyton or even the bull's thigh! In fact, it must rather be a military bag which Mithras is throwing over the Sun's shoulder, and this image must correspond to the consecration of the 'Soldier', the third step in initiation, for the bag features among the symbols of the *Miles* on the mosaic of the Ostian sanctuary known as 'of Felicissimus' (figure 5). Once crowned *Miles*, the Sun is indissolubly linked with Mithras. This alliance is sealed on an altar over which they clasp each other's right hand (*dextrarum iunctio* or *dexiôsis*) and on which is cooking the meat for the meal they will share on the carcase of the victim.

The iconographic surroundings of the bull's sacrifice underline its cosmic dimension. The Sun (as a bust or standing on his quadriga) has as his counterpart the Moon, the source of the humid principle of which the bull is the keeper. The heads of the great winds (Eurus and Zephyr, Notus and Boreas) are frequently shown at the four corners of the panel. The vaulted edge of the grotto is sometimes surmounted by the seven planetary busts, but also the orb of the zodiacal constellations often overhangs or even circles the scene of the sacrifice. Occasionally, seven altars and seven trees or seven knives correspond to the seven planets, perhaps suggesting the celestial repercussions of the bull sacrifice.[79] On a stele from *Interamna* (Terni),[80] seven aligned vases beneath the sacrificial cave match seven juxtaposed altars above the vault: receptacles thought to contain the victim's blood, for which wine would be used as a substitute in Mithraic banquets. Their number matches the seven initiatory steps or grades.

Mithras is regularly flanked by two persons clad like him in Persian style, with trousers, short hitched-up or belted tunic and Phrygian cap. One holds his torch on high, the other lowers his. But there are exceptions: in Noricum, Pannonia and Dacia, rather mediocre stelae have been found on which the dadophori raise their lighted torch symmetrically or in parallel.[81] They are Cautes and Cautopates who, where they are properly in contrast, personify respectively the rising and ascendant sun on the one hand and the setting and descendant sun on the other, according to its daily and annual revolution. Thus the image of the first is often shown below the solar bust and the other below the lunar bust. But there is also a frequent reversal, and this

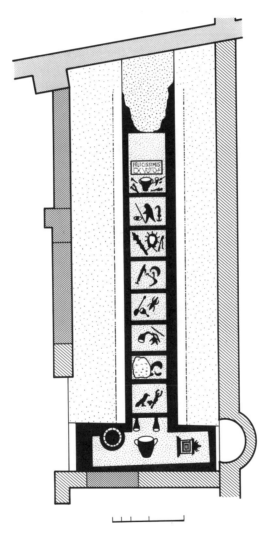

Figure 5 The Mosaic of Felicissimus, Ostia (from G. Becatti, *Scavi di Ostia*, II, *I Mitrei*, p. 107)

detail is not the least of all those that disconcert exegetes of Mithraic iconography. Sometimes the dadophori are shown, one holding a bull's head, the other a scorpion: these signs mark the entry into the hot season and the cold.[82] A whole symbolism of colours emphasized their meanings. Between Cautes and Cautopates, Mithras might appear as the Sun of mid-day or the middle. Plutarch (*Isis and Osiris*, 46, 369 e) describes him as Mesites or 'mediator' between the two worlds of Above and Below, a function that was attributed to Mercury (with whom Mithras was sometimes identified).

Above the bull sacrifice, in the middle of the zodiacal ribbon or among the lighted altars featuring the planets, one can make out (on the Palazzo Barberini fresco and formerly on a relief from the Caelian) a winged god entwined in the coils of a long snake. It was usually recognized as Time or cosmic Eternity (*Aiôn*) who is seen elsewhere endowed with a lion's head (plate 27), breathing fire, holding torches, keys or a sceptre, both feet on an armillary sphere. The example from Arles (which is headless) shows us the twelve signs of the Zodiac between the coils of the scaly reptile. In this instance, the serpent must therefore symbolize the annual circumvolutions of the sun in the ecliptic and its passage through the different constellations (see Macrobius, *Saturnalia*, I, 17, 58ff, 69). The Albani Lionhead, in the Vatican Museum, bears on his chest and thighs only the four signs of the solstices and equinoxes, which seem to have had greater importance in the Mithraic cult: Capricorn, and Cancer, Aries and Libra.

These representations intend to signify that this entire story of salvation belonged in a cycle marked by the courses of the stars. Aries is in the east when Mithras sacrifices the bull. Far from oppressing the world below by astral fatalism, as those in the Gnostic sects were gloomily convinced, the celestial revolutions providentially guaranteed the coming of salvation. The blood shed by Mithras in fact reanimated Creation:

Et nos servasti eternali (sic) *sanguine fuso*

'And us thou hast saved by shedding the eternal blood', was deciphered on a wall of the *Mithraeum* of Santa Prisca.[83] If the epithet *(a)eternali*, whose interpretation remains problematical, was confirmed, this 'eternal' blood would be that of the divine life which irrigates the animal and plant world, like the *pneuma* of the Stoics. The sun's ray striking the Bull-slayer may symbolize the fire which gives nature life, a heat that is as necessary as the lunar moisture, and animates creatures' blood. The two busts of the Sun and the Moon may in this respect illustrate the line from Santa Prisca, since in

Roman iconography the two light-givers precisely represent eternity, particularly on the coins of Vespasian, Domitian, Trajan and Hadrian.[84] Lastly, the breath of the four Winds which often frame the bull sacrifice also shares in the divine *pneuma* which revitalizes creatures.

Basically optimistic and dynamic, Mithraists thus placed their trust in the gods to preserve them from evil and death. Like the *Pronoia* of the Stoics, their providence is in accord with the order and revolutions of the universe. The Neoplatonist Proclus writes that, according to the 'Mithraic mysteries', Themis (divine Justice) coincides with Necessity, that is, with astral destiny.[85]

One then understands why, on some painted panels, Mithras the Bull-slayer's wind-filled cloak is blue as the sky and star-studded like the firmament. The ceiling of several *Mithraea* was decorated to represent that same firmament. That of San Clemente in Rome is pierced by eleven holes, including seven circular ones corresponding to the seven planets. Imagery on some floors and several walls is in accord with this cosmic dimension. In the 'Mitreo delle Sette Sfere' at Ostia, the floor of the central corridor has seven mosaic curves which, equidistant from one another, evoke the interlocking of the planetary spheres; as well as the Sun at chancel level, these are personified by six divinities on the front of the benches; the Moon and Mars, at the entrance, then Mercury and Venus, Jupiter and Saturn. On the rims of the *podis* are the twelve signs of the zodiac, starting with Aries, who always takes first position, as recalled by a line from Santa Prisca:[86]

Primus et hic aries astrictius ordine currit

'Here, too, the Ram runs at the head, strictly in order'. The planetary gods feature on the painted walls of the 'Mitreo delle Sette Porte' at Ostia. The seven grades or stages of initiation were placed under their protection.

To some extent the founding of *Mithraea* was consecrated by the stars. The zodiac occupying the vault of a cultic niche on Ponza (an island opposite Terracina) shows the two Bears and the Dragon which match a disposition of the sky in 212.[87] The planets of the 'Mitreo delle Sette Sfere' can be explained by their position in relation to the sun at dawn on 21 March 172, the day on which the sun entered Aries.[88] A graffito of Santa Prisca dates the consecration of the *Mithraeum* to 20 November 202, when the Bull disappeared shortly before dawn, the Lion remaining high in the sky. Judging by its orientation, it seems that the Königshofen *Mithraeum* was inaugurated on the day of the summer solstice.

Attempts have been made to apply astronomical or astrological exegeses to the pictures of the bull sacrifice.[89] The bull and scorpion, indeed, are in opposition there as in the zodiac, as also in the hands of Cautes and Cautopates. The Scorpion was taken to govern the genital parts, which it pinches precisely in order to suck the victim's sperm. Beside the lion on many Rhine and Danubian stelae the bowl could refer to the constellation *Crater Liberi* or the Cup. Curiously, too, the snake featured between the scorpion and the bowl approximately matches the position of the signs with the same names on the celestial map. But what would be the meaning of the crab placed next to the scorpion on the relief of Ottaviano Zeno, on the Caelian? In this perspective, how is one to interpret the raven and the eagle that are to be seen elsewhere symmetrically perched on the edges of the grotto?

M.P. Speidel tried hard to see in Mithras the constellation of Orion, who was reputed to protect soldiers and officials of the Empire, in short the regular clientele of the Persian cult.[90] The iconography of the Bull-slayer would partly agree with the place occupied *c.* 100 BC along the Equator by several constellations between the Bull and the Scorpion: Orion (= Mithras?), Canis Minor, the Hydra, the Cup (under the Lion), the Raven, the Virgin's Ear of corn. But Greek Fable makes Orion the victim of a scorpion, which does not sit well with the image of the Invincible God. Orion was the son of the Earth, and not born of stone like Mithras. Certainly, he ordered the destiny of people who travelled on official missions or for business, but this horoscope of Orion was deemed maleficent. It is therefore difficult to imagine that Mithraists could have magnified him in their cultic and canonic imagery.

Many other objections arise to rule out this symbolic interpretation. Naturally, bearing in mind the strong astrological permeation of Mithraism under the evident influence of Stoic fatalism, it cannot be denied that some elements of its iconography may be the subject of particular explanations, like those on which certain doctrinaires of the Stoa were so keen, but only secondarily and without in any way giving rise to the inference that they inspired the whole composition of the bull sacrifice.

That composition and the image itself of Mithras striking the bull have very obscure origins.

In the Orient, bulls were sacrificed to obtain the benefits of rain in time of drought. Not so long ago, it seems, Caucasian peasants were still cutting the throats of cattle to moisten the earth with the victims' blood. Curiously, however, the Pahlavian texts ascribe the killing of the primordial bull to Ahriman, and people wondered whether Zoroastrian condemnation of the bloody sacrifice had not caused the spirit of evil to be credited with the bull-slaying for which Mithras had originally been responsible. According to F. Cumont and I. Gershevitch, Ahriman came first, and Mithras only secondarily assumed the role of sacrificer in its quality of promoting life.[91] For H. Lommel, it was the death of Soma in the book of the Vedas – a murder in which Mithras colluded – which lay at the origin of the bull-slaying.[92] As may be seen, the dossier is far from closed! At all events, Mithraism was formed in a Near East imbued with Hittite and Semitic traditions, where the bull embodied the fecundating and fertilizing power of rain magically liberated by slaughter.

As for the imagery of the Bull-slayer himself, it apparently proceeds from the *Nikè* or *bouthutousa* ('sacrificing the ox') 'Victory' which adorned the balustrade of the temple of Athena Nikè on the Acropolis.[93] Figures of this Nikè prospered at the very period when Mithraic art emerged; for example on the frieze of the Ulpian Basilica, in Trajan's Forum, or on the Arch of Benevento. It was an adaptation, but had something symbolic about it since the 'invincible' god took the place of Victory. Nevertheless, the general type of the bull sacrifice became set and complete only gradually. The first dated example (the group offered by the slave Claudius Livanius: plate 24) shows us two minuscule dadophori behind the bull (and not framing the sacrifice), and Cautes, instead of raising his torch, lifts the victim's tail, which one imagines (for it is mutilated) to have been radiating ears of corn. Later, this iconongraphy was enriched and overladen with various motifs relating to the myth or the ritual. It cannot be ruled out that in certain communities a secondary emphasis was put on an astrological set of themes, but there is no verification that such themes fundamentally determined the design that was common to all painted or sculpted bull sacrifices.

In any case, the planetary week, which remains our own and which the Mithraists seem to have adopted, was of astrological origin. It is not certain if they sanctified Sunday, the day of the Sun, as Cumont supposed.[94] But we find busts arranged in the weekly order of today above (stele of Bologna) or below (bronze plaque of Brigetio, Hungary) the bull-slaying Mithras, from the Moon to the Sun or from Saturn to Venus. This order does not match the initiatory grades (Mercury–Venus–Mars–Jupiter–Moon–Sun–Saturn), or that of the planetary spheres, as they were pictured interlocking above the Earth (Moon–Mercury–Venus–Sun–Mars–Jupiter–Saturn). However, initiates were shown a 'ladder with seven doors surmounted by an eighth' in order to explain to them the stages that a soul must climb to reach the heavenly homeland (Origen, *Against Celsus*, VI, 22). The eighth door in fact corresponded to the sphere of the Fixed Stars above which burned the divine fire of the Empyrean.

But the first seven doors were not set out according to the astro-physical schema of the Ancients. They were identified in succession as those of Kronos (Saturn), Aphrodite (Venus), Zeus (Jupiter), Hermes (Mercury), Ares (Mars), Selene (Moon), and lastly Helios. Each door was made of a different metal, from lead for Saturn to gold for the Sun. In other words, Mithraists conceived the gradual return to the celestial light as a great sidereal week in reverse. According to these doctrinaires imbued with Stoicism, the soul could not rediscover or rebecome the divine fire except by way of re-enacting in some sort the entire cycle of the ages, starting with Saturn.

The solar conclusion of the hebdomad obviously makes us think of line 10 of the IVth Eclogue concerning the birth of the Child who embodies the advent of a new golden age, where the Moon is associated with the Sun (as on Mithraic stelae).

Casta, fave, Lucina: tuus iam regnat Apollo.

'Be propitious to him, O chaste Lucina: already thy (brother) Apollo now reigns'. The Neopythagorean Nigidius Figulus in his treatise *On the Gods* (quoted by Servius, *Commentary on the Bucolics*, IV, 10) wrote 'several people also, like the Magi, affirm that the reign of Apollo will be the last'. This reign of Apollo was seen as one of fire, thus the final conflagration of the universe anticipated by the Stoics because of the eternal return to the igneous element. A relief from Dieburg, repre-senting the myth of Phaethon, and the curious exegesis of the orator Dio of Prusa on a hymn of the Magi, gave Cumont the idea that the Mithraists, like the doctrinaires of Stoicism, could have envisaged the periodic reabsorption of the world by celestial fire.[95] Should one interpret in this sense the lion-headed, flame-breathing idol which brandishes torches on a superb marble of the Colonna gardens?[96]

After speaking of the Mithraic ladder in his *True Discourse*, Celsus compares it to the seven 'Archontes' of a Christian gnosis (which Origen identifies with that of the Ophites) and states more exactly: 'The first is pictured in the form of a lion' (Origen, *Against Celsus*, VI, 30), which refers us to the Lion-headed idol of whose existence Celsus must have been aware. The first door of the ladder is that of Kronos (Saturn), who devoured his children, as Chronos (Time) devours days. One may then wonder whether the Mithraists, like the Stoics, believed in the eternal return. On the Danubian stelae, the series of Mithras' exploits ends with the image of a bearded god (like Saturn), around whom a snake is entwined (as around the Lion-head): does this mean that the history of the world which starts with Saturn recommences with him? *Redeunt Saturnia regna*, 'Lo, the reign of Saturn returns', wrote the poet of the IVth Eclogue.

Cumont believed he could throw light on this strange Lion-headed figure as an image of infinite time,[97] as a transcription of the Zervan akarana of the Mazdaeans, already known by Eudemus of Rhodes, a disciple of Aristotle. In fact, if this representation is really of oriental origin, there is nothing precisely Iranian about it. The Lion-headed figure can be seen on Graeco-Egyptian gemstones bearing the caption *abrasax*, which is the isopsephic equivalent, like the name of Mithras (*Meithras*), of the number (365) of days in the year. It is then easy to conceive that the snake undulating between the zodiacal signs on the Arles idol could recall the sinuous and *annual* course of the sun's fire. In point of fact, a Mithraic pedestal from the Giardino della Pigna in the Vatican bears a radiate snake above the dedication (*CIMRM*, 525), and everyone knows that the snake was regarded as the supreme example of igneous creatures, even as an image of the Stoic *pneuma* (to which we shall return). As for the symbolism of the lion, it need not have been borrowed from the Persians. Astrologically speaking, the Lion was held to be the Sun's favourite house, because it was also the first sign in the canicular year. According to Tertullian (*Against Marcion*, I, 13, 5), the 'Lions' of Mithras were an allegory on the theme that was familiar to the Greeks, even outside the caverns, where the initiates of this grade administered the ordeal by fire to the neophytes, as is recalled by an inscription from Santa Prisca:[98]

... per quos consumimur ipsi

(Are we to understand that the ordeal anticipated the great final purification of the universe?)

In Phanes the Orphics honoured eternal Time. A dedication in Rome was consecrated by a Mithraic Father to 'Zeus-Helios-Mithras-Phanes'. Also from Rome must have come a relief preserved at Modena, featuring a young winged and rayed god entwined in the coils of a snake, holding the sceptre and thunderbolt of Zeus between the two halves of an egg from which flames are leaping.[99] This 'Phanes' is set in the oval of a zodiac framed by the busts of the four Winds. The monument cannot and indeed must not have been specially fashioned for a *Mithraeum*. It was however recovered and dedicated by a woman and a 'Father' (though the female name Euphrosyne was hammered out). We must believe at any rate, that this type of image was not unknown to the Mithraists, as a relief from Housesteads (England) shows us the petrogeneous god between the two halves of an egg in the orb of the zodiac. Apparently, the legionaries who frequented the cavern near the Roman fort of *Borcovicium*, on Hadrian's Wall, believed that when Mithras was 'born' he had separated the two parts of the world of which he was henceforth the mediator, between Earth and Heaven, as between the upper hemisphere (sun in the ascendant) and the lower hemisphere (sun in the descendant), between Cautes and Cautopates.

A statue from York which, though decapitated, appears to be entwined by a reptile, bears the name *Arimanius*, and J. Duchesne-Guillemin at first contemplated the identification of the Mithraic Lion-headed idol with Ahriman; the hypothesis aroused passionate argument and he eventually rejected it.[100] The mutilated idol of York remains an isolated instance.[101] But a few rare dedications honouring *Arimanius* raise the problem of dualism in the religion of the caverns. Hardly anyone now subscribes to Cumont's idea that Graeco-Roman Mithraism inherited certain beliefs of ancient Mazdaism. But the foundation of the first *Mithraeum* was dated back to Zoroaster, and he features perhaps in company with Ostanes in the cavern of Dura. That Mithraists harked back to the illustrious Magi certainly does not imply that they preserved their doctrine. But the very name Ahriman presupposes at least a reference to the Persian tradition. Plutarch (*Isis and Osiris*, 47) makes *Areimanios* a sort of tenebrous Pluto. Now, the Lion-headed figure holds the keys to infernal Hecate, and the Castelgandolfo idol shows him flanked by Cerberus. The possibility therefore remains that secondary interpretations were grafted on to this representation to turn it into the image of a fearsome god. Nor is it inconceivable that Mithraists devoted an apotropaic worship to this Arimanius. But generally speaking, the Lion-headed god (who was doubtless the subject of a consecration *Leoni sancto/deo praesenti* in the Barberini *Mithraeum*) rather represented the divine fire from which the world emerged and to which it must one day return, like the souls whose spark, at the end of the sidereal cycle, would rejoin their original element.

Mithraism thus involved a true theo-cosmology, together with a doctrine of the soul, probably in parallel with those of the Stoa, but in a mythico-religious form. In a period like that of the Antonines, when Stoicism had the prestige of an official philosophy, it is not surprising that this cult prospered by recruiting many followers from among the servants of the Empire.[102]

Nevertheless, one is still struck by the epigraphic identification of the Bull-slayer with Zeus and Jupiter, or even Oromasdes (on a denarius where the image of Tarpeia is reinterpreted as a petrogeneous Mithras).[103] Indeed, one receives the impression that the god who is the saviour and in some way restorer of Creation ended by equalling the Creator, or even supplanting him.[104] Thus Porphyry, copying Eubulus and Numenius, makes him a 'demiurge' in the

Cavern of the Nymphs, 6. In fact, after the maleficent anguipeds have been struck by lightning, it is Mithras who is responsible for the creatures of Oromasdes. This is not a unique phenomenon in the history of religions. Does not Christ often tend to overshadow God the Father?

Rituals

An ordinary and perhaps daily liturgy assembled the Mithraists to share a meal, at the hour of the *cena* or dinner, which was customarily taken in the second half of the afternoon or the evening, following public or professional activities and the subsequent relaxation in the Roman baths.

But this meal appears to have been preceded by a session of instruction, as the eucharist in the Christian mass follows a commentated reading of the holy texts or liturgy of the word. In several *Mithraea* bifaced stelae or plaques have been found that could be swivelled according to the various moments of the celebration. Some of these double reliefs bear, on one side, the exploits of the Bull-slayer and, on the other, Mithras and *Sol* at table for the feast of union. These two sides apparently correspond to the two phases of the ceremony. First, the faithful were shown the story of the world saved by Mithras, the liturgy of the picture explained. Then, the stone tablet was turned in order to re-enact the sacramental meal[105] before the gods who had set the example.

What did the Mithraists eat? Did their meal come from a real sacrifice? The discovery of chains (which would have bound the victims), daggers and knives (to cut their throats), and various bones piled in the refuse pits have led to the supposition that bloody slaughter took place in the crypts. But the altars that have been found are not at all suitable for this task. They are often hollow or more deeply hollowed out for lighting effects and do not have the functional structure of sacrificial altars properly speaking; others were used as braziers or bases. In contrast, in several *Mithraea*, below and in front of the cultic idol, tables and counters have been recognized on which the drinks and food intended for the guests could have been arranged and presented.[106] In fact, the Christians who attacked the worshippers of the Persian god blamed them, not for carrying out bloody sacrifices but for performing rites that constituted a kind of diabolical imitation of the eucharistic liturgy. 'Demons have copied this institution in the mysteries of Mithras', laments the apologist Justin (*Ist Apologia*, 66, 4):

> They offer bread and a cup of water, and they pronounce certain phrases which you know or can get to know

he continues, addressing the pagans.

In other words, the bread and water were the object of a consecration, as well as wine no doubt (we know the Mithraists drank it). Significantly, too, Justin (ibid., 67, 3–5) then recalls the two great moments in the Mass (readings from the prophets and the Gospels or Acts of the Apostles, then consecration and sharing of the Eucharist), which Christians celebrate on 'the day of the Sun'. For his part, Tertullian (*Prescription of the Heretics*, 40, 4), whose father must have been an initiate of the Mithraic cult, denounces the 'oblation of bread' among the worshippers of the Bull-slayer: *oblatio* is the precise term applied by Christians to the Eucharist.

In the majority of cases, Mithraists consumed the meat of previously sacrificed victims, like those that other pagans found in the markets. But the possibility remains that in exceptional circumstances animals were slaughtered, like those seen in procession on the painted walls of the *Mithraeum* excavated in Rome under Santa Prisca: pig, bull, cock, ram.[107] The context of the crypts has generally yielded nothing more than the bones of poultry, pigs or goats; very rarely boar, foxes and wolves. Wine mixed with water must also have been consecrated and shared in one of those 'craters' or large bowls held by the 'Lions' of Santa Prisca. On a relief from *Lopodunum* (Ladenburg, Germany),[108] we see Mithras and *Sol* stretched out on the bull's carcase, behind a tripod which carries a bunch of grapes, and again it is a bunch that the Bull-slayer proffers to the Sun on the reverse of the great stele of Heddernheim.[109] In connection with evidence of the Persian cult in Burgundy, E. Thévenot felt able to pose the question, 'Mithras, god of the vine?[110]

The equinoxes and solstices must have been especially sacred. This was verified for the spring equinox of 172, the day when the *Mithraeum* 'of the Seven Spheres', at Ostia, was opened to a new community.[111] The vernal equinox marked the anniversary of the sacrifice that had revived the world. Perhaps at the winter solstice (25 December) they celebrated the birth of Mithras emerging from the rock, which often featured in the crypts' decor. Several *Mithraea* must have been consecrated at the summer solstice or spring equinox, at the hour when the rays of the rising sun fell on the image of the Bull-slayer. But when the cavern was set up in reused premises, it might be oriented towards the south or even south-west. To the south, at the hour when the sun was at its zenith, the direction was appropriate to the median or mediating god, between Cautes and Cautopates; to the west and south-west, it allowed the crypt to be filled with sunshine in the late afternoon, when the faithful gathered to partake of the *cena*.

To take part in these liturgies, it was necessary to be accepted by the group, by way of a cult apprenticeship and ritual tests or ordeals. Integration into the community involved an initiatory hierarchy of seven steps or grades. One became successively 'Raven', 'Bridegroom' or 'Newly-wed' (*Nymphus*), 'Soldier', 'Lion', 'Persian', 'Heliodromos' or 'Messenger of the Sun', and finally, 'Father'. Each of these grades had a matching tutelary planet: Mercury for the Raven, Venus for the *Nymphus*, Mars for the Soldier, Jupiter for the Lion, the Moon for the Persian, the Sun for the Heliodrome, Saturn for the Father. These various stages of the mystery ascent each carried an appropriate ritual.

The initiation of the Ravens marked their entry into the world of the sacred, since this oracular bird who could speak like man belonged to an intermediate race between the lower world and the gods.[112] It may be recalled that the bird served also as the Sun's messenger to tell Mithras that he must sacrifice the bull. In the caverns, the Raven perhaps fitted himself with a mask of the bird whose name he bore (plate 29) to serve the drinks to the mystae, at least judging by certain illustrated monuments.

The candidate to the grade of *Nymphus* had to wear a veil like the *flammeum* of Roman women on their wedding day. At a given moment, his face was unveiled to reveal him to the mystae, with the words:

Look, Nymphus! Hail, Nymphus; hail young light!

which makes one think that he held a lighted lamp.[113] R. Merkelbach explains *Nymphus* as *nymphè*, a Greek name (that has passed into the term 'nymph') for the intermediate stage between the larva and the perfect insect.[114] Aristotle speaks of it following the *psychai* or metamorphoses which result in a butterfly. On the Altieri relief (*CIMRM*, 334), a bee nymph would seem to represent the *Nymphus* above Cautopates, and for Virgil and Porphyry bees symbolize souls. It happens that Love and Psyche were featured in the *Mithraea* of Capua and Santa Prisca. The title *Nymphus* would then refer to the changes in the soul passing through the planetary spheres . . . But at Ostia, on the Felicissimus mosaic (figure 5), the lamp and diadem make allusion to a marriage. Perhaps it was interpreted in relation to the hierogamy of Eros and Psyche, the wedding of the soul.

Tertullian informs us about the Soldier, who bore a mark on his forehead, either tattooed or branded. He was presented with a crown on the point of a sword. But he had to divert it onto his shoulder, saying that Mithras was his true crown (*The Crown*, 15, 3–4). The sword pointed at his forehead with the crown was deemed to put him to the test with a threat of death or one of those mock deaths on which initiatory rituals were so keen. As Mithras had done for the Sun, they had to put on the Soldier's shoulder the symbolic bag that is to be seen beside the helmet and *pilum* on the Ostian mosaic of Felicissimus.

The element of fire dominated the consecration and functions of the Lion. On the above-mentioned mosaic, his grade is illustrated by fire shovel, the sistrum (allusion to Isis-Sothis and thus to the Canicula)

Plate 29 Fragment originating from Rome, *Castra Praetoria* (Mannheim Museum)

and the thunderbolt or heavenly fire. But as this element is the enemy of water, the Lion's hands were washed in honey, and an unction of honey on his tongue purified him from all sin (Porphyry, *The Cavern of the Nymphs*, 15). The honey also recalled the product of bees that were said to have been 'born of the ox' (*bougeneis*), as souls were revived by the blood of the bull. Together with souls, in fact, it was the divine fire that gave life to all creatures. It is possible that the Lions wore a suitable mask (likening them to the lion-headed god) to take part in the liturgies, at least if we are to believe the bifaced relief of Konjič, for the paintings of Santa Prisca show them with their human head. They burned incense and ritually lit the braziers in the *Mithraeum*. They also carried out certain trials of endurance by fire.

The hands of the Persian were also purified with honey, but owing to another symbolism, for the Persian received this unction in the role of 'guardian of the fruits', the honey standing in for preserving sugar, and also because it passed from the Moon to the bull's seed to cause the growth of fuit-bearing plants and trees through the shed blood. Thus the sickle (together with the *harpè* and lunar crescent) was the insignia of this grade on the Felicissimus mosaic (figure 5). Reliefs show Mithras as reaper or fruit-gatherer. The Persian is featured with a Phrygian cap on the Konjič stele.

We know nothing about the initiation peculiar to the Heliodromos. On the Felicissimus mosaic, his symbols are the radiant crown, the torch and the Sun's whip. As for the Father, he wore a richly brocaded cap. Apart from this headdress, which likened him to Mithras, the mosaic gives him the attributes of Saturn's billhook, the libation cup (or a ring?) and the wand of command (figure 5). It may be conjectured that he could be consecrated only by another Father or the 'Father of Fathers', a title to be found at Rome, Ostia and Dura-Europos. The libation cup characterized him as responsible for devotions in the role of *Pater sacrorum* or 'Father of the Mysteries'. It has been supposed that the Father and the Heliodromos played the parts of Mithras and the Sun respectively in the banquets re-enacting the meal that followed the bull sacrifice.

The initiates and their promotion to the various grades were acclaimed:

Hail to the Lions for new and many years!

we read in the Santa Prisca cavern, or:

Hail to the Fathers, from East to West, under the protection of Saturn!

Other acclamations, invocations and exhortations, sung or chanted, gave emphasis to the execution of the rites. The painted walls of Santa Prisca preserve some touching traces for us (the third being an allusion to Mithras carrying the bull):

Chicken livers are certainly delectable, but care rules

We must get through dark times in piety

To the very end I have borne on my shoulders the accomplishment of divine orders

Spring hidden in the rock, thou who of thy nectar hast fed the two brothers.

(The last refers to the miracle of the water that assuages the thirst of the dadophori.[115]) One imagines that these chants accompanied the commentary on the painted or sculpted stories.

The mystae wore costumes with symbolic colours appropriate to their grades (as well as the zoomorphic masks I have mentioned). The frescoes of Santa Prisca give us some idea of them: scarlet cloaks for the Lions, silvery-grey (colour of the Moon) for the Persians, or bright yellow for the 'Bridegrooms'. It is easy to picture the visual effects of this multi-coloured scene in the flickering light of the torches.

In the *Mithraeum* of Capua (Santa Maria Capua Vetere), the front of the benches, which were widened and lengthened in a second phase of rearrangement, had twelve painted scenes, of which nine remain visible. They seem to relate to initiatory ordeals.[116] On the north bench a candidate is thought to be identifiable, walking blindfolded under the guidance of a mystagogue. He then seems to put one knee on the ground before a man who is helmeted like the praetorians (a 'Soldier'?). Then a scene of an embrace can be discerned (the kiss of peace?) and, again, the mysta kneeling beside a sword (?) before the officiating priest, who is clad in a white tunic bordered with red and holds a crown with red ribbons over the head of the one to be initiated.

On the southern bench only three scenes can still be made out: the naked mysta, stretched out on his stomach and with his head lowered, between two persons who extend a hand towards him; facing a man wearing the Phrygian cap, the mysta kneeling and turning his back to a white-clad mystagogue who places his two hands on the mysta's shoulders; lastly, the mysta on his knees, his hands crossed over his chest, before the mystagogue in a white cloak who puts his foot on his calf, facing a priest clad in red, who points his wand at a round loaf placed on the ground. This priest may be identified with the Father. Literary tradition preserves for us a somewhat distorted memory of other rites. According to the *Ambrosiaster*, the candidate, blindfolded, his hands tied with chicken entrails, had to jump over trenches filled with water; after which, a 'liberator' cut his bonds with a sword-stroke.[117] The neophytes would have fasted fifty days, if we are to believe the monk Nonnos. They were said to have been flayed alive then plunged into snow for twenty days. Cosmo of Jerusalem tells of eighty ordeals, including those of hunger and fire. R. Merkelbach claimed to have decoded them in a novel by Iamblichus of which Photius (*Bibliotheca*, 94) recopied or summarized large extracts: the *Babloniacas* . . . [118] But this has not been demonstrated.

The Mithraists have been accused of human sacrifice. Obviously rituals of fictitious killing inspired such accusation. The depiction of the mysta stretched out like a corpse, face downwards, in the Capua *Mithraeum* doubtless corresponds to an ordeal of this kind.[119] In the cavern of Carrawburgh (England), south of the nave, a long stone-faced cavity was discovered, which could hold a lying man. In one of the rooms backing onto the Mithraic nave in Santa Prisca, Rome, was an excavation of similar length. In the Baths of Caracalla, Rome, the floor of the *Mithraeum* opened in the middle of the central corridor onto a vault communicating with a gallery which may have been used for ritual burials.[120]

What was known, or believed to be known, about them gave rise to evil rumours which fourth-century Christians were happy to embroider. Human skulls were said to have been unearthed in a *Mithraeum* in Alexandria where the bishop wanted to build on the ruins. Excavation of the sanctuary of Königshofen yielded half a cranium beside a femur, right against a base of the chancel. It was not necessarily a matter of human sacrifice, any more than in the case of relics consecrated under Christian altars. As for the skeleton found face downwards, its wrists chained, in the *spelaeum* of Sarrebourg, it lay on the debris of the great cultic relief, which had been hammered to pieces by the Christians: the placing of the corpse thus followed the destruction and abandonment of the crypt, and was intended to sully and defame the pagan site.[121]

The psychologically strengthening ordeals of initiation, the stimulating hierarchy founded on a theo-cosmology that elucidated the history of the world as well as the function of men and souls in the universe, were such as to reinforce neophytes' faith in their 'invincible' god. Above all, the perhaps daily, at least weekly, liturgy of the communal meal confirmed their union with the gods and with one another. It seems to have been, first and foremost, a rite of collective invigoration.

The faithful met among men (women being excluded from the cult), soldiers, employees, traders, slaves or freedmen from elsewhere, immigrants and the rootless, all closely bound by the 'mystery' vow to serve the Bull-slayer. The illustrated doctrine in the Persian caverns gave even the illiterate a reason for living and doing things, in a Cosmos where they were never strangers, but creatures saved by the 'eternal blood'. The reverse of the Gnostic, who suffered exile in this world below, the Mithraist, like the Stoic, was at home everywhere in the universe and in society, notably in imperial and cosmopolitan Roman society, where loyalty to the emperor and the consciousness of serving, each in his own position, were in fundamental accord with a religion of 'Soldiers' and the oath, *sacramentum*. In many respects, Mithraism rendered sacred certain constant values of Roman-ness.

Social and Political Impact

A priori, one might think that this religion of small groups, ritually and topographically on the fringe of the public cults, supported on an apparently complex doctrine which incorporated and combined certain elements of Greek astrology and philosophy with the mythical residue of an oriental tradition, would concern only a fairly restricted elite. Indeed we find that its impact outside Rome – Ostia and a few Rhine–Danube sites remained rather sporadic and limited. The exclusion of women was bound to hamper the spread of influence of these closed societies.

That is not to say, however, that they recruited only the flower of distinguished theosophers. Certainly, one could not enter a community without passing through the channels of the initiatory hierarchy, which must have required a minimum of religious instruction for the Ravens. But it has been seen that the theo-cosmology of the Mithraists was summarized and inculcated by means of commentary on pictures, a whole symbolic language of motifs and colours. This audio-visual teaching, opportunely emphasized by the play of light and shadow, was a large part of the attractive strength of the Persian cult, and assured it of a clientele apart from the literate and educated.

The iconographic items are certainly of very uneven aesthetic level; but we are also poor judges. This or that simplistic and crude cippus from a Danubian cavern may have been just as efficacious for the troopers of the place as a stele in the grand style, like those of Osterburken or Königshofen. Mithraic art (as was often the case with

Roman art in general) had nothing to do with art for art's sake. That did not prevent the faithful of Königshofen from importing and employing a team of Italian sculptors to fashion a relief (plate 25) worthy of the best studios in the Urbs.[122] Moreover, at its apogee, Mithraic art had a share in the new breath of life that inspired Roman plastic arts from the time of Marcus Aurelius. A vibrant and moving intensity also characterizes the paintings of Capua and Marino. In sculpture, the stele of the Via Tiburtina (plate 30) shares the same style and temperament.[123] This ardour to communicate, which was singularly in keeping with the spirit of the times, could not fail to facilitate Mithraic preaching.

What it incorporated from philosophy and cosmology derived ultimately from popular or popularized Stoicism, which was a part of the ambient culture, in the widest sense of the term. It therefore reached the most varied strata of Roman society, at least outside rural circles.

The first evidence (shortly before or after AD 90–100) directs us towards freedmen of the imperial court in Rome itself,[124] but also in the legionary camps on the Rhine and Danube, away from the Urbs.[125] This dual component would remain a constant in Mithraic sociology. But, on the one hand, both in the emperor's civilian household and among his officials and in the military class, recruitment tended to expand – in all categories – to every grade on the administrative ladder; and on the other, Mithraism reached further circles, closely or loosely connected with the imperial machine, generally speaking involved with the army and official services through their activity or mobility: traders, business agents, craftsmen, doctors . . .

On the Euphrates, in Africa and Britain, Germania, Pannonia and Moesia, camps and fortified positions had their Mithraic 'cells'. At Dura-Europos and in Dacia, recruits of eastern origin (Commagenians, Syrian and Palmyrenian archers) worshipped and caused others to worship the Bull-slayer. We have seen that he fitted in well with Jupiter Dolichenus and other Syrian gods. Significantly, at Setif Mithras wore the cuirass with lambrequins which likened him (like the Baal of Doliche) to the Roman army officers. In the end he would find followers throughout the hierarchy, from the simple trooper, the legionary clerk, to prefects of the cavalry, legates and high-ranking military governors, by way of centurions. Owing to their postings, they became missionaries. Having become prefect of the legion at Lambaesis (Numidia), Marcus Aurelius Decimus, originally from Carnuntum where Mithraism prospered between AD 100 and 300, hastened to consecrate an altar to the Invincible God. Conversely, a

Plate 30 Bust of Mithras (from the Via Tiburtina; photo. kindly provided by the Director of the Karlsruhe Museum)

centurion of African stock presented Mithras with an altar at Rudchester, near Newcastle. A native of Poetevio (Ptuj) in Pannonia, Marcus Valerius Maximianus offered him one c.180 in the *Mithraeum* of Alba Julia (Romania), before distinguishing himself at Lambaesis by another consecration to the Bull-slayer. Every legion he commanded included Mithraists. He would become suffect consul.

But at Ptuj, revenue employees, free or slaves, also swelled the ranks of the Persian cult.[126] In Noricum, Dalmatia, and Dacia, 'farmers' of the customs, saltworks, iron mines and arms manufacture assiduously attended the crypts. For their part, municipal councillors and local magistrates (often from the army) played a notable role, frequently being the driving or instigating force. But we also find that people of modest social background contributed to the construction, enhancement or restoration of sanctuaries: slaves of the emperor in the tax administration, a farmer of the iron mines of Noricum at Aquileia or a customs farmer in Dalmatia, freedmen accountants, nonranking legionaries.

In urban circles, Mithraism was again not merely a religion of esoteric suppers for intellectuals. At *Elusa* (Eauze, Gers) the Father of the community sold clothes (*CIL*, XIII, 542).[127] A Mithraist *vestiarius* of *Viminacium* (Kostolac, ex-Yugoslavia) was in the same line of business.[128] The bifaced stele of Dieburg was consecrated by a craftsman shoemaker originally from Berry, in partnership with a stonemason and his grandson. At Vieu in Val Romey, a doctor of slave stock carried out his priestly office of Mithraic Father at the same time as his profession, turning to good account a thermal spa which was obviously appropriate to the worship of a god who had slaked the thirst of animal and plant creation.[129]

In the ports, at Arles, Merida or London on the Thames, businessmen, notably Hellenized Orientals, contributed to the setting up or decoration of crypts. At Ostia there is an outstanding example of towmakers who installed a *Mithraeum* in the vaults of their collegial temple. A number of private homes similarly housed devotions to the Bull-slayer. But his cult scarcely gained a foothold in rural areas, apart from a few rocky sites complemented by running water, which were frequented only by peasants.

Did he win over any Caesars? With the exception of Nero, whose 'conversion' to Mithraism under the guidance of Tiridates remains suspect,[130] and Hadrian who – whatever M. Yourcenar's splendid pen may have written – never set foot in a Persian cavern, we must doubtless pay heed for once to the *Augustan History* when it presents Commodus (180–92) as an (unworthy) follower of Mithras. The emperor is said to have polluted his mysteries by a real murder, profiting from the fact that it was customary 'to say or pretend something in order to cause fear'; that is, to test the candidate in a ritual of imaginary killing (*Life of Commodus*, 9, 6). No coins, no public documents obviously confirm that Commodus was initiated. We know, at any rate, that he granted premises to the Mithraists in his imperial residence at Ostia (*CIL*, XIV, 66).

Under Septimius Severus (who called himself the brother of Commodus, greatly scandalizing the Senate), the Invincible God had his chaplain on the Palatine (*CIL*, VI, 2271). But there is no indication that the emperor showed him any special regard. Later, the coins of Tarsus that bore the Bull-slayer on the reverse were no more a sign of the personal devotion of Gordian III, but this occasional publicity must have carried some weight in the opinion of the armies who were then marching against Sassanid Persia. On the great sarcophagus with the battle scene from the old Ludovisi Collection in the Terme (Museo Nazionale), Rome, the victorious horseman who was believed to be Hostilian, the son of Decius Trajan (249–51), bears on his forehead an X, which H. von Heintze considered to be a 'mystery' tattoo. Tertullian certainly writes that Mithras marks (*signat*) his soldiers on the forehead, but with what 'sign'? As for Aurelian, what we know of his reform institutionalizing the solar cult has no bearing on Mithraism.[131]

In fact, the first attestation of an official piety towards Mithras does not appear until 307, at *Carnuntum*, when Diocletian, Galerius and Licinius restored a cavern there, giving the god the title *fautor imperii sui* ('protector of their imperial power'). It is true that this consecration took place in what might be called the 'Mecca' of Mithraism[132] and to assure the Tetrarchs of the support of soldiers who adhered to the Persian cult. 'There was a moment in time when Caesarism appeared on the point of being transformed into a caliphate,' wrote Cumont in this regard:[133] a statement that was without doubt exaggerated and inappropriate. But Galerius may have initiated imperial homage to the Bull-slayer, and it would have been appreciated among his military staff.

Mithras experienced a sort of renewal of favour in Rome itself in the second half of the fourth century among the senatorial 'gentry' who had remained loyal to polytheism. It was at this time that the *'clarissimi'* liked to display their mystery and priestly titles like so many decorations. But in their dedications Mithras rubs shoulders with Cybele, Isis, the three Hecates and Liber Pater. In their eyes he no longer counted except as one manifestation of paganism among others. Apart from Rome and Ostia, the Persian god had long since lost the match.

A few isolated signs of devotion in a spring sanctuary such as Septeuil (Yvelines), between 360 and 385, have little significance.

The Invincible Vanquished

In the time of Commodus (180–92), but chiefly from that of the Severi (193–235), certain Christians had acquired an influential position in the various departments of the court. In the late third century, their faith had reached the executives of the administration and even of the army. Hence the great persecution of 303 ordered by Diocletian, but very likely hatched and organized by Galerius, who must have been alarmed by such infiltration.[134] But official terrorism encouraged neither defections among the Christians nor progress for Mithras, whose expansion seems to have been halted by the third-century crisis. Indeed, his cult remained at one with the imperial religion and its theology of victory, to which the defeat of Valerian, captured by the king of Persia in 260, delivered an almost mortal blow.

After Maxentius was crushed at the Milvian Bridge (312), Constantine's army – and even the rest of the troops – had no option but to tend gradually towards becoming Christian. The emperor having triumphed 'under the inspiration of the divinity' (*instinctu divinitatis*), as we are reminded by the dedication on the arch erected in his honour, the soldiers had to pay homage to the God of the victors. But to begin with, the first Christian emperor also wagered on the ambiguities of the solar cult. The famous vision of 312 was associated with the daystar, and until 320 Constantinian coins promoted *Sol Invictus* as 'companion' (*comes*) of the emperor. Moreover, he had benefited at Grand (Vosges) from an earlier Apollonian epiphany. Much has been written about his alleged hesitations; but he insisted on making the worshippers of *Sol Invictus* – Mithraists or not – understand that there was no other Sun but his God of the Armies.[135]

The repressive laws of Constantine and his sons against paganism did the rest. Even though the Mithraists in their crypts did not carry out bloody immolations, they had neither the right nor the chance to eat the meat of the victims. In Christian eyes, their subterranean or pseudo-subterranean lairs smacked of a cult of shadows in the service of demons. The ban on nocturnal sacrifice was aimed first and foremost at them.[136] In the towns and camps where the Bull-slayer had had the best of his religious followers in the preceding century, the name of Mithras disappeared. His statues were overturned, decapitated, his stelae destroyed with a singular relentlessness. Did not the apologist Firmicus Maternus denounce in Mithras the god of an enemy people – the Persians!

The accession of Julian, known as 'the Apostate', afforded the idolaters some respite. But one may reasonably doubt whether Constantine's nephew was initiated into the liturgies of the caverns,[137] despite a phrase in his *Banquet of the Caesars* (336 c), in which the name Mithras designates the Sun-King to whom Julian has devoted a discourse devoid of any indisputable reference to the Persian cult. The temple created in the imperial palace at Constantinople, of which Libanios writes, housed Julian's devotions to Helios, the god of his ancestor Constantius.

In the *Urbs*, the pagan aristocracy had profited from the good graces of Constantius II (when he visited Rome in 357, dazzled by the monuments of his prestigious past) to make him put the 'avenging sword' of Christian legislation back in its sheath. It has been seen that at this time both Phrygianism and Isiacism had benefited by a renewal in popularity of their festivals. But rites carried out in a small company in the shadows of the crypts were unable to rally so much as a semblance of popular favour; they could not compete with the Hilaria, the Megalesia or the Discovery of Osiris. The militancy of the Christians therefore struck first at Mithraic sanctuaries. The newly converted gave proof of their conviction by sacking them with sword and fire, as for example in 376 or 377, the prefect of the *Urbs*, Furius Maecius Gracchus, whom Saint Jerome praises for having thus merited the grace of baptism (*Letters*, 107, 2). Another Christian commando at Ostia abused the cavern housed in what were known as 'Mithras' Baths'. The Ostian *Mithraeum* of Fructosus was devastated by a fire of criminal origin. In Rome, Santa Prisca received a visit from fervent plunderers who mutilated the statues and defaced paintings with their knives.[138] The Mithras in gilded stucco who was worshipped beneath the future church of Santo Stefano Rotondo was decapitated and the *Mithraeum* shattered. On several occasions wreckers attacked the cultic objects in the sanctuary above which the San Clemente basilica would rise:[139] the altar that was fractured in the first assault seems to have been repaired by the members of the community, who finally had to abandon the premises, at the latest after the victory of Theodosius (394).

In the provinces, the *Mithraea* had long suffered the effects of a deliberate and fanatical violence. The cultic reliefs of Sarrebourg, Mackwiller, and Königshofen were systematically smashed with axes or clubs, even pulverized with hammers for fear that anyone should think of restoring them. The head of the god, removed like those of the saints in French cathedrals during the religious wars or in 1793, was the first to catch the destroyers' attention and actions. Only about half the stele of Königshofen could be put together, of the 360 pieces found.[140] Nothing at all was retrieved of Mithras himself, whose image must have been reduced to tiny fragments and scattered in the vicinity of the crypt. It was believed that by so doing the maleficent powers of the demons could be neutralized.

In the early fifth century, when Macrobius wrote his *Saturnalia* in which he describes the last pagans in Rome, the Bull-slayer appears to have been forgotten.[141] A series of eight chapters defends to the point of puerile paradox the idea that all the gods (Attis, Adonis, Dionysus, Hadad, Jupiter Heliopolitanus, Serapis) were identified with the Sun, but the name of Mithras never emerges.'

Contrary to what E. Renan maintained, there was never the slightest opportunity or danger of the world becoming Mithraist. By excluding women, Mithraism marginalized itself perilously. Furthermore, the very reasons for its success in the civilian and military society of the Antonine era compromised its future in a world undergoing change. The opportunism of officials and officers must always be taken into account. This must have played a part, starting from Constantine's time, but above all during the reigns of his successors.

From the point of view of religion, what held good in paganism and what, in their wise realism, the bishops ended by Christianizing, were the local and naturist cults. Now, with a few rare exceptions, Mithraism remained the religion of the rootless, alien to native soil, at least in the towns where the bulk of its followers were recruited. A few transplants in spring sanctuaries do not fundamentally alter the facts of the problem, for worship survived there without any need of Mithras. But it was in the urban, cosmopolitan milieu, where the god had succeeded so well in the second and third centuries, that Christianity became its victorious rival.

It must be said, finally, that even in towns this religion did not meet the questions, the anguished concerns, of those who, contrary to the Mithraists, suffered by inhabiting a body and aspired only to eternal and spiritual life; those who could not be content with a sacramental meal intended primarily to strengthen the physical health and energy of the 'soldiers', or with an optimism that basically adhered to the order of the Cosmos and that of the Roman Empire. This kind of 'freemasonry' inevitably had to die together with the society which had, if not given it birth, at least furthered and favoured it.

Chapter 5

Horsemen, Mothers and Serpents

MANY other cults – from the Balkans, Asia Minor and the Near
East – made their appearance, or at least asserted themselves
iconographically in the *Orbis Romanus*, but either in very
sporadic fashion outside what might be termed their religious mother-
city, in some instances, or with singular density in this or that sector of
the Empire. By their imagery or symbolism, the typology of their stelae or
idols, several of these cults revealed a kinship with those whose history I
have just outlined, but without ever becoming annexed by them or in
any way suggesting 'syncretism'. In any case, they frequently stemmed
from the same system of beliefs and representations that were characteristic of those times when men lived in a multicultural world – 'civilization
in the Empire was a tapestry' (A.-J. Festugière) – but a world which in
some way breathed the same mental or spiritual air, and where
communication was at a level never previously attained over such a vast
portion of the inhabited universe.

We have seen the case of Mên-Lunus and Mâ-Bellona, who presented such similarities with Attis and Cybele respectively. The first,
as *Menotyrannos*, ultimately lent his crescent to the lover of the Great
Mother, whose cult also effectively established links with Bellona and
the Syrian Goddess. But a number of divinities made unequal progress who, in some respects, resembled the 'stars' of the orientalizing
pantheon without ever being confused with them anywhere, and
many who did not reach the same heights as Mithras, or even
Dolichenus, retain a large share of their mystery for want of the
slightest echo of their cult in literary tradition.

Horsemen Gods

A large number of stelae found in all regions of Thrace highlight, both
artistically and from the religious aspect, a being on horseback who

bears the name 'Hero'.[1] This 'Thracian horseman' advances, sometimes at a walk, sometimes at a gallop, towards an altar erected in front of a tree around which a snake is entwined. We also see him, his chlamys blowing in the wind, leaping forward with a spear in his hand to hunt boar, or astride a lion. Sometimes he holds game – a doe or a hare, for instance – which he has flushed out and killed. A dog usually accompanies him. But, curiously, on occasion this horseman-god holds a lyre in his left hand,[2] and on some monuments a dedication to Apollo expressly designates him as such. Exceptionally, he even appears as a bearded Asclepius, accompanied by a serpent which undulates between his mount's hooves. The serpent, Apollo and Asclepius lead one to think of a healing god, and the tree in juxtaposition to the sacrificial altar seems also to be made sacred by the reptile as the 'tree of life'. Hunting eliminates harmful animals, but also provides man with fortifying food. Sometimes it is possible to make out the motif of an upturned urn on the ground, which relates to the figure of a river-god on a relief at Plovdiv (Philippopolis, Bulgaria),[3] again connected with a theme of health or, at least, health-giving waters. It sometimes occurs that the 'Hero' is three-headed, which obviously implies, like other divine triplicities, an 'omnidirectional' power that is total and absolute.

The majority of stelae of the 'Thracian horseman' are not of the monumental size suitable to sanctuaries (which in any case have not been identified as such anywhere). Many measure between 20 and 30 cm. Those which exceed 50 cm are less numerous. In exceptional cases they reach a height of 1 m. Some come from graves; others must have been venerated in private like kinds of icon.[4]

The 'Thracian horseman' extended his influence over the Black Sea, at Histria, Callatis and Odessos. He is similarly found at Romula, in Dacia, where he is not (as has been supposed) associated with Cybele. At Constantza (Tomi, where Ovid died in exile), the horseman god with his spear is shown winged, like a spirit of death, and in fact it has been demonstrated that the Thracian 'Hero' often had funerary attributes. The stele of Svistov, dedicated to the deceased *Heroni*, shows us the god confronting a kind of enormous dragon which has nothing at all to do with the salutary snake accompanying the 'tree of life', but which must embody death.[5]

Other horsemen gods are encountered in Asia Minor, notably Kakasbos in Lycia, who wears a cuirass and brandishes a club.[6] Like Thrace, Smyrna honoured a mounted Apollo. But the horsemen of Asia Minor do not appear to have been really exported by their local worshippers, unlike the Thracian 'Hero' who is to be found, for example, at Ostia. Two reliefs there show him hunting boar. In one, the beast is emerging from a cavern, as on the sarcophagi illustrating the myth of Meleager; in the other, it charges towards a small altar (to be sacrificed on it?), and the horseman god is accompanied by a squire. The first of these reliefs bears the name of one Aureli(o)s Apronianos, written in Greek, and although it was discovered in a back shop of the theatre at Ostia, it may have been a funerary monument, bearing in mind the prerogatives of the 'Hero' as protector of the dead (the surname of the deceased contains the name for a boar, *aper, apro-*). Several epitaphs for Thracians (more precisely Bessi) have been found at Ostia.[8] Together with the future emperor Maximinus, Septimius Severus must have recruited Thracian horsemen for his personal guard, and they may have imported the cult of their 'Hero'. But that importation had no impact outside their restricted circle (which was probably despised by native-born Romans as much as if not more than the Thracian shepherd who would reign over them between 235 and 238!).

Perhaps the Macedonians too had their 'horseman god',[9] and there has been speculation whether they may have introduced into the Egypt of the Ptolemies a god called *Herôn*, to be found there from the second century BC.[10] This equestrian god was confused with Horus crushing Seth. He was a solar god, like certain horsemen of Asia Minor and like the rider with the lyre identified with Apollo. This image was the forerunner of the mounted saints who, as we know, enjoyed great success in western Christian iconography, notably Saint George vanquishing the dragon.

A horseman Dionysus is known who has something of the Thracian 'Hero'. A relief from Melnik (Macedonia), now in the Brussels Museum, shows him riding among grape-laden vine branches, between Silenus and Pan.[11] On a stele from Plovdiv,[12] the Thracian horseman about to impale a boar features under the cultic image of Sabazius surrounded by Hermes, Pan and Tyche-Fortuna, not to mention the Sun and the Moon whose busts emerge under the acroteria, as they do at the summit of Mithraic plaques. At Thasos, a deceased person is identified with the equestrian Dionysus who makes the Sabazian gesture of the *benedictio latina*, facing a Persephone who offers him the branch of immortality.[13]

This huntsman and saviour god had some affinity with a Mithras on horseback, but as an archer, who can be recognized, for instance, on a fresco from Dura-Europos, on the reverse of the stele of Rückingen, on the relief of Dieburg and on a stele from Neuenheim.[14] Certainly, from these pieces people have erroneously deduced the cynegetic origin of the groups of men from which the initiatory communities of the first Mithraists would evolve.[15] The Roman army

cavalrymen who frequented the caverns doubtless liked to see themselves in this god, galloping through the wild and virgin countryside,
in the company of a snake, a dog, a boar or a lion.

In the Danubian provinces, the troops paid homage to other horsemen
gods whose iconography is more complicated, and whose names we
do not even know. Their cult is mentioned by allusion on stelae that
are similar in shape, format and even the lay-out of reliefs, to certain
Mithraic plaques in those areas.[16]

These 'Danubian horsemen' (as they are called for want of a better
title) feature not only on small stone stelae, but also on lead plaques of
smaller size, even on intaglios that the faithful could carry on or with
them as kinds of amulets. The stone reliefs often have the look of the
Mithraic stelae with a rounded top, of Danubian type; others have a
structured composition like that of the Mithraic reliefs with an arca-
ture or middle niche between two horizontal bases supporting the
busts of the Sun and Moon. These monuments also frequently have a
terracing of registers which are fully comparable to those of the
Mithraica. Obviously the same workshops were meeting the orders of
the various cults entrenched in Pannonia, Moesia and Dacia.

There are many variations which at first sight confound any attempt
at an all-embracing and coherent explanation; but a certain number of
common, or almost common, denominators may be picked out from
this proliferation, which is a sign of vitality.[17] In principle, under the
busts of the two light-givers, *Sol* and *Luna* (though on the odd
example the chariot of Helios dominates the scene), two horsemen are
shown symmetrically on either side of a standing goddess whom they
hail with their right hand. Their horses trample two corpses lying on
the ground; but sometimes a single corpse lies beneath the feet of the
goddess who extends her arms towards the horses, or holds the folds
of her cloak across her stomach. A warrior on the left, a woman on the
right, frame the horsemen. Sometimes a lion accompanies the one on
the left and seems to be attacking the corpse.

Below this to some extent canonical register, one may generally
make out the elements of a scene of sacrifice and ritual meal. A tripod
(which is also found in front of the goddess or even on a level with the
solar bust) can be seen, laden with three receptacles, beside a snake, a
bird, a wine bowl and a lion. On other examples are a ram, a cock
walking towards the altar or a bovine animal beside the tripod, which
bears a fish, or a tree from which hangs the victim with a specialist in
the act of cutting its throat. Occasionally, a person wearing the mask of
a ram or raven (as in the Mithraic banquets) is present at the scene,
unless he is saluting one of the two horsemen.[18]

The skin of the sacrificed animal must have been used in an initiatory rite, to which the lower register of several stelae refers and to which D. Tudor gives the Latin name *occultatio*.[19] A man is shown kneeling behind the victim's carcase, between two of the cult's priests who have the same appearance as the horsemen (chlamys and Phrygian cap). That seems to me to imply that the candidate was supposed to take the place of the victim and that, as in the taurobolic rite, it was a matter of a substitute sacrifice. Two priests with the divine attributes presided over the affair. On a carved stone preserved in the Vienna Museum, the three guests at a banquet are clearly identified with the goddess between the two horsemen. The three balls (of bread?) or the three goblets which several examples show us on the pedestal table, correspond to this triad. Above the goddess and the riders a stele from Terracina shows the lunar bust between two radiate busts, which would lead one to suppose that the goddess possesses the powers of *Luna* and that the horsemen, assimilated to the Dioscuri, symbolize, like their *piloi* or star-spangled caps, the two halves of the sky, i.e. the two annual aspects of the Sun in the austral and boreal hemispheres (like Cautes and Cautopates in the Mithraic system). A small lead plaque from Belgrade shows us the busts of the four Seasons in the areas of the triangular corners separating the central medallion from the quadrangular border.

The fish, the cock and the serpent similarly play an insistent role in this allegorical imagery, whose meaning largely eludes us. Where a cock or eagle surmounts a ram's head, attempts have been made to see the illustration of an oriental myth linked with the worship of a Syrian Baal like Turmasgad, who had a handful of worshippers in Moesia and Dacia.[20] The fish is found under the horses' feet or as an offering in the meal. The snake may flank the goddess, but is also seen (as on Mithraic stelae) approaching the wine-bowl to drink from it. The pair of serpents facing each other around the wine vessel, as may be seen on the lead plaque of Belgrade, is seen again on the Mithraic disc from Salonae (Split Museum). As for the grouping of the lion and the reptile on either side of the wine-bowl, it obviously reminds us of the well-known schema of Mithraic reliefs of the type known as 'Raetio-Rhenish'. But one may well be surprised that this motif does not appear in the Danubian series of 'bull-slaying' stelae. At least, one has every right to doubt that it symbolized the three elements (water between fire and earth), as Cumont supposed.[21]

The basic iconography was also explained as the 'Dioscuri in the service of a goddess', to quote the celebrated title of a thesis by F. Chapouthier.[22] In accordance with a play on words made use of by the Neopythagoreans, Helen (the goddess) was identified with Selene,[23] which could throw light on the presence of the lunar bust above her on the aforementioned stele of Terracina. People have tried to give the name Nemesis to the woman who is sometimes found behind the right-hand horseman; but she is apparently making a gesture of salutation or adoration and could not therefore be a goddess. On the other hand, our Helen-Selene may have been regarded as a Nemesis. Ammianus Marcellinus writes of Adrasteia, 'to whom we give a second name, Nemesis', that 'the sublime authority of this powerful deity, in men's opinion, lives above the lunar circle' (*History*, XIV, 11, 25). Of the Tyche who, in the name of the gods, determines the events in this world below, Julian's friend Sallustius says that 'her power is exerted in the Moon' (*The Gods and the World*, IX, 7). Nemesis also often has the look of an Artemis, who was commonly recognized in the nocturnal star. It is known that Nemesis, iconographically akin to Tyche and Nikè, was relatively popular in the West. She was honoured as 'invincible', 'avenger', 'powerful'. Like many of the major divinities, she also had the epiclesis *Augusta*.

The goddess with the horsemen thus probably personified the omnipotence of celestial Justice, between the Disocuri who represented, there as elsewhere and like the two luminaries, cosmic eternity. Some of her priests masked as rams or ravens participated in a ritual of sacrifice which was the prelude to the incorporation of mystae who were substituted in pretence for the victim after the event. As in the Mithraic liturgy, a repast was probably the crowning act in the admission of candidates and thus consecrated the union of the faithful in commemoration of the banquet which had associated the two horsemen with Helen-Selene.

It is likely that this cult had an essentially military following. But unlike Mithraic segregation, women appear to have been admitted, to judge by those one sees on the plaques rendering homage to the divine triad. These followers transported their devotions to Italy (more precisely, Rome) and Britain (London), but because of special and very limited circumstances. Like the Thracian 'Hero', the Danubian horsemen and their goddess scarcely encroached on the traditional pantheon, or even other oriental gods, outside the regions where this religion was formed and developed, in a fairly restricted circle. Its iconography had a Greek heritage, but was enriched or overladen with disparate elements, perhaps even borrowing from rival cults like those of Mithras or the Thracian horseman (who appears to have influenced some representations). A certain share must therefore be ascribed to what has been called 'cobbling together' in the case of Mithraism. In the Danubian provinces, where so many gods of varied origins and appearance cohabited, liturgies and representational systems could hardly fail to rub off on one another to a certain extent.

Mothers of Ephesus and Aphrodisias

Away from their preserves in Asia Minor and their traditional devotees, the Mothers won over scarcely more followers than the horsemen gods, despite the prestige of their idols and tendencies to syncretism. The singularity of their cultic imagery must have excited the curiosity of the Romans rather than attracted them to become adherents. Like the gods of the Heliopolitan triad, the Artemis of Ephesus and the Aphrodite of Aphrodisias were distinguished by the *ependytes* swathing their body from the bosom to the feet.[24] This hieratic typology is not, as we have seen, of Egyptian origin. On the contrary, it seems to have spread its influence from Anatolia into Syria in the Hellenistic era.

Like the goddess of the Danubian cavaliers, the Ephesian goddess has lunar attributes. She is even shown on a coin of Caracalla between the Dioscuri on horseback.[25] Like Cybele, she has a crown of towers on her head, but sometimes also small storeyed buildings of differing complexity depending on the variations. On the Naples statue, a great nimbus filled with fabulous beasts curves round the shoulders of the goddess, as on the example of Solothurn (which originates from Rome or Naples).[26] Her girdle is generally divided into compartments, like that of Jupiter Heliopolitanus, but instead of the planetary gods she wears the protomes of deer, sheep, cattle, felines, sphinxes or gryphons, bees and flowers, winged busts of women rising from a plant's calyx. She therefore appears as sovereign of the animal world, like so many other Oriental Mothers. Bees were especially consecrated to her. Certain priestesses of Demeter bore the name of the honeybee, *melissai*; but this is not confirmed for the priestesses of Artemis. Like the Great Mother's galli, the Megabyzes or male priests of the Ephesian goddess were eunuchs.

But the best known peculiarity of this Artemis was her polymasty, which has obviously provoked much conjecture.[27] The breasts have been likened to acorns, eggs (ostrich!), bunches of grapes or clusters of dates, even the magic flames of the Virgin's cloak. Quite naturally they have been regarded as an attribute clearly signifying total fruitfulness and motherhood. Comparisons have also been made with the deities laden with the very fruits they are being offered, in gratitude for the harvests they were deemed to have brought about: for instance, the *Botrys* Dionysus of Pompeii whose body is in the form of a bunch of grapes.[28] But whether the polymasty was or was not connected with the breasts that the Amazons cut off (and were supposed to have consecrated on the idol), it is actually external to the body of the goddess. On the best preserved statues, it has in fact been established that the supposedly visible flesh of Artemis (head, neck, hands and feet) was of bronze or dark stone. For the Ephesian goddess was a 'black virgin', like several Mothers of Mediterranean and western Christendom. In its earliest form, the idol must have been carved from a dark wood (ebony or cypress?) or at least darkened by the oil with which it was ritually anointed.

The breasts therefore appear to have been superadded, attached to the corsage or the tunic of the *xoanon*. Originally, there may have been real consecrations of the type ascribed to the legendary Amazons: feminine, or rather anti-feminine, mutilation comparable with the amputation of the male organs for the galli or Megabyzes (rejection of maternity in one case, of paternity in the other). It was supposed that certain devotees – priests or priestesses – donned this polymastic apparel with magical implication to officiate in a liturgy of fertility or fecundity. Polymasty would therefore have established artistically in the iconography of the Ephesian goddess the use of plastrons covered with breasts, as some examples of the idol lead us to suppose. Moreover, such polymasty does not characterize Artemis alone, but also the Zeus of Labraunda, as he was worshipped at Tegea or Mylasa.[30]

The image of the Ephesian goddess does not correspond strictly to that of the Phocaean Artemis who was worshipped at Massalia and might have featured on the reverse of Roman denarii struck in 48 BC in the name of Hostilius Saserna.[31] But a statuette of the classic Ephesian type preserved in the Archaeological Museum of Marseille (and apparently of Roman period) perhaps comes from the soil of the Phocaean colony.[32] A Greek inscription from Autun maybe consecrates the dedication to Apollo of an image of the 'Queen of Ephesus' (*IG*, XIV, 2524). It has been argued that Artemis had travelled up the Rhône valley with Saint Madeleine.[33] But the route of the 'saints, successors to the gods' (P. Saintyves) in the still-pagan Gaul of the Late Empire is very difficult to ascertain. At *Augustodunum*, the cult of the Berecyntian, whose chariot was escorted by dancers like Corybants (Gregory of Tours, *Glory of the Confessors*, 77, 958) doubtless fraternized with that of the Ephesian goddess, if she really did reach the capital of the Aedui.

Replicas and variants, whole or fragmentary, of the many-breasted Artemis have been found at Salonae, Athens, Cos, Caesarea of Palestine, in Cyrenaica, Tripolitania, but above all in Italy: in the port of

Aquileia, where Greeks from Asia Minor worked, at Verona, Liternum, Ostia and Rome, which alone has yielded around fifteen examples.[34] From the *Urbs* comes the splendid statue, made of bronze and alabaster, which I have already mentioned, now in the National Museum of Naples. Where did it stand in ancient times? In the temple of Diana on the Aventine where, according to Strabo (*Geography*, IV, 1, 5), the cult idol recalled the one in Marseille? In the Gallery of the Candelabras, in the Vatican, one may see a statue of similar type which was earlier exhumed in Hadrian's villa at Tivoli.[35] It is not hard to imagine that, just like the Egyptian gods, this exotic Artemis and her strange decor of theriomorphic attributes must have intrigued an emperor as passionate as the *Graeculus* about religious curiosities, *omnium curiositatum explorator* (Tertullian, *Apologetica*, V, 7).

Graeco-Egyptian magic intaglios reproduce variants on her image, which was considered a sort of talisman. On a jasper in the Bibliothèque Nationale, Paris, it is accompanied by the legend (in Greek): 'Productive force for all life'.[36] She was identified with Isis. The Greek novels (*Ephesiaca* by Xenophon, *Leucippus and Clitophon* by Achilles Tatius, *History of Apollonius, King of Tyre*) bear witness to her prestige. Pausanias the Periegete claimed in 173 that 'in the Greek world everyone knows her' and that 'private individuals hold her in special veneration' (*Description of Greece*, IV, 31, 8), but inscriptions relating to the Artemision of Ephesus prove that, in spite of the pomp of the great religious festivals and the mystic sacrifices celebrated by a college of Curetes (Strabo, *Geography*, XIV, 1, 20), attendance there declined in the first two centuries AD. On the whole, apart from her compatriots or Anatolians who honoured Mothers related to the Ephesian, the goddess certainly interested lovers of art or religious exoticism in Italy, but she had very few accredited followers there.

The Aphrodite of Aphrodisias had even fewer.[37] Nevertheless, the future dictator Sulla, whom the Greeks nicknamed Epaphroditos, or Aphrodite's 'darling', had already had dealings with this goddess, whom the oracle of Trophonius had advised him to reward with an axe in order to carry off the victory at Chaeronea (86 BC). The Roman general had then offered her a golden crown, as well as the double-headed axe which qualified her as a warrior Aphrodite (and which was brandished by 'fanatics' of another Anatolian Mother dear to Sulla, Mâ-Bellona). The *imperator* had consecrated the axe, recalling in his dedication: 'I saw thee in a dream exhorting the ranks of my army and fighting with the weapons of Ares' (Appian, *Civil Wars*, I, 97, 455). Moreover, the oracle had emphasized the regard in which Aphrodite held the Romans. So in the imperial era the city of Aphrodisias would have the right of asylum, the status of free town and fiscal immunity.

This Aphrodite was not many breasted like her Ephesian sister. Generally speaking, like her, she wears a mural crown or a *polos*, but on top of a veil. An inverted lunar crescent, sometimes accompanied by the Crab (the zodiacal sign in which the nocturnal star delights), hangs between her breasts above the *ependytes*. The tiered registers of this girdle show us the three Graces, busts of the Sun and Moon, a Nereid (or Aphrodite *Pelagia?*) seated astride a sea monster, and three Cupids. Here again, the two luminaries express the Mother's dominance over the cosmos and eternity. To judge by the examples of the idol found outside her native Caria, the goddess received homage at Athens, but also at the other extremity of the western world, near Beja (Portugal).[38]

Six or seven replicas have been discovered in Rome itself, and she is also found at Parma and Ostia.[39] In Hadrian's time, Aphrodisian sculptors worked in Rome, and others in Ostia. Several of these artists seem to have collaborated on the statuary decoration of the Villa Adriana. The sculptor Zeno of Aphrodisias died in Rome, whence comes his epitaph in verse, now housed in the Vatican Museum.[40] The presence of an Aphrodisian colony in the *Urbs* and at Ostia, where there were many Anatolians, may on its own justify the import of the idol. But most of the replicas inventoried outside Aphrodisias were statuettes suitable for private chapels. The heads, hands and feet appear to have been carved from a different coloured marble, or cast in bronze (only the torsos are preserved).[41]

The goddess does not seem to have enjoyed public worship or a place in public life, although an object in the Vatican reconstructed with a fragment found in the Forum can hardly be interpreted as evidence of a personal cult,[42] unless it was thrown from the top of the Palatine (by fourth-century Christians?): in which case, this object would indicate the devotion of a member of the imperial household, like the little relief mentioned earlier representing the Heliopolitan triad.[43] But is it inconceivable that the Aphrodisian goddess might have been granted a modest idol in the temple of Venus and Rome, which in its monuments glorified the Trojan legend celebrated two centuries before by the oracle of Trophonius in Sulla's favour?

Again from the Roman Forum comes the fragment of a statuette which has been related to the Aphrodisian type. But here it is a goddess with a nimbus like the Ephesian, and the two Victories symmetrically holding her veil refer us rather to the idol of Artemis Leucophryna, 'with the white eyebrows' (those of the star with the silver forehead?).[44] She was worshipped at Magnesia on the Meander.

We know of no other example in the West. Once again, the origin of the fragment raises the problem of the function of the idol to which it belonged. I wonder whether, like the statuette of the Aphrodisian, it bears witness to the private piety of a Carian freedman in service in the Palace of the Caesars.

The Mysteries of Glycon

These Artemises and Aphrodites from Asia Minor have lunar attributes. Artemis was sometimes identified with Anaïtis, as is revealed, for instance, on a famous stele from Leiden, on which the goddess wears the crescent at the nape of her neck, while Apollo has the radiate head of the Sun.[45] Selene perhaps had worshippers at Heraclea of Latmos (south of Ephesus, in Ionia),[46] where people celebrated the myth of the sleeping Endymion, who is to be seen on Roman sarcophagi contemplated by the Moon during his happy slumber.[47] But it is questionable whether real initiations were performed there or that the influence of these problematical mysteries could explain the popularity of this theme in the funerary art of the Urbs.

On the other hand, Selene as well as the handsome Endymion entered into other mysteries, but these were organized, invented and staged from start to finish by a charlatan of genius: Alexander of Abonuteichos.[48] He would not be mentioned if his influence had not reached Rome, and even the imperial power in the person of Marcus Aurelius, a philosopher!

The former minion of a sorcerer who promised 'amorous favours, the summoning of infernal gods against the enemies whose downfall one desires, discovery of treasure or the improper solicitation of legacies', Alexander had learned his craft from a master. He gave the lie to the proverb 'no man is a prophet in his own country'. In fact, he did wonders in his native Paphlagonia where 'a man had only to appear with a player of the flute, timbrel or cymbals, and a sieve to predict the future, when everyone would come running, mouths agape, to hear him, and would gaze at him as if he were an inhabitant of the heavens' (Lucian, Alexander, or the False Prophet, 9). One thinks of the Metragyrtes or the beggar galli of Dea Syria.

At Pella in Macedonia Alexander had seen pet snakes suckled by the women of the region, as in the time when Olympias, the mother of another Alexander – the conqueror of Asia – indulged in the orgies of Bacchus. In the mind of this pastmaster of deception the spectacle sowed the seed of an idea to set up his very own cult. But he needed a divine revelation of the kind that would actually justify the building of a temple. So, with his accomplice Cocconas, in the Apollonian sanctuary of Chalcedon he buried some bronze tablets showing that Asclepius was going to settle in Abonuteichos. The evidently chance discovery of the inscriptions enchanted the inhabitants of the town where people swallowed anything, including serpent's eggs ... The municipality immediately decreed that a temple be erected.

Having donned a purple tunic striped with white (like the robes of the wandering Levantines described by Apuleius (*Metamorphoses*, VIII, 27, 2)) and a white cloak, Alexander returned to his home town. He brandished a long knife with a curved hook, like the *harpè* of Perseus from whom he claimed descent through his mother's line (the importance of the myth of Perseus in the elaboration of certain Anatolian cults may be recalled). He now needed a miracle to establish new mysteries. To this end, he enclosed a new-born snake in a goose egg which he placed by night in the muddy ground where the future temple would stand. The next day, after gesticulating with his *harpè* and tossing his long hair about (like the galli of Cybele and Atargatis or Bellona's fanatics), he prophesied and drew the crowds with him to the site: there he carefully unearthed the famous egg which, when broken, gave birth to the new Asclepius. Everyone acclaimed and saluted the slithering god. The people went wild with joy. The trick had been pulled.

But Alexander had brought back from Pella an enormous snake whose head he concealed in his armpit revealing only a false human face. This was 'Glycon' who would be used in his performances. He held it on his bosom and showed it to astounded visitors, seated on a bed and 'dressed like a god'. He thus predicted the future in the name of the ophidian, 'the grandson of Zeus', and each year, so it seems, delivered tens of thousands of oracles. Alexander had in his service a whole staff of specialized personnel: interpreters, seal-appliers, informers, writers of predictions, archivists, secretaries, accountants and ushers, who turned the oracle into a solid and venerable institution. He organized his publicity so remarkably that its effects were felt as far as the *Urbs*, first of all in senatorial circles. Rutilianus, the governor of Upper Moesia, then proconsul of Asia, went as far as to ask for the hand of Alexander's daughter, 'Selene'. And so this sexagenarian fiancé married the Moon, persuaded that he himself had thus become 'an inhabitant of the heavens' (*Alexander or the False Prophet*, 34).

To round things off, the sorcerer invented mysteries, with processions and liturgies lasting three days. As at Eleusis, the hierophant began with a proclamation excluding not murderers, but atheists, Christians and Epicureans. After these imprecations, a theatrical 'number' recalled the myth of the birth of Apollo and the union of the god with Coronis, the mother of Asclepius. A second day was consecrated to Glycon and his birth (from the goose egg). On the third day there was a representation of the marriage of Podalirius, the son of Aesculapius, with the impostor's mother. This 'Day of the Torches' ended with the love of Selene and Alexander-Endymion, which would engender that other Selene who had become the senator's wife. The pseudo-Endymion was seen lying in the middle of the temple, and from on high descended an imperial official's wife disguised as the Moon who kissed Alexander in full view of her husband! After a lengthy silence, the prophet dressed as hierophant cried: 'Iè, Glycon!', and there was an answering cry from the faithful: 'Iè, Alexander!' (ibid., 38–9).

Even the emperor – although a Stoic without illusions – showed his credulity, because before he marched against the Quadi and Marcomanni on the Danube front, he had two live lions thrown into the river, as Alexander's oracle had invited him to do: the result was disaster. The snaky swindler got out of it by quoting the example of Croesus: the god had predicted a victory, but without specifying which side would win. So, like one of the glories of the town, the image of the coiled Glycon rearing his human head would continue to adorn the coins of Abonuteichos stamped with the imperial effigy. The illustrious man-headed ophidian would also occupy the reverse of coins issued at Nicomedia. He would have dedications in Moesia and Dacia. He would even be confused with a rayed serpent, the Egyptian Chnubis, on intaglios carved in his name, to be used as talismans.[49] The statue of a snake found at Tomi on the shores of the Black Sea perhaps also represents Glycon, whose prodigious popularity throws some light on the mental attitudes of the time. In concocting his cultic drug, Alexander of Abonoteichos had known how to combine the ingredients for which the often perverted religiosity of the Antonine 'age of gold' had such an unhealthy affection.

These stagings of mystery rituals flourished at that time and later still, under the Severi.[50] They persisted even into Christianity and at its expense, in gnostic heresies where the snake dominated the theomythology and sometimes the liturgy of certain sects.

Gnostic Serpents

The Hebrew word for the reptile had given the Naassenes or Naassenians their name, and J. Carcopino believed he could decipher their beliefs and symbolism in the painted hypogeum of the Viale Manzoni in Rome.[51] In fact it must have involved some other sect (Simonians?

Carpocratians?), who incorporated the Neopythagorean dogma of metempsychosis into their system: hence the illustration of the myth of Circe restoring their human bodies to Ulysses' comrades, whom she had previously changed into swine.[52]

The Naassenians recognized in Attis a sort of primordial man, the first-born of the Father, and Hippolytus says they were assiduous in their attentions to the Great Mother. It may be recalled that they interpreted the love of Cybele and Attis, Aphrodite and Adonis, Selene and Endymion as the same allegory of 'beings who yearn for a soul'. But according to Hippolytus, they worshipped the serpent, connecting the Hebrew word *naas* with the Greek *naos* or 'temple', the supreme symbol of consecration. For them the reptile embodied the moist element from which they – like Thales of Miletus – claimed that the world and all life proceeded (Hippolytus, *Philosophoumena*, V, 9).

For another Gnostic sect, the Perates, the 'serpents of the desert' which bit the children of Israel represented the stars whose fatal course oppresses humanity. But they also identified another snake – that of Moses or the 'bronze serpent' – with the Word moving in the matter to which it gives life, rather like the Logos of the Stoics which travels through the world and beings as a fiery breath or *pneuma*. It was because the snake was deemed to be the animal with the most breath and related to fire (Philo of Byblos, quoted by Eusebius of Caesarea, *Praeparatio Evangelica*, I, 10, 45) that it was credited with the power of divination exploited by Alexander of Abonuteichos. It is also why the Mithraic Lionheaded idol is entwined by a snake, which was compared to the helicoidal course of the Sun, the other visible figure of the demiurge-Logos.

The Perates checked their theo-mythology of the Serpent by the constellations in the firmament:

If anyone has fortunate eyes, when he lifts his gaze to the sky he will see the beautiful image of the Serpent coiled at the great beginning of the sky and becoming, for all beings that are born, the principle of all movement ... (Hippolytus, *Philosophoumena*, V, 16)

The Perates recognized their Logos in the Dragon, whose head is flanked by the Crown and the Lyre. A man 'of pitiable appearance' called 'The Kneeling One' and corresponding to Hercules, touches with the tip of his right foot the 'twisting Dragon' spoken of by Aratos (*Phenomena*, 70). But behind this kneeling man another snake approaches to seize the crown and the Serpent-tamer grips it to prevent it from doing so (Hippolytus, loc. cit.). For these Gnostics, whose name means 'emigrants' (an allusion to the passage of the Red Sea, a water of corruption that had to be crossed in order to escape from the lower world of creation), astrology had the value of an irrefutable scientific argument.

It was again a serpent that obsessed the imagination of the Sethians and their predominantly sexual cosmogony. The first serpent, the 'wind of the shadows' or 'first-born of the waters' begets man in order to imprison light in him: this is the demiurge accursed of all Gnostics. But the saviour also wears the snake's appearance, like the Logos of the Perates. 'The perfect Word of the light from above took the monstrous shape of the serpent to penetrate the impure womb' and free the spirit held captive in matter (ibid., 19).

The Ophites, whose name quite clearly reveals their ophidian devotion, held that from the attraction for matter which ensnares Ialdabaoth is born a son in the form of a snake who is none other than Intellect (Irenaeus, *Against Heresies*, I, 30, 5). But Ialdabaoth throws him into the lower world after the damnation of Eve and Adam. Some believed that the serpent had given the gnosis to humankind and identified it with Wisdom. Others detected in the coils of the intestines 'the generative substance of life in the form of a snake' (ibid., 15). But the Ophites about whom the heresiologist Epiphanius of Salamis informs us (*Panarion*, 37, 5) did not cling to phantasmagoria or symbolic explanations. Like the devotees of Glycon or Asclepius, they worshipped a real snake, but for the celebration of their liturgy. The loaves were assembled before summoning the reptile, which emerged from its cage, reached the table and undulated amid the bread to consecrate it, since it was the embodiment of the Word. Only then was the bread broken and pieces distributed to the communicants. Each follower kissed the tame snake on the mouth and prostrated himself before it. The animal was considered to transmit their hymn of praise to the 'Father on high'. There was probably nothing very exceptional about this sect. About fifty years ago H. Leisegang described and commented upon a curious alabaster bowl,[53] inside which is a relief showing an assembly of naked votaries, worshipping around a large snake coiled in the centre of the circle; externally, four Orphic lines can be deciphered inscribed at the base of a colonnade. Even though the bowl is ancient, it is impossible to state definitely that it was used in a ritual of initiatory 'communion'.

The Imagery of Carved Stones

We shall rediscover the serpent in Bacchanalia and the cult of Sabazius. It will be found chiefly in Graeco-Egyptian circles, in the mainstream or on the fringes of official and traditional Nilotic cults. The imagery of the 'magic' intaglios in fact confirms for us the kind of fascination exerted on many minds at that time by the twisting snake. There is no cause to set magic against religion,[54] as was done notably in respect of papyri giving recipes for occult activities (and the accompanying formulae for prayers), unless we accept that only wise men and mystics were genuinely concerned with religion!

On the Graeco-Egyptian gems used as amulets and talismans (which were executed following certain dictates like those preserved for us in the magic papyri) we can recognize the same representations (Isis, Osiris, Serapis, Anubis, Cybele, Artemis of Ephesus, Triple Hecate, Mithras, Jupiter Heliopolitanus, Danubian horsemen . . .) as in the repertoire of figures belonging to Hellenico-oriental worship of the second and third centuries AD. They bear witness to beliefs similar to those expressed in the sanctuaries, confirmed for us by literary or epigraphic tradition. The psychological nuances are all the less important to us, as it happens, because they completely elude us and frequently eluded even the believer himself.[55]

One cannot help but be struck, however, by the place occupied in the bestiary of carved stones by snakes, androcephalous or solar dragons, ophidian or snake-footed monsters of all kinds.

We have seen that the enigmatic idol ritually buried in the 'Syrian' (?) sanctuary on the Janiculum could be explained in the light of the image identified on intaglios as the mummy of Osiris entwined by a helicoidal snake. Helios-*Aiôn*, the Alexandrian god of cyclic eternity, also appears in the form of a snake. A magic papyrus (*PGM*, I, 163ff) advises the operator to use a gem engraved with a lion-headed god entwined by an 'ouroboros' snake (i.e., with its tail in its mouth), before invoking *Aiôn*, the god of gods. The radiate lion-headed god bearing the sign of life (*ankh*) and a sceptre around which a snake is coiled is closely akin to the Mithraic idol of Time and the devouring Fire. On the gems it is found in association with the legend *Iao* or *Abrasax*, which like *Abraxas* is made up of letters whose numerical value is equal to the number of days in a year. These same names (*Iao* and *Abrasax*) designate a spirit with the head of a cock who has two snakes in place of legs.[56] He sometimes has the head of a donkey or a dog. With a Roman-style cuirass, like the Sun he holds a whip, but also a shield in the form of a wheel (the attribute of Fortune or Nemesis). This alectorocephalous anguiped, who apparently simultaneously combines powers over heaven and earth must have been deemed to protect from danger: during life and doubtless after death, for between earth and sky the soul is exposed to the demons of the air whom Abrasax's whip may serve to drive out. One thinks of the seven zoomorphic Archons with the head of a lion, a bear, a dog or a donkey, whom the Ophites imagined as the doorkeepers or customs officers of the sky, in the famous diagram explained by Origen (*Against Celsus*, VI, 30; VII, 40).[57]

A fair number of 'magic' stones also show us a snake twisted in one or more coils, raising a radiate lion's head (with seven or sometimes twelve rays). The name that accompanies it, Knubis (Chnubis) or Chnumis (Chnumos), refers us to the Nilotic god Khnoum, the solar and creator god who is found on other gemstones in association with the Key of the Matrix.[58] But Hellenistic astrology conferred on him a special role of responsibility for a decan of the Crab or the Lion (Cancer or Leo). Hermes Trismegistus was credited with a work describing Chnumis as a god 'with a leonine face, emitting solar rays', but whose 'entire body is that of an upwardly spiralling snake'. His name and function recall Kneph ('he who fulfils his time'), whom Porphyry mentions as a demiurge (Eusebius of Caesarea, *Praeparatio Evangelica*, III, 11, 45–6) and who appeared in the Theban cosmogony as a creator snake.

The Alexandrian Gnostics probably embroidered part of their phantasmagoria onto this Egyptian religious imaginary being. The snake Knubis was considered to heal ills of the stomach. Hence its popularity as a phylactery. On an intaglio in the Bibliothèque Nationale we see it rising from a basket, like the Dionysian snakes, with a leonine face crested with twelve rays.[59] A magician (*PGM*, IV, 939) salutes the serpent and lion as 'the natural principles of fire'. Here we find again a symbolism similar to that from which the Mithraic typology of the Lion-headed god seems to have emerged.

The sign of Knubis can be made out at the centre of a circle formed by the snake with its tail in its mouth, the spatio-temporal symbol of the world and the cyclic course of Helios or the heavens. On our gems, this 'ouroboros' encircles the Matrix closed by a key with seven teeth and surmounted sometimes by the lion-headed snake, or the god Khnoum between Isis and Harpocrates, or Serapis and Thoth, or a scarab.[60] On a magic papyrus (*PGM*, XII, 270ff) concerning a talisman that ensures the protection of the most powerful of the gods (the headless god?), is written:

Let there be a snake with its tail in its mouth, in the shape of a crown, and within the snake a sacred scarab of the radiate kind.

Another papyrus (*PGM*, VII, 580ff) recommends an amulet of an ouroboros snake, bearing within its circle the sacred names of *Aiôn*

and Knephis (the Theban demiurge). 'I am he who causes birth and
death', says an invocation to the headless god or 'Formula of Ieou'
(*PGM*, V, 156); 'I am the beauty of the *Aiôn*. My name is a heart
entwined by a serpent'.[61]

This *Aiôn* is confused in other papyri with the ophidian Agathodaimon, whom Philo of Byblos identified also with Kneph. A gold plate
found in a tomb of the Vigna Codini, in Rome, bears a prayer
inscribed in Greek to the 'reptile Aiôn', assimilated in this instance to
Serapis, to protect the dead man against evil spells (*SEG*, XV, 619). The
snake Agathodaimon, indeed, watched over the deceased. The theme
of the dragon that guards temples and the dead is also well known in
the literature of the Greek alchemists, to which we shall return.

The moults of the snake, which could be taken as the sign of
perpetual rejuvenation, certainly partly explain why it was regarded
as the embodiment of cyclic eternity, the only one commonly conceived by the Ancients, at least in pagan circles. *A priori*, the relationship of the snake with fire is more surprising. Philo of Byblos referred
to a certain Epeeis,[62] an eminent Egyptian hierophant and hier-
ogrammatist, who made a snake the foremost divine creature, a
falcon-serpent (Horus-Apollo?) blazing over creation:

If he opened his eyes, he would fill everything with light
(Eusebius of Caesarea, *Preparatio Evangelica*, I, 10, 49).

Here we may recognize one of those images which filled Gnostic
mythology. Philo of Byblos claimed to have translated a book of
Sanchuniathon on the cosmogony of the Phoenicians, in which he
celebrated the snake as the supreme fiery animal (ibid., 46). If the
name Sanchuniathon does not conceal some fabrication, one may
wonder: did Philo reinterpret the original Phoenician myth with
thoughts of the artistic fire of the Stoics which spread and 'snaked' its
way, so to speak, through the world in order to give it life? The image
of the reptile radiating over creation and animating it, like the Sun in
its annual circumvolutions in the zodiac, mythically transcribed the
physics dear to the philosophers of the Stoa. It is true that Zeno of
Citium, the founder of the School, probably had Phoenician fore-
bears.

Chapter 6
Occultism and Theosophy

O
N THE fringe of the public or 'mystery' ceremonies devoted to divinities that were recognized in various milieux or, geographically speaking, in various sectors of the Roman world, currents of thinking or religiosity developed that were related without however having the same type of liturgy. (The relationship could be in expression, oracular or initiatory style, the gods invoked, operational methods or the very spirit of devotion.) Papyri and literary tradition preserve for us the evidence of those attitudes of mind which germinated and spread owing to the same historical circumstances as the religions of eastern origin, but somewhat anarchically, amid the frustration and dissatisfaction ultimately engendered by the ossified cults of the 'establishment', chiefly among intellectuals and a society of anonymous masses where the individual sought dignity, a personal relationship with the divinity, but also escape – into the supernatural world of magic, alchemy, astrology and, correspondingly, in the mythical Orient of prophets and miracle workers.

Well ahead of the Romantics, Apollonius of Tyana and Plotinus wanted to travel in the Orient. The former went to talk with the Gymnosophists and learn about the philosophy of the Brahmins.[1] In AD 242, at the time when Tarsus was issuing coins of the bull-slaying Mithras type, Plotinus enlisted in the army of Gordian III, to 'acquire firsthand knowledge' of the philosophy reputedly practised by the Persians and Indians (Porphyry, *Life of Plotinus*, 3). At the same instant, Mani was perhaps accompanying Shapur I, in the enemy army; a historic symbol of two worlds in military confrontation, but which advanced to meet each other with the same burning curiosity and the desire to know each other better. Before Gordian III – who marched against the Sassanids in the wild hope of Romanizing Mesopotamia – from Trajan to Caracalla, the emperors had also, in their own fashion, yielded to the temptations of the oriental mirage, dreaming of becoming the new Alexander, or of reincarnating Bacchus, *domitor Orientis*.[2]

This prestige of the East naturally haunted the occult 'sciences' and theosophical literature, the substitutes for cults and philosophy.

Magic and Necromancy

Magic, which played a part in religion (at the same time as medicine and astrology), was held according to Pliny the Elder to have its origins with Zoroaster as the knowledge of the Magi. The Naturalist quotes the more or less legendary names of the Medes Apusoros and Zaratos (otherwise known as Zarathustra and Zoroaster), the Babylonians Marmaros and Arabantiphocos, and the Assyrian Tarmoendas. These were names to conjure with. But written material circulated – notably an 'Octoteuch' – under the pseudepigraphy of Ostanes. The latter had accompanied Xerxes, the Great King, in his war against the Greeks:

> Scattering on his way the seeds of this monstrous art, wherever he had passed he infected the world with it. (Pliny the Elder, *Natural History*, XXX, 8)

In Pliny's time, this world contaminated by magic coincided with the Roman Empire, and it may be recalled that when Tiridates arrived in the *Urbs* to have himself crowned king of Armenia he was said to have initiated Nero to 'magic banquets' (ibid., 17). The emperor claimed 'to command the gods' (ibid., 14), which differentiates magic from religion (though the ritualism of prayers implicitly claims the same kind of efficacy). After having his mother murdered, Nero was supposed to have used the intervention of the Magi to carry out an infernal sacrifice in order to exorcise the shade of Agrippina.[3]

The necromancers drew their inspiration sometimes from Zoroaster, sometimes from the pharaoh Nectanebo. But at all events their operational techniques exhibited a brand image of eastern origin, and the demonology they asserted was reputed to hark back to the teaching of Ostanes.[4] One night, Lucian's Menippus, always vainly running after the truth, decides to go to Babylon to beseech the help of one of those Magi who were the disciples and heirs of Zoroaster:

> For I had heard tell that by incantations and initiations they could open the gates of Hades, take whomever they pleased there and bring them back again safe and sound. (Lucian, *Menippus or Necromancy*, 6)

In fact, these kinds of shaman offered their clientele the prospect of a *katabasia*: a journey into the next world. The actions described in the magic papyri often resemble an escape – ecstasy – into the beyond.

So Menippus contacts a venerable bearded Chaldaean named 'Mithrobarzanus'. For twenty-nine days from the new moon the candidate for the journey below must bathe every morning in the Euphrates, listening to the incantations of certain demons with strange names. The Magus spits three times in his face, purifies him with water and fire, ritually 'armours' him against the phantoms of the dead, then leads him to a sunless place where he invokes Hecate and Persephone, mingling in 'indistinct barbarian words, several syllables long' (ibid., 9). An irresistible efficacy was attributed to these 'barbarian' names of eastern origin. The magic papyri supply a wealth of examples, as do the carved gemstones. Apuleius, defending himself (badly) against an accusation of magic, waxes ironic about words 'drawn from the Egyptian or Babylonian ritual' (*Apologia*, 28, 7).

In fact Egypt, and notably Hermes Trismegistus, also claimed the patronage of both magic and necromancy.[5] In his *Metamorphoses* (II, 25), the same Apuleius brings on stage the 'prophet' Zatchlas, who awakens a corpse to force it to tell the truth. Under Claudius or Nero, the doctor Thessalus makes friends with a priest from Greater Diospolis (Thebes, in Egypt) to have commerce with the gods, and the priest offers to let him converse with the ghost of a dead man.[6] But Thessalus wants to talk to Asclepius. Whatever the branch or variant of the occultism that obsessed so many minds in the imperial era, the ultimate aim was always to enter into contact with the divine (this was also the goal of the mysteries). In this regard Egypt had a well-established tradition.

The Jews, too, had their own, which came from Moses, Jannes and Jambres (the two magicians who had held a real thaumaturgic competition with Moses and Aaron) and Jotapes.[7] Jesus similarly had the reputation of being a magician, or at the least an exorcist.[8] The prestige of Simon Magus had also made him the more or less fabulous inspirer of a Gnostic sect. In papyri and on intaglios, Biblical names often recur, associated with those of pagan and, remarkably, Egyptian gods; Helios-Mithras and the Babylonian Ereshkigal, goddess of the Underworld, appear in the writings of Graeco-Egyptian occultism alongside unintelligible names that smack of an orientalizing abracadabra.

People naturally resorted to magic to relieve the sick or those bitten by vipers. Lucian (*The Friend of Lies*, 11–12) records the story of the wine grower Midas who was saved by a Babylonian ('of those who are known as Chaldaeans'), who drives out the venom by hanging on the unfortunate man's foot a fragment from the stele of a dead young girl (the prematurely dead always have supernatural power). He utters seven sacramental words 'drawn from an old book', purifies the farm with sulphur and fire, summons all the snakes in the place and breathes on them – which instantaneously consumes them all! The dead, especially the victims of violent death (*biaiothanatoi*) or untimely death (*ahoroi*) co-operate in the action of the magicians, for they are held to desire revenge. Here again, the doctrine legitimizing these methods which were condemned by Roman law was ascribed to the Magi, and more precisely, Ostanes. Demons were summoned, too, and a good part of the Christian polemic against these 'unclean' or 'impure' spirits was rooted in an Iranian-type dualism. J. Bidez and F. Cumont trace back to Ostanes (or at least the books put out in his name) a long elaboration by Porphyry (*Abstinence*, II, 37–43) on good and bad demons,[9] a dualism defended (under the same influence?) by the Neoplatonizing antiquary Cornelius Labeo, perhaps in the third century AD.[10] Demonology, which occupies such a large place in Neoplatonism, takes up the best part of Iamblichus' treatise on *The Mysteries of the Egyptians*, justifying occultism.

Alchemy and Astrology

The same illustrious Ostanes was credited with the gnosis of the mysterious properties of bodies which since the Middle Ages has been called alchemy, a word taken from the Arabic *alkimiya*, but adapted from the Greek *chemia*, whose meaning remains enigmatic: the name for Egypt, 'black earth', or 'black' designating the raw material for the transmutation of metals, whitened like silver or yellowed like gold? or the name for 'melting' (*chuma*)? There was doubt even in ancient times, because the discovery of alchemy was attributed to a mythical Chemes, Chimes or Chumes. Ostanes was associated with the celebrated philosopher Democritus, who was credited with a work significantly entitled *Physical and Mystical Teachings*, in which the learned man claimed to have summoned the spirit of the Magus to elicit from him the secrets of the Great Art.[11]

In the second century BC, Bolos of Mendes was inspired by both Ostanes and Democritus in a book of formulas dealing with the sympathies and antipathies of bodies (plants or stones), the tincture of gold and silver, precious stones and purple (*Baphika*). The *Book of Henoch* had already made allusion to these formulas which aroused passions that were not inspired by base interests alone.[12] The *Teachings* of the Pseudo-Democritus probably derive from the work compiled by

270 Occultism and Theosophy

Bolos. Ostanes confessed that his books were hidden in a temple. And in fact, in a Memphite sanctuary, a column which opened in the middle was said to have yielded, among others, the famous formula: 'Like attracts like',[13] which is found applied by Nechepso-Petosiris to astrological medicine in a text datable to the second century BC (Firmicus Maternus, *Mathesis*, IV, 22, 2).

This connection of Ostanes with Egypt in an enlightening account to the glory of alchemy clearly conveys the feeling that the Great Art had a dual ancestry. Other apocrypha took their place in the corpus of the Greek alchemists,[14] whose pseudo-science was attributed either to the Egyptian gods (Hermes, Isis, the snake Agathodaimon) or Cleopatra or the Persian Ostanes, but also to the Jews: King Solomon, Maria, author of a *Treatise on Furnaces*, Theophilus or even, more belatedly, Moses. In fact, at the foundations of the research on which the Greeks expounded lay certain processes of Egyptian craftsmanship which long remained professional secrets, comparable – relatively speaking – with the initiatory traditions of the trades guilds. The intellectuals of Alexandrian Hellenism tended to apply theories of philosophical origin (Platonic and Aristotelian) to empirical formulas or 'grimoires' of Nilotic tradition, turning physics into a kind of metaphysics.[15]

The same dual oriental heritage, laced with Greek philosophy, characterized the astrological schools and literature whose influence so strongly marked some of the great cults mentioned earlier.[16]

In the third century BC, Berosus, a Chaldaean priest, dedicated to the king of Syria, Antiochus I Soter, a history of Babylon extolling the science of the stars which he taught medical students on the island of Cos. But iatromathematics or the 'science' of the relationships uniting the parts of the human body and their physiology with the constellations or planets was held to be an Egyptian discovery (although founded on the principle of universal sympathy dear to the Pythagoreans). Moreover, people readily confused the Chaldaeans with the Magi, and Zoroaster was regarded as the author of astrological books. The Persian reformer was even made out to be an expert astronomer who was supposed to have instructed the Babylonians. However, Hermes-Thoth – the Trismegistus – also claimed the honour of having discovered sidereal mathematics and revealed it to men. A compilation of the second century BC, under the names of the priest Petosiris and the king Nechepso, popularized the elements of a 'hermetic' astrology to be found in the *Salmeschiniaka*, astrological tables that conformed to the principles of the 'chronocratoria'; i.e., a system accepting the influence of the thirty-six horoscopes or decans (as 'masters of time') over each of the thirty-six ten-day periods of the Egyptian year. As in the case of alchemy, the Greeks theorized on the observations recorded for centuries by the Egyptians and Babylonians, refining and systematizing their empirical data. They placed their astronomic geometry and philosophical intellect at the service of that celestial divination which would bear the name *Mathesis*. The Platonizing Stoic Posidonius of Apamea would give it its ideological credentials.[17]

Occultism and Mysterism

In common with the oriental cults, all this occultism did not only have the real or presumed, human or divine, origins of its founders. Like Isiacism, Phrygianism and Mithraism, it had taken on an initiatory form. The magician was a mystagogue. The magic act was a *telete*, a 'consecration' which worked by virtue of a mystery 'tradition' (*paradosis*).[18] The god and his invoker, like the mystae, recognized each other by way of passwords which compelled divine favour: 'Grant my prayer, because I utter mystic symbols,' declares a magician.[19] Like initiation, the whole operation consists of words (*legomena*) and deeds (*drômena*). The papyri designate it a *mysterion* or an ensemble of *mysteria*. As in the instance of Isiac initiation (Apuleius, *Metamorphoses*, XI, 21, 8), one must make oneself worthy of divine grace. When that has been deserved, by making contact with the divinity one is 'consecrated' (*tetelesmenos*), that is, fully initiated. The incantation, the 'consecration' of an intaglio, also bears the name *telete*. The Latin verb *initiare* may equally mean 'to enchant', in other words to put someone in communication with the divine, which was also the objective of candidates to the mysteries.

This religious terminology is just as much characteristic of alchemical literature. The Pseudo-Democritus did not confine himself to *physica*, but from them drew *mystica*. In this regard the title of the pseudepigraph revealed its true colours. Alchemy was a sort of initiatory cult, with its rites, sacrifices, prayers, *symbola* or formulas of consecration which required from the candidate to the Great Art some preliminary instruction and a testing period. It was an esoteric 'knowledge' of which one had to prove oneself worthy, and which one had no right to divulge to the profane. On this point, comparison may be made to the forms of oaths prohibiting the revelation of mysteries to the non-initiated. So the details of operational techniques were transcribed and taught only under the veil of learned enigmas.

Astrology did not escape this initiatory colouring.[20] For Vettius Valens (*Catalogus codicum astrologorum Graecorum*, V, 2, pp. 35, 40, 46, 74, 88, 122 etc.) as for Firmicus Maternus (*Mathesis*, II, 30, 1–2, 14–15;

V, *praef.* 1; VIII, 1, 7), astrology was a sort of mystery gnosis, not fit for common or perverted intellects. By applying one's mind to the study of celestial phenomena, one purged it of passions and initiated it into a real cosmic liturgy. Like the cultic mysteries, astrology demanded a catharsis, a moral and physical asceticism. Like the mystae, the reader or disciple of astrology must take an oath not to reveal anything to non-initiates.

Generally speaking, every kind of access to the supernatural and oracular or oneiric revelation then assumed the mantle of 'consecration' (*telete*). The very contemplation of the world as a myth to be elucidated was therefore likened to an initiation. Cleanthes called the cosmos a 'mystery' (Epiphanius, *Panarion*, 2, 2, 9); Chrysippus gave his theological lessons the title *Consecrations*. Well before the alchemists, Plato had applied the vocabulary of the Eleusinian mysteries to the spiritual journey of the philosopher who is finally illuminated by union with the Beautiful and the vision of Good, like the initiate in the higher grade of the epopts.[21] We know the fortunes of this mystagogy in the Academy and among the Neoplatonists, from Theon of Smyrna to Olympiodorus.

For occultists, it was not simply a matter of a verbal scenario. The astrologer had the feeling that he was entering into contact with the gods of the heavens and living henceforth, like the mysta, in a sort of union or communion with the divine. To know was to be born, reborn, with the gods, for one could know only on condition of being what one wanted to know, according to the old doctrine of Parmenides. Like the alchemist or the magician, the astrologer had access to immortality. Like them, he eluded fate, the liberation promised by Isis to her initiates. According to the alchemist Zosimus (end of the third to beginning of the fourth century AD), Zoroaster stated that 'by the knowledge of all things above and the magic property of corporeal sounds, one averts all the evils of fate' (*On the Letter* Ω, 7).[22] Zoroaster and Hermes Trismegistus claimed this privilege for the 'race of philosophers', i.e., alchemists. Indeed, astral destiny was held to be connected with demons and other powers of the air that the magicians and sorcerers of the Great Work were confident of neutralizing. All these beliefs possessed a distant oriental ancestry.

The practices of occultism certainly differentiated it from cultic mysteries. Yet both alchemy and magic presented similarities to certain rituals in both form and content. In this respect the place occupied by dyeing (*Baphika*) is striking; the baths for metals, stones or fabrics, which gave them a gold, silver, emerald or purple appearance. This method of 'baptism' metamorphosed bodies, as the initiatory bath regenerated the candidate and led him to the new life that the *telete* was deemed to confer on him. As silver was lunar, gold was obviously the metal of the Sun, the star that played a major role in the religion of alchemists as it did in oriental or orientalizing cults. 'It is through the Sun that everything is accomplished' (Berthelot-Ruelle, *Alchimistes grecs*, I, p. 156). Chrysopoea, or the making of gold, symbolized the true transmutation of the soul, when it reincorporates its original being in the divine fire of the Empyrean. The noble metal has the very colour of the light from which it came. With Zosimus, alchemy thus became a religion of salvation. As the metal has to be purified and bathed in order to turn it into gold, the soul is summoned to regain its igneous nature or the gold of its authentic being.

Among the magic papyri, the *Formula for immortality* (*PGM*, IV, 475–732),[23] which A. Dieterich mistakenly called a 'Liturgy of Mithras', is typical of the Graeco-Egyptian circles where people sought a mystic and deifying experience, outside the traditional mystery religions, by means of a kind of psychosomatic regeneration. As in the case of cultic mysteries, the neophyte was deemed to be able to obtain immortality or *apathanatismos* by a sanctification, rebirth or renewal of his individuality, not only physically and bodily but morally and spiritually. He had to pray for a new 'breath' (*pneuma*) to inspire him, then draw to himself from the sun's rays a divine wind to lift and raise him to the ultimate heaven in the presence of Helios-Mithras

a god of immense size, with a face of light, very youthful, with golden hair, clad in a white tunic, a gold turban and broad gaiters, holding in his right hand the shoulder of a golden calf, that is to say, the she-Bear who moves the sky . . . [24]

People have tried to see in this evocation the image of Mithras, opposite the kneeling Sun, brandishing an object which has often (and without good reason) been interpreted as a bull's thigh.[25]

Dazzled by this radiant vision, the mysta then implores the god to dwell henceforth in his soul. Like the initiations of Lucius in Apuleius (*Metamorphoses*, XI, 23, 7), the ecstatic journey to the celestial 'beyond' which anticipates his posthumous ascent results in an illumination, a face-to-face adoration of Helios-Mithras and ends in apotheosis. The great difference is that the *apathanatismos* of the 'Formula' does not proceed, like the consecration of Lucius, from a providential grace confirmed by a liturgy in which a body of priests takes part, but from a technique set in operation materially, in isolation, in a sort of individual secrecy.

Intellectuals like Apuleius who thirsted after mysteries and the supernatural had themselves consecrated to the most varied secret cults, while at the same time flirting with magic or alchemy. But in certain priestly circles, magic and necromancy were denounced as a real imposture, a counterfeit religion. Heliodorus of Emesa (*Ethiopica*, III, 16, 3–4) puts in the mouth of an Egyptian priest all the faults he can find with this 'vulgar science' which, 'in the service of idols, runs around corpses, consumes itself in herbs, is given over to incantations' and 'passes off phantasmagoria for realities'. But there was another science 'the true wisdom whose name the former has usurped', that of the priests and prophets

> which looks upwards to the heavens: the companion of the gods, it partakes of their supernatural power, studies the movement of the stars and thereby acquires foreknowledge of the future. (From a translation by J. Maillon)

Astrology therefore had a right to some respect, for the contemplation of the spheres and the firmament was of a nature to elevate the soul above trivial preoccupations. The same Heliodorus (VI, 14, 7) would recall, after the incantations of a sorceress over the body of his dead son, that the prophets practise their art 'by ritual sacrifices and holy prayers, leaving the profane to crawl over the ground and corpses' (same translation). In the Severan period, Philostratus ascribed a similar vein of language to the Neopythagoreanizing miracle worker Apollonius of Tyana.

Hermes Trismegistus

However, positive religions, or at least the practices of the material cult, were challenged not only by rationalist or moralizing philosophers, but even by a theosophical trend whose teaching harked back to the god Thoth: hermetism.[26]

As early as the Ptolemaic period, an astrological literature had circulated under the name of Hermes, perhaps before the *Salmeschiniaka* which transcribed certain treatises attributed to the god around the third century BC. A *Liber Hermetis* on the decans compiled very old parts that dated back to the time when the Greeks became passionately interested in the Egyptian doctrine of the 'Chronocratoria'. But Hermes-Thoth, the inventor of writing, who had already been celebrated as such by Plato in *Phaedrus* (274 c–e), tended chiefly to appear as a master of wisdom. The priests of Thebes of whom Strabo speaks (*Geography*, XVII, 1, 46) were keenly interested in astronomy and 'philosophy': they made Hermes the patron of their science. In the time of the emperor Domitian (81–96), the poet Martial (*Epigrams*, V,

24, 15) was apparently aware of a theology concerning the god One and All, 'three times One' (*ter unus*). It is true that at the time the Flavian government was dispensing its favours to Egyptian cults: the echo of litanies or sermons heard in the *Iseum Campense*? Some time later, Plutarch (*Isis and Osiris*, 61) cites the books of Hermes on sacred names, and Philo of Byblos salutes the zeal with which Sanchuniathon 'pulled from their hiding-place the treatises of Taaut' or Thoth-Hermes (Eusebius of Caesarea, *Praeparatio Evangelica*, I, 9, 24).

It was during the second century AD that what was to become the *Corpus Hermeticum* must have begun to be formed, a literature of divine revelations on the celestial powers, the world, man and the soul, salvation and piety: dialogues, preachings, cosmogonies, aretalogies, prayers, apocalypses, didactic and theological expositions, but also sometimes mystic evocations, ecstatic experiences of deification comparable to those found in the magic papyri. This *Corpus*, previously known from Byzantine manuscript tradition and quotations or various extracts (notably in the *Anthology* of Stobaeus), has been enriched since 1945 by the discoveries at Nag Hammadi.[27] The most famous text is the *Poimandres*, its cosmogonic myth, anthropology and eschatology curiously recalling the great Gnostic visions.[28] Recent research has demonstrated that a Judaeo-Christian substratum had very probably inspired its composition.

There is no coherence in the doctrine that could justify describing it as a well-defined sect. This gnosis has no unity other than the pseudo-Egyptian colouring of the spokesmen or divine messengers of Hermes. Aside from the differences – often enormous – in the conceptions expressed about the world and the soul, from the religious point of view the *Corpus Hermeticum* presents the notable peculiarity of having been inspired by or in men who apparently derived no satisfaction from the external liturgies of the established cults. Hermetism was more a mysteriosophy than a mystery religion. Its style of devout unction, its literary and intellectual mystagogy met the needs of individuals or circles who were in fact equally unorganized as regards both worship and doctrine. It was an orientalizing religiosity of words and imagination rather than a religion properly speaking. Certainly, those who took delight in it were able, from time to time and in parallel, to participate in rites of pagan practice. But it seems that they could not fully assuage their vaguely spiritualistic aspirations except by a sort of Egyptianizing theosophical dream.[29]

Hermetism had no iconography. The brilliant and celebrated exegesis advanced by J. Carcopino of the mosaic at Lambiridi (Kherbet Ouled Arif, Algeria), which decorates the tomb of Urbanilla, cannot stand up to a thorough critical examination.[30] Nothing genuinely and specifically 'hermetic' can be discerned there. Neither the scene of medical consultation, nor the wine-bowls flanked by ducks, nor the snake-legged spirits typically illustrate the confused and disparate texts of the *Corpus*. Nor, it seems, did the Hermetists have places suitable for sacramental gatherings, which probably never took place.

The *Asclepius*, an augmented Latin translation (or adaptation?) of a *Perfect Discourse* or 'consecration' (*Logos Teleios*), appended to the works of Apuleius in the manuscripts, but datable to the third century AD, reveals the Trismegistus, Tat, Hammon and Asclepius in an Egyptian sanctuary.[31] Following their learned conversation on the cosmos and man who was created to contemplate it, on the imminent death of the gods in men's hearts, on time and eternity, Hermes and his companions emerge 'from the depths of the sanctuary'. Turning towards the south (in the direction of the place where the Sun reaches the lower world, according to the theo-cosmogony of the Egyptians), they pray to God. When Asclepius suggests burning incense and perfumes, Trismegistus replies:

Silence, O Asclepius! When one invokes God it is like a sacrilege to burn incense and all the other things. For he who is All, and in whom All is, lacks nothing. Let us worship him with thanksgiving: that is the finest incense one can offer God. (*Asclepius*, 41)

There could be no better condemnation of a pagan *praxis* which the laws of the Christian emperor Theodosius I, known as 'the Great', would ban in 391. Of course, the same *Asclepius* (23) has earlier glorified man as 'creator of the gods' (*homo fictor est deorum*), with a development on the consecration of statues (24 and 37–8). It also finishes with a reference to a 'pure communion unsullied by any food that ever had life' (41). But under cover of an impeccable logic, Carcopino as always has drawn an arbitrary historical inference: 'no prayers without a religion, no formulas for prayers without a church, even one that is destitute of clergy to set and diffuse them, to prescribe the time and the attitude that give full effectiveness to each prayer . . .'[32] And he goes on to state that the 'Hermetic prayer' uttered at nightfall 'was followed by a ritual meal devised in the fashion of a mystic communion'.

R. Reitzenstein[33] and J. Geffcken[34] also believed in the existence of Hermetic communities. A.-J. Festugière put forward good reasons for doubting it,[35] and the discovery of Hermetic writings in the Gnostic library of Khenoboskion in Upper Egypt does not challenge his argument.[36] One of these texts, entitled *The Ogdoad and the Ennead*, mentions a sort of preliminary training of the candidate for illumination, by means of books and spiritual exercises, before a prayer, a kiss of peace and the contemplation of 'inexpressible profundities'. But this mystico-literary setting does not necessarily imply the life and operation of a sect properly speaking. Hermetism was a theosophical gnosis. For a Hermetist, piety did not consist in rites and practices: it was 'the knowledge of God' (*Corpus Hermeticum*, IX, 4; cf. Lactantius, *Divine Institutes*, II, 15).

As for the famous 'baptism' in the wine-bowl in the IVth treatise, this is a symbolic metaphor proceeding from the meeting of two images: the absorption of the regenerative wine and the purificatory bath.[37] A divine herald invites men to drink and to plunge into the Intellect in order to become 'perfect' (*teleioi*, or 'consecrated'). But it was not a matter of a ceremony of introduction and admission into a circle of initiates. On this subject, the term 'literary mysteries' has rightly been used (by A.-J. Festugière[38]). In this instance, the writer of the treatise has remembered *Proverbs*, 9, 5–6, and perhaps Gnostic themes that can be spotted in the *Pistis Sophia* (142) or, more precisely, in the IInd book of Ieou, which probably inspired him. Confirmed in concrete terms in the case of the Khenoboskion library mentioned above, these links between Christian gnosis and Hermetic gnosis provide much food for thought.

It is nevertheless a fact that the Hermetic *corpus* has a set of themes, a tone and a style that are indisputably initiatory. The XIIIth treatise notably is presented as a *logos* on regeneration.[39] Inititation consists in the transmission (*paradosis*) of a *logos* (like the *hieros logos* of the mysteries), into the process by which a new man is engendered (*genesiourgia*: XIII, 21). This distinction matches that of the *legomena* and *drômena* in the cultic mysteries. The candidate has to observe a 'religious silence' (XIII, 8). As in the Isiac initiation of Lucius in Apuleius, the birth of the new man is a grace of divine mercy (XIII, 8 and 10), obtained by prayers and piety: *novit qui colit* . . . It is also dependent on a purification (XIII, 7, 8, 15). The 'twelve executioners' from whom the votary must be delivered, and whom Hermes relates expressly to the zodiac, recall the twelve robes worn by Lucius (Apuleius, *Metamorphoses*, XI, 24, 1); to me they seem to suggest an imaginary or mystic ascent in sidereal space.

Hermetic initiation aimed to build the Word in the mind of the candidate (XIII, 8: compare Paul, *Galatians*, 4, 19; *Ephesians*, 4, 12). Henceforth God would dwell in man who would recognize himself as a god, the son of God (XIII, 2). It was a 'genesis in God' (XIII, 6). This new man was born in God through the 'will of God' which sowed spiritual wisdom 'in silence' (XIII, 15–21). The votary was renewed in body and soul: another lived in him (cf. Paul, *Galatians*, 2, 20). One thinks of the marriage of the soul united with God, which was akin to initiatory hierogamies.

Absorbing the divine fluid is an illumination for the votary of Hermes Trismegistus. He sees, and is himself the light, because he is light, like the *Nymphus* of Mithraic initiation. The consecration finishes in thanksgivings, a eulogy or hymn of acclamation (XIII, 1521). The regeneration of the votary admits him or reincorporates him into the family of the gods (XIII, 2), as the Eleusinian initiation incorporates the faithful into the *genos* of Demeter. The supernatural experience of the Hermetist, who is identified with the whole of the cosmic elements (XI, 20; XIII, 11 and 20) also recalls the itinerary of Lucius, *per omnia vectus elementa* (Apuleius, *Metamorphoses*, XI, 23, 7). But it apparently has nothing to do with a posthumous purification by the elements – air, fire and water – such as that referred to by Trismegistus in the *Asclepius* (28).[40]

Hermetic initiation was therefore not purely philosophical. It did not consist in 'returning to oneself', but in becoming quite different through absorbing that Total Otherness which is divinity. The votary was 'possessed', like the *Katochoi* of Serapis. His 'salvation' was no longer related to earlier error, but liberated him from astral inevitability and deified him, like the *apanathatismos* in the alleged 'Liturgy of Mithras'.

In many respects, Hermetism agreed with the conception of the mysteries held by the last pagans. For Sallustius, Julian's friend and counsellor in religious matters, 'every initiation tends to unite us with the world and with the gods' (*The Gods and the World*, IV, 6) by a sort of intimate and ineffable sympathy. Iamblichus says no different in his *Mysteries of Egypt* (V, 26). In an extract from Stobaeus (fragment XXIII, 68), Isis speaks of the 'initiators and legislators' of humankind who

> having learnt from Hermes that the things of the lower world have received from the Creator the command to be in sympathy with those of above, have set up on earth the sacred functions that are linked vertically to the mysteries of heaven.[41]

The Hermetists accepted the legitimacy, even the efficacy of institutional cults, but chiefly (like Iamblichus) for the piety of the common herd. Unlike Sallustius,[42] the author of the *Asclepius* did not – any more than Apollonius of Tyana or Porphyry – consider that it was essential for the theosopher to have the mediation of spilt blood, a life sacrificed on the altar, to enter into communion with the divine.

Something extraordinary: Christians (from Tertullian to Cyrillus of Alexandria), and diehard polytheists – even in the period when they were in confrontation regarding worship and doctrine – and alchemists like Zosimus, Neoplatonists and even the thirteenth-century Syrian philosopher Bar Hebraeus (Abû al-Faradj Ibn al-Ibri) commended Trismegistus.[43] About a century ago, he was still filling the imagination of the 'mystic pagan' Louis Ménard.

'The foremost of the leaders of the chrysopoea', wrote Zosimus *Alchimistes grecs*, p. 424, 8ff Berthelot) 'is Hermes Trismegistus'. In fact, was not the great and true chrysopoea the transmutation of the soul into the gold of the divine light? In the very name Trismegistus the mystery of the triadic god was discernible (ibid., p. 132, 19ff). Lactantius, who quotes him assiduously (and seems to have exerted a certain amount of influence over the emperor Constantine) goes as far as to declare:

I do not doubt that Trismegistus arrived in some way at the truth, for on God the Father he has said everything, and on the Son, much of what is implicit in the divine mysteries. (*Divine Institutes*, IV, 27, 20)

It is true that there is nothing exemplary in the orthodoxy of this superficial intellect, lacking in critical capacity and precision. But his reading of the *Hermetica* is evidence of their popularity in intellectual circles at the time when the emperor was becoming Christian. Arnobius had called the devotees of Hermes to witness: *vos, vos appello qui Mercurium . . . sectamini* (*Against the Nations*, II, 13), and no doubt with full knowledge of the facts if, as Carcopino has shown,[44] this belatedly converted Christian had long been associated with Hermetism. What Constantine would have to say in his *Discourse to the Assembly of the Saints* on the Father and the Son,[45] did not flagrantly contradict the doctrine ascribed to Trismegistus. Of course, such Christian quotations may be suspected of tendentious distortion. But conversely, we have seen that some *Hermetica* bear the mark of Judaeo-Christian influence. Whatever the details may be, one gets the feeling that early fourth-century Hermetism represented a meeting-point for pagan henotheism and Christian monotheism.

Chaldaean Oracles and Theurgy

A literature which, by contrast, had nothing ecumenical about it, and whose esotericism enchanted the Neoplatonists, who made it their

280 Occultism and Theosophy

bible, also presented itself as a revelation of oriental origin: the *Chaldaean Oracles*.[46] It has been thought possible to state that they were for Babylonia what the Hermetic *Poimandres* was for Egypt, 'that is to say, indigenous beliefs were highlighted, and seasoned with a heavy proportion of philosophical ingredients' (F. Cumont).[47]

Actually, these 'indigenous beliefs' remain very hard to discern. It must be admitted, however, that the last pagans were receptive to the apocalyptic exoticism of these *Logia*, which were taken to contain the ultimate in the wisdom attributed to the Mesopotamian Magi. At the end of his life, Porphyry took a passionate interest in them, notably in the means they offered for liberating a part of the soul that was likely to regain the astral light. Iamblichus makes reference to them in his *Mysteries of Egypt*,[48] and is said to have devoted twenty-eight books to an in-depth commentary on the *Logia*. As for Proclus, of all the known great texts he claimed to want to remember only the *Chaldaean Oracles* and Plato's *Timaeus*. In both the West and the East we find them quoted directly or indirectly by Christians who had come from Neoplatonism, like Marius Victorinus, Synesius of Cyrene and the Pseudo-Dionysius the Areopagite.[49] The apologist Arnobius, who had sampled Hermetism before he was baptized, seems to have been curious enough to taste this other ambiguous source of theosophic paganism.[50]

These oracles were ascribed to Julian, known as the 'Theurge', who lived in the reign of Marcus Aurelius (161–80). The *Suda* made him the son of a 'Chaldaean philosopher' of the same name, the author of a work on demons. He was said to have contributed by his occult talents to aiding the Roman army on the Danubian front; he was credited with the 'miracle of the rain' which Cassius Dio (71, 8, 4) attributes to the Magus Arnouphis.[51] But the celebrated *Logia* seem to have been forgotten for a century, except perhaps by the Neopythagorean Numenius (although the connections of his doctrine with that of the Chaldaean Oracles remains suspect).[52] Apparently it was Iamblichus who inspired a major renewal of interest in them, and who led Porphyry to take account of them. There is no evident trace of Julian's *Logia* to be detected in the *Philosophy of Oracles*, written and published before Porphyry's meeting with Plotinus. Why this sudden passion for Chaldaeanism at the end of the third century? Iamblichus of Chalcis, who was related to the ancient priestly dynasty of Emesa and willingly played the role of hierophant or thaumaturge, was intent on sacralizing his philosophy. In his *Mysteries of Egypt*, he praises the virtues of theurgy and, like the stelae of Hermes Trismegistus, the *Chaldaean Oracles* served him as 'holy Scriptures', legitimizing his system in the name of the gods.

The *Logia* of Julian the Theurge involve a complex theology whose hierarchic structure is not limpidly clear, at least to judge by the fragments that have come down to us. It is the commentaries of the Neoplatonists, especially Damascius, and above all of a high-chamberlain at the court of Byzantium, Michael Psellus, which help us to reconstruct part of the system. But many enigmas persist. What the Byzantine reveals to us is not always obviously consistent with the letter of the Oracles.[53]

At the summit of the divine hierarchy, the alleged 'Chaldaeans' seem to have conceived a 'transcendental first Fire' (Fr. 5 of the French edition of E. des Places). They call this 'Fire' the 'Father' (Fr. 3, 7, 14), 'Paternal Intellect' (Fr. 39) or 'Hypercosmic Paternal Abyss' (Fr. 18). This Father 'has created all things in perfection': he has conceived them in the intelligible world. But this supreme God is a 'triadic monad' (Fr. 26). He is simultaneously 'one and threefold' (E. des Places), like the God of the Christians. In fact, he dominates the triad which he forms with a second Intellect and an intermediary 'Power', that the Oracles call Hecate (Fr. 32, 35, 50). The second Intellect is the 'craftsman of the igneous world' (Fr. 5, 33), a kind of demiurge of the Empyrean.

The scheme of this 'Father–Power–Intellect' triad, which is typically Chaldaean but of philosophical origin, recurs frequently in the argumentation of the Neoplatonists. The 'Power' of Hecate both unites and dissociates the first and second Fires (Fr. 6), which the Oracles seem to identify respectively with the 'transcendentally One' (*hapax epekeina*) and the 'transcendentally Two' (*dis epekeina*), although Psellus in his *Summary Outline* of the ancient beliefs accepted 'among the Chaldaeans' places this triad after many others,[54] taking his inspiration from an infinitely more complex theology, ascribable to Proclus and perhaps already reconstructed by Iamblichus. There is not even unanimity on the translation itself of the mysterious *hapax* and *dis epekeina*!

After the first triad come intelligible and intellectual triads, the *Iynges* or 'diviners', the 'Assemblers' who unify 'the processions of the plurality of beings' (Psellus) and the *Teletarchs*, 'masters of consecration' or 'perfection', who apparently preside over the perfecting of creation. Psellus subordinates to these triads the 'Source-Fathers' or *Cosmagi* ('guides' or 'conductors of the worlds'), then three 'Implacable ones' (*Ameiliktoi*) and a seventh god who is said to be 'girded below' (*Hypezôkôs*). Next, the 'demiurgic Sources', the generating principles of life, the archangels, the 'azônal' gods established above the visible gods which are the stars, the *Zônaioi* or gods who control the celestial 'girdles' (*zônai*), angels, demons, and heroes occupy different grades of this convoluted chain which fills the vast abyss separating the incarnate soul from the intelligible Father: a hierarchy that reminds us of the demonology set out by Iamblichus in his book of the *Mysteries*.

For the soul that has issued from the paternal Fire (Fr. 115), salvation obviously lies in turning its gaze away from the tangible world, inclining towards the Intelligible by purifying its intellect (Fr. 1) or concentrating it (Fr. 2) towards the light (Fr. 111, 115). Man must be 'consecrated' body and soul (Fr. 135) in order to escape evil demons. Theurgy precisely permits the purification of the 'pneumatic' part of the soul, the irrational breath which serves it as a luminous vehicle to transport it after death across the aerial space separating this lower world from the ethereal places where the angels reign. In Book X of his *City of God*, St Augustine argues copiously about and against Porphyry's *De regressu animae*, in which he speaks of the *teletes* or rites of consecration by the Sun and Moon.[55] These kinds of Chaldaean sacraments insured the 'spiritual' ('pneumatic' in Greek) part of the soul against the demons lying in wait along the celestial route; they made it fit 'to welcome the angels and see the gods'. But Porphyry, who appears to have been somewhat reserved or sceptical about the effects of this theurgy, quoted the instance of a 'Chaldaean' who was foiled by an envious colleague whose action was said to have paralyzed the 'powers conjured up by the sacred prayers' (Augustine, *City of God*, X, 9). However, the 'spiritually' and intellectually purified soul eludes sidereal destiny, like the theurges (Fr. 153).

This theology of fire, and more precisely of fire as 'artist' (Fr. 33), recalls that of the Stoics, the impact of which on Mithraism we have seen. The two Julians, the 'Chaldaean' and the 'Theurge', would seem to have made use of their talents in the Antonine era, that is, at a time when the ideas of the Stoa enjoyed their greatest success and even, with Marcus Aurelius, a kind of imperial blessing. Fire is, so to speak, omnipresent in the Oracles, either as lightning, or the creative and life-imparting breath, or the dazzling or scintillating light in the multiplicity of souls and beings. The allegedly Babylonian origin of the two Julians has suggested that their religious world of imagination might bear the stamp of a country (present-day Iraq, which is so richly petroliferous) where naphtha 'catches fire by the very radiation of light and often burns the intervening air' (Plutarch, *Life of Alexander*, 35, 1).[56] Reading through the preserved fragments of the *Logia*, one glimpses nothing but flames, raging storms, lightning flashes, 'implacable' thunderbolts, sparks, blazes, 'flaring' torches or 'flowers of fire',

gushes and rumblings, floods, torrents, whirlwinds. These visions
have the contrasting bursts of light of a weird, wild moving picture.
The paternal Intellect 'inseminates' in all its works 'the heavy bond
of the fire of Love' (Fr. 39) and spreads it like a 'flower' (Fr. 42). This
image of genital seed giving life to the world like the *pneuma*-fire of
the Stoics is implied in several fragments. The ideas that 'gush out
humming' from the paternal source are compared to swarms which
'gather in abundance the flower of the fire' (Fr. 37). Of course, one
thinks of the bees which, in Virgil (*Georgics*, IV, 220ff), in a passage
heavily tinged with Stoicism, are said to possess a particle of divine
intelligence and an emanation from the Empyrean. One also re-
members Porphyry (*The Cavern of the Nymphs*, 18) who, according to
Numenius (?) identifies the bees born of the bull – as in the *bougonia*
of Aristaeus (Virgil, *Georgics*, IV, 554ff) – with souls that have entered
the world of the creation.[57] The *pneuma* dear to the Stoic philosophers
appears in the Oracles as the imparter of life to beings (Fr. 29) and the
material world (Fr. 216). The Father has 'breathed into the seven
firmaments of the world' (Fr. 57), as if they were so many balloons!

The dualism of the *Logia* and their theology of the Ideas (Fr. 37) that
emanated from the paternal Intellect would seem to refer us rather to
Plato. This mixture of Stoicism and Platonism (in the same way as the
application of universal sympathy in the hieratic art of the theurges)
would steer us in the direction of Posidonius of Apamea, whose
influence on the moderate Platonism of the Antonine period should
not be underestimated. But this oracular literature, in any case,
incorporates a multiple and very composite philosophical heritage,
with a scholastic jargon enhanced by imagery that may have a
religious origin.

The 'Power of the Father', Hecate, is 'girded below' (Fr. 6). This
particular detail of clothing brings to mind the garment which tightly
enwraps the Artemis of Ephesus, and which also has bees on it, those
souls who drink the nectar of the fire flower. A line in the *Logia* says
precisely that 'the flower of the fire has donned a girdle' (Fr. 35, from
the translation by E. des Places), which identifies it with Hecate. This
goddess, whom another line (Fr. 56) seems to confuse with Rhea, is the
source of souls and virtues. Martianus Capella (*Marriage of Mercury
and Philology*, II, 205) calls her 'Spring-Virgin' (*fontana virgo*), which
matches an oracle quoted by Psellus (Fr. 52). But she also bears the
warrior attributes of Athena (Fr. 72), and Martianus Capella (ibid., VI,
571) precisely gives Pallas the title 'flower of the fire' (*flos ignis*). Again,
Martianus Capella (ibid., I, 66) mentions the gleaming veil woven by
Pallas to envelop the head of Jupiter, perhaps symbolizing the luminous firmament of the heavens. Now, the Oracles speak of 'what the

intellective light of the Father had woven' (Fr. 39): was this not the work of the armed Virgin whom Martianus (ibid., VI, 567) extols as the 'source of ethereal light' (*aetherius fomes*)?

Still in the field of pagan imagery, one is tempted to compare the oracles on the *Aiôn*, drawing from the Father the fire and intelligence that give life to the worlds (Fr. 49), or on Kronos (?) from whom are launched the 'implacable thunderbolts' (Fr. 35), with the Mithraic representations of the Lion-head spitting flames. The image of the lion is associated with the thunderbolt in Fragment 147. It is true that the leonine symbolism of fire is not peculiar only to Mithraism or Chaldaeanism.

In any case, on a first reading, the religious imagination of the Oracles has nothing specifically Babylonian or even oriental. The Hurrian-Hittite gods of the thunderbolt have nothing to do with the visions of lightning and storms that permeate them. The iconography of the armed goddess Allat, of the Artemis-Hecate of Ephesus, even the Heliopolitan triad, with its Father-God and Son-God separated by a girdled Atargatis, was probably known to Julian the Theurge. But did he have it in mind when he was compiling the *Logia*? This cannot be stated with any certainty. But intellectuals who were steeped and passionately interested in Greek philosophy, as the Hellenized Orientals of the second century AD inevitably were, could not observe these idols without rethinking them from the doctrinal and allegorical viewpoint, following the approach of Porphyry, a hundred years later, in his treatise on *images* (Περὶ ἀγαλμάτων).[58]

The worship of fire and the dualism, even the demonology, of the Oracles have been laid at the door of Mazdaeism.[59] In fact, there is nothing in the Chaldaean system that cannot be explained according to Greek philosophy. Even the image of the deity girt about below its chest, which I have compared to the girdled idols, is to be found in Philo of Alexandris (*The Descendants of Cain*, 14): God has fastened beneath him (ὑποζεύξας) all the things of becoming without being himself contained by any of them.[60] In the *World* of the Pseudo-Aristotle an antithesis appears between the essence and the power of God who gives life to all that emanates from him: the idea of power, in this sense, is certainly of peripatetic origin.[61] But in the time of Marcus Aurelius Greek philosophy was no longer sufficient unto itself. By then, the syncretic and theosophic constructions that had derived from it required a mysterious oracular consecration and a pseudo-oriental colouring like that of Chaldaean theurgy.

Theurgy was a 'divine action', which 'acted on the gods' because it was divine. It therefore required on the part of those who practised it consecration through piety and purifications which brought them close to the gods, an initiation that would make them fit to enter into contact with those gods. So theurgy was contrasted with magic, with which certain apparent procedures might encourage a comparison. For theurgy did not consist in pure thoughts or mystical prayers:

It is the religious fulfilment of ineffable acts whose results outdo any effort of intellect, as well as the power of mute symbols, heard by the gods alone, which effect the theurgic union. So it is not our thought which carries out these acts; for then their effectiveness would be intellectual and would be dependent on us. Without our thinking about it, indeed, the signs (*synthemata*) themselves, by themselves, effect their own work and the ineffable power of the gods, whom these signs concern, itself recognizes its own images by itself, without being awoken by our thought. (Iamblichus, *The Mysteries of Egypt*, II, 11; from the translation by E. des Places)

In other words, the theurge makes himself known to and recognized by the gods, like the mysta in his initiation, by means of 'symbols', signs or passwords (*synthemata*).[62] It is no longer a matter, as it was for Plato, of reaching and imitating God by the elevation of the mind to pure Ideas. As for Sallustius the *telete* puts us in communion (συνάπτειν) with the gods and the world they mysteriously fill with their power, theurgy was a ritual which caused a current to pass between the human and the divine. Better still, it endowed man with something of the divine. Theurgy, as Iamblichus proceeds to explain to us (ibid., IV, 2), presents a double aspect: it is practised by men, but 'with the support of divine signs [*synthemata*], by their means it rises to the superior beings with whom it unites [συναπτόμενον], the verb used by Sallustius, and takes its direction harmoniously following their command, whereupon it may rightfully assume the form of the gods'. The theurge 'in some way, through the ineffable symbols, dons the hieratic garb of the gods' (ibid.). This 'ceremonial robe-donning' also refers to mystery rituals.

First among the 'symbols' come the divine names. The *synthemata* are sacred phrases of recognition, like those that had to be uttered in order to be consecrated in the initiatory cults or to identify oneself as a mysta among mystae. After death, the soul needs to be recognized by the gods. A *Logion* makes allusion to this:

The paternal Intellect does not receive the will of the soul unless the latter has emerged from forgetfulness and proffered a word, remembering the pure paternal symbol. (Fr. 109)

These *voces mysticae* by themselves have a sovereign efficacy.
'Never change barbarian names', says an Oracle (Fr. 150). In this
respect the *Logia* remained true to oriental traditions. Iamblichus (*The
Mysteries of Egypt*, VII, 5) justifies at length the advantage of 'barbarian' names which are in no way conventional, for the 'language of the
sacred peoples' is secretly, inexpressibly, in harmony with 'the superior beings'. Unlike the Greeks, who were fired by a taste for
innovation

> the barbarians, for their part, being constant in their customs,
> keep solidly to their old ways of talking: so they are looked upon
> kindly by the gods, and offer them speeches which please
> them.

On this point Iamblichus is echoing Origen (*Against Celsus*, I, 24)
who, citing the names Sabaoth, Adonai and 'all the others held in
great veneration among the Hebrews', states that they proceed from a
'mysterious divine knowledge attributed to the Creator of the Universe' and that for the same reason

> these names are effective when they are spoken in a particular
> sequence which interweaves them, in the same way as other
> names uttered in the Egyptian tongue and addressed to certain
> demons . . . or others in the Persian dialect addressed to other
> powers.

In many respects, evidently, pagans and Christians shared the same
convictions.
The *symbola* also included animals, plants, herbs, stones, images,
talismans, *charakteres* or sacred letters (the seven vowels, for example).
A whole system of 'channels' or connections was held to put men in
communication with the gods, the earth with the heavens. Conversely,
a law of antipathies was supposed to be able to thwart a maleficent
influence, like that of the demons of the air who hindered the soul's
return to God. An admirable page *On the Hieratic Art* by Proclus helps
us to understand the enthusiasm that this alchemical theurgy could
arouse:

> Why, indeed, does the heliotrope move in accord with the Sun,
> the Selenotrope with the Moon, both forming a retinue, as far as
> they are able, to the two luminaries of the world? For all beings
> pray according to the rank they occupy; they hymn the leaders
> who preside over their entire range . . . Thus the heliotrope

moves as much as it is capable of moving, and if one could but hear how it beats the air while twisting on its stem, one would realize from the sound that it is offering a sort of hymn to the King, insofar as a plant can sing one ... Do we not see the stones themselves breathe in time with the exhalations of the stars? .... Hence, for example, the large number of heliacal animals, such as the lion and the cock.

The masters of the hieratic art had thus discovered in this network of cosmic and hypercosmic sympathies 'the means of honouring the powers above' by the creation of 'symbols' that were acceptable to the divinity.[63] With its appearances of magic, theurgy at the time seemed like a kind of thanksgiving or act of pantheistic piety. The Chaldaean Oracles gave it their enigmatic backing:

For the Intellect of the Father has sown the symbols throughout the world, he who conceives the Intelligibles which are called inexpressible beauties. (Fr. 108)

Theurgy consecrated men. It also consecrated statues, and by the same processes, so that they were filled with the divine influx. This technique bore the name 'telestic'.[64] It had long been known in Egypt, and the magic papyri bear that out. It claimed to 'animate' idols and penetrate them with a 'divine presence', to use Iamblichus' expression (Photius, *Bibliotheca*, 215, p. 173b), by enclosing in them some sacred name on a gold strip or the residue of a sacrifice, 'sphragids' or magic intaglios of the kind I have mentioned. The *Asclepius* (24) speaks of them as statues

having a soul, conscious, full of the breath of life and which accomplish an infinity of marvels: they know the future, and predict it by means of spells, prophetic inspiration, dreams and many other methods ...

But for the Hermetist, it was a matter of 'terrestrial gods'. Their power resulted from a

composition of herbs, stones and spices which in themselves contain a power of divine efficacy. And if one seeks to please them with numerous sacrifices, hymns, songs of praise, concerts of very sweet sounds that recall the harmony of the heavens, it is so that the celestial element that has been introduced into the idol by the repeated practice of celestial rites may joyfully endure this long sojourn among men. (*Asclepius*, 38)

The ingredients for the hollow idol had to be appropriate to the god or goddess it represented, by virtue of the 'sympathy' which mystically linked them with this or that mineral or plant, in keeping with the system explained by Proclus, following the 'channels' of connection joining the Earth to the Sky. Heraiscus, a Neoplatonist who remained faithful to the very end to his gods of Egypt, claimed to recognize immediately an idol that was 'animated', according to the sensations he felt in its presence.[65]

Clever subterfuges could also impress the credulous. Thus the theurge Maximus of Ephesus was credited with making the statue of Hecate smile, and it seems that her torches caught fire spontaneously.[66] Two centuries earlier, in the Persian sanctuaries of Hierocaesarea and Hypaipa in Lydia, Pausanias (*Description of Greece*, V, 27, 6) had witnessed Magi light altars from a distance by intoning 'barbarian' chants. On this point, it is not inconceivable that the Chaldaean theurges made use of a secret from an ancient oriental tradition. But the example of Maximus (who was from Ephesus) – just like the 'Hecatic' fantasies of Proclus (Marinus, *Life of Proclus*, 28) – confirms for us the preponderance of Artemis-Hecate in these 'mysteries' of Chaldaean Neoplatonism, which seems to have had a liking for light-connected rites.

Telestics had the prestige of a science that put the crown on philosophy. It consecrated idols and men. When Plotinus taught that one must 'sculpt one's own statue' by purifying the soul (*Enneads*, I, 6, 9), he was already evoking something of the theurgy which, starting with Iamblichus, dominated Neoplatonism. The last pagans made much ado of this hieratic art. In vain Nicomachus Flavianus had statues of Jupiter erected on the Alps, 'consecrated by who knows what rites', wrote St Augustine (*City of God*, V. 26), to halt the offensive of the Christian Theodosius. On the other hand, an idol consecrated at Rhegium (Reggio di Calabria) to divert Etna's lava flows was said to have prevented the Visigoth Alaric from getting into Sicily to ravage it (Olympiodorus, in Photius, *Bibliotheca*, 80, p. 58a). The French word 'talisman', derived (through Arabic?) from the Greek *tetelesmena*, preserves the memory of images 'consecrated' by magic and theurgy.

A disturbing text from Proclus (*Platonic Theology*, IV, 9) leads one to think that certain of the theurges' funeral rites could throw light on some as yet ill-explained discoveries.[67] The theurges were said to bury the bodies of some dead people 'except the head in consecrations of the greatest mystery'. It may be recalled that, under the idol of a sovereign god worshipped in the 'Syrian' shrine on the Janiculum, the crown of a skull was found. The upper part of a skull was also discovered in the chancel of the Königshofen *Mithraeum*, under the supports of the cultic stele.[68] One may then wonder whether the theurges practised a similar ceremonial for the consecration of idols. When Constantine initiated the inventory of the temples in 331, 'bones and skulls' were found under the statues of the gods, so it seems (Eusebius, *Life of Constantine*, III, 57).[69] Thirty years later, the Christians in Alexandria exhumed human skulls from the *Mithraeum*, in order to provoke popular indignation.

The Chaldaean Oracles left a profound mark on the great intellects of later Neoplatonism, to a degree that is hard to conceive and whose importance is difficult to measure. It is no surprise to learn that the emperor Julian, greatly enthused by the prestidigitatory talents of Maximus of Ephesus, was an avid reader of the Oracles:

I am wild about Iamblichus in philosophy and my namesake [Julian the Chaldaean or the Theurge?] in theosophy. (*Letters*, 4 = 12, J. Bidez)

It is more surprising, though perhaps wrongly so, to discover that these *Logia* rubbed off strongly on Marius Victorinus – a converted Neoplatonist, it is true – and on the bishop of Cyrene, Synesius, another Christianized Neoplatonist. Synesius quotes them in his *Treatise on Dreams*, and in his reasoning on the luminous spectre of the 'pneumatic' soul, he builds his theory of the glorious body on the basis of a Chaldaean doctrine.[70] He sings to God sublime hymns whose mystic esotericism is studded with Chaldaean expressions.[71]

In the West, the African rhetor Martianus Capella, author of an encyclopaedia of the seven liberal arts which enjoyed a prodigious success throughout the Middle Ages, was absolutely filled with the doctrine and vocabulary of the Oracles. To marry Mercury, Philology submits to the immortalizing rites of theurgy, before reaching the Empyrean by traversing the seven planetary spheres. She invokes the divine triads, the 'transcendentally One' and the 'transcendentally Two', the Spring-Virgin and the 'Flower of the Fire' These prayers are uttered, writes Martianus, *secundum Platonis mysteria*.[72] The Chaldaean Oracles thus served as the *hieros logos* for these 'mysteries of Plato' which theurgy had become.

At the close of the fifth century, Proclus was deemed to have benefited from the luminous epiphanies of Hecate. Using a strap cut from the hide of a sacrificed bull, he shaped a gold rhombus containing a sapphire, made sacred by magic inscriptions, in order to cause rain to fall on the soil of Attica. This Hecatic sphere or top had the name *iunx*.[73]

The Chaldaean writings, or those with Chaldaean leanings, survived Justinian's prohibitions. The whole literature was kept secretly and passionately devoured by good Christians such as Michael Psellus, thanks to whom we know a little more than through scattered quotations and allusions. In the eleventh century, an archbishop is even said to have carried out a 'theagogy' or summoning of the gods (or 'demons' for a Christian), keeping to the rules of Chaldaean theurgy:[74] a singular homage of Byzantium to the 'barbarian' wisdom. With an interval of some six centuries, from Proclus to the archbishop, the religious distance was less, all in all, than from Marcus Aurelius, or even Plotinus, to Iamblichus.[75]

Chapter 7

Dionysus and Sabazius

ALEXANDER'S mother, Olympias, was said to have indulged passionately in Bacchic orgies, in the company of huge tame snakes (Plutarch, *Life of Alexander*, 2, 9), and the story went that one of these reptiles slept with her, making her pregnant with the future conqueror of Asia (Lucian, *Alexander or the False Prophet*, 7). Later, in January 330, Alexander was at the head of a frenzied *komos* that set fire to the royal palace of Persepolis, or so it was said . . . Paradoxically, this arsonist reincarnating the god of drunkenness was transformed into a civilizing hero. It is true that Bacchus had merited apotheosis by spreading the custom of the orgy.

Dionysus was a Greek god, and yet in Greece he appeared as strange and a stranger, always active to disrupt the city's order and routine.[1] In mythical and literary imagination, but also in certain cultic practices, he disquieted, tormented and released pent-up feelings. He sent a wind of madness through the town. But at the same time, homeopathically, by music and shouting, drinking wine and eating raw meat (omophagia), he also healed the deep-seated violence that is ordinarily repressed by family, civic and social discipline. He relieved and let loose not only the instincts, but all the male and female captives in the prison and the gynaeceum. He put worries to sleep through intoxication, but awakened Ariadne from the sleep of abandonment and death. God of the dance and the vital spirit, he also embodied lethargy and languor. Apparently contradictory, and at all events disconcerting, he swooped suddenly with his band of followers like a lightning epidemic, a destroying hurricane, plucking women out of the houses and driving the whole city out of its mind. He was the supreme Stranger, who made men strangers to themselves through ecstasy in the etymological sense of the word, that extraverts the individual and temporarily depersonalizes him to reincorporate him in the divine unity. This ritual depersonalization was a way of

escape from the frustrating and demeaning contingencies and constraints of daily life.

Dionysism notably liberated women, whom Greek tradition condemned even more harshly than Roman tradition to live within four
walls, confined to carrying out household tasks. With Bacchus, they
fled, emigrated, from the home to run wild in the mountains
(oreibasia), leap and whirl in the wooded valleys, commune physically with wild and virgin countryside, 'to forget, to escape for a few
days from the crying baby, the sullen husband, the distaff and the
cooking-pot, to be themselves at last . . . ' (A.-J. Festugière).[3]

The oriental religions that had immigrated into the Roman West
represented *a priori* the selfsame type of disrupting, contagious and
cataclysmic invasion. But though he was an 'epidemic' and revolutionary god, still from elsewhere (even when he returned to his
birthplace of Thebes), Dionysus was the first to shake up Rome in the
wake of the second Punic War. He was Greek (or at least Thracian, like
Orpheus and Sabazius). But it was in the Hellenistic East after
Alexander's conquest that Dionysism really assumed the form of a
mystery religion, with the structures of a genuine initiatory ritual. In
contact with the various peoples affected by the Macedonian invasion
and more or less Hellenized by the domination of the Diadochi,
Bacchus was recognized in several foreign gods. His image spread
throughout the Near East and as far as central Asia. He was identified
with Osiris or Horus-Harpocrates in Egypt and in the Isiac temples of
the Graeco-Alexandrian religious *diaspora*; with Dusares among the
Arabs; with the founder of the sanctuary of the Syrian Goddess,
Atargatis, at Hierapolis-Bambyce, where the god was credited with
having erected the giant phalli holding the precursors of Simeon
Stylites. At Baalbek he was assimilated to the Heliopolitan Mercury.

In Roman Syria, the monetary typology of Apamea, Damascus,
Orthosia, Sidon and Beirut made much room for Dionysism. The
kings of Pergamum were patrons of the dynastic cult of Dionysus
Kathegemon,[4] and under their rule the silver tetradrachm, known as a
'cistophorus' spread the motif of the magic wicker basket from which
a snake sways, inseparable from the thiasus in Bacchic imagery. This
type had a sphere of influence that was all the wider and more
significant, even after the Attalids, because the cistophori played the
role of 'Pan-Asiatic' silver standard, in the same way as the 'owls' of
Athens had formerly. 'Mystery' groups multiplied and prospered in
Roman Anatolia, as the cities' local coinage and epigraphy bear equal
witness. In the reign of Heliogabalus (218–22), coins from Magnesia
near the Meander issued the image of the child Dionysus surrounded
by Corybants. Other towns popularized in their money images of the

newborn Bacchus in the winnowing-basket that served him as a cradle, or of the triumphant god in his chariot drawn by Centaurs, panthers or elephants.[5] This iconography does not date from the Roman era, but reveals an already ancient heritage. In the famous tragedy by Euripides, the god of the Bacchantes proclaims in fact:

I left Lydia with its gold-rich fields, the plains of Phrygia for the plateaux of Persia ... and Arabia *felix* ... and its cities full of Greeks mingled with barbarian races. (1. 13–19)

But it was the Dionysism of the Hellenized East rather than that of Euripides' Bacchae which burst upon Rome in 186 BC with the affair of the Bacchanalia, even though Latin historians reflected certain literary reminiscences on their vision and presentation of the scandal.

Very early on, another god of Thracian origin, Sabazius, made his way in Greece and gained followers even in Athens around the end of the fifth century BC.[6] This god intoxicated with a sort of beer, *sabaia*, as Dionysus intoxicated with wine. In the classical era there was a tendency to identify him with Dionysus. Mocking him, Aristophanes[7] and Demosthenes[8] bear witness to both his marginality and his impact in certain popular milieux. Like that of Bacchus, his cult soon won over part of Asia Minor where corybantism was akin to his ecstatic and cathartic rites. There Sabazius was linked with Cybele as a snake-god. At Sardes, an inscription reworking a contemporary text of the Persian king Artaxerxes II Mnemon (405–359 BC) mentions 'mysteries' celebrated in honour of Sabazius, Agdistis and Mâ.[9] The literary tradition of Hellenistic mythographers incorporates the Thracio-Phrygian god into Graeco-Roman theology. It turns him into an 'ancient' and bearded Dionysus who would later be recognized beside a young and beardless Dionysus in Bacchic iconography.

However, in parallel with this somewhat trivialized imagery, on more precisely Sabazian monuments the god preserves his type and indigenous attributes. The two trends of Dionysus and Sabazius frequently crossed, even joined and became confused in artistic and mythico-cultic imagination, but without being uniformly identified everywhere. Together with Isiacism, Phrygianism and Mithraism, neither was excluded from the religions denounced by the Fathers of the Church as polluting the Roman world. In the fourth century, the renegade Firmicus Maternus enveloped Dionysus and Sabazius in the same opprobrium as the other foreign deities, whether Egyptian, Anatolian, Syrio-Phoenician or Persian.[10] In vain had the old Romans at first rejected and expelled them from the *Urbs*. Dionysus and Sabazius contaminated the city as dangerously as the anubophori with their jackal masks, Cybele's galli or the shadowy and thus diabolical service of the Bull-slayer!

From Orgy to Initiation

Dionysus flourished in the Roman world, both East and West, simultaneously in the form of a mystery religion and in the iconography of mosaics, paintings and sculptures. This imagery does not always, everywhere and necessarily have a cultic significance – far from it. It does not automatically imply that those who commissioned the work were initiates, or that the premises endowed with such adornment were used for initiations. But it carries references to a cult and a myth whose popularity it both reflects and reinforces, because it makes a visual impression. A whole series of figured monuments[11] – frescoes, stuccoes, terracotta plaques known as 'Campana' (in memory of the man who made a marvellous collection of them, purchased in part by Napoleon III for the Louvre Museum, Paris), picturesque reliefs, sarcophagi, mosaic floors – in the imperial period illustrates certain aspects of the initiary ritual, at least allusively or symbolically. But the basic motifs of this repertoire for the most part date back to the time when the religion of Bacchus seems to have undergone a sort of radical alteration, i.e. in the Hellenistic period.

Previously, the term 'mysteries' had been applied specifically to those of Eleusis and, secondarily, those of Samothrace which presented certain similarities to the former. Eleusis gave its initiates guarantees in this world and possibly in the next:

Happy is he who, among the men of this earth, possesses the vision of these mysteries! Conversely, he who is not initiated into the holy rites and he who takes no part in them do not have the same destiny, even once they are dead in the clammy shadows. (*Homeric Hymn to Demeter*, 1. 480–2)

'Happy are those who have contemplated' said Sophocles. The mysta remained 'marked by an imprint' (*tupoumenos*, wrote Aristotle) and as if stamped for life with a divine seal.[12]

In the great upheaval of traditional ideas and values that shook the regime of the Greek city-state during and chiefly after Alexander's conquest, the cults in cities were quickly overtaken, outdated, if not subverted. We have seen that Eleusis held firm, because its mysteries went beyond the horizons of state and even human life. But they suffered from a double handicap. They could be celebrated only in the month of Boedromion (end of September-beginning of October) and in Eleusis itself. The Hellenistic world belonged to an unquiet and restless humanity, people who moved about, displaced and upset by wars, social and political revolutions, new trends or commercial outlets. An entire itinerant population of racketeers, intellectuals, mercenaries and various adventurers of the sword, the word or the pen created active relations in the Mediterranean basin between Greece proper and Asia, Egypt and Italy.

Of course, there were as always the strong spirits and the disillusioned who strove to scorn the vicissitudes of Fortune or Chance, *Tyche*, whose cult flourished in a fairly unbalanced society.[13] The Stoics and Epicureans, the Pyrrhonians and the Sceptics armoured or stiffened themselves doctrinally against reverses of circumstances and the shocks of occurrences that gave rise to error or misfortune. But it is not given to the common run of mortals to persevere to the point of ataraxy and philosophical conversion. The more unstable the world, the greater man's need of a status that ensures him the protection of the gods, associates him with their sacredness, their privilege of happiness and immortality. Without filling the theoretically uncrossable space separating Olympia from the human race, Eleusis promised its faithful divine concern and a better fate in the next world – what was called the 'good hope'.[14] But in the turbulent and upset world of the Diadochi, it would have been impossible to wait for the month of Boedromion each year, or to have to go to Athens on a fixed date to take part in the great procession of Eleusis. People needed to be able to get themselves initiated anywhere, on demand and in any season. Already the mysteries of Samothrace, which were apparently more suitable to the living conditions of sailors and other travellers, were open to passing candidates, at any moment of the year. It was even possible to rise to the grade of epopt immediately after initiation to the first grade, completing everything on the same day, instead of waiting a whole year to become an 'epopt' of Eleusis.

It seems that the Dionysian religion was adapted at that time and, so to speak, restructured to meet the needs and the anguish of Hellenistic humanity. It was not enough to make access easier by the frequency of liturgies and by what might be called the ubiquity of Dionysism. It was profoundly modified in both spirit and practice.

What was the ultimate aim of Dionysism? To become a *Bacchos*, that is to say, to become identified with the god. Prior to the first epigraphic and iconographic evidence referring explicitly to a mystery ritual, namely in the archaic and classical periods, there were two ways of reaching the state of *Bacchos*: Orphic asceticism and the orgy of Maenadism.

The former involved the observance of a way of life, the *bios Orphikos*: daily perseverance, constant effort, until the death of the titanic 'ego' in order to liberate the Dionysian 'id', humanity being the issue of the murderers of Zagreus who had dismembered and devoured him. Orphic asceticism was a personal discipline with intent to change one's life in order to attain the divine life.[15]

Dionysian orgy allowed the Bacchant to emerge from the 'ego' to be united with the god in the ecstatic exaltation of omophagia, dancing and wine. It was the practice of collective and periodic extroversion. Originally it was repeated every two years. This kind of bodily mysticism and psychosomatic liberation had only temporary effects each time – the period of the *ekstasis* – and not the long-term effects of a continuous purification.

But anyway, in neither case was the status of *Bacchos* definitively acquired before death. The strict vigilance of a follower of the 'Orphic life' who wished to 'detitanize' himself finished only with the termination of bodily life, even though charlatans like the 'Orpheotelestes' spoken of by Plato (*Republic*, II, 365a) and Theophrastus (*Characters*, XVI, 11) were quite sure they could purify individuals by 'consecrations': they had nothing at all to do with genuine Orphism. This first way belonged to an elite. The second can be explained by a society which, in putting constraints on individuals or a category of individuals (women, in this instance), needed a safety valve every so often. However, in a period like that of the Diadochi, when the state no longer controlled people so strictly and morally, the problem ceased to be presented in the same terms. Hellenistic man was, in certain respects, 'liberated', and all the more anxious and uncertain. If he was incapable of Orphic asceticism, he was equally unable to be satisfied with temporary mysticism. He wanted to be happy and immortal, like the gods. He needed a guarantee sanctioned by a god or goddess, and that is what ritual initiation was deemed to confer upon him.

Certainly, the Dionysian mysteries preserved some features of the ancient orgy. Their liturgy incorporated the gestural, vestmental, emblematic, symposiac, even omophagic appearances of classic Maenadism: dances, rhythmic swaying of the body and prophecies (*cum iactatione fanatica corporis vaticinari*; Livy, *Roman History*, XXXIX, 13, 11), drunkenness and music, garments of animal skins, the brandishing of staffs wreathed in ivy ... But several ceremonies henceforth had a symbolic ritualism, such as omophagia, which for the new Bacchants of Miletus for example, was reduced to having to put a mouthful of raw meat in the sacred basket.[16] Chiefly, the practice of orgies was an effective technique of depersonalization, whereas initiation was a rite, a ritual substitute for *ekstasis*. The Hellenistic and Roman Dionysian 'consecration' or *telete* had something of a magical and autosuggestive spirit which seems to me essentially foreign to Maenadism, but is essentially in accord with the crisis of conscience of the post-classical period. It was then that, according to F. Nietzsche, 'the tragic conception of the world' (in company with Dionysian art) 'had to take refuge in a kind of subterranean world, where it degenerated into secret cults'; it 'survived in the mysteries, never ceasing, during the course of the most extraordinary metamorphoses and degenerations, to draw to it natures that were given to gravity and seriousness'.[17]

The consecration of the mysta endowed him with a definitive status in this world and the next, through his incorporation into a thiasus by taking on certain attributes, performing certain gestures, formulating certain passwords or 'symbols', swearing an oath, revealing and manipulating objects (*sacra*), witnessing and commenting upon images illustrating a 'sacred discourse' or *hieros logos*. He submitted himself to the scenario laid down by an *ordo* or initiatory form. Everything was regulated in advance. The initiate was passive. He was co-opted, adopted by a group of faithful followers who were legitimized as such by the mediation and ingenious device of a liturgy that allowed the purveying of a kind of 'discount' mysticism, which nevertheless gave a feeling of security and was accessible to all.

This facility, as much as their elasticity in space and time, contributed to the popularization of the mysteries. *Baccheia* were set up anywhere and everywhere, but on private property and away from official sanctuaries. Initiations were carried out several times a year, and even several times a month. Dramatic art dealing with the deeds of Bacchus contained a pathos that suited the Hellenistic temperament. The votaries remained spectators, even if they dressed up or participated sentimentally in the ordeals of Zagreus, dismembered by the Titans; they were not actors like the Bacchantes or Thyiads tearing a fawn to pieces, devouring its hot and still throbbing flesh, or running dishevelled through the woods until they lost their breath. Costumed banquets replaced the drunkenness of the Maenads who roamed far from the towns, among the pine trees and rocks. Even when held out in the countryside, the *Baccheion* or *Bacchanal* did not lend itself, like the wide-open hilly and rocky spaces, to orgiastic outbursts. Certainly, in 186 BC, the Bacchantes on the Aventine rushed down as far as the Tiber, and later, in her gardens, Messalina celebrated Dionysian grape harvests which resembled a mystery performance. But generally speaking, the sacred area of the Bacchic *telete* had nothing to compare with the physical and orchestic field for expansion of the ancient Bassarides: it was always limited and of an artificial nature, with its chapels, grottoes, elegant groves, cultic furnishings, like the landscapes in Campanian painting or so-called 'picturesque' reliefs. In Dionysian initiation of the Roman era, the 'mysticism' was not real, but false or emotional, artificial or affected.

There was never a Dionysian (or Orphico-Dionysian) 'church' properly speaking. But beginning in the third century BC, indications concerning the mysteries multiplied. This was also the period when Orpheus was credited with the founding of the Dionysian mysteries. A poet who was a contemporary of Ptolemy Philopatôr (244–203 BC) wrote of the Thracian minstrel that he 'invented the mystery consecrations of Bacchus'.[18] Hecataeus of Abdera had already attributed to Orpheus the importation into Greece of the Dionysian initiations, supposedly of Egyptian origin. Now, it is precisely in Ptolemaic Egypt that we find the first express emergence of a mystery cult devoted collectively to Bacchus by private companies of people. The fragmentary papyrus of Gouro apparently gives us the text of a formulary (or *hieros logos*) in which are noted both the invocations, the words that must be spoken by the candidate and the detail of the gestures to be performed, and the objects to be handled: *legomena* and *drômena*, words and actions comprised in every telestic liturgy.[19] There we may read the names of Eleusinian divinities (Brimô, Demeter, Eubouleus) and Orphic divinities (Phanes and Protogonos, Erikepaios). There is mention of the playthings with which the Titans were supposed to have amused Zagreus to lull his vigilance, and which Clement of Alexandria (around AD 200) lists among the 'symbols' of Dionysian consecration. The title *boukolos* or 'cattleman' may be made out, typical of the Bacchic throngs. After sacrificing a ram and a he-goat, the mysta participated in a meal of meat. Like the initiates of Eleusis and Cybele, he declared that he had 'drunk' a beverage of a kind not explicitly revealed but which must have been wine. Significantly, he uttered a prayer for his 'salvation' to Brimô, Rhea-Demeter, the Curetes and Dionysus. What kind of 'salvation'? That is another question. But the safeguard requested of the gods at that time did not concern only the posthumous fate of the individual.

It has long been acknowledged that the Gourob papyrus may have been connected with the edict 'of Ptolemy Philopatôr'.[20] It is known that this king of Egypt was a devotee of Bacchus and bore the mark of it on his skin: an ivy-leaf tattoo.[21] Datable to the last quarter of the third century BC, the text of the papyrus is thus probably attributable to Philopatôr. It targets all those 'who consecrate to Dionysus'. The king orders them to come to Alexandria to make a declaration in right and due form. They must state precisely from whom they have received the tradition of the sacred objects (going back as far as the third generation) and submit the text of their *hieros logos* in a sealed envelope to the relevant department. This document presupposes the existence of organized, structured brotherhoods, who applied a set formulary, made candidates ritually handle *sacra* or 'symbols' (like those listed in the Gourob papyrus), and made them repeat or listen to the words written in the 'sacred discourse'. From that time on, it was a matter of a type of *telete* comprising a true mystery ceremonial, and not merely an orgiastic festival as celebrated by the wild female followers of Bacchus in the archaic and classical eras.

Philopatôr would not have thought of taking these measures if the Dionysian brotherhoods had not begun to flourish in the Delta to the point where they interested or worried the Alexandrian government.[22] His edict bears witness to a concern to restrain or control this proliferation, perhaps to unify or homogenize the Dionysian cult under his royal leadership, even to regulate its practice, as there was always a danger that some bands of followers of the 'liberator' (Eleuthereus) or 'releasing' (Lyaios) god might conceal subversive activities. Twenty or thirty years later, the Romans would mercilessly suppress the Bacchanalia.

As revealed to us by the Gourob papyrus, the Bacchic mysteries of Ptolemaic Egypt appear to bear the double stamp of literary Orphism and cultic Eleusinianism, imprints whose mark is still discernible much later, even in the Neoplatonic commentaries of Proclus or Olympiodorus. The Orphic myth of Zagreus would remain fundamental. As for the mysteries of Eleusis, although their fixed location limited their direct sphere of influence, we know that their ritual was the inspiration behind that of both the Isiac and the mother-cult mysteries. We have seen the part played by the Eumolpid Timotheus in the institution of the cult of Serapis and the interest he had shown particularly in the myth of Attis. It is therefore not surprising that Eleusinianism should also have rubbed off to some extent on Alexandrian Dionysism. As early as the fourth century BC Bacchus occupied a growing place in the Eleusinian imagery and cult. In the Little Mysteries of Agrai, which prepared candidates for Eleusinian consecration, either a myth was represented or a rite practised that the Ancients paralleled with those of the Dionysian cult.[23] The purification by the *liknon* or mystic basket had, if not an Eleusinian origin, at least a connection with the ritual of Agrai. In the imperial era, in the priestly hierarchy of the Bacchic thiasoi (at Torre Nova, for instance)[24] the typically Eleusinian titles of hierophant and dadouchos were to be found. One gets the impression that the Great Mysteries served as a matrix for the various Hellenistic mysteries. This was verified in

Egypt in the case of a Dionysian brotherhood. But why first and precisely in Egypt?

Ever since Herodotus, the story of Zagreus had presented too many similarities with that of Osiris – dismemberment followed by rebirth or resurrection – for the Egyptian religion not to encourage Greek immigrants to the Delta ritually to re-enact the Orphic myth. Father Festugière went so far as to state that the legend of Zagreus 'copies that of Osiris',[25] a hypothesis which is difficult to verify, and one which curiously resumes the explanations of Hecataeus of Abdera. At all events, we may believe that the Egyptian contact contributed to strengthen and repopularize in Alexandrian circles the legend of a god torn to pieces by the Titans, and from the cult point of view to place it firmly in the mystery scenarios. Orpheotelestes and other itinerant theosophers perhaps played an effective role and found an attentive clientele among the uprooted Greeks.

Conversely, the Isiac mysteries of the Roman era also bear the mark of Dionysian influences. The two cults interacted in Ptolemaic Egypt before giving each other support in the Roman West. These interactions or forms of osmosis, just as much as the Eleusinian model, prepared the way for, if not actually determined, the crystallization of Dionysian mysteries. They had and would have a hefty impact in the entire eastern Mediterranean world. But it was in Egypt that they took shape as an initiatory religion.

Scandalous Bacchanalia

The same historical conditions that had led the Roman Senate to come to terms with the disturbed religious feeling of a population demoralized by war, by welcoming the Phrygian Great Mother and her frenzied galli, favoured the gradual ascendancy of other cults which were less easy to keep in check by official regulations. The Megalesia were celebrated only once a year, publicly, under the control of the decemviral authorities and the law. But at the same time, on the fringes, there had been a great increase in the number of forms of worship and splinter groups that were alien to both institutional religion and national tradition.

Already in 213 BC, when war was beginning to drag on, the depressed Romans had let themselves be won over by the *externa superstitio*, 'to the point where men or gods seemed to have changed' (Livy, *Roman History*, XXV, 1, 6). 'Sacrificers and soothsayers had gained a hold on people's minds' (ibid., 8): *sacrificuli ac vates*. The same pair of words characterized the mysterious Greek who was said to have imported Dionysian orgies from Etruria (ibid., XXXIX, 8, 3). A senatorial decree immediately commanded 'whoever had books of prophecies, texts of prayers or a sacrificial formulary' to bring them to the praetor before 1 April (XXV, 1, 12). In some respects this edict recalls Philopatôr's, but with the difference that henceforth it categorically forbids sacrifice 'according to a new and foreign rite', but in a public place! In other words, the practices proliferated even more, but in family circles, among private households. Until then, in theory, the state religion was that of the citizens. From then on, a rift of cultic separatism opened up which worsened until the end of the Second Punic War and after victory.

Among the troublemakers of the *externa superstitio* Livy numbers a plebeian peasantry whom insecurity and the ravaging of land had driven to huddle in the town. In this mass of mixed refugees were rural slaves or freedmen from the North and the South. The mentality of these uprooted people, together with the dejection or anxiety of Roman men and women threatened by Hannibal, must have formed a mixture that was propitious to deviations in forms of piety. It must be said that the strict ritualism of national worship left little room for feelings or imagination. It is easy to suppose that in a period of crisis over-excited minds might want to break the floodgates.

But the end of the war, even in Rome's favour, did nothing to seal the cracks in the victors' religious consciousness. As often happens, it had the opposite effect: liberating, releasing instincts that had for too long been tightly bound by the *mos maiorum*. As often happens, too, after a period of restriction and austerity, exoticism seduced the Romans, chiefly perhaps the young and women, but equally those who discovered Hellenism by way of military campaigns and diplomatic or intellectual contact. Furthermore, the *Urbs* continued to witness an influx of all kinds of people who noticeably altered its appearance and ambience: lowly peasants who, after serving in Macedonia or Asia Minor, preferred to live among the clientele of the political class rather than labour on their lands which had remained uncultivated; ruined Campanians who had backed the wrong side in the Punic War; Tuscans who had also been afflicted, both by Roman conquest and the social revolutions which had shattered decadent Etruria; Greeks from southern Italy who came to trade illicitly in the Forum Boarium, not to mention some 30,000 captives brought back from Tarentum in 208 BC. The wars against Philip V of Macedonia, then those of Antiochus III of Syria flooded the market with slaves from the countries where Dionysus had many worshippers.

In 186 BC there erupted the affair of the Bacchanalia,[26] an abscess that had been festering for several years, perhaps even one or two

decades. In fact, the authorities acted as if they had suddenly discovered the existence of a subversive movement, whose noisy and
noctural manifestations the Romans themselves had been noticing for
quite a while in their neighbourhoods or even their own families.
What was it all about?

Not long before, an obscure Greek, a sacrificer and soothsayer
(*sacrificulus et vates*), had infiltrated the *Urbs*, there to become the
instigator of nocturnal and clandestine ceremonies: mystery liturgies
to which men and women were invited. It seems that the votaries
were not content to take part in orgies where wine, good food and
mixed sexes encouraged debauchery. Their sect concealed the worst
possible crimes: falsification of seals and wills, poisonings, murders
diligently perpetrated amid the uproar of cymbals and timbrels which
drowned the victims' voices, the art of cleanly disposing of the bodies.
Here we may recognize all the paraphernalia of malicious gossip
which is ordinarily applied to secret societies and which even Christian reputation would suffer less than three centuries later. Livy
obtained this 'information' in annalistic tradition, transcribing an
official bulletin obviously conceived and composed to justify the
suppression of the Bacchanalia.

The scandal that erupted in 186 BC tends to put flesh on these
accusations. It was suddenly learnt, in fact, that a fine young man, the
son of the knight Aebutius, had had a narrow escape! His mother,
who had remarried with a man who had squandered his stepson's
wealth, wanted to initiate him into the Bacchic mysteries, obviously to
neutralize or get rid of him. But the young Aebutius had a girl-friend,
and as the initiation required a preliminary period of continence (ten
days), he had to warn her. Hispala – the name of the courtesan 'whom
the loftiness of her feelings placed above the profession which need
forced her to continue', and who helped Aebutius to survive despite
the niggardliness of his guardians – made a great fuss: the sanctuary
of the Bacchants was an evil place. She knew what she was talking
about. Hispala was a slave at the time and her mistress had recently
compelled her to accompany her there. But she took care not to return
now that she was free. For two years only under-twenties had been
initiated, so that they could be abused: a real corruption of minors.
Whoever was introduced into that den of iniquity was 'handed over
to the priests as a victim.' Ritual murder? There is no longer any
question of it, properly speaking. But clearly, Aebutius' mistress did
not want her lover to be taken away from her. When his mother
returned to the attack, Aebutius refused. He was driven out and found
shelter with his aunt Aebutia, who advised him to notify the consul.

One gets the feeling that this was just what he was waiting for, and that he already had his own ideas on the subject. But he needed evidence and confessions. He would get them from Hispala's own lips, after a pretty scene (fainting fits and sobs) worthy of the best bourgeois drama. We then learn other details that do not exactly match Livy's first note relating to the *Graeculus* from Etruria. Originally, priestesses were said to have been responsible for the mysteries; they initiated only three times a year; women (and not men); by day (and not at night). A Campanian woman, Annia Paculla, then adapted the conditions of access to the sanctuary in order to meet increasing demand. She initiated her sons, and men, no longer three times a year but up to five times a month! The Bacchanalia then became nocturnal and thus favourable to all homo- or hetero-sexual excesses. They attracted men and women belonging to the best families in Rome, even connected to notabilities in the Senate. Annia Paculla was the one who turned the mysteries into an undertaking for the corruption of the young. If necessary, they were forced (as Aebutius' mother and stepfather attempted to do), and once in the *Bacchanal*, the recalcitrant were tied to a sort of automatic slide (*machinae illigatos*) and precipitated into a secret chasm: they were then said to have been 'carried off by the gods' (*raptos a diis homines dici*).[27] As for the matrons, faithful to the Greek oreibasia, they ran dishevelled in a mad rush down the slopes of the Aventine to the Tiber, where they plunged their flaming torches into the water and drew them out again still blazing, thanks to a coating of chalk mixed with sulphur.

The success of the *aggiornamento* effected by the inspired Paculla seems to have swollen formidably the ranks of the Bacchants who in the mass – over seven thousand – formed almost a 'people' (*alterum iam prope populum*), but a people apart, on the fringe of the *Populus Romanus*, like the Christian church later on: a separatism that was heavy with menace.

All the more so because the movement had ramifications throughout Italy.

Hispala's accusation (which she did not make without reluctance, for by violating the law of the initiatory secrets she was exposing herself to the vengeance of both gods and men; she ran the risk of being dismembered like Pentheus by the Bacchantes) obviously tells us a great deal about the impact of Dionysism on Roman society following the Second Punic War. It also gives us much precise information about the forms of the ritual and the relaxing of the liturgical calendar that was henceforth suited to the influx of neophytes. But if this account does not contradict the first Livian version of the affair, it would be necessary to believe that Annia Paculla reformed the Bacchanalia before the intervention of the Greek from Etruria (?). The Latin historian certainly imputes to this 'sacrificer and soothsayer' the responsibility for the 'unhealthy contagion' of the Bacchanalia. Actually, it is possible and even quite probable that several Dionysian trends converged in the *Urbs*, around the old temple of Ceres, Liber and Libera which was consecrated on the Aventine in 493 BC. This plebeian hill gathered together a partly foreign population, connected with the activities of the river port and the Forum Boarium. The divine triad had not remained impervious to the influences of Magna Graecia (where Demeter and Kore, the 'Mothers', carried such weight in rustic piety), or those of the Eleusinian mysteries (in which Dionysus had played an increasingly significant role since the fourth century).

It is therefore easy to suppose that Campanian and Greek-speaking immigrants practised their forms of worship near a sanctuary that was welcoming to their religious representations and their beliefs, even though these transplanted devotions lived on the fringes of the Roman cult. The intriguing detail is that the Greek incriminated by Livy should have come from Etruria. But we know that Dionysus had his followers in both Tuscania and Tarquinia,[28] where a recumbent female figure on a sarcophagus is suckling a kid (like Euripides' Bacchae) and where, notably, a 'Bacchic' deceased person (*paχana*) is said to be the great-grandson of a Greek. Greek slave-names can also be found in Etruscan epigraphy, such as *Tinusi* (Dionysus) and *Zerapiu* (Serapion). The latter name appears to indicate Alexandrian origin, and it is not inconceivable that certain priests from the Delta might have imported into Roman Tuscany some of those thiasoi whose multiplication was of such concern to the ptolemaic government. In Rome they rediscovered those people from the South where Orphism and Pythagoreanism, Eleusinianism and Dionysism had all helped to impart a religious vitality to what M. Rostovtzeff would call 'mystic Italy'. Like them, they had arrived from regions plagued by wars and social troubles, but also by Rome's domination. This confluence of rather frustrated marginals who, moreover, were perverting and morally contaminating Roman society, were a source of anxiety to the government and *nobilitas*.

One Aulus Postumius had pledged and dedicated the temple of Ceres, Liber and Libera.[29] Because of this, the *Postumia* family must have felt somewhat responsible for anything affecting the worship of Liber, and thus the foreign 'superstitions' that tended to rival it clandestinely. So it is not surprising that a Postumius – the consul alerted by Aebutius – should have taken the matter in hand. But he must have been informed about it for quite a long while, like some of his friends in the Senate. The Bacchanalia made enough racket during the night for the Romans to be aware of their existence. Within families, people must have known and deplored the seductive influence exerted by Dionysism on women and men of the 'new wave', all the more so as several Bacchants apparently had connections with the ruling circles. Duronia, the unworthy mother, was probably related to L. Duronius, the praetor who, in 181, would wipe out the remains of the Bacchic 'conspiracy'[30] in Apulia. As we saw, she had remarried: one T. Sempronius Rutilus, tribune of the plebs in 189! These compromising situations were not of a kind to reassure the leaders of the nobility.

But for what could the Bacchants be blamed? Dionysism was not a crime condemned by law, requiring tribunals. Something else had to be found.

As if by chance, the mother-in-law of the consul Postumius, Sulpicia, was a close acquaintance of Aebutia, the aunt of the honest courtesan's young gallant. It was obviously known that Aebutius' guardian was dishonest and unable to keep his accounts, and was therefore perhaps tempted to falsify them or rid himself of his ward. There Postumius had a good means of incriminating the Bacchants. We know the outcome.

The Senate was convened as a matter of urgency, public opinion terrorized, the town put on a state of alert, if not siege, and combed by the police of the *tresviri capitales*. Measures were immediately taken against nocturnal gatherings and fires (as later against Catiline's accomplices, then when the Christians were suspected of intent to set fire to the town). Comings and goings at the gates of Rome were strictly controlled. Many initiates managed to flee, while others who were subjected to searches and interrogations chose to kill themselves rather than break the rule of silence about the mysteries. Two plebeians (M. and C. Atinius, whose name was found at Pompeii on a Dionysian inscription) were arrested, together with a Faliscan (L. Opiternius) and a Campanian Minius Cerrinius (a theophoric name with the same root as that of Cerrus-Ceres). They were forced to say that the sect was hatching an abominable plot: debauchery and murders, false witness, false wills (and other fraudulent acts useful to insolvent guardians); all these crimes were said to have been included in advance in the oath sworn by the neophytes!

The repression was merciless. Special courts, several thousand charges and sentences (apart from the fate of women and minors who were handed over to family justice), the destruction of all Bacchic shrines in Rome and Italy (excepting ancient altars and idols), a categorical ban on more than five people at a time (two men and three women) meeting to sacrifice, and on holding communal funds, apparently put a surgical end to the movement. The text of the senatus-consultum *De Bacchanalibus*, preserved for us in extraordinary fashion by a bronze table found in 1640 at Tirolo in Bruttium, bears witness to the concern to detect the slightest aftermath anywhere. In 185, the praetor L. Postumius – yet another member of the family connected with Liber Pater and Dionysism – put down a 'conspiracy of shepherds' (*pastores*) in the Tarentum region, who inevitably bring to mind the *boukoloi* of the Bacchic initiations: another 7,000 sentences, but many succeeded in taking to the bush (Livy, *Roman History*, XXXIX, 29, 8–9). A year later, in Rome itself, a poisoning affair earned capital punishment for the 2,000 accused (ibid., 41, 5). Three years later, the praetor L. Duronius again had to act ruthlessly in Apulia (ibid., XL, 19, 9–10). The situation remained disturbed for some time. But public opinion, which had been conditioned, followed suit, if we are to judge by the comedies of Plautus, which reflect its major trends pretty faithfully. There the *Bacchanal* is denounced as a refuge of madmen, the Bacchantes as furies hitting ever harder anyone who has the audacity to oppose them. This popular conformism of the Latin comedy-writer joins the traditionalism of the old Romans, an echo of which can be found in Varro when he taxes the Bacchants with madness (Augustine, *City of God*, VI, 9), and in Cicero in the treatise on *Laws* (II, 37).

Dionysism managed to survive sporadically, at Pompeii for instance.[31] But in the *Urbs* it was stricken from the cultic map until the day when it resurfaced in the imaginations of the Roman aristocracy by way of the aesthetic appreciation of painted or stuccoed decoration.

Dionysian Mysteries in the Imperial Era

According to the 'grammarian' Servius, commenting on Virgil's Vth *Eclogue* and the triumph of Daphnis in a chariot drawn (like that of Bacchus) by 'tigers from Armenia' (1. 29ff), Caesar had been 'the first' to transplant the Dionysian mysteries to Rome. A surprising statement, since one and a half centuries earlier those same mysteries had revolutionized the religious awareness of the *Urbs*, but one which may be explained by admitting that the dictator had been 'the first' to authorize them officially. It must be said that the Caesarian ideology of the universal monarch, conquering and civilizing, matched the Hellenistic image of Dionysus, re-enacted by Alexander's deeds in

Asia and the triumphalist performances of certain Diadochi (Ptolemy Philadelphus, for instance.[32]

Nevertheless, beginning precisely in Caesar's time, the evidence provided by representational archaeology and literary tradition increased. The great frieze in the Villa of the Mysteries at Pompeii is today dated to somewhere in the sixties BC (first phase of the IInd style).[33] Twenty years later, Mark Antony, Caesar's true political heir, entered Ephesus behind a procession of Bacchantes, Pans and Satyrs, to the sound of the Pan-pipes and flutes: he was acclaimed as a New Dionysus, 'bringer of joy and source of peace' (Plutarch, *Antony*, 24, 4). His defeat at Actium and Octavian's Apollonianism by no means prevented Dionysism from making headway, at least in the iconographic environment of wealthy residences. Initiation scenes appeared on stuccoed vaults (Plate 31) and the painted walls in the small salons of the Farnesina, the Transtiberine villa perhaps occupied by Agrippa and Julia, Augustus' own daughter.[34] Then, during the first three centuries AD, the imagery of the mysteries spread and was revealed in pottery, gems, mosaic and funerary art. Literature and epigraphy confirm the success of Bacchic brotherhoods in the Roman world. Despite lacunae and disparities in their informational value, all these data enable us to lift a corner of the veil and obtain a very approximate idea of the ritual.[35]

Theoretically, initiations were performed at night, every two years originally ('trieteric' or biennial periodicity, which has been explained

Plate 31 Stucco from the Farnesina (Rome, Museo delle Terme)

in connection with letting land lie fallow), but several times a year, or even month, in the Bacchanalia suppressed in 186 BC. It is conceivable that the time of the grape-harvest may have been the occasion for mystery-type celebrations. The festival given by Messalina in her gardens in 48, in the company of women dressed in skins and the handsome Silius disguised as Dionysus, presented the spectacle of a *vindemia* in mid-autumn (Tacitus, *Annals*, XI, 31, 4) at the same time as a real Bacchanal, with the possible staging of a sacred marriage.[36]

The Bacchants met most often on the fringe of official and public cults, on private property, in parks or woods rendered sacred by chapels and idols of every kind. The painted, stuccoed or sculpted representations evoke for us a natural environment of trees and rocks, even caverns, to which literary tradition also refers.

Again originally, candidates underwent a self-imposed *castus*; i.e., a time of continence and abstinence. Livy (XXXIX, 9, 4) mentions a purification bath (*pure lautum*, he writes of the candidate) at the end of ten days' preliminary *castimonia*. It is not certain that in the imperial era the strictness of this formulary was always observed. But in certain thiasoi people at least stayed faithful to food taboos like the one concerning eggs (F. Sokolowski, *LSAM*, p. 188): the prohibition that ruled out their consumption in the Bacchants' meals applied *a fortiori* to postulants.

Sacrifices (of a pig or a cock) were the prelude to the consecration of the candidate, to judge by the iconography that is partly confirmed by the Byzantine Tzetzes in his commentary on Aristophanes (*The Frogs*, 338). Certain plants and the contents of the sacred wicker-baskets were blessed beforehand, as seems to be shown by the megalography in the Villa Item (Pompeii) and the reliefs on the sarcophagi, the 'megarian' bowls[37] or a cameo-cup preserved in the Corning Museum of Glass (New York State, USA).[38]

The one to be initiated took the oath, swearing to keep secret the formulary, the verbal or material 'symbols' and the details of the ritual. This *sacramentum* constituted a commitment to serve the god. Livy (XXXIX, 18, 3) speaks of a *carmen sacrum* which had to be pronounced following the dictation of the officiating priest. In the great frieze of the Pompeian Villa known as that 'of the mysteries', we see the veiled candidate listening to a little boy, naked and booted like the infant Bacchus, who is reading the text of a *volumen* under the attentive direction of a priestess.[39]

At that point a sort of investiture took place. The candidate was fitted with a nebris or skin of a fawn, ibex or other similar animal. He was crowned perhaps with ivy, myrtle or other sacred and sacralizing foliage. In his hand were placed attributes such as the thyrsus or a vine branch. In some instances the neophytes were tattooed, for example with an ivy leaf as a sign of belonging to Bacchus. Occasionally the Bacchants put on make-up in memory of the Titans whitened with gypsum.

A representation or painted images on triptychs reminded the candidate of episodes in the myth of Zagreus dismembered by the Titans, probably also celebrated in the communal *hieros logos*, a sort of verbal liturgy.[40] Evocations of the infernal world must have made an impression on the neophytes, if one believes the testimony of Celsus according to Origen (*Against Celsus*, IV, 10; cf. VIII, 48). Dionysian iconography repeats frequently, if not mechanically, the motif of the basket or casket from which a snake rises, frightening the *putti* or little satyrs. The mask of Silenus also plays a notable role in this imagery of fear embodied by several characters in the Bacchanalia: in particular, a terrified woman beside the scene known as the 'lecanomancy' in the megalography of the Villa Item. Whatever may be thought of the interpretations proposed for this representation, it belongs in the series of data showing that candidates had to undergo psychological ordeals, as in the mysteries of Mithras. The officiating priests of the initiatory cult probably donned appropriate disguises for these liturgies.

The consecration by the 'mystic' winnowing basket, as Virgil calls it (*Georgics*, I, 166), but referring to the Eleusinian cult (Little Mysteries of Agrai?), was an important moment, if not the culminating point, of the ceremony. It consisted in holding the veiled basket above the candidate, who bowed his similarly veiled head (plate 32). He then knelt, turning his back and head, his body apparently naked (stucco in the Farnesina and Villa of the Mysteries).[41] Behind him (or her) the contents of the fruit-laden *liknon* were uncovered, including notably a paste phallus, organ and symbol of generation. The unveiling of the mystic basket (plate 31), so often evoked in Dionysian iconography, revealed to the candidate the triumph of life over death, which in the Pompeian frieze of the Mysteries was embodied by a female demon with great black wings, visibly thwarted by the erect phallus of the sacred basket. In vain, therefore, she brandishes her threatening wand, which makes allusion to the punishments of hell. But, contrary to what was and still is believed, there was no flagellation in Dionysian initiation.[42]

'Symbols' or passwords were imparted to the mysta,[43] precisely to enable him to overcome obstacles to eternal happiness in the next world, and to neutralize the infernal demons. He was also given amulets, talismans or figurines to commemorate his initiation, but also to act as phylacteries in this world and the next. Accused of having magic objects about his person, Apuleius (*Apologia*, 55, 8) admits that, having been initiated to several cults in Greece, he carefully preserves their 'symbols and souvenirs'. He then addresses the priests of Liber, saying:

> You know very well what you keep hidden in your homes and venerate in silence, far from all the profane . . .

In some instances, these objects recalled the toys with which the Titans had amused and abused the infant Zagreus. It must not be forgotten that, according to the Orphic myth (which seems to have been very much alive in several Bacchic thiasoi), humanity which issued from the ashes of the Titans struck down by Zeus' thunderbolt also contains something of Zagreus that must be separated and liberated from the Titanic elements.

It is possible, but not certain, that grottoes or caverns were used for mock *katabasia*. In such cases the mysta would have mimed a descent to the Underworld, dying (like the Isiac or Mithraic neophyte) to his previous life before being reborn into a new life. At that point the made-up Bacchants would enact the mysteries of the next world. In the thiasos of Torre Nova 'guardians of the cavern' (*antrophylakes*)

Plate 32 Painting (lost) from the *Domus Aurea*, Rome (after F. d'Olanda)

made their appearance,[44] possibly watching over the maintenance of the place, out of sight of the profane, and guarding against possible damage or defilement. But the natural or artificial grottoes of the *Baccheia* may also have been used as a reminder of the god's birth, and it has even been thought possible to compare them to our Christmas cribs.

The initiation ended in a liturgy of inebriation and dance. Sarcophagi show us the wine-bowl from which the Bacchants drank before enjoying the ecstasies of divine orgy. The eating of raw meat (omophagia) which originally followed the dismemberment of a live bullcalf or goat – like Zagreus torn to pieces by the Titans – assumed the form of a symbolic ritual in the Hellenistic era. Like the wine, the music of the flutes, Pan-pipes, cymbals, castanets and timbrels which enlivened and gave rhythm to frenzied dancing, helped to make the initiate beside himself and turn him into a *Bacchos*. Ecstasy was the therapy for madness, treated by giving madness release. It seems that certain dances mimed episodes from Bacchic deeds, such as the 'passion' of Zagreus (Lucian, *The Dance*, 39). Through the Bacchanalia in which the neophyte could then participate, he was henceforth incorporated into the thiasus and a sort of divine life.

Following the Dionysian associations, he moved on to various grades in an initiatory hierarchy and certain titles which related either to special priestly functions or to stage roles personifying the characters in the myth: Silenus, Bacchus' nurse, the Titans or infernal demons. The great Bacchic inscription in the Metropolitan Museum, New York (found at Torre Nova in 1926) lists the names of some 420 members of a thiasos led by a great lady of the Roman aristocracy, but whose family's ancestry was linked with the isle of Lesbos (where Dionysism had a long tradition);[45] priests and priestesses, hierophants, theophori, phallophori, cistaphori, licnaphori, dadoukoi and 'fire-bearers', 'herdsmen' (*boukoloi*) and 'chief herdsmen' (*archiboukoloi*), *bacchoi* and *bacchai*, not to mention other titles whose exact sense eludes us and who, with the foregoing, make a total of twenty-six different grades! Elsewhere, we find a 'neophant' (responsible for introducing neophytes to the community?), a 'theophant' or one who revealed the god, an 'orgiophant' or initiator to the *orgia*.

These celebrations, crowned by joyous banquets, might frequently resemble jolly masquerades in which theology merely played a rather particular role, which did not prevent them from satisfying a genuinely religious need to escape periodically from secular everyday life.[46]

The liturgy varied more or less perceptibly from one association to another, for there was no central body to regulate its ritual, a fact which facilitated the spread and establishment of thiasoi, but carried the risk of enfeebling cultic ardour and strictness. Whoever founded a community, boasting of a *hieros logos* that was rather concocted, could organize it as he wished, and his successors could reinterpret the formulary or suit it to the circumstances, if not the current whim, of the Bacchants. We have seen this verified already in the case of Annia Paculla. Certainly, every association (religious or not) had to be declared to the Roman state, together with its exact methods of operating. But many *collegia* were not, and seem to have functioned *de facto*, at least temporarily. One gets the impression that in the second century AD, the very liberal regime of the Antonines – despite the strict letter of the law – turned a blind eye to the activities of these people who met together to feast and make merry whether or not in the name of a god or cult.

Many thiasoi had nothing 'mystic' or even 'of mystery' about them. They operated and recruited like some oenophile brotherhoods in Burgundy or Beaujolais, with their grand masters, their enthronement ceremonials, the flashiness of their insignia and costumes. This Dionysism with a middle-class bent, patronized by local notabilities in Italy as in Asia Minor, was a religion of festive euphoria and well-being guaranteed by the Pax Romana. Furthermore, it often went hand in hand with the imperial cult and henceforth lost everything of its earlier revolutionary ferment.

That time also saw an increase in the number of funerary colleges. If Dionysus helped with wine and orgies to allay the anxieties of life here below, he was important above all as protector of the dead, and the guarantor of a happy life hereafter.

Funerary Dionysism

Certain associations had their own cemetery and collectively ensured a cult to the spirits of their dead, like many funerary colleges to which Christians were affiliated. For a long time, people erroneously ascribed to the Dionysian mysteries an inscription from Cumae, dating to the end of the sixth century BC, which excludes from a reserved sector the burial of anyone who has not 'become Bacchos'. In fact, it must belong to an Orphic sect.[47]

In the Roman era, generally speaking, the mysteries united post-humous salvation with the safekeeping of the initiate in this life, and in a sort of biocosmic continuity which is indirectly illustrated, in their own way, by the carved marbles of the tombs. This is particularly true of the Dionysian mysteries.[48]

As a reaction against the Epicureans who denied the ordeals and ills of man after death, Plutarch (*Consolation to his Wife*, 10, 611 D) cites the 'mystic symbols' of Bacchic orgies. If in the initiations the neophyte was shown the torments or perils of the next world, it must be assumed that the ritual was deemed capable of averting them from him. Dionysus, who had brought his mother Semele back from the Underworld, must similarly save initiates from death. He himself was a reborn god who had known several mythical lives. Zagreus, whose story was enacted, represented or narrated in the mysteries was supposed to have been reconstituted and restored to life. Texts tell us of the celebration of an awakening of the god at the *liknon* or 'Liknites', who is to be seen carried in the basket as if in a cradle, on sarcophagi in Naples and Cambridge.[49] On other examples in this range, the same Bacchus is featured both as a young beardless god and an old man, sometimes crowned with the calathus, like Serapis, who also watched over the deceased.[50] These reincarnations of the *Dimorphos*, as Diodorus Siculus calls him (IV, 5, 2), doubtless had a symbolic value. In the Antonine era, the rhetor Aelius Aristides (*Dionysus*, 7) extolled his regenerative power, which restored youth to old men.

On third-century sarcophagi, the god of the orgy is frequently seen in company with spirits personifying the Seasons, and thus the cycle of nature's annual rebirths. Sometimes Dionysus is enthroned side-saddle on a lioness (or other large cat) in the midst of his thiasos, with Silenus and the god Pan, or flanked by large Cupids, each bearing different produce of the year as offerings to the dead. So the god appears as master of animal life and the plant world. The imagery of the Seasons illustrates the idea that the deceased takes part in the periodic renewal of the cosmos and the limitless rejuvenation of its luxuriant vitality.[51]

For nearly two centuries (from Hadrian to the Tetrarchy) the iconography of the Roman sarcophagi repeats the theme of Dionysus triumphing on returning from his campaign in India. The god who civilized and mastered the Orient, to which he brought the benefits of the vine and drunkenness (as wild animals and their savagery were tamed by wine), by his exploits in the company of Heracles he had merited immortality and could therefore promise it to his followers.[52] Passing through Naxos, he had awakened and consoled the fair Ariadne, who had been deserted by Theseus. From the end of the Antonine period, a whole series of sarcophagi shows us Bacchus alighting from his chariot to snatch the daughter of Minos from the sleep of death, personified by a bearded *Hypnos* of Plutonian aspect. On an example from the Borghese Palace in Rome, on one side we

may see an Eros raising his torch before Dionysus, and on the other an
Eros sadly lowering his at Ariadne's bedside: a graphic picture of
temporary death compared with the life embodied by the god of
wine.[53] From the 200s, Ariadne is often portrayed in the likeness of the
dead woman or, at least, her face is outlined with a coiffure in keeping
with contemporary fashion so that the features of the deceased could
be filled in when necessary.

Often, too, the Centaurs pulling the chariots of Bacchus and
Ariadne bear a medallion (*imago clipeata*) of the bust of the one or
more who died. We know that the horse-bodied monsters belong to
the mythical fauna of the next world. Virgil, Seneca and Statius picture
them guarding the gates of the Underworld. On the other hand, for
the Ancients the *imago clipeata* evoked the visible and almost heroized
image of the invisible soul. This iconography of apotheosis, with
which Victories are sometimes associated, thus quite clearly signified
the conviction of triumph over death in the company of the thiasos,
i.e., the initiates.[54]

In the third century many sarcophagi had the form of oval-shaped
vats, like the *lacus* or *lenoi* used for pressing the grape harvest. Certain
literary testimony expressly likens the death of Dionysus-Zagreus,
torn apart by the Titans, to that of the grapes crushed by the
winemakers to produce wine, which these same texts identify with the
god who is reborn to rejoice the hearts of humans.[55] A Pompeian
painting represents a Bacchus in the form of a bunch of grapes or
Botrys, and earlier Euripides (*Bacchae*, 284) made Tiresias say: 'This
god, for all that he is god, flows as an offering to the gods'.

Later, Clement of Alexandria (*Pedagogue*, II, 2, 19, 3) would speak of
the 'grapes pressed for our salvation', and St Cyprian (*Letters*, 69, 5)
would explain John's parable of the vine by making wine the symbol
of a return to unity. In fact, Christian sarcophagi also are known in the
shape of grape-pressing vats. Some Bacchic sarcophagi of this type
were apparently re-used for Christian burials, those who salvaged
them not even taking the trouble to destroy the image of the god or
the Bacchants.

As for the Dionysiasts who ordered or reserved for themselves vats
of this kind (on the anterior face of which sometimes just such a scene
of grape-pressing is featured, in a *lenos* similar to the one that is their
last resting-place), they may have thought that after becoming decom-
posed by death, like the grapes, they would live again like Bacchus,
like wine, in the delights of an eternal orgy. This is merely a hypothesis, justified by the data of textual and archaeological tradition. But
the pagans' idea of an afterlife must in general have been as confused

as the immortality conceived or imagined by many believers even in
these days.

Nevertheless, people envisaged a sort of paradise for initiated
children, like the father who, in a metric epitaph from Philippi in
Macedonia (*CIL*, III, 686), says to his dead son:

> Revived (*reparatus*), thou livest in the flowery meadows of the
> Elysian Fields, where thou art welcomed into the troop of Satyrs
> by the mystae of Bacchus, marked with the sacred seal [possible
> allusion to the initiatory tattooing].

Several children's sarcophagi unfold for us on their facade the
sequence of initiations through which the young Dionysus passed to
serve as an example for his followers, which apparently implies a
parallel, an analogy with the consecration of the deceased who died at
an early age or prematurely (*ahoros*), like Zagreus. The adaptation of
the carved ornamentation to the fate of children, borne out by a good
number of sarcophagi, indicates the concern and the hopes of the
parents.[56]

The considerable quantity of sarcophagi with Dionysian subjects
remains a fact, and is not without good reason. In the range of pagan
myths treated and repeated by Roman monumental masons, the
deeds of Bacchus by far outclassed all the rest. Of all the gods,
Dionysus was the most frequently represented in Roman funerary art,
and he sometimes bore the features of the dead person: this would
tend to confirm the explanation outlined earlier for the *lenoi* where the
deceased was implicitly likened to Dionysus-Zagreus. In *The Golden
Ass* (VIII, 7, 7), Apuleius quotes the instance of a widow who rendered
divine honours to her husband who was featured as Liber Pater, *ad
habitum dei Liberi*. This case must not have been an exception.

Sanctus Sabazius

The Thracio-Phrygian Sabazius, god of the fermented 'juice' (*saba* or
sapa), was related to Dionysus by the corybantic rites of his worshippers and by certain methods in the initiatory ceremonial.

At the beginning of the fourth century BC, in some quarters of
Athens the Sabaziasts created a nocturnal din to which Aristophanes,
and later Demosthenes, bear witness with hostile sarcasm. In his
Speech On the Crown (259–60), the enemy of Aeschines describes their
liturgy in terms which, curiously enough, prefigure those of the
Dionysian mysteries as they would be revealed in the epigraphy and
iconography of the Graeco-Roman world. The young Aeschines, who

in this instance was accompanying his mother, used the nebris and wine-bowl like the Bacchants. He proceeded with the preliminary purification of candidates for consecration by smearing them with mud and bran, before making them repeat the sacramental formula: 'I have escaped evil, I have found good'. The ceremony ended the next day with dances in which 'plump snakes' were brandished, and the mystic winnowing fan was borne aloft to cries of *'Euoi Saboi'* and *'Hues Attes'*. One may wonder whether this ritual influenced that of the Dionysiasts.[57]

Strongly entrenched in Asia Minor, where he established links with Attis and Mên (the Moon god), like them Zeus Sabazius wore a Phrygian cap or at least the conical *pilos*. His attributes were an ivy-wreathed staff and a pine cone. He was represented placing his foot on a ram's head (as Mên did on a bull's head). He was a sovereign god, 'lord', identified with Zeus (sometimes Helios) and associated with the Great Mother or *Meter Hipta*, the native name for a wet-nurse of Bacchus. People feared the wrath of the Lord Sabazius, and several 'confessional' stelae preserve for us the evidence of penitent worshippers, who were often afflicted by a disease of the eyes or other physical trials because, for example, they had cut down the trees in a sacred wood or carried off a temple slave.[58]

In Thrace, Sabazius had affinities with the horseman Hero. His noisy and rather violently festive cult won over certain cosmopolitan circles in the Greek, then Italic, world. There were Sabaziast clubs in Rhodes and Piraeus around 100 BC.[59] In 139 they attracted unfavourable attention by their disturbances, even excesses, which threatened accepted standards of behaviour in Rome itself. The *praetor peregrinus* Cornelius Hispalus included them in the same decree of expulsion as the Jews and Chaldaeans (or astrologers). Valerius Maximus (*Memorable Words and Deeds*, I, 3, 3), who records the event, strangely attributed the worship of Jupiter Sabazius to the former,[60] and there has been speculation as to whether at the time Sabaoth was confused with the Thracio-Phrygian god, as would happen later following some fanciful etymologies. It has been suggested that the Jews then driven from the *Urbs* were from Pergamum, where Sabazius enjoyed a dynastic cult under the Attalids. In fact, the Roman police were in the habit of lumping together groups of undesirables. The Jews would again pay the price under Tiberius with the followers of Isis, and under Claudius with the early Christians. The main thing about this affair was that the nocturnal goings-on of the Sabaziasts were very soon to become a scandal.

Indeed, some hundred years later, Diodorus Siculus (IV, 4) informs us precisely that sacrifices were made by night to Sabazius and 'clandestinely, because of the shame attached to these gatherings'. The flutes, cymbals and timbrels, in this instance, provided the music for a ritual comparable to the orgies of Bacchus (Iamblichus, *The Mysteries of Egypt*, III, 9). The disgraceful drinking bouts and sexual promiscuities hinted at by other sources of information must have contributed to the Sabaziasts' bad reputation.

Nevertheless, their god seems to have made a place for himself in Rome, and even on the Capitol, not far from Jupiter *Optimus Maximus*, whose names and epithets he sometimes bears in Latin dedications. On the slopes of the *Arx* or 'citadel' – where Juno *Moneta* protected the old mint – the Punic goddess *Caelestis*, who had been 'evoked' by Scipio Aemilianus in 146, had a sanctuary which seems to have housed the devotions of the Sabaziasts in the imperial era, at least judging by three inscriptions found in the area.[61] The Carthaginian Tanit, invoked as *Triumphalis* (which went well with a Capitoline cult), sheltered a Sabazius *Invictus* there, which assimilated him to Mithras. The Persian cult had also gained a foothold on the holy hill, in a *Mithraeum* from which the great cultic relief in the Louvre, Paris, came (*CIMRM*, 415/6). On this stele, above the bull which bears the engraved dedication 'to the Sun god, Invincible Mithras', may be deciphered the epigraph NAMA SEBESIO. Because *nama* is a word of Iranian origin meaning 'salvation', people have tried to explain *Sebesio* from *Saoshyant*, the name of the 'saviour' in the Avesta. However, a bronze bust of Sabazius unearthed at Bolsena (*CIMRM*, 659) has the relief of a bull-slaying Mithras on his chest (plate 33), and there is nothing to rule out the dedication on the Louvre stele from having begun with a homage to the father god, Jupiter Sabazius or *Sebesios*, just one variant among several others of the divine name.[62]

Around a century ago, the building of the Victor Emmanuel Monument in Rome brought about the discovery of a marble statuette of a seated goddess, dedicated *Sancto deo Sabazi* 'by the voice of the priest Pegasus', that is to say, very likely at his prophetic instigation.[63] The name Pegasus recalls both that of the 'spring' (*pege*), so dear to the Mithraists, and the myth of Perseus of which they could boast. This 'find' near the *Arx* confirms for us that Sabazius was implanted there, in connection with the Persian cult. In Rome itself, the Thracio-Phrygian god also had worshippers in the barracks of the *Equites Singulares*, the cavalry of the imperial guard, under the basilica of San Giovanni Laterano, and doubtless also in the Trastevere region, where other foreign religions rubbed shoulders.[64]

But the bust of Bolsena proves that the connection between the Sabazian and Mithraic cults did not form a specifically Roman exception. Again at Ostia, a *Sabazeum* linked (as on the Capitol) with the cult of *Caelestis* was ultimately used as a *Mithraeum*. The epigraphy of the site demonstrates that Mithras, in his role of 'Invincible Omnipotent Sun', had the same followers there as Jupiter Sabazius.[65]

However, evidence in Italy remains rather scattered (Praeneste, Suessula connected with Ortona on the Adriatic, Cassino, Luni, Fiano Romano, from where came a remarkable bifaced stele of the Bull-slayer).[66] In Africa, at Henchir el-Fouar, the dedication of an altar to Liber Pater 'at the command of Jupiter Sabazius' once more bears witness to the theological solidarity of the two divinities.[67] According to some traditions, indeed, Dionysus was said to be the son of Zeus Sabazius.

Plate 33 Sabazius of Bolsena (Vatican Museums; photo. kindly provided by M.J. Vermaseren)

People called on Sabazius as a saviour god, *Conservator* (as may be read on an altar in Mainz dedicated by a soldier of Pannonian origin).[68] The safeguarding of physical well-being stemmed from his omnipotence, which is illustrated by several bronze plaques where this Jupiter is flanked by many symbols: the Sun and Moon, thunderbolt and caduceus, the caps of the Dioscuri and other cosmic attributes.[69] On bronze triptychs he is found in association with Castor and Pollux, Cybele, Attis and Mercury. In Gaul, his cult grafted itself onto certain spring sanctuaries, where migrants from the Mediterranean East rubbed shoulders with the natives. In a watering-place such as Vichy, some eighty ex-votos have been recovered. For the most part they are silver plaques: sometimes triangular sheets like those of the Dolichenian cult, in the shape of trilobate palm leaves or stylized branches bearing the image in repoussé of the thunderbolt or Jupiter Sabazius in his temple, accompanied by the eagle. The plant motifs (as well as the palm of triumph) evoke the Bacchic vine – and thus the wine of immortality – or the Dionysian ivy, but more generally the god's omnipotence over flora and fruitfulness, which are so closely bound up with the health-giving waters.[70]

Sabazius does not appear to have had regular temples, or at any rate ones devoted solely to him, in the West, even in Rome. On the other hand, like other Graeco-oriental deities, he had an itinerant following of pilgrims and rootless people. It was not by chance that Apuleius (*Metamorphoses*, VIII, 25, 3) attributed to the mendicant galli of Atargatis the invocation of Bellona, the Great Idaean Mother and *Sanctus Sebadius* (yet another variation of the name Sabazius). It is then very easy to explain the use of the above-mentioned triptychs which assemble the 'icons' of Sabazius, Cybele and Attis. They were folded up in luggage so that they could be conveniently carried and presented for the worship of occasional devotees in one of those mother-cult or Mithraic shrines in whose shadow nomadic or poorly endowed gods were honoured. Some of these triptychs have been retrieved in Rome and Ampurias.

Among the most significant indications of this cult, and the most widely diffused in the Roman world, are notably those bronze hands known as 'pantheistic' (plate 34) making the gesture of the *benedictio latina*, the first three fingers (thumb to middle finger) upright, the last two curved under.[71] These hands are often displayed on a base, but some are hollow and apparently made to be fixed on a shaft. The middle plaque of the triptych discovered at Ampurias shows us an altar flanked by two hands raised on supports of this type.[72]

Several of the hands bear an image of Sabazius above the palm, as a bust or standing, as well as a variety of motifs illustrating the god's cult and the multiplicity of his powers: scales, caduceus, snake, lizard, frog or toad, tree, pine-cone, amphora or wine-bowl, straight and curved flutes, ram's head, round loaf, offertory table, etc. Above all, many examples show a woman suckling a baby in a cavern. The ram's head, wine containers, bread, snake and musical instruments refer to the sacrificial and banqueting rites of the Sabaziasts. But the nursing mother in the grotto? She is sometimes accompanied by an eagle, which obviously suggests Jupiter. It must be the illustration of a myth about which literary tradition provides some information.[73] Indeed, Sabazius was supposed to be the fruit of the love of Zeus and Persephone. Clement of Alexandria and Arnobius deride or wax

Plate 34 Pantheistic hand (Musée d'Avenches)

indignant about the Sabazian mysteries. But Sabazius took on the powers of Zeus, and on several 'pantheistic' hands we see the eagle clutching the thunderbolt of the celestial sovereign. As happens in other religions, the son-god ended by supplanting the father-god, and Sabazius became Jupiter *Sabazius*.

Zeus was said to have mated with Persephone in the form of a dragon. So initiation to the mysteries of Sabazius included a rite of sacred marriage. A metal serpent was placed against the breast of the neophyte: *aureus coluber*, write Arnobius (*Against the Nations*, V, 21).

In the mysteries of Sabazius, the symbol taught to initiates is the god who passes through the breast . . . witness to Zeus' disgraceful behaviour! (Clement of Alexandria, *Protreptikos*, II, 16, 2)

About one hundred Sabazian hands are known. Unfortunately, fewer than two thirds of them are of certain provenance. They have been found in Thrace and Asia Minor, the Danubian provinces, Gaul and Germany, but chiefly in Italy and the offshore islands (Sicily and Sardinia), where about thirty examples that are well situated geographically are attested. Out of this third, around ten originate from Campania, notably Herculaneum and Pompeii where, in a house known as the 'Complesso di riti magici', the centre of a Sabazian sect has been recognized.[74]

This house (II. 1. 12) is sufficiently typical of the new forms adopted by pagan piety in the imperial era to merit a brief pause. We are speaking of a dwelling that was relatively far from the colony's civic centre, and in any case removed from official and public worship. It had only one fairly narrow entrance from the street, and almost 'blind' walls. One entered by a corridor at the end of which a small dining-room was on the left, but which led to a large porticoed courtyard. In line with the entrance stood a very simple altar made of masonry bricks and provided with iron rings to which the poles supporting the 'pantheistic' hands could be fixed. Facing the altar was a covered room, in which a *podium* had been created that was sufficiently deep to be used for theatrical presentations. Around the courtyard or connected with the courtyard was access to rooms whose purpose escapes us. One of these, surrounded by large solid walls, had sufficient capacity to house initiatory gatherings; another with its hearth and sink may have been used as a kitchen. Others must have served as bedrooms.

At the entrance to the covered room containing the *podium* (to which M. della Corte appropriately gave the name *sacellum*),[75] on the left-hand pillar the neuter noun graffito ANTRV[M] has been deciphered; on the right-hand pillar were carved drawings of an ibis (with an inscription in demotic designating the god Thoth) and a naked, ithyphallic dancer holding a timbrel. Near the altar two wine amphorae were unearthed: one decorated with bunches of grapes, snakes, round loaves and other motifs similar to those with which the 'pantheistic' hands are laden. Besides snakes, the other bears medallions with erotic subjects.[76] The facade of the house revealed a Mercury (the equivalent of the Egyptian Thoth), a Bacchus and a Venus, painted on a white background. On the interior surface of the door jamb, a Priapus seemed to invite the habitués of the place to certain specific activities . . . which, like the medallions with erotic subjects and the ithyphallic dancer, would seem to confirm Diodorus' testimony to the 'shame' of the clandestine ceremonies dear to Sabaziasts. Apart from the 'pantheistic' hands,[77] between the altar and the *sacellum* a whole series of lamps were found which were obviously used at their nocturnal meetings.

On the *podium* a founding myth must have been presented to the neophytes. The graffito ANTRV[M] lets us suppose that this referred to the cavern seen on the bronze hands which shelters the birth of Sabazius, suckled by Persephone in the presence of the Jovian eagle. There are no grounds for the commonly held opinion that this cult was of more special interest to women in childbirth. Moreover, we have no knowledge of any Sabazian dedication following upon a 'churching' ceremony, and there is reason to doubt that these Pompeian premises could have been frequented by pregnant women or those who had recently given birth. Venus and Priapus, with Bacchus, served as a sign for the house. Furthermore, what we know of the Sabazian cult leaves us in no doubt about the licentiousness summed up in his own way by the lecherous old man portrayed at the entrance to the sacred cavern. After attending the scenic re-enactment of the myth, the candidate to the mysteries had to take part in a banquet, drink and dance in the courtyard around the altar, on which libations of wine were poured before the sacrifice of a ram. The neophyte was incorporated into the club by a sort of bacchanalia which received as much bad press as the orgies of Bacchus. The Priapus at the entrance door personified a whole programme on his own. Diodorus Siculus (IV, 6, 4) writes of the god of Lampsacus that he was honoured in nearly all the mysteries 'by celebrating him with laughter and games'.

Situated between the amphitheatre and the *Schola armaturarum* (the headquarters of an association that apparently devoted itself to martial arts), house II.1.12 may have had connections with the gladiators, who were often recruited in Thrace where Sabazius had at least part of his roots.[78] Spartacus, whose name may be discerned in a gladiatorial

scene painted on a wall in the house of Amandus (Via dell'Abbon-
danza), was said to have seen a dragon wind round his face when he
arrived in Rome to be sold (Plutarch, *Life of Crassus*, 8, 4), before being
enslaved as a gladiator in the Capua barracks. This 'dragon' was
doubtless connected with the Sabazian cult.[79] It is not out of the
question that Spartacus and his compatriots imported, or at least
reinforced, the cult in Campania.

We know, moreover, that the Pompeian gladiators had supporters
organized in commando gangs who, if the need arose, could wade
into adversaries, as happened in the bloody brawl which the Nucer-
ians had to endure in 59. It was then that the Senate pronounced the
dissolution of the 'colleges' which the Pompeians had set up 'contrary
to the laws' (Tacitus, *Annals*, XIV, 17, 5), i.e., without making a prior
declaration and receiving the consent of the public authorities. This
case is fairly typical of associations to which the Roman state turned a
blind eye until a scandal broke out. In this regard, the precedent of the
Bacchanalia in 186 BC is a good example. Now, concerning the
Sabaziasts, Diodorus Siculus talks of 'clandestine' meetings. Were
those who gathered at house II.1.12 mixed up in the violence of the
clubs suppressed by the Senate in 59? We may well raise the question.

The structure and the location itself of these premises also illustrate
a phenomenon that is characteristic of religious history in the imperial
era. With Sabazius as with Dionysus, piety changed its place and its
form. Part of religious life moved away from public and traditional
areas. It was no longer seen necessarily in or in front of temples,
around the altars of the municipal centre, but in the homes of
individuals or in private clubs like that of house II.1.12. It changed in
form, too, to be expressed in quite a different manner from the family
or civic cult. Certainly, people met to make sacrifices, but away from
indiscreet eyes, and above all to enjoy hours of collective relaxation,
not to mention psychological outlets, far from municipal authorities
and possible intruders.

* * *

Did the Sabaziasts have the prospect of posthumous survival, even
an eschatology? Those who simultaneously worshipped Dionysus,
Cybele and Mithras probably envisaged a celestial immortality in
keeping with the soteriology of their mysteries. But what did the
others think? Or rather, what could they believe?

The paintings adorning the tomb of a Sabaziast priest and a
follower in the Catacomb of Praetextatus (near the Appian Way,

Rome) throw some light and surprise us, while confirming some suspicions.[80] Discovered in the eighteenth century, these frescoes had already caused some surprise, if not shock, and their publication was delayed until 1852. In fact, it was a catacomb that had initially been Christian, but where, perhaps around the late third century but certainly in the fourth, pagans – notably Sabaziasts and Mithraists – occupied four *arcosolia* for burials. It was difficult to understand the crudely profane decoration of these tombs alongside the Christian graves, especially the presence of a Venus *aversa* whom Father R. Garrucci interpreted as the indecent picture of 'the impure Cotytto'.[81] Today we have a better knowledge and understanding of the complexity of religious cohabitations in late Antiquity, in a period when Christians maintained family and socio-professional links with pagans. Other catacombs have yielded examples of funerary hospitality offered to idolaters.

Not far from a tomb housing the remains of two Mithraic priests, facing the one whose vault bears the immodest Venus on its summit, a priest of Sabazius was buried whose life and doctrine were summed up as follows:

Eat, drink, enjoy thyself and come to me. As long as thou livest have a good time: thou wilt carry it with thee!
Here lies Vincentius, priest of the god Sabazius, who with pious heart hath celebrated the divine holy ceremonies.

This mixture of priestly devotion and enjoyable Epicureanism may be disconcerting.[82] It is far less astonishing when one takes Diodorus and the Pompeian evidence into account. But, apparently, Vincentius expected nothing other than the pleasures of his past life.

However, in this same tomb, Vibia, a female worshipper of Sabazius, had herself represented in an after-life where Vincentius takes part in a banquet of immortality. She is first shown being carried off like Proserpine by Pluto and guided by Mercury accompanied by Alcestis to the tribunal of the sovereign of the Netherworld (*Dis Pater*) and *Aeracura* (possible transcription of *Hera Core* or Infernal Juno), before the three deities of Destiny, *Fata divina*. After which, a 'good angel' (*angelus bonus*) takes Vibia by the hand to introduce her to the foliage-crowned guests who have been chosen by the 'judgement of the good' (*bonorum iudicio iudicati*): seated in a semi-circle at the table amid flowers, they will drink and eat like royalty, waited on by charming little boys. Beside this paradise is shown one where, beneath floral garlands, seven priests of Sabazius (and Mithras, as has been supposed?) make merry. Among them Vincentius is recognizable, picked out by name in an inscription, and wearing the same sort of cap as his god. On this priestly table, alongside dishes containing meat, game, fish and pastries, one can make out several round segmented loaves like those carried in relief on the 'pantheistic' hands and the above-mentioned amphora of the Pompeian premises.

So for Vibia and those who had her tomb decorated, Vincentius and his flock were supposed to enjoy the sensual delights of wine and good food for all eternity. Cumont explained these representations in the light of the coarse 'brutal naturalism' which, in his view, remained linked with the rustic devotions of ancient Anatolia.[83] But the joys of banqueting beyond the grave matched beliefs to be found elsewhere and in contexts alien to the 'brutal naturalism' of the rustic cults: for example – and Cumont knew this better than anyone – in Orphico-Pythagorean circles. The imperial era saw an increase in the numbers of colleges of *convictores*, whose members' sole aim was to 'eat together': *qui una epulo vesci solent* (*CIL*, XI, 5244). At that time many others than Sabaziasts gathered to share a meal, for instance Mithraists and Christians. And the latter did not always avoid certain excesses, if we are to believe the apostle Paul and his calls to order (First Epistle to the Corinthians, 6: 12–16; 11: 20–2), to say nothing of some heretic and Gnostic sects where debauchery was standard practice.

Ineluctably, the vision of paradise people had in such instances was merely a prolongation or sublimation of the pleasures of this world.

Literary, Clandestine or Popular Survivals

Even in the fourth century the Fathers of the Church were still waxing indignant about the dissoluteness and horrors of omophagy, but this polemic often smacks of bookish inspiration and seems fiercest when attacking a certain outmoded mythology of the Bacchanalia. This is notably so with Arnobius and Firmicus Maternus. The *Ambrosiaster* similarly feigns offence at the *sacra Liberi*, those 'unseemly' and 'wild' frolics which he had probably never seen; in contrast, he seems to have looked at pictures of Dionysian orgies in the presence of Priapus . . .[84]

However, the festive traditions retained their vitality locally. In his youth St Augustine still saw the decurions and notables of Madaurus, in Africa, run wild in the town streets in honour of Liber Pater.[85] His friend, the philosopher Maximus, to whom the future bishop of Hippo replies, reproached the Christians for their hidden and macabre devotions towards obscure Punic martyrs. For this pagan, God was to be worshipped in the open air and with joy, like Bacchus!

He was therefore no longer a clandestine and mystery god, although he had to become so again when idolatrous practices were definitively banned by the laws of Valentinian II and Theodosius in 391, and those of their successors in 399 and 423. At the close of the fourth century, alongside their Mithraic promotions, 'taurobolic' senators eagerly displayed the titles of hierophant of the Hecates and arch-herdsman of Liber, which presupposes at least the temporary survival of a whole organization of cultic societies that were more or less tolerated by the Christian government. But their activities were carried on in private houses, in Rome itself or in the suburban properties of the 'clarissimi'.

Excavations at Cosa revealed the establishment at a late date (on the edge of the old Republican Forum) of premises where pagans met secretly for nocturnal meals in honour of Dionysus, Sabazius, Venus, the Triple Hecate and yet other gods.[86] Statuettes originally belonging to the decor of private houses were salvaged for use as cultic images. For the ban on sacrifices and the destruction of idols in temples that were henceforth closed forced polytheists to use personal articles for this purpose. In this makeshift sanctuary (imposed by hard times) a foodsafe, benches, a masonry altar and vessels with Sabazian motifs (lizard and snakes) have been recognized. Evidently the house must have been abruptly abandoned after being sacked by Christian activists in the early fifth century AD at the latest.

Popular paganism had a hard time of it, however, and certain naturist solemnities verging on bacchanalia tended to upset the bishops. At Nola, Paulinus (Poems, XIX, 169 ff) deplored the explosion of ritual orgies where Venus got on too well with the god of wine: sociata libido furori ('debauchery in company with madness'). On this topic, L.A. Muratori (Patrologia Latina, 61, col. 523 E) emphasized that the Nola grape harvests in his times gave rise – as elsewhere – to the worst kinds of licentiousness.

In Gaul, in Comminges, the Life of Maurilius (bishop of Angers, d. 453) informs us that the saint had to set fire to the wood crowning a rock where the pagans performed their boisterous farandoles (bacchando) and annually gave themselves up to seven days of bloody madness, going as far as murders (Acta Sanct., Sept. IV, Paris, 1868, p. 74).

Other testimony confirms the occasional manifestations of a recurrent Dionysism. In the time of Gregory of Tours, in the sixth century, a Berrichon attacked in the forest by a swarm of bees or wasps, lost his reason. Out of his mind, clad in animal skins, he went through Provence, then Gévaudan and Velay, prophesying. He claimed to be Christ, accompanied by a woman – whom he called Mary – and a crowd of followers with whom he robbed the region to give to the needy. He had messengers go ahead of him, leaping and dancing in the nude, like members of a dishevelled thiasos. After having him captured and executed, the bishop of Le Puy forced the alleged Mary to confess that this 'Christ' led minds astray by devilish artifices. And Gregory of Tours adds:

Furthermore, at that time there appeared in all the Gauls a number of men who, by similar magic spells, attached to themselves young women who claimed in their orgies [*debacchantes*] that these men were saints. (*History of the Franks*, X, 25).

Other Fathers of the Church, especially Firmicus Maternus (*The Error of Profane Religions*, VI, 6), had accused Dionysus of leading women astray by means of maleficent spells. We should not be surprised. The collective intoxication of the bacchanalia is the equivalent of a permanent temptation for mankind.

Even in these days, using various methods and in historical contexts that have nothing to do with cults of oriental origin, bacchanalia crop up and explode, the manifestation of an eternal Dionysism that upsets established behaviour and religions.

Epilogue

THE *Introduction* researched, listed and analysed the reasons that might explain the apparent success of the oriental cults in the *Orbis Romanus*. Now we must examine the reasons for their failure in the face of Christianity – yet another religion of eastern origin which succeeded and ultimately compelled recognition, but which in the eighth century was rivalled and even supplanted in half the Roman world by one more eastern religion, Islam.

Leafing through the corpus, looking at the map of finds and the mass of epigraphic, iconographic and archaeological evidence of every kind in the various social and geographical sectors of the Roman Empire – to say nothing of the data provided by pagan and Christian literary tradition – one gets the impression of witnessing an overwhelming and almost irresistible tide of eastern cults, at least until the Severan era that marked their apogee. Why did this intense proliferation, reinforced by allegorical interpretations, ambient syncretism and local adaptations, perceptibly decline in the second half of the third century AD, before fading away at the end of the following century?

We must not be misled by the instance of Rome and some other very particular contexts. The pietism displayed by certain 'clarissimi' in the *Urbs* of the Theodosian period, their Isiac and Mother-cult propaganda, the peaceful and well-bred polytheism still evoked in the early fifth century by Macrobius' *Saturnalia*, should not make us forget that in the rest of the Empire the *Mithraea* were then ruined or abandoned; that the last taurobolium attested in Gaul is datable to the reign of Gallienus (253–68) and, in Africa, of Probus (276–82); that in Rome itself the sanctuary of Jupiter Dolichenus on the Aventine gave hardly any further sign of life after Gallienus and Salonina. Here and there, outside Egypt, the Isiac cult seems to have had some extensions of vitality, but they were precarious and had no future. Ammianus

Marcellinus (*History*, XVI, 12, 25) is perhaps alluding to the port of Arles when, regarding the Aleman prince Mederich, he writes that before 357 he had been converted to the Egyptian cult 'in the Gauls', to the point of changing his son's name from Agenarich to 'Serapion'. But no document confirms the survival of Isiacism there at the end of the fourth century. Certainly, we have seen that in 417 people were still celebrating the death and *Discovery* of Osiris at Falerii. But the testimony of Rutilius Namatianus remains an isolated instance, like that of St Paulinus about the Mother-cult solemnities at Nola after 410 (*Poems*, XIX, 181ff). The gods formerly domiciled on the Rhine frontier had been swept away in the third century in the turbulence of the first invasions, at the same time as the fortresses then abandoned by the legionaries; and on the banks of the Danube, the few Persian or Syrian sanctuaries did not hold out for long after the Tetrarchy.

Christianity first made progress in the urbanized centres where in other times the oriental cults had recruited the best part of their clientele, and the anti-pagan laws of Theodosius often did no more than ratify what had already taken place. The scattered survivals in rural paganism had more to do with variations on a naturist and 'neolithic' religion than with the lasting signs of oriental idolatry properly speaking.

There is no reason to attach great importance to the argumentations of Christian apologetics which denigrate the zoomorphic idols of the Delta, the revoltingly bloody rites of the taurobolium or castration, the macabre stories of gods who were mutilated or torn apart, the liturgical and dramaturgical performances. Already exploited and repeatedly trotted out by pagans hostile to the *externa superstitio*, these diatribes had not prevented the Levantine religions from increasing their ascendancy during the first two centuries AD. Moreover, the polemic of the Fathers of the Church was addressed rather to educated and 'enlightened' polytheists, to make them understand that this often primitive and demented paganism had nothing to do with their culture and philosophy. In fact, the *physica ratio* and symbolic exegesis resolved those contradictions for them: so Firmicus Maternus threw all his relentless effort into condemning their artifices. The Christians, too, were adept at going well beyond the letter and interpretation of the Bible. But these controversies scarcely touched the mass of believers who swung from idolatry into the new faith.

In the Antonine period, at the time of Justin Martyr and the philosopher Celsus, the friend of Lucian, we get the feeling that Christianity was in competition with the oriental religions rather than with the old Graeco-Roman paganism. Significantly, apologists were then attacking Isis and Osiris, Attis and, above all, Mithras, and the diabolical imitations forged by demons in their cult. Celsus, who seemingly speaks in the name of a tradition that was rather hostile to foreign liturgies, and of a developed Platonism, appropriate to the eclecticism and occultisms of his generation, likens the Christian preachers 'to the mendicant priests of Cybele and the diviners, the devotees of Mithras and Sabazius', and compares the illusions of which the converted are victims 'to everything that may be encountered, apparitions of Hecate, or this or that demon' (Origen, *Against Celsus*, I, 9). To ridicule Christian beliefs concerning the next world he can find nothing better than a parallel with Bacchic initiations (ibid., IV, 10) and other mysteries (ibid., VIII, 48), among which he probably implicates those of Isis and the corybantic rites of the Sabazian cult (ibid., III, 16). That is also why Celsus invokes against the Christians the example of the mysteries of Samothrace and Mithras (ibid., VI, 23). To which Origen feels obliged to reply:

'Nothing is borrowed from the Persians or Cabirians in what is said by our prophets, or the apostles of Jesus, or the Son of God in person!'

Christians and pagans passed the ball back and forth. The former accused the demons of fraudulent borrowings from their form of worship, and the pagans in their turn imputed the same plagiarism to the disciples of Christ. It was the sign of a rivalry that at the time was vehement and close-fought. The defenders of the polytheistic tradition placed Christianity on the same level as 'barbarian mysteries', to use an expression of Celsus. This type of reaction was to be found two centuries later from the pen of Maximus of Madaurus (St Augustine's correspondent), for whom devotions to the Punic martyrs Miggin, Sanam and Namphano resembled the monstrosities of Egyptian superstition – like Virgil's *latrator Anubis* – battling at Actium against Apollo and the gods of Rome (Augustine, *Letters*, 16). In Rome itself, the last bastion of paganism where the festivals of Attis and Osiris were part of the official calendar, one clan – that of Symmachus – remained rather reserved or reluctant with regard to formerly foreign religions.

Thus polytheism was divided, and even some of the 'clarissimi' whom the Christians did not succeed in converting appeared not to be in favour of the bloody sacrifices, for though pagans, they were more Porphyrians. The diptych of the Nicomachi and Symmachi, on one of its panels (preserved in the Victoria and Albert Museum in London), shows not the old-fashioned immolation of a living victim, but an offering of fruit, wine and incense. That is why in the fourth century

Firmicus Maternus, the *Ambrosiaster* and the author of an anonymous poem *Contra Paganos* direct their attacks more precisely against oriental cults. But outside the *Urbs* and Italy, the match had been won long before. Nevertheless, these cults did not have that 'dogmatic homogeneity' of which Cumont spoke, and even reading Firmicus Maternus, who lumps them all together in the same vengeful reprobation, gives no serious reason for regarding their clergies as the 'congregations' of one and the same 'church'.[1]

In actual fact, neither the rites nor the myths of the oriental religions caused them to lose their followings among the urban masses or the military and administrative circles of the Roman world. We must look elsewhere for the causes, or rather the reasons, for this disaffection. They were simultaneously psychological, historical and theological.

There were psychological causes because even oriental paganism was by its very nature pluralist, disparate and contradictory. Doubtless the devotions of foreign origin tended, each on its own account, towards a more or less pronounced sort of henotheism. Isis dominated Egyptian religion, or Serapis, depending on the sanctuaries. Mithras the Invincible prevailed over Jupiter himself, or in any case annexed his sovereign prerogatives over the cosmos and Creation. The Baals of Heliopolis, Doliche and above all Emesa, were sole rulers on earth and in heaven. But – whatever the *Augustan History* (*Life of Heliogabalus*, 3, 4) may have written about it, though in a passage aimed at Christian proselytism – even the cult of Elagabal did not rule out other gods. Quite the reverse! For a pagan god, the height of prestige was to dominate the others: there was no true sovereignty except in relation to other deities. Temples gloried in housing gods other than the titular divinity. A real oecumenism ensured that Atargatis would receive hospitality from Cybele. One could honour Serapis, Attis, Dionysus, Mercury, even the Gaulish Mercury of travellers, Cissonius, in a Mithraic crypt, or worship Mithras, Isis and Serapis in Jupiter Dolichenus' temple on the Aventine. At Brindisi, a single priest carried out his ministry for the followers of Isis, the Great Mother and the Syrian Goddess (*CIL*, IX, 6099).

But this liberalism, which could turn annexationist in the case of Elagabal, also held the risk of diluting the gods' personality in a vague syncretism, chaotic and undifferentiated. 'At the conclusion,' says R. MacMullen, 'confusion reigned'.[2] Syncretism and the *physica ratio* gave this melting-pot merely a semblance of coherence which it was easy for those in the Christian camp to deride.

In truth, a distinction must be made between several types of syncretisms. One consisted in boosting the standing of a divinity of whom all the others in the world were merely equivalents or different names (as in the case of Isis who, for Apuleius, subsumed all the Mediterranean variants of Juno, Diana and Venus). Another turned to pandemonism and placed all gods on the same level, but their very multiplicity was important to pagans who were anxious to gain favour with the various manifestations of the divine. The first steered piety towards monotheism. The second would result in the worship of the saints. The syncretism of the philosophers who regarded the gods as 'powers' or agents of the supreme god transcended positive religions, without favouring or excluding any. But another form of syncretism belonged to the dabblers or the worriers, those people who, alternately passionate and blasé, sought experiences, new sensations, unprecedented encounters with the divine. In the late second century, the emperor Commodus personified something of this unstable syncretism, when he flirted with Bellona, Isis and Mithras, before claiming to reincarnate Hercules. Thirty years later, Caracalla made pilgrimages and frequented sanctuaries – chiefly those of gods of health, Asclepius or Serapis and it was when he wanted to visit the Moon-god of Carrhae that he got himself assassinated.

The proliferation of mystery cults and initiatory sects, the elaboration of rituals like that of the serpent Glycon, the more or less fantastic extrapolations on myths that were variously salvaged and reinterpreted, all met a demand but without satisfying it in the long term, perhaps because of their very abundance. Here again, Apuleius provides us with an enlightening and precious testimony. He admits having collected all sorts of consecrations, *sacrorum pleraque initia . . . multiiuga sacra et plurimos ritus et varias cerimonias* (*Apologia*, 55, 8–9). Why? *Studio veri et officio erga deos*, in the name of a 'passionate search for truth' and an 'obligation to the gods', with this idea that honours must be paid to all the known gods. This second motivation smacks of the most traditional polytheism. But the first – the quest for truth – is a preoccupation inspiring both the neophytes of oriental cults and those who, having vainly sampled the philosophical schools and the mysteries, ended by converting to Christianity.

In fact, if Apuleius goes from one initiation to another, it is because none of them fully satisfies him or truly answers his profound aspirations. This cultic or spiritual vagabondage in search of the supernatural and decisive revelations characterized a fair number of his contemporaries and a few other representatives of the later generations. The disparities of Graeco-oriental paganism were equalled only by the cacophony of philosophical systems, which were at least partly at one with them in the moral crisis of the Antonine and Severan periods.

We know the story of Justin Martyr who went in turn to a Stoic, an Aristotelian and then a Pythagorean before finding the revelation of Christ in the teachings of an old man.[3] But to judge by the information he give us about Mithraic and Dionysian liturgy, Justin did not meet only philosophers. Like other old pagans whose traditional religion failed to fulfil their inmost needs, he must have at least sounded out the possibilities offered by certain mystery cults. Similarly, Tatianus who became his disciple had 'travelled in many lands', seen the statues of gods, 'taken part in the mysteries and tried out the various cults established everywhere by effeminates and hermaphrodites [an allusion to Dionysism]', before discovering the truth (*Discourse to the Greeks*, 29 and 35); from the translation by A. Puech). After him, Clement, known as 'of Alexandria', but a native of Athens, had himself initiated into the Eleusinian mysteries and other cults of which he speaks apparently with some authority; he travels through the world: Greece, the Orient, Egypt, before meeting Pantenus who 'engendered pure knowledge in the soul of those who heard him' (*Stromateis*, I, 1, 11; from the translation by M. Caster).

With the confession of Cyprian 'the Magus', we have a real novel which grew around the end of the third century on the legend of the bishop of Carthage who was martyred in 258, but which in the same way as the *Homilies of Clement* helps us to understand the spirit of the times.[4] It tells us, in fact, of the religious tribulations of a man who had first been pledged when still a child to the cult of the Pythian Apollo, 'initiated into the dramaturgy of the snake'; then consecrated to Mithras, at the age of seven; to Demeter and Kore three years later, and then to Hera of Argos and the mysteries of Artemis Tauropola. In Phrygia he learned the secrets of divination. In the subterranean sanctuaries of Heliopolis and Memphis, in Egypt, he obtained the revelation of all the mysteries relating to the demons and spirits which animate the world. Naturally, in Chaldaea he was taught astrology, the mysteries of the sky and the aether. But he, too, was ultimately converted.

Another typical example is Arnobius, engrossed in Neoplatonism and Hermetism, just as curious about the slightest methods of archaic Roman ritualism as about Graeco-oriental liturgies: chiefly Eleusinianism, Dionysism, Isiacism and Phrygianism. This assiduous devotee of idols could not see 'a stone polished and rubbed with oil' without prostrating himself and praying to this 'unfeeling block' (*Against the Nations*, I, 29). Like Apuleius, he avidly perused the writings of the theosophers, the Chaldaeans and perhaps the magicians. Exoticism and occultism excited his unhealthy curiosity. But these strayings led him to doubt and despair. He then converted, but following a dream

and struck by Christ's miracles. Like so many others, after drifting in
uncertainty and dissatisfaction on the vast sea of human phantasmagoria he found his God and what the Isiac priest of Cenchreae in
Apuleius' *Metamorphoses* (XI, 15, 1) calls the 'haven of rest', *portus
quietis*: an expression that already has a Christian sound to it. Curiously, moreover, Arnobius (*Against the Nations*, II, 73) compares the
reasons which enabled Romans to adopt new and foreign cults with
those that explain the success of Christianity: disarray in a difficult
situation.

Far from assuaging a basic need to enter into contact with the
divine, the very hotch-potch of pagan, and particularly oriental,
liturgies compromised their credibility. In parallel with the controversies of the learned and the insoluble contradictions of the many
schools and sects, which justified the prevailing atmosphere of scepticism, the jumble of polytheism and its discordant luxuriance con-
founded all those who had a passion for the truth (*studio veri*) and
urgently desired to believe. The *ratio physica* apparently did little more
than reinforce (sometimes ludicrously) the myths whose insignificance
or morbid and macabre indecency were not of a nature to underpin a
true theology. The allegorical rationalization of polytheism also contained the drawback of being hand in glove with more or less
discredited philosophical systems. Often it too closely resembled an
artificial verbal or theoretical patching-up to be able to resolve the real
questions that obsessed the minds of men such as those whose
anguish and concerns are revealed in the gnosis of Valentinus or
Basilides.

Another way of rationalizing mythology was to resort to the
doctrine of demons, as Plutarch did when he ascribed to these mixed
beings the adventures of the gods among men, their 'passions' and
therefore their intervention in the mysteries.[5] But the Christians of the
times were completely at ease in denouncing this intermediate race as
a maleficent pack thirsty for blood and solely interested in tormenting
humans, seizing for their own profit the homage due to the one and
supreme divinity. On this point the Neoplatonist Porphyry joined in
their reproof of sacrifices.[6] But with their suffering gods, the oriental
liturgies were directly targeted by this polemic, and the 'passion' of
the alleged immortals jarred flagrantly with the cosmological allegor-
ies identifying Osiris with water or (like Attis) with the sun.

The traditional cults had no theology. Isiacism and Phrygianism had
one, as did the Dolichenian and Heliopolitan cults, it would seem, but
there was no central church to establish their dogma. Even Mithraism
appears to have contained variants, which are revealed in certain
regional particularities of its iconography, even its epigraphy. Against

the background of a single cult (Isiacism or Phrygianism, for instance) exegeses appeared in anarchic profusion. But chiefly, the disparities between one cult and another had a disorientating effect. Generally speaking, a sort of indifference on the part of idolatries in the matter of theology eventually threatened them with a dogmatic indetermination which had its advantages, because it favoured local adaptations and the vitality of a spontaneous re-creation, but which was not of a kind to give believers a feeling of security and anchor them in the *portus quietis*. In the beginning, oriental religions had brought such security to the anxious, in this world and the next. But their very success and their polymorphous vegetation henceforth presented as frightening a spectacle as G. Flaubert's *Temptation of St Anthony.*

The pagan intellectuals might reply, like Symmachus (*Report on the Altar of Victory,* 10; from the translation by M. Lavarenne):

What matters philosophy through which everyone seeks the truth?
One road alone does not suffice to attain so great a mystery!'

Maximus of Madaurus, St Augustine's correspondent mentioned earlier, justified his pagan eclecticism in the same spirit:

Thus by honouring in various sorts of cults that which we regard as His various members, we worship Himself [God] in His entirety (Augustine, *Letters,* 16)

But this is the very kind of theoretical reasoning whose calm rationality does not touch hearts in search of a total and coherent faith. Porphyry acknowledged the plurality of local and initiatory rites only on account of intelligences that were unfitted for philosophy.[7] But it was precisely among the urban masses who were unfamiliar with Neoplatonism that the oriental mysteries were no longer a success in the fourth century! These cults did not prohibit their respective followers from praying to the god next door. But this wandering polytheism wearied even the dilettantes. In contrast, Christianity categorically and effectively ruled out theological and intellectual chopping and changing.

Beginning with the great crisis in the third century,[8] the historical context seems to have strengthened those psychological conditions that were favourable to a single religion, exclusive of all others.

In 260, when the Alemanni had already forced their way through the Rhine frontier and the governor of Belgica, Postumus, had himself

proclaimed emperor of the Gauls, Valerian was defeated and taken
prisoner by the Persians. The charisma of imperial power and the
theology of victory which was the foundation of its legitimacy col-
lapsed at the same stroke. Then the Goths crossed the Danube, and
invaded Greece and Asia Minor. The plague wreaked havoc on
countries. Usurpations increased in both East and West. Politically,
militarily, socially and economically, everywhere the *Orbis Romanus*
was cracking. During a quarter of a century, Gaul was delivered over
to the devastations of the Germani; its defenceless towns were destroyed, pillaged, depopulated; its rural lands, too, to the point where
Probus (276–82) had to rebuild livestock herds by bringing animals
from across the Rhine, and barbarian colonists had to be settled to
restore the land to a useful state. To build fortifications, defence walls
were then hastily constructed, utilizing everything that was to hand
on the outskirts of cities (remains of tombs and mausoleums, with no
regard for respect or memory of the dead). Even within the towns
themselves, material was randomly taken from public monuments,
including those of the imperial cult and the temples, which lost many
of their 'congregations'. For people no longer believed in gods who
did not protect them, at least in the formerly prosperous large
townships. In contrast, local and rural cults, stones, mountains, trees
and springs held firm through the upheaval, and bishops had to come
to terms with these popular devotions by Christianizing them under
the patronage of the saints.

Similarly, in Africa, the rebellions and inroads of the Moors, epidemics and other scourges put Roman-ness to the test. Elsewhere,
disturbances, secessions, civil wars or foreign invasions threw an all-
enveloping cloud over the last days of the *Pax Romana*. Correspondingly, trade and craftsmanship declined, as did the currency which
lost a great deal of its instrinsic value: there was inflation, and prices
soared. Weakened since the Severan period by tax and military
pressure, the municipal elites who had financed the amenities of
towns and fed the destitute could no longer cope, and abandoned
their responsibilities. The poor became poorer. This economic crisis
may have had effects on the practice of pagan cults. The bloody
sacrifices were expensive, notably the large victims of the taurobolium. Apuleius also admits to us (*Metamorphoses*, XI, 22, 3; 28, 3; 30,
1) that initiation to the mysteries of Isis, then Osiris, involved heavy
expenditure. The crisis necessarily hit the pomp of the oriental liturgies, formerly financed by the generosity of the faithful. But above all,
its effects were demoralizing.

Decius Trajan (249–51), then Valerian (253–60), issued edicts against
the Christians, who had already been treated as scapegoats in the

affair of the martyrs of Lyon (177), a pitiless persecution. Even if Gallienus, after the capture of his father, Valerian, 'reduced to slavery by the barbarians' (Eusebius, *Ecclesiastical History*, VII, 113), repealed the edict of persecution, the Christians continued to explain the misfortunes of the Roman world as a punishment from God. Around the middle of the century, Commodian (*Apologetic Poem*, 805ff) prophesied:[9]

There will be a number of signs to mark the end of this immense ruin. The beginning of the end will be the seventh persecution directed against us. Lo, he is already knocking at our gate, and he is urged on by the sword, he who will swiftly cross the river with a stampede of Goths. They will have with them the Destroyer king [*Apollyon*] . . . He marches on Rome with thousands of men and by the will of God he makes prisoners among the Romans. Then many senators will bewail their captivity. Defeated by the barbarians, they blaspheme against the God of Heaven!

In other words, Kniva, king of the Goths, in this instance embodies for the Christians the exterminating angel of the *Apocalypse*.

Around the same period, Cyprian wrote in his letter *To Demetrianus* (3–4) that the world was growing old and its end approaching. Famines, epidemics, incessant wars and other calamities were the evils that God's wrath inflicted on Romans who were guilty of not worshipping Him, *quod a vobis non colatur Deus*. In the most traditional Roman religion, the idea of divine anger remained alive in the time of Tacitus and probably for another century. Also traditional was resorting to other gods when ancestral rites no longer succeeded in warding off misfortunes. Now, as the gods of the city did not respond to the pagans' appeals, any more than the oriental gods, many polytheists were thrown off balance, and must have been worried, if not shattered, by this talk of divine judgement and the end of the world. Had not Hermes Trismegistus himself in the *Asclepius* (26) predicted 'the old age of the world' at the same time as the twilight of the gods?

Haec et talis senectus veniet mundi: inreligio, inordinatio, inrationabilitas bonorun omnium

'irreligion, disorder, confusion of all good things' (from the translation by A.-J. Festugière). It was, of course, a prophecy *post eventum*, but one which impressed some idolaters all the more after the conversion of the imperial government.

The idea of sin, and above all collective sin, was alien even to oriental paganisms, in which 'penances' were the punishment for ritual misdeeds towards the divinity. But in the light of the miseries of this period, it was able to gain ground in the consciousness of Romans disappointed by the indifference or powerlessness of their 'saviour' gods. They could be resented for turning a deaf ear to the supplications of humans stricken by plague, famine, war and devastation. But the avenging God of the Christians, escaping that accusation, remained the only one who could still be called upon, not to deliver the pagans from the ordeals they were deemed to have deserved, but for their eternal salvation. In the early fourth century, Arnobius, who experienced the utter confusion of the pagans, exhorted them all the more fervently (*Against the Nations*, II, 78; from the translation by P. Monceaux):

Time is pressing. There are many dangers and we are threatened with terrible punishments: let us take refuge with the God of salvation and take no account of the present that is offered to us. When it is a matter of the salvation of souls and our own interest, we must do something, even without a reason, as Epictetus said, according to Arrian.

'Even without a reason', writes Arnobius. In fact the implacable logic of the Last Judgement, as a category in a new philosophy of history, and the urgency of the salvation that was its corollary, ended by imposing itself on the vision of the bewildered idolaters:

Let us fear to see the arrival of the Supreme Day and find ourselves in the gaping jaws of the enemy, death! (ibid.)

The third-century crisis would have lasting effects on the state of minds, even after the very relative Tetrarchic restoration and Peace of the Church (313). For although the imperial government, apart from a few theological misunderstandings, henceforth got on well with the Christians, the Romans' troubles were not at an end.

But Christianity's great strength in the face of oriental or orientalizing polytheism was also, correlatively and fundamentally, its theology.

In the first place, its unwavering monotheism was in accordance with the Constantinian monarchy. The *Ambrosiaster* (*Questions on the*

Old and New Testament, 114, 2) denounces in worship given to inferior gods an absurdity as blameworthy as homage shown to servants or dignitaries of the palace at the expense of the emperor himself. Monarchic loyalism thus implied obedience to a single God. This theologico-political parallelism received a sort of providential blessing when, after the defeat and death of Licinius (324), Constantine remained sole master of the Roman world. Eusebius (*Ecclesiastical History*, X, 9, 6) does not fail to underline that 'the great victor, Constantine, resplendent with all the virtues of his piety', in this way re-established the empire of the Romans 'in its former unity'. The restoration of imperial unity logically demanded conversion to the sole king of heaven who had shown it favour.

However, there was the risk that the celestial monarchy and its transcendence would distance God from men, a gap which classical Greek religion had made uncrossable between the fortunate Immortals and the unfortunate mortals, but which the oriental and mystery cults had tended to fill with their gods who suffered (Dionysus, Attis, Osiris, Adonis) or at least acted in the world (Mithras). In the third century, the major aspirations of Roman paganism had converged in solar henotheism and notably, in the end, in the official cult of *Sol Invictus*, held dear (at least apparently) by Constantine's father himself. For Plato and the Platonists, the Sun was the perceptible image of Good, the supreme god. The second creator god Numenius, the luminous *Nous* who conceived the cosmos, prefigured the second hypostasis of Plotinus, whose triadic scheme answered the same need systematically to hierarchize the action of the divine on and in the world as the Christian trinity. All these simultaneously religious and philosophical trends were to crystallize in the representation of Christ-Helios, remarkably illustrated in a mosaic of the St Peter Necropolis in the Vatican: *Lux mundi*, the visible Word of the invisible God.[10]

The advantage of the Christian trinity, developed in the third century before being established and clarified at the Council of Nicaea (325) against the Arian heresy, was to proclaim a God both transcendent and incarnate in Christ, and at the same time present in this world, until the end of the world, in the Holy Ghost. Thus not only did the divine and hypercosmic monarchy legitimize that of the emperor, but the emperor himself could appear as a permanent reincarnation of divine delegation.[11] 'Whence came the communication of imperial power to a being of flesh and blood?' asked an adulator of the first Christian emperor,[12] and he went on to speak of the Logos spread through the world, as the Stoics had done when speaking of the fiery breath of Zeus. Effigies of Constantine show him raising his eyes heavenwards, like Mithras looking at the Sun to

accomplish his act of universal salvation. Deliberately likened to
Helios, vaunted as the light of the world and drawing the inspiration
for the decrees from the divine will, the mediator-sovereign henceforward extended his influence over his subjects like the Word over
Creation.[13] So soldiers could be expected to show the same fidelity to
the emperor as to a 'present and corporeal god' (Vegetius, *Treatise on
the Military Art*, II, 5). In the time of Justinian, Leontius of Byzantium
would make him the eye of the world:[14]

Between God and him there is no intermediary.

This was what has justly been called 'Caesaropapism'. 'Bishop of the
outside world', as Constantine designated himself, missionary and
representative of Christ, the emperor embodied both the second and
third persons of the Trinity. This logic of the Christian Empire was or
might appear to be incontrovertible.

But the incarnation of the Father in the Son and the organization of
salvation by a suffering and crucified god empowered, even encouraged, men to identify with Him. Their ordeals and sacrifices in the
emperor's service legitimized that identification; that is to say, their
promotion at the same time as their submission. Only the conception
of a God become man so that man could become God could resolve
this squaring of the circle. Neither Osiris nor Mithras was supposed to
have taken on and worn the mantle of suffering and sinful humanity.
Their cult could not therefore mystically base the deification of man
on the redemption of evil through sufferings endured, including
obedience to the earthly vicar of the saviour God.

Even when they were hand in glove with the imperial cult, never
had any of the religions of ancient Africa or Asia benefited from a
theology that was so effectively coherent and appropriate to the
antinomic demands of mankind as the Christian Empire, yet singularly in accord with those of an absolute monarchy by divine right.
The principate may well have had its religion of the sovereign, its cult
of Rome and Augustus, its flamines, pontiffs, augustal seviri and other
official brotherhoods. It even had an ideology, but neither dogmas,
theology, nor a 'state religion'. For the imperial cult was but one
religion among others, and was in no way exclusive. A true state
religion made its appearance with Constantine and the Christian
Empire. Before, the expression had no meaning, so to speak. Persecutions were not carried out in the name of *one* religion, but of civic
traditions involved in loyalty towards the emperor.

The theology of the Trinity consecrated man in a mystic and cosmic
totality, both as an individual and a member of a new state that

prefigured the City of God. It was a far cry from the 'à la carte' pietism offered to the undecided and anxious by the many-hued fascinations of oriental exoticism. Nevertheless, albeit uneven and temporary, the impact of these foreign cults had contributed to a development of mental attitudes and personal or collective modes of piety. On this score, they played their part in what Eusebius called the *Evangelical Preparation*.

Notes

Introduction

1. Who also speaks of 'oriental mysteries' or 'cults': RO^4, passim. Cf. already E. Renan, *Marc-Aurèle et la fin du monde antique*,[3] Paris, 1882, p. 569ff. G. Boissier (*La religion romaine d'Auguste aux Antonins*,[7] I, Paris, 1909, p. 334ff), like the Romans, gives them the generic designation 'foreign religions', while emphasizing the 'oriental cults' (p. 350ff).
2. *Études préliminaires aux religions orientales dans l'Empire romain* (abbr. *EPRO*), from 1961: 112 parts published to date.
3. V. Basanoff, *Regifugium. La fuite du roi*, Paris, 1943, p. 93
4. The evidence is clearly set out in G. Dury-Moyaers and M. Renard, 'Aperçu critique de travaux relatifs au culte de Junon', *ANRW*, II, 17, 1, Berlin-New York, 1981 p. 196ff: *Les divinités de Pyrgi*. Cf. R. Bloch, 'Le culte étrusco-punique de Pyrgi vers 500 avant J.-C.', in *Die Göttin von Pyrgi* (Kolloquium zum Thema . . . , Tübingen, 16–17 Jan. 1979), Florence 1981, p. 123ff.
5. *GgR*, II 2, p. 190; C. Schneider, *Kulturgeschichte des Hellenismus*, II, Munich, 1969, p. 871ff.
6. A.-J. Festugière, *La révélation d'Hermès Trismégiste*, I, *L'astrologie et les sciences occultes*, Paris, 1950 (re-edited), p. 76f.
7. I explained this in 'La soteriologia, dei culti orientali nell'impero Romano', *Atti del Colloquio Internazionale . . . Roma 24–28 Sett. 1979* (*EPRO*, 92), Leiden, 1982, p. XVII and 173ff.
8. M. Yourcenar, *Mémoires d'Hadrien*, Paris, 1951, p. 55f.
9. RO^4, p. 189.
10. Infra, pl. 19.
11. Servius Danielis, *Aeneid*, VIII, 698 (II, p. 302, 20fa Thilo-Hagen).
12. R. Turcan, *Sénèque et les religions orientales* (Coll. Latomus, 91), Brussels, 1967, p. 46ff.
13. Paul, *Sent.*, V, 21, 2: *qui novas sectas vel ratione incognitas religiones inducunt, ex quibus animi hominum moveantur* . . . Cf. *Digest*, 48, 19, 30.

14. Cf. G. Dumézil, *La religion romaine archaïque*, Paris, 1966 (re-edited), p. 412ff; R. Bloch, 'Interpretatio', in *Recherches sur les religions de l'Italie antique*, Geneva, 1976, p. 32ff.

15. R. Turcan, 'Religion et politique dans l'affaire des Bacchanales', *RHR*, 181, 1972, p. 18ff.

16. Valerius Maximus, I, 3, 2. Cf. E.N. Lane, 'Sabazius and the Jews in Valerius Maximus: a re-examination', *JRS*, 69, 1979, p. 35ff.

17. Cf. R. Turcan, *Mithras Platonicus. Recherches sur l'hellénisation philosophique de Mitra (EPRO, 47)*, Leiden, 1975, p. 2–4.

18. 'Isiskult und Umsturzbewegung' Schweizer Münzblätter, 5, 1954, p. 25ff.

19. Tacitus, *Histories*, III, 24, 6: ... *et orientem Solem (ita in Syria mos est) Tertiani salutavere*.

20. Juvenal, *Satires*, VIII, 159–62.

21. *Life of Hadrian*, 22, 10.

22. Xenophon, *Memorabilia*, II, 1, 13.

23. Ovid, *Fasti*, II, 684: *Romanae spatium est urbis et orbis idem*. Cf. R. Turcan, 'Terminus et l'universalité hétérogène ... ', in *Popoli e spazio romano tra diritto e profezia (Da Roma alla Terza Roma, Studi III, 21 April 1983)*, Naples, 1986, p. 51. Varro (*On the Latin Language*, V, 143, p. 95, Collart) makes the *Urbs* into an *orbis* as a circular defence wall traced by the plough furrow.

24. Cf. *Le secret*, texts collected by P. Dujardin, CNRS, Lyon-Paris, 1987, p. 10ff.

25. J. Carcopino, *La vie quotidienne à Rome à l'apogée de l'Empire*, Paris, 1939 (re-edited), p. 34f, 40ff. On Ostia, see F. Pasini *Ostia antica. Insule e classi sociali*, Rome, 1978.

26. Tertullian, *Against the Valentinians*, VII, 3; translation-edition J.-C. Fredouille in the Coll. 'Sources Chrétiennes', Paris, 1980, p. 93 and commentary p. 222f. *Felicles* is a genitive and not the nominative of a man's name.

27. *Deipnosophists*, I, 36, 20 c. Cf. R. Turcan, *Terminus et l'universalité hétérogène* (n. 24), p. 59.

28. H. Jonas, *The Gnostic Religion: The Message of the Foreign God and the Beginnings of Christianity*.

29. *Metamorphoses*, XI, 17, 5; 19, 1; 24, 5 (*inexplicabili voluptate simulacri divini perfruebar*) – 7; 25, 1–6.

30. R. Turcan 'Religion romaine. Les dieux', in *Iconography of Religions*, XVII, 1, Leiden, 1988, p. 6f.

31. M. Meslin, *La ffe des Kalendes de janvier dans l'Empire romain* (Coll. Latomus, 115), Brussels, 1970; R. Turcan, 'Janus à l'époque impériale', *ANRW*, II, 17, 1, Berlin-New York, 1981, p. 374ff, 397ff.

32. Y. Hajjar, *La triade d'Héliopolis-Baalbek. Iconographie, theology, culte et sanctuaires*, Montreal, 1985, p. 179f.

33. R. Turcan, 'Le sacrifice mithraïque', in *Le sacrifice dans l'Antiquité*, Entretiens sur l'Antiquité Classique, Fondation Hardt, 27, Geneva-Vandoeuvres, 1981, p. 363ff.

34. Cf. for example J.p. Alcock, 'The concept of Genius in Roman Britain', in
    Pagan Gods and Shrines of the Roman Empire (M. Henig and A. King eds.),
    Oxford, 1986, p. 116ff.
35. Cf. 'La soteriologia dei culti orientali' (n. 7), p. XVII.
36. Apuleius, *Metamorphoses*, XI, 15, 1, with commentary by J.G. Griffith
    (*EPRO*, 39), Leiden, 1975, p. 245. On the metaphor: B. Andreae, *Studien
    zur römischen Grabkunst* (*RM*, 9. Ergänzungsheft), Heidelberg, 1963,
    p. 136ff.

Chapter 1: The Great Mother and her Eunuchs

1. D. Van Berchem, 'Hercule-Melqart à l'Ara Maxima', *Rend. Pont. Accad.
   Rom. di Arch.*, 32, 1959/60, p. 61ff; idem, 'Sanctuaires d'Hercule-Melqart
   ... ' *Syria*, 44, 1967, p. 73ff; R. Rebuffat, 'Les Phéniciens à Rome', *MEFR*,
   79, 1966, p. 7ff.
2. R. Fleischer, *Artemis von Ephesos und verwandten Kultstatuen aus Anatolien
   und Syrien* (*EPRO*, 35), Leiden, 1973.
3. M.J. Vermaseren, *Cybele and Attis, the Myth and the Cult*, London, 1977,
   p. 13ff.
4. 63 (p. 114, 8 Wuensch).
6. *Lexicon*, II, p. 539, Latte; M.J. Vermaseren, op. cit., p. 23.
7. 'Kuba-Kybele', *Philologus*, 68 (NF, 22), 1909, pp. 122f, 125.
8. M.J. Vermaseren, op. cit., p. 18, pl. 7.
9. Ibid., p. 20f., pl. 10.
10. *Attis, seine Mythen und sein Kult* (*RGVV*, 1), Giessen, 1903 (re-edited
    Berlin, 1967), p. 217f. Cf. H. Graillot, *Le culte de Cybèle, Mère des dieux, à
    Rome et dans l'Empire romain* (*BEFAR*, 107), Paris, 1912, p. 290f.; G.M.
    Sanders, s.v. 'Gallos' in *RAC*, VIII (1972), col. 1025ff; M.C. Giammarco
    Razzano, 'I "Galli di Cibele" nel culto di età ellenistica', *Ott. Miscellanea
    Greca e Romana, Studi pubblicati dall'Istit. Ital. per la Storia Antica*, 33, 1982,
    p. 227ff; G. Sfameni Gasparro, *Soteriology and Mystic Aspects in the Cult of
    Cybele and Attis* (*EPRO*, 103), Leiden, 1985, p. 28.
11. E. Will, 'Aspects du culte et de la légende de la Grande Mère dans le
    monde grec', in *Éléments orientaux dans la religion grecque ancienne* (Col-
    loque de Strasbourg 22–24 May 1958), Paris 1960, p. 95ff; F. Naumann,
    Die Ikonographie des Kybele in der phrygischen und der griechischen Kunst
    (*Istanb. Mitteil.*, Beih. 28), Tübingen, 1983, p. 101ff, 117, 124ff, 130ff; F. Isik,
    *Die Entstehung der frühen Kybelebilder Phrygiens und ihre Einwirkung auf die
    ionische Plastik* (*Jahreshefte d. österr. arch. Institutes in Wien*, 57, Beiblatt),
    1986/7, p. 42ff.
12. Photius, *Lexicon*, s.v. Μητρῷον (I, p. 422 Naber, Leiden, 1864); Cf. Julian,
    Discourse on the Mother of the Gods, 1, 159 a–b.
13. Plutarch, *Life of Nicias*, 13, 3–4.
14. Demosthenes, *On the Crown*, 259–60. Cf. G. Sfameni Gasparro, op. cit.,
    p. 66f; infra, p. 313.

15. 'Une nouvelle inscription de Sardes . . .', *CRAI*, 1975, p. 306ff; Id. in *Bull. épigraphique, REG*, 89, 1976, p. 541f, No. 624, Cf. *CCCA*, I, p. 133, No. 456.
16. *CCCA*, II, p. 92f, No. 308, pl. LXXVIII.
17. *CCCA*, VII, p. 49f, No. 175, pl. CVI.
18. Arnobius, *Against the Nations*, V, 5.
19. Pausanias, *Description of Greece*, VII, 17, 9–12.
20. Cf. M. Meslin, 'Agdistis ou l'androgynie malséante', in *Hommages à M.J. Vermaseren* (*EPRO*, 68), Leiden, 1978, II, p. 765ff; D.M. Cosi, *Casta Mater Idaea. Giuliano l'Apostata e l'etica della sessualità*, Venice, 1986, p. 28ff.
21. *CCCA*, I, p. 233f, Nos 777, 786.
22. R. Fleischer, op. cit., p. 310ff, pl. 138ff.
23. *SIG*, 985; *LSAM*, 20; *CCCA*, I, p. 147f, no. 489. Cf. G. Bardy, *La conversion au christianisme durant les premiers siècles*, Paris, 1949, p. 35f; G. Sfameni Gasparro, op. cit., p. 36.
24. Arnobius, *Against the Nations*, V, 7. Plutarch (*Isis and Osiris*, 28, 362 a) gives Timotheus the title *exegete*.
25. *De mensibus*, IV, 1 (p. 64, 12 Wuensch).
26. *Discourse on the Mother of the Gods*, 13, 173 d.
27. Arnobius, *Against the Nations*, V, 7.
28. Ibid., 5.
29. Cf. M.J. Vermaseren, 'The Miraculous Birth of Mithras', in *Studia Archaeologica G. Van Hoorn oblata.*, Leiden, 1951, p. 98.
30. *CCCA*, VII, p. 44f, No. 158, pl. XCVI; M.J. Vermaseren, *Cybele and Attis*, p. 74, pl. 57.
31. Ibid., p. 25; B.M. Felletti Maj, s.v. 'Cibele' in *Encicl. Ital. dell'arte antica classica e orientale*, II, Rome, 1959, p. 574, fig. 778; E. Schmidt, *Le grand autel de Pergame*, Fr. transl., Leipzig, 1962, p. 15f, 30 and fig. 25; F. Naumann, op. cit., p. 158, 263ff.
32. M.J. Vermaseren, op. cit., p. 35; *CCCA*, II, p. 73ff, Nos 261ff.
33. M.J. Vermaseren, op. cit., p. 98f; J. Carcopino, *Aspects mystiques de la Rome païenne⁶*, Paris, 1942, p. 107f, 154f.
34. Ibid., p. 107; M.J. Vermaseren, op. cit., p. 98; *CCCA*, I, p. 24f, No. 56 (with the earlier bibliography).
35. M.J. Vermaseren, op. cit., p. 38ff; F. Coarelli, 'I monumenti dei culti orientali in Roma', in *La soteriologia dei culti orientali* (*EPRO*, 92) Leiden, 1982, p. 39ff.
36. F. Bömer, 'Claudia Quinta' *RM*, 71, 1964, p. 146ff; *CCCA*, III, p. 45f, No. 218, pl. CXIII.
37. *CCCA*, III, p. 11ff, Nos 14f. Cf. p. Romanelli, 'Magna Mater e Attis sul Palatino' in *Hommages à J. Bayet* (Coll. Latomus, 70), Brussels, 1964, p. 619ff; F. Coarelli, loc. cit., p. 40f; p. Pensabene, ibid., p. 86ff.
38. Arnobius, *Against the Nations*, VII, 49; Prudentius, *Hymns*, X. 156f.
39. Varro, *Menippeae*, 132 (149) = *Eumenides*, XVI, p. 530, 614ff of the translation-edition with commentary by J.-p. Cèbe (Coll. de l'Ec. franc. de Rome, 9, 1977).
40. H. Graillot, op. cit., p. 74ff; M.J. Vermaseren, op. cit., p. 96.

41. Diodorus Siculus, XXXVI, 13; Plutarch, *Life of Marius*, 17, 9–11. Cf. M.J. Vermaseren, op. cit., p. 99.
42. R. Turcan, *Numismatique romaine du culte métroaque* (*EPRO*, 97), p. 13f, pl. VI, 1–3.
43. *De rerum natura*, II, 621, 629ff.
44. Translation-edition with commentary by J.-p. Cèbe (1977), p. 530ff, 562ff.
45. P. Boyancé, 'Une exégèse stoicienne chez Lucrèce', *REL*, 19, 1941, p. 147ff = *Études sur la religion romaine* (Coll. de l'Ec. franc. de Rome, II, 1972), p. 205ff. Discussed by G. Rocca-Serra, 'Les philosophes stoïciens et le syncrétisme', in *Les syncrétismes dans les religions grecque et romaine* (Colloque de Strasbourg 9–11 June 1971), Paris, 1973, p. 22f. When Tertullian (*Against Marcion*, I, 13, 4) mocked the physico-rationalist exegeses applied to the cult of Cybele, he was thinking of Varro and the Stoics, amongst others.
46. Supra, n. 37.
47. Strabo, *Geography*, XII, 2, 3–5, 535–7; 3, 36, 559.
48. Plutarch, *Life of Sulla*, 27, 12.
49. F. Cumont, 'Le taurobole et le culte de Bellone', *Rev. d'Hist. et de Litt. Rel.*, 6, 1901, p. 98f (inscription of Kastell).
50. F. Eichler and E. Kris, *Die Kameen im Kunsthistorischen Museum*, Vienna, 1927, p. 52f; M.J. Vermaseren, op. cit., pl. 58.
51. P. Lambrechts, *Livie-Cybèle, La Nouvelle Clio*, 4, 1952, p. 251ff.
52. *CCCA*, IV, p. 28f., No. 76; M. Guarducci, 'Enea e Vesta', *RM*, 78, 1971, p. 94, 110ff, pl. 68.
53. *CCCA*, III, p. 5f, No. 2, pls IX–XII.
54. Suetonius, *Claudius*, 25, 13; J. Carcopino, *Aspects mystiques de la Rome païenne*, p. 169.
55. R. Turcan, *Vivre à la cour des Césars*, Paris, 1987, p. 298f.
56. *RO*[4], p. 52; H. Graillot, op. cit., p. 115; J. Carcopino, op. cit., p. 51ff.
57. Prudentius, *Hymns*, X, 1076ff. Cf. H. Graillot, op. cit., p. 51ff.
58. Prudentius, *Hymns*, X, 1083ff.
59. W. Schepelern, *Der Montanismus und die phrygischen Kulte*, Tübingen, 1929.
60. R. Turcan, *Les religions de l'Asie dans la Vallée du Rhône* (*EPRO*, 30), Leiden, 1972, p. 86ff.
61. H. Hepding, H. Graillot, R. Pettazzoni, S. Angus, R. Reitzenstein, G. Heuten, etc. ... F. Cumont hesitated between the cults of Attis and Adonis.
62. Cf. my translation-edition with commentary in the Coll. des Universités de France, Paris, 1982, p. 314.
63. *CCCA*, III, p. 119, No. 384, pl. CCXXXIX.
64. Herodian, *Roman History*, I, 10, 5–7. Cf. R. Turcan, *Numismatique romaine du culte métroaque*, p. 37f.
65. Tertullian, *To the Nations*, I, 10, 47 (p. 90f of the translation-edition by A. Schneider and commentary of I, 10, 45 p. 237); idem, *Apologeticum*, 15, 5; Arnobius, *Against the Nations*, V, 35 (p. 243, 7ff, Marchesi) and VII, 33

(p. 384, 21ff). Cf. also, Firmicus Maternus,. *The Error of Profane Religions*, XII, 9 (commentated translation-edition p. 262f).

66. N. Himmelmann, *Typologische Untersuchungen an romischen Sarkophagreliefs des 3. und 4. Jhts n. Chr.*, Mainz, 1973, p. 37ff, pls 56 b, 57 b.

67. R. Turcan, *Les religions de l'Asie* . . . , p. 25ff.

68. Ibid., p. 29f, pls XIV–XV.

69. Ibid., p. 30f, pl. XVI, 2.

70. Ibid., p. 50ff.

71. Op. cit., p. 109ff.

72. *CIL*, XIII, 1751; *CCCA*, V, p. 133f, No. 386. On the taurobolium and the methods implied by certain variations in terminology, see R. Duthoy, *The Taurobolium, Its Evolution and Terminology* (*EPRO*, 10), Leiden, 1969: a useful but controversial work. There is no evidence and it has not been demonstrated that the basic elements of the ritual evolved from the second to the fourth century AD.

73. R. Turcan, *Les religions de l'Asie* . . . , pl. XXV; idem, Les religions orientales en Gaule Narbonnaise . . . ', *ANRW*, II, 18, 1, Berlin-New York, 1986, p. 493, n. 324.

74. 'Le Tarobole et le culte de Anahita', *RA*, 1888, II, p. 132ff; Idem, *Le taurobole et le culte de Bellone* (n. 49), p. 104. Cf. H. Graillot, op. cit., p. 192ff.

75. Hesychius, *Lexicon*, s.v. ὄκκαβος (II, p. 748, 75, Latte). The archigallus of Ostia (*CCA*, III, p. 141ff, Nos 446/8, pls CCLXXXIII/IX) wears a bracelet decorated with the divine image in relief. But often the *occabus* is also considered as a necklace, the word generically designating a 'ring': *Etymologicum Magnum*, s.v. p. 383, 22, Gaisford.

76. R. Turcan, *Numismatique romaine du culte métroaque*, p. 52ff, pls XXXI (2–3)–XXXIII.

77. *CCCA*, III, p. 49ff, Nos 226ff.

78. F. Cumont, 'Le taurobole et le culte de Bellone' (n. 49), p. 104. Cf. R. Turcan, 'Les religions orientales en Gaule Narbonnaise . . . ' (n. 73), p. 493.

79. *CCA*, III, p. 59, No. 242. Cf. G. Sfameni Gasparro, op. cit., 112f.

80. *CCCA*, IV, p. 110, Nos 271/2.

81. R. Turcan, 'Rome éternelle et les conceptions gréco-romaines de l'éternité', in *Roma Costantinopoli Mosca* (*Da Roma alla Terza Roma*, 21 April 1981) Naples, 1983, p. 25ff.

82. *Life of Heliogabalus*, 7, 1. Cf. T. Optendrenk, *Die Religionspolitik des Kaisers Elgabal im Spiegel der Historia Augusta*, Bonn, 1969, p. 30ff; R. Turcan, *Numismatique romaine du culte métroaque*, p. 43.

83. A.-J. Festugière, 'Les mystères de Dionysos', *Rev. Bibl.*, 44, 1935, p. 382 = *Études de religion grecque et hellénistique*, Paris, 1972, p. 48.

84. R. Duthoy, op. cit. (n. 72), pp. 101, 118; M.J. Vermaseren, *Cybele and Attis*, p. 49 and fig. 18; G. Sfameni Gasparro, op. cit., p. 81.

85. 'Sur les mystères phrygiens . . . ', *REA*, 37, 1935, p. 161ff = *Études sur la religion romaine*, p. 201ff.

86. Cf. L. Richard, 'Juvenal et les galles de Cybèle', *RHR*, 169, 1966, p. 51ff.

87. *CCCA*, III, p. 151f, No. 464.
88. Ibid., p. 152f, No. 466, pl. CCXCVIf.
89. Ibid., p. 107ff, No. 362. Alleged *fossa sanguinis*: ibid., p. 110 and pl. CCXXIV.
90. Ibid., p. 123, No. 394, pl. CCXLIV.
91. Ibid., p. 141, No. 446, pl. CCLXXXIIf; supra, n. 75.
92. *CCCA*, IV, pp. 1–57 (maps, p. 2, 39, 50), 69ff (maps, p. 70, 76, 81).
93. Ibid., p. 69ff, No. 174.
94. *CCCA*, III, p. 155f, No. 473. Cf. H. Graillot, op. cit., p. 430.
95. *CCCA*, IV, p. 33ff, Nos 87–91.
96. G. Sfameni Gasparro, *I culti orientali in Sicilia* (*EPRO*, 31), Leiden, 1973, p. 267ff; *CCCA*, IV, p. 61ff, Nos 152–64.
97. *CCCA*, V, p. 17ffa and map (fig. 6).
98. H. Mattingly and E.A. Sydenham, *Roman Imperial Coinage*, IV, 1, p. 69f, 116, No. 193; p. 125, No. 266, pl. 7, 9 and passim. Cf. C. Vermeule, *The Cult Images of Imperial Rome* (*Archaeologica*, 71), Rome, 1987, p. 48 and fig. 10 ('Magna Mater').
99. G. Charles-Picard, *La Carthage de saint Augustin*, Paris, 1965, p. 125f.
100. A. García y Bellido, *Les religions orientales dans l'Espagne romaine* (*EPRO*, 5), Leiden, 1967, p. 42ff. and maps (figs. 2–3); M. Bendala Galan, 'Die orientalischen Religionen Hispaniens . . . ', *ANRW*, II, 18, 1, Berlin-New York, 1986, p. 380ff and map (fig. 4).
101. A. García y Bellido, op. cit., p. 58, No. 6; *CCCA*, V, p. 75, No. 204, pl. LVII.
102. *CCCA*, V, p. 83–163, map p. 84.
103. R. Turcan, *Les religions de l'Asie* . . . , p. 75ff.
104. R. Turcan, *Les religions orientales en Gaule Narbonnaise* . . . , p. 494f.
105. Ibid., p. 511.
106. *Les Martyrs de Lyon (177)*, Colloque International du CNRS (Lyon 20–23 Sept. 1977), Paris, 1978, p. 205f.
107. Unpublished excavations by A. Jacques on the site of the Rue Baudimont. Cf. meanwhile P. Ravera, 'Arras. Un sanctuaire des dieux orientaux', *Archaeologia*, 219 (Dec. 1986), p. 11. Heads of Attis may perhaps be discerned on a pillar from Paris: H. Lavagne, 'Lutèce, le monument aux Amours de Mars', *Cahiers de la Rotonde*, 1987, p. 38ff, p. 48ff.
108. Sulpicius Severus, *Vie de saint Martin*, trans-edn with commentary by J. Fontaine in the Coll. 'Sources Chrétiennes', Paris, 1969, p. 729f, 741ff.
109. M.J. Vermaseren, *Cybele and Attis*, p. 140ff.
110. M.J. Vermaseren, *Der Kult des Kybele und des Attis im römischen Germanien*, Stuttgart, 1979, p. 20 and fig. 25.
111. J. Medini, 'Ein taurobolisches Objekt und das Ritual auf Zecovi', *Archaeologia Iugoslavica*, 20–21, 1980–1 (1983), pp. 96–102 and fig. p. 97.
112. J. Medini, 'Le culte de Cybèle dans la Liburnie antique', in *Hommages à M.J. Vermaseren* (*EPRO*, 68), II, p. 734.
113. Ibid., p. 747 and pl. CLVI. On the cult of the Mothers in the Balkans, cf. M. Tacheva-Hitova, *Eastern Cults in Moesia Inferior and Thracia* (*EPRO*, 95), Leiden, 1983, p. 71ff.

114. E.N. Lane, *Corpus monumentorum dei Menis* (*EPRO*, 19), Leiden, 1971, No. 83; III, Leiden, 1976, p. 79.
115. M. Floriani Squarciapino, *I culti orientali ad Ostia* (*EPRO*, 3), Leiden, 1962, p. 10, n. 2 and pl. IV, 6.
116. Cf. n. 115.
117. *CCCA*, IV, p. 93, No. 224, pl. LXXXVIII.
118. R. Turcan, 'Déformation des modèles et confusions typologiques dans l'iconographie des sarcophages romains', *Annali di Scuola Normale Sup. di Pisa*, 1987, p. 440f.
119. M. Guarducci, 'L'interruzione dei culti nel Phrygianum del Vaticano durante il IV secolo d. Cr.', in *La soteriologia dei culti orientali* (*EPRO*, 92), p. 109ff.
120. *CCCA*, III, p. 56f, No. 239.
121. Aem. Baehrens, *Poetae Latini minores*, III, Leipzig, 1881, p. 287–92; J. Wytzes, *Der letzte Kampf des Heidentums in Rom* (*EPRO*, 56), Leiden, 1977, p. 162ff, especially p. 163, 1. 57ff. The question of precisely which pagan is targeted in this poem continues to be a matter of controversy.
122. R. Turcan, 'L'aigle du pileus', in *Hommages à M.J. Vermaseren*, III, p. 1281ff.
123. *CCCA*, III, p. 54, No. 236.
124. J. Wytzes, op. cit., p. 164, 1. 109.
125. *CCCA*, IV, p. 107ff, No. 268; L. Musso, *Manifattura suntuaria e committenza pagana nella Roma del IV secolo. Indagine sulla lanx di Parabiago*, Rome, 1983. For the contorniate medallions, see R. Turcan, *Numismatique romaine du culte métroaque*, p. 50ff.
126. Damascius, *Dubitationes et solutiones de primis principiis*, 352 (II, p. 214, 6 Ruelle, Paris, 1889).
127. Marinus, *Vie de Proclus*, 33 (p. 168, 9ff, Boissonade, in the Coll. Firmin-Didot, Paris, 1929).
128. Edition E. Vogt (Wiesbaden, 1957), p. 27, 1. 25, and commentary p. 56.
129. *Vie de Proclus*, 19 (p. 160, 47ff, Boissonade).

Chapter 2: Isis of the Many Names, or Our Lady of the Waves

1. Diodorus Siculus, *Bibl. Historica*, I, 23, 2–3, 6–7; 46; IV, 25, 1–4; Eusebius, *Praeparatio Evangelica*, I. 6, 4.
2. *Les mystères d'Eleusis*, Paris, 1914.
3. G. Sfameni Gasparro, *I culti orientali in Sicilia*, p. 6ff; G. Matthiae Scandone, 'Materiali egiziani e egittizanti del Museo di Mozia', *Riv. di Studi Fenici*, 3, 1975, p. 65ff; G. Höbl, *Beziehungen der ägyptischen Kultur zu Altitalien* (*EPRO*, 62), Leiden, 1979; idem, *Ägyptisches Kulturgut im phönikischen und punischen Sardinien* (*EPRO*, 102), Leiden, 1986; M. Bendala Galán, loc. cit., (*ANRW*, II, 18, 1), p. 348ff; J. Padró i Parcerisa, *Egyptiantype documents from the Mediterranean Littoral of the Iberian Peninsula before the Roman Conquest* (*EPRO*, 65), I–III, Leiden, 1980–5; F. de Salvia, 'Un ruolo apotropaico dello scarabeo egizio nel contesto culturale greco-

arcaico di Pithekoussai (Ischia)', in *Hommages à M.J. Vermaseren*, III, p. 1003ff. Reference should be made to the invaluable annual chronicle of J. Leclant ('Découvertes d'objets égyptiens et égyptisants hors d'Égypte') in *Orientalia*; for example 55, 1986, p. 318 (11 b and 12); 56, 1987, p. 386ff.

4. F. Dunand, *Le culte d'Isis dans le bassin oriental de la Méditerranée* (*EPRO*, 26), Leiden, 1973, II, p. 4ff.

5. Ibid., I, p. 27ff.

6. On the cult of Serapis: ibid., I. p. 45ff; J.E. Stambaugh, *Sarapis under the early Ptolemies* (*EPRO*, 25), Leiden, 1972; W. Hornbostel, *Sarapis. Studien zur Überlieferungsgeschichte, den Erscheinungsformen und Wandlungen der Gestalt eines Gottes* (*EPRO*, 32), Leiden, 1973. Sanctuaries: R.A. Wild, 'The Known Isis-Sarapis Sanctuaries from the Roman Period, *ANRW*, II, 17, 4, Berlin-New York, 1984, p. 1739–1851.

7. Plutarch, *Isis and Osiris*, 29 (Phylarchus); Clement of Alexandria, *Stromateis*, I, 21, 106, 3; F. Dunand, op. cit., p. 53.

8. Ibid., I. p. 58. Cf. W. Amelung, 'Le Sarapis de Bryaxis', *RA*, 1903, II, p. 176ff; C. Picard, *Manuel d'archéologie grecque. La sculpture*, IV, 2, 2, Paris, 1963, p. 870ff.

9. At least in the note transcribed by Eustathius in his commentary on Dionysus the Periegete, 255: Stephanus of Byzantium, *Ethica*, p. 571, Meineke, note (Berlin, 1849; republication Graz, 1958).

10. C. Picard, 'Sabazios, dieu thraco-phrygien', RA, 1961, II, p. 129ff; infra, p. 291.

11. Firmicus Maternus, *On the Error of Profane Religions*, XIII, 2.

12. Pausanias, *Description of Greece*, I, 18, 4. Cf. Rufinus, *Ecclesiastical History*, II, 23 (*Patrologia latina*, Migne, 21, col. 529f).

13. W. Amelung, loc. cit.; W. Hornbostel, op. cit.

14. On this question, see generally *GgR*, II², p. 94; F. Dunand, op. cit., I, p. 73f.

15. V. Tran Tam Tinh and Y. Labrecque, *Isis Lactans. Corpus des monuments gréco-romains d'Isis allaitant Harpocrate* (*EPRO*, 37), Leiden, 1973, and in *Hommages à M.J. Vermaseren*, III, p. 1231ff. On the meaning itself of the name 'Isis': F. Dunand, op. cit., I, p. 3.

16. Diodorus Siculus, I, 23, 6–7 and 96, 3–4; Plutarch, *Isis and Osiris*, 35. Cf. A.-J. Festugière, 'Les mystères de Dionysos', *Rev. Bibl.*, 44, 1935, p. 381; H. Jeanmaire, *Dionysos. Histoire du culte de Bacchus*, Paris, 1951 (re-edited), pp. 405, 449.

17. Plutarch, *Isis and Osiris*, 13–19, with commentaries by T. Hopfner (Prague, 1940–1) and J.G. Griffiths (Univ. of Wales, 1970, re-edited).

18. F. Dunand, op. cit., I, p. 94f; p. Bruneau, 'Isis Pelagia à Délos', *BCH*, 85, 1961, p. 435ff; ibid., 87, 1963, p. 301ff; M. Malaise, *Les conditions de pénétration et de diffusion des cultes égyptiens en Italie* (*EPRO*, 22), Leiden, 1972, p. 180f.

19. F. Dunand, op. cit., I, p. 89ff.

20. Ibid., p. 81ff; eadem, *Religion populaire en Égypte romaine. Les terres cuites isiaques du Musée de Caire* (*EPRO*, 76), Leiden, 1979.

21. M. Malaise, op. cit., p. 203ff.
22. Apuleius, *Metamorphoses*, XI, 5, 1, with commentary by J.G. Griffiths, *Apuleius of Madaurus, The Isis-Book* . . . (*EPRO*, 39), Leiden, 1975, p. 145ff; V. Tran Tam Tinh, *Le culte des divinités orientales en Campanie* (*EPRO*, 27), Leiden, 1973, p. 214ff.
23. Diodorus Siculus, *Bibl. historica*, I, 17–18. Cf. H. Jeanmaire, op. cit., p. 361.
24. Ibid., p. 351ff; R. Turcan, *Les sarcophages romains à représentations dionysiaques* (*BEFAR*, 210), Paris, 1966, p. 374, 441ff.
25. F. Dunand, op. cit., II, p. 4ff; R. Garland, *The Piraeus*, London, 1987, p. 126ff.
26. F. Dunand, op. cit., II, p. 17ff, 72ff.
27. P. Bruneau, *Le sanctuaire et le culte des divinités égyptiennes à Erétrie* (*EPRO*, 45), Leiden, 1975.
28. Y. Grandjean, *Une nouvelle arétalogie d'Isis à Maronée* (*EPRO*, 49), Leiden, 1975.
29. F. Dunand, op. cit., III, p. 54ff, 57.
30. Ibid., II, p. 83ff, 106.
31. H. Engelmann, *The Delian Aretalogy of Sarapis* (*EPRO*, 44), Leiden, 1975.
32. M. Malaise, op. cit., especially p. 19 ff.
33. G. Sfameni Gasparro, op. cit., (n. 3), p. 19ff.
34. Ibid., p. 31ff. Cf. the representations of Isis-*Dikaiosynè* in the coinage of Catania: G. Sfameni Gasparro, 'Isisde-Dikaisoyne in une seria monetale bronzea di Catania . . . ', *Studi e Materiali di Storia delle Religioni*, NS 10, 1986, p. 189ff.
35. G. Sfameni Gasparro, op. cit. (n. 3), p. 73ff, 223f, Nos 191–2.
36. Cf. the chronicle of J. Leclant in *Orientalia*, 46, 1977, p. 293f (12 a); 53, 1984, p. 413f (7 a–e); 54, 1985, p. 413 (10 a–c).
37. V. Tran Tam Tinh, *Le culte des divinités orientales en Campanie*, p. 3ff; M. Malaise, *Inventaire préliminaire des documents égyptiens découverts en Italie* (*EPRO*, 21), Leiden, 1972, p. 289ff.
38. V. Tran Tam Tinh, *Le culte d'Isis à Pompéi*, Paris, 1964, p. 30ff; E. La Rocca, M. and A. de Vos, *Guida archeologica di Pompei*², Milan, 1981, p. 159ff.
39. M. Floriani Squarciapino, *I culti orientali ad Ostia*, p. 18ff; M. Malaise, op. cit., (n. 37), pp. 66–95.
40. *Letters to Lucilius*, 77, 1–3; R. Turcan, *Sénèque et les religions orientales*, p. 41.
41. Cf. M. Malaise, *Les conditions de pénétration* . . . (n. 18), p. 363f.
42. M. Malaise, *Inventaire préliminaire* . . . (n. 37), p. 96, No. 4; J. Champeaux, *Fortuna. Le culte de la Fortune à Rome et dans le monde romain*, I (Coll. de l'Ec. Franç. de Rome, 64), Rome, 1982, p. 70, n. 303; F. Coarelli, *Lazio* (Guide Archeologiche Laterza), Bari, 1982, p. 135, 153f.
43. *Metamorphoses*, XI, 30, 5, with the above-mentioned commentary (n. 22) by J.G. Griffiths, p. 343f. On the pastophori: H.B. Schönborn, *Die Pastophoren im Kult der ägyptischen Götter*, Meisenheim, 1976. Their name apparently means 'those who carry the curtain'. It seems that the

pastophors' duty was to close and open the curtains at the entrance to the temple: M. Malaise, *Les conditions de pénétration* ... , p. 129.

44. P. Roussel, *Les cultes égyptiens à Délos du IIIe au Ier siècle av. J.-C.*, Nancy, 1916, p. 62, 152f, 270; F. Dunand, op. cit., II, p. 88 (fig. 5), 106; M. Malaise, op. cit., p. 141; L. Vidman, *Isis und Sarapis bei den Griechen und Römern* (*RGVV*, 29), Berlin, 1970, p. 62, n. 50.

45. M. Malaise, *Inventaire préliminaire* ... , p. 238ff (*Roma*, 443 a–g). Cf. L. Vidman, op. cit., p. 101ff; A.S. Fava, *I simboli nelle monete argentee repubblicane e la vita dei Romani*, Turin, 1969, p. 71, Nos 289–91; p. 76f.

46. A. Alföldi, *Isiskult und Umsturzbewegung* ... , *Schweizer Münzblätter*, 5, 1954, p. 30.

47. F. Coarelli, 'Isis Capitolina, Clodio e i mercanti di schiavi', in *Alessandria e il mondo ellenistico-romano, Studi in onore di A. Adriani*, III, Rome, 1984, p. 461ff; J.-M. Flambard, 'Clodius, les collèges, la plèbe et les esclaves ...', *MEFR(A)*, 89, 1977, p. 115ff.

48. Loc. cit., (n. 46), p. 25–31.

49. H. Crawford, *Roman Republican Coinage*, Cambridge, 1974, I, p. 405, No. 391, 2 (pl. XLIX) = E.A. Sydenham, *The Coinage of the Roman Republic*, London, 1952, No. 788. Cf. P.F. Tschudin, *Isis in Rom*, Aarau, 1962, p. 45, n. 62.

50. M. Malaise, *Les conditions de pénétration* ... , p. 369ff.

51. Ibid., p. 374.

52. Tacitus, *Histories*, III, 74, 1; Suetonius, *Domitian*, 1, 4 (*Isiaci celatus habitu*). Cf. M. Malaise, *Inventaire préliminaire* ... , p. 186.

53. H. Jeanmaire, *La Sibylle et le retour de l'âge d'or*, Paris, 1939, p. 61ff; idem, *Dionysos*, p. 465ff; F. Chamoux, *Marc Antoine*, Paris, 1986, p. 234ff.

54. *RO⁴*, p. 20.

55. S.K. Heyob, *The Cult of Isis among Women in the Graeco-Roman World* (*EPRO*, 51), Leiden, 1975. Cf. G. Boissier, *La religion romaine* ... , I, p. 360ff.

56. L. Bragantini and M. de Vos, *Le decorazioni della villa romana della Farnesina* (Museo Nazionale Romana. Le pitture, II, 1), Rome, 1982, especially p. 128ff.

57. M. Malaise, *Inventaire préliminaire* ... , p. 218f. (*Roma*, 395); F. Coarelli, *Guida archeologica di Roma²*, Milan, 1975, p. 151ff.

58. T. Picard-Schmitter, 'Bétyles hellénistiques', *Monuments Piot*, 57, 1971, p. 43ff, 51ff.

59. G. Carettoni, in *Kaiser Augustus und die verlorene Republik* (Exposition, Berlin 7 June–14 August 1988), Mainz, 1988, pp. 268 and 270, No. 126.

60. M. de Vos, *L'egittomania in pitture e mosaici romano-campani della prima età imperiale* (*EPRO*, 84), Leiden, 1980.

61. R. Turcan, *Vivre à la cour des Césars*, Paris, 1987, p. 299f.

62. *Tiberius*, 36, 1.

63. R. Turcan, *Sénèque et les religions orientales*, p. 8f.

64. R. Turcan, *Vivre à la cour des Césars*, p. 73.

65. I, p. 503, Adler. Cf. M. Malaise, *Les conditions de pénétration* ... , p. 399.

66. Suetonius, *Caligula*, 57, 4.

67. M. Malaise, *Inventaire préliminaire* . . . , p. 110f (*Villa Adriana*, 29).
68. P.W. Vand der Horst, *Chaeremon, Egyptian Priest and Stoic Philosopher* (*EPRO*, 101), Leiden, 1984.
69. M. Malaise, *Les conditions de pénétration* . . . , p. 84, 404.
70. P. Grimal, 'Le *De clementia* et la royauté solaire de Néron', *REL*, 49, 1971, p. 205ff.
71. A. Henrichs, 'Vespasian's Visit to Alexandria', *Zeitschr. f. Papyr. u. Epigraphik*, 3, 1968, p. 51ff; M. Malaise, op. cit., p. 408ff.
72. M. Malaise, *Inventaire préliminaire* . . . , p. 208ff, pl. 19 a; A. Roullet, *The Egyptian and Egyptianizing Monuments of Imperial Rome* (*EPRO*, 20), Leiden, 1972, p. 30 and pl. XV, 22.
73. Supra., n. 52; M. Malaise, *Les conditions de pénétration* . . . , p. 414f.
74. M. Malaise, *Inventaire préliminaire* . . . , p. 206.
75. Ibid., p. 219ff.
76. Ibid., p. 190f and pl. 16.
77. Ibid., p. 101ff (where the function of the Tiburtine Canopus is relativized); F. Coarelli, *Lazio*, p. 67; H. Mielsch, *Die römische Villa. Architektur und Lebensform*, Munich, 1987, p. 105f. It has been conjectured that the grave or a cenotaph of Antinous was in the Canopus of the Villa Adriana: N. Hannestad, 'Über das Grabmal des Antinoos. Topographische und thematische Studien im Canopus-Gebiet der Villa Adriana', *Analecta Romana Instituti Danici*, 10, 1982, p. 69ff; idem, *Roman Art and Imperial Policy*, Aarhus, 1988, p. 209.
78. M. Malaise, op. cit., p. 104ff.
79. Ibid., p. 240f (*Roma*, 444 bis–445).
80. Ibid., p. 326f (*Roma*, 448); idem, *Les conditions de pénétration* . . . , p. 429f.
81. Ibid., p. 430f; idem, *Inventaire préliminaire* . . . , p. 10 (*Aquileia*, 18).
82. M. Malaise, *Les conditions de pénétration* . . . , p. 436, from Cassius Dio, *Roman History*, 73, 15, 3.
83. *Augustan History, Life of Pescennius Niger*, 6, 8.
84. M. Malaise, *Inventaire préliminaire* . . . , p. 242 (*Roma*, 450).
85. Cf. R. Turcan, 'Le culte impérial au IIIᵉ siecle', *ANRW*, II, 16, 2, Berlin-New York, 1978, p. 1037f.
86. Ibid., p. 1059f.
87. M. Malaise, op. cit., p. 180ff (*Roma*, 334–6); F. Coarelli, in *La soteriologia dei culti orientali* . . . (*EPRO*, 92), p. 58f.
88. M. Malaise, op. cit., p. 143 f (*Roma*, 108).
89. Ibid., p. 228f (*Roma*, 415ff).
90. R. Turcan, *Vivre à la cour des Césars*, p. 73, 229f.
91. F.M.D. Darsy, *Recherches archéologiques à Sainte-Sabine*, Monum. dell'Antichità Cristiana (Pont. Istit. di Arch. Crist., II Ser., IX), Vatican City, 1968, p. 30ff; M. Malaise, op. cit., p. 225ff (*Roma*, 410–11); R. Volpe, 'I graffiti isiaci nell'area di S. Sabina a Roma', in *La soteriologia dei culti orientali*, p. 145ff.
92. M. Malaise, op. cit., p. 177ff; F. Coarelli, loc. cit., p. 53ff.
93. M. Malaise, op. cit., p. 78ff; R. Meiggs, *Roman Ostia*², Oxford, 1985, p. 367ff.

354 Notes to pages 95–7

94. V. Tran Tam Tinh, *Le culte des divinités orientales en Campanie*, p. 1–84.
95. M. Malaise, op. cit., p. 6–13; M.-C. Budischovsky, *La diffusion des cultes isiaques autour de la Mer Adriatique* (*EPRO*, 61), I, Leiden, 1977. On the importance of the port of Aquileia: J. Rouge, 'La place de l'Illyrie méridionale et l'Epire dans de système des communications de l'Empire romain', in *L'Illyrie méridionale et l'Epire dans l'Antiquité*, Clermont-Ferrand, 1987, p. 260.
96. M.-C. Budischovsky, op. cit., map. On Isiac expansion, now see M. Malaise, 'La diffusion des cultes égyptiens dans les provinces européennes de l'Empire romain', *ANRW*, II, 17, 3, Berlin-New York 1984, p. 1616ff, 1648ff. Canopic vase of Pozzuoli: A. Maiuri, *Itinerario Flegreo*, Naples, 1983, p. 113f, fig. 9 = *Notizie degli Scavi di Antichità*, 1927, p. 330–2.
97. P. Selem, *Les religions orientales dans la Pannonie romaine partie en Yougoslavie* (*EPRO*, 85), Leiden, 1980, p. 1–75 (6ff, 25ff).
98. Ibid., p. 5f.
99. As at Carnuntum: L. Vidman, *Isis und Sarapis*, p. 118; V. Wessetzky, *Die ägyptischen Kulte zur Römerzeit in Ungarn* (*EPRO*, 1), Leiden, 1961, p. 10ff; K. Póczy, in *Archaeologiai Ertesitö*, 91, 1964, p. 176ff; 93, 1966, p. 272ff.
100. V. Wessetzky, 'Zur Wertung des ägyptischen Totenkultes in Pannonien', *Acta Antiqua Hungar.*, 15, 1967, p. 451ff. On Isis and Serapis in the Balkans: M. Tacheva-Hitova, *Eastern Cults in Moesia Inferior and Thracia* (*EPRO*, 95), Leiden, 1983, p. 3–67.
101. Rutilius Namatianus, *On his Return*, I, 373–6. Cf. J. Carcopino, *Rencontres de l'histoire et de la littérature romaines*, Paris, 1963, p. 249ff.
102. E. Leospo, *La mensa isiaca di Torino* (*EPRO*, 70), Leiden, 1978.
103. V. Tran Tam Tinh, *Le culte des divinités orientales à Herculanum*, p. 7f, 52–5, Pls III–IV.
104. Supra, n. 35.
105. E. Paribeni, *Catalogo delle sculture di Cirene. Statue e rilievi di carattere religioso*, Rome, 1959, especially p. 142ff; R.A. Wild, *The Known Isis-Sarapis Sanctuaries* ... , *ANRW*, II, 17, 4, p. 1770ff. Cf. *RO*[4], pl. V, 3 ('initiate of Isis'); S. Ferri, 'Il Telesterio isiaco di Cirene', *Studi Classici e Orientali*, 12, 1963, p. 5ff.
106. Cf. J. Toutain, *Les cultes païens dans l'Empire romain*, II, Paris, 1911, p. 6f, 10ff, 18f, 31ff; G. Charles-Picard, *Les religions de l'Afrique antique*, Paris, 1954, p. 224ff; M. LeGlay, *Les religions orientales dans l'Afrique ancienne d'après les collections du Musée S. Gsell (Algiers)*, Algiers, 1956, p. 19ff.
107. Loc. cit., pp. 30, 34; op. cit., III, Paris, 1920, p. 4ff, approved by R. MacMullen, *Paganism in the Roman Empire*, New Haven and London, 1981, p. 116. Cf. L. Vidman, *Isis und Sarapis*, pp. 112–14.
108. J.G. Griffith, *Apuleius of Madaurus, The Isis-Book*, passim.
109. A. García y Bellido, *Les religions orientales dans l'Espagne romaine*, p. 106ff; M. Bendala Galan, 'Die orientalischen Religionen Hispaniens ... ', *ANRW*, II, 18, 1, p. 371ff; M.M. Alves Dias, 'Os cultos orientais em Pax Julia', in *Mem. de Historia Antigua*, 5, Oviedo, 1981, p. 33ff; J. Leclant, in *Orientalia*, 56, 1987, p. 386ff.

110. A. García y Bellido, op. cit., p. 135f; M. Bendala Galán, loc. cit., p. 379; F. Coarelli, in *La soteriologia dei culti orientali* . . . , (*EPRO*, 92), p. 56f.

111. A. García y Bellido, op. cit., p. 109f.

112. R. Turcan, 'Les religions orientales en Gaule Narbonnaise', *ANRW*, II, 18, 1, p. 462, 468ff.

113. *Gallia*, 7, 1949, p. 131, figs. 3–4.

114. G. Fouet, *La villa gallo-romaine de Montmaurin (Haute-Garonne)*, XXᵉ Supplement to *Gallia*, Paris, 1969, p. 168f, pl. LII. Cf. a fragment of an ivory plate found in the villa of Saint-Loup-de-Comminges, representing Serapis: G. Fouet and M. Labrousse, in *Monuments Piot*, 48, 1952, p. 117f. On the distribution of images of Serapis, see G.J.F. Kater-Sibbes, *A preliminary Catalogue of Sarapis Monuments* (*EPRO*, 36), Leiden, 1973. The file of *Aegyptiaca* in Roman Gaul is dealt with by M. Malaise, in *ANRW*, II, 17, 3, p. 1651ff.

115. Cf. R. Turcan, loc. cit. (n. 112), p. 464.

116. A. Audin and H. Vertet, 'Médaillons d'applique à sujets religieux des vallées du Rhône et de l'Allier', *Gallia*, 30, 1972, p. 246ff.

117. R. Turcan, loc. cit., p. 471f.

118. S. Ratié, 'Une voie de pénétration alpine des cultes isiaque', *Cahiers du Vieux Conflans*, 32, 1980, p. 42ff; eadem, 'Un oushebti du général Potasimto au Musée d'Annecy', *Rev. Savoisienne*, 104, 1964, p. 37ff.

119. P. Dissard, *Collection Recamier, Catalogue des plombs antiques* . . . , Paris-London, 1905, Nos 465–7; R. Turcan, *Nigra Moneta* . . . , Lyon, 1987, p. 18, No. 3; p. 33, No. 42.

120. J.-J. Hatt, 'Observations sur quelques statuettes gallo-romaines en bronze du Musée de Strasbourg', *RAE*, 12, 1961, p. 116ff.

121. G. Grimm, *Die Zeugnisse ägyptischer Religion und Kunstelemente im römischen Deutschland* (*EPRO*, 12), Leiden, 1969; M. Malaise, in *ANRW*, II, 17, 3, p. 1663ff.

122. K. Parlasca, *Die Isis- und Sarapisverehrungen im römischen Köln, Kölner Jahrbuch f. Vor- und Frühgeschichte*, 1, 1955, p. 18ff; *IBIS*, L-Q, p. 185f, No. 1043.

123. L. Richard, 'Un Harpocrate de bronze en provenance de Corseul', *Annales de Bretagne*, 75, 1968, p. 203ff; *Statuette en bronze d'Osiris provenant de Tronoën (Finistère)*, ibid., 76, 1969, p. 263ff; 'Sur une statuette en bronze d'Osiris découverte près de Saint-Brieuc', *Bull. et Mem. de la Soc. d'Émulations des Côtes-du-Nord*, 97, 1968, p. 82ff; 'Sur trois documents isiaques des Côtes-du-Nord', ibid., 98, 1969, p. 6ff; 'Aegyptiaca d'Armorique', *Latomus*, 31, 1972, p. 88ff.

124. P.-M. Duval, *Paris antique des origines au IIIᵉ-siècle*, Paris, 1961, p. 271; J. Leclant, *Chronique d'Orientalia*, 32, 1963, p. 216ff; 54, 1985, p. 413f (11); *IBIS*, A–D, p. 191 (pl. XXI).

125. See *Archaeologia*, 219, (December 1986), p. 11.

126. J. Leclant, *Osiris en Gaule, Studia Aegyptiaca*, I, Budapest, 1974, p. 263ff.

127. E. and J.R. Harris, *The Oriental Cults in Roman Britain* (*EPRO*, 6), Leiden, 1965, p. 74ff.

128. *Origines de la France contemporaine*, II, *La Révolution*, 3, Paris, 1885, p. If.

356 Notes to pages 104–22

129. M. Malaise, *Inventaire préliminaire* ... , p. 275f.
130. Ibid., p. 187ff.
131. R. Reitzenstein, *Die hellenistischen Mysterienreligionen nach ihren Grundgedanken und Wirkungen*[3] (1927), re-ed. anast. Darmstadt, 1966, p. 197, 200f; F. Dunand, *Le culte d'Isis* ... , I, p. 64; III, p. 57f, 186.
132. *Metamorphoses*, XI, 24, 2, with the commentary of J.G. Griffiths (*EPRO*, 39), p. 310.
133. V. Tran Tam Tinh, *Le culte d'Isis à Pompéi*, p. 34f; M. Malaise, *Inventaire préliminaire* ... , p. 276f.
134. V. Tran Tam Tinh, op. cit., 35f, 136 ff, Nos 30–8, pl. II–V, 2–3.
135. Ibid., p. 138ff, pl. VI.
136. M. Malaise, op. cit., p. 210f.
137. Ibid., p. 197ff, Nos 363, 368; K. Parlasca, in W. Helbig, *Führer durch die öffentlichen Sammlungen klassicher Altertümer in Rom*[4], II, Tubingen, 1966, p. 42f, No. 1194 (Museo Capitolino).
138. M. Malaise, op. cit., p. 211.
139. A. Henrichs, *Vespasian's Visit to Alexandria* (n. 71), p. 65ff; F. Dunand, op. cit., III, p. 128f.
140. V. Tran Tam Tinh, op. cit., p. 43ff; M. Malaise, *Les conditions de pénétration* ... , p. 83f; E. La Rocca- A. and M. de Vos, *Guida archeologica di Pompei*, p. 240ff.
141. M. Malaise, 'Documents nouveaux et points de vue recents sur les cultes isiaques en Italie' in *Hommages à M.J. Vermaseren*, II, p. 685f; *Inventaire préliminaire* ... , p. 202, No. 383; p. 231, No.
142. R. Turcan, *Sénèque et les religions orientales*, p. 49.
143. M. Malaise, *Les conditions de pénétration* ... , p. 217ff.
144. Ibid., p. 119; V. Tran Tam Tinh, op. cit., p. 99.
145. M. Malaise, op. cit., p. 221ff. Cf. R. Merkelbach, *Isisfeste in griechisch-römischer Zeit. Daten und Riten*, Meisenheim, 1963.
146. Firmicus Maternus, *The Error of Profane Religions*, XXVII, 1.
147. M. Malaise, op. cit., p. 228f.
148. Ibid., p. 129.
149. Supra, n. 140. Cf. H. Mielsch, *Die römische Villa*, p. 104.
150. Apuleius, *Metamorphoses*, XI, 21, 4–6, 8 (*magni numinis dignatione*) and the commentary by J.G. Griffiths, p. 279ff; R. Reitzenstein, op. cit., p. 253f.
151. Apuleius, *Metamorphoses*, XI, 24, 1, with the commentary by J.G. Griffiths, p. 308f. See *Ro*[4], p. 283, N. 69 (a less convincing explanation).
152. F. Dunand, op. cit., II, p. 164f; III, p. 153.
153. P. Derchain, 'L'authenticité de l'inspiration égyptienne dans le "Corpus Hermeticum"', *RHR*, 161, 1962, p. 188ff. On the problems posed by the *Asclepius*, cf. D.N. Wigtil, 'Incorrect Apocalyptic: The Hermetic "Asclepius" as an Improvement on the Greek Original', *ANRW*, II, 17, 4, p. 2282ff.
154. Supra, n. 85.
155. M. Malaise, op. cit., p. 447; H.-P. Laubscher, *Der Reliefschmuck des Galeriusbogens in Thessaloniki* (*Arch. Forsch.*, 1), Berlin, 1975, p. 72f, pls 58, 60, 1.

156. M. Malaise, op. cit., p. 449.

157. R. Turcan, 'Trois "rebus" de l'iconographie romaine ou les pièges de l'analogie', in ΕΙΔΟΛΟΠΟΙΙΑ, *Actes du Colloque sur les problèmes de l'image* ... (Lourmarin 2–3 Sept. 1982), Rome, 1985 (= *Archaeologia*, 61), p. 64ff.

158. H. Castritius, *Studien zu Maximinus Daia* (Frankf. *Althist. Studien*, 2), Kallmünz, 1969, p. 24 (n. 4)) and 55 (n. 53); W. Hornbostel, *Sarapis* ... (*EPRO*, 32), p. 326.

159. L. Budde, 'Julian-Helios Sarapis und Helena-Isis', *AA*, 1972, p. 630ff – already very rightly challenged by A. Alföldi, *A Festival of Isis in Rome under the Christian Emperors of the Fourth Century* (Oissert. Pannonnicae, II, 7), Budapest, 1937, p. 7.

160. G.J.F. Kater-Sibbes and M.J. Vermaseren, *Apis* (*EPRO*, 48), III. *Inscriptions, Coins and Addenda*, Leiden, 1977, p. 31ff, Nos 112–49. There have been attempts to discern in this motif the bull of Mithras under the stars of the Dioscori, which I consider must be ruled out.

161. A. Alföldi and E. Alföldi, *Die Kontorniat-Medaillons*, Berlin, 1976, I, p. 32, No. 112 and pl. 38, 5–7.

162. A. Alföldi, 'Die alexandrinischen Götter und die Vota Publica am Jahresbeginn', *Jahrb. f. Antike u. Christ.*, 8/9, 1965/6, p. 58f., pl. IV, 1; M. Malaise, *Inventaire préliminaire* ... , p. 94f.

163. Edition G. von Hartel in the *Corpus* of Vienna (*CSEL*), III, p. 302f; cf. also *CSEL*, XXIII, p. 227ff.

164. A. Alföldi, *A Festival of Isis* ... (n. 159), pp. 30–42; M. Malaise, op. cit., p. 244ff (*Roma*, 454–71); idem, *Les conditions préliminaires* ... , p. 451.

165. *Isis and Osiris*, 71–2, 74–5, with the rich commentaries of J.G. Griffiths.

166. Supra, n. 101.

167. J. Maspéro, 'Horapollon et al fin du paganisme égyptien', *Bull. de l'Inst. Franç. d'Archéol. Orient. du Caire*, 11, 1914, p. 184ff; J. Geffcken, *Der Ausgang des griechisch-römischen Heidentums*, Heidelberg, 1929 (re-ed. anast., Darmstadt, 1963), p. 194f.

168. R. Merkelbach, *Isisfeste* ... (n. 145), p. 55ff.

Chapter 3: The Orontes Pouring into the Tiber

1. M. Hammond, 'Composition of the Senate AD 68–235, *JRS*, 47, 1957, p. 74ff, 79.

2. L. Friedländer, *Darstellungen aus der Sittengeschichte Roms*[10], Leipzig, 1922, I, p. 39.

3. J. Rougé, 1Lyon et l'Aquitaine: à propos de C.I.L. XIII, 24–48. Thaim, fils de Saad', in *96th Congr. Nat. des Soc. Sav.* (Toulouse, 1971), *Archéologie*, I, Paris, 1976, p. 211ff; idem, 'Aspects économiques de Lyon antique', in *Les Martyrs de Lyon (177)*, Colloque international CNRS (Lyon 1977), Paris, 1978, p. 60.

4. Cf. R.A. Oden, *Studies in Lucian's De Syria Dea* (Harv. Sem. Monogr., 15), Missoula Mont., 1977; C.P. Jones, *Culture and Society in Lucian*, Cambridge' Mass., 1986, p. 41ff.

Notes to pages 134–40

See the texts analysed and compared by P.-L. Van Berg, in *Corpus cultus Deae Syriae (EPRO, 28)*, 1, *Répertoire des sources grecques et latines (sauf le De dea Syria)*, Leiden, 1972; 2, *Étude critique des sources mythographiques grecques et latines*, Leiden, 1972. On the Syrian Goddess in general: M. Hörig, *Dea Syria. Studien zur religiösen Tradition der Fruchtsbarkeitsgöttin in Vorderasien*, Neukirchen-Vluyn, 1979; fadem, 'Dea Syria-Atargatis', *ANRW*, II, 17, 3, Berlin-New York, 1984, p. 1536ff; H.J.W. Drijvers, art. 'Dea Syria', in *LIMC*, III, 1 (1986), p. 355ff; R. Fleischer, art. 'Atargatis', ibid., p. 358.

6. E. Will, *Le sanctuaire de la Déesse Syrienne (Exploration archéologique de Délos, 35)*, Paris, 1985. Cf. p. Roussel, *Délos colonie athénienne (BEFAR, 111)* Paris, 1916, p. 252, 259ff, 270, 352ff, and in *Mélanges G. Radet*, Bordeaux, 1940, p. 131ff; P. Lambrechts and P. Noyen, *Recherches sur le culte d'Atargatis dans le monde grec, La Nouvelle Clio*, 6, 1954, p. 258ff.

7. E. Will, op. cit., p. 147.

8. Ibid., p. 140.

9. Ibid., p. 141.

10. W. Otto, *Priester und Tempel im hellenistichen Aegypten*, I, Leipzig-Berlin, 1905, p. 172; *GgR*, II², p. 165.

11. *LSAM*, 17 (1st Century BC). Cf. P. Roussel, 'Règlements rituels', *Mélanges M. Holleaux*, Paris, 1913, p. 265ff.

12. *IG*, II² p. 564, No. 726.

13. G. Sfameni Gasparro, *I culti orientali in Sicilia*, p. 162, 295, No. 358; p. 164, n. 2 (*IG*, XIV, 287). On Astarte in Sicily and Italy: S. Moscati, 'Astarte in Italia', *Riv. di Cultura Classica e Medievale*, 7, 1965, p. 756ff; idem, 'Sulla diffusione del culto di Astarte Ericina', *Oriens Antiquus*, 7, 1968, p. 91ff; chiefly Egyptian objects and statuettes were found at Mount Eryx.

14. Cf. J. Carcopino, *Des Gracques à Sulla*, in the *Histoire Générale* of G. Glotz, *Histoire romaine*, II, 1, Paris, 1952, p. 189; C. Gallini, *Protesta e integrazione nella Roma antica*, Bari, 1970, p. 129ff.

15. Ibid., pp. 130, 135; Diodorus Siculus, XXXVI, 5, 1–2.

16. Plutarch, *Life of Marius*, 31, 2. Cf. R. Turcan, *Numismatique romaine du culte métroaque*, p. 8. On Martha: F. Chamoux, in *Mélanges W. Seston*, Paris, 1974, p. 81ff.

17. T. Mommsen, in *Monumenta Germaniae Historica, Auctores Antiqui*, IX, p. 147 (*templum Iasurae*); P.-L. Van Berg, op. cit., 1, p. 60, No. 93; p. 91 f., No. 116.

18. Supra, p. 113.

19. Lucian, *Loukios or The Donkey*, 35–41.

20. 'Cybèle et la Déesse Syrienne', *REA*, 63, 1961, p. 45ff; *Les religions de l'Asie dans la vallée du Rhône*, p. 118f; 'Les religions orientales en Gaule Narbonnaise', *ANRW*, II, 18, 1, p. 511.

21. E. and J.R. Harris, *The Oriental Cults in Roman Britain*, p. 105f

22. Ibid., p. 104f. (*CIL*, VII, 758).

23. Ibid., p. 104 (*CIL*, VII, 750).

24. Ibid., p. 105 (*CIL*, VII, 272).

25. I. Berciu and C.C. Petolescu, *Les cultes orientaux dans la Dacie méridionale* (*EPRO*, 54), Leiden, 1986, p. 8, 23f, 35, No. 19.

26. V. Tran Tam Tinh, *Le culte des divinités orientales en Campanie*, pp. 133, 158, S. 19.

27. *CIL*, IX, 4187.

28. R. Turcan, *Les religions de l'Asie dans la vallée du Rhône*, p. 120f.

29. *CIL*, X, 1554; V. Tran Tam Tinh, loc. cit.

30. Ibid., p. 161 (*CIL*, X, 1598).

31. F. Coarelli, in *La soteriologia dei culti orientali* ... (*EPRO*, 92, p. 52f. No. 8.

32. H. Stuart Jones, *The Sculptures of the Musei Capitolini*, Oxford, 1912, p. 92, No. 11 a; E. Simon, in W. Helbig, *Führer* ... [4], II, p. 28 f., No. 1180; H.J.W. Drijvers, art. 'Dea Syria' in *LIMC*, III, 1, p. 35, No. 30.

33. P. Gauckler, *Le sanctuaire syrien du Janicule*, Paris, 1912, p. 164ff; C. Pietrangeli, *Musei Capitolini, I monumenti dei culti orientali*, Rome, 1951, p. 17, No. 22; M. Mele and C. Mocchegiani Carpano, eds., *L'area del 'santuario siriaco del Gianicolo'*, Rome, 1982, p. 101, fig. 1.

34. N. Goodhue, *The Lucus Furrinae and the Syrian Sanctuary on the Janiculum*, Amsterdam, 1975; Mele and Carpano, eds., *L'area del 'santuario siriaco del Gianicolo'*, p. 37ff, 75ff.

35. *AE*, 1903, 58; *CIL*, III, 10393, 10574, 10964, 10973. On the 'Lady of Byblos': R. Du Mesnil du Buisson, *Études sur les dieux phéniciens hérités par l'Empire romain* (*EPRO*, 14), Leiden, 1970, p. 58ff.

36. W. Atallah, *Adonis dans la littérature et l'art grecs*, Paris, 1966; B. Soyez, *Byblos et la fête des Adonies* (*EPRO*, 60), Leiden, 1977. See also the article 'Adonis' in *LIMC*, I, 1, (1981), p. 222ff. The brilliant book by M. Detienne (*Les jardins d'Adonis. La mythologie des aromates en Grèce*, Paris, 1972) is irrelevant to the matters that concern us here.

37. W. Atallah, op. cit., p. 222f.

38. J. Bidez, *Vie de Porphyre*, p. 10* = Eusebius, *Praeparatio evangelica*, III, 11, 12; 15; 17; 19; III, 13, 14. A commentator on Theocritus (p. 131, 21ff. Wendel) identifies Adonis with wheat, whose seed spends six months in the earth (with Persephone) and the other six above ground (with Aphrodite).

39. W. Atallah, op. cit., p. 77 and fig. 11.

40. Ibid., p. 225f. Cf. P. Grimal, *Les jardins romains*[3], Paris, 1984, p. 188f; J.-C. Grenier and F. Coarelli, 'La tombe d'Antinoos a Rome', *MEFR(A)*, 98, 1986, p. 228f, 244f (with fanciful hypotheses on the tomb of Antinous on the Palatine and Hadrian's medallions which were reputed to have adorned a monument erected in homage to his memory before they were used to decorate the entrance portico to the *Elagabalium*, then the arch of Constantine; Antinous was said to have been assimilated with Adonis).

41. F. Cumont, 'Les Syriens en Espagne et les Adonies de Séville', *Syria*, 8, 1927, p. 330ff. Cf. W. Atallah, op. cit., p. 248f; A. García y Bellido, *Les religions orientales dans l'Espagne romaine*, p. 102ff; E. Will, 'Le rituel des Adonies', *Syria*, 52, 1975, p. 93ff.

42. Cf. R. Turcan, 'Déformation des modèles ... dans l'iconographie des sarcophages romains', *Annali d. Scuola Normale Sup. di Pisa*, 1987, p. 430f.

43. R. Turcan, 'Les sarcophages romains et le problème du symbolisme funéraire', *ANRW*, II, 16, 2, p. 1721ff.

44. P. W. Lehmann, *Roman Wall Paintings from Boscoreale in the Metropolitan Museum of Art*, Cambridge, Mass., 1953; W. Atallah, op. cit., p. 274ff.

45. *GgR*, II², p. 639; R. Turcan, commentated translation-edition of Firmicus Maternus, p. 314f.

46. Whatever V. von Graeve (in *Jahrb. d. deut. arch. Inst.*, 87, 1972, p. 314ff) and U. Bianchi (in Mele and Carpano, eds., *L'area del 'santuario siriaco del Gianicolo'*, p. 97ff may have written about it: see infra, pp. 191–2.

47. W. Baudissin, *Adonis und Esmun*, Leipzig, 1911, p. 121.

48. Y. Hajjar, *La triade d'Héliopolis-Baalbek. Iconographie, théologie, culte et sanctuaires*, Montreal, 1985, p. 179f.

49. Ibid., p. 116, 178, 195.

50. Ibid., p. 61f.

51. R. Fleischer, *Artemis von Ephesos* ... (*EPRO*, 35), p. 1ff, 146ff, 310ff.

52. Y. Hajjar, op. cit., p. 210.

53. Y. Hajjar, *La triade d'Héliopolis-Baalbek. Son culte et sa diffusion à travers les textes littéraires et les documents iconographiques et épigraphiques* (*EPRO*, 59), Leiden, 1977, I, No. 321; II, pl. CXXVII.

54. Ibid., I, No. 233; II, pls XC–XCI. Cf. idem, *La triade ... Iconographie ...* (n. 48), p. 98.

55. R. Turcan, 'Une allusion de Plotin aux idoles cultuelles' in *Mélanges H.-Ch. Puech*, Paris, 1974, p. 307ff, 313.

56. A.-J. Festugière, *La révélation d'Hermès Trismégiste*, IV, Paris, 1954 (re-ed.), p. 152ff, 176ff.

57. Y. Hajjar, *La triade ...* (n. 53), I, No. 277; II, pl. CIV; Idem, *La triade ... Iconographie ...* (n. 48), p. 58f.

58. Ibid., p. 140ff; R. Fleischer, op. cit., pl. 105 b.

59. Y Hajjar, *La triade ...* (n. 53), I, No. 136; II, pl. L (Fike); ibid., I, No. 293; II, pl. CXIV (Palatin).

60. Y. Hajjar, *La triade ...* (n. 48), p. 159ff.

61. Ibid., p. 281ff, 326f.

62. Ibid., p. 300ff. Several points in this explanation are still much debated. Cf. the paper presented by E. Will to the Collogue International CNRS *Archéologie de l'espace sacrificiel* (Lyon 4–7 June 1988).

63. Y. Hajjar, *La triade ...* (n. 48), p. 273.

64. E. Schwertheim, *Die Denkmäler orientalischer Gottheiten im römischen Deutschland* (*EPRO*, 40), Leiden, 1974, p. 158, No. 122; 318. On the spread of the Heliopolitan cult, cf. generally, Y. Hajjar, *La triade ...* (n. 53). Regarding the cippus of Nîmes, see R. Turcan, *Les religions de l'Asie dans la vallée du Rhône*, p. 109f.

65. Y. Hajjar, *La triade ...* (n. 48), p. 250.

66. V. Tran Tam Tinh, *Le culte des divinités orientales en Campanie*, p. 131ff, 149f, S.12.

67. Ibid., p. 148f, S.11.
68. *Journal Asiatique*, 1873, p. 384.
69. N. Goodhue, op. cit. (n. 34), p. 11ff; F. Coarelli, in *La soteriologia dei culti orientali* (*EPRO*, 92), p. 52, No. 7.
70. Infra, pp. 166–7.
71. Y. Hajjar, op. cit., (n. 48), p. 249f.
72. Ibid., p. 58f.
73. He is found in association with Jupiter Dolichenus: A. Popa and I. Berciu, *Le culte de Jupiter Dolichenus dans la Dacie romaine* (*EPRO*, 69), Leiden, 1978, p. 5. For Upper Pannonia, cf. *CCID*, p. 147, No. 221, and p. 176, No. 274.
74. E. and J.R. Harris, op. cit., p. 68, 104; Y. Hajjar, op. cit. (n. 48), p. 376, No. 363.
75. R. Turcan, op. cit., p. 112.
76. Y. Hajjar, 'A propos d'une main de Sabazios au Louvre', in *Hommages à M.J. Vermaseren*, I, p. 471, pl. LXXXIX.
77. R. Turcan, *Vivre à la cour des Césars*, p. 301.
78. Y. Hajjar, *La triade* ... (n. 48), p. 383.
79. *CCID*, *Epigraphischer index*, p. 403f; M. Hörig, 'Jupiter Dolichenus', *ANRW*, II, 17, 4, p. 2165.
80. *CCID*, p. 17, No. 11, pl. V; M. Maaskant-Kleinbrink, 'Cachets de terre – de Doliché (?)', *Bull. Ant. Besch.*, 46, 1971, p. 38, No. 26, fig. 36.
81. *CCID*, pl. VII, 22.
82. Ibid., pl. VIII.
83. P. Merlat, *Jupiter Dolichenus. Essai d'interprétation et de synthèse*, Paris, 1960, p. 4, 72ff.
84. Ibid., p. 81ff; M. Hörig, loc. cit. (*ANRW*, II, 17, 4), p. 2143f.
85. *CCID*, p. 230 f, No. 512, pl. CVIII.
86. Ibid., p. 231, No. 365, pl. LXXVII; p. 253, No. 386, pl. LXXXVII.
87. Cf. F. Cumont, *Recherches sur le symbolisme funéraire des Romains*, Paris, 1942 (re-ed. 1966), p. 79, 94; R. Turcan, 'Rome éternelle et les conceptions gréco-romaines de l'éternité', in *Roma Costantinopoli Mosca*, Naples, 1983, p. 27.
88. Y. Grandjean, *Une nouvelle arétalogie d'Isis à Maronée*, p. 20, 57ff.
89. F. Cumont, op. cit., p. 92; R. Turcan, loc. cit., p. 29.
90. P. Merlat, op. cit., p. 88ff; M. Hörig, loc. cit. (*ANRW*, II, 17, 4), p. 2144f.
91. P. Merlat, op. cit., p. 168ff; M. Hörig, loc. cit. p. 2170f.
92. A.H. Kan, *De Jovis Dolicheni cultu*, Groningen, 1901, p. 9. Cf. by the same, *Jupiter Dolichenus* ... , Leiden, 1943, p. 24ff.
93. *CCID*, p. 81f, No. 103, pl. XXVI.
94. Cf. P. Merlat, op. cit., p. 174, fig. 25.
95. Ibid., p. 183ff.
96. Ibid., p. 177ff; M. Hörig, loc. cit. (*ANRW*, II, 17, 4), p. 2171f.
97. *CCID*, p. 259f, No. 400, pl. XCII.
98. P. Merlat, op. cit., p. 175, 202ff.
99. *CCID*, p. 241, No. 375; p. 246, No. 381. Cf. p. Merlat, op. cit., p. 202ff.
100. Ibid., p. 192; *CCID*, Nos 373, 375f, 380f.

101. Ibid., p. 312, No. 493.
102. Op. cit., p. 202.
103. Ibid., p. 147ff; CCID, p. 221ff, No. 355, pl. LXIX.
104. R. MacMullen, *Paganism in the Roman Empire*. On Dolichenian communities, cf. p. Merlat, op. cit., p. 190f.
105. CCID, Nos 123 (Barlaha), 3, 154, 363 (Barhadad); 34, 104, 147, 165, 221, 414 (Basus or Bassus).
106. CCID, p. 129f, No. 200. Cf. R. MacMullen, op. cit.; J. Fitz, 'Der Besuch des Septimius Severus in Pannonien ...', *Acta Arch. Acad. Scient. Hung.*, 11, 1959, p. 241ff.
107. P. Merlat, op. cit., p. 24ff.
108. CCID, p. 263ff, Nos 407–16.
109. R. Turcan, *Vivre à la cour des Césars*, p. 301.
110. P. Merlat, op. cit., p. 22f; M. Hörig, loc. cit. (*ANRW*, II, 17, 4), p. 2157ff.
111. CCID, Nos 61, 165, 363, 433. On the above-mentioned inscription (*CIL*, III, 7756), cf. R. MacMullen, *Paganism in the Roman Empire*. The authors of the CCID take no account of it. Indeed, it is not certain whether it concerns Jupiter Dolichenus: A. Popa and I. Berciu, *Le culte de Jupiter Dolichenus dans la Dacie romaine* (*EPRO*, 69), Leiden, 1978, p. 43.
112. P. Merlat, op. cit., p. 209; CCID, Nos 218, 227, 426, 443, 465f (with the earlier bibliography).
113. E. and J.R. Harris, op. cit., p. 106f.
114. A. García y Bellido, op. cit., p. 152ff; M. Bendala Galán, loc. cit. (*ANRW*, II, 18, 1), p. 349ff.
115. V. Tran Tam Tinh, op. cit., p. 136, 153ff, S. 17.
116. E. and J.R. Harris, op. cit., p. 107.
117. V. Tran Tam Tinh, op. cit., p. 137, 156ff, S. 18.
118. Ibid., p. 151f; R. Fleischer, *Artemis von Ephesos*, p. 379f., pl. 167f.
119. CIL, III, 159; 7680. Cf. Y. Hajjar, *La triade* ... (n. 48), p. 243f.
120. Lydus, *Les mois*, IV, 80 (p. 133 Wuensch); M. Floriani Squarciapino, *I culti orientali ad Ostia*, p. 63f; Y. Hajjar, op. cit. (n. 48), p. 189, 230, 271.
121. *Life of Severus Alexander*, 17, 4. Cf. J. Straub, 'Marnas' *Historia-Augusta-Colloquium (Bonn 1963)*, Bonn, 1964, p. 165ff. Proclus invoked Marnas of Gaza and the Asclepius of Ascalon: Marinus, *Life of Proclus*, 19 (p. 161, 7ff of the Boissonade edition in the Coll. Firmin-Didot, Paris, 1929).
122. J. -C. Balty, 'L'oracle d'Apamée' *L'Antiquité Classique*, 50, 1981, p. 8ff.
123. A. Salac, 'ΖΕΥΣ ΚΑΣΙΟΣ', *BCH*, 46, 1922, p. 160ff.
124. P. Chuvin and J. Yoyotte, 'Documents relatifs au culte pélusien de Zeus Casios', *RA*, 1986, p. 41ff.
125. A. García y Bellido, op. cit., p. 100ff.
126. W. Jobst, 'II Id. Juni 172 n. Chr ... ', *Sitzungsber. d. österr. Akad. d. Wiss. in Wien*, Philos. Hist. Klasse, 335, 1978, and in *ANRW*, II, 6, Berlin-New York, 1977, p. 715; M.M. Sage, 'Marcus Aurelius and "Zeus Kasios" at Carnuntum', *Ancient Society*, 18, 1987, p. 151ff.
127. Or 'mountain of the santuary'; J. Stracky, 'Stèle d'Elahagabal' *Musée Saint-Joseph*, 49, 1975/6, p. 514. On Turmasgad in Dacia, cf. I. Berciu and C.C. Petolescu, *Les cultes orientaux dans la Dacie méridionale* (*EPRO*, 69),

p. 37. In Rome, an altar consecrated to this god and found near the Palace of the Chancellery is preserved in the Museo Capitolino: C. Pietrangeli, op. cit., p. 12, No. 8.

128. P. Gauckler, *Le sanctuaire syrien du Janicule*, p. 11f, 47f; Y. Hajjar, op. cit. (n. 48), pp. 190, 358.

129. *CIL*, VI, 36792; *AE*, 1950, 232. Cf. P. Gauckler, op. cit., p. 13ff, 50ff; N. Goodhue, op. cit., p. 13.

130. R. du Mesnil du Buisson, 'Les origines du panthéon palmyrien' *Mélanges de l'Univ. Saint-Joseph*, 39, 1963, p. 169ff; H.J.W. Drijvers, *The Religion of Palmyra Iconography of Religions*, XV, 15), Leiden, 1976; idem, in *La soteriologia dei culti orientali* (*EPRO*, 92), p. 713ff; J. Teixidor, *The Pantheon of Palmyra* (*EPRO*, 79), Leiden, 1979; J. Starcky and M. Gawlikowsky, *Palmyre*, Paris, 1985, p. 89ff. For the iconography, cf. in *LIMC*, I, 1 (1981), p. 298ff; 2, p. 216–21, art. 'Aglibol': III, 1 (1986), p. 90–2; 2, p. 69–71, art. 'Bel'.

131. Cf. H. Seyrig, 'Antiquités syriennes, 93 (Bel de Palmyres)', *Syria*, 48, 1971, p. 89ff.

132. Ibid., p. 104, n. 4 (*IGVR*, 118).

133. *CIL*, VIII, 2498, 2503, 18004, 18007; E. Albertini, 'Inscriptions d'El Kantara', *Rev. Africaine*, 72, 1931, p. 193ff (No. 10); Cf. G. Charles Picard, *Castellum Dimmidi*, Algiers-Paris (n.d.), p. 136f.

134. Ibid., p. 104, n. 4 (*IGVR*, 118).

135. *CIL*, III, 7954/6; J. Toutain, *Les cultes païens dans l'Empire romain*, ii, p. 63; J. T. Milik, *Recherches d'épigraphie proche-orientale*, I (Inst. Fr. d'Arch. de Beyrouth, Bibl. arch. et hist., 112), Paris, 1972, p. 436; A. Popa and I. Berciu, op. cit., p. 43. Cf. R. MacMullen, op. cit., p. 38, p. 162 n. 20.

136. G. Lafaye, *Un nouveau dieu syrien à Rome*, RHR, 17, 1888, p. 219ff.

137. A. Popa and I. Berciu, op. cit., p. 5f, No. 3 (with the earlier bibliography). But M.P. Speidel (*The Religion of Jupiter Dolichenus in the Roman Army* = *EPRO*, 53, Leiden, 1978, p. 50ff No. 28) and the authors of the *CCID* (p. 105f, No. 154) prefer to read *A(e)D(ituus)LEG(ionis)*. In fact, nothing on the stone (pl. XXX) imposes this interpretation. Priest *ad signa*: R. Cavenaille, *Corpus papyrorum Latinarum*, Wiesbaden, 1958, p. 423f, No. 331 (239 A.D.); cf. p. 418f, No. 326. Cf. F. Cumont, *Fouilles de Doura-Europos* (1922–3), Paris, 1926, p. 113.

138. Supra, n. 3; J. Toutain, op. cit., p. 63.

139. F. Cumont, op. cit., p. 44ff, pls XXXI–XLI; H.J.W. Drijvers, *The Religion of Palmyra*, pl. LXXX.

140. Cf. C. Pietrangeli, op. cit., p. 13, No. 11; p. 16, No. 19: sector of the Mattei Gardens.

141. Cf. H. Seyrig, 'Iconographie de Malakbêl', *Syria*, 18, 1937, p. 201, pl. XXXI; idem, *Bêl de Palmyre* (n. 131), p. 101.

142. C. Pietrangeli, op. cit., p. 21f, No. 33; E. Simon, in W. Helbig, *Fügrer⁴*, II, p. 30f, No. 1182; J. Teixidor, *The Pantheon of Palmyra*, p. 47 and pls XV–XVI. Cf. *RO⁴*, pl. X. On the *Galbienses* and the zone of the *Emporium*: F. Coerelli, in *La soteriologia dei culti orientali* (*EPRO*, 92), p. 50ff.

143. Zosimus, *New History*, I, 61, 2 (p. 53 of the translation-edition F. Paschoud in the Coll. des Universités de France, Paris, 1971).

144. R. Turcan, *Héliogabale et le sacre du Soleil*, Paris, 1985, p. 26ff, 67.
145. On the (very relative) expansion of this solar god: G.H. Halsberghe, 'Le culte de Deus Sol Invictus à Rome au 3ᵉ siècle après J.-C.' *ANRW*, II, 17, 4, p. 2182f. For *Intercisa*, cf. J. Fitz, *Les Syriens à Intercisa* (Coll. Latomus, 122), Brussels, 1972, p. 183, 192ff. Religious policy of Heligabalus: M. Pietrzykowski, 'Die Religionspolitik des Kaisers Elagabal', *ANRW*, II, 16, 3, Berlin-New York, 1986, p. 1806ff.
146. G.H. Halsberghe, loc. cit., p. 2183.
147. *Cynegetica*, I, 7; Z. Kadar, 'Julia Domna comme Assyrié Kythereia et Séléne', *Acta, Class. Univ. Scient. Debrec.*, 2, 1966, p. 101ff.
148. R. Turcan, *Héliogable* ..., p. 86ff.
149. F. Castagnoli, 'Su alcuni problemi topografici del Palatino', *Rend. Accad. Lincei*, 1979, p. 331ff.
150. *Augustan History, Life of Heliogabalus*, 3, 4–5; 7, 1 and 5–6. Cf. T. Optendrenk, *Die Religionspolitik des Kaisers Elagabal im Spiegel des Historia Augusta*, Bonn, 1969, p. 14ff; T. Pekary, 'Statuen in der Historia Augusta', *Historia-Augusta-Colloquium (Bonn 1968/9)*, Bonn, 1970, p. 166ff.
151. Cf. R. Turcan, 'Héliogabale précurseur de Constantin?', *Bull. de l'Assoc. G. Budé*, 1988, p. 38ff.
152. E. von Mercklin, *Antike Figuralkapitelle*, Berlin, 1962, p. 154ff, No. 383, figs 729–36.
153. R. Turcan, *Héliogabale* ..., figs 21, 35–6 and p. 122 (plan).
154. A.M. Colini, 'Horti Spei Veteris, Palatium Sessorianum', *Mem. d. Pont. Accad. Rom. di Archeologia*, 1955, p. 137ff.
155. A. García y Bellido, op. cit., p. 96ff; H. Seyrig, 'Le culte du Soleil en Syrie à l'époque romaine', *Syria*, 48, 1971, p. 370f; M. Bendala Galan, 'Die orientalischen Religionen Hispaniens', *ANRW*, II, 18, 1 p. 405.
156. E. Nash, *Pictorial Dictionary of Ancient Rome*, I, 1968, p. 537ff.
157. H. Seyrig, 'Antiquités syriennes, 89 (Les dieux armés et les Arabes en Syrie)', *Syria*, 47, 1970, p. 82.
158. *CIL*, III, 875, 1130–8, 7652; J. Toutain, op. cit., p. 49; Z. Kadar, *Die kleinasiatisch-syrischen Kulte zur Römerzeit in Ungarn* (*EPRO*, 2), Leiden, 1962, p. 23f. On the cult of Aziz: B. Lifshitz, 'Études sur l'histoire de la province romaine en Syrie' *ANRW*, II, 8, Berlin-New York, 1977, p. 21f; H. Seyrig, loc. cit., p. 670ff.
159. H.J.W. Drijvers, art. '*Dusarès*' in *LIMC*, III, 1 (1986), p. 670ff.
160. Ibid., 2, p. 532. Cf. R. Dussaud, *Notes de mythologie syrienne*, Paris, 1903, fig. 39 and in *Rev. Numismatique*, 1904, p. 160ff.
161. V. Tran Tam Tinh, *Le culte des divinités orientales en Campanie*, p. 217ff, 141ff, S. 1–7.
162. Ibid., p. 128.
163. Ibid., p. 144ff, S. 3–5 (bases) and 6 (altar).
164. Ibid., p. 129. n. 3.
165. 'Un monument enigmatique "Dusari sacrum" a Pouzzoles', in *Hommages à M.J. Vermaseren*, II, p. 782ff.
166. 'Mithra et Dusares', *RHR*, 78, 1918, p. 207ff. Cf. F. Cumont, 'The Dura Mithraeum', in *Mithraic Studies*, I, Manchester, 1975, p. 160.

167. Supra, p. 168.
168. On this much debated site: N. Goodhue, op. cit. (n. 34), p. 3ff; M. Mele and C. Mocchegiani Carpano, eds., *L'area del 'santuario siriaco del Gianicolo'*, p. 47ff, 61ff; Y. Hajjar, op. cit. (n. 48), p. 356ff.
169. G. Darier, *Les fouilles du Janicule a Rome* . . . , *Bibliographie chronologique des travaux publiés à leur sujet de 1906 à 1918*, Geneva, 1920. Resumption of the excavations and critical re-examination of the data: J. Calzini-Gysens, in *L'area del 'santuario'* . . . , p. 61ff.
170. P. Gauckler, *Le sanctuaire syrien du Janicule*, p. 83f, 86ff.
171. Ibid., p. 192ff, amended by A. Pasqui, 'Il simulacro siriaco del Gianicolo', *Studi Romani*, 1, 1913, p. 343ff; Y. Hajjar, op. cit., p. 364ff.
172. N. Goodhue, op. cit., p. 8f, 79ff, and in *Pacific Coast Philology*, 10, 1975, p. 29ff.
173. Y. Hajjar, op. cit., p. 361ff.
174. B.M. Felletti Maj, 'Il santuario della triade eliopolitana e dei misteri al Gianicolo', *Bull. Com.*, 75, 1953/5, p. 153f; N. Goodhue, op. cit., p. 62f.
175. Y. Hajjar, op. cit., p. 159ff.
176. *Dubitationes* . . . , 123 bis (I, p. 317, 15ff. Ruelle) = O. Kern, *Orphicorum fragmenta*², Berlin, 1963, p. 130f, No. 54.
177. A. Delatte and P. Derchain, *Bibliothèque Nationale, Les intailles magiques gréco-égyptiennes*, Paris, 1964, p. 73ff, 76, Nos 90–1; p. 134f, No. 172.
178. Ibid., p. 103, No. 129.
179. Cf. Y. Hajjar, op. cit., p. 366.
180. J. Collins-Clinton, *A Late Antique Shrine of Liber Pater at Cosa* (*EPRO*, 64), Leiden, 1977.
181. Y. Hajjar, op. cit., p. 358ff.
182. J. Bidez, *Vie de Porphyre*, p. 14*ff = Eusebius, *Praeparatio evangelica*, III, 11, 30–8.
183. Cf. Z. Kádár, *Die kleinasiatisch-syrischen Kulte zur Römerzeit in Ungarn*, p. 25f; S. Sanie, 'Deus Aeternus et Theos Hypsistos en Dacie romaine', in *Hommages à M.J. Vermaseren*, III, p. 1092ff.

Chapter 4: Beneath the Rocks of the Persian Cavern

1. A. Meillet, 'Le dieu indo-iranien Mitra', *Journal Asiatique*, 1907, p. 143ff; G. Dumézil, *Les dieux souverains des Indo-Européens*, Paris, 1977, p. 82f.
2. Ibid., p. 24f, with the previous bibliography. Text translated in R. Labat et al. *Les religions du Proche-Orient, Textes et traditions sacrés babyloniens-ougaritiques-hittites*, Paris, 1970, p. 505 (M. Vieyra).
3. J. Varenne, *Le Véda*, Paris, 1967, p. 85. Cf. G. Dumezil, op. cit., p. 56ff.
4. Ibid., p. 159ff; idem, *Mitra-Varuna*, Paris, 1940, p. 29ff; idem, *Mythe et épopée*, I², Paris, 1968, p. 274ff.
5. I. Gershevitch, *The Avestan Hymn to Mithra*, Cambridge, 1959; J. Duchesne-Guillemin, *La religion de l'Iran ancien*, Paris, 1962, p. 37. Complete translation in J. Darmesteter, *Le Zend-Avesta*, II, Paris, 1892. Cf.

P. Thieme, 'Mithra in the Avesta, Études mithriaques', in *Acta Iranica*, I, 4, 17 (= Actes du 2ᵉ Congr. Intern., Tehran 1–8 Sept. 1975), Leiden and Tehran-Liège, 1978, p. 501ff.

6. Duchesne-Guillemin, 'Le dieu de Cyrus', in *Acta Iranica*, I, 3 (Hommage Universel), Tehran-Liège, 1974, p. 17.

7. Cf. M. Schwartz, 'Cautes and Cautopates the Mithraic Torchbearers', in *Mithraic Studies* (proceed. of the First Intern. Congr. of Mithraic Studies), II, Manchester, 1975, p. 417f.

8. G. Widengren, *Les religions de l'Iran*, Fr. trans., Paris, 1968, p. 238; I. Gershevitch, 'Die Sonne das Beste', in *Mithraic Studies*, I, p. 85. Resumé in M. Dikran-Tchitouny, *Sassounacan, Épopée populaire arménienne*, Paris, 1942, p. 371. Cf. J.A. Boyle, 'Meher in the Carved Rock', *JMS*, I, 2, 1976, p. 107ff.

9. J. Duchesne-Guillemin, *Le dieu de Cyrus*, p. 16f.

10. Cf. R. Turcan, *Mithras Platonicus* (*EPRO*, 47) Leiden, 1975, p. 17f.

11. A. Dupont-Sommer, 'L'énigme du dieu "Satrape" et le dieu Mithra', *CRAI*, 1976, p. 648ff.

12. On Anahita, cf. R. Turcan, op. cit., p. 95ff.

13. E. Benveniste, *Titres et noms propres en iranien ancien*, Paris, 1966, p. 88ff.

14. *Les mystères de Mithra*³, Brussels, 1913, p. 10ff; *RO*⁴, p. 136.

15. G. Gnoli, 'Politique religieuse et conception de la royauté sous les Achéménides', in *Acta Iranica*, I, 2 (Hommage Universel), Tehran-Liège 1974, p. 133ff.

16. R. Turcan, op. cit., p. 50ff.

17. Cf. D. Ulansey, 'Mithras and Perseus', *Helios*, 1986, p. 46f.

18. J. Bidez and F. Cumont, *Les mages héllénisés. Zoroastre, Ostanès et Hystaspe d'après la tradition grecque*, I–II, Paris, 1938, (re-edited).

19. Ibid., I, p. 91ff; II, p. 142ff (fr. *O* 8).

20. *CIMRM*, 1247.

21. Bidez-Cumont, op. cit., I, p. 39 and pl. I; F. Cumont, 'The Dura-Mithraeum', in *Mithraic Studies*, I, p. 182ff; II, pl. 25.

22. *CIMRM*, 454; M. Guarducci, in 'Mysteria Mithrae', *Atti del Semin. Intern. Roma e Ostia 21–31 March 1978* (*EPRO*), 80), Leiden 1979, p. 171ff.

23. *CIMRM*, 19; R. Turcan, *Mithras Platonicus*, p. 28 (where obviously *Rhodandos* should be read).

24. H. Waldmann, *Die kommagenischen Kultreformen unter König Mithradates I. Kallinikos und seinem Sohne Antiochos I.* (*EPRO*, 34), Leiden, 1973.

25. Cf. P. Beskow, 'The Routes of Early Mithraism', in *Acta Iranica*, I, 4, p. 14.

26. *CIMRM*, 11–12; W. Blawatsky-G. Kochelenko, *Le culte de Mithra sur la côte septentrionale de la Mer Noire* (*EPRO*, 8), Leiden, 1966, p. 14ff, figs 8–10; P. Beskow, loc. cit., p. 14f.

27. G.F. Hill, *British Museum Coins, Lycaonia* ... , London, 1900, p. 213, No. 258, pl. XXXVII, 4; *CIMRM*, 27.

28. *CIMRM*, 408.

29. D. Ulansey, loc. cit. (n. 17), p. 33ff, 40ff.

30. F. Cumont, 'La fin du monde selon les mages occidentaux', *RHR*, 103, 1931, p. 29ff; Bidez-Cumont, *Les mages hellénisés*, I, p. 217ff; II, p. 361ff.
31. *César*[4], in the *Histoire Générale* by G. Glotz (*Histoire Romaine*, II, 2), Paris, 1950, p. 641.
32. F. Cumont, *Les mystères de Mithra*[3], p. 46f; C.M. Daniels, 'The Role of the Roman Army in the Spread and Practice of Mithraism', in *Mithraic Studies*, II, p. 250f.
33. *CIL*, VI, 732; *IGVR*, 179; *CIMRM*, 362. Cf. R.L. Gordon, 'The Date and Significance of *CIMRM* 593', *JMS*, II, 2, 1978, p. 151ff.
34. Ibid., p. 155ff; *CIMRM*, 593/4.
35. F.M. Ahl, 'Statius' Thebaid: a reconsideration', *ANRW*, II, 32, 5, Berlin-New York, 1986, p. 2856f; R.L. Gordon, loc. cit., p. 161f.
36. M.J. Vermaseren, *Mithriaca* (*EPRO*, 16), I, *The Mithraeum at S. Maria Capua Vetere*, Leiden, 1971.
37. Cf. generally R. Turcan, *Mithra et le mithriacisme*, Paris, 1981 ('Que-sais je?', 1929), p. 26f; R. Beck, 'Mithraism since Franz Cumont', *ANRW*, II, 17, 4, p. 2020ff.
38. See the evaluations (exaggerated) of F. Coarelli, in *Mysteria Mithrae* (*EPRO*, 80), p. 75ff.
39. G. Becatti, *Scavi di Ostia*, II, 1: *I Mitrei*, Rome, 1954; F. Coarelli, loc. cit. (n. 38), p. 76.
40. Cf. P. Rancillac, 'L'insuccès du mithriacisme en Afrique', *Bul. Soc. Géogr. et Arch. d'Oran*, 52, 1931, p. 221ff; J. Toutain, op. cit., II, p. 146f. Lambaesis: M. Le Glay, in *JMSI*, 2, 1976, p. 205f. The case of the 'Mitreo' (S. Stucchi, *Divagazioni archeologiche*, I, Rome, 1981, p. 87ff) of Cyrene is discussed: R.L. Gordon, in *JMS*, I, 2, 1976, p. 210ff.
41. A. García y Bellido, op. cit., p. 21ff; M. Bendala Galán, loc. cit. (*ANRW*, II, 18, 1), p. 394ff; J. Alvar, 'El culto de Mitra en Hispania', in *Mem. de Historia Antigua*, 5, Oviedo, 1981, p. 51ff.
42. A. Ziegle, 'Bordeaux. Du culte de Mithra au Couvent des Carmes', *Archaeologia*, 234 (April 1988), p. 42ff (18.40 × 10.30 m.).
43. On Mithras in the Rhône Valley in general: R. Turcan, *Les religions de l'Asie dans la vallée du Rhône*, pp. 1–47, and in *ANRW*, II, 18, 1, p. 499ff.
44. V.J. Walters, *The Cult of Mithras in the Roman Provinces of Gaul* (*EPRO*, 41), Leiden 1974, p. 45f, 95ff.
45. Ibid., p. 149ff. Cf. H. Vertet, in *Hommages à L. Lerat*, Paris, 1984, II, p. 849ff.
46. J.-G. Sainrat, 'Le Mithraeum de Septeuil', in *'Connaître les Yvelines'*, *Histoire et Archéologie*, 1987, pp. 33–40.
47. V.J. Walters, op. cit., p. 138f. On the allegedly Mithraic Sun of Lillebonne: ibid., p. 29f, 124f.
48. E. and J.R. Harris, op. cit., pp. 1–54; R. Beck, loc. cit. (*ANRW*, II, 17, 4), p. 2033f.
49. M.J. Vermaseren, *Der Kult des Mithras im römischen Germanien*, Stuttgart, 1974; R. Beck, loc. cit., p. 2036ff.
50. Ibid., p. 2039ff, 2043–7.
51. V.J. Walters, op. cit., p. 23ff, 108ff.

52. *CIMRM*, 1400. Cf. R. Turcan, 'The Date of the Mauls Relief', *JMS*, I, 1, 1976, p. 68ff.

53. While awaiting publications concerning other sectors, cf. L. Zotović, *Le mithraisme sur le territoire de la Yougoslavie*, Belgrade, 1973; P. Selem, *Les religions orientales dans la Pannonie romaine partie en Yougoslavie*, p. 76ff.

54. E. Will, 'Les fidèles de Mithra à Poetevio', *Adriatica Praehistorica et Antiqua (Miscell. G. Novak)*, Zagreb, 1970, p. 635f; R. Merkelbach, *Mithras*, Meisenheim-Königstein, 1984, p. 162ff.

55. I. Berciu and C.C. Petolescu, *Les cultes orientaux dans la Dacie méridionale*, p. 14ff; R. Beck, loc. cit., p. 2043ff.

56. *CIMRM*, 2268; R.L. Gordon, loc. cit. (n. 33), p. 153f.

57. D.M. Pippidi, 'En marge d'un document mithriaque de Scythie Mineure', in *Hommages à M.J. Vermaseren*, III, p. 967ff.

58. E. Will, *Le relief cultuel gréco-romain (BEFAR, 183)*, Paris, 1955, p. 356ff.

59. *RO*⁴, pl. XIII, 2; *CIMRM*, 1896; R. Merkelbach, *Mithras*, p. 381 (Sarajevo Museum).

60. *Lives of the Sophists* p. 436 in the Wright English translation edition in the Coll. Loeb (1952).

61. P. Beskow, loc. cit. (n. 25), pp. 7–18.

62. W. Radt, *Kapikaya bei Pergamon* ... , in *Mysteria Mithrae (EPRO, 80)*, p. 789ff; St.-Chr. Dahlinger, *Der sogenannte Podiensaal in Pergamon: ein Mithräum?*, ibid., p. 793ff.

63. Infra, p. 273f.

64. R. Pettazzoni, 'La figura mostruosa del tempo nella religione mitriaca', *L'Antiquité Classique*, 18, 1949, p. 265ff; idem, 'Kronos-Chronos in Egitto', in *Hommages à J. Bidez et à F. Cumont* (Coll. Latomus, 2), Brussels, 1949, p. 245ff; A.-J. Festugière, 'Les cinq sceaux de l'Aiôn alexandrin', *Rev. d'Égyptologie*, 8, 1951, p. 63ff = *Études de religion grecque et hellénistique*, Paris, 1972, p. 201ff; E. Will, op. cit., p. 189ff; M.J. Vermaseren, 'A Magical Time God', in *Mithraic Studies*, II, p. 451ff.

65. H. Humbach, 'Mithra in the Kusana Period', in *Mithraic Studies*, I. p. 135ff.

66. *The Decline of the west.*

67. Cf. R. Turcan, 'Les motivations de l'intolérance chrétienne et la fin du mithracisme au IVᵉ siècle ap. J.-C.', *Actes du VIIᵉ Congrès de la F.I.E.C.*, II, Budapest, 1983, p. 220f.

68. A.M. Sgubini Moretti, in *Mysteria Mithrae*, p. 259ff.

69. M. De' Spagnolis, *Il Mitreo di Itri (EPRO, 86)*, Leiden, 1980, p. 7ff.

70. M.J. Vermaseren, *Mithriaca (EPRO, 16, III, The Mithraeum at Marino*, Leiden, 1982, p. 4f.

71. V. Santa Maria Scrinari, in *Mysteria Mithrae*, p. 219ff.

72. E. Lissi-Caronna, *Il Mitreo dei Castra Peregrinorum (EPRO, 104)*, Leiden, 1986.

73. P. Selem, op. cit. (n. 53), p. 78, 93, 125, 144.

74. Cf. R. Turcan, in *JMS*, II, 2, 1978, p. 176f, from information from *Gallia*, 32, 1974, p. 373; 34, 1976, p. 385.

75. F. Coarelli, in *Mysteria Mithrae*, p. 76ff: the figure of 700 *Mithraea* may be 'prudent' ... (?).

76. *CIMRM*, 1292; R. Merkelbach, *Mithras*, p. 350f.

77. *CIMRM*, 985. Cf. V.J. Walters, op. cit., p. 108ff; R. Turcan, *Mithras Platonicus*, p. 78 (n. 127) and 85 (n. 172).

78. M.J. Vermaseren, op. cit. (n. 70), p. 12ff, pls XI–XVI.

79. R. Turcan, 'Le sacrifice mithraique', in *Le sacrifice dans l'Antiquité* (Entretiens sur l'Antiquité Classique, 27), Geneva-Vandoeuvres, 1981, p. 363ff.

80. *CIMRM*, 670 and fig. 191.

81. R. Beck, 'The Mithraic Torchbearers and "Absence of Opposition"', *Echos du Monde Classique/Classical Views*, 26, 1982, p. 126ff; idem, "Four Dacian Tauroctonies ... ", *Apulum*, 22, 1985, p. 45ff.

82. M.J. Vermaseren, *Mithriaca* (EPRO, 16), IV, *Le monument d'Ottaviano Zeno et le culte de Mithra sur le Celius*, Leiden, 1978, p. 38ff.

83. Ibid., p. 30, 45f; R. Turcan, in *La soteriologia dei culti orientali* (EPRO, 92), p. 176.

84. Supra, p. 159.

85. *Sur la République de Platon*, II, p. 345, 4ff. Kroll = Bidez-Cumont, *Les mages hellénisés*, II, p. 155 (fr. 0 9).

86. M.J. Vermaseren-C.C. Van Essen, *The Excavations in the Mithraeum of the Church of Santa Prisca in Rome*, Leiden, 1965, p. 217ff. Cf. M.J. Vermaseren, *Mithriaca* (EPRO, 16), II, *The Mithraeum at Ponza*, Leiden, 1974, p. 27f; R. Turcan, *Mithras Platonicus*, p. 55f, 83ff and in *Knowledge of God in the Graeco-Roman World* (EPRO, 112), Leiden, 1988, p. 249.

87. R. Beck, *Interpreting the Ponza Zodiac I–II*, *JMS*, I, 1, 1976, p. 1ff; II, 2, 1978, p. 87ff.

88. R. Beck, 'Sette Sfere, Sette Porte ... ', in *Mysteria Mithrae*, p. 515ff. On the graffito in Santa Prisca: M. Guarducci, ibid., p. 153ff.

89. S. Insler, 'A New Interpretation of the Bull-Slaying Motif', in *Hommages à M.J. Vermaseren*, II, p. 519ff; A. Baussani, in *Mysteria Mithrae*, p. 503ff; R. Beck, *Planetary Gods and Planetary Orders in the Mysteries of Mithras* (EPRO, 109), Leiden, 1988.

90. *Mithras-Orion, Greek Hero and Roman Army God* (EPRO, 81), Leiden, 1980.

91. I. Gershevitch, op. cit. (n. 5), p. 62f.

92. 'Mithras und das Stieropfer', *Paieduma*, 3, 1949, p. 207ff.

93. E. Will, op. cit. (n. 58), p. 169ff.

94. *Les mystères de Mithra*[3], p. 173.

95. Supra, n. 19–20. Cf. R.L. Gordon, 'F. Cumont and the Doctrines of Mithraism', in *Mithraic Studies*, I, p. 237ff.

96. *CIMRM*, 383; R. Merkelbach, *Mithras*, p. 305.

97. Op. cit., p. 106ff.

98. Vermaseren-Van Essen, op. cit. (n. 86), p. 224ff.

99. *CIMRM*, 695/6; R. Merkelbach, *Mithras*, p. 324f. Cf. F. Cumont, 'Mithra et l'orphism', *RHR*, 109, 1934, p. 64ff.

100. 'Aiôn et le Léontocephale', *La Nouvelle Clio*, 10, 1960, p. 1–8; *La religion de l'Iran ancien*, p. 256f. Contra: idem, in *L'Encyclopédie de la Pléiade, Histoire des religions*, I, Paris, 1970, p. 685. I.F. Legge and R.C. Zaehner had already wanted to recognize Ahriman in the lion-faced monster which the York dedication (*CIMRM*, 833/4) would designate as such: U. Bianchi, 'Mithraism and Gnosticism', in *Mithraic Studies*, II, p. 457ff.
101. *CIMRM*, 833/4; U. Bianchi, loc. cit., p. 460f.
102. Cf. R. Merkelbach, *Mithras*, p. 153ff.
103. *CIMRM*, 837; R. Beck, in *ANRW*, II, 17, 4, p. 2049, pl. XXII.
104. R. Turcan, *Les dieux et le divin dans les mystères de Mithra, Knowledge of God ... (EPRO*, 112), pp. 257, 260.
105. R. Turcan, 'Note sur la liturgie mithriaque', *RHR*, 194, 1978, p. 147ff.
106. R. Turcan, 'Les autels, du culte mithraique,' in *Archéologie de l'espace sacrificiel*, Colloque International CNRS (Lyon 4–7 June 1988).
107. *CIMRM*, 480/3; *Mysteria Mithrae*, Append. 1, pls I–XII. Cf. Vermaseren–Van Essen, op. cit. (n. 86), p. 148ff, pls LIII–LXV.
108. *CIMRM*, 1275 a.
109. *CIMRM*, 1083.
110. *RAE*, 3, 1952, p. 125ff.
111. Supra, n. 88.
112. R.L. Gordon, 'Reality, Evocation and Boundary in the Mysteries of Mithras', *JMS*, III, 1980, p. 25ff.
113. Firmicus Maternus, *On the Error of Profane Religious*, XIX, 1.
114. *Mithras*, p. 88ff.
115. Vermaseren–Van Essen, op. cit., p. 148ff, 179ff.
116. M.J. Vermaseren, *Mithriaca* I, p. 24ff, pls XXI–XXVIII; V. Tran Tam Tinh, *Le culte des divinités orientales en Campanie*, p. 189–93.
117. *Questions sur l'Ancien et le Nouveau Testament*, 114, 11 (p. 308, 18f. of the Souter edition in the *Corpus* of Vienna, 50, 1909).
118. *Roman and Mysterium in der Antike*, Munich, 1962, p. 178ff. Cf. R. Beck, in *La soteriologia dei culti orientali (EPRO*, 92), p. 527ff.
119. M.J. Vermaseren, *Mithriaca* I, pl. XXVI.
120. D.M. Cosi, in *Mysteria Mithrae*, p. 933ff, pls XXVIII–XXX.
121. Cf. R. Turcan, *Les motivations de l'intolérance chrétienne ...* (n. 67), p. 223f.
122. J.-J. Hatt, *Strasbourg, Musée Archéologique, Sculptures antiques régionales*, Paris, 1964, No. 24.
123. Karlsruhe bust reincorporated with the cultic relief housed by the Museum of the Thermae: R.A. Stucky, 'Das Mithrasrelief Rom. Thermenmuseum 164688/ Karlsruhe 76/121', *Hefte des archäol. Seminars d. Universität Bern*, 12, 1987, pp. 17–19, pls 5–6.
124. Supra, n. 33.
125. C.M. Daniels, 'The Roman Army ...', in *Mithraic Studies*, II, p. 250f; M.J. Vermaseren, *Der Kult des Mithras im römischen Germanien*, p. 7f.
126. E. Will, 'Les fidèles de Mithra à Poetevio; (n. 54), p. 633ff; P. Selem, op. cit., p. 154ff.
127. V.J. Walters, op. cit., p. 58f.

128. L. Zotović, *Les cultes orientaux sur le territoire de la Mésie Supérieure* (*EPRO*, 7), p. 82, No. 25.
129. V.J. Walters, op. cit., 84ff; R. Turcan, in *ANRW*, II, 18, 1, pp. 505, 508.
130. Whatever E. Cizek may write about it, *Néron*, Paris, 1982, p. 352, following F. Cumont, 'L'iniziazione di Nerone da parte di Tiridate d'Armenia, *Riv. di Filol. e di Istr. Class.*, NS, 11, 1933, p. 145ff. Cf. also R. Merkelbach, *Mithras*, p. 48f.
131. M. Simon, 'Mithra et les empereurs' in *Mysteria Mithrae*, p. 417.
132. Ibid., p. 415.
133. *Les mystères de Mithra*³, p. VIII: a phrase applied inexactly to Heliogabalus by A. Piganiol (*Histoire de Rome*, Paris, 1949, p. 405).
134. R. Turcan, *Vivre à la cour des Césars*, p. 303ff.
135. T.D. Barnes, *Constantine and Eusebius*, Cambridge, Mass. and London, 1981, p. 36f, 48. Cf. A. Alföldi, *The Conversion of Constantine and Pagan Rome*², Oxford, 1969, p. 48, 54ff.
136. R. Turcan, *Les motivations de l'intolérance chrétienne* ... (n. 67), p. 220ff.
137. R. Turcan, *Mithras Platonicus*, p. 105ff; M. Simon, *Mithra et les empereurs* (n. 131), p. 418ff.
138. Vermaseren–Van Essen, op. cit., p. 241f.
139. F. Guidobaldi, 'Il complesso archeologico di S. Clemente...', in *San Clemente Miscellany II, Art and Archaeology*, Rome, 1978, pp. 256, 260, 283.
140. Supra, n. 122. The Archaeological Museum of Strasbourg also houses fragments of sculptures found on the site of Mackwiller: ibid., Nos 27–37 (with the previous bibliography).
141. On the discredit suffered at that time by Mithras: R. Turcan, *Les motivations de l'intolérance chrétienne* ..., p. 224f.

Chapter 5: Horsemen, Mothers and Serpents

1. Since the work of G. Kazarow, *Die Denkmäler des thrakischen Reitergottes in Bulgarien* (*Dissert. Pannonicae*, II, 14), Budapest, 1938, which cleared the ground, a *Corpus Cultus Equitis Thracii* = *CCET* (*EPRO*, 74) has been published: I, *Monumenta orae Ponti Euxini Bulgariae* (Z. Goceva–M. Oppermann); II, *Monumenta inter Danubium et Haemum reperta* (eidem, 1, 1981, and 2, 1984); IV, *Moesia Inferior* (Romanian Section) and *Dacia* (N. Hampartumian, 1979); V, *Monumenta intra fines Iougoslaviae reperta* (A. Cermanović–Kuzmanović, 1982). On the Thracian Horseman in general and the Danubian Horsemen: M. Oppermann, *Thrakische und Danubische Reitergötter und ihre Beziehungen zu orientalischen Kulten*, in *OrRR*, p. 510ff. On iconographic problems: F. Benoit, *L'héroïsation équestre* (Ann. Fac. Lettres d'Aix, NS, 7), 1954, p. 49ff; E. Will, *Le relief cultuel gréco-romain*, p. 56ff; Z. Goćeva, 'Les traits caractéristiques de l'inconographie du Cavalier Thrace', in *Iconographie classique et identités régionales* (Colloque International 26–7 May 1983), *BCH*, Suppl. XIV, Athens-Paris, 1986, p. 238ff.

2. E. Will, op. cit., p. 117; Z. Goćeva, loc. cit., p. 243 and fig. 9; CCET, 317, 337.

3. G. Kazarow, op. cit., No. 1093, fig. 520; F. Benoit, op. cit., p. 58 (with arguable comparisons).

4. E. Will, op. cit., p. 24ff, 30.

5. G. Kazarow, op. cit., No. 486, fig. 252; CCET, II, 2, p. 128f, No. 674.

6. L. Robert, 'Un dieu anatolien: Kakasbos', *Hellenica*, III, Paris, 1946, p. 37ff; E. Will, op. cit., p. 104f.

7. M. Floriani Squarciapino, *I culti orientali ad Ostia*, p. 67f.

8. Ibid., p. 68 (*CIL*, XIV, 234, 236, 240).

9. O. Picard, 'Numismatique et inconographie: le cavalier macédonien', in *Iconographie classique et identités régionales* (n. 1), p. 67ff.

10. P. Perdrizet, *Negotium perambulans in tenebris. Études de démonologie gréco-orientale* (Publ. Fac. Lettres Univ. de Strasbourg, 6), Strasbourg-Paris, 1922, p. 7ff; A.-J. Festugière, *La révélation d'Hermès Trismégiste*, I. Paris, 1950, p. 255; F. Benoit, op. cit., p. 50ff; E. Will, op. cit., p. 57ff, 121ff.

11. P. Perdrizet, 'Reliefs du pays des Maedes', *RA*, 1904, I, p. 19f; pl. I; R. Eisler, *Orphisch-dionysische Mysterien-Gedanken*, Leipzig-Berlin, 1925, pl. VIII, fig. 38; E. Will, op. cit., p. 117; F. Benoit, op. cit., p. 59.

12. M. Tacheva-Hitova, *Eastern Cults in Moesia Inferior and Thracia* (EPRO, 95), p. 170ff, No. 17 and pl. LVIII; E.N. Lane, *Corpus cultus Iovis Sabazii*, II (EPRO, 100), *The other Monuments and Literary Evidence*, Leiden, 1985, p. 45, D³, pl. XL.

13. F. Benoit, op. cit., p. 60 and pl. IX, 2.

14. CIMRM, 52, 1137, 1247, 1289.

15. R. Merkelbach, *Mithras*, p. 3f, 111.

16. D. Tudor, *Corpus monumentorum religionis equitum Danuvinorum* (EPRO, 13), I, *The Monuments*, Leiden, 1969; II, *The Analysis and Interpretation of Monuments*, Leiden, 1976.

17. E. Will, op. cit., p. 89ff, 312ff.

18. Cf. L Zotović, 'Les éléments orientaux dans le cult des cavaliers danubiens et quelques nouveaux aspects de ce culte', in *Hommages à M.J. Vermaseren*, III, p. 1351ff.

19. Op. cit., II, p. 243ff.

20. D. Tudor, in *Dacia*, 11–12, 1945–57, p. 271f; L. Zotović, loc. cit. (n. 18), pp. 1361f, 1371.

21. E. Will, op. cit., p. 404ff.

22. F. Chapouthier, *Les Dioscures au service d'une déesse* (BEFAR, 137), Paris, 1935, p. 106, 185. Cf. E. Will, op. cit., p. 90; L. Zotović, loc. cit. (n. 18), p. 1369f.

23. Eustathius, Commentary on the *Odyssey*, IV, 121. Cf. J. Carcopino, *La basilique pythagoricienne de la Porte Majeure*[8], Paris, 1944, p. 356; F. Cumont, *Recherches sur le symbolisme funéraire* ... , p. 186; J. Carcopino, *De Pythagore aux Apôtres*[2], Paris, 1968, p. 204.

24. R. Fleischer, *Artemis von Ephesos* ... (EPRO, 35), p. 88ff, 170ff; idem 'Artemis Ephesia und Aphrodite von Aphrodisias', in *OrRR*, p. 298ff,

303, 307ff. On the history of the Ephesian cult: C. Picard, *Ephèse et Claros* (*BEFAR*, 123), Paris, 1922.

25. F. Chapouthier, op. cit., p. 75f, No. 68 and pl. XIII; B.V. Head, *British Museum Coins, Ionia*, London, 1892, p. 85, No. 269 (Caracalla and Geta') and pl. XIV, 2.

26. R. Fleischer, *Artemis von Ephesos* ..., pls 11 and 33.

27. Ibid., p. 74ff.

28. H. Herter, 'Bacchus am Vesuv', *Rhein. Museum*, 100, 1957, p. 101ff. Cf. R. Eisler, op. cit., p. 227 and pl. XVII, plg. 184; R. Kany, *Dionysos Protrygaios*, *Jahrb. f. Anti. u. Christ.*, 31, 1900, p. 6.

29. R. Fleischer, op. cit., p. 3f, pls. 3–4.

30. Ibid., p. 310ff, pl. 138ff.

31. Ibid., p. 137ff, pl. 60 b.

32. Ibid., p. 8, E 21; E. Espérandieu, *Recueil des bas-reliefs, statues et bustes de la Gaule romaine*, I, Paris, 1907, p. 71, No. 84.

33. Cf. J. Bonnet, *Artémis d'Ephèse et la légende des sept dormants*, Paris, 1977, p. 107.

34. R. Fleischer, op. cit., p. 10ff, Nos 30–44.

35. Ibid., p. 12, E 36; C. Pietrangeli, in G. Lippold, *Die Skulpturen des Vatikanischen Museums*, III, 2, Berlin, 1956, p. 167ff, No. 22, pl. 77, 450.

36. A. Delatte and P. Derchain, *Bibliothèque Nationale, Les intailles magiques gréco-égyptiennes*, p. 179ff; p. 182, No. 239.

37. M. Floriani Squarciapino, 'Afrodite d'Afrodisia', *Boll. d'Arte*, 44, 1959, pl. 97–106, and in *Archaeologia Classica*, 12, 1960, p. 208ff; R. Fleischer, op. cit., p. 146ff, and in *OrRR*, p. 306ff.

38. A. García y Bellido, *Les religions orientales dans L'Espagne romaine*, p. 171f (with previous bibliography).

39. M. Floriani Squarciapino, *I culti orientali ad Ostia*, p. 69f.

40. M. Floriani Squarciapino, *La scuola d'Afrodisia*, Rome, 1943, p. 15, No. 23, and p. 37.

41. M. Floriani Squarciapino, *I culti orientali ad Ostia*, p. 69f.

42. M. Floriani Squarciapino, 'Afrodite d'Afrodisia', *Boll. d'Arte*, 44, 1959, p. 99 (fig. 13): R. Fleischer, op. cit., p. 151, A 19.

43. Supra, p. 158.

44. R. Fleischer, op. cit., p. 140 and pl. 61 a–b.

45. Ibid., p. 22, E 71, and pl. 39.

46. A. Dain, *Inscriptions grecques du Musée du Louvre. Les textes inédits*, Paris, 1933, p. 66ff, No. 60. Cf. Pausanias, *Description of Greece*, V, 1, 5; Strabo, *Geography*, XIV, 1, 8, 635.

47. Cf. R. Turcan, 'Les sarcophages romains et le problème du symbolisme funéraires', *ANRW*, II, 16, 2, p. 1705ff, 1708.

48. F. Cumont, 'Alexandre d'Abonotichos et le néo-pythagorisme', *RHR*, 86, 1922, p. 202ff; M. Caster, *Lucien et la pensée religieuse de son temps*, Paris, 1937, p. 255ff; idem, *Études sur Alexandre ou le Faux Prophète de Lucien*, Paris, 1938; C.P. Jones, *Culture and Society in Lucian*, pp. 133–58.

49. A. Delatte and P. Derchain, op. cit., p. 67f.

50. On the phenomenon in general: H. Dorrie, 'Mysterien (in Kult und Religion) und Philosophie', in *OrRR*, p. 341ff.
51. *De Pythagore aux Apôtres*², p. 110ff.
52. R. Turcan, 'Ulysse et les prétendus prétendants', *Jahrb. f. Ant. u. Christ.*, 22, 1979, p. 161ff.
53. 'The Mystery of the Serpent', in *The Mysteries*. *Eranos-Jahrbuch, Papers from the Eranos Yearbooks* (ed. J. Campbell, in *Bollingen Series*, XXX, 2), Princeton Univ. Press, 1978, p. 194ff. Cf. also H. Leisegang, *La gnose*, Fr. transl., Paris, 1951, pl. VIII.
54. A.-J. Festugière, *L'idéal religieux des Grecs et l'Évangile*², Paris, 1981, p. 289ff.
55. On this subject, cf. generally J. Schwartz, 'Papyri Magicae Graecae und magische Gemmen', in *OrRR*, p. 485ff, with pertinent bibliography.
56. A.A. Barb, 'Abraxas-Studien', in *Hommages à W. Déonna* (Coll. Latomus, 28), Brussels, 1957, p. 67ff; M. Philonenko, 'L'anguipède alectorocéphale et le dieu Iao', *CRAI*, 1979, p. 297ff; A. Delatte and P. Derchain, op. cit., p. 23ff.
57. Cf. U. Bianchi, 'Mithraism and Gnosticism', in *Mithraic Studies*, II, p. 464f, and in *Mysteria Mithrae*, p. 36.
58. A. Delatte and P. Derchain, op. cit., p. 54ff, 248ff.
59. Ibid., p. 66, No. 79. Cf. ibid., p. 60, No.62 (nine rays); p. 63, No. 70 (five rays).
60. Ibid., p. 81, 245ff, 251ff.
61. Ibid., p. 49 and passim. Cf. A.-J. Festugière, *La révélation d'Hermès Trismégiste*, IV, p. 182f, 189f, 191f.
62. Cf. A.I. Baumgarten, *The Phoenician History of Philo of Byblos. A Commentary* (*EPRO*, 89), Leiden, 1981.

Chapter 6: Occultism and Theosophy

1. A.-J. Festugière, *La révélation d'Hermès Trismégiste*, I, p. 19ff, 32ff. On Apollonius, cf. E.L. Bowie, 'Apollonius of Tyana: Tradition and Reality', *ANRW*, II, 16, 2, p. 1652ff.
2. R. Turcan, *Les sarcophages romains à représentations dionysiaques*, p. 374f.
3. Suetonius, *Nero*, 34, 8.
4. Bidez-Cumont, *Les mages hellénisés*, I, p. 180ff; F. Cumont, *Lux perpetua*, Paris, 1949, pp. 99f, 320.
5. A.-J. Festugière, op. cit., I, p. 201ff, 283ff.
6. Ibid., p. 56ff; idem, 'L'expérience religieuse du médecin Thessalos', *Rev. Bibl.*, 48, 1939, p. 45ff = *Hermétisme et mystique païenne*, Paris, 1967, p. 141ff.
7. Pliny the Elder, *Natural History*, XXX, 11. Cf. Bidez–Cumont, op. cit., II, p. 14, n. 23–4. Jambres is sometimes called 'Mambres' or 'Membres'.
8. Origen, *Against Celsus*, I, 28 and 68; II 32 and 48f.
9. Op. cit., I, p. 178ff; II, p. 275ff.

10. P. Mastandrea, *Un neoplatonico latino: Cornelio Labeone* (*EPRO*, 77), Leiden, 1979, p. 145ff.
11. A.-J. Festugière, *La révélation d'Hermès Trismégiste*, I, p. 217ff; G. Luck, *Arcana Mundi. Magic and the Occult in the Greek and Roman Worlds*, Baltimore-London, 1985, p. 361ff.
12. A.-J. Festugière, op. cit., I, p. 223 (*Hénoch*, 8, p. 26, 11ff, Radermacher).
13. Ibid., p. 228f; annotated text in Bidez–Cumont, op. cit., II, p. 317ff.
14. While awaiting the complete publication of the Greek alchemists in the Coll. des Universités de France (since 1981), reference may be made to the *Collection des anciens alchimistes grecs* by M. Berthelot and C.-E. Ruelle, Paris, 1887–8.
15. A.-J. Festugière, op. cit., I, p. 260ff: *L'alchimie religion mystique*; G. Luck, op. cit., p. 364f.
16. A.-J. Festugière, op. cit., I, p. 89ff; W. Gundel and H.G. Gundel, *Astrologumena. Die astrologische Literatur in der Antike und ihre Geschichte* (*Sudhoffs Archiv*, Beiheft 6), Wiesbaden, 1966; H.G. Gundel, *Weltbild und Astrologie in den griechischen Zauberpapyri* (*Munch. Beitr. z. Papyrusforschung u. ant. Rechtsgeschichte*, 53), Munich, 1968.
17. W. Gundel-H.G. Gundel, *Astrologumena*, p. 102f.
18. A.-J. Festugière, *L'idéal religieux des Grecs* . . . , p. 303f.
19. Cf. A. Dieterich, 'Die Religion des Mithras', *Bonn. Jahrb.*, 108/9, 1902, p. 32: *Kleine Schriften*, Leipzig-Berlin, 1911, p. 260; idem, *Abraxas*, Leipzig, 1891, pp. 51 and 97.
20. A.-J. Festugière, *L'idéal religieux des Grecs* . . . , p. 120ff; W. Gundel-H.G. Gundel, op. cit., pp. 218 and 229. Cf. F. Cumont, *L'Egypte des astrologues*, Brussels, 1937, p. 154.
21. C. Riedwig, *Mysterienterminologie bei Platon, Philon und Klemens von Alexandrien* (*Untersuch. z. ant. Literatur u. Geschichte*, 26, 1987).
22. A.-J. Festugière's transl. (*La révélation d'Hermès Trismégiste*, I. p. 266).
23. Ibid., p. 303ff.
24. Ibid., p. 307.
25. Cf. R. Beck, 'Mithraism since Franz Cumont', *ANRW*, II, 17, 4, p. 2051.
26. A.-J. Festugière, op. cit., I–IV, Paris, 1950–4 (re-issued 1986); idem, *Hermétisme et mystique païenne*, Paris, 1967, pp. 13–137; J. Doresse, 'L'hermétisme égyptianisant' in *L'Encyclopédie de la Pléiade, Histoire des religions*, II, Paris, 1972, pp. 430–97; A. Gonzalez Blanco, 'Hermetism. A Bibliographical Approach', *ANRW*, II, 17, 4, p. 2240ff. Annotated transl. ed. by A.D. Nock and A.-J. Festugière in the Coll. des Universités de France, I–IV, Paris, 1945–54.
27. J.-P. Mahe, *Hermès en Haute-Egypte*, 1, *Bibliothèque copte de Nag Hammadi*, Quebec, 1978; 2, Louvain-Quebec, 1982; idem, 'Hermès Trismégiste et Nag Hammadi', *Histoire et Archéologie*, 70 (Feb. 1983), p. 34ff.
28. H. Jonas, *La religion gnostique*, Fr. transl., Paris, 1978, p. 196ff; text and transl. by A.-J. Festugière in the Coll. des Universités de France, *Corpus Hermeticum*, I, pp. 1–28; Italian transl. presented and commentated by P. Scarpi, *Ermete Trismegisto, Poimandres*, Venice, 1987.

29. Cf. G. Van Moorsel, *The Mysteries of Hermes Trismegistus. A Phenomenological Study in the Process of Spiritualization in the Corpus Hermeticum and Latin Asclepius*, Utrecht, 1955; K.-W. Troger, *Mysterienglaube und Gnosis in Corpus Hermeticum XIII*, Berlin, 1971.

30. *Aspects mystiques de la Rome païenne*[6], p. 207ff; G. Charles-Picard, *Les religions de l'Afrique antique*, p. 228ff. F. Chamoux recognized the story of Perdiccas and Hippocrates in the scene of the central medallion: 'Perdiccas', in *Hommages à A. Grenier* (Coll. Latomus, 58), I, Brussels, 1962, p. 384ff. Cf. P. Grimal in *Jérôme Carcopino. Un historien au service de l'humanisme*, Paris, 1981, p. 284ff.

31. D.N. Wigtil, 'Incorrect Apocalpytic: the Hermetic "Asclepius" as an Improvement on the Greek Original', *ANRW*, II, 17, 4, p. 2282ff.

32. Op. cit., p. 289.

33. *Poimandres. Studien zur griechisch-agyptischen und frühchristlichen Literatur*, Leipzig, 1904 (re-ed. anast., Darmstadt, 1966), p. 248.

34. *Der Ausgang des griechish-römischen Heidentums*, p. 80.

35. *La révélation d'Hermès Trismégiste*, I, p. 82ff.

36. J.-P. Mahé, loc. cit. (*Histoire et Archéologie*, 70), p. 39: *Le probleme des communautes hermetiques*.

37. A.-J. Festugière, *Hermetisme et mystique païenne*, p. 100–12.

38. *L'idéal religieux des Grecs* ... , p. 116ff.

39. A.-J. Festugière, *La révélation d'Hermès Trismégiste*, IV, p. 211ff. On Hermetic soteriology and eschatology: ibid., III, p. 119ff. and in *Hermetisme et mystique païenne*, p. 58ff; K.-W. Troger, op. cit., p. 103ff.

40. F. Cumont, *Recherches sur le symbolisme funéraire des Romains*, p. 136.

41. A.-J. Festugière, in *Corpus Hermeticum*, IV, p. 22.

42. *Les dieux et le monde*, XVI, 2 (p. 21 of the transl. ed. by G. Rochefort in the Coll. des Universités de France, Paris, 1960).

43. A.D. Nock and A.-J. Festugière, in *Corpus Hermeticum*, IV, pp. 104–13.

44. *Aspects mystiques de la Rome païenne*[6], p. 293ff.

45. Cf. T.D. Barnes, *Constantine and Eusebius*, p. 74f.

46. E. des Places' annotated transl. ed. in the Coll. des Universités de France, 1971. By the same author, see a list of matters in question: 'Les Oracles Chaldaïques', *ANRW*, II, 17, 4, pp. 2299–335.

47. *Lux perpetua*, p. 273f.

48. E. des Places, 'Les "Mystères d'Egypte" de Jamblique et les "Oracles Chaldaïques"' in *Oikoumene*, II, Catania, 1964, p. 455ff; F. W. Cremer, *Die chaldäischen Orakel und Jamblich De mysteriis*, Meisenheim, 1969.

49. E. des Places in *ANRW*, II, 17, 4, p. 2314ff.

50. Ibid., p. 2313f; A.-J. Festugière, *La révélation d'Hermès Trismégiste*, III, p. 50ff.

51. *Suidae lexicon*, s.v.,' Ἰουλιανος (434), II, p. 642, 4ff, Alder (Leipzig, 1931); Michel Psellus, *Scripta minora*, I, p. 446, 22f of the E. Kurtz–F. Drexl edition (Milan, 1936) = E. des Places, *Oracles Chaldaïques*, p. 222. Cf. P. Hadot, 'Bilan et perspectives sur les Oracles Chaldaïques', in H. Lewy, *Chaldaean Oracles and Theurgy*[2], Paris, 1978, p. 703ff.

52. A.-J. Festugière, op. cit., III, p. 53ff; IV, p. 132f.

53. Cf. E. des Places, *Oracles Chaldaïques*, p. 153ff (texts of Psellus); idem, in *ANRW*, II, 17, 4, p. 2327ff; M. Tardieu, 'Un texte négligé de Psellus sur les Oracles Chaldaïques', *Byzant. Zeitschrift*, 73, 1980, p. 12f.

54. In E. des Places, *Oracles Chaldaïques*, p. 198f (6–7).

55. *City of God*, X, 23 = J. Bidez, *Vie de Porphyre*, p. 36*. Cf. H. Lewy, op. cit. (n. 51), p. 455.

56. J. Bidez, *La vie de l'empereur Julien*, Paris, 1930, p. 75.

57. R. Turcan, *Mithras Platonicus*, p. 72ff.

58. J. Bidez, *Vie de Porphyre*, p. 21ff, 1–23*; F. Buffière, *Les mythes d'Homère et la pensée grecque*, Paris, 1956, p. 536ff.

59. F. Cumont, *Lux perpetua*, p. 274, 361. Cf. Bidez–Cumont, *Les mages hellénisés*, I, p. 161.

60. On this text see P. Boyancé, 'Le Dieu très haut chez Philon', in *Mélanges H.-Ch. Puech*, p. 145ff.

61. Ibid., p. 145.

62. Cf. L. Cardullo, *Il linguaggio del simbolo in Proclo. Analisi filosoficosemantica des termini symbolon/eikôn/synthema del commentario alla Repubblica* (*Symbolon. Studi e Testi di Filosofia Antica e Medievale*, 4), Catania, 1985.

63. J. Bidez, *Catalogue des manuscrits alchimiques grecs*, VI, Brussels, 1928, p. 148ff; transl. A.-J. Festugière, *La révélation d'Hermès Trismégiste*, I, p. 134ff.

64. Cf. generally E.R. Dodds, *The Greeks and the Irrational*, Berkeley, 1951, 292ff.; P. Boyancé, 'Théurgie et télestique néoplatoniciennes', *RHR*, 147, 1955, pp. 189–209.

65. *Suidae lexicon*, s.v. Ἡραΐσκος (450), II, p. 579f, Adler.

66. Eunapius, *Lives of the Sophists*, ed. W.C. Wright in the Coll. Loeb, p. 434. Cf. J. Bidez, *La vie de l'empereur Julien*, p. 71ff. On Hecate in the Chaldaean Oracles: J. Aronen, 'Hecate's Share in the Cosmic Order', *Studia Fennica*, 32, 1987, p. 65ff.

67. H.D. Saffrey and L.G. Westerink's annotated transl. ed. in the Coll. des Universités de France, IV, Paris, 1981, p. 30 and 135f, n. 4. This text intrigued A. Dieterich (*Eine Mithrasliturgie*, Leipzig, 1903, p. 163) and E.R. Dodds (*The Greeks and the Irrational*, p. 292, n. 66; *Pagan and Christian in an Age of Anxiety*, Cambridge, 1965, p. 43).

68. R. Forrer, 'Das Mithra-Heiligtum von Königshofen bei Strassburg' *Mitt. d. Gesellsch. f. Erhaltung d. gesch. Denkmäler in Elsass*, II, 24, 1915, p. 75ff.

69. Cf. R. Turcan, 'Les motivations de l'intolérance chrétienne . . .', *Actes du VIIe Congres de la F.I.E.C.*, II, p. 223.

70. C. Lacombrade, *Synésius de Cyrène hellène et chrétien*, Paris, 1951, p. 168f; H.-I. Marrou, in *REG*, 65, 1952, p. 482; E. des Places, *Oracles Chaldaïques*, p. 36.

71. C. Lacombrade's annotated transl. ed. in the Coll. des Universités de France, Paris, 1978. Cf. W. Theiler, *Die chaldaïschen Orakel und die Hymnen des Synesios* (*Schr. d. Königsberger Gel. Gesellsch.*, 18, 1), Halle, 1942 (re-ed.)

72. *Noces de Mercure et de Philologie*, II, 204–5 (p. 77, 6ff, Dick–Préaux, Stuttgart, 1969). Cf. L. Lenaz, *Martiani Capellae De nuptiis Philologiae et*

Mercurii, Liber Secundus, Padua, 1975, p. 33ff; E. des Places, in *ANRW,* II, 17, 4, p. 2318f.

73. Marinus, *Life of Proclus,* 28, (p. 165, 20ff, Boissonade).
74. Michel Psellus, *Scripta minora,* I, p. 237f, Kurtz–Drexl.
75. On the tenacious prestige of the Chaldaean Oracles in the Middle Ages and up to the Renaissance: E. des Places, in *ANRW,* II, 17, 4, p. 2332ff.

Chapter 7: Dionysus and Sabazius

1. H. Jeanmaire, *Dionysos. Histoire du culte de Bacchus,* Paris, 1951 (reissued); E.R. Dodds, *The Greeks and the Irrational,* p. 7ff, 2ff.
2. M. Detienne, 'Dionysos en ses parousies: un dieu épidémique', in *L'association dionysiaque* ... (Table ronde, Rome, 24–5 May 1984 = Coll. de l'Éc. Franç. de Rome, 89), Rome, 1986, p. 53ff.
3. *Études de religion grecque et hellénistique,* Paris, 1972, p. 242.
4. E. Ohlemutz, *Die Kulte und Götter in Pergamon,* Giessen, 1940, p. 90ff; H. Jeanmaire, op. cit., p. 446; M.P. Nilsson, *The Dionysiac Mysteries of the Hellenistic and Roman Age,* Lund, 1957 (re-issues anast., New York, 1975), p. 9f; D. Musti, 'Il dionisismo degli Attalidi   ... ' in *L'association dionysiaque* (n. 2), p. 105ff, 117ff.
5. M. Bernhart, 'Dionysos und seine Familie auf grieceischen Munzen ...' Jahrb. f. Numismatik u. Geldgeschichte, 1. 1949.
6. C. Picard, 'Sabazios, dieu thraco-phrygien: expansion et aspects nouveaux de son culte, *RA,* 1961, II, p. 129ff; R. Fellmann, 'Der Sabazios–Kult', in *OrRR,* p. 316ff; M. Tacheva–Hitova, *Eastern Cults in Moesia Inferior and Thracia,* p. 162ff; S.E. Johnson, 'The Present State of Sabazios Research', *ANRW,* II, 3, Berlin–New York, 1984, p. 1583ff.
7. *Hours,* fr. 566; *Wasps,* 8ff; *Birds,* 876; *Lysistrata,* 387ff.
8. *On the Crown,* 259–60 (debated testimony).
9. Supra, p. 31.
10. *The Error of Profane Religions,* VI; X, 2; XXI, 2; XXVI.
11. I am preparing a corpus intended to illustrate in part a collection of texts relating to Dionysiac initiation.
12. Cf. P. Boyancé, 'Sur les mystères d'Eleusis', *REG,* 75, 1962, p. 461ff (in which *tupoumenos* seems to me to have been too vaguely translated as 'impression'.
13. GgR, II², p. 200ff; C. Schneider, *Kulturgeschichte des Hellenismus,* II, Munich, 1969, p. 460ff, 830ff.
14. F. Cumont, *Lux Perpetua,* p. 401ff.
15. R. Turcan, 'Bacchoi ou bacchants? De la dissidence des vivants à la ségrégation des morts', in *L'association dionysiaque* (n. 2), p. 227–46.
16. M.P. Nilsson, *The Dionysiac Mysteries* ... , p. 6f; A.-J. Festugière, op. cit. (n. 3), p. 110ff.
17. La naissance de la tragédie, Fr. transl. of the *Complete Philosophical Works,* I, Paris, Gallimard, 1977, p. 117 and 120.
18. Damagetus, in *Anthologie Palatine,* VII, 9, 5 (IV, p. 59 in the Coll. des Universités de France, Paris, 1960).

19. In O. Kern, *Orphicorum fragmenta*[2], Berlin, 1963, p. 101f, No. 31.
20. G. Zuntz, in *Hermes*, 91, 1963, p. 228ff. = *Opuscula selecta*, Manchester Univ. Press, 1972, p. 88ff.
21. *Etymologicum Magnum*, s.v. Γαλλος, 220, 19ff, col. 631, Gaisford.
22. Cf. F. Dunand, 'Les associations dionysiaques au service du pouvoir lagide (III[e]- s. av. J.-C.)', in *L'association dionysiaque* (N. 2), p. 85ff, 87f, 97ff.
23. R. Turcan, 'Les sarcophages pamphyliens de Rome, in *Proceed. of the Xth Intern. Congr. of Class. Archaeology*, II, Ankara, 1978, p. 691f.
24. F. Cumont, 'La grande inscription bacchique du Metropolitan Museum', *AJA*, 37, 1933, p. 232ff; J. Scheid, 'Le thiase du Metropolitan Museum' (*IGVR*, I, 160), in *L'association dionysiaque* (n. 2), p. 275ff. Cf. M.P. Nilsson, *The Dionysiac Mysteries* . . . , p. 56f.
25. Op. cit. (n. 3), p. 47.
26. Ibid., p. 89ff. Cf. D.W.L. Van Son, *Bacchanalia: Livius' behandeling van de Bacchanalia*, Amsterdam, 1960; C. Gallini, *Protesta e integrazione nella Roma antica*, pp. 11–90; R. Turcan, 'Religion et politique dans l'affaire des Bacchanales', *RHR*, 181, 1972, pp. 3–28; E. Montanari, *Identità culturale e conflitti religiosi nella Roma repubblicana*, Rome, 1988, p. 119ff. The bibliography on this dossier has considerably increased over the last twenty years.
27. Cf. J.-M. Pailler, '*Raptos a diis homines dici* . . . ' (Livy, XXXIX, 13): les Bacchanales et la possession par les Nymphes' in *Mélanges J. Heurgon* (Coll. de l'Ec. Franç. de Rome, 27), II, Rome, 1976, p. 731ff.
28. J. Heurgon, 'Influences grecques sur la religion etrusque: l'inscription de Laris Pulenas', *REL*, 35, 1957, p. 106ff.
29. Dionysius of Halicarnassus, *Roman Antiquities*, VI, 94; Tacitus, *Annals*, II, 49, 1. Cf. H. Le Bonniec, *Le culte de Cérès à Rome des origines à la fin de la République*, Paris, 1958, p. 213ff, 254ff.
30. Livy, XL, 19, 9–10.
31. Suburban temple of S. Abbondio: A. Mauri, *Pompei*[5], Rome, 1955, p. 102 and fig. 96; R. Etienne, *La vie quotidienne à Pompéi*, Paris, 1966, p. 237f.
32. R. Turcan, 'César et Dionysos' in *Hommages à la mémoire de J. Carcopino*, Paris, 1977, p. 317ff. On Daphnis, cf. J. Perret, 'L'exaltation de Daphnis' in *Hommages à J. Cousin*, Paris, 1983, p. 123ff; R. Merkelbach, *Die Hirten des Dionysos*, Stuttgart, 1988, p. 37ff.
33. A. Maiuri, *La Villa dei Misteri*, Rome, 1947; G. Griego, 'La grande frise de la Villa des Mystères et l'initiation dionysiaque', *La Parola del Passato*, 188/9, 1979, p. 417ff; U. Pappalardo, 'Nuove osservazioni sul fregio della "Villa dei Misteri" a Pompei, in *La regione sotterrata del Vesuvio*, Naples, 1982, p. 611ff. Here again, each space rules out a detailed list of publications concerning the much debated interpretation of the paintings.
34. I. Bragantini–M. de Vos, *Le decorazioni della villa romana della Farnesina*, p. 138f, pls 71–9; p. 193f, pls. 110–20.
35. Cf. F. Matz, ΔΙΟΝΥΣΙΑΚΗ-ΤΕΛΕΤΗ, *Abhand. d. Akad. Mainz*, 1963, 15, pp. 1385–1454; L. Foucher, 'Le culte de Bacchus sous l'Empire romain',

ANRW, II, 17, 2, Berlin–New York, 1981, pp. 684–702. On the iconography of Dionysos as a child initiated into his own mysteries: C. Gasparri, art. 'Dionysos/Bacchus' in *LIMC*, III, 1 (1986), p. 553f.

36. J. Colin, 'Les vendanges dionysiaques et la légende de Messaline,' *Les Études Classiques*, 24, 1956, p. 25ff; A. La Penna, 'I Baccanali di Messalina e le Bacchanti di Euripide', *Maia, NS*, 2, 1975, p. 121ff.

37. M. Bats, 'Dionysiastai. A propos, de cases corinthiens à représentations dionysiaques d'époque romaine', *RA*, 1981, p. 3–26, ig. 1–4.

38. E. Simon, 'Drei antike Gefässe aus Kameoglas in Corning, Florenz und Besançon'. *Journ. of Glass Studies*, 6, 1964, p. 13ff.

39. Cf. A.–J. Festugière, op. cit. (n. 3), p. 107f; E. La Rocca, M. and A. de Vos, *Guida archeologica di Pompei 2*, p. 343.

40. Cf. a stucco from the Farnesina: F. Matz, op. cit. (n. 35), pl. 5; Bragantini–de Vos, op. cit. pl. 120.

41. R. Turcan, 'Pour en finir avec la femme fouettée', *RA*, 1982 (= *Mélanges H. Metzger*), p. 291ff, 297f.

42. R. Turcan, 'La démone ailée de la Villa Item', in *Hommages à M. Renard* (Coll. Latomus, 103), Brussels, 1969, III, p. 586ff.

43. P. Boyancé, 'Une allusion de Plaute aux mystères de Dionysos'. *Mélanges, A. Ernout*, Paris, 1940, p. 29ff; idem, 'Dionysiaca', *REA*, 68, 1966, . 38f.

44. *IGVR*, I, 160, col. III B 28. Cf. F. Cumont, loc. cit., *AJA*, 37, 1933, p. 258ff; P. Boyancé, 'L'antre dans les mystères de Dionysos', *Rend. Pont. Accad. Rom. di Arch.*, 33, 1961, p. 107f; R. Merkelback, *Die Hirten des Dionysos*, p. 63ff.

45. Ibid., p. 17f; supra, n. 24.

46. Cf. M.P. Nilsson, *The Dionysiac Mysteries* ..., pp. 60ff, 74, 115, 131, 146. Many 'mysteries' were in reality public festivals: R. MacMullen, op. cit.

47. R. Turcan, *Bacchoi ou Bacchants?* ... (n. 15), p. 237ff.

48. R. Turcan, *Les sarcophages romains à représentations dionysiaques*, passim; F. Matz, *Die dionysischen Sarkophage*, I–IV, Berlin, 1968–75.

49. R. Turcan, op. cit., p. 394ff.

50. Ibid., p. 391f, 532f.

51. Ibid., p. 595ff.

52. Ibid., p. 464ff, 468ff.

53. Ibid., p. 529ff.

54. Ibid., p. 504ff.

55. Ibid., p. 532f. and in *L'imaginaire du vin* (Colloque de Dijon 15–17 October 1981), Marseille, 1983, p. 49ff.: *Le symbolisme funéraire des lènoi*.

56. *Les sarcophages romains* ..., pp. 405ff, 568ff.

57. H. Jeanmaire, *Dionysos*, pp. 94ff.

58. E.N. Lane, *Corpus cultus Iovis Sabazii* (*EPRO*, 100), Leiden, 1985, p. 14ff, Nos 33, 34, 36, 40.

59. Ibid., p. 22, No. 46; p. 24ff, No. 51; R. Garland, *The Piraeus*, p. 132f.

60. E.N. Lane, 'Sabazius and the Jews in Valerius Maximus: a re-examination', *JRS*, 69, 1979, p. 35ff.

61. M. Guarducci, 'Nuovi documenti del culto di Caelestis a Roma', *Bull. Com.*, 72, 1946/8, pp. 11–25; E.N. Lane, *Corpus cultus Iovis Sabazii*, II, p. 29f, Nos 58–60.

62. Cf. M.J. Vermaseren, 'Ouderlinge betrekkingen tussen Mithras-Sabazius-Cybele', *Medel. van de Koninklijke Academie voor Wetenschappen, Lett. en Sch. Kunsten van Belgie*, 46, 1984, p. 27ff.

63. E.N. Lane, op. cit., p. 29, No. 58 (= *CIL*, VI, 30948).

64. Ibid., p. 28f, No. 57; p. 30, No. 61 (= *CIL*, VI, 429), in which the author mistakenly places the discovery 'in the transtiburtine area' instead of 'transtiberine'.

65. M. Floriani Squarciapino, *I culti orientali ad Ostia*, p. 65f. Cf. R. Meiggs, *Roman Ostia*², p. 376.

66. R. Turcan, 'Feu et sang. A propos d'un relief mithriaque', *CRAI*, 1986, p. 217ff.

67. E.N. Lane, op. cit., p. 35, No. 73.

68. Ibid., p. 36, No. 75.

69. Ibid., pl. XXXII.

70. C. Picard, 'Le dieu thraco-phrygien Sabazios-Sabazius à Vichy', *Rev. Arch. du Centre*, 1, 1962, p. 10ff; idem, 'Sabazius et Bacchus enfant à Vichy', *RA*, 1962, II, p. 71ff; E.N. Lane, op. cit., p. 35, No. 74; J. Corrocher, *Vichy antique*, Clermont-Ferrand, 1981, pp. 252–7.

71. M.J. Vermaseren (with E. Westra and M.B. de Boer), *Corpus cultus Iovis Sabazii (EPRO, 100)*, I, *The Hands*, Leiden, 1983; S.E. Johnson, in *ANRW*, II, 17, 3, p. 1595ff.

72. E.N. Lane, op. cit., p. 40f, No. 85 and pl. XXXV; R. Fellmann, loc. cit. (n. 6), p. 329f.

73. E.N. Lane, op. cit., pp. 47–50.

74. M.J. Vermaseren, op. cit. (n. 71), pp. 6–9, Nos. 14–15 bis, with the previous bibliography. I returned to the problems raised by this site in an address presented to the Convegno Internazionale *Ercolano 1738–1988, 250 anni di ricerca archeologica* (Pompei – Ercolano – Ravello, 30 October–5 November 1988): 'Sabazios à Pompéi'.

75. *Notizie degli Scavi di Antichità*, 1958, p. 121; *CIL*, IV. Suppl. 3, 4 (1970), 10104.

76. M.J. Vermaseren, op. cit., pp. 7–9, No. 15 bis, pls XII–XVII.

77. Ibid., pp. 6–7, Nos 14–15, pls X–XI.

78. As Sabazius had links with Dionysus, it explains why some Pompeian gladiators' helmets had scenes of Bacchic initiation on their crown: F. Matz, op. cit. (n. 35), p. 1392, Nos 6–7, pl. 14. This fact intrigued H. Jeanmaire (*Dionysos*, p. 460).

79. Cf. C. Gallini, op. cit., p. 131. Spartacus was originally from the country of the Maedi, whence comes the relief of Melnik representing an equestrian Dionysus: supra, p. 250.

80. E.N. Lane, op. cit., p. 31f, No. 65 (with part of the former bibliography) and pl. XXVII; A. Ferrua, 'La Catacomba di Vibia', *Riv. di Archeol. Crist.*, 47, 1971, pp. 7–62; M.J. Vermaseren, *Mithras-Sabazius-Cybele* (n. 62), p. 34ff, figs VII–IX.

81. 'Les mystères du syncrétisme phrygien dans les Catacombes romaines de Prétextat (nouvelle interprétation)', in C. Cahier and A. Martin, *Mélanges d'archéologie, d'histoire et de littérature*, IV, Paris, 1856, p. 39. Cf. M.J. Vermaseren, loc. cit., p. 41 and fig. IX.

82. Cf. E. Maass, *Orpheus*, Munich, 1895, p. 207ff, 211.

83. *Lux perpetua*, p. 257.

84. *Questions sur l'Ancien et le Nouveau Testament*, 114, 12 (p. 309, 15f of the Souter ed. in the *Corpus* of Vienne).

85. *Letters*, 17, 4. Cf. P. Mastandrea, *Massimo di Madauros*, Padua, 1985.

86. J. Collins-Clinton, *A Late Antique Shrine of Liber Pater at Cosa* (*EPRO*, 64), Leiden, 1977.

Epilogue

1. *RO⁴*, p. 188ff.

2. *Le paganisme dans l'Empire romain*, p. 164.

3. *Dialogue avec Tryphon*, II, 3ff. Cf. G. Bardy, *La conversion au christianisme durant les premiers siècles*, Paris, 1949, p. 127ff.

4. A.-J. Festugière, *La révélation d'Hermès Trismégiste*, I, p. 38ff, 374ff.

5. P. Decharme, *La critique des traditions religieuses chez les Grecs*, Paris, 1904, p. 454ff; G. Soury, *La démonologie de Plutarque*, Paris, 1942; *GgR*, II², P. 407ff; F.E. Brenk, 'In the Light of the Moon: Demonology in the Early Imperial Period, *ANRW*, II, 16, 3, p. 2117ff.

6. R. Turcan, *Les motivations de l'intolérance chrétienne* . . ., p. 214ff.

7. J. Bidez, *Vie de Porphyre*, p. 91, 101. Cf. Iamblichus, *The Mysteries of Egypt*, V, 15 (p. 170 of the transl. ed. by E. des Places in the Coll. des Universités de France).

8. Only partial studies exist on this period, but there is no in-depth synthesis on the development of intellects sensitive to the Roman crisis. Some useful findings are collected in J. Geffcken, *Der Ausgang des griechisch-römischen Heidentums*, p. 20ff.

9. On this text, which P. Courcelle (*Histoire littéraire des grandes invasions germaniques*, Paris, 1948, p. 128f) unjustifiably dated to the Vth century, cf. S. Mazzarino, *La fin du monde antique. Avatars d'un thème historiographique*, Fr. transl. Paris, 1973, p. 40ff; J. Fontaine, *Naissance de la poésie dans l'Occident chrétien*, Paris, 1981, p. 42f.

10. P. du Bourguet, *Art paléochrétien*, Paris, 1970, p. 117: mosaic dated too early (p. 116) to the 'beginning of the IIIrd century'. Cf. P. Testini, *Le catacombe e gli antichi cimiteri cristiani in Roma*, Bologna, 1966, p. 308 and fig. 196.

11. Cf. M. de Diéguez, *Et l'homme créa son Dieu*, Paris, 1984, pp. 67ff, 309ff.

12. Eusebius, *Eulogy of Constantine*, 4 J.P. Migne, (*Patrologia Graeca*, col. 1333 A).

13. A. Alföldi, *The Conversion of Constantine and Pagan Rome²*, p. 58f, 131, n. 21; G. Dagron, *Naissance d'une capitale. Constantinople et ses institutions de 330 à 451*, Paris, 1974, pp. 38f, 307, 374, 407: Constantine, 'in his city, thinks himself the equal of Christ'.

14. In J.P. Migne *Patrologia Graeca*, 86, 2, col 5 1178, 1183 A.

Suggestions for Further Reading (in English)

General Works and Background Reading

F. Cumont's classic study of 1906 is available in English, with the title *Oriental Religions in Roman Paganism*, New York: Dover Publications 1956 (translated from the second French edition of 1909). On Cumont's work in general see A. Momigliano, *Studies on Modern Scholarship*, Berkeley: California University Press 1994, 323–8.

General books in English on Roman paganism include J. Ferguson, *Religions of the Roman Empire*, London: Thames & Hudson 1970; R. Macmullen, *Paganism in the Roman Empire*, London: Yale University Press 1981; A. Wardman, *Religion and Statecraft among the Romans*, London: Granada 1982.

On ancient mystery religions see above all W. Burkert, *Ancient Mystery Cults*, Cambridge, Mass.: Harvard University Press 1987; notice also J. Godwin, *Mystery Religions in the Ancient World*, London: Thames & Hudson 1981 (a brief introductory synthesis, with good illustrations). For a selection of sources and documents in translation see M.W. Meyer (ed.), *The Ancient Mysteries: a sourcebook*, San Francisco: Harper 1987. R. Reitzenstein, *Hellenistic Mystery Religions*, Pittsburgh: Pickwick Press 1978 (from the German original of 1910; second edition 1927) is still worth consulting. Further references can be found in B. Metzger, "A Classified Bibliography of the Graeco-Roman Mystery Religions 1924–73, with supplement 1974–77", in *ANRW* II. 17, 3 (1984), 1259–1423.

Other works of general relevance include T.R. Glover, *The Conflict of Religions in the Early Roman Empire*, London: Methuen 1909; A.D. Nock, *Conversion*, Oxford: Oxford University Press 1933; E.R. Dodds, *Pagan and Christian in an Age of Anxiety*, Cambridge: Cambridge University Press 1965; H.S. Versnel, *Inconsistencies in Greek and Roman Religion 1: Ter Unus. Isis, Dionysus, Hermes: Three studies in henotheism*, Leiden: Brill 1990.

Regional studies include E. and J.R. Harris, *The Oriental Cults of Roman Britain*, Leiden: Brill 1965 (EPRO 6); M. Tacheva-Hitova, *Eastern Cults in Moesia Inferior and Thracia*, Leiden: Brill 1983 (EPRO 95).

384   Suggestions for Further Reading

Articles on aspects of pagan religion (in various languages including English) can be found in *ANRW* II. 16, II. 17, and II. 18 (1978–95). See also the papers by A.D. Nock, *Essays on Religion and the Ancient World*, 2 vols., Oxford: Oxford University Press 1972, and A. Momigliano, *On Pagans, Jews and Christians*, Middletown, Conn.: Wesleyan University Press 1987.

Monographs on individual cults

On the Great Mother/Cybele: M.J. Vermaseren, *Cybele and Attis: the Myth and the Cult*, London: Thames and Hudson 1977; M.J. Vermaseren, *The Legend of Attis in Greek and Roman Art*, Leiden: Brill 1966 (EPRO 9); G. Thomas, "Magna Mater and Attis", *ANRW* II. 17, 3 (1984), 1500–1535; C. Sfameni Gasparro, *Soteriology and Mystic Aspects in the Cult of Cybele and Attis*, Leiden: Brill 1985 (EPRO 103). On the Taurobolium: J.B. Rutter, "The Three Phases of the Taurobolium", *Phoenix* 22 (1968), 226–49; R. Duthoy, *The Taurobolium. Its Evolution and Terminology*, Leiden: Brill 1969 (EPRO 10).

On Isis: R.E. Witt, *Isis in the Graeco-Roman World*, London: Thames and Hudson 1971; S.K. Heyob, *The Cult of Isis among Women in the Graeco-Roman World*, Leiden: Brill 1975 (EPRO 51); J.G. Griffiths, *Apuleius, The Isis Book (Metamorphoses, Book XI)*, with intr. trans. and notes, Leiden: Brill 1976 (EPRO 39); F. Solmsen, *Isis among the Greeks and Romans*, Cambridge, Mass.: Harvard University Press 1979; R.A. Wild, *Water in the Cultic Worship of Isis and Sarapis*, Leiden: Brill 1981 (EPRO 87); ID., "The Known Isis-Sarapis-Sanctuaries from the Roman Period", *ANRW* II. 17, 4 (1984), 1739–1851.

On Mithras: F. Cumont, *The Mysteries of Mithra*, London: Kegan Paul 1903; M.J. Vermaseren, *Mithras, the Secret God*, London: Chatto and Windus 1963; R.L. Gordon, "Mithras and Roman Society", *Religion* 2 (1972), 92–121; ID., "Reality, Evocation and Boundary in the Mysteries of Mithras", *Journ. Mithraic Studies* 3 (1980), 19–99; ID., "Authority, Salvation and Mystery in the Mysteries of Mithras", in *Image and Mystery in the Roman World: Papers in Memory of Jocelyn Toynbee*, ed. J. Huskison et al., Gloucester: Sutton 1988, 44–88; R. Beck, *Planetary Gods and Planetary Orders in the Mysteries of Mithras*, Leiden: Brill 1988 (EPRO 109); D. Ulansey, *The Origins of the Mithraic Mysteries*, Oxford: Oxford University Press 1991. See also the survey article by R. Beck, "Mithraism since F. Cumont", *ANRW* II. 17, 4 (1984), 2002–2115. An extremely important collection of papers can be found in J.R. Hinnells (ed.), *Mithraic Studies: Proceedings of the First International Congress of Mithraic Studies*, Manchester: Manchester University Press 1975.

On Dionysus/Sabazius: M.P. Nilsson, *The Dionysiac Mysteries of the Hellenistic and Roman Age*, Lund: C.W.K. Gleerup 1957; G. Zuntz, "On the Dionysiac Frescoes in the Villa dei Misteri at Pompeii", *Proceedings of the British Academy* 49 (1963), 177–202; O.J. Brendel, "The Great Frieze in the Villa of the Mysteries", in *The Visible Idea*, Washington, DC: Decatur House 1980, 90–138; R.A.S. Seaford, "The Mysteries of Dionysus at Pompeii" in *Pegasus: Classical Essays from the University of Exeter*, ed. H.W. Stubbs, Exeter University Press 1981, 52–68; S.E. Johnson, "The Present State of Sabazius Research", *ANRW* II.

17, 3 (1984) 1583–1613. On the Bacchanalia affair of 186 BC: J.A. North, "Religious Toleration in Republican Rome", *Proceedings Cambridge Philol. Soc.* 205 (1979), 85–103.

On the Syrian deities: J. Teixidor, *The Pagan God: Popular Religion in the Greco-Roman Near East*, Princeton: Princeton University Press 1977; ID., *The Pantheon of Palmyra*, Leiden: Brill 1979 (EPRO 79); H.J.W. Drijvers, *Cults and Beliefs at Edessa*, Leiden: Brill 1980 (EPRO 82). On Jupiter Dolichenus: M. Speidel, *The Religion of Jupiter Dolichenus in the Roman Army*, Leiden: Brill 1978 (EPRO 63); V. Najdenova, "The Cult of Jupiter Dolichenus in Lower Moesia and Thrace", *ANRW* II. 18, 2 (1989), 1362–96.

Among the vast literature on magic, astrology, occultism, etc. notice especially F. Cumont, *Astrology and Religion among the Greeks and Romans*, New York: G.P. Putnam's Sons 1912. See also A.A. Barb, "The Survival of Magic Arts", in *The Conflict between Paganism and Christianity in the Fourth Century*, ed. A. Momigliano, Oxford: Clarendon Press 1963, 100–125; G. Fowden, *The Egyptian Hermes: a Historical Approach to the Late Pagan Mind*, Cambridge: Cambridge University Press 1986; A. Faraone, D. Obbink (eds), *Magika hiera: Ancient Greek Magic and Religion*, Oxford: Oxford University Press 1991; T. Barton, *Ancient Astrology*, London: Routledge 1994. The best introduction to Gnosticism is K. Rudolph, *Gnosis: The Nature and History of an Ancient Religion*, Edinburgh: T. & T. Clark 1983.

T.J. Cornell

Index